PERSPECTIVES IN SCHIZOPHRENIA RESEARCH

Perspectives in Schizophrenia Research

Editors

Claude F. Baxter, Ph.D.
Chief, Neurochemistry Laboratories
Veterans Administration Medical Center
Sepulveda, California
Professor
Department of Psychiatry
Center for Health Sciences
University of California, Los Angeles
Los Angeles, California

Theodore Melnechuk
Research Associate, Western
Behavioral Sciences Institute
La Jolla, California
Associate
Department of Neurosciences
University of California,
San Diego
San Diego, California

Raven Press ■ New York

Raven Press, 1140 Avenue of the Americas, New York, New York 10036

Made in the United States of America

International Standard Book Number 0–89004–490–2
Library of Congress Catalog Card Number 80–5052

Preface

Traditionally, a symposium volume takes both a retrospective look at past accomplishments and an up-to-date look at the present state of the art. This symposium volume is different. Based on a conference held in 1979 at Harpers Ferry, West Virginia, this symposium volume is concerned primarily with charting strategies for *future* research in schizophrenia. The presentations at the conference were made by scientists and clinicians who had personal knowledge of past successes, failures, and pitfalls in schizophrenia research. They were asked to describe recent experimental approaches, strategies, findings, and theories that might be guideposts for future research. They were encouraged also to voice their personal views and prejudices concerning the kind of research that should be supported to reach a better understanding of schizophrenia and to find more consistently successful treatment modalities for it.

Whereas the approaches recommended by different experts reflected their personal involvement in the biological, behavioral, psychosocial, or clinical sciences, there emerged areas in which they were in substantial agreement. This included the belief that schizophrenia, as presently defined, comprises a family of diseases and that "markers" of these different disease entities require definition and identification before real progress in prognosis and treatment of the diseases can be assured. This volume is organized with this belief in mind.

After an overview of the different approaches to schizophrenia research, a variety of possible biological markers for schizophrenia, and other considerations, are described from the point of view of the neurophysiologist, neuroendocrinologist, psychopharmacologist, neurologist, neurochemist, morphologist, immunologist, and behavioral psychologist.

In the next section of the volume, a more clinically oriented point of view is presented. Schizophrenia research is discussed in terms of experimental design, statistical analysis, drug side effects, placebo effects, patient selection, outcome measurements, and other parameters that may affect the onset and course of the disease. Included are some of the genetic, emotional, and biological factors in the patient's "internal environment," as well as job and living conditions, interpersonal relations, ethnicity, social standing, etc. all of which contribute to the patient's "external environment." Also considered is research that should be conducted to improve the health-care delivery systems for patients with schizophrenia. In a separate chapter, the establishment of a regional brain bank for the collection of brains of deceased schizophrenic and normal individuals is described. Arguments are made for the more widespread utilization of neuropathological tissues in controlled retrospective studies. The discussions that followed most of the presentations have been condensed and follow each chapter.

The reader will find many good ideas contained in these discussions. The final chapter of the volume is an effort, on the part of the editors, to highlight some aspects of the conference and to share some provocative thoughts related to material presented at the conference.

The subject matter of this volume may interest not only researchers and clinicians, but also medical research administrators, legislators and others who make policies and control the funding of schizophrenia research. To help present the gist of the different approaches to people with such responsibilities, each chapter is introduced by a summary for laypersons.

The primary research objective in schizophrenia must be to develop the basic insight into the nature of the disease that will permit a rational approach to prevention and cure. As long as this basic insight is lacking, emphasis must be placed on finding ways to improve the effectiveness of empiric treatment and to reduce the suffering that this disease imposes not only on the patient, but also on the people in his sphere of influence.

In selecting contributors for this volume, we aimed to provide, for the reader, a representative, integrated, interdisciplinary, and updated look at some theoretical concepts, some basic and applied research objectives, and some practical medical problems related to future research and treatment of schizophrenia. We hope that this approach will help to focus attention upon crucial issues that must be addressed in order to advance our primary research objectives and improve patient care.

Claude F. Baxter
Theodore Melnechuk

Acknowledgments

This volume and the conference on which it is based were made possible through financial sponsorship by the Veterans Administration, specifically the Medical Research Service (Research and Development Office) and the Continuing Education and Staff Development Service (Office of Academic Affairs). We thank the following individuals in the Veterans Administration without whose help neither the conference nor this volume would have been possible: for his support, Dr. James C. Crutcher, Chief Medical Director; for their help, sage advice, useful suggestions, and encouragement, Dr. Marguerite T. Hays (Assistant Chief Medical Director for Research and Development), Dr. Betty G. Uzman (Director, Medical Research Service), Dr. Jack R. Ewalt (Director, Mental Health and Behavioral Science Service), and Dr. Earl X. Freed (Deputy Director, Medical Research Service).

We acknowledge with gratitude the administrative support that we received from Dr. Robert Allen (Special Assistant to the Director, Medical Research Service) who, with endless patience, tact, and persistence, saw to it that arrangements for the conference and the publication of this volume were coordinated and had the approval and support of the many V.A. services involved. Our appreciation also goes to the many individuals in the V.A. whose technical support was indispensible for the success of our venture. They include Ms. Tommie Stapleton and Ms. Karen Seitz (Medical Research Services), Ms. Susan Mailheau (Research Service, V.A.M.C., Sepulveda, California), Mr. Luther C. Peevy (Director, Audio Visual Service), and Mr. William Meredith (Audio Visual Service). Finally, we would like to thank Raven Press for their patience and support of this venture.

Contents

An Overview of Strategies in Schizophrenia Research

1 Three Paradigms for Studies on Schizophrenia
A. Yuwiler

Possible Biological Markers of Schizophrenia

Morphological

29 Structural Brain Abnormalities in Chronic Schizophrenia: Computed Tomography Findings
D. R. Weinberger and R. J. Wyatt

43 Quantitative Neurohistology with the Computer Microscope
S. Matthysse and R. Williams

Physiological

61 Computer-Analyzed Electroencephalogram to Predict the Therapeutic Outcome in Schizophrenia
T. M. Itil

81 Predicting Outcome from Measures of Attention and Autonomic Functioning
T. P. Zahn

107 Abnormal Distribution of Cerebral Activity in Chronic Schizophrenia: A Neurophysiological Interpretation
D. H. Ingvar

Endocrinological

131 Psychoendocrine Research on Schizophrenia: A Need for Reevaluation
J. W. Mason and J. P. Docherty

149 Neuroleptic-Induced Elevations in Serum Prolactin Levels: Etiology and Significance
H. Y. Meltzer, D. Busch, R. So, H. Holcomb, and V. S. Fang

177 Diagnostic Classification and the Endorphin Hypothesis of Schizophrenia: Individual Differences and Pharmacological Strategies
M. S. Buchsbaum, G. C. Davis, and D. P. van Kammen

Biochemical

195 Elevation of Brain Neuroleptic/Dopamine Receptors in Schizophrenia
P. Seeman, T. Lee, E. D. Bird, and W. W. Tourtellotte

209 Biological Concepts of Schizophrenia
F. A. Henn

227 Chronic Schizophrenia—Postmortem Studies
J. E. Kleinman, P. Bridge, F. Karoum, S. Speciale, Jr., R. Staub, S. Zalcman, J. C. Gillin, and R. J. Wyatt

237 Biochemical Correlates of Behavior: What Is a Neurochemist to Measure?
J. R. Perez-Polo, C. E. Beck, and M. Blum

Immunological

249 Immunological Components in Schizophrenia
A. L. Goldstein, J. Rossio, G. I. Kilysaskina, L. E. Emory, J. E. Overall, G. B. Thurman, and J. Hatcher

Clinical Considerations

Vulnerability Markers

269 Chronic Schizophrenia from the Standpoint of Vulnerability
J. Zubin

Patient Selection, Outcome Measurements, and Treatment Strategies

297 Clinical Research Methods Applicable to the Study of Treatment Effects in Chronic Schizophrenic Patients
W. T. Carpenter, Jr.

317 Strategies for Applied Research in Chronic Schizophrenia: Choosing the Right Treatment and Measuring Outcome
P. R. A. May

Undesirable Treatment Side Effects

333 Pharmacological Studies of Tardive Dyskinesia: Implications for Future Research
P. A. Berger and K. L. Davis

353 Prevention of Tardive Dyskinesia and Other Drug-Related Adverse Effects
J. O. Cole

365 Clinical Strategies for Antipsychotic Drug Treatment, Tardive Dyskinesia, and the Training of Research Psychiatrists
J. M. Davis, P. G. Janicak, and G. A. Killian

The Placebo Effect

385 Some Thoughts Concerning the Influence of Environmental Factors and Placebo Treatment on Schizophrenia
E. X. Freed

389 The Placebo Effect: From Control to Experimental Condition
N. R. Schooler

National Resource for Neuropathological Studies

401 A Brain Tissue Resource Center to Promote Research in Schizophrenia
E. D. Bird

Summary

425 New Initiatives in Schizophrenia Research
C. F. Baxter and T. Melnechuk

435 *Subject Index*

Contributors and Participants

Robert Allen, Ph.D.
Special Assistant to the Director
Veterans Administration Central Office
Washington, D.C. 20420

Claude F. Baxter, Ph.D.
Chief, Neurochemistry Laboratories
Veterans Administration Medical Center
Sepulveda, California 91343

Caroline E. Beck, M.S.
Research Associate
Department of Human Biological Chemistry and Genetics
University of Texas Medical Branch
Galveston, Texas 77550

Edward Beck, Ph.D.
Research Psychologist
Veterans Administration Medical Center
Salt Lake City, Utah 84118

Philip A. Berger, M.D.
Assistant Professor
Department of Psychiatry and Behavioral Sciences
Stanford University School of Medicine
Stanford, California 94305
and
Director, Stanford Mental Health Clinical Research Center
Veterans Administration Medical Center
Palo Alto, California 94304

Edward D. Bird, M.D.
Department of Pathology
Harvard University
McLean Hospital
Belmont, Massachusetts 02178

Mariann Blum
Department of Human Biological Chemistry and Genetics
University of Texas Medical Branch
Galveston, Texas 77550

Peter Bridge, M.D.
Adult Psychiatry Branch
Division of Special Mental Health Research
Intramural Research Program
National Institute of Mental Health
Saint Elizabeths Hospital
Washington, D.C. 20032

Walter Armin Brown, M.D.
Associate Professor of Psychiatry
Brown University
Providence Veterans Administration Medical Center
Providence, Rhode Island 02908

Monte S. Buchsbaum, M.D.
Chief, Section on Clinical Psychophysiology
Biological Psychiatry Branch
National Institute of Mental Health
Bethesda, Maryland 20205

Daniel Busch, M.D.
Unit Chief, 10 West Research Unit
Illinois State Psychiatric Institute
Chicago, Illinois 60612

Rosa Canoso, M.D.
Department of Medicine
Harvard Medical School
Coagulation Research Laboratory
Veterans Administration Medical Center
Brockton, Massachusetts 02401

William T. Carpenter, Jr., M.D.
Director
Maryland Psychiatric Research Center
Catonsville, Maryland 21228

Jonathan O. Cole, M.D.
Psychopharmacology Program
McLean Hospital
Belmont, Massachusetts 02178

Joseph Collins, Sc.D.
Assistant Chief, Cooperative Studies Program
Veterans Administration Medical Center
Perry Point, Maryland 21902

James C. Crutcher, M.D.
Chief Medical Director
Veterans Administration Central Office
Washington, D.C. 20420

Glen C. Davis, M.D.
Associate Professor of Psychiatry
University of Tennessee School of Medicine
Memphis, Tennessee 38163

John M. Davis, M.D.
Director of Research
Illinois State Psychiatric Institute
Chicago, Illinois 60612

Kenneth L. Davis, M.D.
Associate Professor of Psychiatry
Mount Sinai School of Medicine
Veterans Administration Medical Center
Bronx, New York 10468

John P. Docherty, M.D.
Staff Psychiatrist
Veterans Administration Medical Center
West Haven, Connecticut 06516; and
Assistant Professor of Psychiatry
Yale University School of Medicine
New Haven, Connecticut 06501

Lee E. Emory, M.D.
Department of Psychiatry
University of Texas Medical Branch
Galveston, Texas 77550

Jack R. Ewalt, M.D.
Director, Mental Health and Behavioral Sciences Services
Veterans Administration Central Office
Washington, D.C. 20420

Victor S. Fang, Ph.D.
Associate Professor of Medicine and Psychiatry
Department of Medicine and Psychiatry
University of Chicago Pritzker School of Medicine
Chicago, Illinois 60637

Earl X. Freed, Ph.D.
Deputy Director
Medical Research Service 151F
Veterans Administration Central Office
Washington, D.C. 20420

Eduard Gfeller, M.D.
Chief, Psychiatry Service
Veterans Administration Medical Center
Gainsville, Florida 32602
and
Professor of Psychiatry and Neuroscience
University of Florida
Gainesville, Florida 32602

J. Christian Gillin, M.D.
Adult Psychiatry Branch
Division of Special Mental Health Research
Intramural Research Program
National Institute of Mental Health
Saint Elizabeths Hospital
Washington, D.C. 20032

Allan L. Goldstein, Ph.D.
Chairman, Department of Biochemistry
The George Washington University School of Medicine
Washington, D.C. 20037

Janelle Hatcher
Medical Technologist
Department of Biochemistry
The George Washington University School of Medicine
Washington, D.C. 20037

Marguerite T. Hays, M.D.
ACDM for Research and Development
Veterans Administration Central Office
Washington, D.C. 20420

Fritz A. Henn, Ph.D., M.D.
Associate Professor of Psychiatry
Neurochemical Research Laboratories
Department of Psychiatry
University of Iowa Hospitals and Clinics
Iowa City, Iowa 52242

John F. Hiatt, M.D.
Assistant Clinical Professor of Psychiatry
University of California, San Francisco School of Medicine
Psychiatry Inpatient Unit (116N)
Veterans Administration Medical Center
San Francisco, California 94121

Henry Holcomb, M.D.
Research Physician
Department of Psychiatry
Yale University Medical School
Connecticut Mental Health Center
New Haven, Connecticut 06519

David H. Ingvar, M.D.
Professor and Chief
Department of Clinical Neurophysiology
University Hospital
S-221 85 Lund, Sweden

Turan M. Itil, M.D.
Research Professor and Director
Division of Biological Psychiatry
New York Medical College
New York, New York 10595
and
Chief, Center for Biological Psychiatry
Veterans Administration Health Care Facility
Montrose, New York 10548

Philip G. Janicak, M.D.
Unit Chief
Illinois State Psychiatric Institute
Chicago, Illinois 60612

David S. Janowsky, M.D.
Staff Physician
Veterans Administration Medical Center
San Diego, California 92161; and
Professor of Psychiatry
University of California, San Diego
La Jolla, California 92093

Farouk Karoum, Ph.D.
Adult Psychiatry Branch
Division of Special Mental Health Research
Intramural Research Program
National Institute of Mental Health
Saint Elizabeths Hospital
Washington, D.C. 20032

Grant A. Killian, M.S.
Research Fellow
Illinois State Psychiatric Institute
Chicago, Illinois 60612

Galina I. Kilysaskina, Ph.D.
Institute of Psychiatry of Academy of Medical Science
Zagorodoe Shosse 2
Moscow, USSR

Joel E. Kleinman, M.D., Ph.D.
Staff Psychiatrist
Adult Psychiatry Branch
Division of Special Mental Health Research
Intramural Research Program
National Institute of Mental Health
Saint Elizabeths Hospital
Washington, D.C. 20032

Tyrone Lee, Ph.D.
Assistant Professor
Departments of Pharmacology and Psychiatry
Medical Sciences Building
University of Toronto
Toronto, Canada

John W. Mason, M.D.
Senior Researcher
Veterans Administration Medical Center
West Haven, Connecticut 06516; and
Professor of Psychiatry
Yale University School of Medicine
New Haven, Connecticut 06501

Stephen Matthysse, Ph.D.
Associate Psychobiologist
Mailman Research Center
McLean Hospital
Belmont, Massachusetts 02178

Philip R. A. May, M.D.
Director, Health Services Research and Development Laboratory
Veterans Administration Medical Center, Brentwood; and
Professor of Psychiatry
Neuropsychiatric Institute
Center for Health Sciences
University of California, Los Angeles
Los Angeles, California 90037

Theodore Melnechuk
Research Associate
Western Behavioral Sciences Institute
La Jolla, California 92037; and
Lecturer
Department of Neurosciences
University of California, San Diego
San Diego, California 92122

Herbert Y. Meltzer, M.D.
Professor
Department of Psychiatry
University of Chicago Pritzker School of Medicine
Chicago, Illinois 60637

William Meredith
Audio Visuals Service
Veterans Administration Central Office
Washington, D.C. 20040

Loren Mosher, M.D.
Chief, Center for Studies in Schizophrenia
National Institute of Mental Health
Rockville, Maryland 20857

Henry A. Nasrallah, M.D.
Chief, Psychiatric Service
Veterans Administration Medical Center
Iowa City, Iowa 52240

John E. Overall, Ph.D.
Professor
Department of Psychiatry and Behavioral Science
Baylor College of Medicine
Houston, Texas 77025

J. Regino Perez-Polo, Ph.D.
Associate Professor
Department of Human Biological Chemistry and Genetics
University of Texas Medical Branch
Galveston, Texas 77550

Jeffrey Rossio, Ph.D.
Department of Microbiology and Immunology
Wright State University School of Medicine
Dayton, Ohio 45431

Charles Savage, M.D.
Chief, Psychiatric Service
Veterans Administration Medical Center
Baltimore, Maryland 21218

Nina R. Schooler, Ph.D.
Psychopharmacology Research Branch
National Institute of Mental Health
Rockville, Maryland 20857

Philip Seeman, M.D., Ph.D.
Professor and Chairman
Department of Pharmacology
University of Toronto
Toronto, Ontario, Canada

Karen Seitz
Information Specialist
Medical Research Service
Veterans Administration Central Office
Washington, D.C. 20420

Man Mohan Singh, M.B., B.S., M.R.C.P., M.R.C. Psych, D.P.M.
Chief, Schizophrenia Program
Veterans Administration Medical Center
Memphis, Tennessee 38104

Rebecca So, Ph.D.
Research Scientist II
Illinois State Psychiatric Institute
Chicago, Illinois 60612

Samuel Speciale, Jr., Ph.D.
Adult Psychiatry Branch
Division of Special Mental Health Research
National Institute of Mental Health
Saint Elizabeths Hospital
Washington, D.C. 20032

Richard Staub, B.A.
Adult Psychiatry Branch
Division of Special Mental Health Research
Intramural Research Program
National Institute of Mental Health
Saint Elizabeths Hospital
Washington, D.C. 20032

Gary B. Thurman, Ph.D.
Associate Research Professor
Department of Biochemistry
The George Washington University School of Medicine
Washington, D.C. 20037

Wallace W. Tourtellotte, M.D., Ph.D.
Chief Neurology Service
Department of Neurology
Wadsworth Hospital
Los Angeles, California 90025

Betty G. Uzman, M.D.
Director, Medical Research Service
Veterans Administration Central Office
Washington, D.C. 20420

Daniel P. van Kammen, M.D.
Unit Chief, Section on Neuropsychopharmacology
National Institute of Mental Health
Bethesda, Maryland 20205

Daniel R. Weinberger, M.D.
Staff Psychiatrist
Adult Psychiatry Branch
Division of Special Mental Health Research
National Institute of Mental Health
Saint Elizabeths Hospital
Washington, D.C. 20032

Roser Williams, M.D.
Mailman Research Center
McLean Hospital
Belmont, Massachusetts 02178

Richard Jed Wyatt, M.D.
Chief, Adult Psychiatry Branch
Division of Special Mental Health Research
National Institute of Mental Health
Saint Elizabeths Hospital
Washington, D.C. 20032

Arthur Yuwiler, Ph.D.
Chief, Neurobiochemistry Research Laboratory T-85
Veterans Administration Medical Center, Brentwood
Los Angeles, California 90073

Theodore P. Zahn, Ph.D.
Research Psychologist
Laboratory of Psychology and Psychopathology
National Institute of Mental Health
Bethesda, Maryland 20205

Steven Zalcman, M.D.
Adult Psychiatry Branch
Division of Special Mental Health Research
Intramural Research Program
National Institute of Mental Health
Saint Elizabeths Hospital
Washington, D.C. 20032

Joseph Zubin, Ph.D.
Research Career Scientist
Veterans Administration Medical Center
Pittsburgh, Pennsylvania 15206

Perspectives in Schizophrenia Research,
edited by C. Baxter and T. Melnechuk.
Raven Press, New York, 1980.

Three Paradigms for Studies on Schizophrenia

Arthur Yuwiler

Neurobiochemistry Research Laboratory T-85, Veterans Administration Medical Center Brentwood, Los Angeles, California 90073; and Department of Psychiatry and Brain Research Institute, University of California at Los Angeles, Los Angeles, California 90024

LAYPERSON'S SUMMARY

Three paradigms for studies on schizophrenia are presented: the Gerard paradigm, concerned with diagnosis, the McGuire-Raleigh-Brammer paradigm, concerned with treatment, and the Schapiro paradigm, concerned with etiology.

The Gerard paradigm is based on the assumption that the diagnostic label "schizophrenia" encompasses a variety of diseases of diverse etiology which share final common pathways leading to abnormal affect and mentation. The paradigm attempts to dissociate these component diseases by seeking biological and behavioral commonalities, in addition to clinical symptomatology, between groups of patients. In operation this is accomplished by clustering subjects in accordance with data derived from a variety of biological and behavioral tests. The utility of these clusters is evaluated by their success in facilitating predictions of clinical response to various therapeutic modalities. Some of the problems in test selection, patient sampling, data analysis, and research logistics of this paradigm are discussed and compared with alternate strategies.

The McGuire-Raleigh-Brammer paradigm is concerned with factors contributing to idiosyncratic drug response. More specifically, the paradigm attempts to document and evaluate the influence of social role and environment on drug response using social units of vervet monkeys. In addition, the paradigm is concerned with identifying state- and trait-dependent biological concomitants of social role which might help predict drug sensitivity. Data are presented indicating that social role influences behavioral response to some agents, that drug-induced alterations in the behavior of socially important members of the group affect the behavior of entire social units, and that some biological variables in peripheral tissues correlate with social status in vervet monkey society.

The Schapiro paradigm seeks to determine if neonatal stress exposure leads to biological changes which could interact with genetic propensity and lead to manifest disease. More specifically, the paradigm proposes that chronic exposure of neonate to stress-induced hormones might disrupt normal ontogeny by forcing premature development of hormone-sensitive enzymes. Such precocious development might weaken the tight interdigitation between metabolic systems leading to increased vulnerability of the organism to environmental stimuli. Data are presented showing that treating neonatal rats with stress-released hormones of the adrenal gland alters the development of some brain transmitter systems as well as metabolic processes involved in their regulation.

INTRODUCTION

Medicine is concerned with diagnosis, treatment, etiology, preventive medicine, and, in lieu of effective treatment, custodial care. Its goal is the treatment and prevention of disease and all else are necessary means towards that end. I would like to briefly present several experimental paradigms concerned with diagnosis, treatment, and etiology.

GERARD PARADIGM

The primary function of diagnosis in medicine is identification of treatment groups. Its secondary function is identification for the sake of communication. Diagnosis is essentially a type of classification and, like classification generally, depends on enumeration of relevant features. The choice of what is deemed "relevant" determines the utility of classification. For example, a classification of the animal kingdom based on color is perhaps as reasonable as a classification based on reproductive mechanism, but the former has less utility for biology.

In medicine, presenting symptoms are initially taken as the relevant items in establishing diagnosis, and these items are subsequently clustered into syndromes so as to distinguish variant disorders. The specific items comprising the syndrome are weighted in accordance with frequency and assumed relevance to etiology or prognosis, and this weighting changes with additional information. Such weightings are particularly influenced by information, arising from medical research, related to etiology frequently leading to the identification of new disease states. Thus the number of identified diseases in a 19th century textbook of medicine is considerably smaller than in a contemporary one, and their identification is correspondingly less definitive. Indeed, medical research has identified some variables so closely related to etiology that they make for diagnosis without recourse to symptomatology at all. A positive Wassermann reaction cannot be ignored even in the asymptomatic subject, and biochemical abnormalities in amniotic cells permit a diagnosis even before the very organs to be affected are formed.

Two basic medical strategies are implicit in this simple analysis. The first, and most common, derives from the assumption that the clinical diagnosis, based on presenting symptoms, defines an etiologically homogeneous population. This assumption leads to a search for more objective or efficient measures confirming the diagnosis, and the success of these measures must necessarily be judged by concurrence with the diagnosis. This has two implications: first, the measure cannot do more than completely correspond with the diagnosis; and second, measures only partly corresponding with diagnosis are deemed less important than those corresponding completely. Thus, if a biochemical abnormality occurs in only 10% of a schizophrenic population, it is of little interest even though it occurs in only 0.01% of "matched" controls, whereas a measure showing a 100% correspondence with diagnosis is of great interest even though it occurs in 10% of the general population.

The second approach, first explicated and used deliberately by R. W. Gerard (14) (and hence termed the "Gerard paradigm"), derives from the assumption that similar symptoms may occur through different mechanisms and that clinical diagnosis may encompass diseases of diverse etiology. In order to dissect component subpopulations from a larger group, Gerard proposed a Q-sort, clustering patients in a multidimensional matrix on the basis of the results of a variety of biological, psychosocial, and behavioral measures (12,13).

This approach is illustrated by the idealized diagram in Fig. 1 in which the columns represent tests and the rows, subjects. It is apparent from this figure that categorical features of schizophrenia common to all subjects have little value for this type of analysis. Rather, one of the criteria for variable selection is that of heterogeneity within the population studied. Thus, in contrast to the selection procedure used when etiological homogeneity is assumed, the biological abnormality occuring in 10% of the schizophrenic population and 0.01% of controls is of greater interest to the Gerard approach than is that found in

IDEALIZED CLUSTER DIAGRAM

TEST \ PATIENT	A	B	C	D	E	F	…	M
1	-	-	+	+	-	-		+
2	-	-	+	+	-	-		+
3	+	+	-	-	-	+		-
4	+	+	-	-	-	+		-
5	-	-	+	+	-	-		+
6	+	+	-	-	-	+		-

FIG. 1. Idealized cluster diagram. Patients A, B, and F would fall into one group while C, D, and M would form another.

100% of the schizophrenics. In this manner, variables such as the activities of platelet monoamine oxidase (40) and serum creatine phosphokinase (31), or even the urinary concentrations of bufotenine (37) and 3,4-dimethoxyphenethylamine (9), are all of potential interest precisely because they are reported to be abnormal in some but not all schizophrenics.

Selecting Variables for Measurement

Most test variables are selected because they relate to some hypothesis of causation, and their function, whether single or multiple etiologies are assumed, is to test the hypothesis. However, in the framework of the unitary hypothesis the test is measured by correspondence with diagnosis, whereas in the Gerard strategy it is measured by utility in partitioning the diseased population into distinct subgroups. The various monoaminergic theories of schizophrenia, for example, are competing hypotheses if schizophrenia has a single etiology, and the experimental question becomes which hypothesis corresponds best with diagnosis. If multietiologies are assumed, however, they are complementary hypotheses, none of which are expected to coincide with global symptoms, but any of which may define a separate disease. This is the case, for example, in mental retardation which cannot be biochemically characterized by a generalized defect in phenylalanine hydroxylase, a failure to decarboxylate branched-chain amino acids, or an extra bit of chromosome, although each identifies a specific form of retardation.

Schizophrenia research obviously encompasses many disciplines, and although all disciplines are interrelated, a lexicon of disciplinary equivalents is yet to come. The set of measures used in the Gerard paradigm must therefore be drawn from many disciplines and couched in the units of those disciplines. This poses several practical problems. Biochemical data are largely parametric with a true zero and a continuum of intervals between numbers. Physiological variables such as heart rate are limited to integers. Rating scales are ordinal without a true zero or equal intervals between numbers. Diagnosis is categorical and lacking either a zero, equal intervals between numbers, or even numbers themselves. Variables also differ in their time frame. Social history is invariant, the concentration of a constituent in blood reflects its status at the time of blood drawing, and a urinary measure, at its simplest, yields values integrated over time. Because the Gerard paradigm is dependent on developing patient clusters, these differences in the very nature of the variables employed in that clustering pose problems for the statistician in developing commensurate units which normalize such data without introducing bias.

Still another level of complexity results from trait- and state-dependent characteristics of variables. Some measures maintain constancy within an individual over time and circumstance; others vary widely. In the first category are both primary genetic variables which make for qualitative distinctions between populations as well as quantitative derivatives of the integrated actions of multiple genetic factors. In the second category are the quantitative variations resulting from the interplay between homeostatic mechanisms and environmental challenge. Probing for genetic contributions to the schizophrenias entails a search for qualitative differences such as the aberrant phenylalanine hydroxylase in phenylketonuria. A search for environmental contributions to the schizophrenias targets quantitative variations in adaptive processes. The two of course are interdependent, for genetic expression depends on existing environment and environmental adaptation still requires a genetic substrate. If phenylalanine were a much rarer amino acid in the diet, phenylketonurics might neither excrete phenylketones marking the defect nor show manifest symptoms and the clinical disease would not exist. Similarly, blood serotonin appears to be a trait-dependent marker perhaps reflecting genetic control over platelet half-life, although blood serotonin concentration can be transitorily altered by pharmacological tryptophan loading.

In contrast to these are ACTH, glucocorticoids, growth hormone, and prolactin which respond to environmental challenge and indicate the physiologic and metabolic mechanisms required for adaptation to that challenge. Both hormone release and their adaptive sequelae are state dependent, as is the magnitude of their changes.

In terms of the Gerard paradigm these correlations suggest that repeated measures may be required to establish the nature of the variables under study and that, in some instances, individual variances may be as important to analysis as the measures themselves. Based on these considerations, repeated measures of a variable over time should be included in the Gerard battery and variance in the measure included as well. Further, both static and active measurements may be required. The rise in blood tryptophan after a tryptophan load, or the magnitude of ACTH changes after a repeated stressor, may reveal more about adaptive mechanism than the static measures alone.

Understanding the nature of the variables under study is of obvious importance even to guard against spurious classifications based on disease-linked changes in state-dependent variables. A common example derives from urinary studies (41,42). Conventionally, urinary products are normalized with respect to concentration (quantity/unit volume), rate (quantity/unit time), or some secondary index of organ or body mass.

The daily excretion of creatinine is considered to be directly proportional to muscle mass, and expression of urinary concentrations on a creatinine basis frequently has been used to normalize excretion to body size. Because muscle mass is 36 to 40% of body weight, this is a reasonable correction factor, as long as the relationship between muscle mass and body weight remains constant and provided that the excreted compound is produced by muscle or in proportion to muscle. These conditions are not always met. Hormonal activities may be quite independent of muscle mass; some compounds are excreted in a volume-dependent manner and others in a time-dependent fashion, so that results may be misinterpreted if any basal measure is indiscriminately used without first examining the behavior of both the basal measure and the variable in question and without considering the implications in taking their ratio. For example, urinary creatinine excretion by nonparanoid schizophrenics in the Joint Research Project on Schizophrenia at the University of Michigan and the Ypsilanti State Hospital was negatively correlated with the length of hospitalization. Since creatinine for all groups correlated with muscle mass indices, the creatinine-hospitalization correlation was interpreted as representing a gradual muscular deterioration among the nonparanoid schizophrenics which was not shared by paranoids or hospitalized nonschizophrenics. Indeed, many of the nonschizophrenics, particularly the alcoholics, physically improved; muscle mass increased and creatinine excretion correlated positively with length of hospitalization. Consider, now, the case of some metabolite excreted in such manner that all diagnostic groups eliminate identical quantities per unit time. If comparisons are made only on a creatinine basis, nonparanoid schizophrenics will appear to excrete relatively large amounts because of the decreased creatinine excretion and to differ from other groups. If metabolite production is primarily in muscle or proportional to muscle, this result would be suggestive of a metabolic difference between populations. If the excreted compound is not a muscle metabolite, however, or if the rate of its production is not normally proportional to muscle mass, then a misleading relationship has been introduced by sole reliance on, and misuse of, the creatinine ratio. Similarly, daily urine volume and even urinary creatinine are influenced by emotional state. Metabolites excreted in a volume-dependent fashion are thereby also excreted in parallel with those emotional states influencing urine volume, and this secondary relationship to emotional state and to diagnosis might well be noted and pursued, while the less dramatic primary relationship is overlooked.

Ideally, the measures for use in the Gerard paradigm should be selected because of empirical or theoretical relevance to schizophrenia and because of variance within the schizophrenic population. Both passive and active measures may be required as may multiple determinations.

Weighting Importance and Limiting Variables

Once variables are selected, a decision must be made as to whether measures should be weighted with respect to their assumed importance in the disease. Such weightings are automatic in most of medicine and keyed to complaint. The cardiologist, examining for coronary disease, is generally uninterested in the occurrence of buccal infections, whereas these may be of chief importance to the oral surgeon faced with a tooth extraction. Similarly, it might be argued that a presenting symptom such as paranoia should be given greater weight in defining subpopulation than urinary creatinine, platelet monoamine oxidase, or attention span. On the other hand, the clinical feature of the disease may be a common product of diverse dysfunctions, and excessive weighting might obscure these underlying causes. The choice is thus between risking a group separation which merely reflects initial conceptual bias and generating groups unrelated to schizophrenia itself. For this reason, it may be necessary to assess the stability of the groupings computed with and without weightings and to examine the relative importance of specific variables in subgroup formation. The latter additionally furnishes direction for more specific etiological studies. Even if consciously avoided, however, weightings may be inadvertently introduced by inclusion of related and redundant variables in the analysis. Partly because of this, the number of variables in the test battery should be kept relatively small and should be generic rather than repetitive.

An even stronger reason for limiting the number of variables is to prevent submerging both the investigation and the investigators in a deluge of data that must be screened for meaning. By definition, 100 numerical comparisons between sets of normally distributed numbers will lead to 5 chance differences "significant" at the 0.05 level. This will occur whether the numbers derive from 100 replications of one experiment or single comparisons in 100 experiments, whether carried out by one man or 100, or whether experiments are carried out sequentially or concurrently. Chance differences are to be expected in multivariate studies involving large numbers of variables. Deciding whether they result from the vagaries of chance or the imperatives of nature requires a tedious and careful analysis of the stability of the findings and the pattern of expected cross-correlations. Obviously, the larger the ratio of chance correlations to meaningful ones, the harder the task becomes, so that the fewer and more potentially relevant the variables, the better.

The Gerard paradigm then requires sufficient background information to permit judicious selection of measures relevant to disease. Further, it requires minimizing the selection of measures secondary to dietary, drug, or environmental differences between diseased and comparison populations. Following from this, the strategy requires a population that can be maintained under conditions controlling environmental artifacts. In addition, it requires populations representative of the larger diseased population and not one preselected from it by social, economic, or logistic factors that may later be confused with attributes of the disease.

Environmental and Sociological Controls

The need for controlling disease-associated environmental factors such as drugs, dietary peculiarities, disease-related shifts in sleep-wake cycles, physical activity, and shared intercurrent infections within confined populations has been extensively documented (19,21) and needs no further elaboration. The Gerard paradigm must be carried out under conditions adequately controlling such factors if the resultant dissection into disparate etiologies is not to degenerate into a haphazard division of groups according to environmental artifact. The possible influence of sociological artifact on categorization is more subtle. Voluntary commitment preselects for patients sufficiently disturbed by their problem to seek medical help and sufficiently intact to find it. Involuntary commitment preselects those who disturb others. A middle group may be excluded and the behavioral characteristics of the extremes may weight their division into subgroups. In addition, admission to a particular medical facility involves many factors including those of economics, personal status, and group affiliations. The biological, sociological, and psychiatric correlates of these socioeconomic variables can easily be mistaken for the sociopathology of the disease. In Gerard's Q-sort study carried out in a midwestern hospital, for example, 71% of the experimental population came from families in Hollingshead and Redlich's social classes 4 and 5 (17). Furthermore, 21% were first generation offspring from eastern and southern European immigrants and 30% were from families of southern Negroes who had recently migrated north. Compared to general accepted "norms," the families of the hospitalized population appeared to show considerable sociopathology, but when Helen Fritz, the project sociologist, corrected for the ethnic, cultural, and socioeconomic composition of the population, the bulk of the "sociopathology" was discovered to be more apparent than real. Without such recognition and appropriate correction, groups may be skewed in accordance with ethnic and subcultural customs having little to do with etiology.

In the same project Dr. Charles Ingram *(unpublished observation)* detected a high incidence of physical dysplasias in the hospitalized population as a whole. Among these was a decrease in the androgeny score, an anthropological bone measure devised by Tanner (38) consisting of three times the shoulder width (biacromial distance) minus the pelvic width (bi-iliac distance). This measure was originally devised to distinguish male from female body builds independent of dietary or other environmental influence. Using this measure, Rey and Coppen (33) reported that schizophrenics had a more feminine body build than did normals. This was essentially confirmed by Ingram. Low androgeny scores were not unique to the schizophrenics, however, for there was a high incidence among hospitalized sociopaths as well. Further, a low androgeny score correlated both with the number of hospital readmissions and the length of hospitalization. Based on the correlation matrix, it appeared that the high incidence of low androgeny scores in schizophrenics could best be explained as a sociological artifact. Every group has its scapegoat and election to that office is often by idiosyncratic personality or form. The fat kid and the skinny kid both have their interpersonal troubles, and a feminine physique, especially in lower socioeconomic groups, may identify a victim. In such groups the consequences of dysplasias may be testing, teasing, and horseplay. A normal learns to bear these with acceptable resignation or anger, or to turn them aside. The schizophrenic may well respond in a manner leading to difficulties with authorities and eventually to hospital commitment. Such a subject is treated and discharged only to return to the same socioeconomic environment still carrying the same anthropometric problem, and the cycle repeats until the subject is a permanent resident of the hospital system. Over time, the hospitals gradually fill with such social rejects, and the attributes responsible for hospitalization become accepted as attributes of the disease.

Essentially, these are all problems in dissociating epiphenomena from phenomena and normally are handled by concurrent examination of appropriate controls. Controls are required in the Gerard paradigm too, although, in principle, the strategy of dividing patients into subgroups could be done with patients alone. Establishing appropriate controls, however, is more easily said than done, particularly when dealing with schizophrenia, for what is an appropriate control group for subjects who have been hospitalized for extended periods of time—and exposed to bromides, barbiturates, phenothiazines, hydrazides, shock treatment, hydrotherapy, hypnotherapy, carbon dioxide and insulin coma, psychotherapy, neglect, inactivity, minimal diet, and probably intercurrent and chronic endemic infections, not to mention exposure to social rejection and neglect? Further, controls are used to eliminate, or control for, contributions to the results from sources other than the pertinent variables. But the number and kinds of factors to be controlled increase in proportion to the obscurity of etiology, as does the difficulty in determining whether a disease aspect is an ancillary or etiologically linked feature. Paranoid schizophrenics differed in many ways from the nonparanoid schizophrenics in the studies carried out at the University of Michigan and Ypsilanti State Hospital. Should these differences be regarded as due to different etiologies or to different expressions of a single etiology? Should the different activity level of the paranoid schizophrenic be considered a variable to be controlled or an identifying feature of the disease? In order to at least minimally control for hospitalization, social rejection, population selection, and the like, control groups in Gerard's project included nonpsychotic hospitalized subjects (largely sociopaths), psychotic, nonschizophrenic subjects (largely chronic brain syndrome patients), chronically institutionalized subjects, and "normal" hospital personnel. Even these, however, may be inadequate.

Q-Sort Group Validation

Finally, the Gerard paradigm requires some external criteria to validate the medical significance of the populations separated by the Q-sort. The reason for this is obvious. Any population can be separated into subgroups by any set of variables—hair color, length of nose, high school grades, belt size—and it is essential that there be some means of assessing the utility of the grouping so obtained. It has such utility only if it provides clues to etiology, predicts response to therapy and drugs, or predicts clinical course. Correspondingly, the initial Q-sort is a first step which must be followed by a careful detailing of treatment response, clinical course, and a search for further evidence suggestive of etiological deficits.

With the exception of this last aspect, the various problems and complexities discussed above are not unique to the Gerard paradigm but are inherent in clinical and preclinical studies generally. They are merely more obvious at the onset and more easily detected in the results. The laws of chance operate in the test tube as well as on the ward. Social preselection occurs whether recognized or not, disease-associated artifact contributes to conflicts in the literature of all fields of medicine, and the problem of relating clinical, biological, and behavioral findings is a general one in medical science. The Gerard paradigm simply offers a more coherent and direct approach to the problem of revealing subgroups within a global classification than do results from a multitude of single studies. Its structure also permits detection and specification of subtle sources of artifact that otherwise might linger interminably as conflicting reports in the literature. Further, it provides a means of clarifying the significance of differences between groups and of linking behavioral and biological observations on diseased and normal populations. It does, however, suffer from rigidity, for once the Q-sort has been initiated, a new test cannot be lightly introduced nor old ones dropped without endangering the fabric of the design. Also, the design is somewhat fragile and sensitive to missing data, to variance in assay procedures, and to the scheduling of testing.

On the practical level, the commitments of time, staff, and technical resources required by the Q-sort strategy, as well as its dependence on a stable and well-screened population of subjects, require a facility or consort of facilities geared to screen, select, and maintain a specified number of subjects under controlled conditions for specified periods of time. Testing can be carried out in two ways. On the one hand, testing facilities can be established on site. Although this is the usual pattern, it is expensive and limiting since few single facilities can acquire the number and kind of personnel and equipment needed to carry out all the procedures that might be desired. An alternate procedure is to limit on-site facilities to those for the relatively few tests and procedures requiring direct access to patients while carrying out the bulk of analysis by collaboration with interested investigators already engaged in related studies throughout the country. Although this presents a logistic problem, it has the advantage of recruiting a wide range of expertise at comparatively minor cost.

In summary, Gerard proposed the Q-sort strategy some 20 years ago and attempted to apply it towards defining the nosology of schizophrenia when relatively little was known about the biology of the disease and few tools were available for verification of derived subgroups. Although the bulk of the results of that study are largely unpublished, owing chiefly to the mass of data obtained, seven subgroups of schizophrenics were extracted; their medical significance has yet to be determined. In the ensuing 20 years a great deal has been learned about the biology of the brain, and with this knowledge has come some insight into the biology of the mind and behavior. Of equal importance, pharmacological and behavioral tools which can be used to determine the utility of the approach have become available. The time may now be appropriate for a reapplication of Gerard's approach.

McGUIRE-RALEIGH-BRAMMER PARADIGM

The Gerard paradigm is concerned with diagnosis. The McGuire-Raleigh-Brammer paradigm is concerned with therapy and takes its name from the clinical ethological studies of M. McGuire which have been extended into biochemical-behavioral studies by M. Raleigh and G. Brammer in our laboratory and the Laboratory for Biosocial Pharmacology.

These studies are concerned with the influence of social environment and social role on drug response. It is generally accepted that individuals differ widely in sensitivity to drugs and that individual response can be modified by expectation, as in placebo responses, momentary physical and emotional state, and social environment. More phenothiazine is usually required to break a psychotic episode than control it, and equivalent doses of alcohol consumed during a tense diplomatic dinner produce less inebriation than when taken in solitude. The intraindividual variations suggest that sociology as well as genetics affect metabolism, drug disposition, receptor sensitivity, and neural transactions. The McGuire-Raleigh-Brammer paradigm is concerned with documenting that interaction, establishing markers predictive of drug response, and, ultimately, explicating the mechanisms involved.

The approach assumes that behavior is a manifestation of state- and trait-dependent neural interactions, that these interactions influence, and are influenced by, the biology of peripheral organs, and that the status of both central and peripheral biology determines response to therapeutic interventions, be they psychosocial or pharmacological. These premises have led to two sorts of experiments: one examining the effect of social setting and social role in drug response, and the other concerned both with apportioning transmitter contributions to specific behaviors and with using these behaviors to test for peripheral correlates of such transmitter activity.

The bulk of these studies have been carried out in the vervet monkey which, like man, lives in a social network but in a simpler, more stable one in which the individual plays a limited number of social roles. Their behavioral repertoire is large but not excessive, well characterized, and can be quantified. Colony life is partly oriented around a dominant alpha-male whose position is based largely on overt behavior and not size, strength, or aggression *per se.* The social position of other group members similarly seems to reflect their individual behavior.

Effect of Social Setting and Social Role on Drug Responses in Vervet Monkey

The characteristics of this social system are well suited for experimentally examining some major questions about social-pharmacological interaction. First, is it true that pharmacological response is tempered by social environment? Does the alpha-male, for example, respond differently from other males to pharmacological agents? If so, is this because of the biological consequences of the social role or because of the innate biological characteristics which determined assumption of that role? That is, is the altered response due to state-dependent or innate trait-dependent factors? Do these trait- and state-dependent factors alter the biology of peripheral tissue? Can these be detected and used to identify like characteristics in man where they may be hidden by the complexity of human society and the consequent multiplicity of social roles played by the individual? Further, can such markers identify appropriate therapeutic interventions and predict clinical response? Because social systems are interactive, does a successful therapeutic intervention alter the behavior of significant others, and do such alterations, in their turn, modify the response of the subject to subsequent therapy? That is, to what extent must therapy be group oriented rather than individual oriented?

Our current studies provide tentative answers to some of these questions and, hopefully, will furnish information on the others as well. Our data suggest, for example, that social role does indeed influence pharmacological response. In one set of experiments we examined the behavioral effects of a battery of pharmacological agents affecting the serotonin system, among which was tryptophan. Vervets given tryptophan (Fig. 2) show an increase in behaviors associated with socialization and a decrease in behaviors accompanying fear or anxiety. Although the response is general among all animals, the magnitude of the response varies and appears related to social rank. This is illustrated in Fig. 3 which compares the changes in one of these behaviors, approach, in alpha-males ($N = 6$) and males of intermediate status ($N = 12$) as a function of treatment times. Approach is defined as moving within 0.5 meters of another animal and remaining within that distance for 5 sec or longer. Behavioral observations were made 2 hr after daily i.p. administrations of tryptophan 20 mg/kg. As seen from this figure, both groups exhibited the same basal frequency of this behavior and the frequency increased for both upon tryptophan treatment. The magnitude of the increase, however, was significantly greater for the alpha-males. Nor are the effects of treatment limited to the medicated animal alone, particularly when that animal is a "significant other." This is illustrated in Fig. 4, which depicts the changes in the ongoing behavior of six groups of six animals each when either an alpha-male or a male of indifferent rank was treated daily with *p*-chlorophenylalanine (PCPA) at a dose of 80 mg/kg. This agent is a long-acting irreversible inhibitor of serotonin biosynthesis, and, as might be expected, it produces behavioral changes which are largely opposite in direction from those produced by tryptophan. Animals treated with PCPA, for example, are more withdrawn, restless, vigilant, irritable, and aggressive than under baseline conditions (see Fig. 2). Such conduct by an alpha-male markedly disturbed social grooming behavior by untreated animals and the disruption increased with time. In contrast, the agitated behavior of a male, other than alpha, initially produced a small transient interruption of group behavior which quickly normalized despite continued aberrant behavior by the treated animal.

Although our data are more limited, treatment of the entire group produces

	TREATMENT				
	TRYPT	PCPA	5-HTP	CHLORG	PCPA+5-HTP
	CRITERIA				
5HT	△	▽	△	△	△
5HT-CA	△	▽	△ ○	△ ○	△ ○
CA-5HT	△	▽	▽ ○	▽ ○	▽ ○
CA-some 5HT	○	▽	▽	▽	▽
Not 5HT	○	○			
	BEHAVIORS				
GROOMING	△	▽	△	△	△
APPROACH	△	▽	○	△	△
REST	△	▽	○	○	○
EAT	△	▽	○	○	○
LOCOMOTION	▲	▼	○	○	○
SOLITARY	▲	▼	○	▲	▼
AVOID	▲	▼	○	▲	▼
VIGILANCE	▲	▼	▼	▼	○
AGGRESSION	○	▼	▼	○	▽
HUDDLE	○	▽	○	○	○
SEX	○	○	○	○	○

FIG. 2. Summary of behavioral effects of pharmacological agents. The upper portion of the figure outlines the criteria for assigning transmitter contribution to a behavior. The apex of the triangle points in the direction of expected change if serotonin is arbitrarily taken as increasing a behavior. A circle designates no effect on the behavior. The lower portion of the figure shows the observed statistically significant ($p < 0.05$) behavior changes accompanying treatment of vervet monkeys in social groups. To maintain continuity with the pattern for criteria, all changes produced by tryptophan point up; filled triangles, however, designate an observed change in the opposite direction from that initiated by the triangle. Compounds were administered i.p., daily over a 2-week period. Behavioral observations were made 2 hr after treatment. The dosages employed were L-tryptophan (20 mg/kg); DL-*p*-chlorophenylalanine (PCPA) (180 mg/kg); L-5-hydroxytryptophan (5-HTP) (40 mg/kg); chlorgyline (10 mg/kg). In the last column PCPA was given for 2 weeks followed by concurrent PCPA and 5-HTP over the subsequent 2-week period.

alterations in social structure which appear to continue for some time after treatment. For example, when the entire group was given tryptophan, social bonds appeared to increase and the behavior of all animals seemed more easygoing and accepting. The alpha-male began to tolerate normally unacceptable behavior, such as beta-males sampling preferred foods, and the epsilon-animal,

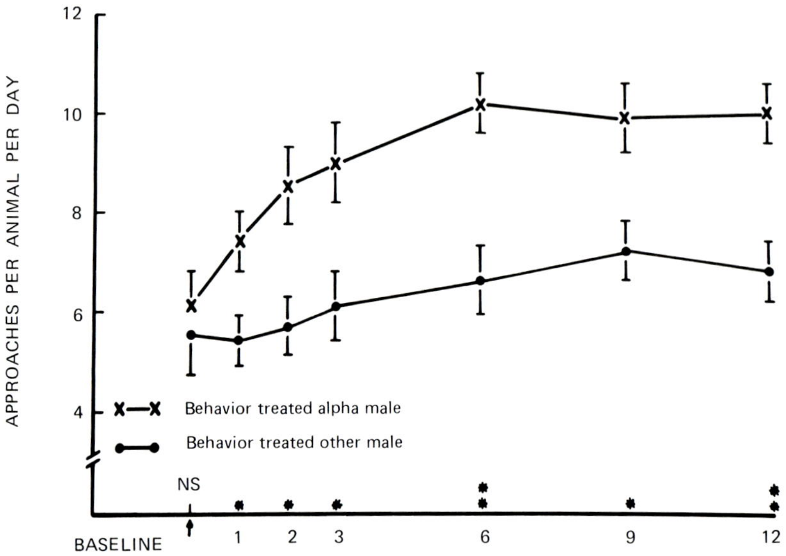

FIG. 3. Alterations in approach behavior produced by tryptophan administration to alpha- and non-alpha-male vervet monkeys. Animals were maintained in open colonies and treated daily with i.p. L-tryptophan (20 mg/kg). Behavioral observations were made 2 hr after treatment. The integer on the axis denote days. Asterisks indicate statistically significant ($p < 0.05$) differences between groups. Bars denote standard errors.

who usually remains outside the group structure, received group acceptance and participated in social grooming. This cohesiveness appeared to last beyond the time that the behaviors of singly treated animals revert to normal.

Social Factors and Drug Responses: Possible Relationships to Man

While these results are preliminary, their potential application to man is clear. Who is treated and in which social context may be important to the therapeutic efficacy of the "what" he is treated with. Additionally, untreated members within a social unit may also respond to the pharmacological treatment of a group member, and that interaction and its consequences are also of importance to therapy. The situation, then, is much like that described for impairment of function caused by brain lesions, in which not only the size and the location of the lesion determine the extent of disability, but also to whom it occurs and the social surroundings of that individual.

In order to make such data applicable to man, objective measures of the factors involved in the expression of psychological and social role are required. However, human society is so complex and the individual's role in that society so variable that internal and external status may be hard to define. That ancient statesman, Pericles, reportedly remarked that while Athens ruled the world

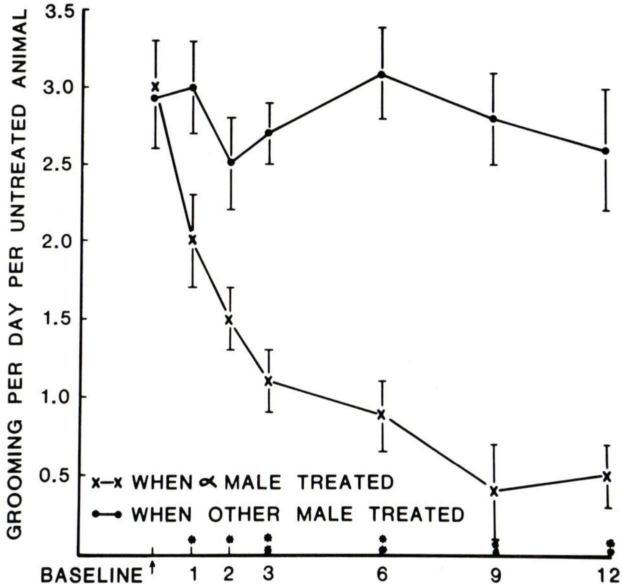

FIG. 4. Effects of drug treatment on behaviors of nontreated vervet monkeys maintained in social groups. The axis denotes the grooming activity of initiated monkeys maintained in colony conditions when either an alpha- or non-alpha male was treated daily with *p*-chlorophenylalanine (80 mg/kg) over a 2-week period. The bars denote standard errors. The numerals along the ordinate indicate days of treatment while the asterisks indicate significant differences in group grooming behavior.

and he ruled Athens, his wife ruled him and his infant son ruled her. If therapeutic response is modified by social milieu and internal image, would Pericles, the general, respond differently from Pericles, the husband, or would the constancy of internal self-image and its associated biochemistry produce the same results in both situations? To answer this, we have sought for state- and trait-dependent markers of social status in peripheral tissues of monkeys in the belief that equivalent measures in man might help predict therapeutic response. Two kinds of measures on monkeys may be applicable to man. The first are behavioral ethological signals of the kind used by McGuire and Polsky (29) in their studies predicting clinical outcome of manic-depressive subjects, for although the behavioral vocabulary of man and monkey differ, some translation between them is possible. The second are biological markers of social rank and social behaviors since both man and monkey probably share many basic biological attributes. Our studies in this area are just beginning, but, of the variables examined to date, blood serotonin appears to be a trait-dependent marker in both man and monkey with a remarkably small intraindividual variance over long time periods. In the monkey, blood serotonin also appears to be a marker for the alpha-male. Thus, in 10 groups of animals, alpha-males had a mean blood serotonin

(5-HT) level of 838 ng/ml (standard error of 24) as compared to a mean of 635 ± 25 for 24 non-alpha-males. The difference was statistically significant at the 0.00002 level. Indeed, relative blood serotonin concentrations have allowed for correct prediction, in a limited number of cases, as to which of two males would attempt to assume the dominant role. Whether such successful prediction was due to chance or to a true biological-behavioral linkage must be determined by more systematic study.

To date, we have examined only monkeys in stable groups. As a result, differentiation between state- and trait-dependent properties has rested heavily on intraindividual stability over time and return to pre-existing baselines after pharmacological manipulations. Similarly, inferences on the relationship between social role and pharmacological sensitivity derive largely from their correlation. Fortunately, the nature of vervet society permits more rigorous examination of these propositions by manipulation of group composition and social and biological status. For example, removal of the alpha-male is followed in several weeks by emergence of a new alpha from the group. From the biological status of this animal before and after its social elevation, trait-dependent characteristics involved in establishing its alpha position can be discriminated from state-dependent characteristics resulting from the demands of the new social role. Similarly, trait-dependent characteristics of the original alpha-male should persist independent of social milieu while state-dependent characteristics should change. Reintroduction of the original alpha back into the home group allows a further examination of the biological-behavioral interactions and so on through a variety of experimental sociological manipulations.

Biological Substrates of Specific Behaviors

A second aspect of the McGuire-Raleigh-Brammer strategy is that it permits a broad search for biological substrate of specific behaviors and provides a means of examining the validity of meaures, in peripheral tissues, thought to reflect the status of transmitter systems in brain. The importance of this latter aspect has already been discussed under the Gerard paradigm.

The approach is relatively straightforward and consists essentially of three interrelated steps. The first is an examination of behavioral responses produced by batteries of pharmacological agents, each of which is designed to primarily manipulate one transmitter system. The second is an examination of the correlation between basal behaviors and biological variables in peripheral tissues thought to relate to particular transmitter systems. The last step consists of first selecting those peripheral markers which correlate with behaviors that appear to relate to a particular transmitter system on the basis of pharmacological manipulations and then to assess the utility of these markers in defining status and subsequent drug response.

That is, it is assumed that any behavior is the end resultant of interactions between several transmitter systems. Further, behavior is a *functional* output of those systems. The first step in this approach, then, is designed to parcel out the relative contributions of different transmitter systems to particular behavioral outputs. However, few pharmacological agents are specific for one transmitter system alone, and manipulation of any one system will invariably influence linked systems. As a result, the pattern of responses to a battery of pharmacological agents, rather than response to one agent alone, allows for an evaluation of transmitter involvement in a particular behavior on the basis of pharmacological consistency. Further, involvement of other specific transmitters is implicated by response inconsistencies compatible with known pharmacological overlap between systems. These inferences concerning transmitter contributions to behavior can be then tested, first, by predicting the effects of other agents on the behaviors, second, by systematically examining interactions between agonist and antagonist within one transmitter system, and, third, by predicting the effects of combinations of agents affecting different transmitter systems. As an example, Fig. 2 describes the behavioral effects of a small battery of pharmacological agents employed to manipulate the serotonin system. This battery consisted of tryptophan and PCPA which are relatively specific, 5-HTP and chlorgyline which are progressively less specific, and a combination of PCPA and 5-HTP. The upper portion of the figure illustrates the criteria used to assign serotoninergic contributions to a behavior. The apex of the triangle represents the direction of behavioral change and was arbitrarily constructed to indicate an increase caused by tryptophan. If the system is largely driven by serotonin, PCPA, a tryptophan hydroxylase inhibitor, should produce effects opposite to those of tryptophan, while 5-hydroxytryptophan and the monoamine oxidase inhibitor chlorgyline should resemble tryptophan in their effects. However, if catecholamines act in opposition to serotonin in mediating a behavior, chlorgyline may show effects opposite to those of tryptophan, since it elevates catecholamines as well as indoleamines, and 5-HTP, which can act as a false transmitter in catecholaminergic neurons, may show such opposite effects as well.

The lower part of the figure shows the changes in particular behaviors produced by these agents. These data were derived at only one dosage level for each pharmacological treatment and inferences are correspondingly tentative. From the results, however, grooming behavior appears to have strong serotoninergic input whereas vigilance has a much smaller one. The frequency of huddling behavior and sex were too small to permit any conclusions regarding serotoninergic involvement in their mediation. On the other hand, vigilance and aggression are likely to be largely catecholaminergic, and eating and locomotion are probably mixed.

As discussed, this transmitter assignment can be tested in several ways. First, one can predict the effects of other agents manipulating the serotoninergic system. For example, fluoxetine and quipazine should simulate tryptophan, the one because it is a serotonin reuptake blocker and the other because it is reported to serve as an agonist. Second, one can predict which behaviors should be affected by compounds in the norepinephrine and dopamine batteries and, from the nature of the pharmacological agent, the direction of change. For example, treatment with L-tryptophan (20 mg/kg) decreases locomotion, amphetamine increases it. Pretreatment with L-tryptophan attenuates the amphetamine response on the first day but by the second day the amphetamine response is the same as in animals not pretreated. Concomitant treatment with both tryptophan and amphetamine leads to a slow decline in the amphetamine effect. Pretreatment with tryptophan followed by combined treatment with tryptophan and amphetamine markedly attenuate the amphetamine effect. Third, one can play an agonist or antagonist in one series against the corresponding antagonist or agonist in another and by dose response relationships more quantitatively assess interactions. We have only begun to do this recently, and, to date, the few predictions we have made appear to be borne out experimentally.

Identifying transmitter contributions to particular behaviors is only the first step in this approach, however. The second step is to use this information to identify peripheral markers of functional transmitter activity in brain, for if the presumed marker does indeed reflect the functional state of a central transmitter system, it should correlate with behaviors regulated by that system. This approach differs from the ones currently in use which rely heavily on similarities between brain and peripheral tissues in cellular contents (platelet 5-HT) or enzymic complement (red cell COMT, platelet MAO), on shared metabolites (MHPG, VMA, 5-HIAA) or essential precursors (choline, tryptophan) in body fluids, or on materials released into such fluids as a result of neural activity (pituitary hormones, free fatty acids, norepinephrine). These potential markers at best reflect the general activity of neural systems and even then cannot distinguish between functional and nonfunctional activity. Markers derived from behavior, however, necessarily represent the functional output of specific neurons and, in addition, the ones relevant to those neuronal activities involved in psychiatric symptoms.

The final stage in this strategy is to determine whether these markers can predict social rank, pharmacological response, and the functional status of transmitter systems, first in the monkey and then in man. Together, these studies should expand information on the intrinsic physiological and behavioral effects of drugs and on the influence of personality and social interactions on drug response. In this manner, it may be possible to more clearly define conditions maximizing therapeutic success and minimizing dosage for each individual patient suffering from schizophrenia or other diseases.

SCHAPIRO PARADIGM

The final approach to be discussed concerns the etiology of mental disease, and arose from joyous arguments with the late Shawn Schapiro. The arguments were over the meaning of stress and over the mechanisms which might enduringly affect biological systems. From the debate evolved the proposition that early stress exposure loosened the integration of metabolic and cellular processes by disrupting the programmed sequence of maturational events. The agents for the disruption were stress-related hormones, their mode of action was through premature induction of hormone-sensitive processes, and their consequence was increased vulnerability to environmental disturbance. Family, twin, cross-foster, and worldwide incidence studies have resulted in convincing evidence of genetic contributions to the incidence of mental disease (23), but neither monogenetic theories with partial penetrance nor polygenetic theories satisfactorily explain why one identical twin may have schizophrenia while his sibling may not. As Kety (22) cogently noted, what seems to be inherited is not schizophrenia but vulnerability to that disease. But what converts vulnerability into manifest symptoms and what is the substrate for "vulnerability"? One suggestion is that unspecified genetic defects make neural structures particularly sensitive to physical compromise during childbirth. A strong case for this comes from prospective studies of children at risk in which histories of pregnancy and birth complications occurred more often among children developing schizophrenia than among those who stayed well (29). Yet not all subjects with manifest disease had such histories nor was the absence of birth complications a guarantee of health. Further, complications of pregnancy and birth trauma are not physiologically identical and it is unclear if anoxia, toxemia, generalized stress, or physical damage are most important to disease development.

The corresponding hypothesis, that stress caused mental disease, enjoyed wide popularity for many years and only the postulation of an interaction with a genetically weakened constitution need be added to the original formulation to make it compatible with current genetic data. So phrased, the hypothesis is both intuitively attractive and sufficiently vague to be untestable. The vagueness resides in identifying the psychogenic stressor and specifying the constitutional weakness it acts upon. Socioeconomic, societal, familial, parental, and individual stresses have all been postulated to initiate the disease process (3), but none appear sufficient. The schizophrenogenic family, the schizophrenogenic mother, the ambiguities of the double bind, and the complexities of developmental psychosexuality all make nice theoretical constructs, but none seem consistently associated with the incidence of schizophrenia and none seem to be able to clearly differentiate between the sib that becomes ill and the sib that does not.

In retrospect, this could have been anticipated. It is not what happens to a man that is important but rather what he thinks happens to him. What he thinks happens to him, in turn, is based on individual recognition and categorization of events, and these are derived from an individual's unique store of experiences and the equally unique organization of his mind. Because of this, the search for a specific stimulus common to all schizophrenics seems as futile as the search for rainbow's end, since both shift with individual perspective. But although the stimulus cannot be specified by its overt appearance, it is possible that it may be identified by the response it elicits.

Stressors, Corticoid Release, and Other Biological Consequences

Whatever the stimulus, it must have a physiological expression if it is to act upon a genetic substrate. In 1956 Selye (36) demonstrated that a variety of diverse noxious stimuli led to activation of the pituitary adrenal system. This established an operational definition of stress. Later demonstrations, that adrenocortical hormones could increase the activity of a variety of enzymes (1,2,5,18,25,43), provided a possible mechanism for corticoid-mediated adaptation to stressors. Since some enzymes involved in tryptophan and tyrosine metabolism are corticoid sensitive and these essential amino acids are precursors, respectively, to the indoleamine and catecholamine neurotransmitters, corticoid induction of these enzymes might produce metabolic changes leading to altered neurotransmitter balance and altered behavioral set. The indoleamine system might be particularly sensitive to stressors since the rate-limiting step in serotonin biosynthesis, tryptophan hydroxylation, is both enzyme and substrate limited (10), and both might be affected by stressors. Thus, 4 hr after administration of glucocorticoids to rats, hepatic tryptophan oxygenase activity is elevated. Concomitant with this rise is a fall in brain serotonin presumably reflecting the diversion of tryptophan through the kynurenine pathway and away from the serotonin pathway (4,45). Similarly, tryptophan aminotransferase activity is increased by glucocorticoids. On the other hand, the serotonin biosynthetic enzymes tryptophan hydroxylase and 5-HTP decarboxylase are also induced by corticoids under some conditions, and the balance between these various systems may be of importance in modulating tryptophan metabolism.

Not all stressors are thought equally potent in altering subsequent behavior, although, by definition, all must stimulate corticoid release. If corticoid induction of enzymes is evoked as a potential mechanism for enduring behavioral change, patterns of enzyme induction must differ between stressors and must differ from the full pattern produced by pharmacological doses of corticoids. This appears to be the case. For example, whereas corticoids are elevated in the rat 18 hr after fasting and remain elevated for 48 hr, tryptophan oxygenase is not elevated even after 48 hr of fasting (44). Similarly, corticoids are elevated in the adult rat by the "psychological" stress of shaking, but tyrosine transaminase activity is not (34,35). Both enzymic activities, of course, are increased by administered corticoids (11).

The behavioral literature also places primacy on stressors during development rather than in later life as being important to subsequent behavior. Maternal rejection in infancy, for example, is thought to be more important than maternal rejection in adulthood. Given this, age dependency in enzymic response to stressors might be expected if enzyme induction is important to subsequent behavior. This too appears true, at least in specific cases. For example, tyrosine transaminase is not induced in adult rats by shaking but is induced in infant rats (35). Both the stress and age specificity of enzymic response to endogenous corticoid release may be related to interactions between glucocorticoids and other hormonal systems responding to particular stressors although, as clearly shown by Nemeth et al. (32), corticoids play a determining role in the induction of some enzymes by some stressors.

Most information on the biological effects of stressors derives from studies using relatively acute stressors. However, the types of trauma thought to contribute to schizophrenic symptomatology are chronic environmental stressors such as constant exposure of the infant to double binds, ridicule, guilt, disparagement, or overprotection. Not only do those differ in duration from most experimental stressors but they are directed at the neonate and they involve dynamic social interactions which are difficult enough to replicate in man and nearly impossible to devise for animals. Perhaps the experimental studies which most directly examine the effects of adverse environments on subsequent development are the maternal deprivation studies in monkeys (15) and the stimulus deprivation studies in weanling rats (27).

Stressor Effects on the Neonate and on the Adult

A more indirect approach is to examine the consequences of chronic treatment of neonates with hormones released by stressors. Although such studies cannot pinpoint the changes produced by a particular stressor, they can circumscribe the types of changes chronic exposure to stress-released hormones could produce. For example, if noxious environments serve as true stressors, they must, by definition, elicit activation of the adrenocortical system. The possible consequences of such an activation can be simulated by exposing the neonatal rat to exogenous corticoids and, indeed, such treatment produces profound developmental effects.

As a generalization, neonatal exposure to glucocorticoids results in the retardation of a number of developmental processes including growth, formation of dendritic spines on pyramidal neurons of the visual cortex, appearance of visual and auditory evoked potentials, development of coordinated motor movement, and development of the adrenal response to stress and the adrenal circadian rhythm (7,8,34,39).

Because the monoamines appear to be involved in moderating emotional state, their response to chronic corticoid treatment of the newborn is of particular interest. As indicated above, acute tryptophan administration to the adult rat results in an induction of tryptophan oxygenase, the major catabolic enzyme in tryptophan metabolism (47). Normally, this enzyme does not make its ontogenic appearance until the 12th day after birth (26). Because tryptophan is essential for protein synthesis, both as limiting substrate and as a stabilizer of polysomes, this delay in tryptophan degradation probably serves to facilitate rapid growth of the neonate. However, in response to a single subcutaneous injection of hydrocortisone acetate on the first day of birth, the enzyme can be induced to appear as early as day 3. Concomitantly with this premature induction of tryptophan oxygenase is a retardation in the developmental increase of brain serotonin which, while statistically significant, is considerably smaller than might be expected from the massive increase in tryptophan oxygenase activity (47). This could be taken to indicate that brain serotonin biosynthesis is relatively independent of the rate of tryptophan degradation through the tryptophan oxygenase pathway. Alternately, hormonal treatment might activate a mechanism counteracting the increase in tryptophan degradation. Some evidence suggests the latter. Corticoid treatment not only prematurely induces tryptophan oxygenase but also increases brain tryptophan hydroxylase activity as well (47). Tryptophan hydroxylase is the rate-limiting enzyme in serotonin biosynthesis, and because serotonin formation is both enzyme and substrate dependent, a decrease in substrate may be partly overcome by an increase in enzyme (10). Perhaps even more important, however, neonatal corticoid treatment delays maturation of the neutral amino acid carrier system of the blood-brain barrier (47) so that tryptophan enters more freely into the brain of the corticoid-treated animal over a longer period of development than is the case for the normal animal. This could reflect a delay in the formation of tight junctions between the epithelial cells of the brain capillary plexus rather than a delay in the formation of the neutral amino acid carriers themselves. Whatever the mechanism, this increased permeability may well compensate for the decrease in available tryptophan.

The delayed development of the blood-brain barrier following corticoid treatment may have consequences for other transmitter systems as well. This suggestion arises from the effects of neonatal corticoid treatment on the maturation of the pineal gland which, although outside the blood-brain barrier, nonetheless has often served as a model for examining aspects of noradrenergic innervation. In this system norepinephrine released from an innervating branch from the superior cervical ganglion stimulates a beta receptor on the pinealocyte coupled to adenylcyclase. The resultant rise in cyclic AMP leads, by still poorly defined mechanisms, to a 20- to 100-fold increase in the activity of serotonin-*N*-acetyltransferase (SNAT), and this large signal makes the pineal such a useful tool for the study of the noradrenergic system (24). Functionally, SNAT *N*-acetylates endogenous serotonin in the pinealocyte to *N*-acetylserotonin, which is acted on by pineal hydroxyindole-O-methyl transferase to form melatonin.

The activity of serotonin-*N*-acetyltransferase undergoes a daily fluctuation reflecting a circadian rhythm in norepinephrine release from the superior cervical ganglion. In the adult rat activity is very low during the day and high at night. In the newborn, however, daytime levels are intermediate between the adult high and low and this level is only slightly increased at night. The difference between the day and night values slowly increases with age until the adult pattern is reached during the second week after birth (6).

The characteristic intermediary activity of pineal *N*-acetyltransferase in the infant rat appears due to inefficient norepinephrine reuptake and a resultant exposure of the infant pinealocyte receptor to circulating catecholamines (46). For example, the infant responds to stressors releasing catecholamines with a rise in SNAT activity which is not seen in the adult unless pretreated with a norepinephrine reuptake inhibitor such as desmethylimipramine. Among these stressors, incidentally, is inadequate mothering, which leads to elevated day and night levels of SNAT activity in cross-fostered pups (46).

The maturational change from infant to adult pineal rhythms is delayed by neonatal glucocorticoid treatment, and this is largely attributable to a delay in development of efficient reuptake. This delay is evidenced both by a decreased incorporation of labeled norepinephrine into isolated pineal glands, from steroid-treated animals, cultivated *in vitro,* as well as by the attenuated response of steroid-treated animals to desmethylimipramine administration *in vivo.* A more important consequence of this maturational delay, however, is its effects on the postsynaptor receptor.

It is now well recognized that increased stimulation of catecholamine receptors leads to a decrease in their sensitivity (37a), and such is the case for the pineal system as well (G. Brammer and A. Yuwiler, *unpublished*). Indeed, the desensitization of the infant pineal upon continuous exposure to circulating catecholamines appears to account for the attenuated night time rise accompanying nocturnal release of norepinephrine from the superior cervical. Not only does neonatal glucocorticoid administration delay maturation of the reuptake system and the appearance of the adult serotonin-*N*-acetyltransferase rhythm, but it also leads to desensitization of postsynaptic noradrenergic receptors in pinealocytes. This is manifest both in a decreased sensitivity to noradrenergic agonists of pineals maintained in organ culture for 48 hr (a time sufficient for degeneration of associated nerve terminals) and in lowered baselines in 24- to 26-day-old hydrocortisone-treated animals (G. Brammer and A. Yuwiler, *unpublished*).

Although the pineal system is outside the brain proper, a hormone-induced delay in maturation of the blood-brain barrier could expose developing catecholamineregic receptors in the central nervous system to circulating catecholamines; increases in such circulating catecholamines during emotional stress might well lead to long-term desensitization. Further study will determine if this possibility corresponds to reality.

Although the marked effects of hormonal treatment of neonates do not demonstrate that exposure to social stressors in infancy accounts for conversion of genetic propensity into mental disease, they do indicate a mechanism whereby such could occur and, correspondingly, provide a basis for more direct studies in man. Nor has this brief overview touched on all of the metabolic changes that might occur from exposure to noxious environments. Only some of the effects of adrenal corticoids have been recounted, and it is clear that other hormones are also released in response to particular stressors. These, too, have potentially important effects. For example, simple removal of the mother from infant rats is reported to affect the infant's ability to respond to growth hormone (28) with a rise in ornithine decarboxylase, a necessary reaction for polyamine-stimulated growth, whereas neonatal exposure of the female rat to androgens results in later masculinization of behavior (16). The Schapiro paradigm, thus, not only has potential relevance to schizophrenia and other mental diseases such as depression but also has implications for delineating the effects of early environment on normal development as well.

SUMMARY

Three paradigms have been presented: the Gerard paradigm geared to discriminating subpopulations with a diagnostic category, the McGuire-Raleigh-Brammer paradigm concerned with the effects of personality and social role on drug response, and the Schapiro paradigm examining the effects of hormonal factors on the development of the neonate. Each is relevant to research on schizophrenia and beyond that to the human condition generally.

REFERENCES

1. Azmitia, E. C., Jr., and McEwen, B. S. (1969): Corticosterone regulation of tryptophan hydroxylase in midbrain of the rat. *Science,* 166:1274–1276.
2. Azmitia, E. C., Jr., and McEwen, B. S. (1974): Adrenocortical influences on rat brain tryptophan hydroxylase activity. *Brain Res.,* 78:291–302.
3. Clausen, J. A., and Kohn, M. I. (1960): Social relations and schizophrenia. In: *Etiology of Schizophrenia,* edited by D. Jackson, pp. 295–323. Basic Books, New York.
4. Curzon, G., and Green, A. R. (1968): Effect of hydrocortisone on rat brain 5-hydroxytryptamine biosynthesis. *Life Sci.,* 7:657–663.
5. Davis, V. E. (1963): Effect of cortisone and thyroxine on aromatic amino acid decarboxylation. *Endocrinology,* 72:33–38.
6. Ellison, N., Weller, J. L., and Klein, D. C. (1972): Development of a circadian rhythm in the activity of pineal serotonin N-acetyltransferase. *J. Neurochem.,* 19:1335–1341.
7. Erskine, M. S., Geller, E., and Yuwiler, A. (1980): Effects of neonatal hydrocortisone treatment on pituitary-adrenocortical response to stress in young rats. *Neuroendocrinology (in press).*
8. Erskine, M. S., Geller, E., and Yuwiler, A. (1980): Modification of pituitary-adrenal feedback sensitivity in young rats by neonatal treatment with hydrocortisone. *J. Endocrinol. (in press).*
9. Freidhoff, A. J., Park, S., Schweitzer, J. W., Burdock, E. I., and Armour, M. (1977): Excretion of 3,4-dimethoxyphenethylamine (DMPEA) by acute schizophrenics and controls. *Biol. Psychiatry,* 12:643–654.
10. Friedman, P. A., Kappelman, A. H., and Kaufman, S. (1972): Partial purification and characterization of tryptophan hydroxylase from rabbit hindbrain. *J. Biol. Chem.,* 247:4165–4173.
11. Geller, E., Yuwiler, A., and Schapiro, S. (1964): Comparative effects of a stress and cortisol on some enzymic activities. *Biophys. Acta,* 93:311–315.
12. Gerard, R. W. (1963): The nosology of schizophrenia. *Am. J. Psychiatry,* 120:16–29.
13. Gerard, R. W. (1964): Nosology of schizophrenia: A cooperative study. *Behav. Sci.,* 9:311–333.
14. Gerard, R. W., and Mattsson, N. B. (1963): The classification of schizophrenia. In: *The Diagnostic Process,* edited by J. A. Jaquez, pp. 81–101. University of Michigan, Ann Arbor, Michigan.
15. Harlow, H. F., and Harlow, M. K. (1965): The affectional systems. In: *Behavior of Nonhuman Primates, Vol. 2,* edited by A. M. Schrier, H. F. Harlow, and F. Stollnitz, pp. 287–334. Academic Press, New York.
16. Harris, G. W., and Levine, S. (1965): Sexual differentiation of the brain and its experimental control. *J. Physiol. (Lond.),* 181:379–400.
17. Hollingshead, A. B., and Redlich, F. C. (1953): Social stratification and psychiatric disorders. *Am. Sociol. Rev.,* 18:163–169.
18. Holton, D., and Kenney, F. T. (1964): Regulation of tyrosine α-ketoglutarate transaminase in rat liver. VI. Induction by pancreatic hormones. *J. Biol. Chem.,* 242:4372–4377.

19. Horwitt, M. K. (1956): Fact and artifact in the biology of schizophrenia. *Science,* 124:429–430.
20. Kenney, F. T. (1967): Regulation of tyrosine α-ketoglutarate transaminase in rat liver. V. Repression in growth hormone treated rats. *J. Biol. Chem.,* 242:4367–4371.
21. Kety, S. S. (1959): Biochemical theories of schizophrenia. Parts I and II. *Science,* 129:1528 and 1590.
22. Kety, S. S. (1972): Toward hypotheses for a biochemical component in the vulnerability to schizophrenia. *Semin. Psychiatry,* 4:233–238.
23. Kety, S. S., Rosenthal, D., Wender, P. H., and Schulsinger, F. (1968): The type and prevalence of mental disease in biological and adoptive families of schizophrenics. In: *The Transmission of Schizophrenia,* edited by D. Rosenthal and S. S. Kety, pp. 345–362. Pergamon Press, New York.
24. Klein, D. C., and Weller, J. L. (1973): Adrenergic-adenosine 3′,5′-monophosphate regulation of serotonin N-acetyltransferase activity and the temporal relationship of serotonin N-acetyltransferase activity to synthesis of ^{3}H-N-acetylserotonin and ^{3}H-melatonin in the cultured rat pineal gland. *J. Pharmacol. Exp. Ther.,* 186:516–527.
25. Knox, W. E. (1963): The adoptive control of tryptophan and tyrosine metabolism in animals. *Trans. N.Y. Acad. Sci.,* 35:503–512.
26. Knox, W. E., and Auerbach, V. H. (1956): The hormonal control of tryptophan peroxidase in the rat. *J. Biol. Chem.,* 241:307–313.
27. Krech, D., Rosenzweig, M. R., and Bennett, E. L. (1962): Relations between brain chemistry and problem-solving among rats raised in enriched and impoverished environments. *J. Comp. Physiol. Psychol.,* 55:801–807.
28. Kuhn, C. M., Butler, S. R., and Schanberg, S. M. (1978): Selective depression of serum growth hormone during maternal deprivation in rat pups. *Science,* 201:1034–1036.
29. McGuire, M. T., and Polsky, R. (1980): An ethological analysis of schizophrenic disorders. *J. Nerv. Ment. Dis. (in press).*
30. Mednick, S. A. (1970): Breakdown in individuals at high risk for schizophrenia: Possible predispositional perinatal factors. *Ment. Hygiene,* 54:50–63.
31. Meltzer, H. Y. (1975): Neuromuscular abnormalities in the major mental illnesses. I. Serum enzyme studies. In: *The Biology of the Major Psychoses: A Comparative Analysis,* edited by D. X. Freedman, pp. 168–188. Raven Press, New York.
32. Nemeth, S., Strakova, A., and Vigas, M. (1973): The role played by adrenal hormones in the increase of liver tyrosine aminotransferase activity in rats subjected to trauma. *Horm. Metab. Res.,* 5:204–207.
33. Rey, J. H., and Coppen, A. J. (1959): Distribution of androgyny in mental patients. *Br. Med. J.,* 11:1445–1447.
34. Schapiro, S. (1971): Hormonal and environmental influences on rat brain development and behavior. In: *Brain Development and Behavior,* edited by M. G. Sterman, D. J. McGinty, and A. M. Adinolfi, pp. 307–344. Academic Press, New York.
35. Schapiro, S., Yuwiler, A., and Geller, E. (1966): Maturation of a stress-activated mechanism inhibiting induction of tyrosine transaminase. *Science,* 152:1642–1643.
36. Selye, H. (1956): *The Stress of Life.* McGraw-Hill, New York.
37. Spaide, J., Tanimukai, H., Bueno, J. R., and Himwich, H. E. (1968): Behavioral and biochemical alterations in schizophrenic patients. *Arch. Gen. Psychiatry,* 18:658–665.
37a. Sulser, F. (1978): Functional aspects of the norepinephrine receptor coupled adenylate cyclase system in the limbic forebrain and its modification by drugs which precipitate or alleviate depression: Molecular approaches to an understanding of affective disorders. *Pharmakopsychiat. Neuropsychopharmakol.,* 11:43–52.
38. Tanner, J. M. (1951): Current advances in the study of physique. Photogrammetric, anthropometry and an adrogyny scale. *Lancet,* 1:574–579.
39. Ulrich, R., Yuwiler, A., and Geller, E. (1976): Neonatal hydrocortisone effect on the development of the stress response and the diurnal rhythm of corticosterone. *Neuroendocrinology,* 21:49–57.
40. Wyatt, R. J., Murphy, D. L., Belmaker, R., Cohen, S., Donnelly, C., and Pollin, W. (1973): Reduced monoamine oxidase activity in platelets: A possible genetic marker for vulnerability to schizophrenia. *Science,* 173:916–918.
41. Yuwiler, A. (1965): Psychopathology and 5-hydroxyindoleacetic acid excretion. *J. Psychiatr. Res.,* 3:125–131.

42. Yuwiler, A. (1969): Basal biochemical measures and their possible influence on biochemical test for schiozphrenia. In: *Schizophrenia: Current Concepts and Research,* edited by D. V. Siva Sankar, pp. 600–613. PJD Publications, New York.
43. Yuwiler, A. (1971): Stress. In: *Handbook of Neurochemistry, Vol. 6,* edited by A. Lajtha, pp. 103–171. Pergamon Press, New York.
44. Yuwiler, A., Geller, E., and Schapiro, S. (1969): Response differences in some steroid-sensitive hepatic enzymes in the fasted rat. *Can. J. Physiol. Pharmacol.,* 47:317–328.
45. Yuwiler, A., Geller, E., and Wetterberg, L. (1972): Relationship between alternate routes of tryptophan metabolism following administration of tryptophan peroxidase inducers or stressors. *J. Neurochem.,* 18:593–599.
46. Yuwiler, A., Klein, D. C., Buda, M., and Weller, J. L. (1977): Adrenergic control of pineal N-acetyltransferase activity: Developmental aspects. *Am. J. Physiol.,* 233:141–146.
47. Yuwiler, A., Simon, M., Bennett, B., Plotkin, S., Wallace, R., Brammer, G., and Ulrich, R. (1978): Effect of neonatal corticoid treatment on tryptophan and serotonin metabolism. *Endocrinol. Exp.,* 12:21–31.

Discussion

Singh: As shown by the experience you cite of Dr. Gerard, it is difficult but possible to do a longitudinal, multidimensional study of schizophrenia in a defined environment, like the one we began 10 years ago, which had included prospective diagnostic and prognostic evaluations and elaborate measures of psychopathology, psychophysiological function, cognitive function, and ethological attributes. Without benefit of large computers we have resolved schizophrenic heterogeneity into three major types. One is the paranoid type as defined by British psychiatry. Of the two nonparanoid types, one shows a dysphoric response to neuroleptic treatment and a poor treatment outcome; the other, nondysphoric type has a good prognosis. These findings are not definitive but they suggest a framework for conducting the kind of study you described.

Yuwiler: Dr. Gerard found seven subgroups, two of which consisted of paranoid and the remaining two of nonparanoid patients. Unfortunately the work remains unpublished so I can't cite a reference but I have the data. The problem lies in testing the medical significance of those defined groups. That could be done now by determining if the groupings predict drug response or general prognoses.

Melnechuk: Your mention of the correlation between high blood serotonin and alpha males reminds me of the claim that dogs can smell the extra adrenalin we secrete when we're afraid, which in turn suggests mentioning substances that exemplify one aspect of Gordon Tomkins' notion that early in evolution hormones originated as intracellular messengers and then became extracellular messengers. I'm referring to pheromones. Can you comment on studies of pheromones in schizophrenics?

Yuwiler: There have been many reports of volatile materials in schizophrenics over the last 20 years, ranging from the "sweat" substance (*trans*-3-methyl-2-hexenoic acid) (1) to materials that attracted mosquitoes. I don't know what the current status of the sweat substance is but as for the mosquito pheromone, it turned out to be lactic acid and disappeared with better hygiene. I don't think there's good evidence for a pheromone characteristic of schizophrenics. As for Tompkin's view on evolutionary shifts in the localization of hormones, it is certainly true that nature is parsimonious and uses the same materials to accomplish different tasks. The English nettle contains norepinephrine, serotonin, acetylcholine, and dopamine, which serve as irritants, and presumably evolved to keep the nettle from being eaten. The same irritants in the long, thin, epithelial cells called neurons serve as a communication system.

REFERENCE

1. Smith, K., Thompson, G. F., and Koster, H. D. (1969): Sweat in schizophrenic patients: Identification of the odorous substance. *Science,* 166:398–399.

Perspectives in Schizophrenia Research,
edited by C. Baxter and T. Melnechuk.
Raven Press, New York, 1980.

Structural Brain Abnormalities in Chronic Schizophrenia: Computed Tomography Findings

Daniel R. Weinberger and Richard Jed Wyatt

Adult Psychiatry Branch, Division of Special Mental Health Research, National Institute of Mental Health, Saint Elizabeths Hospital, Washington, D.C. 20032

LAYPERSON'S SUMMARY

It has long been suspected that the brains of schizophrenic patients are structurally different from the brains of normal individuals. Until recently, however, this suspicion has been difficult to confirm or dismiss.

A new approach to the problem is the use of computed tomography (CT), an innovation in clinical radiology that permits visualization of internal brain structures during life. CT is safe and noninvasive, requiring only that a patient lie still for approximately 10 min while pictures of the internal structure of his brain are produced.

In controlled studies of chronic schizophrenic patients evaluated by this method, four abnormalities of brain structure have been described. These include enlargement of the cerebral ventricles, dilatation of several fissures on the surface of the brain, apparent atrophy of a portion of the cerebellum, and atypical asymmetries between various aspects of the cerebral hemispheres. The first three of these findings suggest subtle degeneration of brain tissue. The fourth finding has also been associated with various cognitive disorders, such as autism and dyslexia. Approximately two-thirds of the chronic schizophrenic patients studied have at least one of these abnormalities. However, many patients have only one abnormality, and some have none.

These findings support the notion that schizophrenia is not a unitary disease entity but a heterogeneous collection of abnormalities of higher brain function that may result from various causes. To answer vital questions about cause and clinical effect, prospective, long-term studies of chronic schizophrenic patients who have undergone CT scanning are required. The VA hospital system is in a unique position to accomplish such a study cost-effectively and with no compromise in clinical care.

INTRODUCTION

One of the oldest issues in schizophrenia research is whether the brains of schizophrenic patients are morphologically different from the brains of normal individuals. Despite 70 years of research, the question remains unresolved. It has been approached from three directions—the examination of postmortem brain tissue, pneumoencephalographic studies of living patients, and recently, the study of living patients using computed tomography (CT).

Postmortem histopathology studies, most of which were done before 1950, have been widely regarded as inconclusive because they suffered from many methodological problems (5,6,37). Few of them used controls, even fewer were done blindly, and most used poorly standardized methods of tissue processing and staining. In addition, these studies were guided by the assumption that schizophrenia was a specific disease entity which should have a specific pathological anatomy. Nonspecific or variable findings were not considered relevant. Although most studies found abnormalities in the brains of schizophrenic patients, the findings were either inconsistent between studies, nonspecific, or they revealed abnormalities that were found occasionally also in the brains of control subjects (27).

Pneumoencephalography has been used to study cerebral morphology in schizophrenic patients during life. With few exceptions, pneumoencephalographic studies found structural abnormalities in schizophrenic patients, usually ventricular enlargement and cortical atrophy (2,13,14,25). Why these reports have been virtually ignored by American psychiatrists is difficult to understand. Certainly, pneumoencephalography, because of its frequent morbidity, is ill-suited to the study of large populations of psychiatric patients. Furthermore, it is inappropriate for the study of normal individuals necessary as controls. Such problems have made it difficult to continue this line of research.

The advent of computed tomography in 1972 (12) introduced a new approach to the study of brain morphology in schizophrenia. Computed tomography is a radiological technique for visualizing gross brain structure during life that is reliable and virtually free of uncontrollable artifact. The technique is safe and noninvasive. As a result, it can be used with large numbers of patients and appropriate control subjects, including asymptomatic individuals. In this chapter, we will discuss the application of computed tomography to the study of brain morphology in schizophrenia.

COMPUTED TOMOGRAPHY SYSTEM

Like conventional radiological methods, computed tomography produces visual images of internal structures by virtue of the attenuation of X-rays transmitted through a density. The CT image, however, is not derived from a photographic plate. Instead, a scintillation crystal detects the attenuated X-rays, generating voltages which are converted into digital readings and stored. This process of X-ray transmission and detection (i.e., scanning) is performed through a 180° arc as both X-ray source and detector move in a designated plane of section. Readings are also taken at various angles to the scanning plane. Thus thousands of X-ray readings (i.e., "attenuation coefficients") are derived for each section scanned. The readings are processed by a computer into a visual image that represents the distribution of densities in the plane examined. Most head CT scanners in current use complete a series of horizontal cross sections in under 15 min, providing pictures in the form of either self-developing prints or transparencies. The radiation exposure is approximately that of a routine skull X-ray series.

CT FINDINGS IN SCHIZOPHRENIA

Controlled CT studies have found that structural brain abnormalities are associated with chronic schizophrenia. The abnormalities described thus far can be classified into four categories: ventricular enlargement, abnormalities of cortical sulci, reversals of usual neuroanatomical asymmetries, and atrophy of the anterior cerebellar vermis. The findings are relatively subtle and, with the exception of the cerebellar abnormality, require quantitative methods. Atrophy of the vermis is determined by qualitative interpretation of the scans.

Ventricular Enlargement

In 1976 Johnstone and colleagues (18) published the first controlled CT study of schizophrenic patients. They compared the size of the lateral ventricles as measured by planimetry of 17 chronic schizophrenic patients to those of eight similarly aged healthy volunteers. Ventricular size in the group of schizophrenics was significantly greater than in the controls ($p < 0.01$). Included among the schizophrenic patients were four subjects who had never received phenothiazines and seven who had never been treated with electroconvulsive therapy (ECT). These patients also had significantly enlarged ventricles. Thus ventricular enlargement did not appear to have been the result of somatic treatment. Johnstone's study had two major problems in addition to the use of small samples. The first was the age of the patient population (mean = 58 years). Starting around the seventh decade of life, the size of the lateral ventricles in normals is significantly more variable than during earlier years (4). The second problem was that the patients had been institutionalized for extensive periods (mean = 30 years). This raised the criticism that the findings represented the effects of institutionalization (17,24).

At NIMH, we have studied ventricular size in a larger number of schizophrenic patients and asymptomatic volunteer subjects, all under age 50. In our initial report (34), we compared ventricular size in 73 psychiatric patients diagnosed by Research Diagnostic Criteria (31), 58 of whom were chronic schizophrenics, to that in 56 healthy volunteers. To determine ventricular size, we selected the CT section that showed the bodies of the lateral ventricles at their largest and measured their area and the area of the inner table of the skull by planimetry. Ventricular size was expressed as the percentage of the intracranial space occupied by lateral ventricle—the ventricular-brain ratio (VBR). A more complete discussion of this method is provided elsewhere (34). We chose this method of determining ventricular size because it has been shown to be almost as valid and reliable as computer-derived volume (26). Linear measurements popular among neuroradiologists [e.g., Huckman's measure (15)] take considerably less time but do not correlate well with ventricular volume and are less reliable, especially when evaluating modest increases in ventricular size (26,38).

We found the size of the ventricles in the 58 chronic schizophrenic patients to be significantly greater (two-tailed *t*-test, $p < 0.0001$) than in the controls. This difference could not be explained by age, sex, race, alcohol abuse, or treatment with ECT. To assess the roles of neuroleptic drug treatment and institutionalization, we tried to correlate ventricular size with length of illness and length of hospitalization. It was impossible to determine more reliably the amount of drug therapy. Neither of these variables correlated significantly with ventricular size. We concluded, therefore, that mild ventricular enlargement is related to chronic schizophrenia, and not to its treatment, and that it does not appear to be significantly progressive in this age group.

Figure 1 shows the sizes of the ventricles for the chronic schizophrenic and control subjects examined to date. A comparison of ventricular size between these groups, both of which have a mean age of 29, reveals not only a highly significant difference, but that 37% of the chronic schizophrenic patients are entirely outside of the control range and 52% are beyond two standard deviations of the control mean.

It is important to appreciate the subtle nature of the ventricular enlargement in the schizophrenic patients. Mean ventricular size of these patients is within the normal range for individuals approximately 70 years old (4). This may explain why most of the scans were interpreted subjectively by two neuroradiolo-

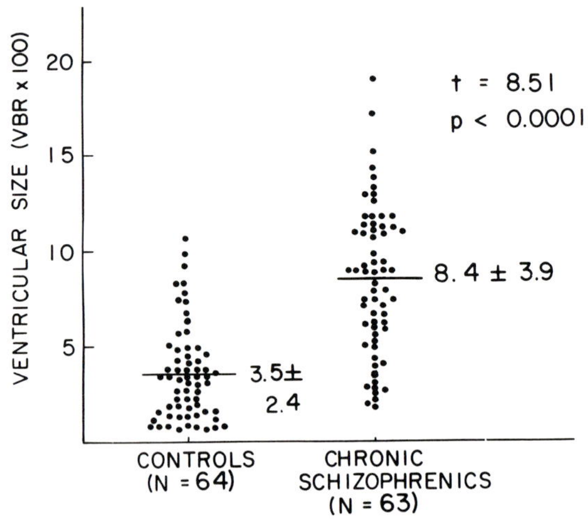

FIG. 1. Ventricular sizes for control subjects and chronic schizophrenic patients.

gists as being "within normal limits." This degree of enlargement is much less dramatic than that seen in dementia. Synek et al. (32) found that patients with dementia of various etiologies, excluding "hydrocephalus," had a mean ventricular-brain ratio of approximately twice that of the schizophrenic group. The mean VBR in patients with hydrocephalic dementias tends to be around four times greater (16,32).

We have also evaluated 20 psychiatric patients with other diagnoses. In three of four subacute and one of four acute schizophrenic patients, and two of five schizoaffective patients, ventricular size exceeded two standard deviations of the control mean. In none of these patients did it exceed the control range. The seven other patients (six—affective disorders; one—mental retardation) were well within the control range. Finally, the two patients with the largest ventricles were further evaluated by radionuclide cisternography. In one patient, the study was normal except for evidence of mild dilatation of the sylvian fissures. The second patient had two uninterpretable studies. On both occasions, no radioactivity could be detected in the ventricular system at 24 hr.

Abnormalities of the Cerebral Cortex

Further evidence of cerebral atrophy, the presumed cause of ventricular enlargement found in the absence of CSF obstruction, might also be observed in the cerebral cortex. With this in mind, we measured blindly the widths of the sylvian fissure, the interhemispheric fissure, and the three broadest cortical sulci of 75 patients and 62 controls (35). This involved choosing the cut from each subject's CT scan series that showed these structures at their widest. In selecting a cut for the cortical sulci, it was important to avoid an apical image that showed distorted sulci, because this may represent an artifact (7). A more complete discussion of this method is provided elsewhere (35). When the chronic schizophrenic patients were compared to the controls, the groups differed significantly in the proportion of widths for the sylvian fissures ($p < 0.005$, Fisher exact test), for the interhemispheric fissure ($p < 0.05$), and for the mean width of the cortical sulci ($p < 0.01$). Figure 2 illustrates this comparison for the sylvian fissures.

We defined an abnormality in an individual as a structure width outside the control range. By this definition, 32% of the chronic schizophrenic patients had at least one abnormality. It is interesting to note that more patients (eleven) had an abnormality of the sylvian fissure than of any other structure. None of the 15 patients with other diagnoses in this study had an abnormality.

As in the case of ventricular enlargement, we were unable to relate these findings to other variables. Again, age, sex, race, alcohol abuse (only seven patients), length of illness or hospitalization, and ECT could not explain the findings. Therefore, we concluded that mild cortical atrophy that is neither markedly progressive nor an apparent effect of treatment is also found in some chronic schizophrenic patients.

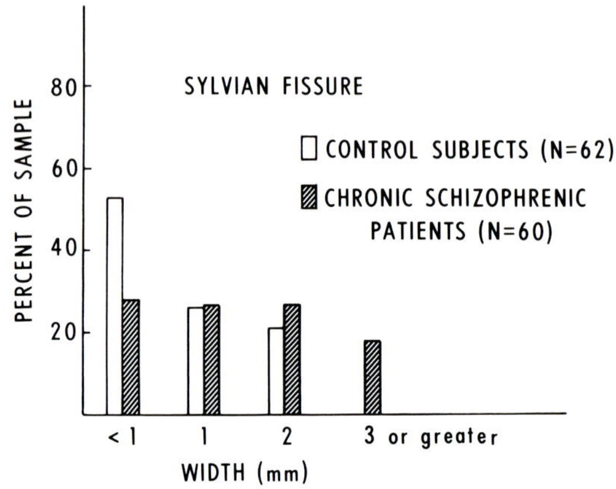

FIG. 2. Comparison of sylvian fissure widths for chronic schizophrenic and control subjects. Fisher exact test $p < 0.005$.

TABLE 1. *Relationship between cortical abnormalities and ventricular enlargement*

	Patients with cortical abnormalities	Patients without cortical abnormalities	Totals
Patients with enlarged ventricles (VBR > 8.1)[a]	10	21	31
Patients without enlarged ventricles	9	20	29
Totals	19	41	60

[a] VBR, ventricular-brain ratio.
$\chi^2 = 0.01$, not significant.

A surprising finding in this study was that cortical abnormalities did not correlate significantly with ventricular enlargement (Table 1). If a single degenerative process were at work in these patients, ventricular enlargement and cortical atrophy probably would have been correlated. The failure to find such a correlation suggests that the process responsible for these changes is heterogeneous and of more than one etiology. Finally, Johnstone et al. (19) did not find cortical sulci abnormalities in their sample of older patients. This may be a function of the patients selected, or possibly that subtle structural changes in older patients are obscured by the effects of aging.

Reversals of Neuroanatomical Asymmetries

Neuroanatomical asymmetries are frequently found in the brains of normal individuals (8). With CT scanning it is possible to see hemispheric asymmetries during life. For example, LeMay and colleagues (20,21) have shown that on CT scans, normal right-handed individuals tend to have wider right frontal and left occipital lobes. Reversals of the usual asymmetries have been observed in several putative disorders of higher cortical function, including autism (10), developmental dyslexia (11), and delayed speech onset (28). In light of the numerous reports of disorders of lateralization in schizophrenic patients, it is relevant to examine neuroanatomical asymmetries in these patients.

For this investigation, we used the CT scans of 57 right-handed patients diagnosed with either schizophrenia or schizoaffective disorder (23). We determined lateral asymmetries by a modification of the method of LeMay (20). This involved placing over the appropriate CT image a cross hair with millimeter calibrations, aligning the vertical hair with the interhemispheric fissure. The extent of the frontal and occipital lobes in both lateral directions from a designated position on the midline was measured on the horizontal hair. When the results were compared to established normals (21), we found a significant increase in the frequency of both frontal (33% in the schizophrenics versus 13% in the normals, $p < 0.001$) and occipital (25% versus 9%, $p < 0.01$) reversals of the usual asymmetry. This increased frequency of reversals discriminated between schizophrenic patients with other CT scan abnormalities and those without them. The 29 patients without other structural abnormalities had an increase in the frequency of left frontal predominance (52%, $p < 0.0001$) and right occipital predominance (38%, $p < 0.001$), whereas the frequency of these reversals in the 28 schizophrenic patients with other abnormalities was not different from that in the controls. This is further evidence for the notion that structural abnormalities in schizophrenic patients are etiologically heterogeneous.

Atrophy of the Cerebellar Vermis

An unexpected finding in our CT scan series was a subgroup of 10 patients among those diagnosed with chronic schizophrenia who had apparent atrophy of the anterior cerebellar vermis (36). This diagnosis was based on blind interpretation by a neuroradiologist and on objective criteria described in the literature (1). The finding is easily missed if the appropriate CT cut is not studied. Vermal atrophy could not be explained in these patients on the basis of other known causes, and evidence of significant impairment in cerebellar function was not found clinically. In three of the patients, this finding did not overlap with other structural abnormalities, reaffirming that these abnormalities probably involve multiple etiologies.

Atrophy of the anterior vermis is a surprising finding in that the cerebellum has not been widely considered as an anatomical site relevant to the problem of schizophrenia. Few postmortem studies examined the cerebellum. However, there is emerging now a body of research demonstrating a link anatomically, physiologically, and neurochemically between the anterior vermis and areas of the limbic system that have been implicated in schizophrenia (9,29,30). We have recently completed a small but carefully controlled postmortem study using brains from the Yakovlev Collection of the Armed Forces Institute of Pathology in which we have confirmed the finding of reduced size of the anterior vermis in a subgroup of chronic schizophrenic patients (33). These observations suggest that pathological anatomy of the vermis is relevant to the problem of schizophrenia.

IMPLICATIONS FOR FUTURE RESEARCH

The results of the studies reviewed indicate that, contrary to clinical lore, structural abnormalities of the brain are associated with chronic schizophrenia and can be observed in many patients by the CT scanning technique. This fact alone has far-reaching implications for our understanding and treatment of chronic schizophrenia. The findings also appear to involve multiple etiologies, supporting the notion that schizophrenia is not a unitary disease entity, but a heterogeneous collection of abnormalities that may contribute to disordered brain function. Future research should focus on the following questions: What are the etiologies of these findings, and how are the findings clinically significant?

The question of etiology will have to be approached from many directions. It would seem advisable to separate chronic schizophrenic patients into subgroups defined by the type of structural abnormality found or at least by the presence or absence of any of the abnormalities described. This subdivision process should reduce the heterogeneous population of patients with the diagnosis of chronic schizophrenia into more homogeneous subgroups, an approach to schizophrenia research now widely advocated (3). Studying the various subgroups along genetic, biochemical, and developmental lines may provide clues to etiology. For example, our own preliminary data suggest that patients with evidence of atrophy have a different HL antigen (HLA) profile than those without such findings (22). Other biological and psychosocial parameters believed relevant to schizophrenia should also be considered in relation to these findings.

Although the structural abnormalities do not seem to have been the result of neuroleptic drug treatment or of chronic institutional care, these possibilities cannot be conclusively discounted. In order to do so, a prospective study involving first-break patients who have never received such treatment would be ideal. An alternative, although less conclusive, approach would be to use as controls other chronically institutionalized patients or patients who have received chronic neuroleptic therapy for other indications.

A long-term prospective study of randomly selected acutely psychotic patients will help resolve many of the questions about clinical significance. The VA hospital system is in a unique position to carry out such a study. Patients could be scanned shortly after admission, after their acute symptoms have resolved, and then followed with repeat scans at 5-year intervals. Such a design might answer the following questions: What are the frequencies of the abnormalities in an unselected population of psychotic patients, are they found only in schizophrenics, are they present early in the course of the illness or do they develop, do they progress, are they reversible, and finally, do they have prognostic significance? Our data suggest that these findings have at least prognostic significance. They appear to be found in highest frequency among chronic, unremitting patients. In addition, we have preliminary data to suggest that patients with large ventricles respond less well to drug therapy than do other chronic schizophrenic patients (D. R. Weinberger, L. B. Bigelow, J. E. Kleinman, S. Klein, and R. J. Wyatt, *unpublished*). Also, the patients with evidence of atrophy perform significantly worse on Halsted-Reitan neuropsychological tests, suggesting that they are a more impaired population (D. R. Weinberger, E. Donnelly, I. Waldman, and R. J. Wyatt, *unpublished*).

We are also looking at the neurophysiological implications of these findings using the evoked-response EEG technique. Numerous other approaches are possible and should be encouraged. The VA Medical Center System could accomplish much of this effort with no compromise in clinical care. The potential for further insights into the nature and treatment of schizophrenia is great.

REFERENCES

1. Allen, J. H., Martin, J. T., and McLain, L. W. (1979): Computerized tomography in cerebellar atrophic process. *Radiology,* 130:379–382.
2. Asano, N. (1967): Pneumoencephalographic study of schizophrenia. In: *Clinical Genetics in Psychiatry. Problems in Nosological Classification,* edited by H. Mitsuda, pp. 209–219. Igaku Shoin Ltd., Tokyo.
3. Baldessarini, R. J. (1977): Schizophrenia. *N. Engl. J. Med.,* 297:988–995.
4. Barron, S. A., Jacobs, L., and Kinkel, W. R. (1976): Changes in size of normal lateral ventricles during aging determined by computerized tomography. *Neurology (Minneap.),* 26:1011–1013.
5. Dastur, D. K. (1959): The pathology of schizophrenia. *Arch. Neurol. Psychiatry,* 81:601–614.
6. David, G. B. (1957): The pathological anatomy of the schizophrenias. In: *Schizophrenia: Somatic Aspects,* edited by D. Richter, pp. 93–130. Pergamon Press, Oxford.
7. Dichiro, G., Brooks, R. A., and Dubal, L. (1978): The apical artifact: Elevated attenuation values toward the apex of the skull. *J. Comput. Assist. Tomogr.,* 2:65–70.
8. Galaburda, A. M., LeMay, M., Kenger, T. L., and Geschwind, N. (1978): Right-left asymmetries in the brain. *Science,* 199:852–856.
9. Heath, R. G., Dempsey, C. W., Fontana, C. J., and Myers, W. A. (1978): Cerebellar stimulation: Effects on septal region, hippocampus and amygdala of cats and rats. *Biol. Psychiatry,* 13:501–529.
10. Hier, D. B., LeMay, M., Rosenberger, P. B. (1978): Autism: Association with reversed cerebral asymmetry. *Neurology (Minneap.),* 28:348–349.
11. Hier, D. B., LeMay, M., Rosenberger, P. B., Perlo, V. P. (1978): Developmental dyslexia: Evidence for a sub-group with reversal of cerebral asymmetry. *Arch. Gen. Neurol.,* 35:90–92.
12. Hounsfield, G. N. (1973): Computerized transverse axial scanning (tomography): Part 1. Description of system. *Br. J. Radiol.,* 46:1016–1022.
13. Huag, J. O. (1962): Pneumoencephalographic studies on mental disease. *Acta Psychiatr. Scand.* [*Suppl. 165*], 38:1–114.
14. Huber, G. (1957): *Pneumoencephalographische und Psychopathologische Bilder Bei Endogen Psychosen.* Springer-Verlag, Berlin.
15. Huckman, M. S., Fox, J., and Topel, J. (1975): The validity of criteria for the evaluation of cerebral atrophy by computed tomography. *Radiology,* 116:85–92.
16. Jacobs, L., and Kinkel, W. (1976): Computerized axial transverse tomography in normal pressure hydrocephalus. *Neurology (Minneap.),* 26:501–507.

17. Jellinek, E. H. (1976): Cerebral atrophy and cognitive impairment in chronic schizophrenia. *Lancet,* ii:1202–1203.
18. Johnstone, E. C., Crow, T. J., Frith, C. D., Husband, J., and Kreel, L. (1976): Cerebral ventricular size and cognitive impairment in chronic schizophrenia. *Lancet,* ii:924–926.
19. Johnstone, E. C., Crow, T. J., Frith, C. D., Stevens, M., Kreel, L., and Husband, J. (1978): The dementia of dementia praecox. *Acta Psychiatr. Scand.,* 57:305–324.
20. LeMay, M. (1976): Morphological cerebral asymmetries of modern man, fossil man, and non-human primates. *Ann. N.Y. Acad. Sci.,* 280:349–366.
21. LeMay, M., and Kido, D. K. (1978): Asymmetries of cerebral hemispheres on computed tomograms. *J. Comput. Assist. Tomogr.,* 2:470–476.
22. Luchins, D. J., Torrey, E. F., Weinberger, D. R., Zalcman, S., Delisi, L., Johnstone, A., Rogentine, N., and Wyatt, R. J. (1980): HLA antigens in schizophrenia: Difference between patients with and without brain atrophy. *Br. J. Psychiatry,* 136:243–248.
23. Luchins, D. J., Weinberger, D. R., and Wyatt, R. J. (1979): Schizophrenia: Evidence for a sub-group with reversed cerebral asymmetry. *Arch. Gen. Psychiatry,* 36:1309–1311.
24. Marsden, C. D. (1976): Cerebral atrophy and cognitive impairment in chronic schizophrenia. *Lancet,* ii:1079.
25. Nagy, K. (1963): Pneumoencephalographische befunde bei endogen psychosen. *Nervenarzt,* 34:543–548.
26. Penn, R. D., Belanger, M. G., and Yasnoff, W. A. (1978): Ventricular volume in man computed from CAT scans. *Ann. Neurol.,* 3:216–223.
27. *Proceedings of the First International Congress of Neuropathology* (1952), *Vol. 1,* pp. 465–674. Rosenberg and Sellier, Torino.
28. Rosenberger, P. B., and Hier, D. B. (1980): Cerebral asymmetry and verbal-intellectual deficits. *Neurology (Minneap.) (in press).*
29. Snider, R. S., Maiti, A., and Snider, S. R. (1976): Cerebellar pathways to ventral midbrain and nigra. *Exp. Neurol.,* 53:714–728.
30. Snider, S. R., and Snider, R. S. (1977): Alterations in forebrain catecholamine metabolism produced by cerebellar lesions in the rat. *J. Neural Transm.,* 40:115–128.
31. Spitzer, R. L., Endicott, J., and Robins, E. (1977): *Research Diagnostic Criteria (RDC) for a Selected Group of Functional Disorders, 3rd Ed.* Biometrics, New York.
32. Synek, V., Reuben, J. R., and Duboulay, G. H. (1976): Comparing Evans' index and computerized axial tomography in assessing relationship of ventricular size to brain size. *Neurology (Minneap.),* 26:231–233.
33. Weinberger, D. R., Kleinman, J. E., Luchins, D. J., Bigelow, L. B., and Wyatt, R. J. (1980): Cerebellar pathology in chronic schizophrenia: A controlled, post-mortem study. *Am. J. Psychiatry,* 137:359–361.
34. Weinberger, D. R., Torrey, E. F., Neophytides, A. N., and Wyatt, R. J. (1980): Lateral cerebral ventricular enlargement in chronic schizophrenia. *Arch. Gen. Psychiatry,* 36:735–739.
35. Weinberger, D. R., Torrey, E. F., Neophytides, A. N., and Wyatt, R. J. (1980): Structural abnormalities in the cerebral cortex of chronic schizophrenic patients. *Arch. Gen. Psychiatry,* 36:935–939.
36. Weinberger, D. R., Torrey, E. F., and Wyatt, R. J. (1979): Cerebellar atrophy in chronic schizophrenia. *Lancet,* ii:718–719.
37. Weinstein, M. R. (1954): Histopathological changes in the brain in schizophrenia. *Arch. Neurol. Psychiatry,* 71:539–553.
38. Wolpert, S. M. (1977): The ventricular size on computed tomography. *J. Comput. Assist. Tomogr.,* 1:222–226.

Discussion

Meltzer: You may have given me a new way to look at the skeletal muscle abnormalities in neuromuscular dysfunction that I've been investigating in schizophrenic patients over the years. Virtually everything that I've reported in the peripheral motor nerves and skeletal muscle fibers of psychotic patients is consistent with the concept of a 70-year-old brain affecting the alpha motor neurons of a 20- to 40-year-old body. The decreased functional activity in the motor cortex, together with a cerebellar dysfunction, acting through the trophic influence of the central nervous system (CNS) in maintaining alpha-motor-neuronal function, may be responsible for the abnormalities of motor nerve and skeletal muscle fibers I have observed (4). Your work also suggests a possible relationship between the dilated cerebral ventricles and mental retardation repeatedly found in patients with Duchenne-type muscular dystrophy and the dystrophic changes in skeletal muscle (6).

Ingvar: Do you attribute what you see to atrophy or to neuronal loss?

Weinberger: On the basis of the studies, it is impossible to determine the pathogenesis of the findings. The few pneumoencephalographers who studied patients over time never found any reversal of the changes, although most of them noted that the changes seemed to correlate best with severity of illness rather than with actual length of illness. We're now looking at older patients as a means of differentiating trait-dependent from state-dependent changes. Older schizophrenics may get much more demented than younger patients do because they have much less brain tissue left to lose. The CAT scans of 70-year-old chronic schizophrenics often show dramatic changes. It's remarkable that they're not more demented than they are. Thus, dementia may relate not only to extent of atrophy but also to dynamic factors such as rate of atrophy. Alzheimer's disease is a very rapidly progressing atrophy.

Ingvar: Have you any information on the third ventricle and thalamic contours?

Weinberger: No, but we've looked at the fourth ventricle, and find it is usually enlarged in patients with a cerebellar abnormality.

Uzman: Have you correlated these changes according to the subjects' sex?

Weinberger: We do not find significant sex differences.

Brown: How did you decide what structures to look at?

Weinberger: We began with the suspicion that something morphological was wrong with schizophrenic brains. In a very early stage, we found a patient with enlarged ventricles, and we turned to the pneumoencephalographic literature, which is unknown to most American psychiatrists. According to that literature, schizophrenic patients as a group have enlarged ventricles. That's why we chose ventricles, although they also visualize well on CAT scans. We looked at cortical structures because some of the patients had obvious dilatations.

Buchsbaum: More structures will be measurable now with the new scanners that clearly show white and gray matter, details of the basal ganglia, and cortical thickness. The next generation of CT scanners will allow us to measure 80 to 100 structures instead of the few that have been done.

Uzman: How many ways to measure ventricle size are there?

Weinberger: Several. We chose the technique of Barron et al. (1), whose study is the only other one of asymptomatic normal human volunteers evaluated by tomography. Barron et al. studied asymptomatic people between the ages of 9 months and 90 years, 15 in each decade of life. We used his data as a reference to confirm that our sample was normal. There are four or so other samples of "normals" but they are symptomatic normals: people who were scanned because they had symptoms such as headaches, but who had no confirmed neurological abnormality. These were the kind of controls who were available to pneumoencephalographers. Barron took the cut through the brain that showed the lateral cerebral ventricles at their largest and determined by planimetry what percentage of the brain space was occupied by lateral ventricle. The results of that method correlate well with computer-derived ventricular volumes. The computer method is of course the best way and the program is available; it would be easy for any of your hospitals to use.

Matthysse: It would be an excellent topic of investigation for the VA system. I hope that genetic studies would not be left out because of the phenomenon that young schizophrenic twins can have normal siblings.

Could you measure shape to find out which part of the brain is suffering the hypoplasia?

Weinberger: There's a wealth of data, since this material is all in digital form.

Buchsbaum: A patient of Dr. Dan van Kammen was found by CT scan to have another neuroanatomical abnormality—a thinness or hole in the middle of the corpus callosum. This was a woman who met all of the RDC criteria and was clinically indistinguishable from other schizophrenics. She had interesting findings on some lateralized psychological tests, and an abnormal offspring with a peculiar head they were unable to test. There probably are many other different kinds of anatomical lesions awaiting investigation.

Nasrallah: We did a postmortem study (5) of about 65 postmortem brains from a mixed group—schizophrenic, affective disorders, organic brain syndrome, and undiagnosable. We found a difference that approaches significance (0.08) between late-onset paranoid schizophrenics and early-onset, poor-prognosis schizophrenics. The difference was in the thickness of the corpus callosum, which was thicker in the early-onset than in the late-onset or the organic brain syndrome groups. We had divided the entire group arbitrarily into onset before the age of 30 and after 30, which is probably why the results only approached but did not achieve significance.

Beck: Can your scans determine changes in cortical density?

Weinberger: The machine we have used does not have the resolution to do that.

Beck: I ask because formerly it was claimed that Golgi stains showed defoliation of the apical dendritic forest of cortical pyramidal neurons.

Weinberger: I'm fascinated by the neuropathology literature of schizophrenia. Most controlled studies reported significantly more abnormalities in schizophrenic brains than in normal controls, one notable exception in English being Dunlap's (3) 1923 study. These findings were ignored because they were also found in patients with diabetic encephalopathy, Huntington's disease, or multiple infarctions.

Beck: Yes, even Papez, who gave us the notion of the limbic system, i.e., Papez's loop, was laughed at during an American Psychiatric Society meeting because he thought schizophrenia had an anatomical correlate or basis.

Weinberger: We don't know yet whether or not there are nonspecific degenerative changes in schizophrenic brains. It may not be the pathology that is specific but rather when, how, and to whom it occurs, what else is going on at the time, and how the patient copes with the deficit, which may have a great influence on the behavior of schizophrenics.

We find no significant association between ventricular enlargement and the cortical-sulcal abnormalities. They are randomly assorted, although some cases overlapped, again suggesting that the abnormalities in schizophrenia are heterogeneous. Along related lines, Davison and Bagley noted in their extensive review (2) that a tumor in almost any part of the brain can cause schizophreniform symptoms.

Melnechuk: The late Hans-Lukas Teuber (7) once concluded that although no known anatomical brain lesion would reproduce the entire syndrome of schizophrenia, focal brain lesions in many parts of the brain produced behavioral or psychological states similar to or indistinguishable from some aspects of schizophrenia.

Beck: Syphilis can also mimic schizophrenia.

REFERENCES

1. Barron, S. A., Jacobs, L., and Kinkel, W. R. (1976): Changes in size of normal lateral ventricles during aging determined by computerized tomography. *Neurology,* 26:1011–1013.
2. Davison, K., and Bagley, C. R. (1969): Schizophrenia-like psychoses associated with organic disorders of the central nervous system. In: *Current Problems in Neuropsychiatry,* edited by R. N. Herrington. *Br. J. Psychiatry (Suppl. 4),* x:113–184.
3. Dunlap, C. B. (1924): Dementia praecox: Some preliminary observations in brains from carefully selected cases and a consideration of certain sources of error. *Am. J. Psychiatry,* 3:403–421.
4. Meltzer, H. Y. (1976): Neuromuscular dysfunction in schizophrenia. *Schizophr. Bull.,* 2:106–135.
5. Nasrallah, H. A., Bigelow, L. B., Rauscher, F. P., and Wyatt, R. J. (1979): Corpus callosum thickness in schizophrenia. *Am. Psychiatric Assoc. New Res. Abstracts,* May:15.
6. Rosman, N. P. (1970): The cerebral defects and myopathy in Duchenne muscular dystrophy: A comparative clinicopathological study. *Neurology,* 20:329–335.
7. Teuber, H.-L. (1972): Effects of focal brain lesions. In: *Prospects for Research in Schizophrenia,* edited by S. S. Kety and S. Matthysse, pp. 381–384. *Neurosci. Res. Program Bull.,* 10:369–507 + vii.

Perspectives in Schizophrenia Research,
edited by C. Baxter and T. Melnechuk.
Raven Press, New York, 1980.

Quantitative Neurohistology with the Computer Microscope

Steven Matthysse and Roger Williams

Mailman Research Center, McLean Hospital, Belmont, Massachusetts 02178

LAYPERSON'S SUMMARY

The computer microscope is a powerful new tool that can be used to study the architectural geometry in the fine structure of the central nervous system. Some data are presented to illustrate how this instrument can be used to detect and analyze geometric patterns. Examples are given in which characteristic repetitive branching patterns of trees are compared to similar patterns that can be discerned with the computer microscope in the branching of dendrites in the nervous system. Just as disease alters the pattern in trees, disease might also alter the pattern of dendrites branching in the nervous system. Computer analysis permits geometric pattern recognition and quantitation. Until the advent of this technical development, such recognition and analyses were impossible. It is suggested that pattern analyses in postmortem tissues may show differences in the brains of schizophrenic patients that could be characteristic of the disease and differentiate some of them from mentally healthy controls.

NEUROHISTOLOGY WITH THE COMPUTER MICROSCOPE

It is possible to review in a few sentences what is known about the neuropathology of schizophrenia. The changes most commonly reported by the classic neuropathologists were nerve cell loss, especially in supragranulayer layers of the frontal and temporal lobes, cytoplasmic changes in neurons such as swelling and pigmentation, rarefaction of intracortical and subcortical myelin, and mild astrogliosis. For the most part, the neuropathological community has regarded these findings as indistinguishable from artifacts. As pointed out forcefully by Dr. Weinberger elsewhere in this volume, however, a new perspective, which emphasizes heterogeneity, might be somewhat kinder to findings which are not universally replicated.

If there are neuropathological changes in schizophrenia, they may be at a much finer structural level than we are used to examining. Schizophrenic patients are largely normal from a neurological perspective, so gross neuroanatomical abnormalities would not be expected. Many severely mentally retarded individuals seem to have normal brains when examined by classic techniques, even though some structural defect is almost certainly present. Our working hypothesis is that computer-assisted quantitative histologic methods will permit a more precise and objective examination of neural structure than has been possible before. We hope to apply these methods to brain tissue from schizophrenic patients in the relatively near future.

Certain studies in the literature suggest that quantitative analysis of neurohistological fine structure in diseases of obscure etiology might be revealing. Most of these studies utilize the Golgi method, which is able to impregnate the axonal and dendritic processes of entire neurons. For example, in Figure 1, taken from Berry and Bradley (1), a normal Purkinje cell is at the lower right. The dendrites are richly branched and contained in a single plane. The two other cells illustrate how the dendritic arbor is altered by changes in the synaptic milieu during development (irradiation, middle cell; lesion of the cerebellar nuclei, left cell). Figure 2, from Purpura (6), is a Golgi preparation of a biopsy from a severely retarded 10-month-old child. The only abnormality apparent is that the dendritic spines are unusually long and tortuous (right) compared to normal (left). In both these examples, the changes in morphology are convincing in Golgi preparations, but they would not be apparent in the cell and with fiber stains employed conventionally in neuropathology laboratories.

The billions of neurons in the central nervous system can be divided into a

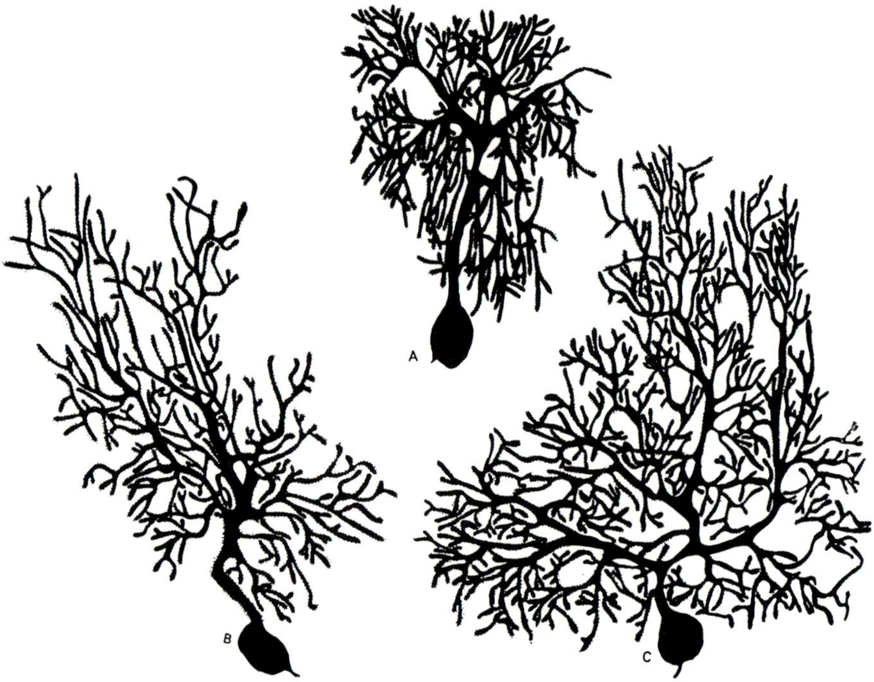

FIG. 1. Morphology of normal and abnormal Purkinje cells.

FIG. 2. Dendritic spines in normal cortex *(1)* and in a retarded child *(2)*.

finite number of morphological subspecies based on similarities and differences in the shape of their axonal and dendritic processes. These branching patterns are exceedingly complex, and their final form is governed by the interaction of many factors, many of which are largely unknown. Some insights may be gained from botany, a field where the classification of the shapes of branched structures has received attention for a long time.

> Trees growing in a sunny or windy position are more branched, shorter and less straight, and in general mountain trees have more knots than those that grow in plains, and those that grow in dry spots more knots than those that grow in marshes. (Theophrastus, Enquiry Into Plants, c.350 B.C.)

It is possible for field workers to tell that the tree in Figure 3 has suffered damage, because of its bayonet-shaped branches (2). When the apical meristem, which is the growing tip of a plant, is damaged, a lateral meristem takes over and starts off at right angles, then begins to curve upward in order to reach the light. We postulate that the dendritic tree will be a permanent record of the environmental life history of the cell, just as it is in the woody tree.

FIG. 3. Tree trunk showing morphologic abnormalities caused by injury.

We believe that computer analysis is essential for descriptions of neuronal geometry, because of the problem of subjective bias. Figure 4, from Mandelbrot (4), is a randomly generated pattern of lines, completely isotropic with respect to angles. If one had a preconceived expectation about the predominant directions in this set of lines, this ambiguous diagram could easily be construed as confirming it. The human brain is a wonderful pattern recognizing machine, so good that it even finds patterns when they are not there.

A complementary limitation of subjective pattern recognition appears in Figure 5 (5). Somewhere in this pattern, a change occurs. In the outer portion, the angles are randomly selected from a uniform distribution between zero and 180°. In the inner portion of the square, the angles are random but not uniform;

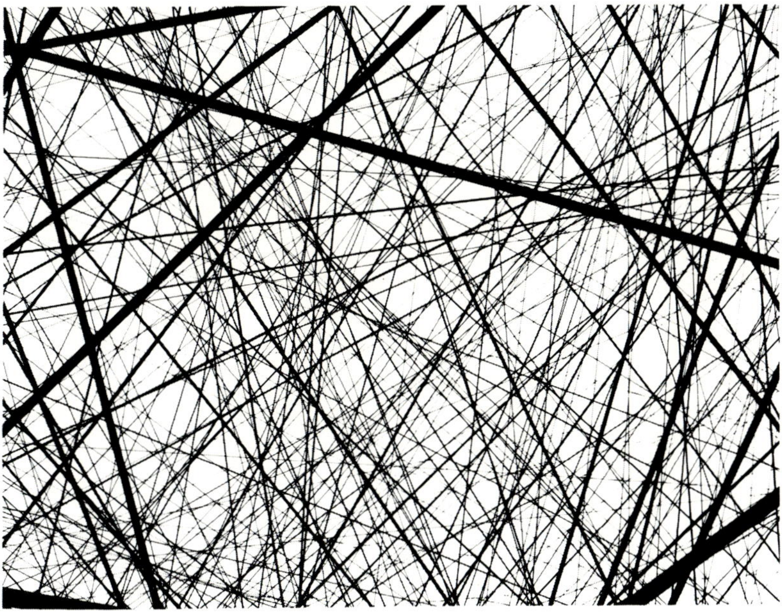

FIG. 4. Random pattern of lines, susceptible to bias in pattern recognition.

they are restricted to 60°, 120°, or 180°. Nevertheless, no zone of demarcation appears in the diagram. The computer readily ascertains that the histogram of angles is different inside than outside, but the human pattern recognizing machine is not programmed to make that discrimination. Similarly, there may be structure and orderliness in the nervous system that fails to impress us subjectively. Thus there are two pitfalls to avoid: false positives—finding order where there is none, and false negatives—failing to find order where it does exist.

Our work to date has been largely concerned with the quantitative analysis of the dendritic structure of hippocampal granule cells in the mouse. After we have studied the sensitivity of this system to pathological changes, we will be in a position to apply the method to human brain specimens. We are grateful to Dr. Richard Sidman for making the computer microscope in his laboratory available to us.

Figure 6 is a drawing of a typical hippocampal granule cell, as viewed in Golgi preparations. It shows the characteristic "wineglass" shape. In order to express this form in quantitative terms, we have to decide what the crucial parameters are. In view of the cylindrical symmetry of the cell, we define an "ideal axis" by computing a unit vector in the direction of the vector sum of all the branches. This vector represents the general tendency of the outward growth of the cell. Now we are in a position to ask how strict the axis of

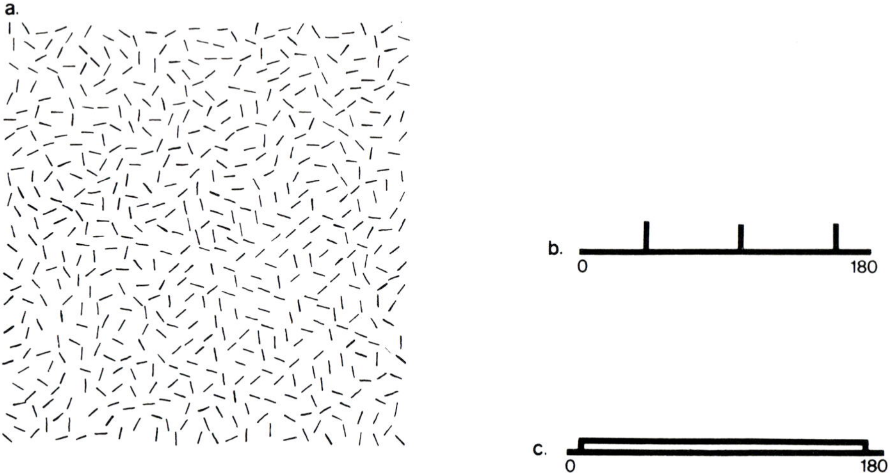

FIG. 5. Angular pattern not detectable by human pattern vision.

symmetry is. If the symmetry is exact, any cross section perpendicular to the ideal axis will have the axis intersection as its geometric center.

Figure 7 shows five planes, perpendicular to the ideal axis, and occupying successively higher levels of the molecular layer. These planes are reconstructed from the microscope data by computer. The X's represent the intersections of

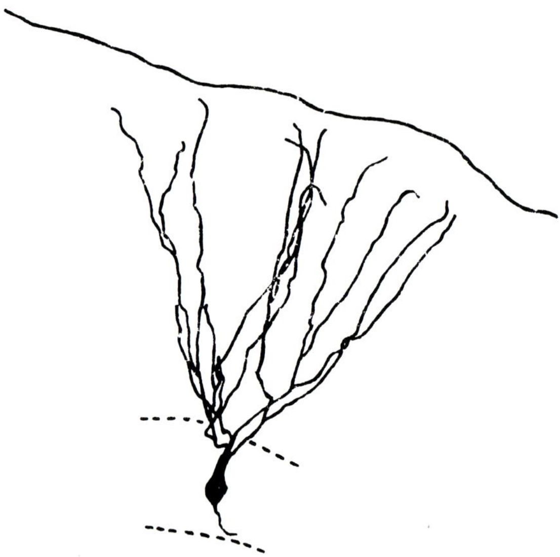

FIG. 6. Normal mouse hippocampal granule cell.

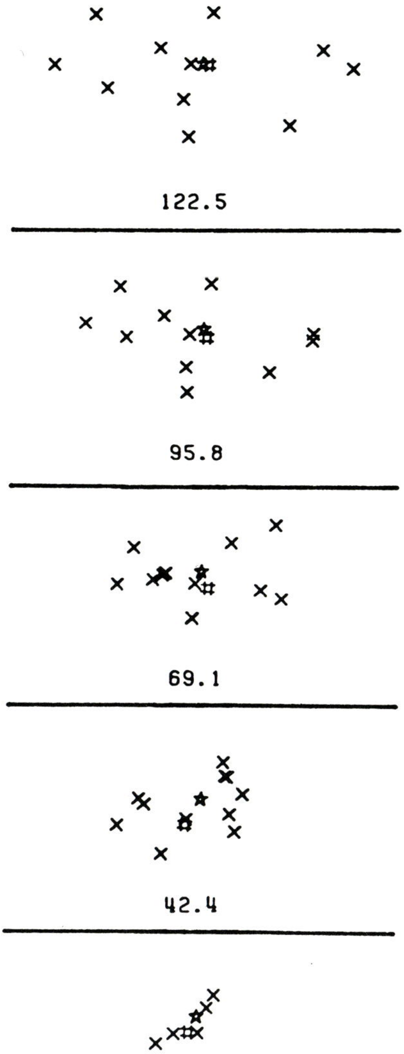

FIG. 7. Serial cross sections of hippocampal granule cell dendrites.

the dendritic segments with the plane of the cross section. The stars represent the geometric center of these intersections. The number symbols represent the intersection of the ideal axis with the plane. As the dendritic arbor grows outward, it gets larger, but this particular cell remains axial: the geometric center and the ideal axis almost coincide in every plane. This arbor also has a simple ellipsoidal form in the outer layers. In our experience, most mouse hippocampal granule cells are strongly axial, and this ellipsoidal shape is often seen in the outer layers, although sometimes the configuration is more planar.

We have preliminary results on 27 granule cells in the normal mouse hippocampus. The *planar angle* is defined as the angle of inclination of the plane of the daughter branches with respect to the main axis of the cell. As shown in Figure 8, it is strongly concentrated around zero. The *bisector angle* indicates whether, within their plane, the daughter branches emerge symmetrically or asymmetrically with respect to the central axis. Figure 9 indicates that the bisector angle is also concentrated around zero. These two regular features—

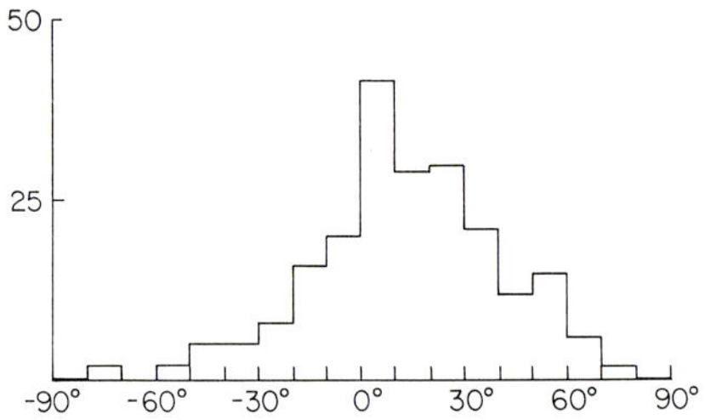

FIG. 8. Distribution of planar angles of normal mouse hippocampal granule cells.

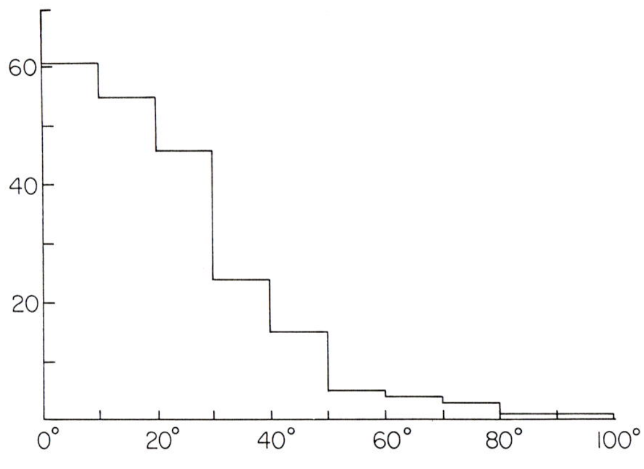

FIG. 9. Distribution of bisector angles of normal mouse hippocampal granule cells.

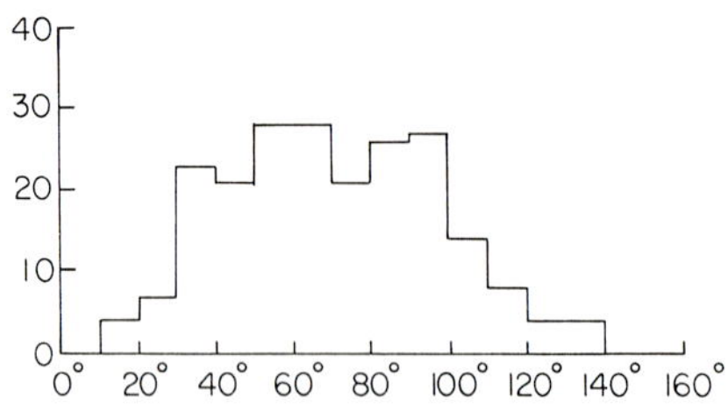

FIG. 10. Distribution of daughter angles of normal mouse hippocampal granule cells.

the planar angle and the bisector angle—give rise to the characteristic wineglass shape of the hippocampal granule cell. The angle between the daughter branches *("daughter angle")* is much more variable (Fig. 10). It is as if the angle between the daughters were less crucial in preserving the characteristic shape than the angle their bisector makes with the main axis of the cell. Lindsay and Scheibel (3) obtained similar results on daughter angles in pyramidal cells from the adult rat neocortex. It seems that globally rather than locally defined angles will be the most likely to reveal orderly relationships.

In view of our ambition to apply these methods to the study of schizophrenia, it is fortunate that the Golgi method can be used with human postmortem material under favorable conditions. Figure 11 is from a study by Williams et al. (8) on the effect of postmortem time on Golgi preparations. The left specimen was fixed at 5 min post-mortem, the middle one at 6 hr, and the right at 24 hr. The 24-hr preparations are not very useful, but at 6 hr, while fewer cells are stained, the quality of the impregnations of individual cells is good. Using

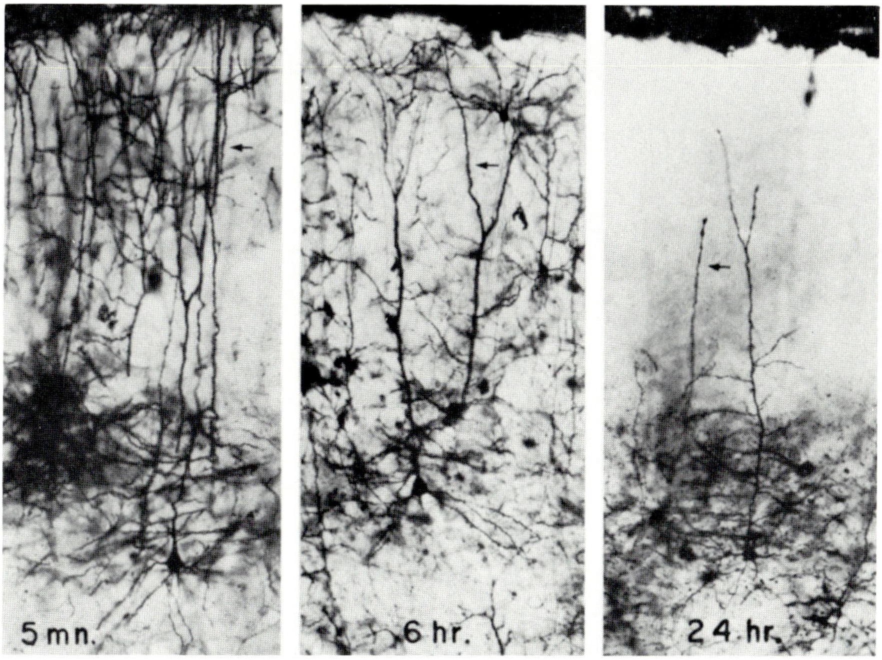

Fig. 11. Effect of postmortem time on Golgi preparations. Low-power photomicrographs of layers 1–5 of the adult mouse neocortex as seen with fixation within 5 min, 6 hr, and 24 hr of death. Silver chromate precipitate is seen at the pial surface. In tissue fixed by immersion within minutes of death, or after latencies of up to 6 hr, most impregnated cells are completely impregnated. The apical shafts of pyramidal neurons *(arrows)* are well demonstrated where they arborize in the superficial layers. With fixation latencies of 24 hr, few cellular elements are impregnated in the superficial layers. The apical shafts of pyramidal neurons impregnated in the deep layers appear truncated and are varicose (× 240).

these methods, it should soon be possible to carry out quantitative analysis of dendritic geometry in specimens from patients with neuropsychiatric diseases.

Some interesting geometrical information can also be obtained using ordinary Nissl-stained brain specimens. Figure 12 is area 4a from the von Economo (7) atlas of normal human brain. The cells are not arranged at random, but rather in columns, with the long axis of the Betz cells oriented parallel to the flow. Parallel order is a feature that has been overlooked in the description of pathologi-

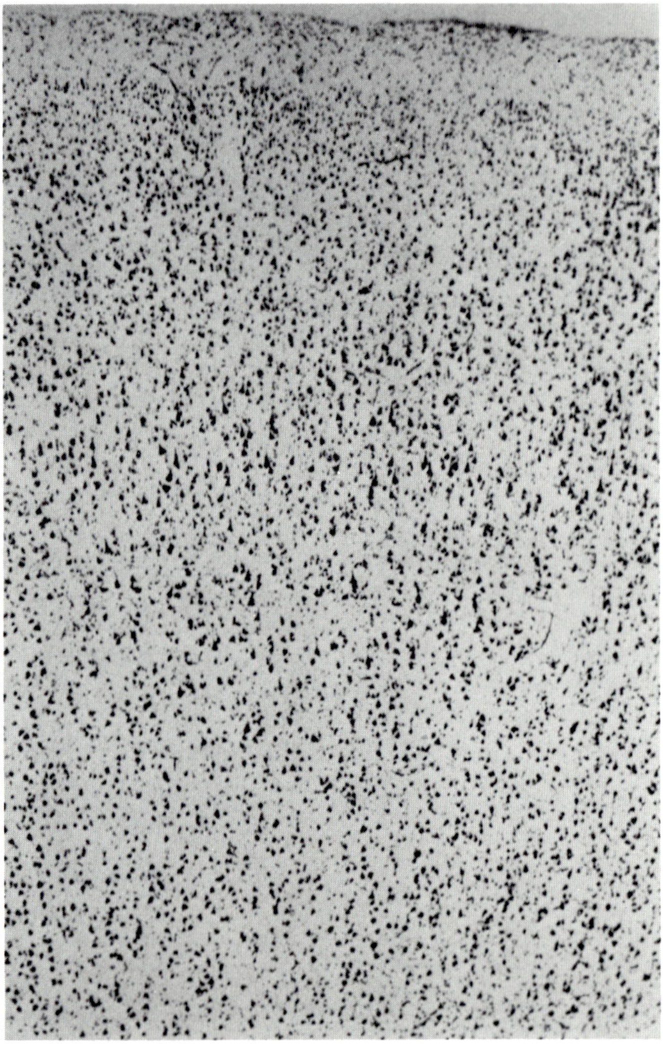

FIG. 12. Columnar organization of normal human neocortex. Area 4a of the human brain. Toluidine blue. From von Economo and Koskinas (7). Magnification about 45:1.

cal material, perhaps because of the difficulties of quantitating it. Figure 13 is area 4 gamma from the same atlas; it illustrates local rather than global parallelism, since the alignment is parallel in any small region, but the predominant direction changes from place to place. Figure 14, from area 6, illustrates a third variant of parallelism, in which the columns of cells seem to fan out from a central point. We would like to ask: In mental retardation, schizophrenia, and other neuropsychiatric diseases, will there be changes in the orderly arrange-

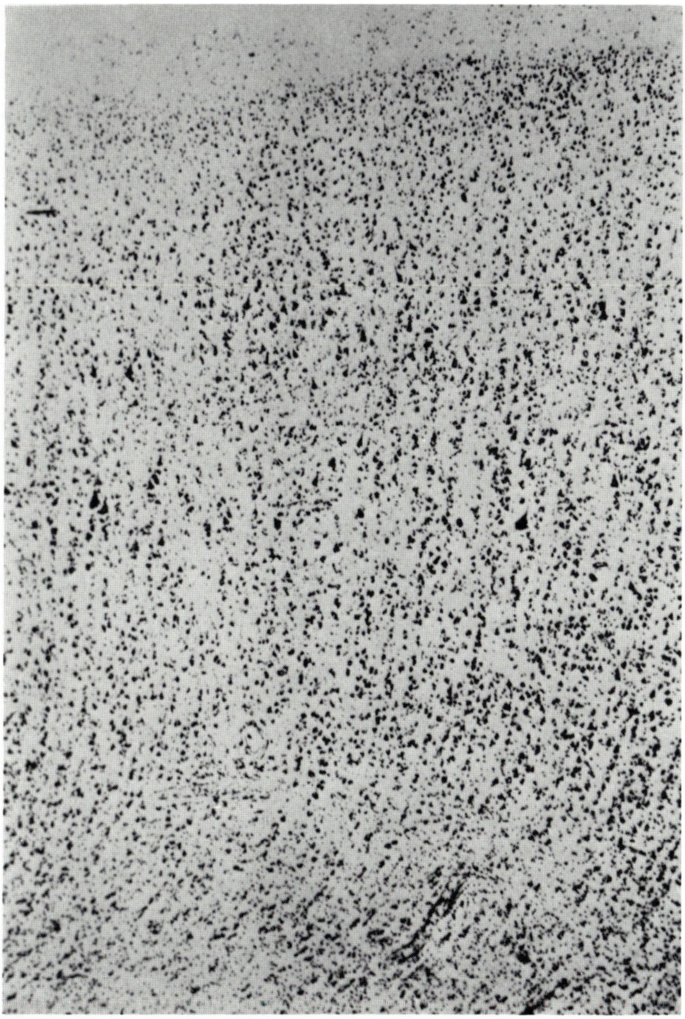

FIG. 13. Columnar organization of normal human neocortex. Area 4γ of the human brain. Toluidine blue. From von Economo and Koskinas (7). Magnification about 45:1.

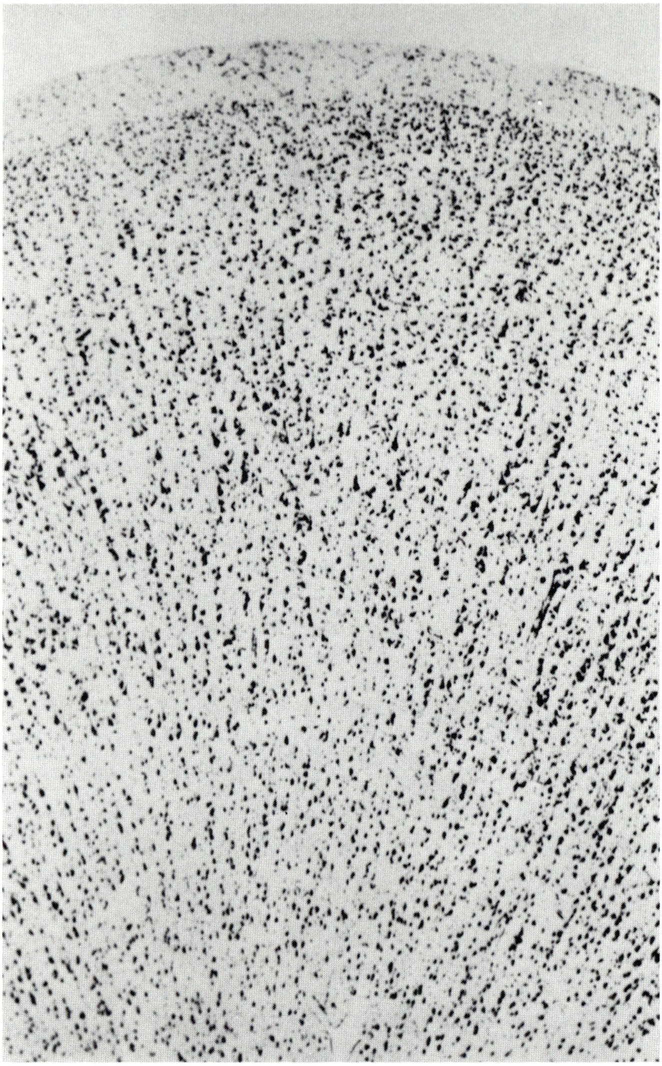

FIG. 14. Columnar organization of normal human neocortex. Area 6 of the human brain. Toluidine blue. From von Economo and Koskinas (7). Magnification about 45:1.

ment of the cells? This question is attractive because it requires only conventional staining methods.

As these illustrations suggest, the problem of subjective bias is particularly troublesome in making judgments of local and global parallelism. To circumvent this difficulty, we have implemented a computer algorithm based on the Fourier transform. It is analogous, in the spatial domain, to the transform in the time

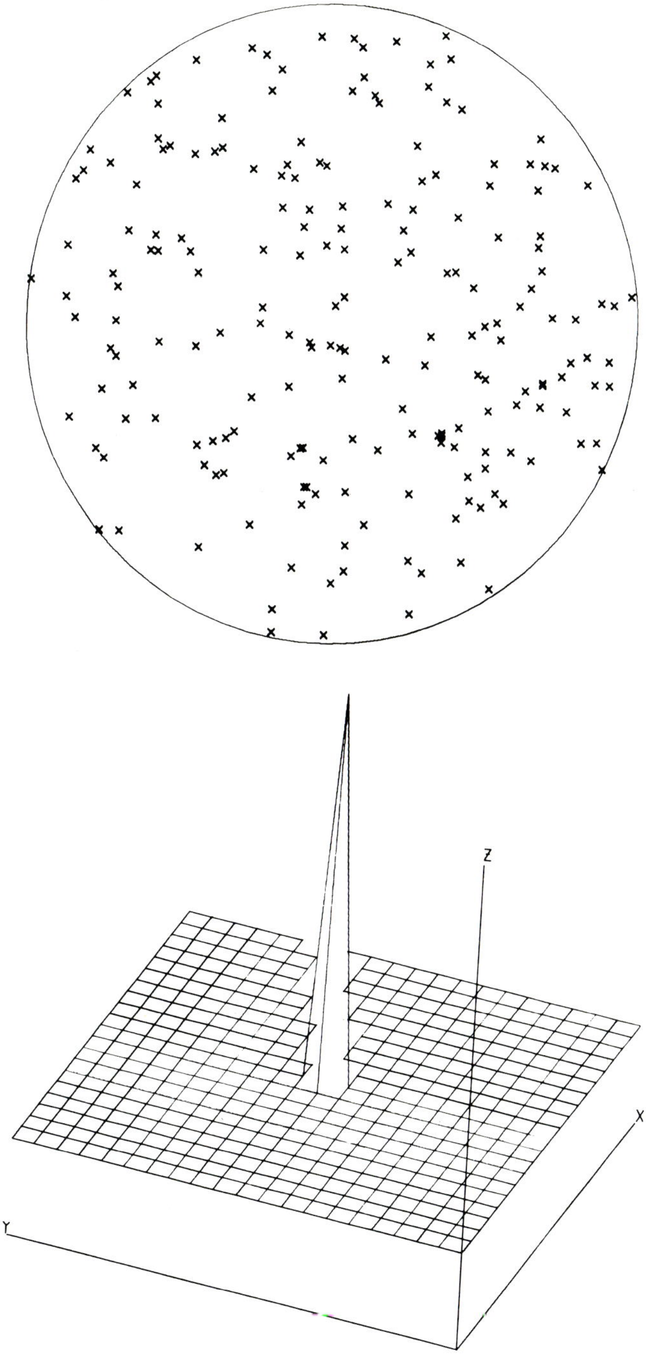

FIGS. 15 and 16. Random point pattern and its spatial Fourier transform.

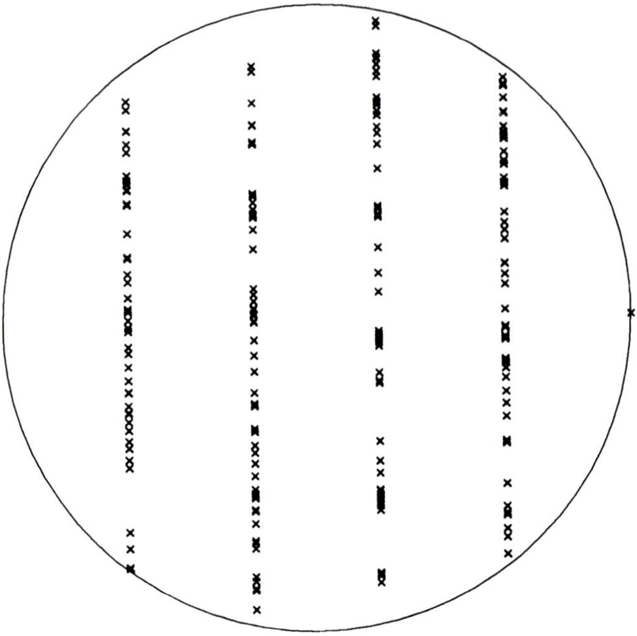

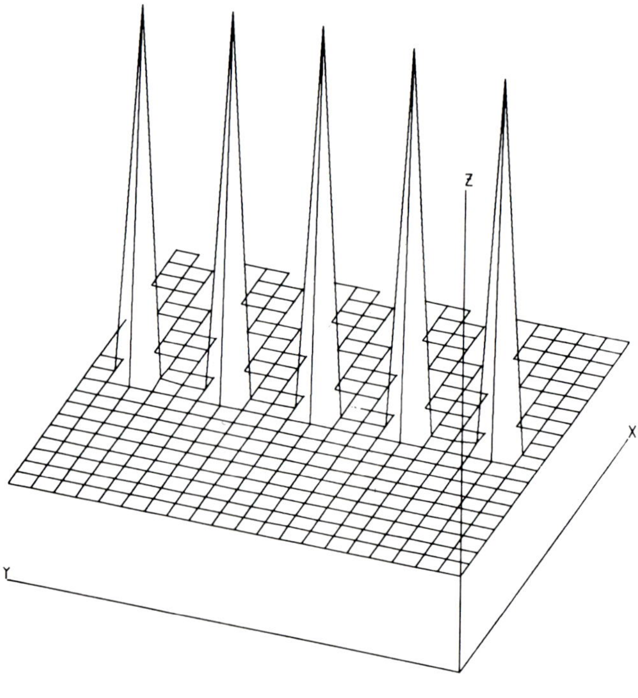

FIGS. 17 and 18. Perfectly ordered point pattern and its spatial Fourier transform.

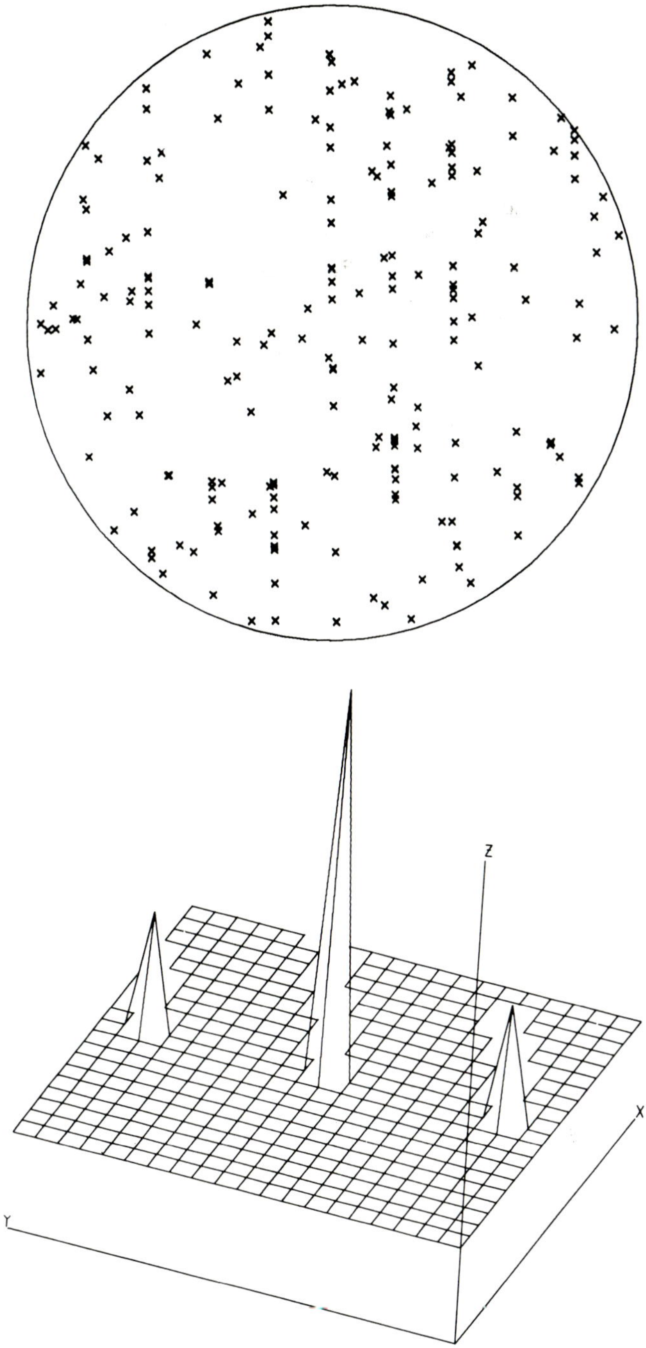

FIGS. 19 and 20. Partially ordered point pattern and its spatial Fourier transform.

domain which reveals the frequency components of auditory signals. Peaks in the spatial Fourier transform occur whenever there is a spatially repetitive pattern. The height of the peak indicates the degree of orderliness of the repetition, and the spacing of the peaks is inversely proportional to the width of the repeating pattern. The technique is illustrated in Figures 15 through 20.

Figure 15 is a computer-drawn pattern of points, randomly arranged in space. The corresponding spatial Fourier transform has one peak, at the origin; this peak is always present (Fig. 16). Figure 17 is a perfectly ordered arrangement of points in columns. The corresponding Fourier transform displays a regular set of peaks (Fig. 18). Figure 19 is an arrangement where half the points are random and half are arranged in regular columns. This is the kind of pattern that the human observer might feel uncertain about classifying. The Fourier transform of this pattern (Fig. 20) gives, in addition to the peak at the origin which is always present, peaks half as high as those in the previous transform, indicating that half the points are arranged in an orderly pattern. We believe that this type of analysis will overcome the problem of subjective bias, and make possible quantitative comparisons of order and disorder in neuropathologic material.

Since our studies in quantitative neurohistology have only just begun, we are not able to present data and conclusions. We are hopeful, however, that this approach will prove useful in the study of schizophrenia.

REFERENCES

1. Bradley, P., and Berry, M. (1976): The effects of reduced climbing and parallel fiber input on Purkinje cell dendritic growth. *Brain Res.*, 109:133–151.
2. Halle, F., Oldeman, R. A. A., and Tomlinson, P. B. (1978): *Tropical Trees and Forests: An Architectural Analysis.* Springer-Verlag, Berlin.
3. Lindsay, R. D., and Scheibel, A. B. (1974): Quantitative analysis of the dendritic branching pattern of small pyramidal cells from adult rat somesthetic and visual cortex. *Exp. Neurol.*, 45:424–34.
4. Mandelbrot, B. B. (1977): *Fractals: Form, Chance and Dimension.* W. H. Freeman, San Francisco.
5. Marr, D. (1977): Representing visual information. M.I.T. Artificial Intelligence Monograph 415.
6. Purpura, D. P. (1974): Dendritic spine 'dysgenesis' and mental retardation. *Science*, 186:1125–1128.
7. Von Economo, C., and Koskinas, G. N. (1925): *Die Cytoarchitektonik der Hirnrinde des erwachsenen Menschen.* Julius Springer, Vienna.
8. Williams, R. S., Ferrante, R. J., and Caviness, V. S., Jr. (1978): The Golgi-rapid method in clinical neuropathology: I. Morphologic consequences of suboptimum fixation. *J. Neuropathol. Exp. Neurol.*, 37:1333.

Discussion

Yuwiler: The very strength of the Golgi, which is that it stains some but not all neurons, has also been a source of concern, because without knowing the basis for its selectivity, one is not sure he isn't just looking at an atypical subpopulation of cells. Are there any new ideas on the mechanism for selectivity of the Golgi?

Matthysse: It's still a mystery.

Yuwiler: Of course, if the population stained in schizophrenic brain has abnormal morphology, that still may be an important clue even if the abnormalities are limited to a subpopulation of cells.

Baxter: If a tree has, say, a wineglass shape, you can justify its shape in terms of its need to maximize the capture of light energy and optimize photosynthesis. Could a wineglass shape of a neuron be justified in functional terms?

Matthysse: I feel sure that it's possible. In the cerebellum, it seems likely that the planar nature of Purkinje cell dendritic trees is related to its reception of information from the parallel fibers. I think we can come to grips with this problem by doing deafferentation experiments.

Meltzer: Many factors must be taken into account before what you are discovering can be considered representative of the de novo situation. For example, catecholaminergic neurons are turned on and off, perhaps for a long time, by drugs. Alpha motor neurons are exquisitely sensitive to their environment, particularly to adjacent nerve cells, such that the activity or malfunction or death of one affects its neighbors. They are not static; they continuously branch and sprout, so that the analogy of neurons to trees has also been used in muscle-disease studies to describe the terminal branching of motor neurons. I invite you to look at our preparations of subterminal motor nerves of psychotic patients, where we found characteristic increased branching and sprouting and abnormalities in terminal arborization.

Matthysse: I'd be delighted to accept. I don't think it would be too difficult to analyze the branching of alpha motor neurons. The analytical process is both an art and a science. One might begin by taking a good look, just artistically, at the cells, seeing what seems to be present—not double blind!—and then processing the tissue blind.

Perspectives in Schizophrenia Research,
edited by C. Baxter and T. Melnechuk.
Raven Press, New York, 1980.

Computer-Analyzed Electroencephalogram to Predict the Therapeutic Outcome in Schizophrenia

Turan M. Itil

Division of Biological Psychiatry, New York Medical College, Valhalla, New York 10595; and Center for Biological Psychiatry, V.A. Health Care Facility, Montrose, New York 10548

LAYPERSON'S SUMMARY

Two important findings were established in recent years:

1. A group of patients with schizophrenia have different brain function from that of a matched control group of healthy subjects when the brain function is evaluated based on the scalp-recorded and computer-analyzed electroencephalogram (CEEG). Surprisingly, a group of psychotic children and a group of children of schizophrenic parents (so-called high-risk children) also have a different CEEG pattern from that of control groups. The types of CEEGs (low voltage, fast EEG with sporadic occurrence of very slow waves) of the "sick" groups (adult schizophrenics, psychotic children, high-risk children) show certain similarities to each other and to those seen after administration of hallucinogenic compounds.
2. All drugs effective in schizophrenic syndromes (major tranquilizers or neuroleptics) produce, after single test dosages or during multiple administration, systematic EEG alterations. The CEEG effects of neuroleptics are characterized by an increase of slow and decrease of fast frequencies. These effects are diametrically opposite to the EEG pattern of schizophrenic and hallucinogenic drugs.

Based on these findings, two hypotheses were developed to determine the therapeutic outcome in schizophrenia:

1. Patients with "typical" schizophrenia EEG pattern (low voltage, dysynchronized fast activity) have a better response to neuroleptic drugs in conventional dosages than those patients with slow EEG, or particularly with high-voltage, rhythmical synchronous, slow alpha EEGs. The latter type of EEG pattern reflects an "inhibition" of the stimulatory effects of reticular activating system of the brainstem on the cortical functions.
2. There is a close relationship between the CEEG response of a patient to a single test dose neuroleptic and the therapeutic response after multiple dosages: whereas schizophrenia patients who show a good outcome to neuroleptic treat-

ment demonstrate the "typical" CEEG response to a neuroleptic (neuroleptic CEEG profile), patients with poor outcome do not show any response, or they do show response as normal subjects with response to a psychostimulant.

Accordingly, based on the test dose procedures using computer-analyzed EEG, it may be possible to tailor the type of the drug treatment and the dosage for each individual patient. A "typical" CEEG response of a schizophrenic patient to a neuroleptic compound indicates that this drug is adequately absorbed, properly metabolized, penetrated through the blood-brain barrier, and has noticeable effects on the brain function of this particular patient. Whether these types of effects also have a significant relationship to therapeutic outcome requires further well-controlled studies.

INTRODUCTION

One of the major goals in schizophrenia research is to predict the therapeutic outcome based on objective criteria. Specialized electroencephalographic (EEG) investigations in recent years with child and adult schizophrenics, "high-risk" children, and antipsychotic (neuroleptic) drugs suggest that computer-analyzed EEG (CEEG) can be used to predict the outcome, particularly when the modality is treatment by pharmaceuticals. This report will summarize some highlights of our own CEEG investigations. Other investigators' work can be found in previously published review articles (4,24,39).

QUANTITATIVE EEG FINDINGS IN SCHIZOPHRENIA

No pathognomonic quantitative EEG characteristics were established for schizophrenia. Neither was it possible to use CEEG for a diagnostic tool in schizophrenia. Nevertheless, systematic differences in EEG pattern between schizophrenic patients and a matched control group of normals were established.

CEEG in Adult Schizophrenia

A large study was conducted to answer the question of whether the CEEG pattern of adult schizophrenic patients is different from that of normals (26). Multiple shortcomings of the previous studies were overcome, to wit: (a) the sample size was large enough to have statistical evaluation (100 schizophrenics versus 100 matched normal controls); (b) diagnosis was established based on a variety of rating scales and by at least two psychiatrists; (c) matching with normals was done carefully and the EEG was analyzed by two different quantitative methods (power spectrum and period analysis). Analog frequency analyzer data demonstrated that schizophrenics showed a significantly higher power in slow and very fast frequencies, but low power in alpha bands ($p = 0.05$–0.01, analysis of variance and two sample t-tests) as compared with normals. Digital computer period analysis indicated that the schizophrenic patients had significantly (analysis of variance and two sample *t*-tests) more slow delta waves (1.3 to 3.5 cps, $p < 0.05$) and significantly more superimposed high-frequency waves (40 to 50 cps first derivative) ($p < 0.01$) than normal volunteers. On the other hand, schizophrenics showed significantly less 13 to 20 cps activity in the primary wave analysis and significantly more over 20 cps activity in the first derivative measurements (all at the $p < 0.01$ level of significance). Multiple discriminant analysis showed that the group of schizophrenic patients could be clearly differentiated from the normal group based on both methods of analysis (at the level of $p < 0.005$ significance discriminant analysis) (28).

The further question arose as to whether these findings, which were the result of a single EEG recording, might be due to chance. For this reason we conducted CEEG investigations in one group of schizophrenics at weekly intervals and in another group of schizophrenics at monthly intervals. Both groups were matched with the normal control subjects. The results demonstrated that regardless of whether the subjects were recorded at weekly or monthly intervals, the schizophrenics did have a different CEEG pattern from those of a matched group of normals (29). The differences were stable. CEEG of schizophrenics was characterized by a low-voltage "desynchronized" fast beta activity. These "stability" investigations, as we named them, confirmed that the CEEG pattern of a group of adult schizophrenics is significantly different from those of a matched group of normal volunteers.

CEEG in Schizophrenic Children

The CEEG study of a group of psychotic children (the majority were diagnosed as schizophrenic) and a matched group of normal children indicated that the CEEG profiles of both groups were significantly different (30). Psychotic children are characterized by more slow waves (3.5 to 5.5 cps) and more high-frequency waves (about 20 cps in the primary wave measurements, and about 30 cps waves in the first derivative measurements) than the control group of subjects. Interestingly, although the frequency distribution of children and adults differs, the differences in EEG pattern between psychotic children and controls are very similar to those seen in adult schizophrenics and normal controls.

CEEG Findings in Children at "High Risk" for Schizophrenia

As mentioned, in our previous studies we overcame many of the weaknesses inherent in earlier EEG-schizophrenia studies. Still, the basic methodological approach had the weakness of being a "retrospective" study model. Within the "prospective" schizophrenia research program of Mednick and Schulsinger (35), we investigated the CEEG pattern of a group of children at high risk for schizophrenia (26). Results of the data analysis demonstrated that the high-risk children, in contrast to the control group, were characterized by an increase of very slow and particularly very fast beta waves in both primary wave and first derivative measurements, and a decrease of alpha activities in the 10 to 13 cps range. High-risk children have significantly higher average frequencies in the first derivative and higher frequency deviations in the primary wave and first derivative measurements than do the control subjects. High-risk children showed significantly less amplitude variability. Both groups could be differentiated significantly ($p < 0.01$ discriminant analysis) from each other by CEEG measurements. A striking result of this study was that the differences in CEEG measurements between high-risk children and the control group were similar to those seen in the studies of adult schizophrenics and psychotic children.

Sleep CEEG Findings

In order to test whether the increase of fast beta activity in the resting EEG of schizophrenics originates in muscle, a finding suggested by some investigators, a series of all-night sleep studies were conducted. Using digital computer analysis of all-night sleep EEG, based on the "sleep print" method and on automatic classification of the sleep stages, we found that when schizophrenic patients were compared with nonpsychotic subjects, the former had significantly fewer deep sleep stages (stages 2, 3, and 4) and more light sleep stages and awakening periods (25). The evaluation of the computer-analyzed EEG variables during rapid eye movement (REM) periods demonstrated that schizophrenics have more superimposed, very fast activity, fewer slow delta waves, less frequency deviation, lower amplitude variability, and average absolute amplitude than nonpsychotic subjects. Thus these findings confirm the data from the awakening EEG studies. Since the muscle potential decreased during REM periods, we could postulate that the presence of fast activity in schizophrenia cannot be linked to the increase of muscle potentials.

CEEG FINDINGS AFTER HALLUCINOGENIC COMPOUNDS

Chemicals that produce experimental hallucinations such as LSD-25, bufotenine, and mescaline also produce systematic changes in human EEG. Using analog frequency analyzer and digital computer methods, our results demonstrated that LSD-25 significantly increases desynchronous fast potentials and decreases slower wave forms in scalp-recorded human EEG (1). In contrast to indole hallucinogens (LSD-25, bufotenine, and mescaline), anticholinergic hallucinogens such as *N*-ethyl-3-piperidyl phenylcyclopentylglycolate (Ditran ®) and (1-12-diethylaminoethyl) phenobarbital (Hexamid ®) produce not only more fast waves but also very slow potentials (19). Accordingly, the EEG changes induced by indole hallucinogens, particularly anticholinergic hallucinogens, bear a strong resemblance to the EEG pattern of schizophrenics (Fig. 1).

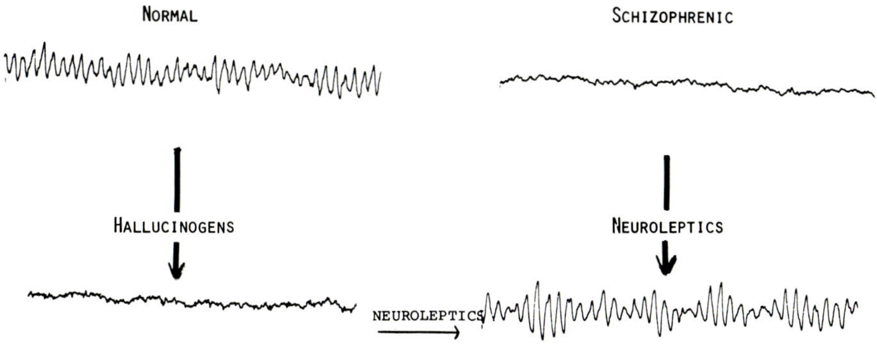

FIG. 1. EEG pattern of normals, schizophrenics, and effects of psychotropic drugs. EEG pattern of schizophrenics is characterized by low-voltage desynchronized fast activity. Similar records are seen after hallucinogenic compounds in normal subjects. Neuroleptics decrease fast activities and increase alpha waves and slower potentials. Thus reversal EEG findings are observed after neuroleptics both in schizophrenics and in hallucinogenic-induced psychosis.

CEEG OF NEUROLEPTICS

According to clinical EEG investigations, it was found that all chronically administered neuroleptics produce systematic changes in scalp-recorded human EEG, which is characterized by a decrease of fast waves and an increase of rhythmical and synchronous slow alpha waves and/or accentuation of the slower potentials (2,9,18,22) (Fig. 1). Also, all-night sleep investigations indicated that the neuroleptics produce systematic EEG changes. Neuroleptics with strong sedative properties produce more sleep stage 4 and less sleep stage 1 and awakening periods, whereas neuroleptics with potent extrapyramidal side effects produce less stage 4 sleep (21). In recent years, we established that neuroleptics also cause systematic CEEG changes when only one single dose is administered orally in normal volunteers. The decrease of fast potentials and an increase of slow waves in both primary wave and first derivative measurements are the most characteristic changes associated with neuroleptic compounds (23).

BEHAVIOR-EEG CORRELATIONS

According to our studies, which have been corroborated by other investigators, there are close correlations between changes in EEG and behavior if the changes occur in a fast and marked degree, and if the evaluation of EEG and behavior is done quantitatively. In a large study, we established that the more we observed a decrease of high-frequency beta activity and the more we noted an increase of slow waves and alpha waves in EEG during drug treatment, the more frequently we could expect psychopathological improvement (27). There was statistically significant correlation between a decrease of high-frequency fast activities

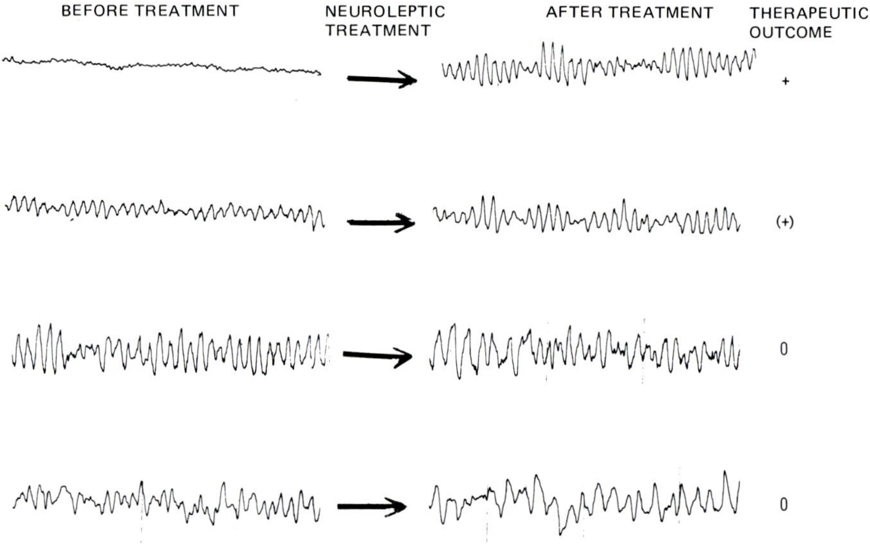

FIG. 2. EEG behavior relationship in schizophrenia. According to the quantitative EEG studies, the type (increase of slower potentials and decrease of fast activities) and the degree of the changes in EEGs are correlated with the therapeutic outcome during drug treatment in schizophrenic patients. The more fast activities are prevalent in pretreatment EEG records of schizophrenics, the more improvement in psychopathology is expected.

and the improvement of global psychiatric symptomatology during the neuroleptic treatment of schizophrenic patients. Furthermore, it was found that the more fast activity a patient has in pretreatment EEG, the better is the therapeutic outcome to a subsequent drug treatment (Fig. 2). Patients who have more slow alpha activity, fewer fast beta waves, and higher amplitudes or abnormal potentials with slow waves, epileptic activities in pretreatment EEG, have poor therapeutic outcomes (therapy-resistant patients). The cluster analysis has clearly identified that schizophrenic patients with a marked degree of acute (florid) psychotic symptoms (responsive patients) also have lower amplitudes, fast beta EEGs, and a lesser degree of alpha activity (27).

TEST DOSE CEEG RESPONSES IN PREDICTION OF OUTCOME

In recent years we have established that therapeutically equivalent compounds (for example, all neuroleptics) even after a single oral dose produce identifiable systematic and statistically significant changes within 3 to 6 hr after administration. Surprisingly, the mean CEEG changes (group CEEG profile) found after a single-dose neuroleptic in a group of normal volunteers strikingly resemble those seen in a group of schizophrenics (mean of the group) after repetitive dose administrations (Fig. 3) (23). Furthermore, it was observed that only 4

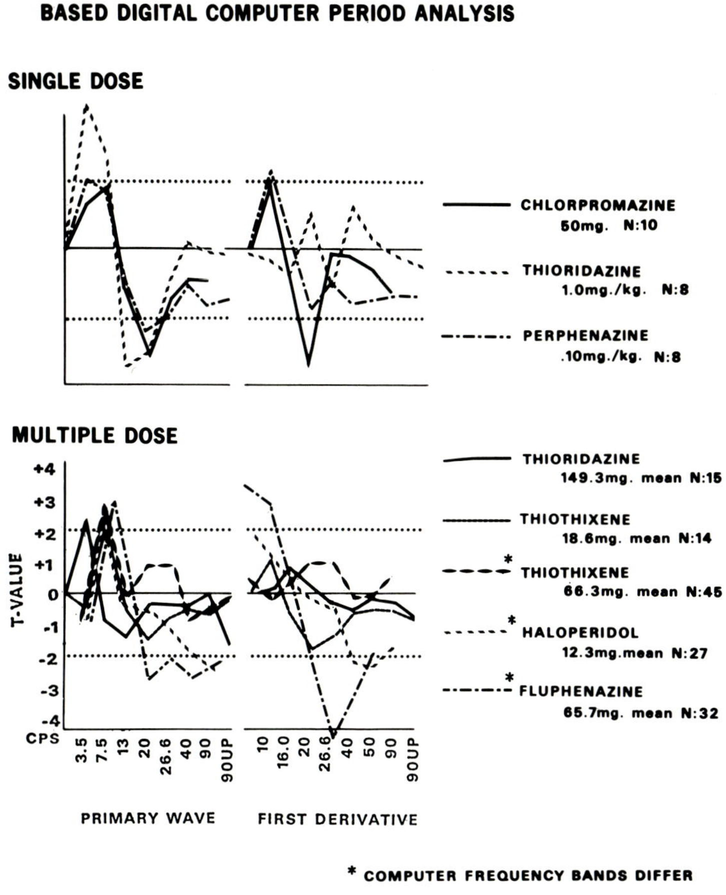

FIG. 3. CEEG profiles of major tranquilizers. In the abscissa, 16 frequency bands of the digital computer period analysis; in the ordinate, changes from pre-drug administration in terms of *t*-values. In the upper part of the figure, the CEEG profiles of chlorpromazine, thioridazine, and perphenazine are seen after single oral test dose in normal volunteers. In the bottom part of the figure, the CEEG profiles of thioridazine, thiothixene (in 2 studies), haloperidol, and fluphenazine are seen after multiple dose, chronic administration of neuroleptics in schizophrenic patients. The EEG records were done before and 3 hr after single test dose administration in normals *(upper figure),* and before and 1 month after chronic treatment in schizophrenics.

As seen, the CEEG profiles of neuroleptics are similar in temporal shape whether they are administered single dose in normal volunteers or multiple dose in schizophrenic patients. Overall, the CEEG profiles of neuroleptics are characterized by an increase of slow waves and decrease of faster potentials in both primary wave and first derivative measurements.

Thioridazine, in comparison to other neuroleptics, produces more slow waves after single dose in normals and multiple dose in schizophrenics.

to 8 out of 10 to 16 normal subjects in each study show the "typical" neuroleptic EEG response (CEEG profile); these individuals apparently influence the group's CEEG profile. The rest have no noticeable response or have different responses (paradoxical response) (Fig. 4). A "typical" response to a neuroleptic compound is characterized by an increase of slower potentials (including slow alpha waves) and a decrease of fast waves in both primary waves and first derivative measurements. After a single test dose, some schizophrenics also show the "typical" or "good" response (characteristic neuroleptic CEEG profile), some no response, and some other paradoxical response (Fig. 5). The correlation statistics demonstrated that when more low-voltage fast beta waves are present in a pre-drug EEG, the more "typical" neuroleptic CEEG response (profile) to a neuroleptic can be expected.

In a recent study we investigated the CEEG response of chronic, therapy-resistant schizophrenics (20) to some of the well-known neuroleptics such as haloperidol, thiothixene, fluphenazine hydrochloride, and molindone. None of the 14 investigated patients showed any "typical" neuroleptic response to any of the administered neuroleptics. In general, this group of schizophrenic patients responded to neuroleptic compounds as a majority of normals would respond to a psychostimulant compound (Fig. 6). Accordingly, two possibilities existed: (a) the bioavailability of neuroleptics in this group of schizophrenics (chronic, therapy-resistant schizophrenics) was inadequate in the dosages administered; or (b) in comparison to the normal volunteers and "responsive" schizophrenic patients, in the "therapy-resistant" schizophrenic patients neuroleptics produced different biochemical effects, thus the associated electrophysiological response also deviated. The question whether or not to have "typical" CEEG response to a single test dose neuroleptic correlated with the blood levels of the compound—and/or therapeutic effects, side effects, or both—is now being studied in part in collaboration with Dr. May. It is obvious that the correlation of clinical and/or blood level data with the "typical" CEEG response to a test dose neuroleptic will provide important objective information for the treatment of schizophrenic patients.

FIG. 4. CEEG response profiles of normals to clozapine. The CEEG profiles of test dose neuroleptics may vary from subject to subject. For example, in this study only 5 of 15 subjects exhibited the "typical" neuroleptic CEEG profile. We call these subjects "good" responders (increase of slow and decrease of fast activities in both primary wave and first derivative measurements). Moderate responders do not exhibit an increase of slow waves in the first derivative measurements and decrease of fast potentials in both primary wave and first derivative measurements as much as do the good responders. As a matter of fact, they may show some increase of fast activities, particularly in the first derivative measurements. Poor responders do not exhibit any noticeable and systematic alterations in CEEG frequencies. Paradoxical responders exhibit different types of CEEG profiles than neuroleptic CEEG profiles. For example, the CEEG profile of subject 13 is similar to those seen after psychostimulants such as dextroamphetamine in the majority of the population. Subjects 9 and 10 showed CEEG profiles which are similar to those of tricyclic antidepressants.

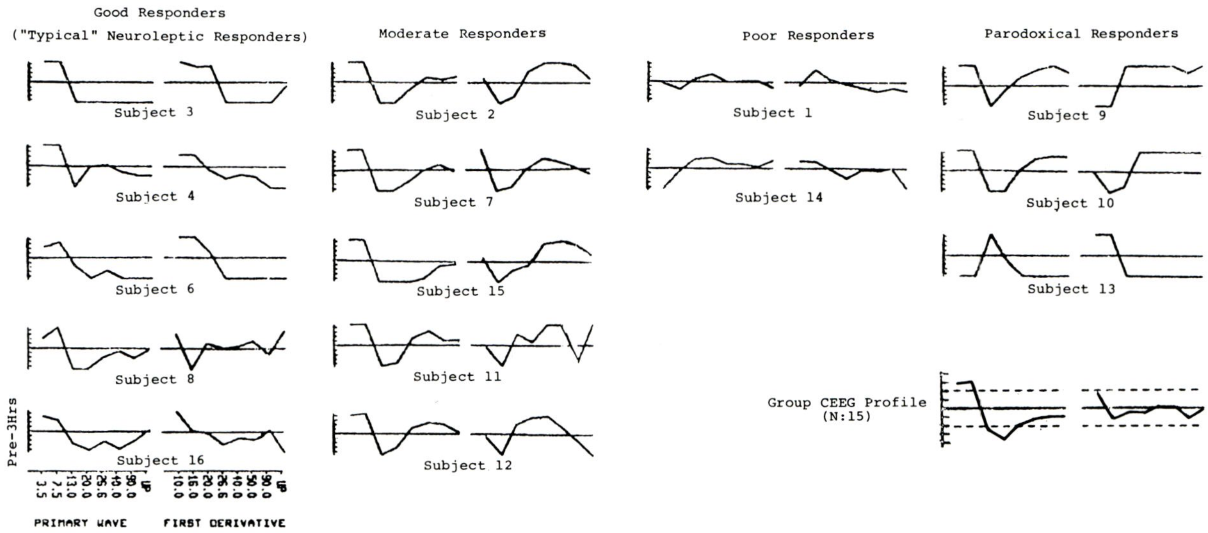

Good Responders
("Typical" Neuroleptic Responders)
Moderate Responders
Poor Responders
Parodoxical Responders
Subject 3
Subject 2
Subject 1
Subject 9
Subject 4
Subject 7
Subject 14
Subject 10
Subject 6
Subject 15
Subject 13
Subject 8
Subject 11
Group CEEG Profile
(N:15)
Pre-3Hrs
Subject 16
Subject 12
3.5
7.5
13.0
20.0
25.6
40.0
90.0
UP
10.0
16.0
20.0
26.6
40.0
50.0
90.0
UP
PRIMARY WAVE
FIRST DERIVATIVE

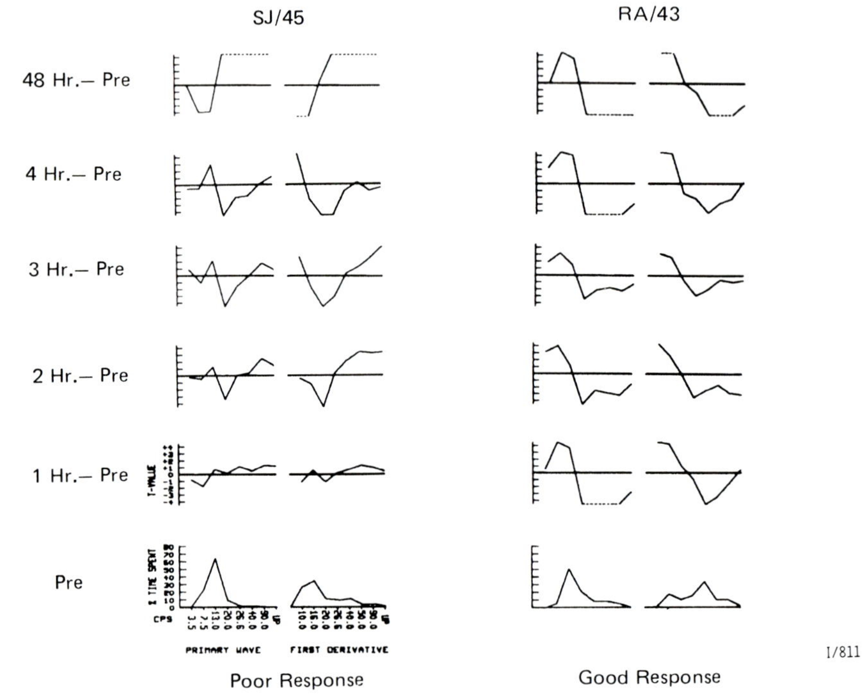

FIG. 5. CEEG Response profiles of two schizophrenic patients to thiothixene (20 mg single dose). The CEEG profiles of neuroleptics may vary from one patient to another. After a single test dose of thiothixene, patient RA responded as the majority of normal subjects would respond (increase of slow waves and decrease of fast activities in both primary wave and first derivative measurements). However, subject SJ did not show any significant changes up to 3 hr, and even after that, the type of the changes is not "typical" for thiothixene. This subject is a poor responder to test dose. (Figures are derived from the collaborative program with Dr. P. May.)

DISCUSSION

The lack of alpha waves and the presence of low-voltage fast beta activity in the EEG of schizophrenics was described as early as 1936 by pioneers in psychiatric EEG research. Lemere (32) reported in 1936 that "the apathy and affective deficiency of the schizophrenic is the feature of the illness most clearly related to an absent or 'poor' alpha rhythm." The same author published in 1938 (33) that "although electroencephalograms obtained from schizophrenic patients fall within normal limits, there is a definite tendency towards a weak alpha (10 per sec.) rhythm in this disorder." Even Berger (3) described that "in many mental disturbances one finds, predominantly, certain beta waves." Later, Gibbs (14) found that the schizophrenics had less alpha and more fast activity than normal subjects. Davis (6) confirmed that a large number of schizo-

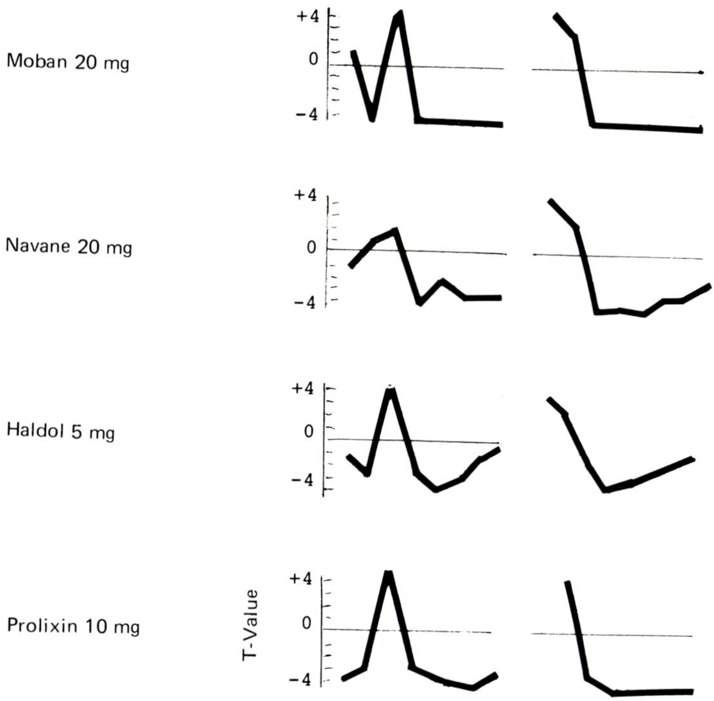

FIG. 6. CEEG response profiles of a therapy resistant schizophrenic to different neuroleptics. Therapy-resistant schizophrenic patients do not show "typical" CEEG profile to neuroleptics. This patient exhibited "psychostimulant" type CEEG profile to four different neuroleptics.

phrenics (61%) showed low-amplitude, disorganized, accelerated EEG tracings, which he called "choppy activity." In subsequent years, however, these findings were rejected by a majority of investigators. Depending on the study, abnormal EEGs were reported occurring in 15 to 80% of the schizophrenic patients (41). Colony and Willis (5), in the largest population studied (1,000 schizophrenic patients), failed to show differences in the incidence of abnormalities between patients and controls. Thus the existence of definite pathologically applicable EEG changes in "genuine" schizophrenic syndromes was denied. The abnormal EEG changes were frequently related to an existing brain injury and/or the sequelae of a purposeful biological (organic) treatment. The presence of a low-voltage fast beta EEG with an absence of alpha activity in schizophrenic patients, as described earlier, was also not generally accepted. Since the use of quantitative analytical techniques of EEG, more and more investigators report that schizophrenic patients, in contradistinction to normals, show less alpha activity and/or more non-alpha activity (13,14,28,31,38,40). Goldstein and his associates (15) found a reduced variability of time in EEG amplitude in schizophrenic patients.

Our studies confirmed both qualitative (3,6,32,33) as well as quantitative EEG findings (13,14,31,38), concerning the presence of more fast beta and less-organized alpha activity in schizophrenics than controls. Furthermore, and most strikingly, we established that the psychotic children and children at high risk for schizophrenia also have different EEG patterns than the matched group of controls. The EEG patterns of high-risk children, psychotic children, and adult schizophrenics are characterized by having less alpha waves, more high-frequency beta activity, and also more very slow low-voltage delta waves in the frequency of 1.3 to 3.5 Hz. Based on these findings, we hypothesized that "desynchronized high-frequency beta activity may be the electrophysiological representation of the genetic predisposition of the schizophrenia" (22). Lemere (33) has already suggested that a "poor cortical neuron synchronization is an inherent neurophysiological characteristic of schizophrenic patients."

The high-frequency, low-voltage fast beta activity in the EEG has been attributed to the presence of continuous intense abnormal activation of the cortex by subcortical mechanisms (16). It has been postulated that the desynchronized fast activity in schizophrenia is "a reflection of the modulation of cortical activity by a specific subcortical system" (34). Desynchronized fast beta activity in the EEG may be induced by stimulation of the reticular activating system in the brainstem of animals (37). A similar EEG pattern may be seen after administration of hallucinogenic compounds. Qualitative, but particularly quantitative, EEG investigations demonstrated that both indole hallucinogens as well as anticholinergic hallucinogens decrease alpha waves and increase fast beta activity (8,11). Whereas indole hallucinogens such as LSD-25 produce predominantly only fast beta activity, anticholinergic hallucinogens such as Ditran ® induce both very fast beta activity and very slow delta waves (19). Thus the EEG pattern of schizophrenics resembles predominantly the effects of anticholinergic hallucinogens. Accordingly, EEG findings of schizophrenia primarily support Friedhoff's biochemical hypothesis (12) that in schizophrenia a genetically determined imbalance between dopaminergic and cholinergic systems exists. Secondarily, among the existing hypotheses of the biochemistry of schizophrenia (36), the dopamine hypothesis is probably in closest harmony with the quantitative EEG study results.

All drugs effective in schizophrenia (neuroleptics or major tranquilizers), whether administered in single dosages in normal volunteers or in repetitive dosages in schizophrenic patients, produce slow waves (including slow alpha waves) and decrease fast activities. These EEG patterns are almost diametrically opposed to those seen in schizophrenia or after hallucinogenic drugs in normals. There are close correlations between psychopathological changes and EEG alterations during the drug treatment of schizophrenic patients. The more fast activity decreases, the more clinical improvement is seen (27). Thus behavior and EEG correlations during the neuroleptic treatment of schizophrenia resemble those seen with other organic therapies such as ECT (7,10).

Our investigations also suggest that the pretreatment EEG pattern may be predictive for the outcome of the therapeutic treatment in schizophrenia (27). The more fast activities present in the EEG of a schizophrenic patient, the better is the therapeutic outcome. Nonresponsive schizophrenic patients exhibit more slow, high-voltage alpha activity with synchronization and rhythmical tendency than we see in responsive patients (17,20).

Investigations in recent years indicate that the EEG response to a test dose of a neuroleptic compound may be used to predict the therapeutic effects of these compounds. The "typical" CEEG response to a test dose neuroleptic (decreased fast waves and increased slow waves) is indicative that the orally administered compound has been properly absorbed, then metabolized, then distributed in the peripheral "compartments," passed through the blood-brain barrier, and finally had its effect on the CNS. The replicability of the "typical" CEEG profiles of neuroleptics with different chemical structures, pharmacological profiles, and biochemical properties in different populations indicate that neuroleptic drugs, even after one single oral dose, produce common biochemical alterations accompanied by "typical" physiological changes (similar CEEG profiles). We do not have enough data yet to decide whether these "typical" CEEG responses to a test dose neuroleptic have any predictive value for the therapeutic outcome when the patient is treated with the same neuroleptic. However, our studies demonstrated that the chronic, therapy-resistant schizophrenic patients do not show the "typical" neuroleptic CEEG response to neuroleptics. In contrast, therapy-refractory patients showed "psychostimulant" type CEEG response (such as dextroamphetamine) to neuroleptic drugs (such drugs as molindone, haloperidol, thiothixene, and fluphenazine hydrochloride). Accordingly, a resting CEEG pattern along with the active test dose CEEG response (CEEG profiles) may be developed as an objective method to predict the prognosis and to select the best effective drug and dosage for each individual patient.

SUMMARY

Qualitative and quantitative EEG investigations suggest that the electrophysiological correlates of schizophrenia may be the presence of desynchronized fast activity and the absence of alpha waves. EEGs of this type are produced after stimulation of the reticular activating system of the brainstem in animals, and after the administration of certain hallucinogenic drugs in man. All antipsychotic (neuroleptic) drugs reverse these EEG patterns, demonstrating decreasing fast waves, increasing slow waves, and slow alpha activity. There are close correlations between EEG and behavior changes. The more decreased fast waves and increased slower potentials during a drug treatment of schizophrenic patients, the more improvement in psychopathology is observed. Patients with low-voltage fast EEG activity in pre-drug treatment EEG recordings have a better therapeutic response to subsequent treatment than is seen in patients with heightened alpha activity and slower EEGs. The patients known to be resistant to neuroleptic drug treatments (therapy-refractory schizophrenics) do not show a "typical" neuroleptic response to a test dose neuroleptic. In contrast, they show a response which is similar to that seen after psychostimulant administration in normal subjects. The CEEG response to a test-dose neuroleptic may be indicative of the therapeutic response resulting from subsequent repetitive dose treatment with the same compound. Patients with a "typical" CEEG response to a test-dose neuroleptic may also show the best therapeutic benefit after repetitive dose treatment with the same compound. Thus, utilizing resting EEG profiles and test-dose CEEG responses, a more scientific appraisal may be arrived at to help select the drug of choice in the treatment of schizophrenic patients.

REFERENCES

1. Akpinar, S., Itil, T. M., Marasa, J., and Marrazzi, A. (1972): Blocking effect of chlorpromazine on LSD-25 induced clinical and digital computer analyzed EEG changes. *Clin. Electroencephalogr.*, 3(4):224–232.
2. Arnold, O. H., Collard, J., Deniker, P., Ginestet, D., Hippius, H., Itil, T. M., Labhardt, F., Leeds, A., Montanini, R., Morozov, G., Simon, P., and Villeneuve, A. (1970): Definition and classification of neuroleptics. The neuroleptics. *Mod. Probl. Pharmacopsychiatry,* 5:141–147.
3. Berger, H. (1969): A note of correction (Published in *Arch. Psychiatr. Nervenkr* 1937b, 106:508). Hans Berger on the Electroencephalogram of man. *Electroencephalogr. Clin. Neurophysiol.* [*Suppl.*], 28:289.
4. Buchsbaum, M. S. (1977): The middle evoked response components and schizophrenia. *Schizophr. Bull.,* 3:93–104.
5. Colony, H. S., and Willis, S. E. (1956): EEG studies of 1,000 schizophrenic patients. *Am. J. Psychiatry,* 13:163.
6. Davis, P. A. (1940): Evaluation of the EEG of schizophrenic patients. *Am. J. Psychiatry,* 96:851.
7. Fink, M. (1957): Unified theory of action of psychodynamic therapies. *J. Hillside Hosp.*, 6:197–206.
8. Fink, M. (1959): EEG and behavioral effects of psychopharmacologic agents. *Neuropsychopharmacology,* 1:441.
9. Fink, M. (1964): A selected bibliography of electroencephalography in human psychopharmacology. *Electroencephalogr. Clin. Neurophysiol.* [*Suppl. 23*].
10. Fink, M. (1969): The human electroencephalogram: Index of clinical activity of new psychoactive agents. The Thioxanthenes. *Mod. Probl. Pharmacopsychiatry,* 2:106–110.
11. Flügel, F., and Itil, T. (1962): Klinisch-elektroencephalographische Untersuchungen mit Verwirrstheit hervorrufenden Substanzen. *Psychopharmacologia,* 3:79.
12. Friedhoff, A. M. (1973): Biogenic amines and schizophrenia. *Biol. Psychiatry,* 113–129.
13. Giannitrapani, D., and Kayton, L. (1974): Schizophrenia and EEG spectral analysis. *Electroencephalogr. Clin. Neurophysiol.,* 36:377.
14. Gibbs, F. A. (1939): Cortical frequency spectra of schizophrenic, epileptic and normal individuals. *Trans. Am. Neurol. Assoc.,* 65:141.
15. Goldstein, L., Murphree, H. B., Sugerman, A. A., Pfeiffer, C. C., and Jenney, E. H. (1963): Quantitative electroencephalographic analysis of naturally occurring (schizophrenic) and drug-induced psychotic states in human males. *Clin. Pharmacol. Ther.,* 4:10.
16. Hill, D. (1956): *Electroencephalography.* MacDonald, London.
17. Igert, C., and Lairy, G. C. (1962): Prognostic value of the EEG in the course of the development of schizophrenics. *Electroencephalogr. Clin. Neurophysiol.,* 14:183.
18. Itil, T. M. (1969): Definition and classification of neuroleptics from the EEG point of view. In: *Reprints of the Interdisciplinary Week on Neuroleptiques,* edited by D. P. Bobon, pp. 167–169. Universitie de Liege, Liege.
19. Itil, T. M. (1969): Quantitative EEG and behavior changes after LSD and Ditran. In: *Neurophysiological and Behavioral Aspects of Psychotropic Drugs,* edited by A. Karczmar and W, Koella, pp. 62–71. Charles C Thomas, Springfield, Ill.
20. Itil, T. M. (1973): Drug treatment of therapy-resistant schizophrenic patients. In: *The World*

Biennial of Psychiatry and Psychotherapy, edited by S. Arieti, pp. 246–264. Basic Books, New York.

21. Itil, T. M. (1973): The effects of minor and major tranquilizers on digital computer sleep prints. In: *The Nature of Sleep,* edited by U. J. Jovanovic, pp. 78–87. Gustav Fischer Verlag, Stuttgart.
22. Itil, T. M. (1974): Computerized EEG findings in schizophrenia and effects of neuroleptic drugs. In: *Biological Mechanisms of Schizophrenia and Schizophrenia-like Psychoses,* edited by Mitsuda, Hisatoshi, and Fukuda, Tetsuo, pp. 196–207. Igaku Shoin Ltd., Tokyo.
23. Itil, T. M. (1974): Quantitative pharmaco-electroencephalography. Psychotropic drugs and the human EEG *Mod. Probl. Pharmacopsychiatry,* 8:43–75.
24. Itil, T. M. (1977): Qualitative and quantitative EEG findings in schizophrenia. *Schizophr. Bull.,* 3:61–79.
25. Itil, T. M., Hsu, W., Klingenberg, H., Saletu, B., and Gannon, P. (1972): Digital computer-analyzed all-night sleep EEG patterns (sleep prints) in schizophrenics. *Biol. Psychiatry,* 4:3.
26. Itil, T. M., Hsu, W., Saletu, B., and Mednick, S. (1974): Computer EEG and auditory evoked potential investigations in children at high risk for schizophrenia. *Am. J. Psychiatry,* 131:892.
27. Itil, T. M., Marasa, J., Saletu, B., Davis, S., and Mucciardi, A. N. (1975): Computerized EEG: Predictor of outcome in schizophrenia. *J. Nerv. Ment. Dis.,* 160(3):188–203.
28. Itil, T. M., Saletu, B., and Davis, S. (1972): EEG findings in chronic schizophrenics based on digital computer period analysis and analog power spectra. *Biol. Psychiatry,* 5:1–13.
29. Itil, T. M., Saletu, B., Davis, S., and Allen, M. (1974): Stability studies in schizophrenics and normals using computer-analyzed EEG. *Biol. Psychiatry,* 8:321–335.
30. Itil, T. M., Simeon, J., and Coffin, C. (1976): Qualitative and quantitative EEG in psychotic children. *Dis. Nerv. Syst.,* 37(5):247–252.
31. Kennard, M. A., and Schwartzman, A. E. (1957): A longitudinal study of electroencephalographic frequency patterns in mental hospital patients and normal controls. *Electroencephalogr. Clin. Neurophysiol.,* 9:263.
32. Lemere, F. (1936): The significance of individual differences in the Berger rhythm. *Brain,* 59:366–375.
33. Lemere, F. (1938): Effects on electroencephalogram of various agents used in treating schizophrenia. *J. Neurophysiol.,* 1:590–595.
34. Lester, B. K., and Edwards, R. J. (1966): EEG fast activity in schizophrenic and control subjects. *Int. J. Neuropsychiatry,* 2:143.
35. Mednick, S. A., and Schulsinger, F. (1965): Children of schizophrenic mothers. *Bull. Int. Assoc. Appl. Psychol.,* 14:11–27.
36. Meltzer, H. Y. (1976): Biochemical studies in schizophrenia. *Schizophr. Bull.,* 2(1):10–18.
37. Moruzzi, G., and Magoun, H. W. (1949): Brain stem reticular formation and activation of the EEG. *Electroencephalgr. Clin. Neurophysiol.,* 1:455.
38. Rodin, E., Grisell, J., and Gottlieb, J.: (1968): Some electrographic differences between chronic schizophrenic patients and normal subjects. *Recent Adv. Biol. Psychiatry,* pp. 194–204.
39. Shagass, C. (1976): An electrophysiological view of schizophrenia. *Biol. Psychiatry,* 11:3–30.
40. Shagass, C. (1977): Early evoked potentials. *Schizophr. Bull.,* 3:80–92.
41. Small, J. G., and Small, I. F. (1965): Re-evaluation of clinical EEG findings in schizophrenia. *Dis. Nerv. Syst.,* 26:345.

Discussion

Meltzer: Do typical antipsychotics, such as clozapine and sulpiride, act in the same manner?

Itil: Yes. Clozapine, especially in lower dosages, produces some changes like those effected by Mellaril which are called neuroleptic-type CEEG profiles (6). With sulpiride there is tremendous biological variability. We have not had enough subjects in our studies with sulpiride to establish a typical EEG profile.

Singh: What effects do anxiolytics have on the EEG patterns in schizophrenics?

Itil: Anxiolytics have significant effects on the EEG that are different from those of the neuroleptics.

Singh: Don't they make fast beta rhythms disappear?

Itil: They do make the very fast beta (above 70 cps) disappear, but they increase beta activity of 20 to 40 cps, in a higher amplitude and spindle form.

Hiatt: And, in addition, an opposite effect on delta?

Itil: Yes.

Singh: What are the effects of antimuscarinic agents on the EEG, what interactions do they have with neuroleptics in terms of EEG parameters, and what would you predict the antipsychotic activity of neuroleptics would be when combined with antimuscarinics?

Itil: Antiparkinsonism drugs like Ditran (2) and atropine at dosages up to 10 mg produce a tremendous simultaneous increase of slow and superimposed fast activity, especially Ditran. Every drug that produces confusion produces these kinds of EEG changes (5). As for antiparkinsonism-anticholinergic drugs, we have published that some of them block the slowing effects of the neuroleptics, but we haven't studied these systematically.

K. Davis: We (17) found that physostigmine produces the same pattern as do anticholinergics—decreased alpha and increased beta rhythms. It is a nonspecific finding; you see it with hallucinogens, with anticholinergics, with almost any delirium-producing agent—the same pattern you described in schizophrenia. Yet you do not see schizophrenic behavior associated with these drugs; you see delirious behavior.

Itil: The EEG correlates of delirium induced by drugs (10) or by illness (18) are very different from those EEG patterns characteristic for schizophrenia (13). Granted that in schizophrenia there is also some slow wave activity, but it is much less than in delirium, and also with much lower amplitudes. Whereas delirium is characterized by generalized high-voltage slow waves with superimposed faster potentials, the EEG pattern of schizophrenia is characterized by low-voltage dysynchronized fast waves with poor alpha activity and only some low-voltage slow waves.

K. Davis: The dose-response pattern must be considered. Low doses of anticholinergics like physostigmine produce a wave pattern much more like what you described as the schizophrenic pattern than like what you described as the delirious pattern.

Itil: That is correct. The low-dosage anticholinergic compounds also produce slower waves, but much less than those produced by high dosages or the activities induced by anticholinergic hallucinogens. Also, psychopathological changes induced by low-dosage anticholinergics are different from those of delirium induced by high-dose anticholinergics.

Carpenter: Have you looked at the effects of phenothiazines that do not have antipsychotic activity?

Itil: We did large studies with promethazine, a well-known antihistamine-anticholinergic phenothiazine without antipsychotic or other potent psychotropic properties (4). The EEG changes induced by promethazine are characterized by low-voltage slow potentials with superimposed low-voltage, fast beta activity, and sporadic alpha waves.

These EEG changes, which are called the "promethazine type" EEG reaction (3), are different from those of schizophrenia (which has more fast and fewer slow waves), and resemble a spontaneous drowsiness-like pattern (fewer slow waves than stage I sleep). Clinically, subjects after promethazine also demonstrate drowsiness-like behavior.

Carpenter: One of your slides suggests that desynchronous activity or theta activity might identify a subgroup of atypical psychoses, like those of Mitsuda (15) or Monroe (16).

Itil: You saw correctly that patients given high dosages of anticholinergic drugs (or better with anticholinergic hallucinogens) may show the typical EEG correlates of delirium or toxic psychosis (high-voltage, very slow EEG with superimposed fast beta waves), as described by Romano and Engel (18) more than 25 years ago. These EEG alterations and associated psychopathological syndromes are seen after Ditran more frequently than after atropine.

Carpenter: Is there a normalization of the schizophrenic EEG when behavior normalizes?

Itil: Yes. A decrease in hallucinations, thought disorders, and agitation are associated with an increase of alpha waves and a decrease of fast beta waves in the EEG. However, the majority of the chronic schizophrenics in the VA and state hospitals have a stable psychopathology and a stable EEG pattern. The slight changes in psychopathology may not be reflected in the EEG, particularly if the EEG is not analyzed quantitatively with computers. As a matter of fact, most of the EEG correlations of the behavior and/or EEG changes induced by drugs can be established only if the EEG is analyzed quantitatively and the behavior is evaluated by sophisticated behavioral evaluation techniques (12).

Nasrallah: Are there EEG differences between psychotic and nonpsychotic epileptics?

Itil: We haven't studied that recently because we don't have an epileptic population.

Nasrallah: Have you observed any EEG differences between the two hemispheres, with leads on both?

Itil: We've never studied both hemispheres, simply for financial reasons.

Nasrallah: Why did you pick the right occipital lead?

Itil: By chance, even though the occipital site is good because it avoids the muscle and eye-movement artifacts.

Hiatt: The brain may fluctuate during wakefulness as it does during sleep, with 16 cycles per day. Therefore some individual differences in the response to a single dose of a drug may reflect an initial-value effect that depends on where in that cycle the patient is when given the drug, at a high or a low point on a certain parameter. Perhaps those performing studies of single-dose effects should take samples over a period of time.

Itil: The computer EEG response to a neuroleptic, but particularly to an anxiolytic or antidepressant, is very stable. In studies we (14) made at the VA, seven subjects were given a benzodiazepine (Valium) 10 times at weekly intervals, and, despite lack of controls on food intake and life style, the similarity coefficient from one week to the next was $0 + .95$. In studies we (8) made in Turkey, Germany, Italy, Great Britain, and in the United States, a single dose of benzodiazepine always produced the same EEG effect, although in some populations the dosage may have had to be greater or smaller.

Hiatt: In EEG sleep studies I've done, schizophrenic patients when in a psychotic state almost always have gross cognitive distortions about what was going on when the EEG was being recorded, with fears of being electrocuted, so it seems possible that some EEG findings relate not to schizophrenia but to anxiety. For the remainder of this conference I am going to try to relate findings not to diagnoses but to the state of the patient.

Itil: We never say that the low-voltage, fast activity, is an indicator of schizophrenia.

What we say is that the low-voltage, fast EEG pattern seems to be the neurophysiological correlate of schizophrenia (9). For an outburst of schizophrenic illness, additional factors are needed.

Beck: In support of Dr. Hiatt, I can relate the following. Many years ago I (1) had 30 nurses as a control group in an EEG study. We ran these at night. I couldn't find any alpha rhythm in the records of the nurses; they had low-voltage, fast activity—perhaps because Dr. Boswell and I were young doctors, and the recording room was dark. The nurses were anxious. The state of the subject is important; and psychotic patients *are* anxious.

Itil: It is true that an acute anxiety state may be associated with an increase in fast activity and a decrease in alpha waves. Thus the EEG pattern of an anxiety state has some similarity to the EEG pattern of schizophrenia. We hypothesized that the low-voltage, fast EEG pattern is the neurophysiological correlate of schizophrenia. Any condition that increases the low-voltage, fast EEG pattern also increases the risk of becoming a schizophrenic outburst. Among others, acute stressful conditions, conflict reactions, and hyperarousal states may potentiate schizophrenic outbursts. We speculated, therefore, that a schizophrenic breakdown may be prevented if the low-voltage, fast EEG pattern can be modified to an alpha pattern (7). Thus, if high-risk children (children of schizophrenic parents) are taught to relax, for example by using meditation, yoga, alpha training, or biofeedback, and if their fast EEG pattern is reduced, they may not develop schizophrenic illness (11). Even elimination of stressful environmental conditions alone may decrease fast EEG patterns; thus it may be preventive for the development of schizophrenia.

Beck: Have you indeed done that?

Itil: It is being done on the island of Mauritius.

REFERENCES

1. Dustman, R. E., and Beck, E. C. (1965): Phase of alpha brain waves, reaction time, and visually evoked potentials. *Electrocenphalogr. Clin. Neurophysiol.,* 18:433–440.
2. Flugel, F., and Itil, T. M. (1962): Klinisch-elektroencephalographische Untersuchungen mit "Verwirrtheit" hervorrufenden Substanzen. *Psychopharmacologia (Berlin),* 3:79–98.
3. Itil, T. M. (1961): Elektroencephalographische Befunde zur Klassifikation neuro- und thymoleptischer Medikamente. *Med. Exp. (Basel),* 5:347–363.
4. Itil, T. M. (1964): *Elektroencephalographische Studien bei Psychosen und Psychotropen Medikamenten.* Ahmet Sait Matbaasi, Istanbul.
5. Itil, T. M. (1966): Quantitative EEG changes induced by anticholinergic drugs and their behavioral correlates in man. In: *Recent Advances in Biological Psychiatry,* Vol. 8, edited by J. Wortis, pp. 151–173, Plenum Press, New York.
6. Itil, T. M. (1968): Electroencephalography and pharmacopsychiatry. In: *Clinical Psychopharmacology: Modern Problems of Pharmacopsychiatry, Vol. 1,* edited by F. A. Freyhan, N. Petrilowitsch, and P. Pichot, pp. 163–194. Karger, Basel/New York.
7. Itil, T. M. (1974): Computerized EEG findings in schizophrenia and effects of neuroleptic drugs. In: *Biological Mechanisms of Schizophrenia and Schizophrenia-like Psychoses,* edited by H. Mitsuda and T. Fukuda, pp. 196–207. Igaku Shoin, Tokyo.
8. Itil, T. M. (1975): Transcultural psychopharmacology from the EEG point of view. In: *Transcultural Neuropsychopharmacology,* edited by T. M. Itil, pp. 39–45. Bozak, Istanbul.
9. Itil, T. M. (1976): Novel neurophysiological findings in schizophrenia. In: *Schizophrenia Today,* edited by D. Kemali, G. Bartholini, and D. Richter, pp. 203–210. Pergamon Press, Oxford/New York.
10. Itil, T. M., and Fink, M. (1969): EEG and behavioral aspects of the interaction of anticholinergic hallucinogens with centrally active compounds. In: *Progress in Brain Research, Vol. 28: Anticholinergic Drugs,* edited by P. B. Bradley and M. Fink, pp. 149–168. Elsevier, Amsterdam.
11. Itil, T. M., Hsu, W., Saletu, B., and Mednick, S. (1974): Computer EEG and auditory evoked

potential investigations in children at high risk for schizophrenia. *Am. J. Psychiatry,* 131:892–900.
12. Itil, T. M., Marasa, J., Saletu, B., Davis, S., and Mucciardi, A. N. (1975): Computerized EEG: Predictor of outcome in schizophrenia. *J. Nerv. Ment. Dis.,* 160:188–203.
13. Itil, T. M., Saletu, B., and Davis, S. (1972): EEG findings in chronic schizophrenics based on digital computer period analysis and analog power spectra. *Biol. Psychiatry,* 5:1–13.
14. Itil, T. M., Schneider, S. J., and Fredrickson, J. (1979): Reliability of EEG assessment of the effects of psychotropic drugs: Diazepam. (Abstr.) *Psychophysiology, (in press).*
15. Mitsuda, H., and Mukuda, T., editors (1974): *Biological Mechanisms of Schizophrenia and Schizophrenia-like Psychoses.* Igaku Shoin, Tokyo.
16. Monroe, R. R. (1970): *Episodic Behavioral Disorders.* Harvard University Press, Cambridge, Massachusetts.
17. Pfefferbaum, A., Davis, K. L., Coulter, C. L., Mohs, R. C., and Kopell, B. S. (1979): Electrophysiological effects of physostigmine in humans. In: *Brain Acetylcholine and Neuropsychiatric Disease,* edited by K. L. Davis and P. A. Berger, pp. 345–360. Plenum Press, New York.
18. Romano, J., and Engel, G. L. (1944): Delirium: 1. EEG Data. *Arch. Neurol. Psychiatr.,* 5:356.

Perspectives in Schizophrenia Research,
edited by C. Baxter and T. Melnechuk.
Raven Press, New York, 1980.

Predicting Outcome from Measures of Attention and Autonomic Functioning

Theodore P. Zahn

Laboratory of Psychology and Psychopathology, National Institute of Mental Health, Bethesda, Maryland 20205

LAYPERSON'S SUMMARY

This chapter proposes that attention and autonomic nervous system (ANS) activity, impairment of which is frequently thought to be fundamental in the schizophrenic disorder, be measured more often in clinical studies of schizophrenia.

In a recent study of acute schizophrenics, under medication-free conditions 3 weeks after hospitalization, the short-term outcome of a schizophrenic episode was predictable from attentional functioning as measured by a reaction time technique and from ANS functioning as measured principally by palmar sweat gland activity (skin conductance) and heart rate. Specifically, patients whose clinical state showed minimal improvement over a subsequent 4-month hospitalization had poor attention, high ANS activity ("arousal") at rest, slow habituation of skin conductance responses elicited by innocuous stimuli, and smaller ANS effects of meaningful and demanding stimuli and situations. Good outcome patients were significantly more alike to normals. Two other studies have found similar prognostic value in measurements of attention and ANS functioning.

The deviant functioning is not merely a transient accompaniment of the psychotic state, as indicated by findings that the two outcome groups had equal-rated psychopathology at the time of the tests, and that minimal changes in the pattern accompanied marked clinical improvement. Thus these laboratory measures may reflect longer lasting traits which have considerable clinical significance.

This conclusion is supported by several studies with remitted schizophrenics and with first-degree relatives of schizophrenics from which it can be surmised that attention deficits may be more closely related to a vulnerability to schizophrenia than to current clinical state. ANS studies of the offspring of schizophrenic parents suggest that slow habituation may be a potential genetic marker indicating risk of schizophrenia. Correlational studies and studies of the effects of drugs suggest that ANS activity is related to biogenic amines and to enzyme activities which are thought to play important etiological roles in schizophrenia.

The evidence, then, suggests that attention and ANS functioning may be partly biologically determined traits with etiological and prognostic significance. It is suggested that the studies on outcome be replicated and extended to a more heterogeneous sample and be designed to answer questions such as: Can predictions of improvement on specific drug regimens or without drugs be validated? Are optimal ANS effects of drugs related to optimal clinical benefit? Can length of remission under minimal or no medication be predicted? Can imminent relapse be predicted from tests given periodically during the remission period?

INTRODUCTION

Disturbances of attention and autonomic nervous system (ANS) functioning are well documented in schizophrenia, especially in chronic schizophrenia, and the assumption is frequently made that they are fundamental features of schizophrenia which underlie many or most of the psychotic symptoms themselves. Most of the evidence which demonstrates the differences in functioning comes from studies comparing schizophrenic and normal subjects or subgroups of schizophrenics at one point in time. Relatively few of what we shall call "clinical" studies—studies of clinical course, of the effects of therapy, or of outcome—have included assessment of these basic psychophysiological processes. Nor has much attention been given to the possibility that these types of laboratory measures might actually be useful in treatment decisions. This chapter will review evidence on (a) the relationship of measures of attentional and autonomic functioning to subsequent clinical course (i.e., outcome) in both unmedicated patients and those taking antipsychotic drugs; (b) changes in psychophysiological functioning in relation to clinical changes, comparing changes occurring in unmedicated patients with those attributable to drugs; and (c) other relevant evidence on possible genetic and neurochemical determinants of the attentional and ANS deficits in schizophrenia. It will be my contention that this research area is sufficiently promising as to be worth pursuing, and suggestions will be offered in this regard.

Two general purposes can be served by this approach. The first is theoretical. The often observed and well-confirmed disorders of attention and, to a lesser extent, autonomic functioning are considered by many investigators to be fundamental aspects of schizophrenia in the sense that they lie in an implicitly causal chain of events between basic cellular processes and the overt symptoms of schizophrenia. It seems reasonable that these intermediate processes may relate more directly and specifically to the neurochemical events thought to be etiologically significant than do the more molar symptoms which are more complex and may be more subject to present and recent environmental influences. The types of clinical studies dealt with in this chapter can, along with genetic, family, and high-risk studies, help determine whether attentional and ANS disturbances are accompaniments of the ups and downs of the psychotic state or more permanent dispositions (traits) which are relatively independent of clinical changes.

A second advantage of including laboratory measures of functioning in clinical studies is practical. Regardless of how basic these attributes turn out to be, they may serve as useful markers of potential or actual clinical course. If their validity can be established they would have the advantage of being simpler and more objective than most predictors of prognosis or indicators of clinical condition.

ATTENTION

Impairment of attention as measured by reaction time (RT) and vigilance techniques is probably the best documented psychological deficit in schizophrenia (28). One of the most widely used RT techniques for studying attention has been the "set index" procedure devised over 40 years ago by Huston and Shakow and their colleagues (18). In this method RT is measured as a function of the length of the preparatory interval (PI—interval between a warning signal and the imperative stimulus) under constant PI and variable PI conditions. In addition to having much slower overall RT, schizophrenics have been found to be disproportionately slow on longer PIs (> 4 sec) under constant PI conditions—attributed to an inability to maintain attention—and are also disproportionately slow on the shorter PIs (< 4 sec) under variable PI conditions. The latter finding may be due to slowness in shifting attention or set since the effect is influenced strongly by the length of the PI on the preceding trial. This pattern of PI variations distinguishes schizophrenics from other groups with slow RTs such as neurological patients (29). It occurs in acute as well as chronic schizophrenics (but in differing degrees). The original findings on chronic schizophrenics have stood up over the years in studies done in various countries and with modifications in the technique (2). Its robustness recommends the method for use in clinical studies.

Studies of Outcome

The set index technique was included in a recent study of predictors of outcome in acute schizophrenics (53) at NIMH. Since various results of this study will be a major focus of this chapter, and since the design of the project has many useful features for studies of this type, the overall design is presented in Fig. 1. Patients diagnosed acute schizophrenic with good prior social and work functioning were recruited from local community hospitals and transferred to a 12-bed research ward at NIMH. They were taken off drugs for a 3-week evaluation period followed by an "admission" test week in which a Present State Examination (PSE) was given, global ratings of psychopathology were made by ward psychiatrists and nurses, and various research procedures were performed. This was followed by a 2½- to 3-month "treatment" period in which psychosocial therapies were emphasized (these went on during the other parts

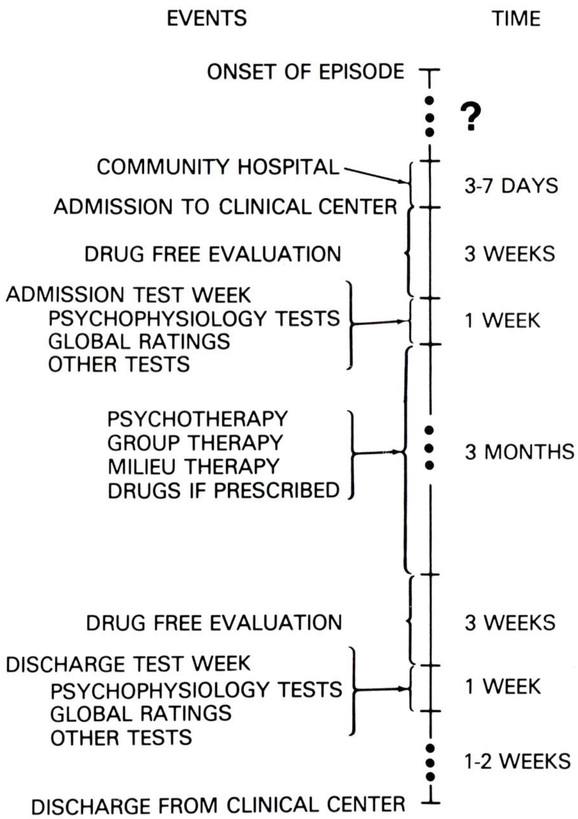

FIG. 1. Chronology of a hospitalization for a typical patient admitted to the NIMH research unit.

of the hospitalization as well), but about half of the patients received drugs. Following this was a "discharge" test week in which global ratings were made and research procedures were repeated. Diagnosis of acute schizophrenia followed DSM II (7a) guidelines, and its stringency was increased by a flexible system of criteria (6).

The design permits data collected during the "admission" test week to be evaluated as predictors of clinical course. In our study using the admission and discharge ratings, we compared patients who showed definite clinical improvement and substantial remission of symptoms ($N = 18$) with those whose improvement was minimal ($N = 17$). We have labeled these groups Improved (I) and Not Improved (NI). It is important to note that neither the global ratings nor symptom profiles derived from the PSE differed for the two groups at admission so that they differ only on subsequent clinical course and not on current clinical state. Drugs (usually chlorpromazine) were used during the treatment period in 44% of the I group and 53% of the NI group, a nonsignificant difference. Evaluation of the effects of clinical state was accomplished by comparing discharge test results in patients grouped just on the basis of discharge ratings into "Well" and "Sick." There was minimal deterioration in clinical state in the final drug-free period, so the ratings can be taken to reflect the optimal treatment effect.

Using the classic set index paradigm, we found that on admission the I patients had significantly faster RTs under virtually all conditions than the NI group. However, the relationships of RT with the PI and preceding PI (PPI) under constant and variable conditions previously shown to be important in schizophrenia were not statistically different, although they showed trends in the expected direction. On the discharge test the Sick patients not only had slower RTs than the Well group but differed significantly in the schizophrenic direction on most of the more subtle features of the procedure (i.e., the PI and PPI had greater effects in the Sick patients). The change from admission to discharge in the I patients was not striking for the group as a whole; only I patients whose performance was exceptionally poor at admission tended to improve markedly in RT performance. The main effect of symptom remission was to reduce the variability of the I group.

The conclusion, then, is that most patients who will achieve a quick remission from a psychotic episode compared to slower remitters have less impaired attention, as measured by RT performance, despite equal rated psychopathology. For most patients, the effects of good prognosis are the same as the effects of good clinical condition.

Similar results were obtained in a study by Cancro et al. (3) who measured simple RT to a series of lights and tones in 30 newly admitted drug-free schizophrenics. With this method schizophrenics have been found to have disproportionately slow RT when the stimulus on the preceding trial was of a different modality (e.g., Tone-Light) compared to ipsimodal sequences (e.g., Light-Light). The method thus presumably measures ability to shift attention quickly (40). Cancro et al. found that RT was correlated significantly to clinical course over the next 3 years as measured by total nights spent in any mental institution. As in our study it was the RT level rather than the more subtle cross-modal effects that carried the bulk of the predictive load.

Evidence for Attention Deficits As Traits

The independence of RT and clinical state in the admission phase of our study, and the lack of a general effect of clinical improvement on RT suggest that attention deficits may have properties of traits and that these traits may have important consequences in terms of future clinical course. This conclusion is supported by findings of more pronounced RT attentional deficits in process compared to reactive patients (2). Several studies have tested the trait hypothesis by assessing attention in remitted patients. Salzman, Klein, and Strauss (35) studied pendulum eye tracking in remitted schizophrenic women. They found that poor eye tracking as measured by velocity arrests and by an overall rating was not correlated with the current psychiatric ratings of their subjects but was positively and significantly correlated with the severity of the psychosis during the previous hospitalization. Deficits in eye tracking performance are thought to be due to some sort of disorder of attention (15). Thus remitted schizophrenics with attentional problems may be more vulnerable to severe psychotic episodes than those with better attention.

Two other studies of attention in remitted schizophrenics have used the Continuous Performance Task (CPT), a test of vigilance, given both with and without distraction. Wohlberg and Kornetsky (47), using carefully chosen medication-free female ex-patients who had maintained remission status for at least 1 year and who had had only one brief prior hospitalization, found significant CPT impairment (increased errors) both with and without distraction compared to a control group. On a repeat of the no-distraction condition, the patients improved in errors to almost the control level, but interestingly this was accompanied by an increase in response time. This suggests that these patients were able to adapt to their attentional deficit by slowing down their behavior. In a similar study, with medicated outpatients whose prognosis was poorer, and using an easier form of the CPT, Asarnow and MacCrimmon (1) found minimal impairment under nondistraction conditions, but marked impairment with distraction. Under the latter condition the remitted group performed as poorly as currently psychotic inpatients.

The remission studies show that an impairment of attention outlasts the schizophrenic symptomatology and thus has the characteristics of a long-lasting disposition or trait. This conclusion is supported by findings of subtle attentional deficits in several studies of children at risk for schizophrenia by virtue of having a schizophrenic parent, recently reviewed by Garmezy (9). Abnormal eye tracking has been found in first-degree relatives of schizophrenics (14,16). Kornetsky and Orzack (20) found that schizophrenics with family histories of mental illness were more likely to have poor CPT performance than were those without family histories. These studies suggest that the trait of attentional capacity may have a genetic basis. However, Van Dyke and Rosenthal (43) using the adoptive strategy to separate genetic from environmental factors found that rearing by a schizophrenic parent rather than genetic background accounted for RT deficits.

Effects of Clinical State

The foregoing evidence that attentional capacity has characteristics of a trait suggests an alternate interpretation of findings of substantial correlations between attentional performance and global psychiatric condition in schizophrenic groups. Rosenthal et al. (33) found a rank correlation of 0.89 between RT performance and rankings of schizophrenic disorganization in a heterogeneous group of unmedicated chronic schizophrenics using a sensitive ranking method.

In an unpublished replication of this in our laboratory correlating the global psychopathology rating from the Inpatient Multidimensional Psychiatric Scale (IMPS) with the same RT measure in unmedicated schizophrenics, a correlation of 0.70 was obtained. Using a more differentiated measure of clinical state based on the IMPS and nurses ratings, Goldberg et al. (10) found RT in medicated patients to be correlated with withdrawal symptoms but not with paranoid symptoms. Although the correlations are consistent they rarely exceed 0.3. These relatively low values might be due to the medication (i.e., interferences produced by extrapyramidal side effects) or the fact that the data came from regular clinical services in several hospitals rather than a single research unit.

Similarly, as described previously for the discharge test in our recent study, two groups of patients differing in clinical state also differed in RT. But this difference, to only a slightly lesser degree, was present also at admission when these patients were not clinically distinguishable. Therefore, variations in attentional capacity may reflect a potential for varying degrees of psychopathology, in terms of severity or length of episode or chronic state; but the psychopathology may fluctuate so as not always to be in close concordance with attentional performance.

Effects of Drugs

If attentional capacity is a trait which remains essentially the same in the face of clinical improvement under drug-free conditions, then it should be unaffected by antipsychotic medication as well. From a review of several studies of the effects of phenothiazines on RT, Neuchterlein (28) concluded that these drugs could not be shown to affect RT. However, Orzack et al. (30) found positive effects of carphenazine on the CPT which paralleled a gradual clinical improvement. In a large study Schooler and Goldberg (36) found a marked and highly significant decrease in RT over a 5-week period after initiation of phenothiazine treatment, but no further improvement over the next 21 weeks. The change in RT closely paralleled the change in ratings of withdrawal.

Recently in a carefully controlled study, Spohn et al. (38) found that chlorpromazine improved RT and other indices of attention in comparison to placebo. This improvement was significantly correlated with clinical improvement. There was a gradual improvement over an 8- to 12-week period after subjects began medication.

This evidence that medication which improves clinical state in chronic schizophrenics also leads to improved attentional performance suggests that attention may be a capacity that is both state and trait related. In our study (53), despite a finding of no significant change in RT for the I group as a whole, 5 of the 6 I patients whose admission RT was impaired showed improvement at discharge, sometimes quite marked. In drug studies such as those described above, which include more chronic and poor prognosis patients, one might expect more poor "pre" scores and therefore more opportunity for improvement.

A possible conclusion from this is that although there is good evidence that attentional capacity is, to some extent, trait related, it is affected by the psychotic state in some patients, but only minimally in others. The data suggest that minimal state effects are more likely to occur in acute good prognosis patients and perhaps in paranoids. It would seem to be important to define the factors determining this state-relatedness.

AUTONOMIC NERVOUS SYSTEM ACTIVITY

In contrast to the near unanimity of the findings on attentional deficits in schizophrenic patients, there is less agreement on the distinguishing features of autonomic nervous system activity. One reason for this might be that there are real differences in ANS activity among subtypes of patients (13) so that differences in sampling are more critical. In addition, there are many more problems of measurement (e.g., effect of base levels on response amplitude) and effects of the conditions of testing (e.g., subjects' expectancies or activity required of the subjects). The effect of medication is a serious problem and the difficulty of obtaining random samples of drug-free subjects has seriously hindered good research in this area.

Nevertheless, based on reviews of the literature and findings from our laboratory (49,50,54), three features of ANS activity in unmedicated chronic schizophrenics stand out as reasonably well confirmed.

1. High ANS "arousal" or activation under resting conditions. This is indicated by such variables as heart rate (HR), skin conductance level (SCL), and frequency of spontaneous skin conductance responses (SCRs) among others. High electrocortical activation seems to characterize chronic schizophrenics as well (45). Itil's *(this volume)* finding of low level fast EEG activity in resting schizophrenics can be interpreted in this way.
2. Low phasic and tonic ANS reactivity to meaningful or "demanding" stimuli. This is shown by relatively smaller and less frequent SCRs to, say, imperative stimuli in an RT task or less of an increment in SCL or HR during task performance.
3. Slow adaptation and habituation. One indicant of this is a slower decrease in SCL during the initial rest period in an experiment (54). This can be seen as following from the first two features: a flatter curve would be produced by a small response to a novel situation with a return to a higher endogenous activity level. Another indicant is slow habituation of the SCR component of the "orienting" response (OR) to simple sensory stimuli. The considerable controversy about the OR in schizophrenia and its habituation (13,46,51) is beyond the scope of this chapter. In our laboratory we have consistently found slow habituation, as defined below, in unmedicated chronic schizophrenics who respond at all.

Studies of Outcome

The extent to which this pattern of ANS activity also characterizes acute schizophrenics was investigated in the recent study from our laboratory (56) the design of which was described earlier. The patients and a group of normal controls were tested in two sessions in which skin conductance, HR, and skin temperature were recorded continuously. In the first session a 5-min rest period was followed by presentation of 20 mild tones (72 db, 500 Hz) at irregular 30- to 60-sec intervals. For the second session a reaction time procedure consisting of 20 trials—10 with a 3 sec PI and 10 with a 10 sec PI—was followed by a 3 min rest period, a mental arithmetic "stress" procedure, and another rest period.

The acute, largely good prognosis schizophrenics, as a group, showed significant ANS differences from normal in the same direction as previously found in chronic patients (although seemingly to a lesser degree for the most part). This result was due primarily to the marked deviations from normal in patients who subsequently showed a poor clinical outcome (NI group). The I patients were much less different from normal on most of the variables indexing the "schizophrenic pattern" described above.

Specifically, the NI patients were significantly higher than both controls and I patients on two activation indices: resting HR and spontaneous SCR frequency. The I patients were nonsignificantly higher than controls on these measures. The NI group had a lower resting skin temperature than the I patients suggesting greater peripheral vasoconstriction.

The NI group showed a slower decline (adaptation) in SCL during an initial rest period than I patients or controls. Habituation of the SCR orienting response also was slower in the NI group as shown in Fig. 2 when assessed by several indices of habituation which control for differences in responsivity as has been customary in this laboratory (54). These analyses show that the NI patients are relatively less reactive on early trials and more reactive on later trials in the series than are the other groups. This was related to a tendency in these patients, as in chronic schizophrenics, to give an erratic stop-and-go pattern of responding rather than responding on every trial until habituation occurs. I patients were not different from controls on any of these habituation indices.

ANS reactivity to meaningful stimuli and situations was assessed by measuring phasic responsivity to the reaction time situation and tonic reactivity to the mental arithmetic task. Here again the NI patients deviated from the I patients and controls. The NI group had fewer SCRs to both the ready signal and the imperative stimulus of the RT task, and their SCRs to the latter stimulus had longer latencies. A particularly striking deficit in reactivity in the RT situation shown by NI patients is illustrated in Fig. 3 which shows HR averaged during and after the 10 sec PI. The I patients and controls show the typical HR slowing in anticipation of the imperative stimulus (21) to an equal degree while the

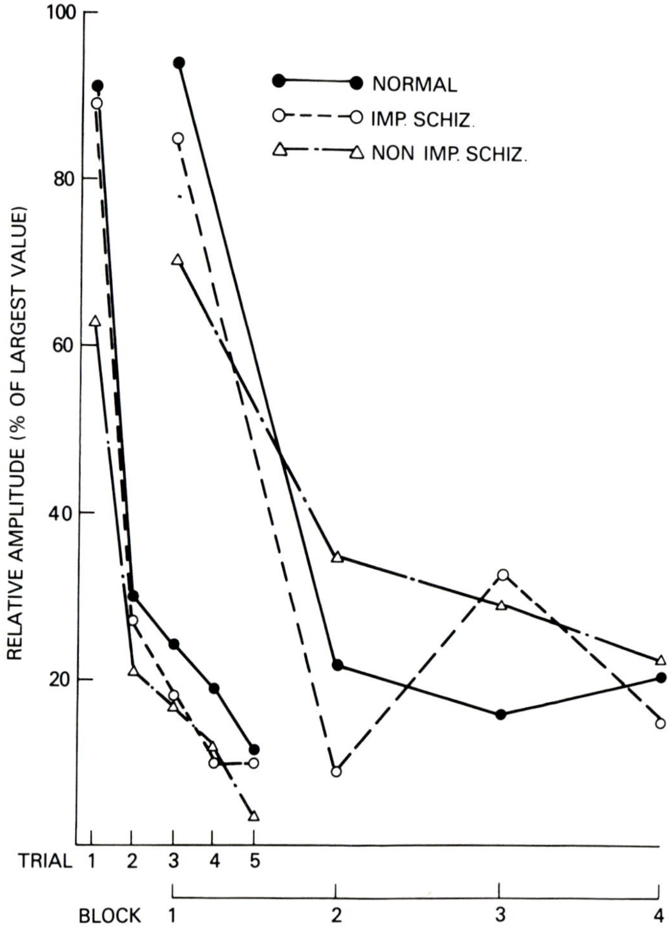

FIG. 2. Habituation of the skin conductance orienting response.

NI group decelerates significantly less. This gives some support to the deficient preparatory set hypothesis of the schizophrenic RT deficit.

Another manifestation of low reactivity by the NI patients was a smaller increase in SCR frequency during the mental arithmetic procedure, particularly during the instruction period preceding the task itself.

In summary, two groups of medication-free acute schizophrenic patients, delineated on the basis of subsequent clinical course, did not differ on global ratings of clinical state shortly after hospital admission, but did differ in ANS and attentional functioning at that time. According to our measures, patients with a poor clinical course were more like chronic schizophrenics in showing high ANS activation, slow habituation, and low reactivity to "demanding" stimuli and situations; whereas good outcome patients were similar to controls. It should

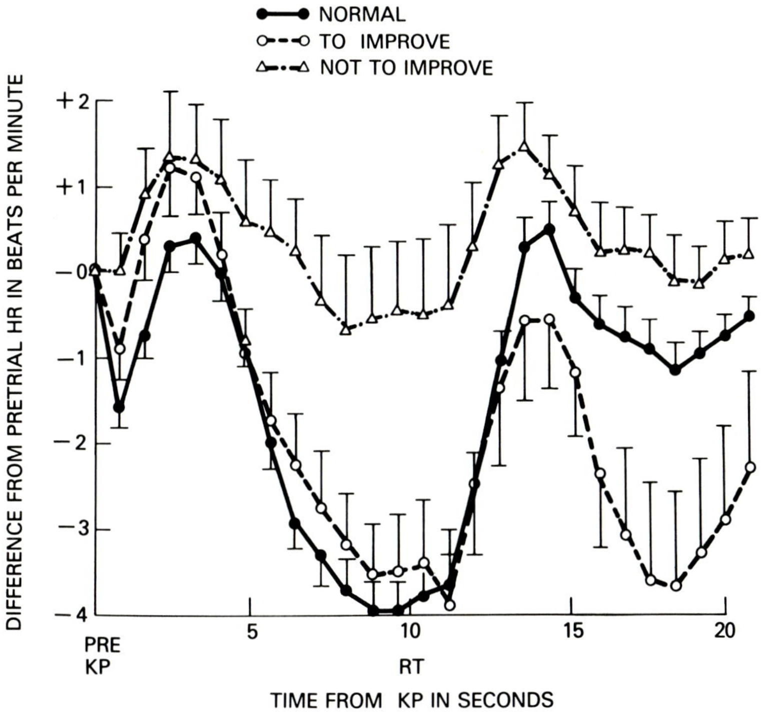

FIG. 3. Averaged heart rate for 10 reaction time trials with 10-sec preparatory intervals.

be pointed out that it was only the male I and NI patients who were clearly different on the SC response to demand, both I and NI females giving a smaller response than control females. Nevertheless, a discriminant analysis, shown in Table 1, using just ANS variables, correctly identified 84% of the I and NI patients.

Only two other studies in which ANS activity was related to a direct measure

TABLE 1. *Discriminant analysis of improved vs not improved patients from admission psychophysiology*

Actual group	Predicted group: Improved	Predicted group: Not improved
Improved	16	2
Not improved	3	11
Normals	93	26

Patients correctly classified = 84.4%

Variables: 1. Habituation of orienting SCR
2. HR deceleration in RT
3. Spontaneous SCR response to stress

of outcome are known to the author. Stern et al. (39) tested schizophrenic patients 1 to 3 days after hospital admission (before treatment) on SC responsiveness to a series of tones and during a word association test. They were retested 5 weeks later during phenothiazine treatment. Patients who were in treatment at the 5-week test were separated into good and poor outcome groups on the basis of whether they were able to be discharged by 7 weeks (good) or not (poor). No differences were found between the groups on the admission test. Several methodological differences between this study and ours might be responsible for the differences in results. Testing patients so soon after hospital admission, although advantageous in maximizing the chances of the patients being at the height of an acute episode, does not control for possible prehospitalization medication, and the psychological and biological effects of a recent change in environment (22) are added to the effects of the schizophrenic episode *per se.* The 7-week outcome measure is based on a considerably shorter period of time than in our study, and hospital discharge might be influenced by many other factors besides psychiatric condition.

Results similar to ours have been obtained recently by Frith et al. (8) who recorded the SCRs to a series of 14 moderately intense (85 db, 1000 Hz) tones in schizophrenics who had suffered an acute exacerbation of their psychosis but had been free of regular medication for at least 4 weeks. The patients were then treated with either α-flupenthixol (which blocks dopamine receptors but not norepinephrine receptors), β-flupenthixol (which does not block dopamine receptors), or placebo on a random double-blind basis for 4 weeks. Frith et al. found that clinical improvement as assessed by global ratings was significantly greater for those patients who received α-flupenthixol than for those who received the other treatments. Improvement was also greater in patients whose SCR to the tones habituated or who failed to respond (46%) compared to patients who failed to habituate (54%). There was no interaction between these predictor variables—habituators improved more regardless of what treatment they were on. The reduction in psychopathology rating due to the SC variable (2.52 on a 5-point scale) was actually better than that of the medication variable (2.31). Other SC variables such as SCL and spontaneous SCR frequency were significantly related to habituation status and showed nonsignificant relationships to outcome in the same direction.

These findings lend support to the results of our study that a pattern of high SC activation and slow habituation is predictive of poor short-term outcome. The difference in the actual habituation measures that related to outcome in the two studies is probably due to the much more intense stimuli used by Frith et al.

ANS Change in Relation to Clinical Change

The finding that a "schizophrenic pattern" of ANS functioning differs in patients who will later differ in outcome but who do not differ in global clinical state at the time of the test suggests that the ANS pattern is trait rather than state related. This question was investigated further in our study by comparing ANS functioning at admission with that shortly before discharge in the 15 I and 15 NI patients. Both groups of patients were tested on both occasions.

Taken as a whole the data showed minimal ANS changes accompanying the substantial clinical improvement in the I patients. Of the base "arousal" measures, HR decreased reliably in the I group but not in the NI group. SCL decreased for both groups combined but not significantly for either group separately. Assessment of changes in responses to the RT and mental arithmetic tasks was complicated by the presence of sex differences. The general pattern of these variables was that the I females who, it will be recalled, showed moderate deficits in reactivity at admission, showed significant increases in ANS responsivity at discharge; whereas the I males, who tended to be mildly hyperresponsive at admission, showed modest and nonsignificant declines in reactivity. Thus these measures of ANS reactivity to demanding stimuli and situations seem to have a state-related component which in turn is related to gender. Women have attenuated reactivity during an acute psychotic episode and men, if anything, change in the opposite direction.

When patients who were in a fair state of remission just before hospital discharge ("Well"; $N = 21$) were compared with those who remained psychotic ("Sick"; $N = 19$), the differences in ANS functioning were somewhat more marked than at admission and sex differences were largely absent. The Sick group had higher resting HR and spontaneous SCRs, showed slower adaptation and habituation, was less reactive to the RT stimuli with both SCRs and HR, and had smaller tonic ANS reactions to the arithmetic task. Patients in remission were at normal levels for all of those variables. Well patients were distinguished from controls primarily by low SCL and a low frequency of orienting SCRs to the tones.

The two other outcome studies, cited above, also found low orienting SCRs in some patients on a second test (while patients were in treatment), but their results differ somewhat from ours and from each others. Stern et al. (39) (whose patients were all receiving phenothiazines) found that only the good prognosis group decreased in responsivity. Frith et al. (8) found that patients receiving the dopamine blocker α-flupenthixol had reduced SCRs but patients who improved did not decrease significantly in responsivity. The latter result might be expected on the basis of the fact that the good outcome group was already low in responsivity prior to treatment.

Do ANS Disturbances Reflect Traits?

The data from our study and those from Frith et al. suggest that many of the ANS disturbances found in schizophrenics are not merely secondary consequences of the psychotic state but may reflect more permanent dispositions which have important clinical consequences in terms of outcome. A possible implication is that the ANS differences index a fundamental typology of schizophrenia which has been referred to in various ways as acute versus chronic, reactive versus process, or schizophreniform versus nuclear. If this is true, then there should be some correspondence between other indices of these types, outcome measures, and ANS activity.

Frith et al. (8) found that patients whose psychotic episode had an insidious onset showed less clinical improvement than those with an acute onset, but this was independent of the SCR frequency measure. Thus acuteness of onset and SCR habituation were independently related to outcome and thus are presumably reflecting different prognostically significant processes.

In our study, where it should be kept in mind that patients were selected for relatively good prior social and work functioning, there were about twice as many patients scoring in the "good premorbid" range of the Phillips scale of premorbid social adjustment (31) as those who scored "poor" in both outcome groups. Further, when ANS activity was compared in the two premorbid groups very few differences were found, no more than would be expected by chance. This is consistent with the negative and inconsistent results reported in the literature on ANS activity in relation to the process-reactive dichotomy reviewed by Klorman et al. (19). However, extant studies on this problem are beset with methodological difficulties such as small samples, lack of control over medication, and mixtures of acute and chronic patients. Our study, too, is not a fair test of the hypothesis because of the lack of patients with insidious onset. Thus, although deviant ANS functioning cannot be shown to relate to conventional typologies based on premorbid history, the relationship has not been well tested.

Can the deviant ANS pattern be discriminating patients on the basis of a genetic predisposition for more chronic or nuclear forms of schizophrenia? This hypothesis is suggested by the ANS similarity of our patients with poor outcome to that of chronic schizophrenics together with the fact that chronic schizophrenia and ANS functioning are to some extent genetically determined. If it is true, there should be a similarity between the deviant ANS pattern found in our study and that found in "high-risk" studies of the offspring of schizophrenic parents. Unfortunately, no consistently confirmed findings have emerged from these studies (34,52). However, large SCRs to simple tones and slow habituation or adaptation have been found in several studies. SCR amplitude to tones did not distinguish our acute schizophrenic groups from each other or from controls, but was larger than normal in a previous study with unmedicated chronic patients (54). Mednick and Schulsinger (25) and Van Dyke et al. (44) both found statistically reliable slow habituation in high-risk subjects at some point in their procedures. Whereas Salzman and Klein (34) reported a nonsignificant trend for more trials to habituation to a series of tones in their high-risk group, their data on SCR amplitude show that—despite a lower initial level—the low-risk subjects declined at 4 times the rate of the high-risk group from the first to the second trial block. Since slow habituation (in a relative sense) strongly and consistently distinguished our two outcome groups and has been found in chronic schizophrenia as well (54), it would seem to be a good candidate for a genetic ANS marker.

However, negative evidence on this point was found in a study on discordant monozygotic (MZ) twins carried out in our laboratory as part of a larger study (32). The most striking results were markedly low phasic and tonic ANS reactivity to demanding stimuli and situations by the index twins, but normal reactivity in their nonschizophrenic co-twins (50,52). The co-twins also were not remarkably different from normal on "arousal" measures nor in habituation. Thus no ANS marker of a schizophrenic genotype is apparent from this evidence. This, of course, does not militate against possible ANS markers of vulnerability to schizophrenia based on nongenetic factors or a combination of genetic and nongenetic factors. Mednick's (23) findings of a high rate of pregnancy and birth complications in his genetic high-risk children having an early psychiatric breakdown (who also showed ANS differences from other high-risk subjects) are consistent with this view. The differences between the discordant MZ twins mentioned above might be related to the fact that the schizophrenic twins had lower birth weights than their nonschizophrenic co-twins (32). In addition, ANS markers of risk for schizophrenia have been shown to be highly influenced by familial factors (24). Thus high-risk and twin studies might not be expected to yield similar results with respect to potential ANS markers.

Monoamine Oxidase Activity and ANS Activity

One potential biological marker for schizophrenia which has been suggested is low monoamine oxidase (MAO) activity. In contrast with data reported for chronic samples, this was not lower than normal in our group of acute schizophrenics (5), nor did the activity of this enzyme distinguish the subgroups of patients reliably. However, MAO activity did correlate with certain aspects of ANS activity. Table 2 shows partial correlations (controlling for sex differences) between MAO activity and several representative ANS variables. In addition

TABLE 2. *Correlations between MAO activity and RT with psychophysiological variables for admission (ADM) and discharge (DIS) tests*

Variable	MAO ADM ($N=34$)	MAO DIS ($N=37$)	RT ADM ($N=39$)	RT DIS ($N=37$)
Resting SCL	0.11	0.39[a]	−0.11	0.08
SCR amplitude—RT stimuli	0.28	0.36[a]	−0.35[a]	−0.45[b]
Spontaneous SCR stress response	0.11	0.52[b]	−0.36[a]	−0.43[b]
Overall stress response	0.10	0.40[a]	−0.39[a]	−0.46[b]

[a] $p < 0.05$.
[b] $p < 0.01$.

to resting SCL, phasic and tonic reactivity to demanding stimuli and situations were positively correlated with MAO activity at discharge. At admission the relationships are not significant, suggesting interference by state factors, although males with high MAO were significantly more responsive to the RT stimuli ($r = 0.67$). The correlations with RT, shown for comparison purposes, are about the same at both admission and discharge, which would be expected if state factors were affecting both RT and the correlated ANS variables in the same way.

These correlations suggest that low MAO activity may be related to the "pathogenic" low ANS response to demand in schizophrenia. The direction of the correlations is surprising if it is assumed that skin conductance responsivity should be positively related to catecholaminergic activity, and this in turn is reduced to a greater extent in persons with high MAO activity. However, MAO-ANS relationships in the same direction have been found in our laboratory in a large group of normal subjects (55), and MAO inhibitors have been shown to reduce heart rate and blood pressure in depressives (27).

In addition, the assumption that ANS activity is positively correlated with catecholaminergic activity may be questioned. Table 3 shows product-moment correlations of urinary catecholamines and their metabolites with SC and HR "arousal" measures under resting and task conditions in a group of MZ twins most of whom were discordant for schizophrenia (32). It can be seen that almost all correlations are negative and several are highly significant. Although these correlations are from a mixed group of index and control twins ($N = 34$), separate analyses of twins with and without a diagnosis of schizophrenia produced similar correlations for each group. The general trend of these data has also been shown in a recent finding of significant negative correlations ranging

TABLE 3. *Correlations of skin conductance level (SCL) and heart rate (HR) with urinary biogenic amines and their metabolites*

	Variable and condition				
Amine or metabolite	SCL rest (N=34)	SCL task (N=33)	Spontaneous SCR frequency rest (N=34)	HR rest (N=36)	HR task (N=33)
Epinephrine	−0.01	0.01	−0.25	−0.22	−0.33
Norepinephrine	−0.32	−0.30	−0.41[a]	0.09	0.00
Dopamine	−0.54[b]	−0.09	−0.46[b]	−0.17	−0.21
Metanephrine	−0.37[a]	−0.23	−0.43[a]	−0.45[b]	−0.61[b]
Normetanephrine	−0.56[b]	−0.40[a]	−0.15	−0.04	−0.32
Vanillylmandelic acid (VMA)	−0.18	−0.20	−0.14	−0.22	−0.19

Note: The amines and their metabolites were from 72-hr samples and evaluated per gram of creatinine.

[a] $p < 0.05$.

[b] $p < 0.01$.

from −0.62 to −0.84 between both SCL and HR with urinary vanillylmandelic acid (VMA) and 3-methoxy-4-hydroxyphenylglycol (MHPG) in chronic schizophrenics (7). This result is just the opposite of what one would expect, however, from the positive relationship between ANS and MAO activity together with the finding that MAO inhibitors in depressives reduce MHPG and VMA in urine (26). The apparent conflict in these studies may be due to different interrelationships between the ANS, MAO activity, and catecholamines in schizophrenics, depressives, and normals, or to inherent difficulties comparing results from correlational studies with those from MAO inhibition studies. Certainly the regulation of ANS activity depends on other mechanisms and enzymes as well. The evidence is presented mainly to show that ANS activity may be importantly determined by some of the biological factors thought to be etiologically important in schizophrenia, and to suggest the possibility that these relationships might be different in different subgroups of patients. The measurement of enzyme activity, catecholamines and their metabolites, and ANS activity in the same carefully described individuals at the same time is necessary to resolve the issue.

Effects of Antipsychotic Drugs

The question of the neurochemical determinants of ANS activity can also be approached by consideration of the effects of drugs. In addition, it may be instructive to compare drug-produced improvements in clinical state with "spontaneous" clinical changes (or clinical differences under medication-free conditions).

Phenothiazines have generally been found to lower the "arousal" indicators of SCL, spontaneous SCRs, and blood pressure (38,42), but these effects are sometimes quite marginal. In contrast, HR is increased by phenothiazines, a result sometimes attributed to the drugs' hypotensive effects through compensatory reflex mechanisms. These drugs have been found consistently to lower reactivity in all the above autonomic systems as well as in pupillary activity (38,42). This reduction in reactivity is quite general; it occurs in spontaneous activity and in tonic and phasic reactivity elicited by all types of stimuli. No adequate placebo-controlled studies seem to have been done concerning the effects of phenothiazines on habituation independent of responsivity. Since the primary action of phenothiazines is to block the catecholamine receptors, this system is implicated in the ANS disturbances in schizophrenics. Frith et al. (8) found a significant reduction in SCR-orienting responses and marginal decreases in other SC arousal measures in patients receiving a dopamine receptor blocker, so the dopamine system is more specifically implicated. This conclusion is supported by findings in parkinsonian patients that L-DOPA increased SCL, spontaneous SCRs, SCR amplitude, muscle tension, and systolic blood pressure and slowed habituation of the orienting SCR (17).

A more important question is whether there is a relationship between the drug-produced ANS changes and clinical changes. It is clear that ANS changes produced by conventional antipsychotic drugs do not correspond to those found in our study in patients who showed clinical improvement when tested and rated under drug-free conditions. The trend was for decreases in HR and a selective increase in the tonic and phasic SC response just to demanding stimuli and situations in the remitting patients (this latter effect in female patients). Similarly, Frith et al. found that there was no effect of clinical improvement on SCR frequency independent of the effect of the active drug. Unfortunately, the opportunity to show ANS changes in patients who improve off drugs is limited by their already minimal ANS dysfunction when psychotic.

Nevertheless, it is clear that antipsychotic drugs do not completely "correct" the abnormal ANS pattern that seems to be a general characteristic of schizophrenics and particularly of patients not likely to remit quickly without such medication. The general decrease in arousal measures is in the "right" direction; but the opposite trend for HR, although possibly a peripheral effect, is real and might present patients with conflicting cues from different arousal systems. The other major demonstrated effect of most antipsychotic drugs—a general reduction in ANS responsivity—is equivocal in significance. The good news is that the drugs may reduce the overreactivity many schizophrenics show to innocuous and unimportant stimuli. The bad news is that the drugs also attenuate the schizophrenics' hyporeactivity to important and demanding situations. It can be speculated that this may have some relationship to the persistence of affective blunting in many phenothiazine-treated patients.

There is some evidence that these "unfavorable" drug effects may have a bearing on the treatment outcome. Singh and Kay (37) found that patients with an unfavorable therapeutic response to neuroleptic medication (haloperidol or chlorpromazine) had higher HR during the medication than those with a favorable outcome, a result confirmatory of earlier observations (42). Stern et al. (39) found that patients who improved on phenothiazines also had significantly reduced SCRs to meaningless tones, but also to a word association test while poor drug responders did not. Although this study did not have a normal control group, unmedicated schizophrenics have been found to have lower SCR responsivity to a word association test (50). Thus the ANS response to neuroleptics is related to therapeutic outcome, but ANS changes accompanying good outcome are not necessarily in the direction of "normalization."

If the ANS data reflect incomplete therapeutic reversal of symptoms, then perhaps some different or additional drug which changes the ANS pattern more favorably might also be therapeutically beneficial. A recent study (48) has shown that the addition of propranalol to chlorpromazine led to significant clinical improvement to chronic schizophrenics with a long history of phenothiazine resistance. Propranalol causes a reduction in HR through its β-adrenergic receptor-blocking actions, and this effect was confirmed in the patients. In this same series of studies, Gruzelier (11) found marked effects on the skin conductance orienting response as well. Gruzelier typically finds with his method that most schizophrenics taking phenothiazines are either under- or overreactive in their orienting SCRs to tones. He reports that the combination of phenothiazines and propranalol "normalized" both groups, increasing the responsiveness of nonresponders and reducing that of hyperresponders. This striking result should be interpreted with caution because of serious methodological difficulties (some patients were tested twice and some once, blind and open trials were mixed, etc.), but it suggests that a therapeutic regimen which produces better clinical improvement than that produced by conventional phenothiazine therapy also produces more normal ANS patterns as well.

IMPLICATIONS FOR FUTURE RESEARCH

The preceding discussion has attempted to make the point that ANS and attentional functioning is intimately and perhaps fundamentally related to the schizophrenic process. If this is indeed the case, it should be useful to include tests of such functioning in clinical trials of neuroleptic medication. A general goal of the proposed research is to test the utility of these methods in helping to choose the best treatment for individual patients. This would include the important alternative of psychosocial treatment alone since one way to prevent the side effects of neuroleptic drugs that are discussed in this volume, is to minimize drug use. An inevitable spinoff of this research would be increased basic knowledge about the psychophysiology of schizophrenia.

Direct evidence has been presented that in patients hospitalized for an acute schizophrenic episode, favorable outcome independent of active neuroleptic medication is related to more normal functioning on these variables or to a less active ANS under conditions of low demand. These studies need replication and extension. They need to be repeated on samples which include more process, insidious onset cases. The ability of attentional and ANS variables to discriminate between patients who need drugs (including which ones) and those who do not should also be investigated. A suitable research protocol would be similar to the one presented in Fig. 1, with one or more double-blind medication trials (with a counterbalanced placebo period) occurring during the treatment period. The final discharge test may not be necessary for this purpose. This design is advantageous for testing the predictions of outcome under various treatment regimens from admission test data, and could possibly lead to identification of subgroups of patients for whom it could be determined early in their hospitalization which therapy would be most likely to have a beneficial effect. This type of protocol would be most appropriate with new admissions or readmissions. Of course, prediction equations need not be confined to psychophysiological data, but could include social history data, presenting symptoms, etc., as well.

The potential of this approach should be strengthened if wide individual differences among patients are taken into account. For example, despite the evidence cited in this chapter that schizophrenics as a group are autonomically overaroused, there are wide individual differences. Gruzelier and Venables (13) found about half of their medicated patients to be abnormally underaroused and unresponsive to simple sensory stimuli. This is probably an overestimate of the true size of this group if the patients had been unmedicated, but nevertheless, there seems to be a substantial subgroup of schizophrenics with unusually low ANS activity even when unmedicated. Despite the evidence of dopaminergic involvement in electrodermal activity, one cannot infer that these patients have an underactive dopamine system, but this group would be of particular interest in pharmacological studies.

Psychophysiological testing during the treatment periods would provide a controlled experiment on the ANS and attentional effects of drugs, and the relationships between changes in these parameters and clinical changes under various conditions. It is important that a randomized counterbalanced order of conditions be maintained to control for adaptation to the test situation (or, indeed, to the hospital setting), effects of familiarization with the tasks, etc. It should be pointed out that these "research" protocols are not incompatible with good clinical practice. There is evidence of a subgroup of schizophrenics for whom neuroleptic therapy might not be the optimal treatment (4), and the proposed research design should allow identification of these patients solely on clinical grounds in addition to testing the hypothesis that they can be identified better with the aid of ANS and attention measures. In general, controlled double-blind trials may be the best way of choosing a treatment regimen for the individual patient.

A related question that deserves attention is whether treatments which "normalize" ANS functioning improve clinical state. The studies by Gruzelier (11) and Yorkston et al. (48), previously cited, suggest this possibility. A more detailed knowledge of drug effects on psychophysiology and the mechanisms involved, derived from clinical studies, particularly those in which biogenic amines and enzymes have been measured, will probably be necessary before much progress can be made on this problem.

A final area in which assessment of ANS and attentional functioning may be useful in clinical decisions is in the prediction of relapse in remitted patients. There are two aspects to this problem. One involves prediction of patients who can "survive" for a considerable period of time without neuroleptic medication. This is, of course, closely related to the problem of predicting who can recover without medication. However, there may be patients who need drugs to recover but who can subsequently be maintained without them. If ANS and attention measures can be useful in the first case, they should be of value in the second.

A second researchable question is whether changes in ANS and attentional functioning can predict an impending psychotic episode. There is some indirect evidence from our study on acute schizophrenics that this might be feasible. One possible explanation of the relatively less-impaired laboratory functioning of the Improved patients at admission, despite high psychopathology ratings, is that these patients were already undergoing a process of recovery in which attentional capacity and ANS changes preceded the later clinical improvement. It is well known that the clinical effects of starting or stopping neuroleptic medication usually require several weeks, although Gruzelier and Hammond (12) found that maximum ANS effects occurred within a week of onset or after cessation of chlorpromazine treatment. Therefore, it may be that schizophrenics have to live with an altered biological substrate for some period of time before clinical change occurs and that these changes are detectable by the methods on which this chapter is focused.

Thus, through periodic monitoring of ANS and/or attentional activity during periods of remission, impending psychotic episodes might be able to be detected before full-blown clinical symptoms occur. At this point intervention with pharmacological and/or psychosocial methods could be instituted.

Recent research suggests that familial climate ("expressed emotion" in relatives) can influence relapse rate which, in turn, can be improved by drugs and removal of the social stressors. Evidence suggests that these effects might be mediated by—or at least indicated by—ANS activity (41). Although in this study the ANS effects occurred only under very specific conditions, other sources of life stress might precipitate more general and prolonged ANS reactions. Little is known about the temporal course of changes in ANS activity in relation to the clinical course of the psychosis. Monitoring remitted patients periodically might help answer this question, should help determine the state versus trait issue, and could lead to development of an "early warning system" for impending psychotic episodes.

Finally, there is a continuing need to apply the rapid advances in information processing, cognitive psychology, and psychophysiology to the understanding of schizophrenia. The studies of outcome and of other clinical problems reviewed in this chapter have focused on attention and ANS activity, partly because these processes have been shown to have particular relevance in schizophrenia. Measures of perceptual, cognitive, or information transmission processes might also be fruitful in such studies if they have survived a shakedown period in more basic studies of schizophrenics versus normals or other comparison groups.

ACKNOWLEDGMENTS

I am indebted to John Strauss and William Carpenter who designed and administered the clinical research program on acute schizophrenics at NIMH and who provided an excellent system of clinical evaluation and a highly favorable research climate.

REFERENCES

1. Asarnow, R. F., and MacCrimmon, D. J. (1978): Residual performance deficit in clinically remitted schizophrenics: A marker of schizophrenia? *J. Abnorm. Psychol.*, 87:597–608.
2. Bellissimo, A., and Steffy, R. A. (1972): Redundancy-associated deficit in schizophrenic reaction time performance. *J. Abnorm. Psychol.*, 80:299–307.
3. Cancro, R., Sutton, S., Kerr, J., and Sugerman, A. (1971): Reaction time and prognosis in acute schizophrenia. *J. Nerv. Ment. Dis.*, 153:351–359.

4. Carpenter, W. T., Jr., McGlashan, T. H., and Strauss, J. S. (1977): The treatment of acute schizophrenia without drugs: An investigation of some current assumptions. *Am. J. Psychiatry,* 134:14–20.
5. Carpenter, W. T., Jr., Murphy, D. L., and Wyatt, R. J. (1975): Platelet monoamine oxidase activity in acute schizophrenia. *Am. J. Psychiatry,* 132:438–440.
6. Carpenter, W. T., Jr., Strauss, J. S., and Bartko, J. J. (1973): A flexible system for the identification of schizophrenia: A report from the International Pilot Study of Schizophrenia. *Science,* 182:1275–1278.
7. Deakin, J. F. W., Baker, H. F., Frith, C. D., Joseph, M. H., and Johnstone, E. C. (1979): Arousal related to excretion of noradrenaline metabolites and clinical aspects of unmedicated chronic schizophrenic patients. *J. Psychiatr. Res.,* 15:57–65.
7a. *Diagnostic and Statistical Manual of Mental Disorders (DSM-II)* (1968): American Psychiatric Association, Washington, D.C.
8. Frith, C. D., Stevens, M., Johnstone, E. C., and Crow, T. J. (1978): Skin conductance responsivity during acute episodes of schizophrenia as a predictor of symptomatic improvement. *Psycholog. Med.,* 8:1–6.
9. Garmezy, N. (1978): Attentional processes in adult schizophrenia and children at risk. *J. Psychiatr. Res.,* 14:3–34.
10. Goldberg, S. C., Schooler, N. R., and Mattson, N. (1968): Paranoid and withdrawal symptoms in schizophrenia: Relationship to reaction time. *Br. J. Psychiatry,* 114:1161–1165.
11. Gruzelier, J. H. (1978): Propranolol acts to modulate autonomic orienting and habituation processes in schizophrenia. In: *Propranolol and Schizophrenia,* edited by E. Roberts and P. Amacher, pp. 99–118. Alan R. Liss, New York.
12. Gruzelier, J. H., and Hammond, N. V. (1974): The effect of chlorpromazine upon the psychophysiology of chronic schizophrenics. Presented to the Psychophysiology Group, British Psychological Society, London.
13. Gruzelier, J. H., and Venables, P. H. (1972): Skin conductance orienting activity in a heterogeneous sample of schizophrenics—Possible evidence of limbic dysfunction. *J. Nerv. Ment. Dis.,* 155:277–287.
14. Holzman, P. S., Kringlen, E., Levy, D. L., Proctor, L. R., and Haberman, S. (1978): Smooth pursuit eye movements in twins discordant for schizophrenia. *J. Psychiatr. Res.,* 14:111–120.
15. Holzman, P. S., Levy, D. L., and Proctor, L. R. (1978): The several qualities of attention in schizophrenia. *J. Psychiatr. Res.,* 14:99–110.
16. Holzman, P. S., Proctor, L. R., Levy, D. L., Yasillo, N. J., Meltzer, H. Y., and Hurt, S. W. (1974): Eye-tracking dysfunctions in schizophrenic patients and their relatives. *Arch. Gen. Psychiatry,* 31:143–151.
17. Horvath, T. B., and Meares, R. A. (1974): L-Dopa and arousal. *J. Neurol., Neurosurg. Psychiatry,* 37:417–421.
18. Huston, P. E., Shakow, D., and Riggs, L. A. (1937): Studies of motor function in schizophrenia. II. Reaction time. *J. Gen. Psychol.,* 16:39–82.
19. Klorman, R., Strauss, J. S., and Kokes, R. F., (1977): Premorbid adjustment in schizophrenia: concepts, measures, and implications. Part IV. Some biological approaches to research on premorbid functioning in schizophrenia. *Schizophr. Bull.,* 3:226–239.
20. Kornetsky, C., and Orzack, M. H. (1978): Physiological and behavioral correlates of attention dysfunction in schizophrenic patients. *J. Psychiatr. Res.,* 14:69–79.
21. Lacey, B. C., and Lacey, J. I. (1974): Studies of heart rate and other bodily processes in sensorimotor behavior. In: *Cardiovascular Psychophysiology,* edited by P. A. Obrist, A. H. Black, J. Brener, and L. V. Di Cara, pp. 538–564. Aldine, Chicago.
22. Mason, J. W., Sachar, E. J., Fishman, J. R., Hamburg, D. A., and Handlon, J. H. (1965): Corticosteroid responses to hospital admission. *Arch. Gen. Psychiatry,* 13:1–8.
23. Mednick, S. A. (1970): Breakdown in individuals at high risk for schizophrenia: Possible predispositional perinatal factors. *Ment. Hygiene,* 54:50–63.
24. Mednick, S. A. (1978): Berkson's fallacy and high risk research. In: *The Nature of Schizophrenia,* edited by L. C. Wynne, R. L. Cromwell, and S. Matthysse, pp. 442–452. John Wiley & Son, New York.
25. Mednick, S. A., and Schulsinger, F. (1973): Studies of children at high risk for schizophrenia. In: *Schizophrenia: The First Ten Dean Award Lectures,* pp. 247–293. Edited by S. R. Dean. MSS Information Corp., New York.

26. Murphy, D. L., Brand, E., Goldman, T., Baker, M., Wright, C., van Kammen, D., and Gordon, E. (1977): Platelet and plasma amine oxidase inhibition and urinary amine excretion changes during phenelzine treatment. *J. Nerv. Ment. Dis.,* 164:129–134.
27. Murphy, D. L., Lipper, S., Slater, S., and Shiling, D. (1979): Selectivity of clorgyline and pargyline as inhibitors of monoamine oxidases A and B in vivo in man. *Psychopharmacology* 62:129–132.
28. Neuchterlein, K. H. (1977): Reaction time and attention in schizophrenia: A critical evaluation of the data and theories. *Schizophr. Bull.,* 3:373–428.
29. Olbrich, R. (1972): Reaction time in brain-damaged and normal subjects to variable preparatory intervals. *J. Nerv. Ment. Dis.,* 155:356–362.
30. Orzack, M. H., Kornetsky, C., and Freeman, H. (1967): The effects of daily administration of carphenazine on attention in the schizophrenic patient. *Psychopharmacology (Berl.),* 11:31–38.
31. Phillips, L. (1953): Case history data and prognosis in schizophrenia. *J. Nerv. Ment. Dis.,* 117:515–525.
32. Pollin, W., and Stabenau, J. R. (1968): Biological, psychological and historical differences in a series of monozygotic twins discordant for schizophrenia. In: *The Transmission of Schizophrenia,* edited by D. Rosenthal and S. S. Kety, pp. 317–332. Pergamon Press, New York.
33. Rosenthal, D., Lawlor, W. G., Zahn, T. P., and Shakow, D. (1960): The relationship of some aspects of mental set to degree of schizophrenic disorganization. *J. Pers.,* 28:26–38.
34. Salzman, L. F., and Klein, R. H. (1978): Habituation and conditioning of electrodermal responses in high risk children. *Schizophr. Bull.,* 4:210–222.
35. Salzman, L. F., Klein, R. H., and Strauss, J. S. (1978): Pendulum eye-tracking in remitted psychiatric patients. *J. Psychiatr. Res.,* 14:121–126.
36. Schooler, N. R., and Goldberg, S. C. (1972): Performance tests in a study of phenothiazines in schizophrenia: Caveats and conclusions. *Psychopharmacology (Berl.),* 24:24–81.
37. Singh, M. M., and Kay, S. R. (1979): Dysphoric response to neuroleptic treatment in schizophrenia: Its relationship to autonomic arousal and prognosis. *Biol. Psychiatry,* 14:277–294.
38. Spohn, H. E., Lacoursiere, R. B., Thompson, K., and Coyne, L. (1977): Phenothiazine effects on psychological and psychophysiological dysfunction in chronic schizophrenics. *Arch. Gen. Psychiatry,* 34:633–644.
39. Stern, J. A., Surphlis, W., and Koff, E. (1965): Electrodermal responsiveness as related to psychiatric diagnosis and prognosis. *Psychophysiology,* 2:51–61.
40. Sutton, S., Hakerem, G., Zubin, J., and Portnoy, M. (1961): The effect of shift of sensory modality on serial reaction-time: A comparison of schizophrenics and normals. *Am. J. Psychol.,* 74:224–232.
41. Tarrier, N., Vaughn, C., Lader, M. H., and Leff, J. P. (1979): Bodily reactions to people and events in schizophrenics. *Arch. Gen. Psychiatry,* 36:311–315.
42. Tecce, J. J., and Cole, J. O. (1972): Psychophysiologic responses of schizophrenics to drugs. *Psychopharmacology (Berl.),* 24:159–200.
43. Van Dyke, J. L., and Rosenthal, D. (1975): Schizophrenia: Effects of inheritance and rearing on reaction time. *Can. J. Behav. Sci.* 3:223–236.
44. Van Dyke, J. L., Rosenthal, D., and Rasmussen, P. V. (1974): Electrodermal functioning in adopted-away offspring of schizophrenics. *J. Psychiatr. Res.,* 10:199–215.
45. Venables, P. H. (1966): Psychophysiological aspects of schizophrenia. *Br. J. Med. Psychol.,* 39:289–297.
46. Venables, P. H. (1977): The electrodermal psychophysiology of schizophrenics and children at risk for schizophrenia: Controversies and developments. *Schizophr. Bull.,* 3:28–48.
47. Wohlberg, G. W., and Kornetsky, C. (1973): Sustained attention in remitting schizophrenics. *Arch. Gen. Psychiatry,* 28:533–537.
48. Yorkston, N. J., Gruzelier, J. H., Zaki, S. A., Hollander, D., Pitcher, D. R., and Sergeant, H. G. S. (1977): Propranolol as an adjunct to the treatment of schizophrenia. *Lancet,* ii:575–578.
49. Zahn, T. P. (1964): Autonomic reactivity and behavior in schizophrenia. Psychiatric Research Report 19, American Psychiatric Asociation, Washington, D.C.
50. Zahn, T. P. (1975): Psychophysiological concomitants of task performance in schizophrenia. In: *Experimental Approaches to Psychopathology,* edited by M. L. Kietzman, S. Sutton, and J. Zubin, pp. 109–131. Academic Press, New York.

51. Zahn, T. P. (1976): On the bimodality of the distribution of electrodermal orienting responses in schizophrenic patients. *J. Nerv. Ment. Dis.,* 162:195–199.
52. Zahn, T. P. (1977): Autonomic nervous system characteristics possibly related to a genetic predisposition to schizophrenia. *Schizophr. Bull.,* 3:49–60.
53. Zahn, T. P., and Carpenter, W. T., Jr. (1978): Effects of short term outcome and clinical improvement on reaction time in acute schizophrenia. *J. Psychiatr. Res.,* 14:59–67.
54. Zahn, T. P., Rosenthal, D., and Lawlor, W. G. (1968): Electrodermal and heart rate orienting reactions in chronic schizophrenia. *J. Psychiatr. Res.,* 6:117–134.
55. Zahn, T. P., Schooler, C., and Murphy, D. L. (1977): Relationships between monoamine oxidase activity and autonomic activity in normal subjects. Presented at annual meeting of the Society for Psychophysiological Research, Philadelphia, Pa.
56. Zahn, T. P., Carpenter, W. T., Jr., and McGlashan, T. H. (1980): Autonomic nervous system activity in acute schizophrenia. *Arch. Gen. Psychiatry.* (In press)

Discussion

K. Davis: How did your parameters differentiate degrees of psychopathology?

Zahn: At admission tests, they didn't; at discharge, they did. But at discharge, patient type is confounded with clinical state, so it's hard to distinguish between them.

Meltzer: Would this study predict clinical response *with* medication versus nonresponse *to* medication?

Zahn: Since the patients were off medication in both test periods, our variables may predict only unmedicated outcome. However, one of the studies (1) to which I alluded found that medication with a dopamine blocker and habituation of the orienting response both predicted good outcome, and these two factors were independent, so that the psychophysiological predictor indicated improvement in both the medicated and the unmedicated patients. I think that's true of our studies also, although I haven't compared patients who were given medication with those who weren't. But since about half of each group were given medication, we probably have a general predictor of outcome rather than specifically of medicated or unmedicated outcome.

Mosher: In terms of the state versus trait question, are the discordant identical-twin data relevant?

Zahn: The data bear on that issue. Basically, I found some things that look like trait differences and some that look like state differences. The response to the meaningful stimuli looks like a state effect, with a clear discrimination between discordant identical twins, whereas on some of the baseline measures, index and control twins seemed to have the same levels. It probably differs according to the variable observed.

Hiatt: What's the relationship between the *size* of the changes you observed in the improved and unimproved group and the *standard deviations* of the changes you observed?

Zahn: Isn't that implicit in the data? For if mean changes are relatively small compared with variance changes, the results are not statistically significant. Similar to what Dr. May reports, in some of our admission variables a few people were almost off the scale. There seems to be "noise" in those data: It wasn't always the same patient on each variable. But in the discharge data, one effect of clinical improvement was to reduce the variance of the group, so that the discharge data are more significant. Perhaps what the early period of psychosis does is to affect some patients such that the variance of the group is increased.

Hays: What accounts for the difference between men and women with regard to improvement in reaction time?

Zahn: Women seem to be more affected by being in a psychotic state than are men. I don't know why that trend appears. It might have been different with a female experimenter.

Ewalt: In alcoholism, the genetic data apply only to men, not to women, so there are some sexual differences we don't understand.

Perez-Polo: On the monoamine oxidase (MAO) differences you found, you said there was no significant difference between schizophrenics and nonschizophrenics, yet you said there was a correlation with your psychophysiological findings.

Zahn: Yes, there were correlations within the schizophrenic group, but just at discharge, possibly because of the "noise" in the admission data that I mentioned earlier.

Ingvar: Where in the nervous system do you place these disturbances—at the level of the cortex, or perhaps of the brainstem?

Zahn: There aren't enough data to pin this down. Some people think these are limbic in location because you find the same sort of disturbances in monkeys with hippocampal lesions, which make them hyperreactive while slowing down their habituation. Lesions of the amygdala produce opposite effects. But the brainstem can't be ruled out. In a study (Zahn and Fedio, *unpublished observations*) we did some years ago, patients with cingulum lesions made for intractable pain showed an absence of skin conductance response. The location is unclear at this time.

Singh: Over the last 10 years we have been conducting longitudinal studies of acute and subacute schizophrenics that have prospective diagnostic and prognostic evaluations and periodic multidimensional assessments both when patients are drug-free and when they are receiving medications. We found that the nonparanoids fell into two groups. One group had an initially raised pulse rate that progressively rose over the period of neuroleptic treatment with haloperidol or chlorpromazine. This pulse rate increase was associated with the emergence of a dysphoric state and a poor therapeutic outcome—both short-term and long-term. This group had relatively mild sleeplessness. The other group had a much higher initial pulse rate and marked sleeplessness, both of which decreased with treatment. This group did not develop dysphoria and had good therapeutic outcome. The paranoids differed significantly from the nonparanoids in having lower, relatively normal pulse rate associated with a fair amount of sleeplessness. The pulse rate in those patients increased first with treatment and then plateaued and eventually returned to the baseline. Sleeplessness disappeared completely with treatment. Thus a persistently increased pulse rate or autonomic arousal seems not to be a universal feature of schizophrenia but is only a feature of the dysphoric, poor-outcome, nuclear, nonparanoid patient (4).

Cole: Were they dysphoric before or after they received the drug?

Singh: Nondysphoric responders were dysphoric in the baseline. Their dysphoria decreased with neuroleptic treatment. The reverse was the case with dysphoric responders. They were nondysphoric in the baseline but became dysphoric after receiving treatment. To answer Dr. Nasrallah's question to Dr. May about the placebo response and dysphoria, the dysphoria states in these patients persisted throughout the course of neuroleptic treatment.

In studies of interactions between neuroleptics and anticholinergic drugs, we (3,5) found that the resting pulse rate decreased but sleeplessness increased in good prognosis, nonparanoid patients when anticholinergics were added to neuroleptic treatment. At the same time, the therapeutic response to neuroleptics was decreased or reversed in these patients. In other studies, we (2; and *unpublished data*) found the opposite pattern during a wheat gluten challenge; resting pulse rate increased and sleeplessness decreased. The clinical condition worsened during the challenge period but patients involved were mostly of poor prognosis type.

REFERENCES

1. Frith, C. D., Stevens, M., Johnstone, E. C., and Crow, T. J. (1978): Skin conductance responsivity during acute episodes of schizophrenia as a predictor of symptomatic improvement. *Psychol. Med.*, 8:1–6.
2. Singh, M. M., and Kay, S. R. (1976): Wheat gluten as a pathogenic factor in schizophrenia. *Science,* 191:401–402.
3. Singh, M. M., and Kay, S. R. (1978): Nosological and prognostic distinctions in schizophrenia: Pharmacological validation in terms of therapeutic antagonism between anticholinergic anti-Parkinsonism drugs and neuroleptics. *Neuropsychobiology,* 4:288–304.
4. Singh, M. M., and Kay, S. R. (1979): Dysphoric response to neuroleptic treatment in schizophrenia: Its relationship to autonomic arousal and prognosis. *Biol. Psychiatry,* 14:277–294.
5. Singh, M. M., and Kay, S. R. (1979): Therapeutic antagonism between anticholinergic anti-Parkinsonism agents and neuroleptics in schizophrenia: Implication for a neuropharmacological model. *Neuropsychobiology,* 5:74–86.

Perspectives in Schizophrenia Research,
edited by C. Baxter and T. Melnechuk.
Raven Press, New York, 1980.

Abnormal Distribution of Cerebral Activity in Chronic Schizophrenia: A Neurophysiological Interpretation

David H. Ingvar

Department of Clinical Neurophysiology, University Hospital, Lund, Sweden; and the Laboratory of Cerebral Metabolism, National Institutes of Mental Health, Bethesda, Maryland 20014

LAYPERSON'S SUMMARY

The measurement of blood flow in a specific region of the brain is an indirect measure of the amount of work performed by nerve cells in that region of the brain. This is because nerve cell activity controls the blood vessels of the brain and thereby regulates the blood flow. By using many flow meters simultaneously, it is possible to measure the regional distribution of nerve cell activity. Regions of high blood flow correspond to regions with high nerve cell activity, and vice versa.

In normal human subjects there is, at rest, a typical "hyperfrontal" activity distribution. The activity is considerably higher in frontal parts of the cortex than in parietal and temporal parts. This pattern is often less conspicuous in chronic schizophrenics. In fact, the pattern may even be reversed in such patients with high activity in parietal and temporal regions and low activity in the frontal regions.

We have also found that the more inactive, mute, and autistic the patients were, the lower was the flow in the frontal regions of their brains. The more evidence there was of cognitive disturbance, the higher was the flow in parietal and temporal regions of their brains.

There is at present no theory of schizophrenia that would account for the abnormal distribution of brain function as found in the schizophrenics, and how this abnormality relates to the symptoms of the psychosis. It seems likely, however, that the abnormal distribution of blood flow (nerve cell activity) is caused by some defect in nerve cell pathways which lead from the deeper structures in the brain to the cerebral cortex.

INTRODUCTION

To a clinical neurophysiologist the following facts concerning schizophrenia appear highly significant:

1. *Brain morphology.* Until now, no major specific morphological change has been demonstrated at autopsy in the brains of chronic schizophrenic patients, not even in severely deteriorated cases with a duration of several decades (5, 46,50). This shows clearly that this disorder, in contrast to, for example, organic dementia, is in principle "functional" in nature, i.e., caused by malfunction of neuronal systems in the brain which, when studied by conventional morphological techniques (D. Weinberger, *this volume*), appear normal.

2. *Brain metabolism.* The total mean cerebral blood flow and oxygen uptake, measured with the Kety technique, is normal in chronic schizophrenia (13,39). The mental abnormalities in schizophrenia thus do not affect the net cerebral metabolism. This observation does not exclude, however, that the "functional" abnormality (see "brain morphology" above) underlying the disorder may alter cerebral activity and metabolism regionally, changing the distribution of function in the brain in a manner which cannot be detected by global techniques.

3. *Sensory-motor functions and brainstem mechanisms.* In chronic schizophrenia, basic sensory and motor functions are normal. The primary transmission of sensory stimuli to the cerebral cortex is normal. The motor pathways, spinal reflexes, etc., also function normally. Furthermore, lower brainstem mechanisms regulating sleep and wakefulness, electrolytes, body temperature, as well as those controlling vasomotor activity and respiration, also function—on the whole—normally. Admittedly, abnormalities of autonomic functions are observed in schizophrenics (T. P. Zahn, *this volume*), but, by and large, it has not been demonstrated that they play a primary role for the characteristic mental symptoms.

Since basic sensory and motor, as well as most basic brainstem, mechanisms appear essentially normal in chronic schizophrenia, the characteristic perceptual and behavioral symptoms of this disease must be "located" at a high level, most likely in the cerebral cortex. According to this view, abnormal cortical events are assigned a most important role for the pathogenesis of schizophrenia; but this does not exclude the possibility that subcortical mechanisms which project to the cortex in an abnormal fashion may be of great importance (see Discussion).

4. *Psychiatric symptoms.* From the neurophysiological point of view, two primary categories of symptoms characterize chronic schizophrenia. On the *afferent* (sensory-gnostic) side there are, often at the onset of the disease, perceptual disturbances that lead to overinclusion phenomena, disorders of attention, sensory overflow, etc. On the *efferent* (motor-behavioral) side there is a reduction of the behavioral and affective repertoire, with loss of goal-directed intentional behavior, indifference, inactivity, withdrawal, anhedonia, speech disorganization, and symptoms of catatonia. Chronic schizophrenia thus appears to affect both the selection of sensory stimuli in cortical regions which subserve afferent sensory-gnostic functions, and also regions subserving efferent motor-behavioral functions, including emotional expressions.

To the neurophysiologist the enumerated facts suggest that the abnormalities in the brain which underlie chronic schizophrenia should be studied with a method which fulfills two basic criteria:

1. It should measure the functional level in the cerebral cortex, simultaneously in regions which subserve afferent and efferent functions.
2. It should be so exquisitely sensitive that it can record physiological events in the brain related to mentation.

At present, there is only one clinically applicable technique which can meet these criteria, the multiregional ^{133}Xenon clearance technique. Other methods such as EEG or the three-dimensional methods to measure cerebral glucose uptake in man (47) (see Discussion) either suffer from inherent limitations as to localization, or are simply not yet available for studies in larger groups of patients.

In this chapter studies with the multiregional ^{133}Xenon method are summarized. It will be demonstrated that in chronic schizophrenia there is an abnormal distribution of the activity in the cerebral cortex which correlates with both the characteristic perceptual-cognitive and the motor-behavioral symptoms. This finding will be given an interpretation in neurophysiological terms.

PRINCIPLE OF MEASUREMENT

When the neurons of the brain become more active, this leads to metabolic changes which, in turn, cause a dilatation of the cerebral blood vessels. Thus the increased metabolic demands can be met by an augmentation of the blood flow in the active region. Conversely, the blood flow is reduced when the neuronal activity goes down. This so-called "metabolic regulation" (28) of the regional cerebral blood flow can be utilized to measure indirectly the functional level in a circumscribed part of the brain by recording its regional cerebral blood flow (rCBF) with the ^{133}Xenon clearance technique. With multiregional flow measurements the functional activity in many cerebral regions is measured simultaneously and thus the blood flow distribution, i.e., the distribution of cerebral function is measured. In recent years we have developed multidetector devices, coupled to computers and color displays, which yield "functional landscapes" of the hemisphere. Mean landscapes can also be calculated for groups of patients suffering from the same disorder and studied under similar conditions.

During the last 10 years we have carried out multiregional rCBF studies in groups of patients with neurologic and psychiatric disorders (20,29), including 40 patients diagnosed as chronic schizophrenics (13,14,23). This chapter summarizes the abnormalities found in the cerebral functional landscapes of the schizophrenics. Interpreted in neurophysiological terms, the findings support the notion that one fundamental defect in this mental disease might consist of a defective selection of significant sensory stimuli, leading to abnormally high neuronal activity in postcentral sensory-gnostic cortical regions. At the same time, there may be a defective production of goal-directed motor-behavioral responses, leading to an abnormally low neuronal activity in frontal cortical regions.

The studies to be discussed below have been published in detail (13,14,23,24).

MATERIAL AND METHODS

The main group of chronic schizophrenics consisted of 31 patients of whom 11 were young (four women and seven men, mean age 25 years) and 20 were old (nine women and eleven men, mean age 62 years) (Table 1) (13). In the young group, the duration of the illness was between 8 months and 15 years (mean 5 years). In the old group most of the patients were permanently institutionalized, and the mean duration of the illness was about 35 years. All of the patients had uneventful histories as far as severe somatic disorder, head injury, cerebrovascular disease, etc. were concerned. The somatic findings and laboratory data at the time of the study were normal in all patients, except in five of the old men who showed moderate hypertension.

Independently of the cerebral blood flow studies, the patients were examined by psychiatrists and nurses who rated their symptoms with the aid of the Rockland-Pollin (RP) scale (49) and other similar instruments (25). Thus disturbances of behavior, affectivity, and cognitive activity were assessed. All patients represented classical cases of chronic schizophrenia with distinct symptoms of varying severity of perceptual disturbances and behavioral abnormalities. Many of the old patients were severely deteriorated, and were in a state often labeled as "schizophrenic dementia." Their symptoms included pronounced inactivity, mutism, lack of contact, and clear signs of hallucinatory activity. The older patients, therefore, especially the old women, showed high scores of abnormality.

At the time of the study, only two of the patients were drug free. The others had conventional therapy with phenothiazines and butyrophenones. In addition, several of the patients were taking antiparkinson medication. As discussed in the original publications (13,23), we found no evidence to suggest that the medication could have been of importance for the main finding: the abnormal distribution of function in the cerebral cortex of schizophrenic patients. Additional evidence supports this notion: we have observed a small series of patients undergoing psychopharmacological treatment with positive result. The clinical amelioration was accompanied by some normalization of the cortical activity distribution (25).

The reader should consult the original publications for a discussion of the age factor and the influence of hospitalization *per se* (13). These factors also were found to have no importance for the main findings. The characteristic abnormalities of schizophrenia were found to a varying degree both in young and in old patients in whom the length of hospital treatment varied from only months to several decades.

1. *Ethical considerations* (13). Prior to the investigation of the chronic schizophrenics, considerable experience had been gained for the use of the intra-arterial

TABLE 1. *Main groups of chronic schizophrenics*[a]

Groups	*N*	Age (range)	Total RP points ± SD	Hemisphere mean blood flow (ml/100 g/min ± SD)	
				"Initial" flow	"Gray" flow
Young patients (4 females, 2 males)	11	25 (17–33)	34 ± 6	55 ± 14	75 ± 17
Old men	11	64 (52–70)	57 ± 20	49 ± 9	71 ± 12
Old women	9	61 (49–72)	81 ± 5	56 ± 6	74 ± 6
Total and means	31	49 (17–72)		53 ± 10	73 ± 13
Control (males)	10	39 (29–49)		57 ± 7 N.S.	73 ± 9 N.S.

[a] Age, RP ratings, and mean hemisphere blood flow calculated in ml/100 g/min as "initial" flow from the initial part of the ^{133}Xenon clearance curves, or as "gray" flow from biexponential analysis of the same curves (16).

^{133}Xenon clearance technique with various groups of patients suffering from organic brain disorders. The risks pertaining to the method were assessed by collecting information on complications in about 3,000 studies carried out in several laboratories in many countries (27). The overall risks were found to be small, almost nil in patients who were not suffering from severe organic brain disorders.

Permission was obtained from each patient to carry out the study, and if the patient could not be contacted, the permission of the next of kin was obtained. The whole project was carried out with financial support from the Swedish Medical Research Council and was under the supervision of the Committee of Ethics of the Medical Faculty of the University of Lund, Sweden.

To summarize the ethical considerations: The studies were undertaken with schizophrenics since their disorder is still highly enigmatic and still carries a grave prognosis in many cases. Therefore, we felt it was unethical not to use a new diagnostic tool which carries a very low risk in itself. So far this tool has proven to be the only means by which events related to mental activity of normal and abnormal character can be measured directly in the brain.

2. *Measurements of regional cerebral blood flow (rCBF).* Measurements of regional cerebral blood flow were carried out using the intra-arterial ^{133}Xenon clearance technique (40). A thin polyethylene cathether was placed in the left internal carotid artery for bolus injections of 3–5 ml saline in which 2–4 mCi of ^{133}Xenon was physically dissolved. Originally a battery of 32, and later 64, detectors were placed at the side of the head, and recorded the sudden arrival and subsequent slower clearance of the isotope from the injected hemisphere. Due to absorption of radiation, superficial hemisphere structures, i.e., the cerebral cortex, are seen more clearly than deeper structures. The rCBF for each region was calculated in terms of ml/100 g brain/min by a computer coupled to the battery of detectors. Various display systems, including color TV sets, were used to obtain two-dimensional maps of the rCBF distribution in the hemispheres studied. With the aid of superimposition of individual flow charts, mean hemisphere flow distributions were calculated and thus mean "functional landscapes" in color were produced for the whole group of patients and for subgroups of patients representing different levels of severity of the disease. Control subjects also were included.

Groups of patients with normal neurological and neuroradiological findings, as well as normal psychometric scores, were used as controls. These groups included patients with epilepsy, headache, and alcoholism (studied in a dry state) (13).

RESULTS

1. *RP ratings.* The RP ratings showed high scores of abnormality, especially in the old women (mean total points 81), and the old men (57). In general, the younger group showed lower scores (Table 1). Most of the abnormality in

the RP ratings was found for items scoring abnormal behavior and cognition. The abnormal scores for affectivity were less pronounced.

2. *Mean hemisphere rCBF values.* The mean hemisphere rCBF values, i.e., the mean hemisphere blood flow was calculated from all the regional measurements; this value is comparable to that obtained with the Kety technique, and was found to be normal in all the patient groups (Table 1). This confirms previous measurements with the Kety technique in chronic schizophrenics (39) that showed the overall cerebral metabolism and blood flow in this disorder to be normal.

In some of the older men who showed signs of slight hypertension, a slight reduction of the hemisphere mean rCBF was found. This could have been due to the fact that they suffered from hypertension and subclinical cerebrovascular disease.

In eight of the old men the cerebral metabolic rate of oxygen ($CMRO_2$) was calculated from the mean rCBF and measurements of the cerebral arteriovenous oxygen difference. $CMRO_2$ was found to be low (2.6 $\pm$ SD 0.5), but not significantly different from the normal value (3.3 $\pm$ SD 0.4 ml/100 g/min). This reduction could have been due to the fact that some of the old men had hypertension.

3. *The rCBF distribution in the controls and the chronic schizophrenics.* Our control patients when examined at rest (i.e., with silence in the laboratory, with a pad over their eyes, and no disturbance by touch or speech) all showed a typical hyperfrontal resting rCBF pattern with a high flow rate in the range of 50 to 80 ml/100 g/min in regions anterior to the sylvian and the rolandic fissures. Lower flow rates, in the range of 35 to 50 ml/100 g/min, were found in regions postcentrally in the parietal, occipital, and temporal areas (Fig. 1). As discussed elsewhere (13,20–22,28,32), the normal hyperfrontal activity landscape of the cerebral cortex signals that the resting conscious brain, when awake and undisturbed, is highly active in frontal motor-behavioral cortical regions and much less active in postcentral sensory-gnostic areas.

In the schizophrenics, the rCBF distribution at rest was often found to be hypofrontal, i.e., the blood flow in frontal regions was relatively low and the flow postcentrally relatively high (24,40). Since the total mean flow rate in the hemisphere was within normal limits, the hypofrontal pattern shows that chronic schizophrenia was accompanied by an abnormal distribution of cerebral (cortical) function (Fig. 2).

4. *rCBF distribution versus RP ratings.* The patients were divided into groups based on the severity of their psychosis determined by the RP ratings. When the RP points were examined as a function of the rCBF frontality index (percentual relation between frontal and postcentral mean rCBF), significant correlation coefficients ($p < 0.01$) were obtained for hypofrontality (low index) versus total RP points, (Fig. 3) versus RP points for behavioral abnormalities ($r = -0.658$), and versus RP points for cognitive abnormality ($r = -0.709$). These negative correlations imply that the lower the flow in frontal regions, the more overt

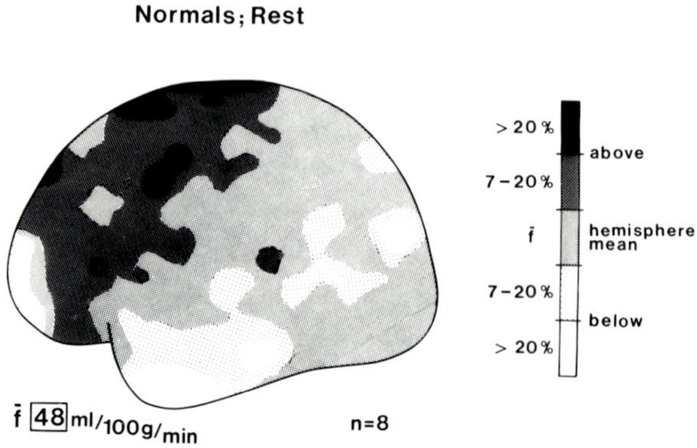

FIG. 1. Normal "hyperfrontal" distribution of the cortical blood flow in the resting conscious state. Mean distribution of regional cerebral blood flow (rCBF) measured with the ^{133}Xenon method in 8 normal left hemispheres. The measurements were carried out in the resting conscious state (see text). The diagram was replotted from a color-TV display of 8 superimposed individual flow distributions in which the mean hemisphere flow (shown as numbers in square) was used as reference (100%). Flow rates above and below the mean (ml/100 g/min) are denoted in accordance with the gray scale to the right.

Note distinct predominance of high blood flows in frontal structures, and low blood flows in parietal, occipital, and especially in temporal regions (see refs. 13,20–22,29,30,32). The hyperfrontal resting pattern is easily changed by means of sensory, motor, and mental activation (refs. 20–22,29–31,41,48).

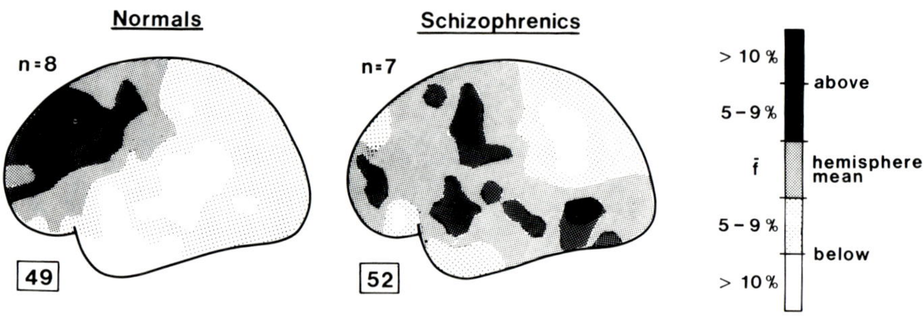

FIG. 2. Distribution of cerebral blood flow at rest in 8 normals and in 8 highly psychotic chronic schizophrenics. The diagrams were replotted from computer-generated color-TV displays (see Fig. 1 and ref. 14). Flow rates above and below the hemisphere mean (shown in squares in ml/100 g/min) are illustrated in accordance with the scale to the right.

Note the normal hyperfrontal resting flow distribution in the 8 normals (see Fig. 1). The 7 schizophrenics were selected from the main series of 31 patients. These patients showed an RP rating of 53, i.e., a high score indicating severe symptoms of psychosis (14).

Note that both groups showed about the same mean hemisphere flow rates (49 and 52 ml/100 g/min, respectively). However, the distribution of the flow rates is different, the schizophrenics showing relatively low flow rates in frontal regions (the "hypofrontal" pattern) and several regions of high flow rates in postcentral and temporal regions.

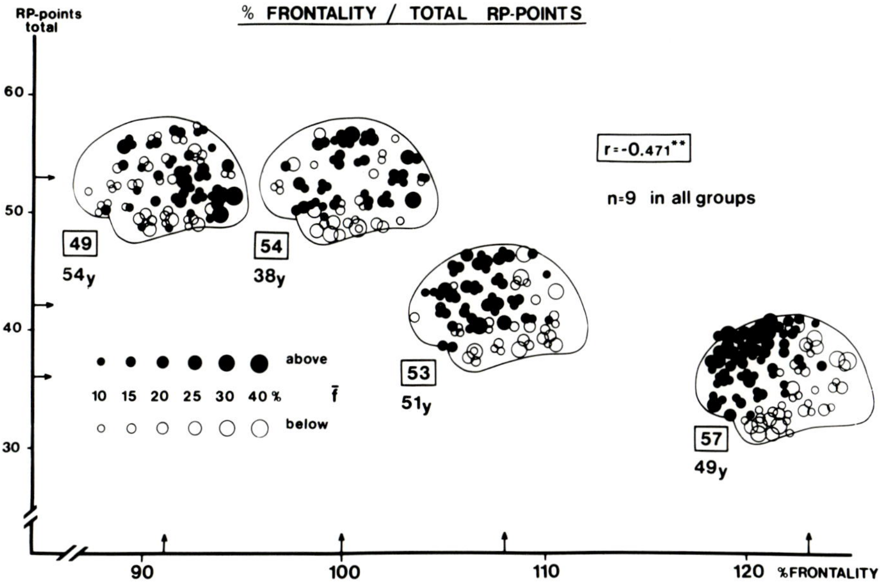

FIG. 3. Distribution of the cerebral blood flow in chronic schizophrenia, related to severity of psychosis. The diagram contains 4 groups of schizophrenics with 9 patients in each group. Mean flow in ml/100 g/min, and mean age is given for the different groups. Black dots indicate flow rates above the hemisphere mean, and open circles indicate flow rates below the mean. On the abscissa percent frontality is indicated, i.e., the quotient relationship between flow rates in frontal regions as related to those in postcentral and temporal regions expressed as a percentage. On the ordinate the total number of RP points is shown as rated by the Rockland-Pollin scale (3).

The group to the right with the highest frontality index (122%) with a "hyperfrontal" flow distribution at rest showed the lowest number of RP points (18). The other 3 groups showed lower frontality indices (108%, 100%, and 92%, respectively) and increasing numbers of total RP points (42, 53, and 53, respectively).

There was a significant negative correlation between the total RP points and percent frontality. This means that the more psychotic the patients were (high RP points), the more hypofrontal was the flow pattern. Replotted from Franzén and Ingvar (ref. 14).

signs of inactivity, autism, indifference, and mutistic tendencies were shown by the patients. The higher the flow was in postcentral regions, the more signs did the patients show of cognitive disturbance including hallucinatory activity. The elevated postcentral flow level in occipitoparietotemporal regions in the old women, the most deteriorated group, showed an especially high negative correlation of hypofrontal flow with the ratings for cognitive disturbance (23).

5. *Activation studies.* In most of the above patients, rCBF measurements were made not only at rest but also during a picture test (14). The patients were asked to identify simple objects in pictures from a weekly magazine. Although most of the young patients cooperated well in this test, several of the deteriorated older patients did not respond at all, or only monosyllabically in spite of intense

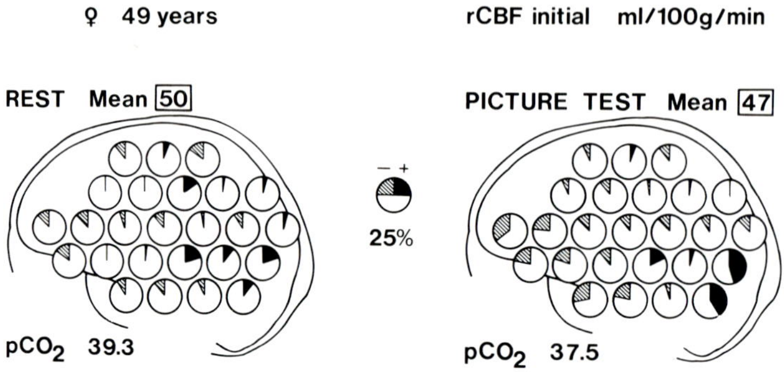

FIG. 4. Absence of activation during "picture test" in a chronic schizophrenic patient. This 49-year-old woman had shown classic symptoms of schizophrenia for 31 years with thought disturbance, bizarre behavior, and hallucinations. At the time of the study she was autistic, absent-minded, and showing evidence of ongoing hallucinations, muttering to herself.

The mean resting hemisphere flow rate was normal (50 ml/100 g/min). The flow distribution was of the hypofrontal type in the 25 fields measured (see Fig. 2). Values above the mean are denoted in black, and below the mean in a gray shade in accordance with the clock symbol between the hemispheres.

When the patient was asked to identify pictures in a weekly magazine her reluctant cooperation required a highly encouraging attitude before answers could be obtained. In normal subjects this test resulted in an increase of the cortical blood flow in various fields including some in the frontal lobe. In this patient hardly any changes in flow rate were induced. (From Ingvar and Franzén, ref. 23).

verbal urging. In other schizophrenics, cutaneous electrical stimulation was applied to the thumb region, contralateral to the hemisphere measured, to stimulate two levels of intensity representing either "touch" or "slight pain."

In normals both types of activation produced specific alterations of the resting functional landscape in the cortex. A picture test raised the flow in the postcentral regions and also frontally. Touch and pain increased the blood flow especially in frontal regions, and with the application of the pain stimulus. In several of the chronic schizophrenics, the activation attempts changed the rCBF landscape only to a limited extent (14). Some of the most deteriorated patients showed hardly any rCBF changes at all when they were shown pictures (Fig. 4). The rCBF change following pain stimulation was less pronounced than in the normals (30) (Fig. 5).

DISCUSSION

Technical Considerations

Three important limitations of the ^{133}Xenon method should be mentioned here. First, it measures only one side of the brain at a time. In the present studies it was the left hemisphere and the results, therefore, apply only to the

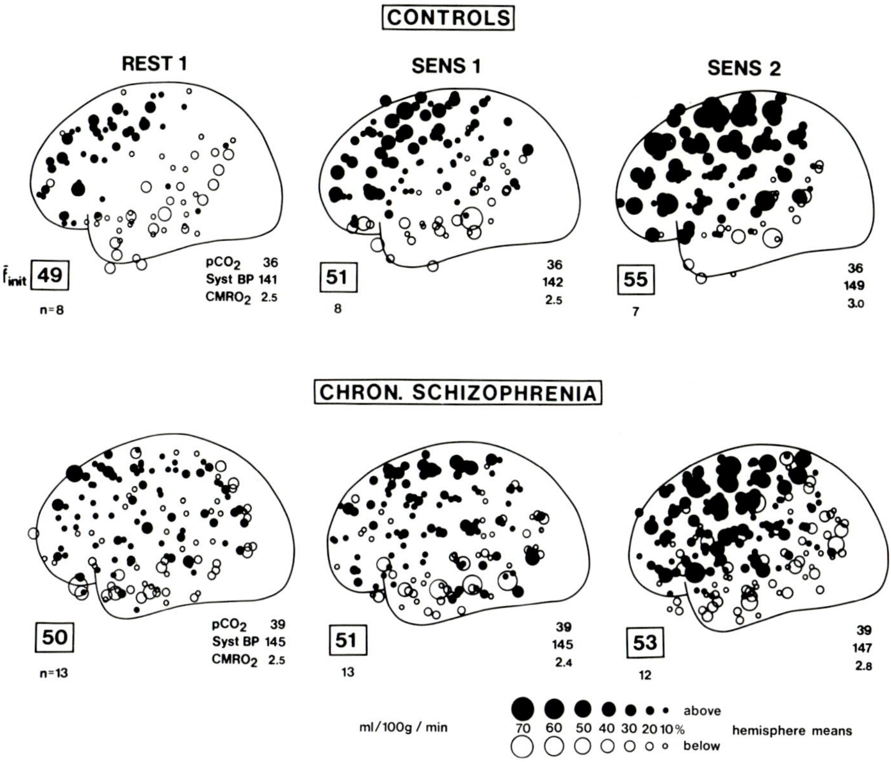

FIG. 5. Distribution of rCBF in 8 normals and in 13 chronic schizophrenics at rest and during touch and slight pain stimulation. All diagrams were plotted with the mean resting flow rate as the 100% reference (49 ml/100 g/min for the 8 normals, and 50 ml/100 g/min for the 13 schizophrenics). Values above the mean are denoted in black, and values below the mean by open circles. The size of the symbols increases with increased changes in flow rate. The scale is shown in the lower right corner. Mean values for arterial P_{CO_2} and systolic blood pressure are given in mmHg. The $CMRO_2$ (in ml oxygen/100 g/min) was calculated from the mean hemisphere flow rate and arteriovenous differences (30,31).

At rest the subjects were studied with silence in the laboratory with a pad over their eyes. During "touch" (SENS 1), weak electrical stimuli were applied to the contralateral thumb. During "slight pain" (SENS 2), the intensity of the stimuli was augmented to a level where the experience was slightly uncomfortable.

Note that at rest the normals showed the typical hyperfrontal distribution (see Fig. 1). In the schizophrenics the distribution of filled and open circles denotes the lack of hyperfrontality (see Fig. 2). During touch the mean blood flow rate per hemisphere increased modestly in the normals but the $CMRO_2$ did not change in either group. The hyperfrontality in the 8 normals became slightly more evident, while there was no definite change in the flow distribution in the schizophrenics. During slight pain a significant fairly widespread increase of the mean flow and $CMRO_2$ ($p < 0.05$) took place in the normals with a clear predominance in frontal regions in which hardly any low flows *(open circles)* were recorded. Only a small, statistically insignificant change of the mean flow and $CMRO_2$ was recorded in the schizophrenics. A number of open circles, i.e., low flow rates, persisted in frontal regions in the schizophrenics, indicating a difference in the central elaboration of a nociceptive stimulation in this disorder (30,31).

dominant "verbal" hemisphere, which is thought to be more involved in schizophrenia than the nondominant, "nonverbal" one (1). Possibly, the nondominant hemisphere is more responsible for affective components of the disorder. This might explain why low and insignificant correlations were obtained for RP ratings with affectivity.

Second, with the present placement of the detectors lateral to the head, the ^{133}Xenon method emphasizes superficial hemisphere structures. Due to tissue absorption they are seen about three times as well as tissues in the deeper structures. The following discussion, therefore, concentrates on the cortex. However, deeper telencephalic structures, such as the basal ganglia, may have been included (to some extent) in flow measurements over the lower middle part of the hemisphere.

Third, the isotope injection was made into the carotid system. Hence circulation in posterior parts of the hemisphere, which are irrigated by the vertebral system, were not measured.

Evidence that rCBF measurements closely reflect the functional level in the regions in which the blood flow is being measured has been presented and discussed elsewhere (28,48). There is good evidence that the functional landscapes obtained with multidetector rCBF devices reflect the distribution of neuronal activity primarily in superficial cortical structures of the hemisphere. Hence, there is reason to conclude that in chronic schizophrenic patients showing the hypofrontal rCBF pattern, the neuronal activity is abnormally low in frontal cortical regions and abnormally high in postcentral areas. Again, as pointed out above, this abnormal distribution does not affect the total mean cerebral blood flow or oxygen uptake, which in the present studies (13) and in previous investigations with the Kety technique (39) were found to be within normal limits.

Normal Resting Functional Landscape of the Cortex

In order to interpret the hypofrontal activity in the chronic schizophrenics, it is necessary first to give a brief account of the interpretation of the normal landscape of resting consciousness (Fig. 1).

A main feature of the normal hyperfrontal resting landscape is its fairly sharp division into an anterior, mainly frontal, area with high flow rates and a postcentral one with low flow rates in occipital, parietal, and temporal regions. In many frontal regions the flow rate is twice as high as in temporal and parietal areas. This is so even though the neuronal and capillary densities in the respective regions are essentially the same.

The dividing line between the high and low flow regions in the resting landscape appears to follow the anterior part of the sylvian fissure and the rolandic fissure up towards the vertex. It is well known that this line of division separates the cerebral cortex into an anterior frontal part in which motor-behavioral functions predominate. Functions with increasing complexity are located in the more anterior regions. Sensory functions of primary, secondary, and higher orders (i.e., functions which may be termed sensory-gnostic) are localized in the postcentral regions.

The normal resting conscious state is thus accompanied by a high neuronal activity in frontal motor-behavioral cortical regions—even though no motor activity or behavioral responses are produced. At the same time, there is a much lower activity in sensory-gnostic areas. Evidence from introspection (see ref. 7), as well as clinical observations on rCBF landscapes in patients with augmented, reduced, or loss of consciousness (see below), suggests that the normal conscious state is accompanied by a general inhibition of the sensory input. When resting awake, immobile, and conscious in a silent laboratory, one is aware only intermittently and often to a small extent of the sensory stimuli which impinge on one's nervous system. At the same time one's mind is highly active and aware, thinking of the actual situation, of previous experiences retrieved from memory, and indeed also of different possible alternative events in the future. From a neurophysiological point of view, the resting conscious state thus appears to be accompanied by a general inhibition of the sensory input, since trivial signals from the surroundings do not enter into awareness. At the same time, the mind is highly active programming alternative motor-behavioral responses based on previous experiences, making hypotheses concerning the future. This anticipatory programming, or inner "simulation of behavior" (22), provides the nervous system with a repertoire of responses to stimuli from the outside world and from the body. From this repertoire the most adequate and optimal response may then be chosen in order to secure survival. According to this view, the resting conscious state is accompanied by a high activity in cortical regions subserving motor-behavioral programming and a low activity in sensory-gnostic areas.

As discussed in greater length elsewhere (14,19–22,32,41), the hypothesis concerning the resting conscious state outlined above is strongly supported by clinical observations. States of reduced or absent consciousness (general anesthesia and coma) show a disappearance of the hyperfrontal rCBF distribution (26). States of increased awareness during increased cognitive activity, induced by pain stimulation (31), by searching for a solution to a difficult intellectual problem (48), etc., show a more marked hyperfrontality that can be seen at rest. In addition, numerous observations during various forms of activation with sensory stimulation, motor activity, speech, reading, and problem solving, etc., show that normally afferent sensori stimuli are translated into motor-behavioral responses in many fashions which can be traced as a multitude of cortical functional patterns (1,30). Such patterns often show quite clearly how specific sensory signals reach the cortex and interact with frontal motor-behavioral centers, also causing a general frontal activation, to produce an adequate response to the stimulus.

Several workers, including Head (17), Freud (15), Cannon (8), Broadbent (4), Jasper (35), and Shakow (53), have pointed out that the central nervous system must be "protected" from the constant barrage of the enormously rich flow of sensory impulses streaming in from the peripheral receptors. Inhibitory "filter" mechanisms, subserving this protection, have been identified at many levels in the central nervous system, including in the spinal cord (10). Teleologically speaking, such mechanisms should allow only "significant" information to reach awareness, i.e., information which can optimize behavior. Such an optimization can be achieved only if the brain has access to a vast repertoire of well-rehearsed programs for alternative behavioral responses.

Resting Functional Cortical Landscape in Chronic Schizophrenia

In chronic schizophrenia the hypofrontal distribution of activity in the cerebral cortex, and the correlations to the clinical symptomatology reviewed above, indicate that a fundamental defect is present which alters the way in which the brain handles sensory information and the way in which it programs behavior. This defect appears to involve the processing of both exteroceptive information from the outside world, as well as interoceptive signals from the body itself. The relatively high activity recorded in the schizophrenics in postcentral sensory-gnostic regions suggests that the normal control of sensory input systems is defective. This may be related to the well-known fact that, often, at the onset of the disease, chronic schizophrenia is accompanied by a change in the awareness to the outside world, as well as to the body itself. Trivial sensory signals—auditory, visual, and somatosensory—interfere constantly with awareness, which leads to abnormal distractibility, interruption of the flow of thoughts, and confusion. Even proprioceptive stimuli which usually never reach consciousness may be perceived with abnormal intensity. The highly increased sensory input may lead to sensory overflow, intense anxiety and catastrophe reactions. To judge from our findings in the old, highly deterioriated female schizophrenics, the increased activity level in postcentral cortical regions may furthermore be related to the clear-cut symptoms of hallucinatory activity which many of these patients showed. The blood flow studies thus appear, for the first time, to have recorded cerebral correlates to hallucinations, i.e., perceptual phenomena without sensory input correlates. This conclusion is supported by observations in patients with alcohol hallucinosis of auditive type (J. Risberg, *personal communication*). In such patients foci of high blood flow in the temporal cortex can be seen to disappear when adequate treatment is given.

The relatively low resting activity found in the hyperfrontal schizophrenic landscape in motor-behavioral cortical areas signals a reduction of the normal inner "simulation of behavior" which leads to a diminution of the available behavioral repertoire. This interpretation seems to fit well with the motor-behavioral (including the affective) symptoms which often become so apparent at an early stage of the disease. Initially there may just be a tendency to withdrawal, later signs of general inactivity, autism, indifference, stereotyped motor behavior, anhedonia, disorganized speech, and, in advanced cases, general catatonia and abulia. Admittedly, not all patients diagnosed as chronic schizophrenics show clear-cut symptoms of this type. Productive symptoms, often bizarre, of motor hyperactivity can be seen often early in the development. Possibly, such overactivity and similar symptoms may be secondary reactions to the altered awareness described above. In the present context a primary pathogenetic role is attributed to the altered awareness. The number of patients tested was too small to allow a subdivision of them into paranoid, hebephrenic, and other variants of the disorder. However, there was a tendency for the most outspoken hypofrontality to be present in the most autistic and "burned out" patients, while patients with active, sometimes paranoid symptoms were less hypofrontal, or even showed a fairly normal cortical activity distribution of the hyperfrontal type.

The existence of a hypofrontal activity distribution in the brain of one chronic schizophrenic patient was confirmed recently by Farkas (12). Measurements with emission tomography were made of the regional glucose uptake by the ^{18}F-fluorodeoxyglucose method of Reivich et al. (47,56). It was shown that prior to treatment, when the patient showed classic symptoms of schizophrenia, the glucose uptake in frontal structures was subnormal. Following psychopharmacological treatment the mental state of the patient improved markedly and the frontal glucose uptake also was augmented.

A number of other studies with schizophrenics can be cited which signal a defective cortical elaboration of the sensory input. Numerous investigations have established disorders of attention in this disease (53), as well as a general reduction of the capacity to habituate to the sensory milieu (Zahn, *this volume*). It would seem likely also that the postulated basic defect on the input side must have consequences for autonomic functions which in schizophrenics often do not show a normal adaptation to sensory signals (18,53; Zahn, *this volume*).

Electrographic Studies

It is pertinent to mention investigations in chronic schizophrenia made with EEG and evoked potential techniques. These electrophysiological methods record regional mass activity in the human cerebral cortex, although the generators of EEG potentials and of the various components in evoked potentials are still by and large unknown.

Ever since the original observations of Hans Berger (3), EEG studies in schizophrenia have shown repeatedly that the production of alpha activity is diminished in this disorder (Itil, *this volume*) (53). It may be recalled that the mean frequency of the EEG correlates to the cerebral blood flow (measured by the ^{133}Xenon technique) (33). The normal hyperfrontal functional landscape therefore appears to be reflected in the normal resting EEG in which the lowest frequencies, the alpha activity, are recorded in postcentral occipito-parieto-temporal regions, while higher frequencies are recorded in frontal parts. The relatively high activity found in postcentral regions in the present flow studies in the schizophrenics agrees with the increase in fast frequencies in the EEG recorded with this disease.

The situation is less clear concerning evoked potentials. Several abnormalities in the components of such responses have been reported in schizophrenia (9,51). Notable among these are changes in the premotor-frontal contingent negative variation (CNV) response, the "expectancy wave" of Walter et al. (58). Such responses are reduced in schizophrenics and this is believed to indicate a diminished capacity to form conditioned behavioral responses to a given stimulus. This interpretation agrees with a reduced activity in motor-behavioral programming regions in the postcentral cortex. Also studies of conventional visual, auditory, and somatosensory evoked potentials in schizophrenics suggest a fundamental disturbance in the sensory input in the form of a reduced filtering capacity (6,51).

ROLE OF SUBCORTICAL MECHANISMS

It seems likely that the abnormal activity distribution in the cortex found in the chronic schizophrenics was related to some abnormality in one or several cortico-subcortical projection systems (18,53). Of the many possibilities, two will be discussed.

First, the intralaminar thalamocortical projection system of Jasper and Droogleever-Foutuyn (35,36) should be mentioned. A vast, mainly electrophysiological, literature from the last decades has demonstrated the "diffuse" character of the system's projections which reach primarily frontal parts of the cortex via the medial forebrain bundle. Electrical stimulation of intralaminar thalamic nuclei produces widespread so-called recruiting responses in the cortex. These were the first described by Morison and Dempsey (1939) (45). The intralaminar system has been assigned various fundamental roles, including the one as pacemaker for the rhythmical cortical electrical activity (2). Jasper (34,35) has suggested that the intralaminar system might be of importance for attention mechanisms. However, there is still insufficient knowledge to make a definite statement concerning its function in man.

Second, the catecholaminergic projections to the cortex should be considered. Noradrenergic pathways to the cortex ascend from the locus coeruleus via the medial forebrain bundle mainly to the frontal and cingulate cortex (57). The medial and lateral parts of the dopaminergic axons, originating in the mesencephalon, project via the medial forebrain bundle to frontal cortical regions (11, 16,42). In recent years, much clinical and experimental evidence has been published to suggest that malfunctioning of the catecholaminergic systems, notably the dopaminergic one, is of primary importance for the development of schizophrenia (38,43,44,55). Several studies have shown that biochemical interference with the catecholaminergic transmission to the cortex may profoundly alter behavior in animals including creating a state of catatonia.

It is impossible, at present, to correlate the evidence on frontal projections from different subcortical systems with the present findings in the schizophrenic patients. It is not known, for example, how—and if—the intralaminar and the catecholaminergic systems interact. However, both systems enter the cortex via fibers passing through the medial forebrain bundle. A transitory blockage in this region of the cat by means of a cold probe alters behavioral and probably also perceptual functions in a most dramatic way (54). While the cold blockage lasts, the animals lose their normal intentional and goal-directed behavior. They become highly distracted by trivial sensory stimuli, walking around aimlessly, sniffing and grooming. At the same time, cortical evoked potentials increase in amplitude, a fact suggesting an increased disinhibited afferent cortical input. In addition, the recruiting responses diminish in amplitude and in cortical distribution. It is noteworthy that this transient and profound change of the animal's behavior and handling of sensory information is due to a reversible lesion in the medial forebrain bundle and takes place without any alteration of the state of wakefulness or primary locomotion. The remarkable similarity between this experimentally produced state in the cat and the defects of afferent and efferent functions which appear to be present in chronic schizophrenics has been pointed out in other publications (13,23,24).

To summarize: The abnormal cortical activity distribution in chronic schizophrenics may be related to some, as yet unknown, malfunction of subcortico-cortical projection systems, possibly involving the thalamus as well as the basal ganglia (37). In all likelihood, the latter is connected to the cortex via the medial forebrain bundle. These systems appear to be involved in setting the functional level in afferent sensory-gnostic regions of the cortex, as well as in efferent motor-behavioral areas (37,43). If they cannot function normally, possibly due to some transmission defect, the normal selection of significant stimuli and the translation of these stimuli into an adequate behavior does not take place. According to this notion, it seems urgent to conduct further studies on the projection systems mentioned above and on their relationship to the abnormal distribution of cortical function demonstrated for chronic schizophrenia.

REFERENCES

1. Alpert, M., and Martz, M. J., Jr. (1977): Cognitive views of schizophrenia in light of recent studies of brain asymmetry. In: *Psychopathology and Brain Dysfunction,* edited by C. Shagass, S. Gershon, and A. J. Friedhoff, pp. 1–13. Raven Press, New York.
2. Andersen, P., and Andersson, S. (1973): *The Origin of the Alpha Waves.* Tavistock, London.
3. Berger, H. (1932): Über das Elektrenkephalogramm des Menschen. Fünfte Mitteilung. *Arch. Psychiatr. Nervenkr.,* 98:321–354.
4. Broadbent, D. E. (1958): *Perception and Communication.* Pergamon Press, New York.
5. Brozer, K. (1949): Hirngewicht und Hirnprozess bei Schizophrenie. *Arch. Psychiat. Nervenkr.,* 182:439–449.
6. Buchsbaum, M. (1977): Psychophysiology and schizophrenia. *Schizophrenia Bull.,* 3:7–14 (see contribution to this volume).
7. Buser, B., and Rougeul-Buser, M. (eds.) (1978): *Cerebral Correlates of Conscious Experience.* Elsevier, Amsterdam.
8. Cannon, W. B. (1932): *The Wisdom of the Body.* W. W. Norton, New York.

9. Dongier, M., Dubrovsky, B., and Engelsmann, F. (1977): Event-related slow potentials in psychiatry. In: *Psychopathology and Brain Dysfunction,* edited by C. Shagass, S. Gershon, and A. J. Friedhoff, pp. 339–353. Raven Press, New York.
10. Eccles, J. C. (1979): *The Human Mystery.* Springer International, New York.
11. Ernson, P. C., and Lindvall, O. (1979): Distribution of putative neurotransmitters in the neocortex. *Neuroscience,* 4:1–30.
12. Farkas, T. (1979): Application of fluorinated deoxyglucose and positron emission tomography in the study of psychiatric disorders. Symposium on Cerebral Metabolism and Neural Function, National Institute of Health, May 21–23, 1979. To be published.
13. Franzén, G., and Ingvar, D. H. (1975): Abnormal distribution of cerebral activity in chronic schizophrenia. *J. Psychiatr. Res.,* 12:199–214.
14. Franzén, G., and Ingvar, D. H. (1975): Absence of activation in frontal structures during psychological testing in chronic schizophrenia. *J. Neurol. Neurosurg. Psychiatry,* 38:1027–1032.
15. Freud, S. (1920): *Beyond the Pleasure Principle, Standard Edition,* edited by J. Strachey, pp. 1–64. Hogarth Press, London.
16. Fuxe, K., Hökfelt, T., Johansson, O., Jonsson, G., Lidbrink, P., and Ljungdahl, A. (1974): The origin of the dopamine nerve terminals in limbic and frontal cortex. Evidence for mesocortico-dopamine neurons. *Brain Res.,* 82:349–355.
17. Head, H. (1920): *Studies in Neurology, Vol. 1.* Oxford University Press, London.
18. Hoskins, R. G. (1946): *The Biology of Schizophrenia.* W. W. Norton, New York.
19. Ingvar, D. H. (1975): Patterns of brain activity revealed by measurements of regional cerebral blood flow. In: *Brain Work,* edited by D. H. Ingvar and N. A. Lassen, pp. 397–413. Munksgaard, Copenhagen.
20. Ingvar, D. H. (1976): Functional landscapes of the dominant hemisphere. *Brain Res.,* 107:181–197.
21. Ingvar, D. H. (1977): L'Ideogramme cérébral. *Encephale,* 3:5–33.
22. Ingvar, D. H. (1980): Hyperfrontal man. Consciousness reconsidered. *Neuroscience (in press).*
23. Ingvar, D. H., and Franzén, G. (1974): Abnormalities of cerebral blood flow distribution in patients with chronic schizophrenia. *Acta Psychiatr. Scand.,* 50:425–426.
24. Ingvar, D. H., and Franzén, G. (1974): Distribution of cerebral activity in chronic schizophrenia. *Lancet,* ii:1484–1485.
25. Ingvar, D. H., and Franzén, G. (1979): Clinical course and symptomatology in chronic schizophrenia related to the activity distribution in the dominant hemisphere. A follow-up study of seven patients. Proc. III Int. Congr. Biol. Psychiatry, Barcelona, September 1978.
26. Ingvar, D. H., and Gadea Ciria, M. (1975): Assessment of severe damage to the brain by multiregional measurements of cerebral blood flow. In: *Outcome of Severe Damage to the Central Nervous System,* edited by B. Jennett and F. Plum, pp. 97–120. Elsevier, Amsterdam.
27. Ingvar, D. H., and Lassen, N. A. (1973): Cerebral complications following measurements of regional cerebral blood flow (rCBF) with the intra-arterial 133 Xenon injection method. *Stroke,* 4:658–665.
28. Ingvar, D. H., and Lassen, N. A. (eds.) (1975): *Brain Work.* Munksgaard, Copenhagen.
29. Ingvar, D. H., and Lassen, N. A. (eds.) (1977): Cerebral circulation, metabolism and function. *Acta Neurol. Scand.* [*Suppl. 64*], 56.
30. Ingvar, D. H., and Lassen, N. A. (1978): Kartläggning av hjärnbarkens funktioner med mätning av dess regionala blodflöde. *Läkartidningen,* 75:3439–3447.
31. Ingvar, D. H., Rosén, I., Eriksson, M., and Elmqvist, D. (1976): Activation patterns induced in the dominant hemisphere by skin stimulation. In: *Sensory Functions of the Skin,* edited by Y. Zotterman, pp. 549–557. Pergamon Press, London.
32. Ingvar, D. H., and Schwartz, M. (1974): Blood flow patterns induced in the dominant hemisphere by speech and reading *Brain,* 97:273–288.
33. Ingvar, D. H., Sjölund, B., and Ardö, A. (1976): Correlation between mean EEG frequency, cerebral oxygen uptake and blood flow. *EEG Clin. Neurophysiol.,* 41:268–276.
34. Jasper, H. H. (1949): Diffuse projection systems: The integrative action of the thalamic reticular system. *EEG Clin Neurophysiol.,* 1:405–420.
35. Jasper, H. H. (1958): Recent advances in our understanding of ascending activities of the reticular system. In: *Reticular Formation of the Brain,* pp. 319–331. edited by H. H. Jasper, L. D. Proctor, R. S. Knighton, W. C. Noshay, and R. T. Costello. Churchill, London.
36. Jasper, H. H., and Droogleever-Fortuyn, J. (1946): Experimental studies on the functional anatomy of petit mal epilepsy. *Res. Publ. Assoc. Nerv. Ment. Dis.,* 26:272–298.

37. Jung, R., and Hassler, R. (1959): The extrapyramidal motor system. In: *Handbook of Physiology, Vol. 2,* edited by J. Field, pp. 863–927. Williams & Wilkins, Baltimore.
38. Kety, S. S. (1967): Current biochemical approaches to schizophrenia. *N. Engl. J. Med.,* 276:325–331.
39. Kety, S. S., Woodford, R. B., Harmel, M. H., Freyham, F. A., Appel, K. E., and Schmidt, C. F. (1948): Cerebral blood flow and metabolism in schizophrenia. *Am. J. Psychiatry,* 104:765–770.
40. Lassen, N. A., and Ingvar, D. H. (1972): Radioisotopic assessment of regional cerebral blood flow. *Prog. Nucl. Med.,* 1:376–409.
41. Lassen, N. A., Ingvar, D. H., and Skinhöj, E. (1978): Brain function and blood flow. *Sci. Am.,* 239:62–71.
42. Lindvall, O., and Björklund, A. (1974): The organisation of the ascending catecholamine neuron systems in the rat brain as revealed by the glyoxylic acid fluorescens method. *Acta Physiol. Scand.* [*Suppl. 412*], 1–48.
43. Mathysse, S. (1974): Schizophrenia: Relationships to dopamine transmission, motor control and feature extraction. In: *The Neurosciences, Third Study Program,* edited by F. O. Schmitt and F. G. Worden, pp. 733–737. MIT Press, Cambridge.
44. Mathysse, S. (1974): Implications of catecholamine systems of the brain in schizophrenia. *Res. Publ. Assoc. Nerv. Ment. Dis.,* 53:305–314.
45. Morison, R. S., and Dempsey, E. W. (1942): A study of thalamocortical relations. *Am. J. Physiol.,* 135:281–292.
46. Peters, G. (1938): Zur Frage der pathologischen Anatomie der Schizophrenie. *Z. Ges. Neurol. Psychiat.,* 160:361–380.
47. Reivich, M., Kuhl, D., Wolf, A., Greenberg, J., Phelps, M., Ido, T., Casella, V., Fowler, J., Hoffman, E., Alavi, A., Sow, P., and Sokoloff, L. (1979): The ^{18}F-fluorodeoxyglucose method for the measurement of local cerebral glucose utilization in man. *Circ. Res.,* 44:127–137.
48. Risberg, J., and Ingvar, D. H. (1973): Patterns of activity in the grey matter of the dominant hemisphere during memorization and reasoning. *Brain,* 96:737–756.
49. Rockland, L. H., and Pollin, W. (1965): Quantification of psychiatric mental status. *Arch. Gen. Psychiatry,* 12:23–28.
50. Rosenthal, R., and Bigelow, L. B. (1972): Quantitative brain measurements in chronic schizophrenia. *Br. J. Psychiatry,* 121:259–264.
51. Shagass, C. (1972): *Evoked Brain Potentials in Psychiatry.* Plenum Press, New York.
52. Shagass, C. (1977): Twisted thoughts, twisted brain waves? In: *Psychopathology and Brain Dysfunction,* edited by C. Shagass, S. Gershon, and A. J. Friedhoff, pp. 353–378. Raven Press, New York.
53. Shakow, D. (1967): Some psychophysiological aspects of schizophrenia. In: *The Origins of Schizophrenia,* edited by J. Romano, pp. 54–69. Excerpta Medica, Amsterdam.
54. Skinner, J. E., and Lindsley, D. B. (1973): The non-specific mediothalamic frontocortical system: Its influence on electrocortical activity and behaviour. In: *Psychophysiology of the Frontal Lobes,* edited by K. H. Pribram and A. R. Luria, pp. 185–234. Academic Press, New York.
55. Snyder, S. H. (1972): Prospects for research on schizophrenia. *Neurosci. Res. Program Bull.,* 10:433–435.
56. Sokoloff, L., Reivich, M., Kennedy, C., de Rosiers, M. D., Potlak, C. S., Pettignew, K. D., Sokurada, O., and Shinohara, M. (1977): The ^{14}C-deoxyglucose method for the measurement of local cerebral glucose utilization: Theory, procedure and normal values in the conscious and anesthetized albino rat. *J. Neurochem.,* 28:897–916.
57. Ungerstedt, U. (1971): Stereotaxic mapping of the monoamine pathways in the rat brain. *Acta Physiol. Scand.* [*Suppl.*], 367:1–48.
58. Walter, W. G., Cooper, R., Aldridge, V. J., McCallum, W. C., and Winter, A. L. (1964): Contingent negative variation: An electrical sign of sensorimotor association and expectancy in the human brain. *Nature,* 203:380–384.

Discussion

Buchsbaum: Using positron emission tomography, Drs. Farkas and Wolf at Brookhaven Laboratory on Long Island have found that the first schizophrenic they've looked at has markedly diminished glucose utilization in the frontal cortex, as assessed by 18-fluro-deoxyglucose. This is a striking confirmation of your findings.

Bird: Have you been able to study any families or siblings before your subjects manifested schizophrenia?

Ingvar: No. Our experience with schizophrenia is limited to 40 patients, but they range in age from 17 to 72 years.

Baxter: The pictures you showed appeared to be the composite average of more than one patient. What is the error of the method?

Ingvar: About 5 to 7% for individual measurements when you make repeated examinations. The error is higher with the Kety method. Some of the pictures you saw were means; others were individual cases.

Beck: Have you studied hemispheric asymmetries?

Ingvar: Not in schizophrenia. In normals, other groups have shown that if you give verbal tests, blood flow in the left hemisphere will increase more than if you give nonverbal tests.

Beck: And if you ask the patient to visualize you see more circulation in the right hemisphere?

Ingvar: Yes.

Nasrallah: What is the right hemisphere like?

Ingvar: We know little about it except for some information in speech. There, the patterns are quite similar.

Perez-Polo: Have you looked at patients who have brain tumors?

Ingvar: Yes. Both local and remote flow abnormalities have been shown by Endo et al. (1).

Perez-Polo: Have you looked at any patients with tardive dyskinesia?

Ingvar: No.

Perez-Polo: Schizophrenics seem to range more widely around means than normals do. If you were to plot standard deviations from the mean in each of your picture areas, would it make a difference?

Buchsbaum: That's an intriguing question from the standpoint of heterogeneity.

Ingvar: We found some heterogeneity even among the young patients. Some of the inactive hebephrenic youngsters had unusually low flows, and some of the active paranoid cases had high flows. In the old women, also, those who had the lowest mean flows were the most inactive and autistic.

Carpenter: Did paranoids have higher flow in frontal areas?

Ingvar: One patient did especially. Dr. Hoyer (2) in Germany has found that the more active the psychosis, the higher the mean blood flow and oxygen uptake.

Nasrallah: What about the good-prognosis schizophrenics?

Ingvar: Some young patients—with productive paranoid symptoms—had a higher frontal flow, whereas the inactive, mutistic, catatonic patients had lower blood flow in the frontal lobe. The typology behind this should be studied more. Dr. Risberg (4) has shown some interesting correlations with the different cognitive strategies of different personalities. If a patient takes a problem seriously, the flow change is marked. In other subjects, who find the tests easy, there is only little change as they solve the problem.

Zubin: Psychologists deal with the distinction between data-driven and conceptually driven behavior. Does cerebral blood flow differentiate between a patient's responses to simple stimuli and that patient's responses to stimuli that require categorization?

Ingvar: I think data-driven responses would be impeded in a schizophrenic brain because it would always be so busy with trivial sensory information. Incoming data would not be easily evaluated as significant or insignificant. That may be why the schizophrenic response is pathological. These patients may have a defect of the behavioral programing related to the low activity in the frontal lobes. That may be the cause of the stereotyped behavior.

Henn: I'm surprised that chronic schizophrenics have such a high occipital flow, because these are not people you'd expect to have visual hallucinations.

Ingvar: The high occipital flow may be related to a defect on the afferent side. The high flow may be a correlate to hallucinations. Very high flows were recorded in patients with evident signs of hallucination—looking around and talking to invisible entities. Another piece of evidence about toxic hallucinations comes from a case studied by Dr. Risberg (4). It was that of an alcoholic young man who had been drinking for 3 weeks and then stopped. He was admitted with auditory hallucinations: He heard a large choir singing the Swedish national anthem continuously. A flow study showed a hyperemic area in the temporal region. After haloperidol treatment, the hyperemia and the hallucinations disappeared.

Henn: In that case the cortical representations are what one would expect with that type of hallucination. In schizophrenic cases, where ordinarily we think first of auditory, and less frequently of visual, and still less frequently of tactile hallucinations, the correspondence isn't so good.

Ingvar: As far as I know, schizophrenics often also have a change in their body awareness. The proprioceptive input from their own movements is experienced in a strange way, giving rise to feelings of stiffness, and so forth.

Melnechuk: The incidence of schizophrenia in the relatives of patients has suggested that the vulnerability is caused by more than one, and perhaps by many, genes. Dr. Matthysse (3) has summarized the arguments. Assuming that vulnerability is multigenic, I've heard a speculation that in a person expressing fewer than all of the genes, the partial deviance might take the form not of schizophrenia but of conceptual innovations or artistic creativity. To help settle that unlikely sounding claim, have you studied mathematicians while abstracting, or composers while composing, or poets while versifying, and if so have you found an intermediate flow level, or perhaps even a series of flow levels that might correlate with different degrees of schizophrenic expression? Do you find a low or a high blood flow when someone is being imaginative?

Ingvar: We have not studied artists at work. But my Danish colleagues have played Mozart and Brahms to some patients and seen how the auditory area and the frontal lobe (at least on the left side) is lit up by good music.

Beck: Have you ever recorded during a seizure?

Ingvar: Yes. Some high flows in the focal region are caused by epileptic processes. Sometimes, abnormal perceptual phenomena are associated with that sort of pathological focal hyperemia.

Zubin: There is some evidence that N1, the early component in the evoked potential that is involved in stimulus set, as opposed to response set, does not habituate in schizophrenia (5). Does the cerebral blood flow change associated with moving the hand or anything else habituate?

Ingvar: The inhalation technique has permitted habituation studies, which show that the frontal activation during problem solving habituates. It is as if the first time you are presented with a given problem you mobilize your brain and frontal lobes. The second time you perform as well with less frontal activation.

Zubin: Does the habituation continue for any great length of time?

Ingvar: This problem has not been studied.

Meltzer: Does the inhalation technique produce as good results as the carotid injection technique?

Ingvar: The inhalation technique is not as accurate. With the intraarterial technique you see isotope only in the brain, but with inhalation you see isotope in the whole body and head, so that the cerebral blood flow curve is contaminated by recirculation of isotope in extracerebral tissues, making it difficult to calculate the rapid clearance from the cortex.

Meltzer: What is the half-life of radioactive xenon?

Ingvar: About 6 days. The biological half-life is 10 min, because the xenon is eliminated in the lungs.

Meltzer: What was the lesion in the animal model?

Ingvar: It was in the anterior thalamus, in the inferior thalamic peduncle, where there are pathways to the frontal lobe. We can't as yet correlate this to present knowledge about dopaminergic systems.

Matthysse: Where do the causal phenomena lie? Can a normal person change his cortical blood flow pattern intentionally? Suppose actors, after careful study of schizophrenic thinking and behavior, tried to mimic them; would they then show schizophrenic blood flow patterns?

Ingvar: I would enjoy working with actors—and actresses. I don't think they would be able to generate this important symptom. Schizophrenics are open to input; they are distracted by any trivial thing that happens to them, and have high distractibility. I think this is difficult to imitate even by very good actors.

Henn: To get at what I think Dr. Matthysse was driving at in another way: you've studied some patients with affective disorders, some of whom were also psychotic. What were their patterns?

Ingvar: We have made about five intraarterial studies during acute manic episodes. They were difficult to make because the patients were restless and uncooperative. They showed a marked hyperfrontal flow distribution, probably related to their high degree of activity. But we don't have enough data to say whether this is a constant phenomenon in the manic phase. Risberg and his colleagues Nilsson et al., cited in (4), have found increased activity in the frontal lobes of paranoid psychotics, indicating that the paranoia itself is accompanied by mental work caused by the abnormal interpretation of the surroundings.

Cole: What do depressives show?

Ingvar: Studies on patients with depression are just starting. It appears that blood flow measurements can be used to study the prognosis of ECT treatment; see (4) for the work of Silverskiöld et al.

Brown: Returning to Dr. Matthysse's first question, do schizophrenics possess their characteristic symptoms because of these characteristic kinds of blood flow, or vice versa?

Ingvar: Blood flow is an index of function; schizophrenia is not a vascular disease. The blood flow abnormalities in schizophrenia are secondary to one or several defects in certain subcortical-cortical projection systems, as it appears, which are responsible for selective attention.

REFERENCES

1. Endo, H., Larsen, B., and Lassen, N. A. (1977): Regional cerebral blood flow alterations remote from the site of intracranial tumors. In: *Cerebral Function, Metabolism and Circulation,* edited by D. H. Ingvar and N. A. Lassen, pp. 524–525. Munksgaard, Copenhagen.
2. Hoyer, S., and Oesterreich, K. (1977): Blood flow and oxidative metabolism of the brain in the course of acute schizophrenia. In: *Cerebral Function, Metabolism and Circulation,* edited by D. H. Ingvar and N. A. Lassen, pp. 534–535. Munksgaard, Copenhagen.

3. Matthysse, S. (1976): Differences in incidence rates predicted by the single major locus and multifactorial models. In: *Frontiers of Psychiatric Genetics,* edited by F. G. Worden, B. Childs, S. Matthysse, and E. S. Gershon, pp. 69–72. *Neurosci. Res. Program Bull.,* 14:1–107 + v.
4. Risberg, J. (1980): Regional cerebral blood flow measurements by 133 Xe-inhalation: Methodology and applications in neuropsychology and psychiatry. *Brain Lang.,* 9:9–34.
5. Tueting, P., and Levitt, R. A. (1979): Long-term changes of event-related potentials in normals, depressives, and schizophrenics. In: *Cognitive Components in Cerebral Event-Related Potentials and Selective Attention,* edited by J. E. Desmedt, pp. 265–279. Karger, Basel.

Perspectives in Schizophrenia Research,
edited by C. Baxter and T. Melnechuk.
Raven Press, New York, 1980.

Psychoendocrine Research on Schizophrenia: A Need for Reevaluation

John W. Mason and John P. Docherty

VA Medical Center, West Haven, Connecticut 06516; and Department of Psychiatry, Yale University School of Medicine, New Haven, Connecticut 06510

LAYPERSON'S SUMMARY

Two bodies of literature relevant to current research on biological factors in schizophrenia are reviewed. The first involves a substantial amount of early clinical psychoendocrine research reported between about 1910 to 1950. This work represents a rich source of leads and guidelines on the role of hormones in the pathophysiology of schizophrenia. It has, however, been neglected in recent years and has not been reexamined with modern experimental methods. More recent basic psychoendocrine research has provided another source of guiding principles and concepts which also appear to have considerable relevance for research on schizophrenia. A general outline is presented of ways in which principles derived from these two bodies of research can be applied in innovative biological approaches to the study of schizophrenia, including the investigation of biological correlates of course and outcome of illness, biological vulnerability or risk factors, and biological differentiation of patient subgroups. Particular strategic importance is attached to the need to consider stage of illness variables in developing improved criteria for reducing the heterogeneity of schizophrenic patient populations which has probably been a confounding factor in this field of research.

INTRODUCTION

A primary purpose of this chapter is to bring together several past lines of clinical and basic research which have remained curiously overlooked in recent years although their relevance to schizophrenia, particularly for the development of innovative biological research approaches, seems rather promising and appealing. The more deeply one examines the early history and the rationale for psychoendocrine research on schizophrenia, the more puzzling it is that this field should be so much left out of the current hypotheses dealing with possible biological factors involved in schizophrenia. It appears that, far from being competitive with other biological approaches in schizophrenia, psychoendocrine strategies should complement current neurochemical and neuropharmacological research on schizophrenia. An outline of the historical background contributing to the above impression will be presented, along with some suggestions for future lines of psychoendocrine research on schizophrenia.

BACKGROUND

Clinical Psychoendocrine Research on Schizophrenia

There is a large body of early clinical psychoendocrine research which presents a source of intriguing concepts and leads which have not yet been reexamined with the benefit of modern experimental methods. The claims emerging from this early work, however, appear to be potentially too important to be dismissed lightly without experimental reevaluation.

Historically, it appears that attention was first called to a possible relationship between schizophrenia and endocrine function, especially gonadal activity, by Kraepelin in 1881 (15,23). During the period from about 1910 to 1930, there were a remarkable number of clinical reports reflecting the popular conviction that endocrine abnormalities somehow played an important role in the etiology of schizophrenia (11,23). The basis for this belief appeared to arise from at least three general sources:

1. Observations on the incidence in schizophrenic patients of stigmata of clinical endocrinopathies, e.g., girdle obesity, infantile constitution, amenorrhea, goiter, genital hypoplasia, and masculinization of females. Even as late as 1958, Hans Kind (14), from Bleuler's Clinic, was reporting observations along these lines, contending that relationships between "the acromegaloid body constitution" and a subgroup of schizophrenic patients were worthy of further study, since family research indicated a marked correlation between the two states and because the endocrine stigmata almost always became manifest before the schizophrenia (14).
2. Observations on pathological changes in endocrine glands from schizophrenic patients at autopsy. Such reports were quite numerous and, though often conflicting, tended to agree that extensive endocrine changes, mostly of a degenerative nature, often were found in schizophrenic patients (11,23). Statistical comparisons with control patient populations, however, were rarely included in these studies nor apparently were other variables, such as nutrition, taken into consideration.
3. Observations on the administration of glandular extracts, which indicated widely varying results, but in some cases dramatic therapeutic improvement was reported (11).

In a review in 1929, Hoskins (11) pointed out that, because of the lack of rigorous research design and reliable methodology, the validity of the great bulk of these observations could be questioned. He apparently regarded the findings suggesting gonadal abnormalities as the most credible at that stage of research in the field (12).

Subsequently, much more substantial contributions in this field were made by Max Reiss and his colleagues, culminating in a rather compelling series of reports in 1958 (26). Reiss and his group collected a large mass of data, using the improved but still relatively crude laboratory methods of endocrine assessment available at that time, and established a much firmer basis for taking seriously a role of endocrine factors in schizophrenia. Although he had methods only for the assessment of the thyroid, adrenal cortical, and gonadal systems, he developed a number of important insights, concepts, and research leads which clearly represent promising, but so far largely neglected, guidelines for future work in the psychoendocrine study of schizophrenia. It should be emphasized that the primary focus of Reiss' work was on the possible pathogenetic role of hormonal effects on the brain, although he recognized that brain-endocrine interactions were bidirectional.

It is not possible to review the work of Reiss and his contemporaries in detail here, but a few examples will be given of some of the observations and views which emerged from their pioneering efforts.

Some General Views

First, it was recognized that the long-standing popular quest for a single, specific, primary endocrine cause for schizophrenia was almost certainly futile, and the implications of the historical pattern of research on different endocrine glands in schizophrenia became evident. First the thyroid and subsequently the gonadal hormones became the focus of similar historical research cycles. Initial reports of striking successes with hormonal treatment of schizophrenia were followed by widespread and indiscriminate treatment of large heterogeneous patient populations on the basis of psychiatric rather than endocrine diagnosis, resulting in many more therapeutic failures than successes. The final outcome was dismissal of the work as irrelevant since it did not demonstrate a single, universal, primary endocrine abnormality in schizophrenia, or lead to the simple, universal cure that was being sought. The work with adrenal cortical extracts apparently varied only somewhat from this pattern. Although a great number of authors reported encouraging successes with adrenal cortical extracts, the discovery of cortisone and its psychopathological effects in some patients receiving huge doses for arthritis cut short further work with crude adrenal cortical extracts. Thus the promising beginnings were forgotten (27).

Reiss recognized the folly of the simplistic, two-dimensional, cause-effect thought pattern of the time and placed emphasis on his data suggesting a multidimensional approach. He demonstrated that multiple and varying hormonal abnormalities occurred in relation to schizophrenia and that it is probably the overall "endocrine equilibrium" which needed to be considered as the most relevant dimension in psychoendocrine studies (27). He emphasized the complexity of the interplay between different endocrine systems and between endocrine systems and the brain, calling attention to the primary and secondary character of various hormonal changes and particularly to the concept of a "vicious circle" developing in brain-endocrine interrelationships (1,27).

Reiss discovered also that underfunction or overfunction of the thyroid, gonads, and adrenal cortex could represent clinically significant disruptions of the endocrine equilibrium in schizophrenic patients (27).

A number of workers reported that instances of clear and lasting clinical improvement were increased when hormonal therapy was rationally based on laboratory assessment of specific endocrine disturbances in individual patients (2,5,6,10,27). A guiding principle, then, was that endocrine therapy needed to be based on specific endocrine deviations and not on the similarity of mental disturbances of different patients. According to Reiss, any given mental disturbance may be associated with a variety of different patterns of endocrine imbalance which must be diagnosed by laboratory methods before rational treatment can be started. He pointed to postpartum mental disorders as one example illustrating this point, since endocrine disturbances were not restricted to ovarian function but also involved changes in levels of thyroid or adrenal cortical hormones with patterns varying in different patients (27). As another example, Reiss cited some patients with recurring monthly psychotic episodes which were related to their menstrual cycle. Such patients experienced striking clinical recovery following treatment of thyroid disorders and did not require treatment that related directly to ovarian function (27).

Emphasis was placed by Reiss on observations that "intermediate" hormonal changes within the "normal range" could play a significant role in influencing mental disorders and that full-blown clinical endocrinopathies were not required for pathogenetic significance, or for influencing the course of illness (5,27). Reference was made also for the need to consider conditions under which the sensitivity of body tissues to hormone might be altered and for which more elaborate diagnostic techniques may be required (5).

Another step forward was the recognition of the importance of a broad multifactorial view of the pathogenesis of schizophrenia. Endocrine factors became recognized as only one of several sets of influences in the etiology of schizophrenia; other influences included precipitating life events or situations and the premorbid personality pattern, presumably reflecting genetic and developmental factors. Reiss viewed these three major factors as pathogenetic influences that were necessary but insufficient individually, and regarded onset of schizophrenia as occurring only when multiple co-determinants were present in proper combination. In view of his more holistic, multifactorial concept of pathogenesis (27), he seriously questioned the "defeatism" emerging during that period from research on genetic factors in mental illness.

Reiss grasped the importance of the confounding problem of the heterogeneity of schizophrenic patient populations and of the priority which should be given to greater refinement in the definition of psychiatrically homogeneous groups, in terms of both diagnostic category and clinical state at the time of psychoendocrine study. He recognized the importance of heterogeneous patient populations in relation to the variable and often conflicting results reported from different laboratories, as well as the fundamental importance of understanding the heterogeneity as a prerequisite for the effective use of the scientific method in this type of clinical research (27).

Reiss also had at least partial insight into a related fundamental principle which has been elaborated more fully and more recently by Reiser (25), namely, that in viewing the possible pathogenetic significance of any set of factors, it must be considered that their role may be that of exerting either a long-term predisposing influence, a short-term precipitating influence, or a modifying or perpetuating influence affecting the course of illness after its onset. The observations of Reiss and his co-workers suggested the probable significance of psychoendocrine mechanisms in all three of the above categories in relation to schizophrenia and that future research strategy in this field would have to take this fact into consideration (1,27).

Some Specific Observations

A few examples of more specific epidemiological and clinical observations which drew attention to endocrine factors in schizophrenia during this period are given below:

1. The long-recognized relationship between onset of puberty and onset of schizophrenia (1).
2. The high incidence of women suffering from acute psychoses who were admitted to the hospital during the premenstrual phase, coupled with observations of a different pattern of clinical symptomatology in premenstrual versus postmenstrual psychoses (16).
3. The association of androgen administration, or of certain adrenal cortical adenomata, with paranoid symptoms (1).
4. The association of an immaturity syndrome in the male—involving wide open inguinal canals, testicles high in the scrotum which easily slip back into the canal, decreased beard growth, absence of chest hair, and female pubic hair border—with a predisposition to schizophrenia (2,6,27).
5. A number of studies relating endocrine function to response to treatment by drugs, insulin coma therapy, or psychotherapy. The immaturity syndrome described above, for example, was found to contraindicate insulin coma treatment, which could lead to "permanent invalidism" in adolescents or young adults with this endocrine disorder. Persistently high or low thyroid activity or ketosteroid excretion was similarly a bad prognostic sign for insulin coma treatment (13). Signs of immaturity or disturbance in gonadal function were

regarded as a strong contraindication to chlorpromazine treatment (28). Other evidence indicated that normalization of the endocrine equilibrium can make patients more responsive to psychotherapy (27,32). Reiss also pointed out that the potent effects of psychoactive drugs such as chlorpromazine on hormone secretion of multiple endocrine systems had not been adequately considered in assessing the mechanism of action of such drugs on the brain. Instead, it had been generally assumed that the effects were due solely to direct local action of the drugs on central neurochemical systems (27,28).

6. A particularly fruitful approach emerged from intensive longitudinal studies of both clinical and endocrine parameters during the course of recovery from acute schizophrenic episodes. For example, a comparison of the timing of the normalization of hormonal equilibrium with phases of clinical improvement revealed that under some conditions, the former preceded the latter. One practical implication of such studies, for example, was the indication that assessment of endocrine balance during the initial phase of hospitalization was helpful in predicting which patients would be most likely to recover "spontaneously" with only a change in environment and ordinary hospital care and attention (27). Observations were also made indicating that under certain conditions endocrine balance could be predictive of subsequent response to drug or other therapeutic programs (27).

In summary, although the work of Reiss and his contemporaries was in some respects relatively crude and questionable by present day scientific standards, they built a substantial foundation for psychoendocrine research in schizophrenia. They recognized many pitfalls to be avoided, discerned some important issues of research strategy, and foresaw some of the future directions psychoendocrine research must take when the principal obstacle which confronted them, namely, the lack of reliable, sensitive, specific, practicable methods for measuring hormone levels of the many neuroendocrine systems, could be overcome (27,29).

During the past 20 years, the area of psychoendocrine research, opened up by Reiss and his colleagues, has received little sustained or systematic attention, except for the limited recent work, mostly on prolactin, which has been largely linked to neuropharmacological and neurochemical hypotheses (3,4,9,24,30). The great impact of neuropharmacological advances in psychiatric treatment during these past two decades may be one of the important factors accounting for the neglect of psychoendocrine research as related to the pathogenesis of schizophrenia, despite the encouraging progress in this area from about 1940 to 1955. The relatively slow pace of refinements in hormone assay methodology until the recent breakthroughs with radioimmunoassays is certainly another factor. In any event, in reviewing the compelling clinical observations of many early workers, one develops a certain sense that a careful, systematic reevaluation of this area of psychoendocrine research is overdue, particularly in view of the relatively sophisticated endocrinological and psychiatric methods that are now available.

Basic Psychoendocrine Research

Recent basic research in psychoendocrinology has provided another source of concepts which appear to have important implications for research on mental disorders. First of all, it is now recognized that the neuroendocrine apparatus represents a third effector or motor system of the brain, along with the skeletal-muscular and autonomic nervous systems. As such, it can provide a useful "window" through which to view the inner functions of the brain in the intact organism. By means of hormonal reflections one can view the operation of psychological, neural, neurochemical, or neuropharmacological mechanisms (17).

A guiding principle of particular strategic importance is that the many neuroendocrine systems tend to respond, not singly, but in concert to psychological or physical stimuli, with resultant broadly organized patterns of response which appear to be distinctive for the specific stimulus involved. A substantial body of data now indicates that the principles underlying the organization of neuroendocrine responses unfold more clearly as we move in the direction of studying the neuroendocrine apparatus more as a whole, whenever possible by measuring multihormonal patterns or profiles of change (17–19).

Figure 1 presents a schematic view of a broad assemblage of interdependent neuroendocrine systems, in order to indicate the scope of such systems that are known to be responsive to psychological influences as well as other natural stimuli. It is now clear that the levels of hormones such as cortisol, epinephrine, norepinephrine, thyroxine, growth hormone, prolactin, testosterone, estradiol, estrone, insulin, and aldosterone are sensitive to psychological influences (17, 20,22). Some hormones, such as vasopressin and oxytocin, along with other hormones not included in the figure, such as renin, glucagon, progesterone, and parathyroid hormone, have not, as yet, been adequately studied in psychoendocrine experiments.

The complexity of an organized pattern of psychoendocrine responses, in terms of both multiple systems being simultaneously involved and the differing dynamics of response from one hormonal system to the next, is shown in Figure 2. This is the pattern of acute hormonal change during the first 6 hr following the capture and initial experience of chair restraint in a rhesus monkey. Whereas prolactin levels peaked in 20 min, growth hormone in 40 min, and cortisol in 4 hr, the thyroxine change was much slower to develop and more enduring, remaining high even at 48 hr. Levels of other hormones, such as insulin and testosterone, were lowered by the stimulus, with an indication that the testosterone response may be biphasic, in that a brief initial elevation preceded the prolonged suppression of levels (22). It is clear how simplistic it would be to try to account for the effects of this stimulus on metabolic functions throughout the body or to understand the brain's role in physiological integration in this situation by looking at only one, or a small subset, of hormones.

Figure 3 summarizes schematically the patterns of hormonal response in mon-

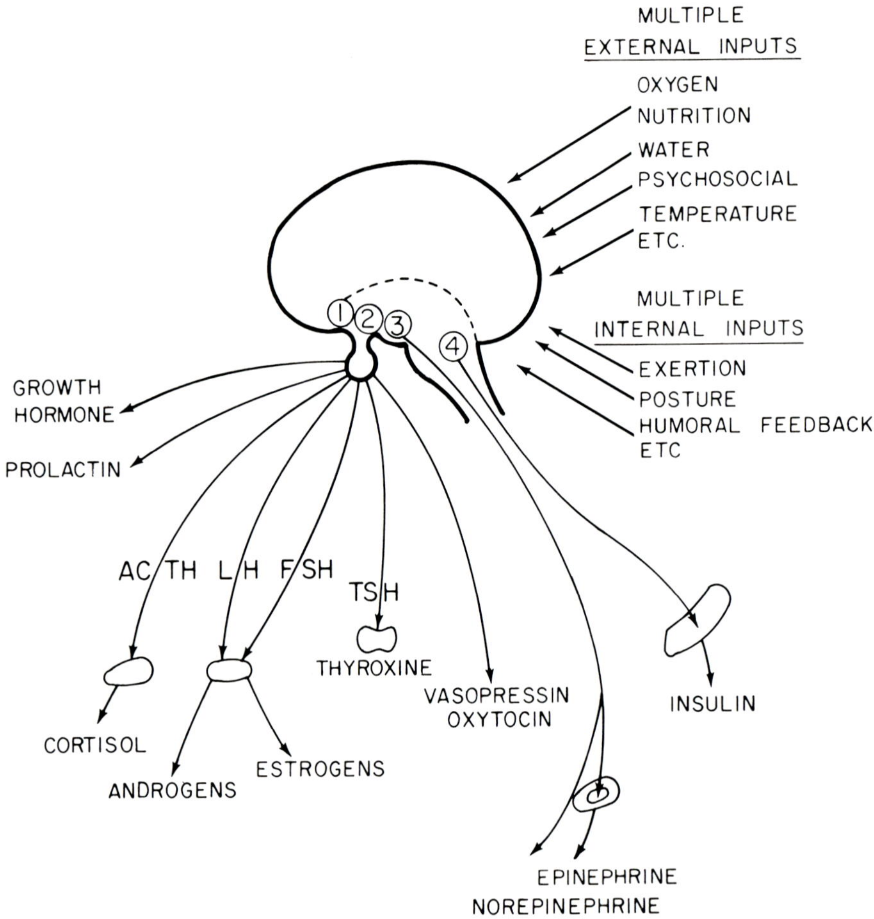

FIG. 1. The assemblage of interdependent neuroendocrine systems.

keys or humans to a variety of other natural stimuli. The figure compares the initial direction of response (↑–rise, ↓–fall, 0–no detectable change) of seven different hormones to stimuli such as exercise, cold, heat, and fasting, as well as both conditioned and unconditioned emotional disturbances. As the multihormonal response patterns are viewed in each vertical column, it is evident that their organization is generally distinctive for the stimulus or stimulus class in question. The contrasts between response patterns for heat versus cold, or fasting versus all-carbohydrate diet, for example, are quite striking. Further details of these studies are discussed at length elsewhere (18).

The foregoing data dealt generally with the first of two major concepts in psychoendocrine research, namely, the influence of the brain on hormonal levels and hormones reflecting processes going on within the brain. A second concept

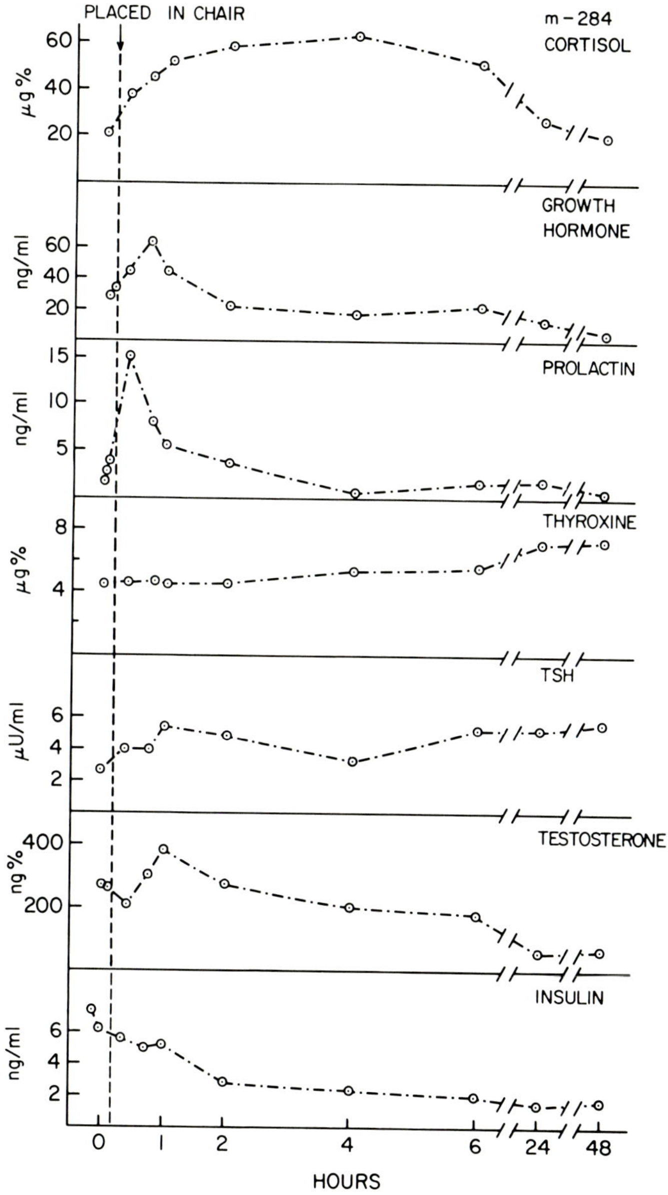

FIG. 2. Pattern of plasma hormonal responses of a monkey to capture and chair restraint.

	ACUTE AVOIDANCE	ACUTE RESTRAINT	MOD. EXERCISE	SEVERE EXERCISE	MOD. HEAT	MOD. COLD	FASTING	CHO DIET	HYPOXIA
17-OHCS	↑	↑	0	↑	↓	↑	0	↑	↑
EPINEPHRINE	↑	↑	↑	↑	↓	↑	↑	↓	↑
NOREPINEPHRINE	↑	↑	↑	↑	↓	↑	↓	↑	0
TESTOSTERONE	↓	↓	↑	↑	↓	↑	↓	↓	0
THYROXINE	↑	↑	↑	↑	↓	↑	↑	↑	
INSULIN	↓	↓	↓	↓	↑	↓	↓	↓	↓
GROWTH HORMONE	↑	↑	↑	0		↑	↑	↑	↑

FIG. 3. Specificity in the organization of patterns of multihormonal responses to various natural stimuli. Tentative summary based largely on pilot experiments.

is that hormones act on the brain as one of their target organs. Hormones act on target units in a highly interdependent fashion, often being aligned in antagonistic or synergistic interactions. The net result at the metabolic level is a function of the overall balance of forces. It is clear, therefore, that no matter from which direction we view brain-endocrine interactions, we are led towards consideration of the pattern or equilibrium involving multiple hormones.

The relevance of this basic work for clinical research lies in the way it clarifies ground rules for the study of neuroendocrine machinery. It is of course, useful and necessary to study individual endocrine systems in depth, but the evidence for multiple hormones responding and working together as co-determinants of events at the cellular level provides hope for a new level of understanding of the integrative machinery as we move stepwise in the direction of dealing with neuroendocrine organization on a broader scope. This conceptual approach has shown considerable predictive power in basic research, and it seems reasonable, now, to extend its application to clinical problems.

In addition, other recent basic psychoendocrine research has revealed that hormonal measurements are useful not only in the study of changing emotional states, but also reflect more enduring personal characteristics such as styles of psychological defense and neurotic processes (21). It has been found, for example, that the extreme use of the psychological defense of denial can be associated with chronic suppression of adrenal cortical hormone levels (21). There is preliminary evidence that styles of handling anger may be reflected in patterns of hormonal change involving epinephrine, norepinephrine, and testosterone levels (19). The implications of basic psychoendocrine findings along these lines remain largely to be explored for the leverage they may provide in the study of psychotic processes.

FUTURE DIRECTIONS

Principles derived from the foregoing background work can readily be applied to both longitudinal and cross-sectional studies of schizophrenic patients. A model that would provide an opportunity to reevaluate many of the leads and hypotheses emerging from older clinical psychoendocrine research would be the intensive longitudinal study of individual patients from the point of hospital admission to maximal clinical improvement. In such an approach it would be important to assess reliably both state and trait factors, and particularly to assess the distinct stages of psychological recompensation during the recovery process in relation to patterns of change in multiple endocrine systems.

A model providing a framework for intensive longitudinal psychoendocrine study of schizophrenic patients, and for relating hormonal levels to clearly defined stages of illness during clinical improvement with milieu therapy in acute schizophrenic reactions, has been reported by Sachar et al. (31). In this study, close correlations were observed between urinary 17-hydroxycorticosteroid (17-OHCS) levels and rather sharply demarcated phases of clinical change, with a clear tendency for 17-OHCS levels to be high during "turmoil" and "depression" phases when affective distress was high, as compared with the lower levels during phases of relatively stable psychotic equilibrium or eventual clinical improvement (31). At the time of this early study, suitable assay methods were not yet available for measuring a broad, multihormonal pattern of change of the type indicated by more recent basic research. There has also been a recent refinement in the systematic classification and methods of assessing distinct stages of decompensation and recompensation in schizophrenic patients that should facilitate future work along these lines (8). This longitudinal model could be applied to the study of the natural course of recovery from psychosis, as well as that under the conditions of drug or placebo treatment.

Such an approach would allow the evaluation of important questions such as the following:

1. Are there characteristic hormonal changes associated with distinct clinical stages of recovery from schizophrenic psychosis?
2. Are multiple endocrine systems involved in these stages of change?
3. Do hormonal changes precede, coincide with, or follow onset of stages of clinical change? Do specific hormones within the profile differ in this respect?
4. Does the pattern of hormonal change during recovery differ depending on treatment modality?
5. Is it possible to predict which patients are likely to recover without drug treatment on the basis of hormonal assessment during the first week or two of hospitalization?
6. Is it possible to predict subsequent response to drug therapy on the basis of hormonal assessment during the initial period of hospitalization?
7. Can endocrine testing criteria be developed to provide contraindications

for the use of specific drugs, to aid in selecting drug of choice, or to predict high risk for side effects, such as tardive dyskinesia?

8. Does the multihormonal balance after maximal clinical improvement give evidence of any persistent endocrine disturbances which may represent predisposing high-risk factors for relapse?

In addition to longitudinal approaches such as those briefly outlined above, psychoendocrine approaches of a cross-sectional nature are clearly indicated in the future development of this work. The marked heterogeneity of the patient population diagnosed as schizophrenic has long been recognized as a major obstacle to investigation, as well as management, of this disorder. The use of multihormonal patterns as a possible biological basis for identifying and classifying subtypes of schizophrenic patients would appear worthy of exploration, especially in conjunction with a variety of recent, innovative psychiatric approaches to subtyping. The latter would include (a) methods based on multiple symptom clusters, such as the classical subtypes or the International Pilot Study of Schizophrenia subtypes (7); (b) methods based on symptom dichotomies, such as paranoid versus nonparanoid, or affective disorder versus no affective disorder; (c) methods based on course of illness, such as premorbid adjustment, acute versus chronic, or hospitalization patterns; (d) methods based on outcome of treatment, especially those dealing with multiaxial levels of function.

Correlations could be sought between the above patient subtype categories and chronic mean levels of individual hormones or the configuration of multihormonal patterns. This approach could be supplemented by the use of endocrinological probe or challenge tests, such as tryptophin-releasing hormone (TRH) injection or insulin hypoglycemia, or by more naturalistic evoked reactions, such as in the study of the pattern of hormonal responses during interpersonal confrontations in individual, group, or family therapy sessions. This latter approach has received little, if any, attention so far although it would seem a promising means of exploring abnormal or idiosyncratic patterns of psychoendocrine response. Because of the greater complexity of cross-sectional studies such as these, the research approach is more difficult than in the proposed longitudinal studies, but it appears that exploratory studies along these lines are certainly worth considering because of the great practical importance of dealing with more homogeneous patient groups as future research develops in this field.

REFERENCES

1. Batt, J. C., and Reiss, M. (1958): The changing concepts of the role of endocrine function and treatment in psychiatry. In: *Psychoendocrinology,* edited by M. Reiss, pp. 41–51. Grune & Stratton, New York.
2. Bradley, J. J. (1958): Clinical observations on the action of chorionic gonadotrophin in adult male psychiatric patients. In: *Psychoendocrinology,* edited by M. Reiss, pp. 76–81. Grune & Stratton, New York.
3. Brambilla, F., Guastalla, A., Guerrini, A., Rovere, C., Legnani, G., Sarno, M., and Riggi, F. (1976): Prolatcin secretion in chronic schizophrenia. *Acta Psychiatr. Scand.,* 54:275–286.

4. Brambilla, F., Guerrini, A., Rovere, C., Guastalla, A., Riggi, F., and Recchia, M. (1975): Growth hormone secretion in chronic schizophrenia. *Neuropsychobiology,* 1:267–276.
5. Bullmore, G. H. L., Kay, W. W., Smith, D. W., and Stott, H. J. (1958): Investigations of thyroid function of mental patients, and possible use of some results for rational treatment procedure. In: *Psychoendocrinology,* edited by M. Reiss, pp. 52–62. Grune & Stratton, New York.
6. Bullmore, G. H. L., Reiss, M., and Smith, D. W. (1958): Endocrine investigations in a juvenile psychiatric unit. In: *Psychoendocrinology,* edited by M. Reiss, pp. 63–75. Grune & Stratton, New York.
7. Carpenter, W. T., Bartko, J. J., Carpenter, C. L., and Strauss, J. S. (1976): Another view of schizophrenic subtypes. *Arch. Gen. Psychiatry,* 33:508–516.
8. Docherty, J. P., Van Kammen, D. P., Siris, S. G., and Marder, S. R. (1978): Stages of onset of schizophrenic psychosis. *Am. J. Psychiatry,* 135:420–426.
9. Ettigi, P., Nair, N. P. V., Lal, S., Cerrantes, P., and Guyda, H. (1976): Effect of apomorphine on growth hormone and prolactin secretion in schizophrenic patients, with or without oral dyskinesia, withdrawn from chronic neuroleptic therapy. *J. Neurol. Neurosurg. Psychiatry,* 39:870–876.
10. Gornall, A. G., Eglitis, B., and Stokes, A. B. (1958): Endocrine studies and hormonal effects in periodic catatonia. In: *Psychoendocrinology,* edited by M. Reiss, pp. 152–167. Grune & Stratton, New York.
11. Hoskins, R. G. (1929): Endocrine factors in dementia praecox. *N. Engl. J. Med.,* 200:361–369.
12. Hoskins, R. G. (1949): Sex-hormone relationships in schizophrenic men. *Psychosom. Med.,* 11:102–109.
13. Kay, W. W. (1958): The endocrinology of deep insulin coma therapy. In: *Psychoendocrinology,* edited by M. Reiss, pp. 138–151. Grune & Stratton, New York.
14. Kind, H. (1958): Investigations on endocrine stigmatized schizophrenics and their families. In: *Psychoendocrinology,* edited by M. Reiss, pp. 120–128. Grune & Stratton, New York.
15. Kraepelin, E. (1910): *Geschlachtliche verirrungen und volksvermehrungpsychiatrie.* J. A. Barth, Leipzig.
16. Mall, G. (1958): On the hormonal treatment of pre- and postmenstrual ovarian psychoses. In: *Psychoendocrinology,* edited by M. Reiss, pp. 96–103. Grune & Stratton, New York.
17. Mason, J. W. (1968): Organization of psychoendocrine mechanisms. *Psychosom. Med.,* 30:565–808.
18. Mason, J. W. (1974): Specificity in the organization of neuroendocrine response profiles. In: *Frontiers in Neurology and Neuroscience Research,* edited by P. Seeman and G. Brown, pp. 68–80. University of Toronto Press, Toronto.
19. Mason, J. W. (1975): Emotion as reflected in patterns of endocrine integration. *Karolinska Symposium on Parameters of Emotion,* edited by L. Levi, pp. 143–181. Raven Press, New York.
20. Mason, J. W. (1975): Psychological stress and endocrine function. In: *Topics in Endocrinology,* edited by E. Sachar, pp. 1–18. Grune & Stratton, New York.
21. Mason, J. W. (1975): Clinical psychophysiology: Psychoendocrine mechanisms. In: *American Handbook of Psychiatry, Vol. IV,* edited by M. Reiser, pp. 553–582. Basic Books, New York.
22. Mason, J. W., Maher, J. T., Hartley, L. H., Mougey, E. H., Perlow, M. J., and Jones, L. G. (1976): Selectivity of corticosteroid and catecholamine responses to various natural stimuli. In: *Psychopathology of Human Adaptation,* edited by G. Serban, pp. 147–171. Plenum Publishing Corp. New York.
23. McCartney, J. L. (1929): Dementia praecox as an endocrinopathy with clinical and autopsy reports. *Endocrinology,* 13:73–87.
24. Meltzer, H. Y. (1976): The effect of neuroleptics on serum prolactin in schizophrenic patients. *Arch. Gen. Psychiatry,* 33:279–286.
25. Reiser, M. (1975): Changing theoretical concepts in psychosomatic medicine. In: *American Handbook of Psychiatry, Vol. IV,* edited by M. Reiser, pp. 477–500. Basic Books, New York.
26. Reiss, M. (ed.) (1958): *Psychoendocrinology.* Grune & Stratton, New York.
27. Reiss, M. (1958): Psychoendocrinology. In: *Psychoendocrinology,* edited by M. Reiss, pp. 1–40. Grune & Stratton, New York.
28. Reiss, M. (1958): Influence of chlorpromazine on endocrine function. In: *Psychoendocrinology,* edited by M. Reiss, pp. 182–197. Grune & Stratton, New York.

29. Reiss, M. (1967): Neuroendocrinology and psychiatry. *Int. J. Neuropsychiatry,* 3:441–463.
30. Sachar, E. J. (1975): Hormonal changes in stress and mental illness. *Hosp. Pract.,* 49–55.
31. Sachar, E. J., Mason, J. W., Kolmer, H. S., and Artiss, K. L. (1963): Psychoendocrine aspects of acute schizophrenic reactions. *Psychosom. Med.,* 25:510–537.
32. Strauss, E. B., and Stevenson, W. A. H. (1958): A note on the treatment with diandrone of eight women patients. In: *Psychoendocrinology,* edited by M. Reiss, pp. 104–114. Grune & Stratton, New York.

Discussion

Perez-Polo: It's clear that the nervous system reacts to everything, that a fantastic homeostatic inertia is at work. This appears to be a difficult obstacle to overcome, especially in looking at neuroleptic drugs. As we are largely limited to looking at them pharmacologically, the masking problem is serious. Have you any suggestions for how to get around that?

Mason: I would suggest two research strategies in this connection. The first is the use of intensive, longitudinal studies of individual patients through the course of their illness, in which the fine time relationships between changes in social environment, clinical symptomatology, and biological factors, including endocrine profile, are assessed concurrently. With this approach, it may be possible to dissect out the sequence and direction of relationships in these interacting variables. A model for longitudinal psychoendocrine studies of schizophrenic patients along these lines has been reported by Sachar et al. (4).

A second approach would be to conduct such longitudinal studies under different treatment conditions in patients not requiring drug treatment, in patients on drug therapy, and perhaps a placebo subgroup from the first group. This should help tease apart the role of the multiple factors involved in the recovery process.

Melnechuk: Estrogen therapy for human breast cancer takes two forms—additive, in which estrogen is given, and ablative, in which the ovaries, adrenals, or pituitary are removed. Both therapies can be effective if the cancer is estrogen-dependent. Assaying the levels of estrogen receptors in the cancers gives good predictions of the outcome (3).

Mason: Since one of the problems in work with multihormonal profiles is dealing with the data statistically, your point about breast cancer reminds me of a hopeful lead in this regard. Once we (2) did a prospective study looking for pre-illness hormonal differences between army recruits who would develop viral illness and those who wouldn't. With several combinations of hormones plotted two-dimensionally, we found that those destined to become ill tended to have either extremely high or extremely low levels and to fall out in the periphery of the plot whereas the control group fell closer to the area around the intersection of the means for hormonal pairs. This finding fits beautifully with the notion that it is endocrine equilibrium, balance between hormonal systems, rather than absolute levels in single systems, that may count the most. This concept needs to be examined in schizophrenia, especially now that we know that enduring psychological mechanisms can cause hormone levels to be either too high or too low.

Brown: We know that all of these hormones cross the blood-brain barrier, that they concentrate in specific brain areas, that many of the steroids inhibit MAO and affect neurotransmitter synthesis, and so forth. Have you any notions of how to integrate that degree of complexity into an understanding of the schizophrenic process?

Mason: You envision what seems to me to be a logical later stage of inquiry once we know more about the scope of hormonal changes in schizophrenia. A related point, however, is that drug-induced hormonal changes may play a role in the therapeutic effects of such drugs because of the relationships you mention. I know of relatively little data yet on the responses of a broad range of neuroendocrine systems to the major neuroleptic drugs. Most of the work has been concentrated on prolactin or growth hormone and perhaps a few others. Also, there is particularly little information on how response to drug treatment may relate to pre-treatment hormonal baselines. The possibility that neuroleptic drugs act not only through primary neuronal effects, but also through secondary hormonal changes, and that their effects can be influenced by ongoing hormonal equilibrium, seem to be questions worthy of investigation.

Meltzer: Actually, we have been doing some of this work, and so have the groups of Dr. Robert Rubin and of Dr. Brambilla but I don't think we have been sophisticated enough for you, for we have looked at only five or six hormones for only 2 or 3 hr after neuroleptic treatment, whereas you want to bring the preceding hormonal output to bear, which no one has looked at in that context. Through the window I just mentioned, we see the neuroleptics causing relatively limited changes in any hormones but prolactin.

Yuwiler: Perhaps a look further downstream from the initial hormonal responses to either stressors or drugs might contribute information on how and whether environmental stressors might act on genetic vulnerability to produce manifest disease. As Dr. Mason has shown, different stressors elicit release of different sets of hormones although by definition all stressors release corticoids. Hormonal induction of enzymes is also well known and with such induction there are alterations in metabolism. Further, there are known instances of hormonal effects on enzyme induction so that, for example, growth hormone inhibits corticoid induction of tyrosine transminase but augments corticoid induction of tryptophan oxygenase. Each stressor then can be pictured as eliciting a metabolic melody played against a corticoid base note and, as with a melody, there are time and emphasis parameters. The time parameters come from the nature of the processes. For example, adrenocorticotropin (ACTH) release takes seconds, corticoid release takes minutes, induction of tyrosine transaminase or tryptophan oxygenase takes 4 to 6 hr, and corticoid induction of alanine transaminase takes a day. The time that hormones must be elevated to affect enzyme induction provides the basis for emphasis. If schizophrenics differ from normals in the proportions of hormones released by different stressors, in the duration of release, or in the sensitivity of systems to the inductive effects of hormones, these should be reflected in downstream metabolic adjustments. That is, perhaps, we should look at metabolic adjustments occurring hours or days after exposure to a stressor in addition to looking at the immediate hormonal response to see if schizophrenics and normals are differentially responsive to stimuli.

Perez-Polo: It's clearer now at least to me that in looking at the effects of various neuroleptics, you must do your measurements in the same sample—i.e., one and the same individual. Otherwise, we'll never make sense of compensatory biochemical mechanisms. Only in one individual can you see what goes up while other things go down, and what sequence of events takes place.

Baxter: If the levels of hormones in the blood change with each hour of the day, the complexity of the system is even greater than indicated by Dr. Mason. Automated sampling techniques might reduce the mathematical complexity and simplify the problem of obtaining average daily levels. One could visualize an implanted automatic sampling device that would withdraw blood samples at preset time intervals throughout the test period. Samples could be stored separately or pooled to form integrated samples. Perhaps the compounds to be studied in each sample could be adsorbed onto a resin pellet, similar to the way in which it is being done by some automatic amino acid analyzers.

Meltzer: There exist portable blood-withdrawal pumps for human use, worn around the chest, that will remove blood at whatever interval you set them for. They have proved useful in endocrine studies for getting an average prolactin level over a 6-hr period.

Mason: I think it is possible to overestimate as well as underestimate the level of complexity of integrative approaches. In some ways, the experience in basic research on multihormonal response profiles yielded less complex data than might have been expected, data not requiring highly complicated sampling or statistical approaches. The first step is to find out how complex the hormonal changes really are in schizophrenia. Relatively simple types of profile analysis may conceivably be sufficient for making useful clinical distinctions. I think the important principle to explore is whether or not we can gain unique insight into the underlying principles of brain integration by looking into hormonal pattern organization, which takes into account the interdependence of neuroendocrine systems. This can be approached in stages and the degree of complexity required for useful clinical application can only be a matter of conjecture at present.

Melnechuk: Current research on the polypeptide hormones seems to be arriving at coherent structural and functional patterns. First, several hormones share amino acid sequences conserved in evolution, supporting the argument that they have differentiated from a single precursor, which suggests a possible link between their evolved functions. Second, several are biosynthesized together as parts of a much larger precursor, a fact that also suggests links between their functions. For example, a 31,000-dalton glycoprotein, called "big ACTH" or "pro-opiocortin," yields by enzymatic cleavage not only an ACTH prohormone and then ACTH, and not only the pituitary hormone beta-lipotropin and then beta-endorphin and met-enkephalin, but also melanotropin (MSH). This has suggested to Dr. Sidney Udenfriend that the ensemble of hormones constitutes a multipurpose response to stress, each with its own target. Third, of the many intestinal hormones recently found to be neuroactive, at least one serves the same biological purpose in the brain that it serves in the periphery, albeit another aspect. Thus, luteinizing hormone-releasing factor (LH-RH or LRF), which, in the periphery, ultimately evokes the release of ova, in the brain increases libido. That is, it serves the purpose of procreation, wherever it acts. Of course not all such biological purposes are as immediately obvious as that one, and there is much to be learned about the "natural dimensions" in terms of which our biology is organized and that unify the seemingly disparate actions of hormones active centrally and peripherally. Yet the three types of pattern I mentioned raise hopes for the possibility of an eventual synthesis of current specifics (1).

REFERENCES

1. Bloom, F. E., editor (1980): *Peptides, Integrators of Cell and Tissue Function.* Raven Press, New York.
2. Mason, J. W., Buescher, E. L., Belfer, M. L., Mougey, E. H., Taylor, E. D., Wherry, F. E., Ricketts, P. T., Young, P. S., Wade, J., Early, D. C., and Kenion, C. C. (1967): Pre-illness hormonal changes in Army recruits with acute respiratory infections. *Psychosom. Med.,* 29:545.
3. Melnechuk, T. (1978): Steroid resistance in breast cancer and leukemia. In: *Cell Receptor Disorders,* pp. 57–66. Western Behavioral Sciences Institute, La Jolla, California.
4. Sachar, E. J., Mason, J. W., Kolmer, H. S., and Artiss, K. L. (1963): Psychoendocrine aspects of acute schizophrenic reactions. *Psychosom. Med.,* 25:510–537.

Perspectives in Schizophrenia Research,
edited by C. Baxter and T. Melnechuk.
Raven Press, New York, 1980.

Neuroleptic-Induced Elevations in Serum Prolactin Levels: Etiology and Significance

*,**Herbert Y. Meltzer, **Daniel Busch, **Rebecca So, **Henry Holcomb, and †Victor S. Fang

*Departments of *Psychiatry and †Medicine, University of Chicago Pritzker School of Medicine, Chicago, Illinois 60637; and **Illinois State Psychiatric Institute, Chicago, Illinois 60612*

LAYPERSON'S SUMMARY

Current theories of the etiology of schizophrenia and the mechanism of action of antipsychotic drugs emphasize the importance of the neurotransmitter dopamine (DA). Since DA affects prolactin and growth hormone secretion, both of which can be readily measured in small serum samples, there have been a large number of both clinical and basic studies of these hormones, whose purpose has been to obtain information useful for the study of schizophrenia. Although most investigators believe excess DA in the limbic region or frontal cortex of the brain may be responsible for some aspects of schizophrenia, the effects of DA on prolactin and growth hormone occur in other brain regions and in the pituitary gland. It is hoped that the endocrine studies will provide information useful to understanding other DA systems that may be more pertinent to the etiology of schizophrenia or the mechanism of action of antipsychotic drugs.

Unmedicated schizophrenic patients appear to have normal prolactin and growth hormone levels in serum with the possible exception of reduced growth hormone levels during sleep. The antipsychotic drug-induced increase in serum prolactin levels as well as the increase due to inhibition of DA syntheses by a drug, α-methyl-P-tyrosine (AMPT), appear to be comparable in schizophrenics and normal controls. Apomorphine, a DA agonist, also produces a comparable decrease in serum prolactin levels in schizophrenics and normal controls. However, the increase in serum growth hormone in schizophrenics ill less than 4 years has been found to be greater than that of controls, whereas the reverse is true for those schizophrenics ill more than 4 years. This finding may reflect altered sensitivity of hypothalamic DA receptors. Modification of DA receptor sensitivity, as part of the disease process or the treatment of schizophrenics, is one of the many hypotheses of interest to schizophrenia investigators which can be investigated by neuroendocrine methods.

A series of studies are reviewed concerning the correlation between serum prolactin levels and clinical improvement after several weeks of neuroleptic treatment. The results are mixed, but methodologic differences may account for the failure to find such a correlation in some studies. A negative correlation was found between serum prolactin response to a single intramuscular injection of chlorpromazine and clinical response after 1 week of treatment. A possible explanation for this result is proposed which, if correct, would indicate this may be a useful method to identify patients with DA-dependent psychoses.

Finally, some preclinical endocrine research which sheds new light on the mechanism of action of various psychotropic drugs, including sulpiride, metoclopramide, and LSD, is discussed. It is demonstrated that atypical antipsychotic drugs such as sulpiride and metoclopramide may stimulate prolactin release by a novel mechanism. LSD was shown to have potent DA-like action at the pituitary, an additional indication that its effects on DA may underlie its psychotomimetic effects.

INTRODUCTION

The demonstration that prolactin secretion from the anterior pituitary gland of man and laboratory animals is under direct dopaminergic inhibition (50,63) proved of considerable importance for biological psychiatry because of the great importance dopamine (DA) has to current theories of the etiology of schizophrenia, mania, and depression (32,70,82,92). Since prolactin levels in blood and cerebrospinal fluid are readily studied in man, this new insight into the function of DA led to an extensive series of clinical investigations concerning dopaminergic function in schizophrenia and the effect of psychotropic drugs on DA neurons and receptors. Growth hormone (GH) secretion is regulated by DA, norepinephrine (NE), and serotonin (5-HT) (51 for review). The determination of GH levels in blood has also been used as a tool to evaluate monoaminergic function in schizophrenia and to study the mechanism of action of psychotropic drugs, but it has not been employed for these purposes as extensively as prolactin secretion.

This chapter will review selected studies of prolactin and GH secretion which we believe are particularly relevant for the planning of research strategies in schizophrenia. Specific topics to be covered, after briefly discussing the central mechanism for the regulation of prolactin and GH secretion in man and laboratory rodents, are (a) assessment in schizophrenics of basal dopaminergic activity in the hypothalamic tuberoinfundibular dopaminergic (TIDA) neurons, the source of DA which tonically inhibits prolactin secretion by the pituitary; (b) assessment of DA receptor sensitivity by studies of the prolactin and GH response to DA agonists such as apomorphine and bromocriptine; (c) the relationship between clinical response to antipsychotic drugs and their effect on prolactin secretion; and (d) prolactin secretion as a means of studying various aspects of the action of classic neuroleptics, atypical neuroleptics such as sulpiride and metoclopramide, other antipsychotic drugs such as alpha-methylparatyrosine (AMPT), nondopaminergic, potential antipsychotic drugs such as trebenzomine, and psychotomimetic drugs such as LSD, amphetamine, and methylphenidate.

REGULATION OF PROLACTIN AND GROWTH HORMONE SECRETION

The secretion of most anterior pituitary hormones is regulated by hypothalamic peptidergic hormones which act as releasing factors or inhibiting factors at the pituitary after they are transported to the pituitary by the pituitary portal circulation (41). It has been known for many years that the primary hypothalamic means of regulating prolactin secretion is via an inhibitory factor (PIF) since hypothalamic ablation or severing the pituitary stalk caused a marked enhancement of prolactin secretion (4,39). The discovery that drugs which increase dopaminergic activity such as DA itself, L-DOPA, or DA agonists such as apomorphine and bromocriptine inhibit prolactin secretion whereas drugs which diminish dopaminergic activity such as the neuroleptics, reserpine, and AMPT increase serum prolactin levels (50,52,63) led to a prolonged inquiry into whether DA itself was the sole PIF, or a major PIF, acting at DA receptors in the pituitary. The majority of evidence supports the latter hypothesis (50). The demonstration that infusions of dopamine intravenously in man lower serum prolactin levels (45,63) and that there are high-affinity DA agonist binding sites on pituitary membranes (15) are more recent pieces of evidence in support of the direct DA action on the pituitary. Other neurotransmitters—such as serotonin, norepinephrine, and acetylcholine—their agonists and antagonists, sex steroids, and prostaglandins, enkephalins, endorphins, and vitamins (e.g., pyridoxine) have been demonstrated to inhibit or stimulate prolactin release *in vivo* in man and laboratory animals. Some of these substances, especially estrogens, appear to act through the dopaminergic regulation of prolactin secretion, but the physiologic significance of the other substance in regulating prolactin secretion is not known. It is beyond the purpose of this chapter to review these topics, most of which are exhaustively covered in the volume by Muller, Nistico, and Scapagnini (73).

Growth hormone secretion is controlled by two hypothalamic hormones, growth hormone releasing hormone (GHRH) and growth hormone release inhibiting hormone (GIH), somatostatin. The secretion of GIH and GHRH is, in turn, regulated by neurotransmitters (29,51,72). There is strong evidence that NE, DA, and 5-HT stimulate GH secretion in man (51). The action of DA on GH secretion appears to be in the hypothalamus, not at the pituitary or median eminence, since intravenous DA does not increase GH secretion in man (72,100). However, it should be noted that not all investigators agree on this latter issue (44).

BASAL PROLACTIN LEVELS AND RESPONSE TO DA ANTAGONISTS IN SCHIZOPHRENIA AND RELATED CONDITIONS

One of the first questions to be asked regarding DA function in schizophrenia was whether prolactin secretion is decreased in unmedicated schizophrenic patients. Since the DA hypothesis posits that there is increased activity of some dopaminergic neurons in some schizophrenics or increased sensitivity of at least some DA receptors (70,92), decreased serum prolactin levels might be expected if there was increased dopaminergic activity in the TIDA neurons or supersensitivity of pituitary DA receptors. Indeed, because of the possibility of decreased monoamine oxidase (MAO) activity in some schizophrenics (74), there is further reason to expect decreased plasma or serum prolactin levels because DA is a substrate of type A MAO (102). However, there is no evidence of decreased serum prolactin levels in single early morning samples from unmedicated schizophrenics (9,34,38,40,56,66,67,76,106). However, single early morning samples can be misleading, since prolactin secretion is episodic and is elevated during the latter part of sleep (80). As part of studies of the effect of initial drug administration on endocrine secretion, we have measured mid-morning serum prolactin levels. Three blood samples were obtained over a 20-min period, via an indwelling catheter, from unmedicated acute and chronic schizophrenic subjects as well as from normal controls (Table 1). There was no significant difference in mean serum prolactin levels between the three groups. Several of the acute schizophrenic females had very high prolactin levels. We attributed this to stress since early morning serum prolactin levels in the same subjects were within normal limits. Similar data have been reported by Ettigi et al. (27) and Rotrosen et al. (84). Furthermore, prolactin samples obtained at 30-min intervals over a 4- to 18-hr period in six unmedicated schizophrenics did not differ from those of comparable normal controls (63). Rather than decreased prolactin levels, some studies have found slight increases in serum prolactin levels in unmedicated, newly admitted schizophrenic patients (34,38,65). Elevated prolactin levels in early morning blood samples from newly admitted psychiatric patients may be due to the persistent effects of neuroleptic drugs, sleep-induced prolactin elevations, stress, or a primary pituitary abnormality such as an adenoma.

TABLE 1. *Catheter study baseline serum prolactin levels in unmedicated schizophrenic patients*

Group	Serum prolactin levels (ng/ml)	
	Males	Females
Controls	27.9 ± 14.0 (13)[a]	23.0 ± 5.5 (12)
Chronic schizophrenics	24.5 ± 14.8 (21)	31.5 ± 23.0 (14)
Acute schizophrenics	35.5 ± 9.8 (2)	37.5 ± 30.8 (10)

[a] Number of subjects.

A comparison of the effects of 50 mg (approximately 0.6–1.1 mg/kg) of intramuscular (i.m.) chlorpromazine (CPZ) on serum prolactin levels provides additional evidence that there is not excessive dopaminergic activity in the TIDA neurons of schizophrenics (Fig. 1). The increase in serum prolactin levels was not significantly different in male schizophrenics and male normal controls. Had increased dopaminergic activity been present in the patients, we should have found a smaller increase in serum prolactin levels in the patients. These results are in agreement with previous data of ours (63) and of Gruen et al. (35), who gave their subjects 25 mg of i.m. CPZ. However, recent work by our group (54) indicates no difference in prolactin secretion after 25 and 50 mg of i.m. CPZ, suggesting that 25 mg of i.m. CPZ produces maximal prolactin stimulation in most subjects.

It is possible that smaller doses of CPZ, in combination with an analysis of effective levels of the drug in blood, may reveal differences in prolactin response between patients and controls. Even if there is no increased dopaminergic activity in the TIDA neurons, this does not rule out increased dopaminergic activity in other DA neurons, such as the mesolimbic and mesocortical DA neurons, which have been specifically implicated in the pathophysiology of schizophrenia (94).

GH levels have been found to be within normal limits in unmedicated schizophrenics (27,56,79,85,97; H. Y. Meltzer, D. A. Busch, and V. S. Fang, *unpublished data*).

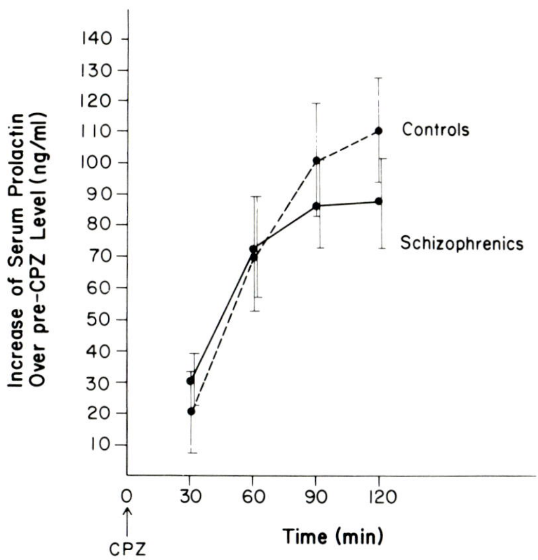

FIG. 1. Effect of 50 mg chlorpromazine (CPZ) on serum prolactin levels. Increase in serum prolactin levels over baseline following injection of CPZ 50 mg, i.m., at $t = 0$ in 14 male chronic schizophrenics and 6 normal controls.

There have been only limited studies of serum prolactin and GH levels in schizophrenics during sleep. There is strong evidence of sleep cycle-related increases in both GH and prolactin secretion in man (80,81). Unmedicated chronic schizophrenic patients have been reported to have no sleep-related GH increase, whereas one acute schizophrenic did have the expected increase (16,101). GH secretion during sleep has also been reported to be flat in patients with endogenous depression (89). We have reported a normal sleep-related prolactin rise and a flat GH curve in two chronic schizophrenic patients treated with fluphenazine decanoate (63). However, Syvälahti and Pekkarainen (95) reported that, of 10 chronic schizophrenics treated with neuroleptics, 4 had a high sleep-induced GH response, 4 had a moderate peak GH response, and 2 had no response. It is conceivable that neuroleptic treatment normalized GH secretion during sleep in the latter study. Takahashi et al. (96) have previously reported that a low dose of CPZ, 30 mg, did not inhibit the sleep-related rise in GH levels in plasma.

Pharmacologic studies of the neurotransmitter systems which regulate the GH and prolactin surges during sleep are few and do not provide a coherent picture of which neurotransmitters are involved (see 98 for refs.); thus only limited speculation is possible about the cause(s) of the flat GH curve during sleep which has been found in some unmedicated and medicated schizophrenic patients. GH secretion during sleep was not markedly influenced by intravenous infusion of L-DOPA to 6 normal volunteers, whereas the episodic release of prolactin and rapid eye movement sleep was suppressed. Thus it is unlikely that dopaminergic mechanisms play an important role in the genesis of sleep-related GH secretion (18). Acute haloperidol had no effect on the increase in GH secretion during sleep (20). Results of studies of the effect of 5-HT on GH secretion in sleep are conflicting, e.g., cypropheptadine decreases whereas methysergide enhances the sleep-related GH secretion (18,71). Although both drugs are serotonin receptor blockers, both have multiple other effects. Therefore, these drugs may not be considered definitive probes. Tryptophan, 100 mg/kg for 2 to 4 days, had no effect on GH secretion during sleep in normal controls or schizophrenics (16). There is some evidence that gonadal steroids (48) and free fatty acids (47,48) can inhibit GH secretion during sleep.

In summary, studies of early morning, midmorning, and continuous sampling of serum prolactin and GH levels in unmedicated chronic and acute schizophrenics provide little if any evidence for abnormalities of the TIDA neurons or those hypothalamic and pituitary DA receptors which are relevant to prolactin and GH secretion. No further investigation of this issue seems warranted. However, investigation of basal serum prolactin levels in relation to issues of stress, psychopathology, and eventual response to neuroleptic drugs may prove of interest. Furthermore, a study of the effect of low doses of neuroleptics, e.g., 0.20 mg/kg of CPZ i.m., is required for a more valid study of prolactin output following DA receptor blockade in schizophrenics and controls. Ideally, blood levels of the neuroleptic and major active metabolites should also be measured.

The preliminary evidence that GH secretion is abnormal during sleep in some schizophrenics also seems worthy of further investigation along with neuropharmacologic studies to understand the mechanism of sleep-related GH surges in man. This information might illuminate which, if any, neurotransmitters are abnormal in schizophrenics in those neural systems which regulate the GH surges during sleep.

DOPAMINERGIC AGONISTS AS PROBES IN NEUROENDOCRINE STUDIES

Measurement of the prolactin and GH response following the administration of direct DA agonists such as apomorphine, the indirect DA agonist, *d*-amphetamine, or the precursor of DA, L-DOPA, to schizophrenic patients and controls may permit the assessment of a variety of dopaminergic parameters. The magnitude of the decrease in prolactin levels following apomorphine may reflect the sensitivity of pituitary DA receptors. The prolactin response to *d*-amphetamine may, in addition, reflect the intactness of the mechanisms of release of newly synthesized DA from neurons and the metabolism of DA following its release. The prolactin response to L-DOPA may further reflect the absorption of L-DOPA, its decarboxylation to DA, and the release and metabolism of DA. Pituitary stores of prolactin, prolactin clearance rates, and activity of other neurotransmitters may also influence the net decrease in prolactin following these drug treatments and might be either the partial or entire cause of any abnormalities found or serve to compensate for any abnormalities in dopaminergic mechanisms. Similar considerations apply to the effect of these drugs on GH secretion in schizophrenia with the following modifications: (a) the DA receptors related to changes in GH levels are present in the hypothalamus rather than the pituitary; (b) the increase in GH due to *d*-amphetamine appears to be based on a noradrenergic mechanism rather than a dopaminergic mechanism (87,88).

There have been several studies comparing the effect of apomorphine on serum GH and prolactin secretion in schizophrenics and normal controls. In a pilot study we reported that the effects of a subcutaneous injection of 0.75 mg apomorphine on peak GH levels and the nadir of serum prolactin was not significantly different in 7 unmedicated chronic schizophrenic patients from that of 10 normal controls (53).

Ettigi et al. (27) studied a group of chronically hospitalized chronic schizophrenics. Of 17 patients, 8 showed an inadequate GH peak (< 6 ng/ml) following 0.75 mg apomorphine. All 21 control subjects showed a peak GH response of > 9 ng/ml. Four schizophrenic subjects with tardive dyskinesia showed essentially no GH response to apomorphine. Ettigi found a significant relationship between GH peak and duration of previous neuroleptic treatment ($r = 0.48$, $p < 0.10$). There was no difference in serum prolactin response to apomorphine between schizophrenics and control subjects in this study.

Rotrosen et al. (84–86) studied GH and serum prolactin response to apomorphine and L-DOPA in a group of recently admitted, floridly psychotic chronic schizophrenics. They found no difference in mean GH peak, after 0.50 mg of apomorphine, between 22 schizophrenics and 9 control subjects. However, the distribution of responses in the two groups differed significantly, with controls tending to cluster about the mean and schizophrenics tending toward a bimodal distribution. As in the Ettigi study, Rotrosen et al. (84) found a negative correlation between GH response to apomorphine and years of neuroleptic treatment, although they did not state whether this finding is statistically significant.

After apomorphine, Rotrosen et al. (86) found that serum prolactin suppression was of lower magnitude in 17 chronic schizophrenics than in 10 control subjects.

Tamminga et al. (97) examined the effect of 0.75 mg of apomorphine and 500 g of L-DOPA on GH and prolactin in controls and in chronic schizophrenics, many with tardive dyskinesia, after a 5-day drug-free period. GH response to apomorphine tended to be lower in the chronic schizophrenics than in controls. After L-DOPA, 7 of 9 schizophrenic subjects had an abnormally low GH response to L-DOPA (< 5 ng/ml) compared with 2 of 11 controls ($p < 0.02$). Prolactin suppression after apomorphine was greater than 20% in 3 of 11 chronic schizophrenics and 5 of 5 controls ($p < 0.02$). The suppression in prolactin secretion after L-DOPA was greater than 50% in 0 of 9 schizophrenics and 6 of 6 controls.

Pandey et al. (79) studied GH response to 0.75 mg of apomorphine in a group of acute and chronic schizophrenics and normal controls. The patients had been drug free for 2 to 3 weeks at the time of the study. The mean GH peak was significantly higher in 21 acute schizophrenics than in 14 chronic schizophrenics ($p < 0.01$) or in 16 normal controls ($p < 0.01$). There was essentially no difference in GH response of controls and chronic schizophrenics.

Brambilla et al. (10) reported no GH response to apomorphine in 3 chronic schizophrenics, but they obtained their blood samples 12 hr after administration, which is too long for evaluation of the response.

We have now studied serum prolactin and GH levels in 15 normal controls and 18 schizophrenic patients who received 0.75 mg of apomorphine. Patients involved in the study were for the most part newly admitted, floridly psychotic acute and chronic schizophrenics by Research Diagnostic Criteria. In our study, the magnitude of the GH response was considered to be the area between the base-line and the 3-hr postapomorphine serum GH curve. The magnitude of the prolactin response was considered to be the area between the base-line and the 3-hr postapomorphine serum prolactin curve. For prolactin, all values for each subject were divided by the mean of three preapomorphine serum prolactin values for that subject before calculation of area under the curve.

We found no significant difference between control subjects, acute and chronic schizophrenics in prolactin or GH response to apomorphine. However, we found that among the chronic schizophrenics, there was a significant correlation between GH response and years since onset of illness ($r = 0.67$, df $= 11$, $p < 0.05$). When we reexamined the data by dividing the schizophrenic subjects into two groups, those ill less than 4 years and those ill 4 or more years, an analysis of variance showed significant group differences: mean GH response was 13.9 ± 12.6 (SD) for 15 controls; 30.5 ± 23.2 for 11 patients ill less than 4 years, and 7.3 ± 5.1 for 7 patients ill 4 years or more ($F = 5.33$, $p < 0.05$). Post hoc testing revealed that GH response was significantly greater in schizophrenics ill less than 4 years than in those ill 4 years or more. There was a strong trend for schizophrenics ill less than 4 years to have a larger GH response than controls, whereas those ill 4 or more years tended to have a smaller GH response than controls. These data agree with those obtained by Pandey et al. (79) who found that the GH response to apomorphine was greater in acute schizophrenics than in controls. They agree also with those published by Ettigi et al. (27) who found GH response in a group of chronic schizophrenics with long duration of illness to be less than that in controls.

Many hypotheses could explain these findings. One possibility is that schizophrenics with illness of shorter duration have supersensitive DA receptors, whereas the more chronically ill schizophrenics have subsensitive DA receptors. This hypothesis fits well with reports concerning the effect of DA agonists on the clinical status of acute and chronic schizophrenics. DA agonists such as amphetamine, methylphenidate, and L-DOPA have been reported to exacerbate psychotic symptoms in acutely psychotic patients (3,12,36). Other investigators have reported improvement in mainly chronic schizophrenics with defect symptoms following L-DOPA, with or without a peripheral decarboxylase inhibitor (2,10,19,30,31). There was also a large number of Japanese studies with similar findings which we have reviewed elsewhere (70). Further studies are required to determine if the clinical state, and the GH response to DA agonists, which appears to be a function of duration of illness, are, in fact, correlated with each other, perhaps on the basis of altered receptor sensitivity.

Postmortem studies on chronic schizophrenics argue against decreased DA receptor sensitivity in chronic schizophrenics. Increases in the number of ^{3}H-neuroleptic binding sites in the striatum and nucleus accumbens of decreased chronic schizophrenics have been reported (46,78). This is consistent with a DA receptor supersensitivity, possibly the consequence of chronic administration of neuroleptics. No comparable studies of hypothalamic or pituitary DA receptors in schizophrenics have been published.

There is thus conflicting evidence as to whether some types of schizophrenics have some DA receptors which are supersensitive or subsensitive, or perhaps a mixture of both (along with the DA receptors of unchanged sensitivity). Major problems here are associated with interpretation of cause and effect, drug effects, and adaptation to other neuronal changes in these studies. It is possible that the apparently favorable clinical response of some chronic schizophrenics to L-DOPA may reflect basic deficiencies of DA, on the basis of which DA receptors in the caudate and nucleus accumbens become more sensitive. Hypothalamic

DA receptors which mediate the apomorphine effect on GH may become subsensitive in chronic schizophrenics, leading to the lower GH response; the opposite may be true for acute schizophrenics.

SERUM PROLACTIN LEVELS AS A PREDICTOR OF CLINICAL RESPONSE

It is unquestionably desirable to have laboratory methods which can predict the optimal dose of an antipsychotic agent for a given patient. Such methods could be utilized to determine when optimal dosage had been achieved, or to indicate that no further clinical benefit would be attained by a further increase in dosage, even if a full clinical response was not apparent. This goal has been achieved for lithium carbonate, in that the therapeutic range of serum levels for the treatment of mania has been defined.

There is some evidence that steady-state plasma levels of neuroleptics and clinical response may be correlated (104), but there is also evidence to the contrary (24). The concentrations of active metabolites derived from the metabolism of most neuroleptics are not measured in most studies relating blood levels to antipsychotic effect. This is one factor which may contribute to the difficulty in obtaining expected results in such studies. Another factor may be the wide range of drug levels that may be therapeutic for different individuals.

We have felt it would be worthwhile to explore serum prolactin levels as a predictor of clinical response to neuroleptic drugs for several reasons: (a) the methodology for prolactin determination is readily available in major hospitals and commercial laboratories (these assays are reasonable in cost, and more reliable, at least within laboratories, than the determination of neuroleptic levels in plasma); (b) the changes in prolactin levels in plasma represent a physiological response to neuroleptics by the subject and thus give more information than just measuring the level of the drug itself; (c) since all active metabolites of a drug will stimulate prolactin secretion, an index of all relevant metabolic species, not just the parent compound, is obtained. Thus it is reasonable to determine whether changes in serum prolactin levels during treatment with neuroleptics will correlate with the extent of clinical improvement.

We have administered CPZ 50 mg intramuscularly to 40 schizophrenic patients. The peak prolactin levels in males and females following this dose were not significantly different. The correlations between peak prolactin levels following these injections and early morning prolactin levels while receiving CPZ 200 mg b.i.d. were not significant for either males ($N = 18$) or females ($N = 22$) ($r = 0.06$, and 0.03, respectively). The peak increase in serum PRL levels following 50 mg CPZ was significantly correlated with the decrease in total score of the Brief Psychiatric Rating Scale (BPRS) (77) ($r = -0.42$, $N = 32$, $p < 0.05$) following one week of treatment with chlorpromazine, 200 mg p.o. One possible explanation of the negative correlation between prolactin response and clinical response to neuroleptics may be related to the likelihood that a lower prolactin response reflects increased DA release from the TIDA. This could be correlated with increased dopaminergic activity in the mesolimbic and limbic cortical dopaminergic pathways. Such patients might be the ones whose psychotic symptoms are most responsive to neuroleptics. Patients without marked excesses of limbic dopaminergic activity might be psychotic on a nondopaminergic basis and therefore be less likely to improve on neuroleptics. Such studies are likely to be meaningful provided that the dose of neuroleptic does not exceed 600 mg CPZ or its equivalent and that the data for males and females are considered separately (see Fig. 2).

With classic neuroleptics of the phenothiazine and butyrophenone series, there

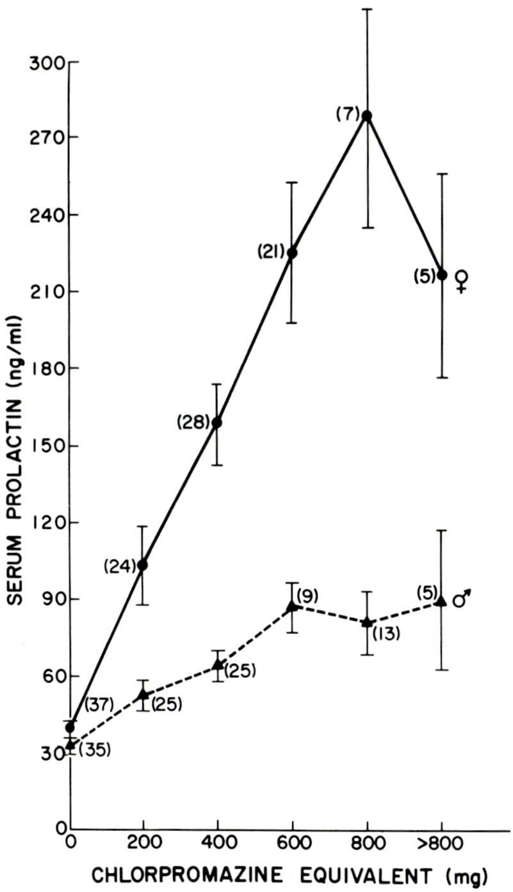

FIG. 2. Dose-response curve for neuroleptic-induced increase in morning serum prolactin levels. Patients were treated with chlorpromazine, thioridazine, fluphenazine, or haloperidol on a b.i.d. schedule. Blood levels of prolactin were obtained after at least 1 week at each dose level, 12 hr after the last dose. All dosages were converted to CPZ equivalents according to Davis (23). Number of subjects is in parentheses.

is a good dose-response relationship between morning serum prolactin levels and neuroleptic doses up to 600 mg/day of CPZ or its equivalent (63) (Fig. 2). These serum prolactin levels were obtained 11 hr after the last drug dose which was one-half the total daily dose. Identical results have been reported by Wode-Helgodt et al. (106). Other investigators have concluded that the prolactin system is totally disinhibited by doses of neuroleptics that are far below therapeutic levels (35). Usually these conclusions were based on acute studies in which serum prolactin levels were monitored for 2 to 6 hr after oral or intramuscular administration. Our studies are based on chronic administration of drugs and examination of the prolactin levels at steady state prior to the next oral dose. This is standard practice in most clinical pharmacological studies. In clinical practice, 600 mg CPZ or its equivalent is a therapeutic dose for most hospitalized schizophrenic patients. Thus serum prolactin levels can be utilized in most schizophrenics to follow their response to almost all dosage levels of neuroleptics.

Since there is a good correlation between serum prolactin levels and blood levels of classic neuroleptics (57), there is reason to expect that serum prolactin levels may be useful as a means of relating blood levels of neuroleptics to clinical response.

A positive correlation has been found in one study between clinical response and serum prolactin levels for males but not for females (56), and a significant correlation between improvement in psychosis levels and serum prolactin levels in another study (8). Wode-Helgodt et al. (105,106) randomly assigned newly admitted schizophrenic patients to CPZ in fixed doses of 200, 400, 600 mg/day and found a good correlation between dose and prolactin levels for males and females. All three doses were equally effective, but there were fewer dropouts and a more rapid response to the higher dose. Clinical response and plasma levels of CPZ were not well correlated. It is probable that prolactin levels were better correlated than blood levels of CPZ with clinical response because the prolactin response is affected not only by CPZ but also by the active metabolites of CPZ (58). In a study of the antipsychotic efficacy of thiethylperazine in 10 newly admitted schizophrenic patients, Rotrosen et al. (84) found the lowest serum prolactin in two patients who failed to respond ($25.0 \pm$ SD, 3.6 ng/ml) and much higher levels (46.3 ± 18.6 ng/ml) in 8 patients who showed marked improvement. Öhman and Axelsson (76) reported that there was a significant correlation between antipsychotic effect and relative serum prolactin levels in 23 schizophrenic patients when prolactin levels and clinical response were expressed as a percentage of the total change, but a poor correlation was obtained when absolute prolactin levels and change in psychosis ratings were compared. Cotes et al. (22) found a weak correlation between clinical change and prolactin levels following α-flupenthixol treatment, but these investigators combined the data from males and females and from four dosage levels of drug treatment. This pooling of data could easily have confounded any existing relationship between the two parameters of interest. Gruen et al. (34) compared change in serum prolactin (from a baseline level) at 3 and 6 weeks of treatment with changes in total BPRS scores. They found no significant correlation in 15 and 12 patients at 3 and 6 weeks, respectively. This study differs from those of Meltzer and Fang (56) and Wode-Helgodt et al. (106) in that fixed doses were not employed and the doses used in the nonresponders were sufficiently large that they were likely to disinhibit maximally prolactin secretion (e.g., 75 to 150 mg loxapine and 40 to 60 mg butaperazine).

Although serum prolactin levels appear to be useful for predicting clinical responses, further studies with lower fixed doses of neuroleptics are needed. Specifically early morning prolactin levels and the prolactin AUC should be studied as potential correlates of clinical response after the oral administration of CPZ in doses no higher than 200 to 300 mg (one-half total daily dose). If a strong correlation were found, such studies might be valuable in indicating whether further treatment with neuroleptics is likely to lead to additional clinical improvement.

It is also desirable to be able to predict optimal dosage levels of drugs after a test dose. It has been possible to do this with lithium carbonate (21), and there is some evidence (25,33) that by monitoring drug levels after a test dose of neuroleptics, one can predict the average plasma drug level during continuous drug treatment. However, there is no evidence that blood levels of neuroleptics after a test dose can predict optimal dose of the drug or clinical response.

It is worth exploring whether changes in serum prolactin levels after a test dose of neuroleptic can predict the degree of clinical response or optimal dosage during continuous neuroleptic treatment.

PROLACTIN SECRETION AS A TOOL FOR STUDYING PSYCHOTROPIC DRUG ACTION

The ability of single intramuscular injections of antipsychotic DA receptor blockers—namely, haloperidol, thiothixene, fluphenazine, perphenazine, trifluoperazine, prochlorperazine, and chlorpromazine—to stimulate prolactin secretion is highly correlated with their antipsychotic potency ($r=0.95$, $p<0.01$) (43).

We have reported similar data following chronic administration of many of these drugs (63) and that the effect of 10 neuroleptics on rat prolactin secretion is significantly correlated with their antipsychotic effect ($r=0.865$, $p<0.05$) (63). These results are consistent with the hypothesis that antipsychotic action of the neuroleptics is based on DA receptor blockade.

There are, however, some quantitative relationships between prolactin secretion and antipsychotic potency which deviate from the relationship described above. Thus clozapine stimulates prolactin secretion in the rat *in vivo* (55), but its potency is weaker than would be expected from its clinical potency. In man, clozapine has an extremely limited ability to stimulate prolactin secretion (69). Similarly, RMI-81,528, which is a morphanthridine chemically related to clozapine, has potent antipsychotic effects and like clozapine has a diminished ability to stimulate prolactin secretion in man compared to classic neuroleptics (68). Melperone is a butyrophenone whose antipsychotic potency in comparison with its ability to stimulate prolactin secretion in man exceeds that of thiothixene, a typical neuroleptic (5). Finally, trebenzomine is an antipsychotic drug which has no antidopaminergic properties in various animal models and also does not stimulate prolactin secretion in man (59). It has a slight effect on rat prolactin secretion. Conversely, sulpiride and metoclopramide, two substituted benzamide-type drugs which are very weak DA receptor blockers, have documented antipsychotic activity albeit at relatively high doses (comparable to chlorpromazine) (93) but can stimulate prolactin secretion maximally at far lower doses than are necessary for their antipsychotic effect (69).

We have found a significant correlation between the effect of neuroleptic drugs on rat prolactin secretion and their ability to displace ^{3}H-spiroperidol from specific binding sites in the rat pituitary (Fig. 3) (69). However, it is apparent that sulpiride and metaclopramide, and to an extent loxapine, are far more potent in stimulating rat prolactin secretion *in vivo* than would be anticipated by their ability to displace ^{3}H-spiroperidol from specific binding sites. The ability of the other drugs studied, including clozapine and RMI-81,582, to stimulate rat prolactin secretion is correlated with their ability to displace ^{3}H-spiroperidol from specific binding sites.

These clinical and laboratory results suggest that there are significant differences in the potency of antipsychotic drugs for different DA receptors. Some DA receptor blocking drugs (e.g., sulpiride and metoclopramide) appear to be relatively more potent at the pituitary DA receptor than in the basal ganglia, mesolimbic region or mesocortical region, whereas other drugs (melperone, clozapine, RMI-81,582) have weak effects at the pituitary and basal ganglia (as evidenced by low extrapyramidal effects) but are relatively much more potent antipsychotic agents (6,7,64,90). It is possible that at least some drugs (such as trebenzomine) may achieve their antipsychotic effect or their ability to stimulate prolactin secretion via a mechanism other than their ability to block DA receptors.

Neuroendocrine studies have contributed to the testing of the DA hypothesis of schizophrenia by utilizing the effect of neuroleptics on prolactin secretion for measuring the time course of DA receptor blockade. We demonstrated (56) that pituitary DA receptor blockade was maximal shortly after initiating treatment with neuroleptics and that blockade of that DA receptor was terminated rapidly (within 2 to 4 days at most) after halting neuroleptic treatment. These findings have been confirmed by many investigators, and most likely apply to limbic and striatal DA receptors as well. The rapidity of onset and cessation of DA receptor blockade contrasts with a much slower remission of psychotic symptoms in most patients after starting treatment with neuroleptics and the much slower relapse rate when neuroleptics are discontinued. If limbic DA receptors became supersensitive in man during neuroleptic treatment and if

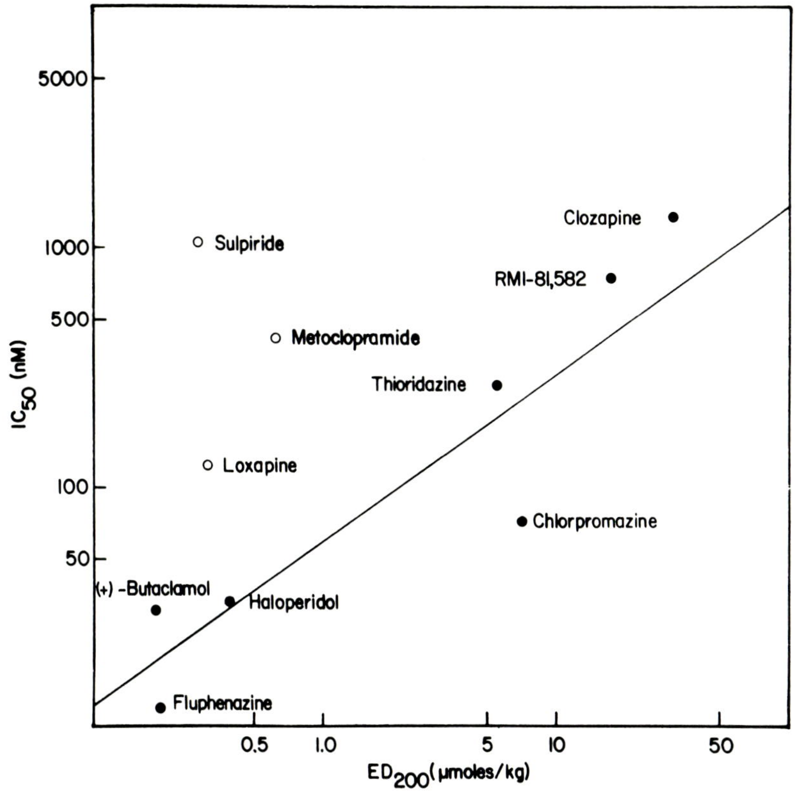

FIG. 3. Relationship between increase in plasma prolactin *in vivo* and ability to displace ^{3}H-spiroperidol from rat anterior pituitary. Correlation between the neuroleptic dose which doubles rat plasma prolactin levels (ED_{200}) and concentration of neuroleptic which produces 50% inhibition of ^{3}H-spiroperidol binding to rat anterior pituitary membranes (IC_{50}).

there were a persistent increase in DA turnover in limbic DA neurons following cessation of neuroleptic treatment, one would expect to find marked exacerbation of psychosis shortly after termination of treatment with neuroleptics. The near universal absence of this occurrence strongly argues against the relevance of the animal studies implicating dopaminergic neurons for a functional explanation of schizophrenia in man. This is not to deny the importance of reducing dopaminergic activity in treating schizophrenics. These considerations suggest only that DA receptor blockade is insufficient to explain the antipsychotic effect of neuroleptics and point up the need to study how interference with dopaminergic function affects other brain processes.

In support of the importance of DA to psychosis, we have confirmed the findings of Carlsson et al. (14) that AMPT can enhance the antipsychotic effect of neuroleptics. Similarly, we found that AMPT can potentiate the effect of neuroleptics on serum prolactin levels (65) (Fig. 4). AMPT, by inhibiting DA synthesis, may prevent the compensatory increase in DA turnover that occurs after neuroleptic treatment (13). The use of AMPT or the development of other tyrosine hydroxylase inhibitors as an adjunctive therapy to neuroleptic treatment is a strategy for the treatment of schizophrenia we believe should be vigorously investigated.

The effect of a single dose of AMPT, 1.0 g p.o., on serum prolactin levels in schizophrenics and normal controls was not significantly different, although there was a tendency for schizophrenics to have a somewhat higher prolactin response (Fig. 5). These results suggest that there is no marked difference in tyrosine hydroxylase activity in the TIDA neurons of schizophrenics and controls. Were there to be excessive amounts of tyrosine hydroxylase in the schizophrenics, we would have expected to find a smaller increase in serum prolactin levels after a standard dose of AMPT. Instead, the slight tendency for a larger increase is perhaps additional evidence that some schizophrenics may have diminished dopaminergic activity in some neural pathways.

In rats, there is a clear-cut difference in the effects of LSD, *d*-amphetamine, and methylphenidate on plasma prolactin on the one hand and indole hallucinogens such as *N,N*-dimethyltryptamine (*N,N*-DMT), mescaline, and 2,5-dimethoxy-4-methylamphetamine (DOM) on the other. LSD has a profoundly inhibitory effect on rat prolactin secretion through what appears to be a direct DA

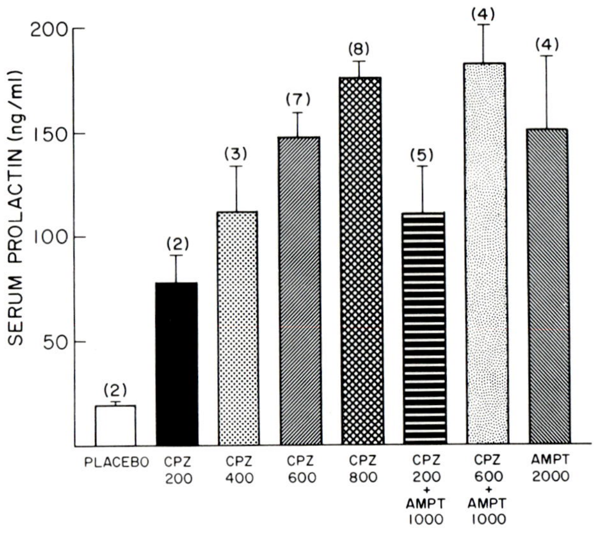

FIG. 4. Effect of chronic treatment with AMPT or CPZ or both on morning serum prolactin levels. Morning prolactin levels in a subject studied on placebo, 4 doses of CPZ alone (200–800 mg), CPZ + alpha-methylparatyrosine (AMPT) (1,000 mg), and AMPT alone (2,000 mg). Samples during drug treatment were obtained after at least 1 week on that regimen. (The number of samples obtained under each condition is in parentheses.)

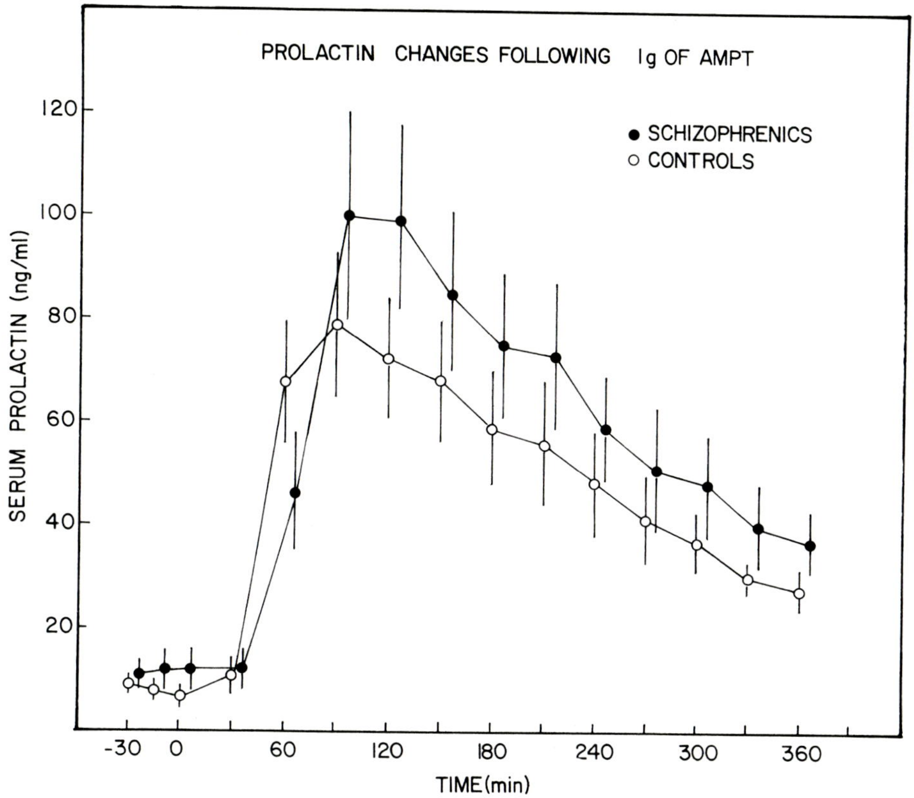

FIG. 5. Effect of AMPT on serum prolactin levels. The effect of a single dose of AMPT, 1.0 g p.o., on serum prolactin levels in schizophrenics and normal controls.

agonist mechanism (59). This is additional evidence that the psychotomimetic effects of LSD may be mediated by a dopaminergic mechanism rather than through 5-HT as had been concluded from previous studies (107). *d*-Amphetamine and methylphenidate also decrease rat plasma prolactin levels but by an indirect dopaminergic mechanism (60,83). On the other hand, the indole hallucinogens stimulate rat prolactin secretion through a direct serotonergic mechanism (61,62).

In man, there have been limited studies of the effect of these drugs on serum prolactin levels and the results are conflicting. Slater et al. (91) and Van Kammen et al. (99) reported that *d*-amphetamine increased serum prolactin levels in depressed patients and schizophrenics, respectively. We have administered 0.1 mg/kg *d*-amphetamine i.v. to 3 chronic drug abusers and 3 depressed patients (Meltzer and Fang, *unpublished data*). Very small decreases in serum prolactin were noted in 3 of the 6 subjects; none had increased serum prolactin levels. The discrepancies between these studies may be the result of subject differences, stress effects, or inadequate prolactin assays. In any event, further study is necessary to resolve the differences. Methylphenidate has been reported to produce no effect on serum prolactin in man (37). LSD, 0.1 mg i.v., also had no effect on serum prolactin levels in man (Meltzer, Goode, and Fang, *unpublished observations*). These last two findings, if replicated, indicate that the effects of direct and indirect DA agonists on prolactin secretion may be species dependent and differ significantly in man and rat.

There is good evidence that *d*-amphetamine can increase GH secretion in normal volunteers and that the GH response to *d*-amphetamine in schizophrenics does not differ from that of normal volunteers (42). The GH response to *d*-amphetamine has been reported to be reduced in endogenous depression (42), but the response to methamphetamine was found to be normal (17). The effect of *d*-amphetamine on GH secretion is believed to be due to its ability to stimulate NE release (88). Methylphenidate also increases GH serum levels in man (11). No data are available on the effect of methylphenidate on serum GH hormone in schizophrenia. We have found that LSD, 0.1 mg i.v., stimulated serum GH in 3 drug-using volunteers. The latter effect may be the result of LSD acting as an agonist for DA or 5-HT. Both of these effects have been described for LSD (see 60 for refs.) and either mechanism can stimulate GH secretion (51). Studies with LSD and specific DA or 5-HT receptor blockers could be useful in determining if either or both effects are involved.

The use of neuroendocrine responses to elucidate drug action will continue to be explored in the foreseeable future as a strategy for an understanding of the etiology of schizophrenia and its treatment. Only rarely will this approach provide definitive information about neurotransmitter mechanisms because of the many factors, known and unknown, which regulate the secretion and clearance of various hormones. However, the effect of drugs on the output of various hormones will permit us to determine the similarities and differences of many psychotropic drugs such as amantadine (28) and bromocriptine (26). Such information is vital for both clinical and theoretical purposes.

CONCLUSIONS AND RECOMMENDATIONS

Some of the neuroendocrine studies aimed at understanding the physiology of various neuronal systems in schizophrenics and the mechanism of action of psychotropic drugs have been reviewed. We have focused exclusively on what could be learned from pituitary hormone secretion, and indeed, have discussed only studies related to prolactin and growth hormone secretion. Other pituitary hormones such as thyrotropin stimulating hormone (TSH), adrenocorticotrophic hormone (ACTH), the gonadotrophins (FSH and LH), melanocyte stimulating hormone (MSH), oxytocin, and vasopressin have been omitted. At the present time, there is little important information concerning TSH, ACTH, FSH, LH, MSH, oxytocin, and vasopressin in schizophrenia. As the secretion of these substances is known to be centrally regulated, they too have the potential to be utilized to explore CNS physiology and the pharmacology of drug action in schizophrenics. Another frontier which is just beginning to be explored concerns the effect of hypothalamic releasing factors and anterior pituitary hormones on neuronal function and behavior (75). Whether any of the behavioral abnormalities of schizophrenia may be directly or indirectly related to the central actions of endocrine-related peptides is unknown. Insofar as the endorphins may be considered to be endocrine-related peptides, the great interest around their role in schizophrenia may be considered an example of the potential importance of further investigations in this area (103).

We have demonstrated in this review that prolactin and GH studies with schizophrenic patients already have yielded considerable information. Further investigations are clearly indicated to further define the prognostic value of the apomorphine-induced increase in GH secretion, the usefulness of prolactin secretion as a predictor or corollary of neuroleptic blood levels and clinical response, and to help illuminate the mechanism of action of atypical antipsychotic drugs and of psychotomimetic drugs. No other biological measures can so readily yield information in man regarding dopaminergic and possibly other neurotransmitter systems. It must, however, be kept in mind that this information is indirect and subject to influence by many factors. In this, neuroendocrine research is not alone. All clinical research has much the same limitations which accounts in no small measure for the enormous effort required to achieve even limited new information concerning schizophrenia.

ACKNOWLEDGMENTS

This work was supported in part by USPHS Grants MH29206 and MH30938 and by the State of Illinois, Department of Mental Health. H.Y.M. is recipient of RCSA MH47808.

REFERENCES

1. Aghajanian, G. K., and Haigler, H. I. (1975): Hallucinogenic indoleamines: Preferential action upon presynaptic serotonin receptors. *Psychopharmacol. Comm.,* 1:619–629.
2. Alpert, M., Friedhoff, A. J., Marcos, L. R., and Diamond, F. (1978): Paradoxical reaction to L-DOPA in schizophrenic patients. *Am. J. Psychiatry,* 135:1329–1332.
3. Angrist, B., Sathananthan, G., and Gershon, S. (1973): Behavioral effects of L-DOPA in schizophrenic patients. *Psychopharmacologia,* 31:1–12.
4. Arimura, A., Dunn, J. D., and Schally, A. V. (1972): Effect of infusion of hypothalamic extracts on serum prolactin levels in rats treated with Nembutal, CNS depressants, or bearing hypothalamic lesions. *Endocrinology,* 90:378–383.
5. Bjerkenstedt, L., Eneroth, P., Härnyrd, C., and Sedvall, G. (1977): Effects of melperone and thiothixene on prolactin levels in cerebrospinal fluid and plasma of psychotic women. *Arch. Psychiatr. Nervenkr.,* 224:281–293.
6. Bjerkenstedt, L., Gullberg, B., Härnryd, C., and Sedvall, G. (1979): Monoamine metabolite levels in cerebrospinal fluid of psychotic women treated with melperone or thiothixene. *Arch. Psychiatr. Nervenkr.,* 224:107–118.
7. Bjerkenstedt, L., Härnryd, C., Grimm, B., Gullberg, B., and Sedvall, G. (1978): A double-

blind comparison of melperone and thiothixene in psychotic women using a new rating scale, the CPRS. *Arch. Psychiatr. Nervenkr.*, 226:157–172.
8. Bowers, M. B., Jr., Heninger, C. R., and Meltzer, H. Y. (1979): Cerebrospinal fluid (CSF) homovanillic acid (HVA), cyclic adenosine mono-phosphate (cAMP), prolactin and serum prolactin in acute psychotic patients at two points during early chlorpromazine (CPZ) treatment. In: *Catecholamines: Basic and Clinical Frontiers. Vol. II,* edited by E. Usdin, I. J. Kopin, and J. Barchas, pp. 1893–1895. Pergamon Press, New York.
9. Brambilla, F., Guastalla, A., Guerrini, A., Rovere, C., Legnani, G., Sarno, M., and Riggi, F. (1976): Prolactin secretion in chronic schizophrenia. *Acta Psychiatr. Scand.*, 54:275–286.
10. Brambilla, F., Scarone, S., Ponzano, M., Maffei, C., Nobile, P., Rovere, C., and Guastalla, A. (1979): Catecholaminergic drugs in chronic schizophrenia. *Neuropsychobiology,* 5:185–200.
11. Brown, W. A., Corriveau, D. P., and Ebert, M. A. (1978): Acute psychologic and neuroendocrine effects of dextroamphetamine and methylphenidate. *Psychopharmacology,* 58:189–195.
12. Calil, H. M., Yessavage, J. A., and Hollister, L. E. (1977): Low dosage levodopa in schizophrenia. *Commun. Psychopharmacol.*, 1:593–596.
13. Carlsson, A., and Lindquist, M. (1963): Effect of chlorpromazine or haloperidol on the formation of 3-methoxytyramine and normetanephrine in mouse brain. *Acta Pharmacol. Toxicol.*, 20:140–144.
14. Carlsson, A., Persoon, T., Roos, B. E., and Walinder, J. (1972): Potentiation of phenothiazines by α-methyltyrosine in treatment of chronic schizophrenia. *J. Neurol. Transm.*, 33:83–90.
15. Caron, M. G., Beaulieu, M., Raymond, V., Gange, B., Drouin, J., Lefkowitz, R. J., and Labrie, F. (1978): Dopaminergic receptors in the anterior pituitary gland: Correlation of (^{3}H)dihydroergocryptine binding with the dopaminergic control of prolactin release. *J. Biol. Chem.*, 253:2244–2253.
16. Cerone, B., Murri, L., Fantasia, L., Muratorio, A., Frioli, F., and Isidor, A. (1974): Effect of tryptophan on human growth hormone release in sleep. 2nd Europ. Cong. Sleep Res., Rome, pp. 332–335.
17. Checkley, S. A. (1979): Corticosteroid and growth hormone responses to methyamphetamine in depressive illness. *Psycholog. Med.*, 9:107–115.
18. Chihara, K., Kato, Y., Maede, K., Ohgo, S., and Imura, H. (1976): Suppressive effects of L-DOPA on human prolactin release during sleep. *Acta Endocrinol. (Kbh.),* 81:19–27.
19. Chouinard, G., and Jones, B. D. (1978): Schizophrenia as dopamine deficiency disease. *Lancet,* 2:99–100.
20. Clarenbach, P., Prunkl, R., Riegler, M., and Cramer, H. (1978): Effects of haloperidol on afternoon sleep and on the secretion of growth hormone in man. *Neuroscience,* 3:345–348.
21. Cooper, T. B., Bergner, R. E. E., and Simpson, G. M. (1973): The 24-hour serum lithium level as a prognosticator of dosage requirements. *Am. J. Psychiatry,* 130:601–603.
22. Cotes, P. M., Crow, T. J., Johnstone, E. C., Bartlett, W., and Bourne, R. C. (1978): Neuroendocrine changes in acute schizophrenia as a function of clinical state and neuroleptic medication. *Psychol. Med.,* 8:657–665.
23. Davis, J. M. (1974): Dose equivalence of the anti-psychotic drugs. *J. Psychiatr. Res.,* 11:65–69.
24. Davis, J. M., Erickson, S., and Dekirmenjan, H. (1978): Plasma levels of antipsychotic drugs and clinical response. In: *Psychopharmacology: A Generation of Progress,* edited by M. A. Lipton, A. Mascio, and K. F. Killam, pp. 905–916. Raven Press, New York.
25. Davis, J. M., Janowsky, D. S., Sekerke, H. J., Maniei, H., and Khaled el-Yousef, M. (1974): The pharmacokinetics of butaperazine in serum. In: *The Phenothiazine and Structurally Related Drugs,* edited by I. S. Forrest, C. J. Carr, and E. Usdin, pp. 433–443. Raven Press, New York.
26. DiChiara, G., Porceddu, M. L., Vargiu, L., Argiolas, A., and Gessa, G. L. (1976): Evidence for dopamine receptors mediating sedations in the mouse brain. *Nature,* 264:564–567.
27. Ettigi, P., Nau, N. P. V., Lal, S., Cervantes, P., and Guyda, H. (1976): Effect of apomorphine on growth hormone and prolactin secretion in schizophrenic patients, with or without oral dyskinesia, withdrawn from chronic neuroleptic therapy. *J. Neurol. Neurosurg. Psychiatry,* 39:870–876.
28. Farnebo, L., Fuxe, K., Goldstein, M., Hamberger, B., and Ungerstedt, U. (1971): Dopamine and noradrenaline releasing action of amantadine in the central and peripheral neurons systems: A possible mode of action in Parkinson's disease. *Eur. J. Pharmacol.,* 16:27–38.

29. Ganong, W. F. (1975): Brain amines and the control of ACTH and growth hormone secretion. In: *Hypothalamic Hormones,* edited by M. Motta, P. G. Crosignani, and L. Martini, pp. 237–248. Academic Press, New York.
30. Garfinkel, P. E., and Stancer, H. C. (1976): L-DOPA and schizophrenia. *Can. Psychiatr. Assoc. J.,* 21:27–29.
31. Gerlach, J., and Luhdorf, K. (1975): The effect of L-DOPA on young patients with simple schizophrenia, treated with neuroleptic drugs. *Psychopharmacologia,* 44:105–110.
32. Germer, R. M., Post, R. M., and Bunney, W. E., Jr. (1976): A dopaminergic mechanism in mania. *Am. J. Psychiatry,* 133:1177–1180.
33. Gottschalk, L. A., Dinovo, E., Bener, R., Birch, H., Syben, M., and Noble, E. P. (1976): Plasma levels of mesoridazine and its metabolites and clinical responses in acute schizophrenia after a single intramuscular drug dosage. In: *Pharmacokinetics of Psychoactive Drugs,* edited by L. A. Gottschalk and S. Merkis, pp. 171–189. Spectrum Publications, New York.
34. Gruen, P. H., Sachar, E. J., Altman, N., Langer, G., Tabrizi, M. A., and Halpern, F. S. (1978): Relation of plasma prolactin to clinical response in schizophrenic patients. *Arch. Gen. Psychiatry,* 35:1222–1227.
35. Gruen, P. H., Sachar, E. J., Langer, G., Aman, N., Leifer, M., Frantz, A., and Halpern, G. S. (1978): Prolactin response to neuroleptics in normal and schizophrenic subjects. *Arch. Gen. Psychiatry,* 35:108–116.
36. Janowsky, D. S., and Davis, J. M. (1974): Dopamine, psychomotor stimulants, and schizophrenia: Effects of methylphenidate and the stereoisomers of amphetamine in schizophrenia. In: *Neuropsychopharmacology of Monoamines and Their Regulatory Enzymes,* edited by E. Usdin, pp. 317–323. Raven Press, New York.
37. Janowsky, D. S., Leichner, P., Parker, D., Judd, L., Huey, L., and Clopton, P. (1978): Methylphenidate and serum prolactin in man. *Psychopharmacology,* 58:43–47.
38. Johnstone, E. C., Crow, T. J., and Mashiter, K. (1977): Anterior pituitary hormone secretion in chronic schizophrenia—an approach to neurohumoral mechanisms. *Psychol. Med.,* 7:223–228.
39. Kanematsu, S., and Sawyer, C. H. (1973): Elevation of plasma prolactin after hypophyseal stalk section in the rat. *Endocrinology,* 93:238–241.
40. Kolakowska, T., Wiles, D. H., Gelder, M. G., and McNeilly, A. S. (1976): Clinical significance of plasma chlorpromazine levels. III. Plasma levels of the drug, some of its metabolites and prolactin in patients receiving long-term phenothiazine treatment. *Psychopharmacology,* 49:101–107.
41. Krulich, L., and Fawcett, C. P. (1977): The hypothalamic hypophysiotropic hormone. *Int. Rev. Physiol. Endocrine Physiol.,* 16:35–92.
42. Langer, G., Heinze, G., Rerin, B., and Matussek, N. (1976): Reduced growth hormone responses to amphetamine in "endogenous" depressive patients. *Arch. Gen. Psychiatry,* 33:1471–1475.
43. Langer, G., Sachar, E. J., Gruen, P. H., and Halpern, F. S. (1977): Human prolactin responses to neuroleptic drugs correlate with antischizophrenic potency. *Nature,* 266:639–640.
44. Langer, G., Sachar, E. J., and Halpern, F. S. (1978): Effect of dopamine and neuroleptics on plasma growth hormone and prolactin in normal men. *Psychoneuroendocrinology,* 3:165–169.
45. LeBlanc, H., Lacheliu, G. C. L., Abu-Fadil, S., and Yen, S. S. C. (1976): Effects of dopamine infusion on pituitary hormone secretion in humans. *J. Clin. Endocrinol. Metab.,* 43:668–674.
46. Lee, T., Seeman, P., Tourtellotte, W. W., Farley, I. J., and Hornykeiwicz, O. (1978): Binding of ^{3}H-neuroleptics and ^{3}H-apomorphine in schizophrenic brains. *Nature,* 274:897–900.
47. Lepman, R. L., Taylor, A. L., Schenk, A., and Mintz, D. H. (1972): Inhibition of sleep-related growth hormone release by elevated free fatty acids. *J. Clin. Endocrinol. Metab.,* 35:592–594.
48. Lucke, C., Adelman, N., and Glick, S. M. (1972): The effect of elevated free fatty acids (FFA) on the sleep-induced human growth hormone (HGH) peak. *J. Clin. Endocrinol. Metab.,* 35:407–412.
49. Lucke, C., and Glick, S. M. (1971): Effect of medroxyprogesterone acetate on the sleep-induced peak of growth hormone secretion. *J. Clin. Endocrinol.,* 33:851–853.
50. MacLeod, R. M. (1975): Regulation of prolactin secretion. In: *Frontiers in Neuroendocrinology,* edited by L. Martini and W. F. Ganong, pp. 169–194. Raven Press, New York.
51. Martin, J. B. (1976): Brain regulation of growth hormone secretion. In: *Frontiers in Neuroendo-*

crinology, Vol. 4, edited by L. Martini and W. F. Ganong, pp. 129–168. Raven Press, New York.

52. Meites, J., and Clemens, J. A. (1972): Hypothalamic control of prolactin secretion. *Vitam. Horm.,* 30:165–221.
53. Meltzer, H. Y., Goode, D. J., Fang, V. S., Schyve, P., and Young, M. (1976): Dopamine and schizophrenia. *Lancet,* 2:1142.
54. Meltzer, H. Y., Busch, D. A., Creese, I. A., Snyder, S. H., and Fang, V. S. (1980): Comparison of effects of chlorpromazine on serum prolactin levels in schizophrenic patients and normal controls: Correlation with serum neuroleptic levels. Submitted for publication.
55. Meltzer, H. Y., Daniels, S., and Fang, V. S. (1975): Clozapine increases rat serum prolactin levels. *Life Sci.,* 17:339–342.
56. Meltzer, H. Y., and Fang, V. S. (1976): The effect of neuroleptics on serum prolactin in schizophrenic patients. *Arch. Gen. Psychiatry,* 33:279–286.
57. Meltzer, H. Y., Fang, V. S., Fessler, R., Simonovic, D., and Stanisic, D. (1977): Neuroleptic-stimulated prolactin secretion in the rat as an animal model for biological psychiatry I. Comparison with anti-psychotic activity. In: *Animal Models of Mental Illnesses,* edited by E. Usdin and I. Hanini, pp. 443–455. Pergamon Press, New York.
58. Meltzer, H. Y., Fang, V. S., Simonovic, M., and Paul, S. M. (1977): Effect of metabolites of chlorpromazine on prolactin secretion in rats. *Psychopharmacology,* 51:181–183.
59. Meltzer, H. Y., Fessler, R. G., Simonovic, M., Doherty, J., and Fang, V. S. (1977): Lysergic acid diethylamide: Evidence for stimulation of pituitary dopamine receptors. *Psychopharmacology,* 54:39–44.
60. Meltzer, H. Y., Fessler, R. G., Simonovic, M., Doherty, J., and Fang, V. S. (1979): Effect of *d*- and *l*-amphetamine on rat plasma prolactin levels. *Psychopharmacology,* 61:63–69.
61. Meltzer, H. Y., Fessler, R. G., Simonovic, M., and Fang, V. S. (1978): The effect of mescaline, 3,4-dimethoxyphenethylamine and 2,5-dimethoxy-4-methyl-amphetamine on rat plasma prolactin: Evidence for serotonergic medication. *Life Sci.,* 23:1185–1192.
62. Meltzer, H. Y., Fessler, R. G., Simonovic, M., and Fang, V. S. (1978): Stimulation of rat prolactin secretion by indolealkylamine hallucinogens. *Psychopharmacology,* 55:255–260.
63. Meltzer, H. Y., Goode, D. J., and Fang, V. S. (1978): The effect of psychotropic drugs on endocrine function. I. Neuroleptics, precursors and agonists. In: *A Review of Progress,* edited by A. Dimascio and M. Lipton, pp. 509–530. Raven Press, New York.
64. Meltzer, H. Y., Goode, D. J., Schyve, P. J. Young, M., and Fang, V. S. (1980): Effect of clozapine in human serum prolactin levels. *Arch. Gen. Psychiatry (in press).*
65. Meltzer, H. Y., Holcomb, H., Young, M., Busch, D., and Fang, V. S. (1979): Alpha-methylpara-tyrosine and schizophrenia: Clinical and neuroendocrine studies. In: *Syllabus and Scientific Proceedings,* p. 61. American Psychiatric Association, Chicago.
66. Meltzer, H. Y., Sachar, E. J., and Frantz, A. G. (1974): Serum prolactin levels in unmedicated schizophrenic patients. *Arch. Gen. Psychiatry,* 31:564–569.
67. Meltzer, H. Y., Sachar, E. J., and Frantz, A. A. (1974): Serum prolactin levels in acutely psychotic patients: An indirect measurement of central dopaminergic activity. In: *Neuropsychopharmacology of Monoamines and Their Regulatory Enzymes,* edited by E. Usdin, pp. 299–316. Raven Press, New York.
68. Meltzer, H. Y., Simonovic, M., Fang, V. S., Piyakalamala, S., and Young, M. (1978): A comparison of the effects of anti-psychotic drugs on pituitary, striatal and limbic system post-synaptic dopamine receptors. *Life Sci.,* 23:605–610.
69. Meltzer, H. Y., So, R., Miller, R. J., and Fang, V. S. (1980): Comparison of the effects of substituted benzamides and standard neuroleptics on the binding of ^{3}H-spiroperidol in the rat pituitary and striatum with *in vivo* effects on rat prolactin secretion. *Life Sci. (in press).*
70. Meltzer, H. Y., and Stahl, S. (1976): The dopamine hypothesis: A review. *Schizophr. Bull.,* 2:19–76.
71. Mendelson, W. D., Jacobs, L. S., Reichman, F. D., Othner, E., Cryer, P. E., Trivedi, B., and Daughaday, W. H. (1975): Methysergide: Suppression of sleep-related prolactin secretion and enhancement of sleep-related growth hormone secretion. *J. Clin. Invest.,* 56:690–697.
72. Muller, E. E., Luizzi, A., Cochi, D., Panerai, A. E., Oppizzi, G., Locatelli, V., Mantegazza, R., Silvestrini, F., and Chiodini, P. G. (1977): Role of dopaminergic receptors in the regulation of growth hormone secretion. In: *Nonstriatal Dopaminergic Neurons,* edited by E. Costa and G. L. Gessa, pp. 127–138. Raven Press, New York.

73. Muller, E. E., Nistico, G., and Scapagnini, U. (1971): *Neurotransmitters and Anterior Pituitary Function.* Academic Press, New York.
74. Murphy, D. L., and Wyatt, R. J. (1972): Reduced monoamine oxidase activity in blood platelets from schizophrenic patients. *Nature,* 238:225–226.
75. Nemeroff, C. B., and Prange, A. J., Jr. (1978): Peptides and psychoneuroendocrinology, *Arch. Gen. Psychiatry,* 35:999–1010.
76. Ohman, R., and Axelsson, R. (1978): Relationship between prolactin response and antipsychotic effect of thioridazine in psychiatric patients. *Eur. J. Clin. Pharmacol.,* 14:111–116.
77. Overall, J. E., and Gorham, D. R. (1962): Brief Psychiatric Rating Scale (BPRS). *Psychol. Rep.,* 10:799–812.
78. Owen, F., Crow, T. J., Poulter, M., Cross, A. J., Longden, A., and Riley, G. J. (1978): Increased dopamine-receptor sensitivity in schizophrenia. *Lancet,* 2:223–225.
79. Pandey, G. N., Garver, D. L., Tamminga, C., Ericson, S., Ali, S. I., and Davis, J. M. (1977): Post-synaptic supersensitivity in schizophrenia. *Am. J. Psychiatry,* 134:518–522.
80. Parker, D. C., Rossman, L. G., and Vanderlaan, E. F. (1974): Relation of sleep-entrained human prolactin release to REM-non REM cycles. *J. Clin. Endocrinol., Metab.,* 38:646–651.
81. Parker, D. C., Sassini, J. F., Mace, J. W., Gotlin, R. W., and Rossman, L. G. (1969): Human growth hormone release during sleep: Electroencephalographic correlation. *J. Clin. Endocrinol. Metab.,* 29:871–874.
82. Randrup, A., Munkvad, I., Fog, R., Gerlach, J., Molander, L., Kjellberg, B., and Scheel-Kruger, J. (1975): Mania, depression, and brain dopamine. *Cur. Dev. Psychopharmacol.,* 2:206–248.
83. Ravitz, A. J., and Moore, K. E. (1977): Effects of amphetamine, methylphenidate and cocaine on serum prolactin concentrations in the male rat. *Life Sci.,* 21:267–272.
84. Rotrosen, J., Angrist, B., Clark, C., Gershon, S., Halpern, F. S., and Sachar, E. J. (1978): Suppression of prolactin by dopamine agonists in schizophrenics and controls. *Am. J. Psychiatry,* 135:949–951.
85. Rotrosen, J., Angrist, B. M., Gershon, S., Sachar, E. J., and Halpern, F. S. (1976): Dopamine receptor alteration in schizophrenia: Neuroendocrine evidence. *Psychopharmacology,* 51:1–7.
86. Rotrosen, J., Angrist, B., and Paquin, J. (1978): Neuroendocrine studies with dopamine agonists in schizophrenia. *Psychopharmacol. Bull.,* 14:14–16.
87. Sachar, E. J. (1978): Neuroendocrine responses to psychotropic drugs. In: *Psychopharmacology: A Generation of Progress,* edited by M. A. Lipton, A. D. Mascio, and K. F. Killam, pp. 499–507. Raven Press, New York.
88. Sachar, E. J., Gruen, P. H., Altman, N., Halpern, F. S., and Frantz, A. G. (1976): Use of neuroendocrine techniques in psychopharmacological research. In: *Hormones, Behavior and Psychopathology,* edited by E. Sachar, pp. 161–176. Raven Press, New York.
89. Schilkrut, R., Chandra, O., Osswald, M., Ruther, E., Baarfussen, B., and Matussek, N. (1975): Growth hormone release during sleep and with thermal stimulation in depressed patients. *Neuropsychobiology,* 1:70–79.
90. Shopsin, B., Klein, H., Aaronsom, M., and Collora, M. (1979): Clozapine, chlorpromazine, and placebo in newly hospitalized, acutely schizophrenic patients: A controlled, double-blind comparison. *Arch. Gen. Psychiatry,* 36:657–664.
91. Slater, S., de la Vaga, C. E., Skyler, J., and Murphy, D. L. (1976): Plasma prolactin stimulation by fenfluramine and amphetamine. *Psychopharmacolog. Bull.,* 12:26–27.
92. Snyder, S., Banerjee, S. P., Yamamura, H. I., and Greenburg, D. (1974): Drugs, neurotransmitters and schizophrenia. *Science,* 184:1243–1253.
93. Stanley, M., Lantin, A., Rotrosen, J., and Gershon, S. (1979): Antipsychotic efficacy of metoclopramide: Do DA neuroleptic receptors mediate the action of antipsychotic drugs. *IRCS Med. Sci.,* 7:322.
94. Stevens, J. R. (1973): An anatomy of schizophrenia? *Arch. Gen. Psychiatry,* 29:117–189.
95. Syvalahti, E., and Pekkarainen, A. (1977): Serum growth hormone levels in schizophrenic patients during sleep. *J. Neural Transm.,* 40:221–226.
96. Takahashi, Y., Kipnis, D. M., and Daughaday, W. H. (1968): Growth hormone secretion during sleep. *J. Clin. Invest.,* 47:2079–2090.
97. Tamminga, C. A., Smith, R. C., Pandey, G., Frohman, L. A., Davis, I. M. (1977): A neuroendocrine study of supersensitivity in tardive dyskinesia. *Arch. Gen. Psychiatry,* 36:1199–1203.
98. Valverde, R. C., Pastrana, L. S., Ruz, J. A., Solis, H., Jurado, J. L., Sordo, C. M., Fernandez-

Guardiola, A., and Maisterrena, J. A. (1976): Neuroendocrine and electroencephalographic sleep changes due to acute amphetamine ingestion in human beings. *Neuroendocrinology,* 22:57–71.

99. Van Kammen, D. P., Docherty, J. P., Marder, S. R., Siris, S. G., and Bunney, W. E., Jr. (1978): d-Amphetamine raises serum prolactin in man: Evaluations after chronic placebo, lithium and pimozide treatment. *Life Sci.,* 23:1487–1492.
100. Verde, G., Oppizzi, G., Colussi, G., Gremascoli, G., Botalla, L., Muller, E. E., Silvestrini, F., Chiodine, P. G., and Liuzzi, A. (1976): Effect of dopamine infusion on plasma levels of growth hormone in normal subjects and in acromegalic patients. *Clin. Endocrinol.,* 5:419–423.
101. Vigneri, R., Pezzino, V., Squatrit, S., Calandra, A., and Maricchiolo, M. (1974): Sleep-associated growth hormone (GH) release in schizophrenia. *Neuroendocrinology,* 14:356–361.
102. Waldmeier, P. C., Delini-Stula, A., and Maitre, L. (1976): Preferential deamination of dopamine by an A type monoamine oxidase in rat brain. *Naunyn-Schmiedeberg's Arch. Pharmacol.,* 292:9–14.
103. Watson, S. J., Akil, H., Berger, P. A., and Barchas, J. D. (1979): Some observations on the opiate peptides and schizophrenia. *Arch. Gen. Psychiatry,* 36:35–40.
104. Wode-Helgodt, B., Borg, S., Fyro, B., and Sedvall, G. (1978): Clinical effects and drug concentrations in plasma and cerebrospinal fluid in psychotic patients treated with fixed doses of chlorpromazine. *Acta Psychiatr. Scand.,* 58:149–173.
105. Wode-Helgodt, B., Eneroth, P., Fyro, B., Gullberg, B., and Sedvall, G. (1977): Effect of chlorpromazine treatment on prolactin levels in cerebrospinal fluid and plasma of psychotic patients. *Acta Psychiatr. Scand.,* 56:280–293.
106. Wode-Helgodt, B., Fyro, B., Gullberg, B., and Sedvall, G. (1977): Effect of chlorpromazine treatment on monoamine metabolite levels in cerebrospinal fluid of psychotic patients. *Acta Psychiatr. Scand.,* 56:129–142.
107. Wooley, D. W., and Shaw, E. A. (1954): A biochemical and pharmacological suggestion about certain mental disorders. *Proc. Natl. Acad. Sci. U.S.A.,* 40:228–231.

Discussion

Henn: Congratulations on cracking the dopamine hypothesis a bit. I'd like to confirm the peculiarity of tardive dyskinesia in another way. We've been studying not endocrine system but presumably limbic system manifestations of supersensitivity. In the first 12 cases we've looked at retrospectively (which unfortunately isn't the best way), we've seen absolutely no indication that increased psychosis results during a phase when you see the development of increased motor side effects. The supersensitivity is inconsistent.

Meltzer: Did their mental status change in the patients with tardive dyskinesia who were given apomorphine or bromocriptine?

Henn: No.

K. Davis: Dopamine receptors probably don't all become supersensitive at the same time. Striatal elevations of homovanillic acid (HVA) decrease before there are changes in mesolimbic HVA. Your data would be consistent with the elevation of prolactin going down after a much longer administration of neuroleptics than we have in the striatum. It should not be assumed a priori that patients with tardive dyskinesia have abnormalities in tuberoinfundibular or mesolimbic dopamine systems that correlate with supersensitivity. That may occur later on in their course.

J. Davis: Carol Tamminga and I (3) studied several patients who had tardive dyskinesia after 10 to 20 years of neuroleptics. They were not supersensitive; rather, they were clearly subsensitive, in terms of their prolactin and growth hormone responses to both dopa and apomorphine. That's consistent with your findings and with those of several other groups.

K. Davis: Another possibility is again that all dopamine receptors may not be alike. It's possible that in the tuberoinfundibular system, an auto receptor might become supersensitive before a postsynaptic receptor. If that happened, one would expect to see subsensitivity before seeing supersensitivity.

Meltzer: By now there is considerable evidence that there are no autoreceptors on the tuberoinfundibular neurons.

Nasrallah: On chronic treatment and the return to normal, we (2) were once studying a chronic schizophrenic group most of whom were on 1,000 mg a day of chlorpromazine for several years. Their prolactin was rather low—for many of them, down to 10 or 12 ng/ml, but the chlorpromazine level in their blood was very low as well. What were the neuroleptic blood levels in the group you cited?

Meltzer: In collaboration with Ian Creese and Solomon Snyder, we measured serum levels of chlorpromazine and its active metabolites, using a radioreceptor assay, in 10 males and 10 females, who each received chlorpromazine 100 mg b.i.d. for 1 week and 200 mg b.i.d. for a second week. At the end of the second study week, blood samples were obtained 11 to 12 hr after the evening dose. Serum chlorpromazine equivalents ranged from 21 to 161 ng/ml in the females (mean 59.6 ± S.D. 50.5 ng/ml). For the males the range was 1.5 to 31 ng/ml (mean 15.9 ± S.D. 29.4 ng/ml). Of the total sample studied, five of ten females and nine of ten males had serum chlorpromazine equivalents below 50 ng/ml. Serum chlorpromazine equivalents were significantly higher in the females than in the males. Even after accounting for differences in body weight, serum chlorpromazine equivalents were still higher in females than in males. There was no significant correlation between clinical response and serum chlorpromazine equivalents in either males or females.

Brown: We've found that tolerance develops to the prolactin-elevating effects of neuroleptics. It can't be accounted for by changes in neuroleptic level. Patients differ in the degree of tolerance: In some, prolactin levels are lowered by more than 50 to 100%, whereas in others they are lowered much less. Those who develop the profound tolerance may constitute a biochemically interesting subgroup of patients.

You showed a slide of our testosterone results. We've found that of the drugs we studied only Mellaril suppresses testosterone; neither haloperidol nor bromperidol, another butyrophenone, suppress it. This is consistent with the findings of Beaumont (1), who found that a mixed group of neuroleptics suppressed testosterone. There may be specificity in the neuroleptics that do this.

In those studies of supersensitivity and dyskinesia, the supersensitivity was elicited by giving a dose of a dopamine agonist, and then the neuroendocrine response was measured. The dose of dopamine agonist used, which was usually something like 0.75 mg of apomorphine, may have produced a maximal response, which would make it impossible to know whether or not there was supersensitivity.

Meltzer: We have found chronic schizophrenics who have been ill for 4 or more years have a decreased growth hormone response to 0.75 mg apomorphine subcutaneous. While it is difficult to conclude anything from a single-dose study, it suggests subsensitivity rather than supersensitivity. I suggest that a range of doses of dopamine agonists need to be studied in schizophrenics with and without tardive dyskinesia and normal controls.

Berger: Dr. Brown, what about the effect of clozapine on testosterone?

Brown: We haven't looked at that. I don't know whether or not anyone else has.

Hiatt: While doing sleep research, we found that many hormones are secreted in a pulsatile fashion. Did you take frequent measurements over the day—say, every half-hour—and any by night?

Meltzer: We have studied unmedicated, acutely psychotic patients throughout the day, taking 15-min samplings with indwelling catheters. In those psychotics who sleep, who are a subgroup in themselves, we found secretory patterns that are indistinguishable from those of untreated controls. Prolactin and growth hormone changes were normal.

Hiatt: Did the medication produce a qualitative change?

Meltzer: No. In our hands, neuroleptics have not changed the typical nocturnal pattern of prolactin—a late increase prior to waking.

Janowsky: Recently, Dr. Robert Neborsky, I, and colleagues gave acute psychotics either high-dose or low-dose haloperidol, using a rapid neuroleptization technique. We gave an average of 40 mg of haloperidol to 10 people, and 10 mg to other people, giving either 10 mg or 2 mg intramuscular doses during the first 24 hr. After that we gave the dose given during the 24 hr in oral form on a b.i.d. or t.i.d. administration schedule. While the blood levels of haloperidol correlated highly with the dose levels we gave, the prolactin levels did not correlate.

Meltzer: Haloperidol 0.5–0.75 mg i.m. will produce maximal prolactin secretion if you are interested in the 6 hr following injection.

Janowsky: So we probably attained that. We also found that the patients who best responded to rapid neuroleptization had a relatively low prolactin response; the nonresponders had a large prolactin response.

Meltzer: That would be consistent with what Daniel Busch and I observed with regard to apomorphine. I think the apparently conflicting data about prolactin levels and clinical response requires careful scrutiny of the nature of the population, the neuroleptic treatment, the times at which prolactin and clinical state are determined in relation to the course of neuroleptic treatment, and the time after the last dose of neuroleptic. We've not been doing the same experiment.

Janowsky: We also gave methylphenidate to another group of schizophrenics, and our drug-responsive schizophrenics had blunted growth hormone responses, which also fits your findings. Another item against the dopamine hypothesis is that methylphenidate, which increases psychotic symptoms if you're an actively ill schizophrenic, does not significantly decrease prolactin levels in people who are off drugs unless the prolactin is elevated to start with.

Meltzer: We have been unable to replicate Van Kammen's (4) report that amphetamine raises serum prolactin levels; I'm not surprised that Ritalin also doesn't raise it.

Carpenter: When you found prolactin predicting response, was it predicting inadequacy of the drug dose or distinguishing between drug-responsive and unresponsive patients?

Meltzer: We found the growth hormone response to apomorphine to be predictive, not of dose, but of clinical change. We examined the relationship between the serum prolactin and growth hormone responses to apomorphine and degree of psychopathology at admission and discharge. There were no significant correlations between the prolactin and growth hormone area under the curve after apomorphine and admission ratings of psychosis, anxiety, or depression. The same was true with regard to discharge ratings and prolactin response. However, we did find significant negative correlations between the growth hormone response to apomorphine and discharge ratings of psychosis ($r = -0.47$, $p < 0.05$), anxiety ($r = -0.55$, $p < 0.05$), and depression ($r = -0.056$, $p < 0.05$) among the 18 schizophrenic patients studied. Thus, the growth hormone response to apomorphine may weakly predict short-term response to neuroleptic treatment or the degree of remission that will occur.

Carpenter: Could you determine if nonresponders would have benefited from a larger dose of the drug?

Meltzer: The patients were receiving relatively high doses, up to 600 or 800 mg/day of chlorpromazine. It is possible that they would have improved further with higher dosages.

Carpenter: For you and Dr. Brown: With regard to tolerance, do those patients who have reduced prolactin levels with chronic drug administration go lower than a drug-free baseline or after drug withdrawal?

Brown: Yes, they drop a bit, but not as much on a percentage basis as when you stop the drug.

Carpenter: If you resume the drug, is the prolactin response robust?

Brown: Yes.

Berger: Dr. Brown, what about the response to treatment of those patients with a decreased endocrine response to apomorphine?

Brown: We haven't done that. We did find, in our original series of patients, that those who showed the greatest degree of tolerance—that is, those who had relatively low prolactins while on neuroleptics—were the ones who tended to relapse immediately when taken off neuroleptics, whereas those who had higher prolactin levels on neuroleptics tended not to relapse within the first few weeks. We're checking this with a larger series now.

Yuwiler: Since many patients are treated with neuroleptics before the challenge, how much time must pass after the last drug dose before the receptor returns to its basal state? You need to know this in order to test the dopamine hypothesis by procedures challenging the dopamine receptor.

Meltzer: We have some first-break patients who've never been treated with neuroleptics and some who were more typically treated chronically anywhere from a week to a month prior to the apomorphine challenge. We find no difference between the groups.

Yuwiler: So you think that a couple of weeks is enough.

Meltzer: Yes.

May: Be cautious about calling the people with low prolactin poor responders. One must watch out for artifact when not using a constant-dose schedule, because you can safely predict that when people are given "doctor's choice," you will find that the more treatment a patient gets, the worse his response—because doctors always give more drug when a patient doesn't respond. You can therefore count on finding a negative correlation.

Meltzer: All of the patients I reported on in the 2-week study of relating prolactin levels and clinical response received the same dose of chlorpromazine, 400 mg.

REFERENCES

1. Beumont, P. J. V., Corker, C. S., Friesen, H. G., et al. (1974): The effects of phenothiazines on endocrine function. II. Effects on men and postmenopausal women. *Br. J. Psychiatry,* 124:420–430.
2. Nasrallah, H. A., et al. (1977): Inhibition of dopamine synthesis in schizophrenia. *Arch. Gen. Psychiatry,* 34:649–655.
3. Tamminga, C. A., Smith, R. C., Pandey, G. N., Frohman, L. A., and Davis, J. M. (1977): A neuroendocrine study of supersensitivity in tardive dyskinesia. *Arch. Gen. Psychiatry,* 34:1199–1203.
4. Van Kammen, D. P., Docherty, J. P., Marder, S. R., Siris, S. G., and Bunney, W. E. Jr. (1978): *d*-Amphetamine raises serum prolactin in man: Evaluations after chronic placebo, lithium, and pimozaide treatment. *Life Sci.,* 23:1487–1492.

Perspectives in Schizophrenia Research,
edited by C. Baxter and T. Melnechuk.
Raven Press, New York, 1980.

Diagnostic Classification and the Endorphin Hypothesis of Schizophrenia: Individual Differences and Psychopharmacological Strategies

M. S. Buchsbaum, *G. C. Davis, and D. P. van Kammen

Biological Psychiatry Branch, National Institute of Mental Health, Bethesda, Maryland 20205

LAYPERSON'S SUMMARY

Each new brain chemical discovered by neuroscientists opens the possibility that its shortage or excess could be the cause of schizophrenia. Each new functional measure of brain function developed by biomedical engineers is a candidate for the ultimate diagnostic test. Many such potential breakthroughs are tested on small populations of patients and few receive any widespread support. Such a research strategy assumes a single biological cause of all cases of schizophrenia. If, instead, schizophrenia is a syndrome contributed to by a wide variety of biological factors, different ones in different patients, then this research paradigm cannot succeed. In its place, new strategies aimed at isolating biologically homogeneous subgroups need to be used. In this chapter we review the endorphin hypothesis of schizophrenia as a case history of research, as a target for psychophysiological and neuropharmacologic approaches, and as a potentially viable but limited factor in mental dysfunction.

INTRODUCTION

In its simplest version, the endorphin hypothesis of schizophrenia suggests that the symptoms result directly from an excess of these opiate-like peptides and implies that opiate (and hence endorphin) antagonists could not only be used as a test of the hypothesis but also provide effective treatment. The initial success with six hallucinating schizophrenics (29) encouraged at least nine other research teams to launch clinical trials of opiate antagonists in schizophrenic patients [see review by Davis et al. (14)]. The aggregate negative result (6 of 10 studies) has somewhat dissipated investigator enthusiasm, and research ward physicians are bracing for the next new neurotransmitter antagonist to appear.

* Present address: Department of Psychiatry, University of Tennessee School of Medicine, Memphis, Tenn. 38163.

This regular boom and bust cycle partly reflects the desperation of physicians hoping to ameliorate intractable suffering in their patients. But it may also result from the false assumption that all schizophrenia results from the same biological causes and responds to the same pharmacological treatments. In this chapter we review evidence linking the endorphin system to schizophrenia, evaluate the immense variability in schizophrenic patients, and discuss strategies for approaching biological heterogeneity in the schizophrenia syndrome. The discovery of new neurotransmitter systems and the postulation of corresponding etiologies of schizophrenia will be a hallmark of the 1980s: development of correspondingly powerful research strategies is critical to avoid a wilting series of possible false negative results and to find those particular schizophrenics, if any, for whom each new neurotransmitter discovery might bring succor.

DIRECT EVIDENCE FOR THE ENDORPHIN HYPOTHESIS IN SCHIZOPHRENIA

Two available possibilities for demonstrating the endorphin hypothesis of schizophrenia are (a) the measurement in plasma and cerebrospinal fluid of endorphins, the measurement of endorphin metabolites or even the number or sensitivity of endorphin receptors; and (b) the clinical response to narcotic antagonists. Given the technical difficulties of assessing endorphins in man, investigators have largely concentrated on the opiate antagonist strategy. These antagonists such as naloxone or naltrexone act by blocking opiate receptors in the brain. Naloxone and naltrexone have been shown *in vivo* and *in vitro* to block and reverse the effects of endorphins (such as beta-endorphin and leucine- and methionine-enkephalin).

The 10 studies reported up to the time of this meeting (April 1979) have been reviewed elsewhere in detail (14). At least seven groups have used short-acting parenterally administered naloxone in schizophrenics, and three groups have used the longer acting naltrexone in clinical trials lasting from 2 to 8 weeks. In each of these studies only a small number of schizophrenic patients have been used (median $N = 7.5$ patients per study) and several diagnostic criteria applied. Behavioral rating instruments such as the Brief Psychiatric Rating Scale (BPRS) or symptom-specific scales (100 mm global hallucination self-rating lines) have been commonly used as outcome measures. A minority of the studies were double-blind and counterbalanced with similar placebo procedures. Only 4 of 10 reported statistical tests, whereas 6 of 10 actually reported group data. However, the negative studies (6 of 10) do not rule out a role for endorphins in schizophrenia.

First, the behavioral effects of such an excess may be the consequences of subsequent actions of endorphins and not easily modified in the acute experiment. Possible therapeutic effects might depend on changes, homeostatic compensations, or drug actions that take time to develop (14). Most of the therapeutic agents used in psychiatry (tricyclic antidepressants, lithium, neuroleptics) require more than a single dose and more than 1 day for their target effects. Three studies have used the orally administered narcotic antagonist naltrexone, which provides continuous receptor blockade with single-day dosing. All three studies were single-blind and, appropriate to the small sample size, no statistical analysis was reported. Longer trials of naltrexone with larger samples will be necessary to address the endorphin hypothesis.

Second, concurrent drug administration may complicate interpretation of opiate antagonist trials. In the earliest report (29) patients were stabilized on various neuroleptics and then concurrently given the narcotic antagonist naloxone. Some of the subsequent replication attempts were done with the patients drug free and others with the patients on maintenance neuroleptics, an experimental design we have termed an "additive trial." An inevitable disadvantage of the additive trial is the difficulty in assessing the significance of results in the absence of a trial of naloxone alone, placebo, neuroleptic alone, and neuroleptic plus naloxone in a crossover design. In addition, patients of investigators using the additive trial design are characteristically on a variety of types and doses of neuroleptics, which further complicates the interpretation of results.

Third, psychiatric symptoms are difficult to assess quantitatively. Even the best measures have problems with reliability, reproducibility, and lack of specificity. Measures tend to be of two types: global measures of severity of psychosis (10), or dimensional, semi-quantitative measures such as used in the BPRS (44). These measures are useful in longitudinal studies in which random changes in ratings and variables influenced by rater variability may be minimized by averaging over days and weeks to more accurately reflect symptom improvement or deterioration. However, these measures have less reliability for repeated use in acute studies (e.g., BPRS where naloxone might be given intravenously and the patient closely observed for a short period every 30 min for 3 hr). Items such as somatic concern, guilt feelings, grandiosity, and hostility, which are based solely on patient reports, are particularly difficult to rate frequently since even very ill patients may not spontaneously report these feelings every 30 min. A nonspecific decrease in verbalization may spuriously produce the appearance of improvement. With a structured interview technique in which specific probe questions are asked, repeated questioning over short time intervals may elevate artificially positive responses. Such high rating levels may not produce a systematic advantage for drug or placebo, but the higher variances created may diminish the power of statistical comparison. In addition, the many symptom scores which are produced give the investigator a chance to make a series of statistical comparisons—one or more of which may produce an isolated significant effect. Thus with 20 rating scales we expect one significant $p < 0.05$ result by chance alone. Lowering of the p value necessary to reject the null hypothesis is sometimes recommended by statisticians [e.g., use of the Bonferroni criterion (32)] but is not really suitable in such small n drug studies. Each patient is an expensive addition to the study, and huge numbers of patients might be necessary to get any significant finding; a corresponding increase in false negative statistical errors and a general discouragement to use new measures (which would lower the necessary *p* value) would result. If narcotic antagonists affect only a limited symptom cluster, limiting the results to a single scale, use of standardized multiscale rating instruments may always provide this statistical problem. Therefore, replication in a second group of patients is often advantageous.

INDIRECT EVIDENCE FOR A ROLE OF ENDORPHINS IN SCHIZOPHRENIA

As opiates and endorphins have been shown to play an important role in pain appreciation, the measurement of pain sensation with psychophysical, psychophysiological, and behavioral tests could provide a useful index of endorphin effects.

Pain Sensitivity

The relative insensitivity of schizophrenic patients to clinical pain has long been noted. Bleuler (3) observed that schizophrenics were undistracted by distension of the rectum and bladder or by uncomfortable positions. Diminished pain has been reported in myocardial infarcts, acute perforated peptic ulcers, acute appendicitis, and other surgical disorders in psychotic patients (27,41,42,50). Geschwind (26) noted that the absence of acute pain may complicate diagnosis of acute surgical conditions and suggested excess endorphins as a possible cause. Decreased headache after lumbar puncture in schizophrenics as compared to controls also has been noted (1,52).

Although it might be argued that denial or avoidance of the sick role (see 50) or depersonalization (36) reduces the reporting of clinical pain in schizophrenics, studies with experimental pain have yielded similar results. Malmo and Shagass (40) found that a subgroup of off-medication schizophrenics were less able to discriminate intensities of thermal stimulation than normals or patients in other psychiatric diagnostic groups. A higher threshold to thermal pain (40), diminished pain reactivity (31), and diminished blood pressure response to the cold pressor test in schizophrenics (19) also have been reported.

At the NIMH, we studied 17 patients with schizophrenia (16) and 64 patients with primarily affective illness (13). All patients had been off medication for 2 weeks or more and were living on NIMH research wards at the time of testing. Age- and sex-matched normal controls were compared with each patient group. All subjects participated in an identical first testing session which included the measurement of visual and auditory evoked potentials (EPs), psychophysical pain testing, and the recording of somatosensory EPs using electrical pain stimuli. The psychophysical pain rating procedure used has been described (12). Brief electrical stimuli were administered to the skin of the left forearm with a computer-controlled constant current stimulator. A total of 93 stimuli (ranging from

1 to 31 mA) were applied and categorized by the subject as "noticeable," "distinct," "unpleasant," or "very unpleasant." Those judged "unpleasant" and "very unpleasant" were counted and the total termed "pain counts." A second index, termed "insensitivity," is a measure of the overlap or variation in judgments of noticeable-distinct with unpleasant-very unpleasant. It is reported as percent error and indicates confusion of the distinct/unpleasant distinction (12). We have developed this measure as a nonparametric analogue of the signal detection analysis measure, d′. Decreases in sensitivity (increased error) have been associated with analgesia from nitrous oxide (11), aspirin (6), and morphine in humans (15) and rats (28).

Schizophrenic patients were significantly more insensitive than normal controls whether assessed by "pain counts" or by the methodologically more rigorous insensitivity measure (15). The distribution of "pain counts" (Fig. 1) reveals schizophrenics who have a wider range of pain count scores than normals,

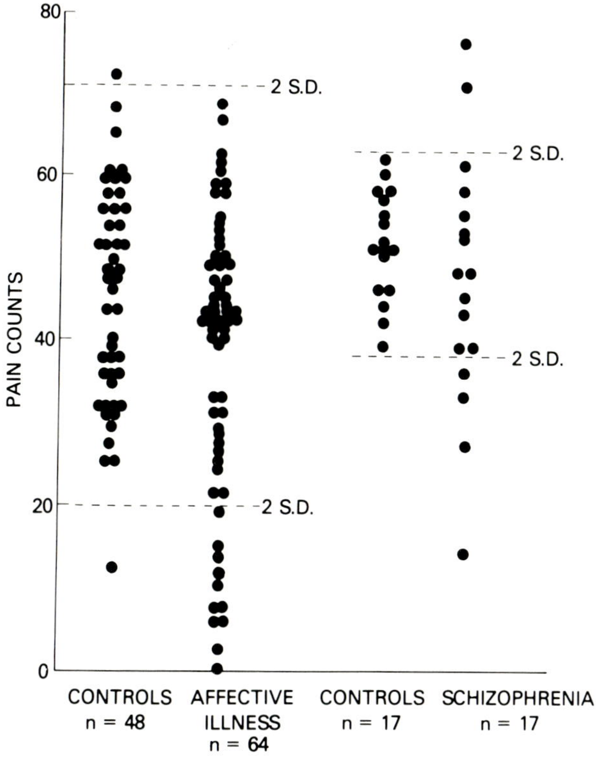

FIG. 1. Decreased pain sensitivity in functional psychoses. Pain count scores (see text) of 64 off-medication patients with affective illness, 17 off-medication patients with schizophrenia, and their individually age- and sex-matched controls. Note extended range in patient groups and the increased incidence of patients more than 2 SD lower on the pain score in both groups.

with four schizophrenics or about 25% showing lower pain counts than any matched control; insensitivity scores showed a similar group of four. Thus the distribution suggests not a generalized analgesia but a subgroup of schizophrenics with unusual hyposensitivity.

Electrophysiological Measures of Sensory Sensitivity

A wide variety of psychophysical studies have been reported in which visual, auditory, and olfactory perceptual abnormalities in schizophrenics were observed (see review 24,25,53). Therefore it is not surprising that the normal perception of pain appears disturbed in schizophrenia. Given the "endorphin excess hypothesis," one might expect diminished perception not only of pain, but of other sensory modalities as well. Indeed, even before the discovery of the opiate receptor and endorphins, it was proposed that schizophrenics develop a kind of "behavioral analgesia" to diminish sensory input (2). Many writers have advanced various concepts of input dysfunction in schizophrenia (49,53,54). However, it can always be argued that diminished motivation and cooperation might account for a large share of the observed perceptual abnormalities. The use of cortical evoked potential correlates of perceptual processing allows us to bypass overt motor responses and examine the perceptual attentional process at a specific electrophysiological stage.

In schizophrenics, most researchers have found lower amplitude EPs than in normal subjects for auditory, visual, and somatosensory stimuli (4). EP studies using high levels of sensory stimulation, provided by rapid rates of stimulus presentation and by novel, paired, or intense stimuli, seem to be especially successful in differentiating schizophrenics from normals. Thus no differences between schizophrenics and normals in EP amplitude could be found for weak stimuli, but significant differences were observed at high stimulus intensities (16,35,47). In our studies with somatosensory stimuli, ranging from barely perceptible up to unpleasant or very unpleasant (16), schizophrenic patients showed markedly lower amplitude EPs to stimuli rated "unpleasant," but were no different from normals in the "noticeable" range.

Opiate Antagonists and EP Amplitude

This diminution is evoked responses to high-intensity stimuli in schizophrenics is consistent with the theories of input dysfunction mentioned above, and perhaps suggestive of dysfunction in the apparently pain-oriented endorphin system. This link between diminished EP amplitude and the endorphin excess hypothesis was explored in EP studies of the effect of chronic naltrexone treatment in a small group of schizophrenics (16).

In all of our EP studies of pain, we have used four intensities of electrical stimulation ranging from barely noticeable to unpleasant, and presented 64 times each in a randomized sequence (12) to the dorsal surface of the left forearm.

EEG is recorded from somatosensory cortex (C4) and responses to each intensity averaged separately. EP amplitude was enhanced by naltrexone treatment, especially for the maximum intensity response. This effect was strongest for the amplitude of a particular EP component, N120 (Fig. 2), which we have previously demonstrated to be increased by naloxone in pain-insensitive normals (7) (Fig. 3). We have observed also this same component to be reduced in amplitude, especially at the highest or "very pleasant" intensity by morphine (15) in a double-blind crossover study with normal volunteers.

The use of the EP as a correlate of pain sensitivity allows us to study opiate antagonist responses in patients who might not otherwise produce interpretable behavioral responses. One recent case dramatized this:

L.B., a 30-year-old woman with a 9-year history of chronic undifferentiated schizophrenia, participated in three somatosensory EP trials following placebo and naloxone treatment (8 and 20 mg, respectively). On the days of EP testing, L.B. was quite delusional; she believed that her mother was being tortured and held hostage by the staff of the hospital. She was preoccupied with the notion of illegitimate children and further believed that she had killed someone. Her paranoid delusions also included thoughts about the CIA, Kremlin, Brezhnev, and the Kennedy murders. She had continuous auditory hallucinations, poor concentration, disorganized thinking, and was negativistic and withdrawn. During her NIMH stay she requested lumbar puncture and other minor medical procedures without local anesthesia. There was no evidence of peripheral neuropathy, and the results of a neurologic examination were within normal limits.

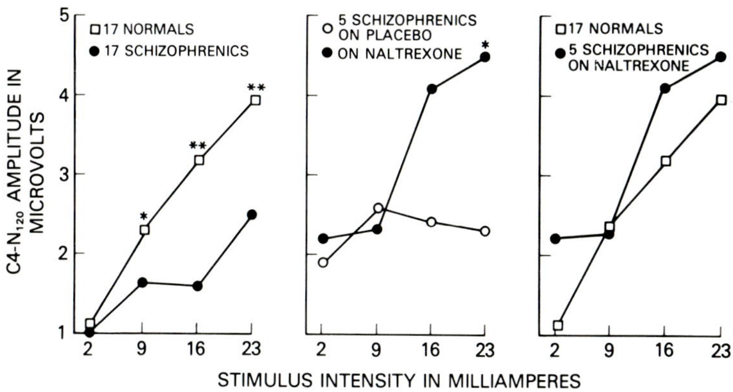

FIG. 2. Evoked potentials in normals and schizophrenics. **Left:** Somatosensory EP amplitude in 17 schizophrenics and 17 age- and sex-matched normal controls for 4 intensities of stimulation. Significant differences in EP amplitude are indicated (*$p < 0.05$; **$p < 0.01$, one-tailed). A two-way ANOVA, 1, 30 df group by linear trend effect interaction is also demonstrated at $p < 0.05$ level (for other EP components). **Middle:** Somatosensory EP amplitude in 5 schizophrenics tested on and off naltrexone (*$p < 0.05$, t = test, on amplitude, one-tailed, t = 2.42.) **Right:** Data from 17 normals and 5 schizophrenics on naltrexone superimposed to illustrate normalizing effect.

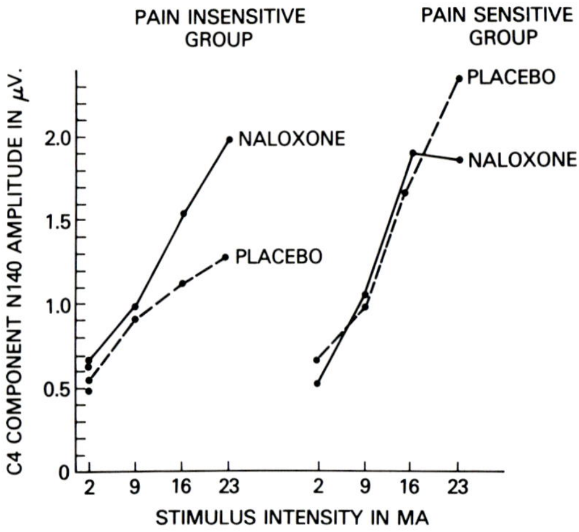

FIG. 3. Mean evoked potential amplitude in μV for negative peak at about 140 ms (N120) at four stimulus intensities for pain-sensitive and -insensitive subject groups. Note EP differences at highest stimulus intensities. Data were analyzed using a three-way ANOVA with repeated measures for the intensity and drug dimensions and independent groups for the third dimension; linear trend analysis was used on the intensity dimension. Group differences were statistically confirmed (group $\times$ drug $\times$ intensity interaction, $F = 4.45$, 1, 17 df, $p < 0.05$). EP differences between sensitive and insensitive groups on placebo can also be seen.

She showed no burn scars on her fingers or other signs or history of laceration or self-mutilation.

The patient was given naloxone (8 mg)–placebo–naloxone (20 mg) i.v. on 3 separate days. Not only did the patient's poor concentration, delusions, and negativism raise questions about her potential performance as a perceptual observer, but the patient always mantained that she could not feel any electric shock, even at the highest stimulus intensity, so no psychophysical rating data were ever collected. EP recordings, however, showed clear hyperalgesic response to naloxone on each day she received the drug and clear hypoalgesia on the placebo day. We recorded EPs as described earlier and calculated the rate of amplitude increase as a function of the four intensities of stimulation, using least-squares regression for the N120 component. The amplitude/intensity slope values in microvolts/mA were 0.15 (8 mg naloxone), −0.05 (placebo), and 0.15 (20 mg naloxone). The comparable value in a population of 26 controls age- and sex-matched to our schizophrenic population was 0.16 + 0.12 (SD); the EP results obtained indicate that the patient was 1.67 SD below normal in pain sensitivity and was restored to almost exactly average by i.v. naloxone. Thus from the EP records we confirmed the patient's pain insensitivity as well as an operative (even hyperactive) endorphin system; from the psychophysical data we could have concluded nothing.

SPECIFICITY OF PAIN INSENSITIVITY FINDINGS FOR SCHIZOPHRENIA

Pain insensitivity has also been reported in patients with affective disorders. Using heat pain (31,33), a pressure algometer (in females only) (43), or electrical stimulation (55,56), it was found that depressed patients have higher pain thresholds and pain tolerance than normals. We obtained similar results in a population of 64 off-medication patients with primary affective disorders (13). As with the schizophrenics, the range of pain count scores is greater and a subgroup of 25% have lower pain count scores than all but one normal (Fig. 1). And, EP amplitude/intensity slopes for the N120 component were significantly lower than in age- and sex-matched normal controls (8). Does the finding of an unusually pain-tolerant subgroup in both schizophrenic and affective groups merely suggest the discovery of a nonspecific correlate of hospitalization or stress? Or might the diagnostic criteria be equally ambiguous? The respective symptom clusters of these major categories of psychiatric illness are far from mutually exclusive (46); pain insensitivity may well indicate a more homogeneous grouping for neuropharmacological approaches to endorphin abnormalities than symptom-based diagnostic approaches. Indeed, a report has appeared (38) that a fraction of both schizophrenics and affective disorder patients have elevated CSF endorphins. Other biological findings which appear in some patients with schizophrenic and affective disorders include low platelet monoamine oxidase (58) and velocity arrests in smooth-pursuit eye movements (34). Both of these abnormalities also might target these specific groups of patients for other, possibly nonendorphinergic therapeutic approaches.

Premature Rejection of New Hypotheses of Schizophrenia

The story of endorphin research in schizophrenia is a case example of a major current research strategy in biological psychiatry. A new pharmacological strategy such as the use of opiate antagonists is introduced, and several clinical tests are made to determine if an improvement in symptoms occurs. Results are obtained in a small patient group, often 20 or less, and then placebo and drug responses are compared by *t*-test. Investigators' results differ from one university center to another, and in a review of the field, the new treatment and its assumed underlying neurochemical mechanisms may be dismissed as irrelevant to psychiatric disease. Statistical problems inherent in tests with a small number of patients and methodological problems with biological heterogeneity may create a bias which encourages many false negative conclusions. The small sample size used in the opiate antagonist trials (median $N = 7.5$) leaves the investigator open to a "type II" error, in which a failure to find a statistically significant drug effect is uncritically interpreted as if it were a satisfactory demonstration that the drug administration was without effect. Recently

71 negative randomized controlled drug trials were surveyed, and it was found that 50 (71%) had greater than a 10% chance of missing even a 50% patient improvement (22). But what if only 25% of schizophrenics have their disease on the basis of high endorphins? If one assumes random occurrence of "hyperendorphinism" in hospitalized schizophrenics, we can use the binomial expansion to predict how likely an investigator would be to draw a hyperendorphinergic schizophrenic. Calculating on the basis of a drug trial sample size of 7 schizophrenics [median 7.5 in review of recent studies by Davis et al. (14)], about half the investigative teams would have two or more such schizophrenics. If 100 investigative teams did studies with seven patients, only seven teams would have a majority of four out of seven schizophrenics with "hyperendorphinism" in their sample population (predicted on the basis of a cumulative binomial distribution). Subgroup analysis, for example, comparing hallucinating with non-hallucinating schizophrenics for naloxone response versus no response (in a 2 by 2 comparison) would yield too few subjects in each of the four categories for adequate statistical assessment by chi-square. For 95% of the research teams to obtain at least five "hyperendorphinergic" schizophrenics requires a sample size of $N = 35$ with this model. Thus, as expected by Davis et al. (14), from these statistical arguments [with the exception of the initial Gunne et al. (29) report], the largest N studies produced the significant results (20, $N = 20$; 17, $N = 14$; 57, $N = 10$).

This same problem of sample size applies, for example, to a measurement of levels of endorphins in the CSF in groups of normal and schizophrenic subjects. This has been done and significant results obtained by Domschke et al. (18), and high but nonsignificant results by Lindstrom et al. (38) and Emrich et al. (21). We have examined the probability of achieving statistical significance in group comparisons, given various degrees of heterogeneity (9). Using a computer simulation we developed the power curves shown in figure 4. The curves show the percent of "success," that is, getting a significant (two-tailed, $p < 0.05$) result of research teams doing t-test comparisons of schizophrenics and normals. In constructing the model, it was assumed that an abnormality such as "high levels of endorphins" was to be found in only a fraction of the schizophrenic population. The control population was normally distributed; the "schizophrenic" population was constructed to consist of some fraction with "normal endorphins" (drawn from the same distribution as the controls) and the remainder having "endorphin excess disease or hyperendorphinism" drawn from a population with a mean level of 2 standard deviations above the normal. The computer then simulated the efforts of 1,000 research teams doing studies with schizophrenic and control groups of equal sample size. It is shown in figure 4 that if only 25% of schizophrenics have high endorphin disease, it takes a sample size of over 40 before even 50% of the research teams report a statistically significant t-value, and over $N = 125$ before there is 95% unanimity in the field. Even deficits with an incidence as high as 70% in the schizophrenic population require a sample size of nearly 20 to achieve such unanimity in

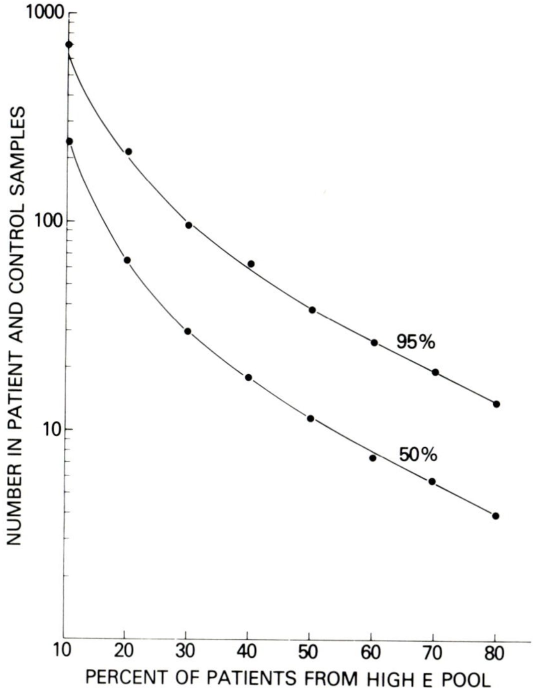

FIG. 4. Percentage of significant *t*-tests, given various sample sizes and various percentages of patients with high "compound E." Percentage of significant *t*-tests ($p < 0.05$, two-tailed) from a simulated cohort of 1,000 research teams comparing samples of "normals" with "schizophrenics" (equal sample sizes) of which only a certain percentage are drawn from a pool with high "compound E," a hypothetical neurochemical abnormality.

the scientific literature. Thus, if one wishes to question the validity of the leucine endorphin hypothesis advanced by Palmour et al. (45), it is insufficient to find the absence of leucine-endorphin in the hemofiltrate of two patients (37), no matter how "well characterized" the diagnosis of these two patients. It should also be noted that statistical tests other than the *t*-test may be more suitable for testing group differences when a subgroup contributes to the difference. The Gail-Green test (23) allows the testing of group differences with a post hoc best result criterion. If this test is applied to the CSF endorphin level data obtained by Terenius et al. (51) and by Gunne et al. (30), a p of 0.05 is obtained using an upper limit of 0.5 pmole/ml endorphins in the CSF as the dividing line between schizophrenics and normals.

NEW STRATEGIES

Phenotypic subtyping is usually the first approach used to deal with the problem of heterogeneity. One may sample a group of schizophrenics who share certain phenomenological features, and then compare them to other schizophrenics, or to a group of normal controls, on some chosen dependent variable. Frequent examples of this have appeared in the literature, the most common being the selective sampling of chronic (process, poor premorbid) schizophrenics or of paranoid schizophrenics. Thus Watson et al. (57) used hallucinating schizophrenics in their study of naloxone.

If selection of a subgroup of schizophrenics on the basis of some symptomatic variable significantly increases the biological homogeneity of the group, then obviously the power of the *t*-test with relatively small samples also increases. However, since symptomatic similarity may not correspond to biologic similarity, this method does not alter the uncertainty surrounding a negative result of such a group comparison. Much of the study of schizophrenia has of necessity proceeded by careful identification and classification of symptoms. Complex behaviors such as the symptoms of schizophrenia are no doubt the expression of a multiplicity of neuronal events. Symptoms may be the final common expression of various etiologies. Further, classic diagnostic symptom clusters have been developed on theoretical bases not related, for example, to the cluster of behavioral effects of the opiates (e.g., euphoria, analgesia, drowsiness). Thus our careful attention to symptoms may be misleading and not yield biologically homogeneous subgroups.

In other words, failure to find a deficit on some biological variable, even when the sample of schizophrenics is selected to be symptomatically homogeneous, does not rule that variable out as an etiological factor in some portion of those schizophrenics.

Screening

Watson et al. (57) screened over 1,000 clinical cases to find 11 patients with very frequent auditory hallucinations, suggested by Gunne, Lindstrom, and Terenius (29) as a key target symptom. This strategy yielded a patient group which showed significant improvement on naloxone.

Selection on the basis of a biological variable has been termed by one of us the "biochemical high-risk strategy" (5). It uses the biological abnormality as the independent variable and psychopathology as the dependent variable, a reversal of the usual clinical research procedure. If there is a significant pathogenic influence of the biological abnormality, then this method will detect an increase in the rate of psychopathology, given an adequate sample size and appropriate controls. Another significant advantage of the method is that it allows for variation in the psychopathological outcome. If the biological factor produces a vulnerability to psychiatric symptoms or disordered behaviors of many types (i.e., a spectrum), these may be detected.

Single-trial screening may be a powerful psychopharmacological strategy. A single dose of a drug such as naloxone can be administered to a large group of patients and clinical response or psychophysiological variables measured.

This is especially applicable to endorphin studies because narcotics affect a large number of physiological parameters including pupillary diameter, respiration, pituitary function, thermal regulation, EEG, gastrointestinal function, and others which can all be monitored objectively, with existing technology. "Responders" on a chosen measure and/or extreme nonresponders may then be admitted to a double-blind placebo-controlled crossover trial for behavioral assessment. This strategy may be especially appropriate in large hospitals where patients with a variety of illnesses may be screened, even on an additive trial basis, and then a small number recruited for further study.

Genetic Strategies

Once a biological or behavioral indicator of endorphin dysfunction has been found, the question remains whether it is an etiologically significant trait variable, a homeostatic response to psychosis, or an artifact of neuroleptic treatment, hospitalization, or some other concomitant of chronic psychiatric illness. If patients can be identified using the screening strategies described above, their relatives can be examined and compared with relatives of other patient populations. Several alternative results are informative. If only the psychiatrically ill relatives of "endorphin dysfunction" probands also have the biological abnormality, credence is produced for a genetic and etiological role for endorphins in this subgroup of schizophrenics. The implications of this and other genetic patterns are discussed elsewhere (48).

These strategies are all aimed at identifying subgroups who are presumptive candidates for "hyperendorphinism" and a potential target population for trials of opiate antagonists and studies of endorphinergic mechanisms. But these are equally applicable to the next new neurotransmitter system to be discovered, as well as the last one to lose glamour (dopamine).

REFERENCES

1. Ballenger, J. C., Post, R. M., Sternberg, D. E., van Kammen, D. P., Cowdry, R. W., and Goodwin, F. K. (1979): Letter to the editor. *N. Engl. J. Med.,* 301:110.
2. Bharucha-Reid, R. P. (1962): The internal modulating system and stress: A neurophysiological model. *J. Gen. Psychol.,* 66:147–158.
3. Bleuler, E. (1950): *Dementia Praecox or the Group of Schizophrenias.* International Universities Press, New York.
4. Buchsbaum, M. S. (1977): The middle evoked response components and schizophrenia. *Schizophr. Bull.,* 3:93–104.
5. Buchsbaum, M. S., Coursey, R. D., and Murphy, D. L. (1976): The biochemical high risk paradigm: Behavioral and familial correlates of low platelet monoamine oxidase activity. *Science,* 194:339–341.
6. Buchsbaum, M. S., and Davis, G. C., (1979): Application of somatosensory event related potentials to experimental pain and the pharmacology of analgesia. In: *Human Evoked Potentials,* edited by D. Lehmann and E. Callaway, pp. 43–54. Plenum Publishing Corp., New York.
7. Buchsbaum, M. S., Davis, G. C., and Bunney, W. E., Jr. (1977): Naloxone alters pain perception and somatosensory evoked potentials in normal subjects. *Nature,* 270:620–622.
8. Buchsbaum, M. S., Davis, G. C., Goodwin, F. K., Murphy, D. L., and Post, R. M. (1980):

Psychophysical pain judgements and somatosensory evoked potentials in patients with affective illness and normal adults. In: *Recent Advances of Biological Psychiatry,* edited by C. Perris and L. von Knorring. S. Karger AG, Basel *(in press).*

9. Buchsbaum, M. S., and Rieder, R. O. (1979): Biological heterogeneity and psychiatric research: Platelet MAO as a case study. *Arch. Gen. Psychiatry,* 36:1163–1172.
10. Bunney, W. E., Jr., and Hamburg, D. A. (1963): Methods for reliable longitudinal observation of behavior. *Arch. Gen. Psychiatry,* 9:280–294.
11. Chapman, C. R., Murphy, T. M., and Butler, S. H. (1972): Analgesic strength of 33 percent nitrous oxide: A signal detection theory evaluation. *Science,* 179:1246–1248.
12. Davis, G. C., Buchsbaum, M. S., and Bunney, W. E., Jr. (1978): Naloxone decreases diurnal variation in pain sensitivity and somatosensory evoked potentials. *Life Sci.,* 23:1449–1460.
13. Davis, G. C., Buchsbaum, M. S., and Bunney, W. E., Jr. (1979): Analgesia to painful stimuli in affective illness. *Am. J. Psychiatry,* 136:1148–1151.
14. Davis, G. C., Buchsbaum, M. S., and Bunney, W. E., Jr. (1979): Research in endorphins and schizophrenia. *Schizophr. Bull.,* 5:244–250.
15. Davis, G. C., Buchsbaum, M. S., Naber, D., and van Kammen, D. P. (1980): Effect of opiates and opiate antagonists on somatosensory evoked potentials in patients with schizophrenia. In: *Recent Advances in Biological Psychiatry,* edited by C. Perris and L. von Knorring. S. Karger AG, Basel *(in press).*
16. Davis, G. C., Buchsbaum, M. S., van Kammen, D. P., and Bunney, W. E., Jr. (1979): Analgesia to pain stimuli in schizophrenics reversed by naltrexone. *Psychiatry Res.,* 1:61–69.
17. Davis, G. C., Bunney, W. E., Jr., Defraites, E. G., Kleinman, J. E., van Kammen, D. P., Post, R. M., and Wyatt, R. J. (1977): Intravenous naloxone administration in schizophrenia and affective illness. *Science,* 197:74–77.
18. Domschke, W., Dickshas, A., and Mitznegg, P. (1979): CSF-beta-endorphin schizophrenia. *Lancet,* 1:1024.
19. Earle, A., and Earle, B. (1955): The blood pressure response to pain and emotion in schizophrenia. *J. Nerv. Ment. Dis.,* 121:132–139.
20. Emrich, H. M., Cording, C., Piree, S., Kolling, A., v. Zerssen, D., and Herz, A. (1977): Indication of an antipsychotic action of the opiate antagonist naloxone. *Pharmakopsychiatrie,* 10:265–270.
21. Emrich, H., Hollt, V., Kissling, W., Fischler, M., Laspe, H., Heinemann, H., v. Zerssen, D., and Herz, A. (1980): Beta-endorphin-like immunoreactivity in cerebrospinal fluid and plasma of patients with schizophrenia and other neuropsychiatric disorders. *Pharmakopsychiatr. Neuropsychopharmakol. (in press).*
22. Freiman, J. A., Chalmers, T. C., Smith, H., and Kuebler, R. R. (1978): The importance of beta, the type II error and sample size in the design and interpretation of the randomized control trial. *N. Engl. J. Med.,* 299:690–694.
23. Gail, M. H., and Green, S. B. (1976): A generalization of the one-sided two-sample Kolmogorov-Smirnov statistic for evaluating diagnostic tests. *Biometrics,* 32:561–570.
24. Garmezy, N. (1977): The psychology and psychopathology. *Schizophr. Bull.,* 3:360–369.
25. Garmezy, N. (1978): Attentional processes in adult schizophrenia and in children at risk. *J. Psychiatr. Res.,* 14:3–34.
26. Geschwind, N. (1977): Insensitivity to pain in psychotic patients. *N. Engl. J. Med.,* 296:1480.
27. Gowdy, J. M. (1979): Letter to the editor. *N. Engl. J. Med.,* 301:110–111.
28. Grilly, D. M., and Genovese, R. F. (1979): Assessment of shock discrimination in rats with signal detection theory. *Perception and Psychophysics,* 25(6):466–472.
29. Gunne, L. M., Lindstrom, L., and Terenius, L. (1977): Naloxone-induced reversal of schizophrenic hallucinations. *J. Neural Transm.,* 40:13–19.
30. Gunne, L. M., Lindstrom, L., and Widerlov, E. (1979): Possible role of endorphins in schizophrenia and other psychiatric disorders. In: *Endorphins in Mental Health Research,* edited by E. Usdin, W. E. Bunney, Jr., and N. S. Kline, pp. 581–593. Macmillan, New York.
31. Hall, K. R. L., and Stride, E. (1954): The varying response to pain in psychiatric disorders: A study in abnormal psychology. *Br. J. Med. Psychol.,* 27:78–60.
32. Hays, W. L. (1963): *Statistics for Psychologists.* Holt, Rinehart and Winston, New York.
33. Hemphill, R. E., Hall, K. R. L., and Crookes, T. G. (1952): A preliminary report on fatigue and pain tolerance in depressive and psychoneurotic patients. *J. Ment. Sci.,* 98:433–440.
34. Holzman, P. S., and Levy, D. L. (1977): Smooth pursuit eye movements and functional psychoses: A review. *Schizophr. Bull.,* 3:15–27.

35. Landau, S. G., Buchsbaum, M. S., Carpenter, W., Strauss, J., and Sacks, M. (1975): Schizophrenia and stimulus intensity control. *Arch. Gen. Psychiatry,* 32:1239–1245.
36. Levitan, H. (1977): The relationship between mania and the memory of pain. *Bull. Menninger Clin.,* 41(2):145–161.
37. Lewis, R. V., Gerber, L. D., Stein, S., Stephen, R. L., Grosser, B. I., Velick, S. F., and Udenfriend, S. (1979): On beta-Leu-5-endorphin and schizophrenia. *Arch. Gen. Psychiatry,* 36:237–239.
38. Lindstrom, L. H., Widerlov, E., Gunne, L. M., Wahlstrom, A., and Terenius, L. (1978): Endorphins in human cerebrospinal fluid: Clinical correlations to some psychotic states. *Acta Psychiatr. Scand.,* 57:153–164.
39. Malmo, R. B., and Shagass, C. (1949): Physiologic studies of reaction to stress in anxiety and early schizophrenia. *Psychosom. Med.,* 11:9–24.
40. Malmo, R. B., Shagass, C., and Smith, A. A. (1951): Responsiveness in chronic schizophrenia. *J. Pers.,* 19:359–375.
41. Marchand, W. E. (1955): Occurrence of painless myocardial infarction in psychotic patients. *N. Engl. J. Med.,* 253:51–55.
42. Marchand, W. E., Sarota, B., Marble, H. C., Leary, T. M., Burbank, C. B., and Bellinger, M. J. (1969): Occurrence of painless acute surgical disorders in psychotic patients. *N. Engl. J. Med.,* 260:580–585.
43. Merskey, H. (1965): The effect of chronic pain upon the response to noxious stimuli by psychiatric patients. *J. Psychosom. Res.,* 8:405–419.
44. Overall, J. E., and Gorham, D. R. (1962): The brief psychiatric rating scale. *Psychol. Rep.,* 10:799–812.
45. Palmour, R., Ervin, F., Wagemaker, H., and Cade, R. (1979): Characterization of a peptide from the serum of psychotic patients. In: *Endorphins in Mental Health Research,* edited by E. Usdin, W. E. Bunney, Jr., and N. S. Kline, pp. 581–593. Macmillan, New York.
46. Pope, H. G., Jr., and Lipinski, J. F., Jr. (1978): Diagnosis in schizophrenia and manic-depressive illness: A reassessment of the specificity of "schizophrenic" symptoms in the light of current research. *Arch. Gen. Psychiatry,* 35:811–828.
47. Rappaport, M., Hopkins, H. K., Hall, K., Belleza, R., and Hall, R. A. (1975): Schizophrenia and evoked potentials: Maximum amplitude, frequency of peaks, variability and phenothiazine effects. *Psychophysiology,* 12:196–207.
48. Rieder, R. O., and Gershon, E. S. (1978): Genetic strategies in biological psychiatry. *Arch. Gen. Psychiatry,* 35:866–876.
49. Silverman, J. (1968): A paradigm for the study of altered states of consciousness. *Br. J. Psychiatry,* 114:1201–1218.
50. Talbott, J. A., and Linn, L. (1978): Reactions of schizophrenics to life-threatening disease. *Psychiatr. Q.,* 50:218–227.
51. Terenius, L., Wahlstrom, A., and Johansson, L. (1979): Endorphins in human cerebrospinal fluid and their measurement. In: *Endorphins in Mental Health Research,* edited by E. Usdin, W. E. Bunney, Jr., and N. S. Kline, pp. 581–593. Macmillan, New York.
52. Torrey, E. F. (1979): Letter to the editor. *N. Engl. J. Med.,* 301:110.
53. Venables, P. H. (1964): Input dysfunction in schizophrenia. *Prog. Exp. Pers. Res.,* 1:1–47.
54. Venables, P. H. (1973): Input regulation and psychopathology. In: *Psychopathology,* edited by M. Hammer, K. Salzinger, and S. Sutton, pp. 261–284. John Wiley & Sons, New York.
55. Von Knorring, L. (1978): An experimental study of visual averaged evoked responses (V. AER) and pain measures (PM) in patients with depressive disorders. *Biol. Psychol.,* 6:27–38.
56. Von Knorring, L., Espvall, M., and Perris, C. (1974): Averaged evoked responses, pain measures, and personality variables in patients with depressive disorders. *Acta. Psychiatr. Scand.,* 255:99–108.
57. Watson, S. J., Berger, P. A., Akil, H., Mills, M. J., and Barchas, J. D. (1978): Effects of naloxone and schizophrenia: Reduction in hallucinations in a subpopulation of schizophrenics. *Science,* 201:73–76.
58. Wyatt, R. J., and Murphy, D. L. (1976): Low platelet monoamine oxidase activity and schizophrenia. *Schizophr. Bull.,* 2:77–89.

Discussion

Itil: The first part of your talk made me enthusiastic because you were the first to show a direct effect of naltrexone on human brain function, but the second part depressed me because you mentioned all the variabilities that can occur and said that the positive results may not be significant.

Buchsbaum: With morphine we found a clear-cut analgesia, on both the evoked response and the psychophysical measures. With naltrexone given to five schizophrenics already analgesic, we found a statistically significant hyperalgesia, again on both the evoked potential and the psychophysical measure. In the larger group of normals, we seemed to see the endorphin system in different states or at different levels. When we administered naloxone to those individuals who were particularly pain-tolerant, they showed hyperalgesia. So the endorphin system seems to play a variable modulatory role in pain perception. We did consider our results positive, showing a naloxone hyperalgesia in the people who could show it—perhaps those whose endorphin system was active enough to exhibit reversal. Our results have just been replicated in Japan by Dr. Satoh's (4) group. They found that rats that were particularly pain-tolerant also showed large effects of opiate antagonists.

Janowsky: What happened when your affect-disorder patients and your schizophrenic patients who were analgesic or hyperalgesic were administered naloxone or naltrexone—were they behavioral responders?

Buchsbaum: We are frustrated by having only five schizophrenics tested on naltrexone, which isn't enough to do that kind of individual-difference analysis.

Janowsky: How about something dramatic, like getting well?

Buchsbaum: No one got well, although some did improve. But to evaluate the relationship between analgesia and soft variables like rating scale changes, a 50-patient study is needed, which is a kind of study difficult to do at the clinical centers of the NIH, where we just don't have that many people.

Janowsky: Dr. Lewis Judd and I have been giving methadone to four schizophrenics (and would like to give it to affective patients, who are rare in the VA system), and they do vomit. Perhaps your concepts can be applied. With naloxone and naltrexone, corticoid levels triple, and LH probably rises also; thus, if we are turning off schizophrenia or mania with naloxone, is it a primary or a secondary effect? We could be hitting nonopiate systems.

Buchsbaum: The opioid response might be secondary to the distress and depression associated with schizophrenia. There may be an adaptation, so that when you feel sick, you produce a lot of endorphins, which might ameliorate your schizophrenia somewhat, but also produce side effects. When we administer an opiate antagonist, it might eliminate some of those side effects, but exacerbate the schizophrenia. It might also be that there are endorphin supersensitive as well as subsensitive people, and the supersensitive people might be the target for studies of methadone or beta-endorphin as opposed to the opiate antagonists.

Nasrallah: Euphoria is another effect of opiate-like compounds, and might be usable in discriminating the population you want to study. Have you found anhedonics to be different from non-anhedonics in terms of endorphins and the naloxone response?

Buchsbaum: I don't think the scales relevant to mood showed statistically significant relationships. Dr. Kleinman, do any of the data analyses answer that question?

Kleinman: Not all of the data have been analyzed yet.

Zubin: The Chapman scale of anhedonia has been given to college students by the Chapmans (2) with some interesting findings.

Buchsbaum: That scale might be useful as a screening measure.

Itil: How do you explain the therapeutic effect, if any, of naloxone or naltrexone, as well as of opiates, on schizophrenia? If endorphins are involved, there shouldn't be this similar kind of effect of opiate agonists and antagonists.

Buchsbaum: There may be more than one kind of opiate system abnormality. Recall our graph with 17 schizophrenics, four *below* two standard deviations from normal, and two *above* two standard deviations. Those in the middle might have trouble with dopamine, GABA, ventricular enlargement, or other intriguing possibilities suggested at this meeting.

Kleinman: With this type of study, both positive and negative results should be viewed with caution. Intravenous infusions can easily lead to negative results, but positive results are suspect too, as I'll demonstrate with this anecdote. Dr. Weinberger and I were studying a woman who had chronic auditory hallucinations and who satisfied clinical diagnostic criteria for schizophrenia but who lacked a formal thought disorder. We gave her naloxone and placebo in a double-blind crossover-type study and she improved dramatically—on placebo. We tried again, five times. The fifth time she fooled us, but until then we were beginning to wonder whether naloxone was blocking the placebo response.

Mosher: Has anyone done a double-blind study of morphine?

Berger: I have prepared a review (1) of the literature on naloxone, endorphins, and opiates in psychiatric disorders, and have found no double-blind studies with any opiate agonist, including morphine, in the treatment of schizophrenia.

Cole: Albert Kurland (3) studied some opiate in schizophrenia at Spring Grove about 15 years ago. The opiate failed to help in any way. Rumors from the New York Medical College Addict Program claim that schizophrenic addicts do better on methadone and worse on cyclasazine. Maybe Dr. Itil suspects that people who don't respond to neuroleptics might do well on methadone.

Itil: We designed an experimental program for treating therapy-resistant chronic schizophrenics with methadone. If it had passed our institutional review board, it could have started in a month.

REFERENCES

1. Berger, P. A. (1978): Investigating the role of endogenous opioid peptides in psychiatric disorders. In: *Peptides and Behavior: A Critical Analysis of Research Strategies,* edited by J. C. Liefeskind, R. K. Dismukes, J. L. Barker, P. A. Berger, I. Creese, A. J. Dunn, D. S. Siegal, L. Stein, and W. W. Vale. *Neurosci. Res. Program Bull.,* 16:490–635.
2. Chapman, L. F., and Chapman, J. P. (1979): Scales of traits of the schizophrenia-prone. *Psychopharmacol. Bull.,* 15:9–10.
3. Kurland, A., and Gruenwald, F. (1962): Phenazocine (Prinadol) in the treatment of psychotic patients. *Bull. Drug Addict. Narcot.* (*Appendix* 8):2791–2808.
4. Satoh, M., Kawajiri, S., Yamamoto, M., Makino, H., and Takagi, H. (1979): Reversal by naloxone of adaptation of rats to noxious stimuli. *Life Sci.,* 24:685.

Perspectives in Schizophrenia Research,
edited by C. Baxter and T. Melnechuk.
Raven Press, New York, 1980.

Elevation of Brain Neuroleptic/Dopamine Receptors in Schizophrenia

*Philip Seeman, *Tyrone Lee, **E. D. Bird, and †Wallace W. Tourtellotte

**Department of Pharmacology, University of Toronto, Toronto, Ontario, Canada; **Department of Pathology, Harvard University, McLean Hospital, Belmont, Massachusetts 02178; and †Department of Neurology, Wadsworth V.A. Medical Center, Los Angeles, California 90025*

LAYPERSON'S SUMMARY

The antidopaminergic actions of the neuroleptic drugs provide a strategy for searching for dopaminergic abnormalities in schizophrenia brain tissue. In order to test the dopamine hypothesis of schizophrenia, the neuroleptic/dopamine receptors in three dopamine-rich regions of 53 postmortem normal human brains and 42 schizophrenic brains were measured using ^{3}H-haloperidol and ^{3}H-spiperone. The binding of 2 nM ^{3}H-haloperidol was significantly elevated in the caudate nucleus (90 $\pm$ 10%) and the putamen (61 $\pm$ 6%) from schizophrenic brains. The binding of 1 nM ^{3}H-spiperone was also elevated by 50 $\pm$ 7% in schizophrenic caudate and 47 $\pm$ 8% in the putamen. The nucleus accumbens from schizophrenic brains revealed an enhanced binding of 110 to 115%. In those schizophrenic patients who had no history of being treated with neuroleptic drugs, the brain regions also exhibited significantly higher (29 to 80%) binding of the ^{3}H-neuroleptics. The results are compatible with the hypothesis that schizophrenia may be associated with an overactivity of post-synaptic dopamine receptors.

INTRODUCTION

The clinical effectiveness of the antipsychotic drugs provides a new strategy for unlocking the chemical mysteries of schizophrenia. An important rationale, therefore, is to try to understand how these drugs work, and this understanding might lead to a knowledge of where in the brain schizophrenia might be triggered. Knowing the locations of disease in the brain could then lead to new and better treatment.

The dopamine hypothesis of schizophrenia essentially states that schizophrenia may be associated with an overactivity of dopamine synapses (2,7,14,30–32, 45,46,49). Although there is no evidence directly demonstrating such an overactivity, there is wide circumstantial support for the hypothesis. For example, neuroleptic drugs effectively block dopamine synapses (1,8,10,45) and receptors (12,20,25,39–41,43,44,48), as well as block the psychotomimetic effects of dopamine-mimetic drugs [amphetamine (45) and apomorphine (10,19,37)].

Dopaminergic hyperactivity may arise, among other possibilities, from either an increased amount of brain dopamine, an increase in the number or sensitivity of the postsynaptic dopamine receptors (22–24,42,47), or a decrease in the number of presynaptic dopamine receptors (24,36). The dopamine content of various brain regions in the postmortem brains from schizophrenic patients has been reported to be normal (17) or elevated (4) in the nucleus accumbens, whereas the content in the striatum is the same as normal (4,17). No difference was found between the dopamine-sensitive adenylate cyclase in the striatum between schizophrenic and control tissues (9).

In order to test for the presence of abnormal properties of dopamine receptors, we have been measuring the binding of ^{3}H-neuroleptics to dopamine-rich regions in postmortem brains from patients who had schizophrenia (22–24,42,47). The present report extends these previous data up to a total of 53 neurologically normal controls and 42 schizophrenic postmortem brains.

Postmortem human brain tissues were obtained from the Wadsworth V.A. Hospital (Los Angeles; Dr. W. W. Tourtellotte), Addenbrookes Hospital (Cambridge, England; Drs. E. D. Bird and E. G. Spokes), the Clarke Institute of Psychiatry (Toronto; Dr. O. Hornykiewicz), and the Toronto Western Hospital (Toronto; Dr. J. Deck). Control human brains were those from individuals who had died suddenly of non-neurological causes such as car accidents, myocardial infarction, or pneumonia. Informed consent was obtained from the next of kin. The criteria used for diagnosis of schizophrenia in this study have been outlined (4).

The average age of the control subjects was 54 years (range 19 to 88). The average age of the schizophrenic patients was 52 years (range 17 to 92). The interval between death and freezing of the brain (autolysis time) for control tissues was 30 hr and for schizophrenic tissues was 37 hr.

As shown in Fig. 1, the specific binding of 2 nM ^{3}H-haloperidol (custom-prepared for this laboratory in 1974 by I. R. E. Belgique) to schizophrenic caudates was 90% higher than normal ($p < 0.001$; two-tailed Student's *t*-test). The average increase in schizophrenic putamens was 61% ($p < 0.001$). The specific binding of 1 nM ^{3}H-spiperone to schizophrenic caudates was elevated by about 50% and that for the schizophrenic putamen was 47% higher ($p < 0.001$). There were also large increases in the specific binding of these ^{3}H-neuroleptics to the schizophrenic nucleus accumbens: 110% increase for ^{3}H-haloperidol binding and 115% increase for ^{3}H-spiperone binding (Fig. 2).

Of the 42 schizophrenic cases, 11 of them had apparently never (as far as we could ascertain) received any neuroleptic drugs in the course of the disease or at least in the last year before death. The average (± SEM) ^{3}H-neuroleptic binding of these "non-neurolepticized" brains is shown in Fig. 3. Both the drug-

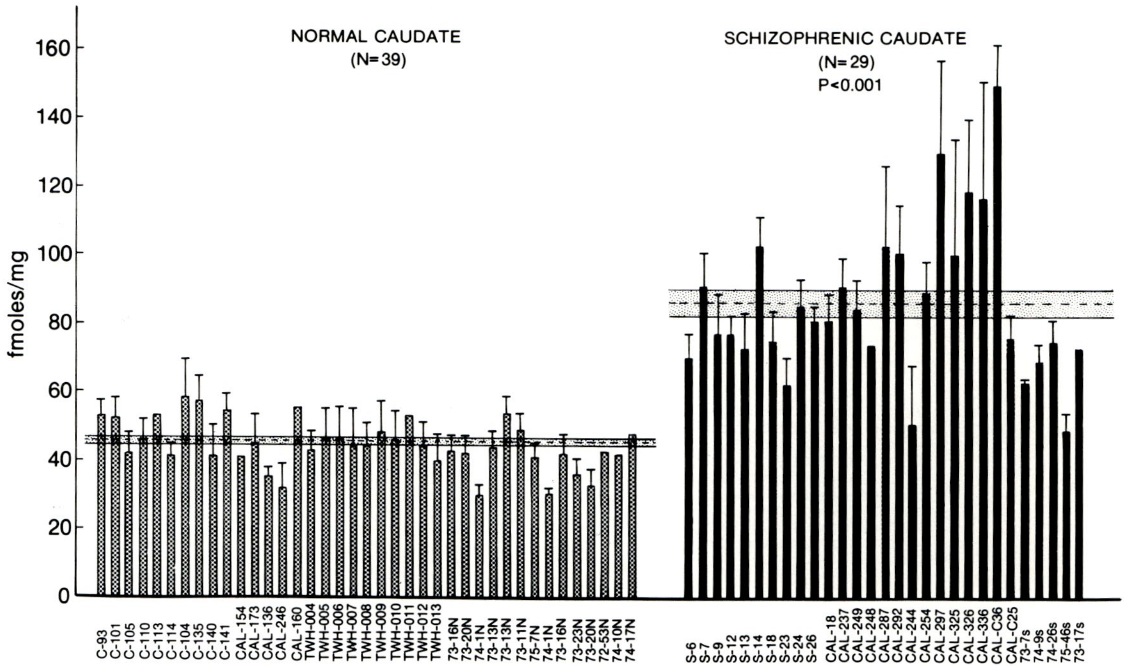

FIG. 1. The specific binding of ^{3}H-haloperidol to homogenates of schizophrenic caudates *(dark columns)* is higher than to control caudates *(light gray columns)*. Each column indicates an average of 4–10 separate assays (in sextuplicate) for each patient's brain region; vertical bars represent SEM. The horizontal lines, interrupted and solid, indicate the mean and SEM, respectively, for each group. Tissues were obtained from 4 different sources. The specific binding of ^{3}H-haloperidol in the schizophrenic caudate was higher by 90% ($p < 0.001$).

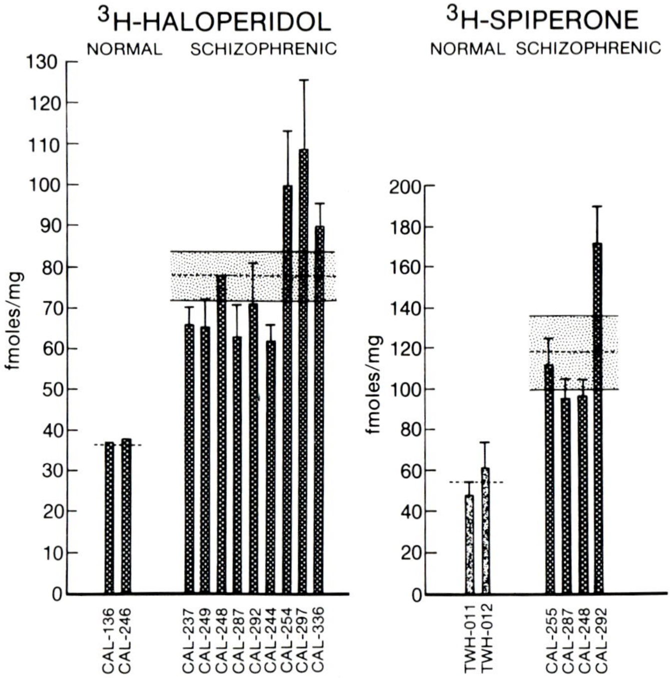

FIG. 2. ^{3}H-Neuroleptic binding in nucleus accumbens from normal and schizophrenic brains. Columns with vertical bars represent average of 4–10 separate assays (in sextuplicate) with SEM. The horizontal lines, interrupted and solid, indicate the mean and SEM, respectively. The specific binding of ^{3}H-haloperidol in the schizophrenic nucleus accumbens was higher by 110%. The specific binding of ^{3}H-spiperone in the schizophrenic nucleus accumbens was higher by 115%.

treated and untreated schizophrenic groups showed significant elevation ($p < 0.001$) in ^{3}H-haloperidol as well as ^{3}H-spiperone binding. However, there was no significant difference ($p > 0.1$) between the drug-treated and untreated groups.

The present results confirm our previous findings that there is an increase in ^{3}H-neuroleptic binding in schizophrenic brains.

Of the schizophrenic brains, 11 of them (74–9s, 74–26s, 75–46s, S–4, S–14, S–15, S–21, S–22, S–27, S–40, S–42) were from patients who had apparently not received any neuroleptics or at least not any during the last year before death. These "untreated" tissues also exhibited an increase in ^{3}H-neuroleptic binding in both the caudate and the putamen. Although there is a limited number of untreated brains assayed, the data indicate that it may be unlikely that the increase in binding is totally drug-induced. Long-term administration of massive neuroleptic doses to animals generally results in an increase of less than 30% (34,35).

The larger difference between normal and schizophrenic tissues found using

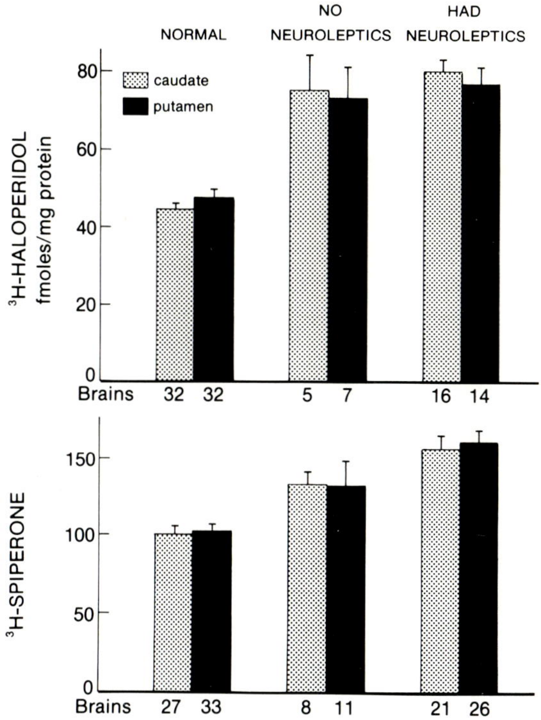

FIG. 3. Binding of ^{3}H-neuroleptics to caudates and putamens from patients who did receive and who did not receive neuroleptic drugs. The binding was significantly higher in both treated and untreated groups when compared to the controls ($p < 0.001$). No significant difference was found between the treated and untreated schizophrenic groups ($p < 0.1$). The untreated patients were 74–26s, 75–46s, 74–9s, S–4, S–14, S–15, S–21, S–22, S–27, S–40, and S–42.

^{3}H-haloperidol (compared to ^{3}H-spiperone) is not surprising because it is known that ^{3}H-spiperone also has a high affinity for serotonin sites (13,26,27).

Owen et al. (38) and Crow et al. (15) have recently confirmed (22–24,42,47) a 50% elevation of ^{3}H-spiperone binding (at 0.8 nM) in 19 schizophrenic caudates and putamens. Mackay et al. (29), however, found no significant difference in ^{3}H-spiperone binding to the schizophrenic nucleus accumbens, but their method was somewhat different; more recently, however, these workers did find an increase in ^{3}H-spiperone binding (Mackay, Iversen, Creese, and Snyder, presented at the Monte Carlo conference on long-term effects of neuroleptics, 1979).

The present results are compatible with previous literature (5,6,21,29,33,50) indicating some association between striatal and psychological abnormalities. The increased ^{3}H-neuroleptic binding may also partly explain the dopaminergic supersensitivity of tardive dyskinesia (3,11,34,35). Finally, it may be possible to use "desensitization therapy" (with L-DOPA or bromocryptine) to reduce the number of ^{3}H-neuroleptic/dopamine receptors in schizophrenic patients (16,18,28).

ACKNOWLEDGMENTS

We thank Dr. E. G. Spokes of Addenbrookes Hospital, Cambridge, Dr. O. Hornykiewicz of the Clarke Institute of Psychiatry, Toronto, and Dr. J. Deck of the Toronto Western Hospital for postmortem tissues. This work was supported by the Ontario Mental Health Foundation and the Medical Research council of Canada (MT-2951).

REFERENCES

1. Andén, N. E. (1972): Dopamine turnover in the corpus striatum and the limbic system after treatment with neuroleptic and anti-acetylcholine drugs. *J. Pharm. Pharmacol.,* 24:905–906.
2. Baldessarini, R. J. (1977): Schizophrenia. *N. Engl. J. Med.,* 297:988–995.
3. Baldessarini, R. J., and Tarsy, D. (1976): Mechanisms underlying tardive dyskinesia. In: *The Basal Ganglia,* edited by M. D. Yahr, pp. 433–446. Raven Press, New York.
4. Bird, E. D., Barnes, J., Iversen, L. L., Spokes, E. G., Mackay, A. V. P., and Shepherd, M. (1977): Increased brain dopamine and reduced glutamic acid decarboxylase and choline acetyl transferase activity in schizophrenia and related psychoses. *Lancet,* ii:1157–1159.
5. Birkmayer, W., Jellinger, K., and Riederer, P. (1977): Striatal and extrastriatal dopaminergic functions. In: *Psychobiology of the Striatum,* edited by A. R. Cools, A. H. M. Lohman, and J. H. L. Van den Bercken, pp. 141–153. Elsevier/North Holland Biomedical Press, Amsterdam.
6. Bowen, F. P. (1976): Behavioural alterations in patients with basal ganglia lesions. In: *The Basal Ganglia,* edited by M. D. Yahr, pp. 169–180. Raven Press, New York.
7. Bowers, M. B. (1974): Central dopamine turnover in schizophrenic syndromes. *Arch. Gen. Psychiatry,* 31:50–54.
8. Bunney, B. S., Walters, J. R., Roth, R. H., and Aghajanian, G. (1973): Dopaminergic neurons: Effect of antipsychotic drugs and amphetamine on single cell activity. *J. Pharmacol. Exp. Ther.,* 185:560–571.
9. Carenzi, A., Gillin, J. C., Guidotti, A., Schwartz, M. A., Trabucchi, M., and Wyatt, R. J. (1975): Dopamine-sensitive adenylyl cyclase in human caudate nucleus. A study in control subjects and schizophrenic patients. *Arch. Gen. Psychiatry,* 32:1056–1059.
10. Carlsson, A. (1978): Antipsychotic drugs, neurotransmitters and schizophrenia. *Am. J. Psychiatry,* 135:164–173.
11. Christensen, E., Møller, J. E., and Faurbye, A. (1970): Neuropathological investigation of 28 brains from patients with dyskinesia. *Acta Psychiatr. Scand.,* 46:14–23.
12. Creese, I., Burt, D. R., and Snyder, S. H. (1975): Dopamine receptor binding: Differentiation of agonist and antagonist states with ^{3}H-dopamine and ^{3}H-haloperidol. *Life Sci.,* 17:993–1002.
13. Creese, I., and Snyder, S. H. (1978): ^{3}H-Spiroperidol labels serotonin receptors in rat cerebral cortex and hippocampus. *Eur. J. Pharmacol.,* 49:201–202.
14. Crow, T. J., Deakin, J. F. W., Johnstone, E. C., and Longden, A. (1976): Dopamine and schizophrenia. *Lancet,* ii:563–566.
15. Crow, T. J., Johnstone, E. C., Longden, A. J., and Owen, F. (1978): Dopaminergic mechanisms in schizophrenia: The antipsychotic effect and the disease process. *Life Sci.,* 23:563–568.
16. Ezrin-Waters, C., and Seeman, P. (1978): L-DOPA reversal of hyperdopaminergic behavior. *Life Sci.,* 22:1027–1032.
17. Farley, I. J., Price, K. S., and Hornykiewicz, O. (1977): Dopamine in the limbic regions of the human brain: Normal and abnormal. *Adv. Biochem. Psychopharmacol.,* 16:57–64.
18. Friedhoff, A. J., Bonnet, K., and Rosengarten, H. (1977): Reversal of two manifestations of dopamine receptor supersensitivity by administration of L-DOPA. *Res. Commun. Chem. Pathol. Pharmacol.,* 16:411–423.
19. Janssen, P. A. J., and Allewijn, F. T. N. (1969): The distribution of the butyrophenones haloperidol, trifluperidol, moperone, and clofluperol in rats, and its relationship with their neuroleptic activity. *Arzneim. Forsch.,* 19:199–208.
20. Kebabian, J. W. (1978): Multiple classes of dopamine receptors in mammalian central nervous system: The involvement of dopamine-sensitive adenylyl cyclase. *Life Sci.,* 23:479–484.

21. Klawans, H. L. Jr., Goetz, C., and Westheimer, R. (1972): Pathophysiology of schizophrenia and the striatum. *Dis. Nerv. Syst.*, 33:711–719.
22. Lee, T., and Seeman, P. (1977): Dopamine receptors in normal and schizophrenic human brains. *Soc. Neurosci. Abstr.*, 3:433.
23. Lee, T., and Seeman, P. (1978): Enhanced ^{3}H-neuroleptic binding in the post-mortem schizophrenic brains. *Soc. Neurosci. Abstr.*, 4:496.
24. Lee, T., Seeman, P., Tourtellotte, W. W., Farley, I., and Hornykiewicz, O. (1978): Binding of ^{3}H-neuroleptics and ^{3}H-apomorphine in schizophrenic brains. *Nature,* 274:897–900.
25. Leysen, J. E., Gommeren, W., and Laduron, P. M. (1978): Spiperone: A ligand of choice for neuroleptic receptors. 1. Kinetics and characteristics of in vitro binding. *Biochem. Pharmacol.*, 27:307–316.
26. Leysen, J. E., and Laduron, P. M. (1977): A serotonergic component of neuroleptic receptors. *Arch. Int. Pharmacodyn. Ther.*, 230:337–339.
27. Leysen, J. E., Niemegeers, C. J. E., Tollenaere, J. P., and Laduron, P. M. (1978): Serotonergic component of neuroleptic receptors. *Nature,* 272:168–171.
28. List, S., and Seeman, P. (1979): Dopamine agonists reverse the elevated ^{3}H-neuroleptic binding in neuroleptic-pretreated rats. *Life Sci.*, 24:1447–1452.
29. Mackay, A. V. P., Doble, A., Bird, E. D., Spokes, E. G., Quik, M., and Iversen, L. L. (1978): ^{3}H-Spiperone binding in normal and schizophrenic post-mortem human brain. *Life Sci.*, 23:527–532.
30. Matthysse, S. (1973): Antipsychotic drug actions: A clue to the neuropathology of schizophrenia? *Fed. Proc.*, 32:200–205.
31. Matthysse, S., and Lipinski, J. (1975): Biochemical aspects of Schizophrenia. *Annu. Rev. Med.*, 26:551–565.
32. Meltzer, H. Y., Sachar, E. J., and Frantz, A. G. (1974): Serum prolactin levels in unmedicated schizophrenic patients. *Arch. Gen. Psychiatry,* 31:564–569.
33. Mettler, F. A. (1955): Perceptual capacity, functions of the corpus striatum and schizophrenia. *Psychiatr. Q.*, 29:89–111.
34. Muller, P., Bowles, J., and Seeman, P. (1977): Dopaminergic and cholinergic receptors in striatal and limbic regions after chronic haloperidol. *Soc. Neurosci. Abstr.*, 3:459.
35. Muller, P., and Seeman, P. (1978): Dopaminergic supersensitivity after neuroleptics: Timecourse and specificity. *Psychopharmacology,* 60:1–11.
36. Nagy, J. I., Lee, T., Seeman, P., and Fibiger, H. C. (1978): Direct evidence for pre-synaptic and post-synaptic dopamine receptors in brain. *Nature,* 274:278–281.
37. Niemegeers, C. J. E., and Janssen, P. A. J. (1978): *In vivo* competitive interaction between haloperidol and apomorphine. Proc. 11th Colleg. Int. Neuropsychopharmacol, Vienna.
38. Owen, F., Crow, T. J., Poulter, M., Cross, J., Longden, A., and Riley, C. J. (1978): Increased dopamine-receptor sensitivity in schizophrenia. *Lancet,* ii:223–226.
39. Seeman, P., Chau-Wong, M., Tedesco, J., and Wong, K. (1975): Brain receptors for antipsychotic drugs and dopamine: Direct binding assays. *Proc. Natl. Acad. Sci. U.S.A.*, 71:4376–4380.
40. Seeman, P., Lee, T., Chau-Wong, M., Tedesco, J., and Wong, K. (1976): Dopamine receptors in human and calf brain, using ^{3}H-apomorphine and an antipsychotic drug. *Proc. Natl. Acad. Sci. U.S.A.*, 73:4354–4358.
41. Seeman, P., Lee, T., Chau-Wong, M., and Wong, K. (1976): Antipsychotic drug doses and neuroleptic/dopamine receptors. *Nature,* 261:717–719.
42. Seeman, P., Titeler, M., Tedesco, J., Weinreich, P., and Sinclair, D. (1978): Brain receptors for dopamine and neuroleptics. *Adv. Biochem. Psychopharmacol.*, 19:167–176.
43. Seeman, P., Wong, M., and Lee, T. (1974): Dopamine receptor-block and nigral fiber impulse-blockade by major tranquilizers. *Fed. Proc.*, 33:246.
44. Seeman, P., Wong, M., and Tedesco, J. (1975): Tranquilizer receptors in rat striatum. *Soc. Neurosci. Abstr.*, 1:405.
45. Snyder, S. H. (1976): The dopamine hypothesis of schizophrenia: Focus on the dopamine receptor. *Am. J. Psychiatry,* 133:197–202.
46. Steven, J. R. (1973): An anatomy of schizophrenia? *Arch. Gen. Psychiatry,* 29:177–189.
47. Timnick, L. (1977): *Los Angeles Times,* Vol. XCVI, November 9, 1977.
48. Titeler, M., Tedesco, J., and Seeman, P. (1978): Selective labeling of pre-synaptic receptors by ^{3}H-dopamine, ^{3}H-apomorphine and ^{3}H-clonidine; Labeling of postsynaptic sites by ^{3}H-neuroleptics. *Life Sci.*, 23:587–592.

49. Van Praag, H. M. (1977): The significance of dopamine for the mode of action of neuroleptics and the pathogenesis of schizophrenia. *Br. J. Psychiatry,* 130:463–474.
50. Yarden, P. E., and Discipio, W. J. (1971): Abnormal movements and prognosis in schizophrenia. *Am. J. Psychiatry,* 128:317–323.

Discussion

Carpenter: Are there any other illnesses or clinical syndromes where an increase in postsynaptic binding sites is thought to be primary rather than secondary?

Seeman: When patients with Parkinson's disease walk into the clinic for the first time they are already supersensitive to dopamine, having abnormally more postsynaptic dopamine receptors in the lesioned striatum, as a compensation for the massive depletion of released dopamine that follows the loss of pigmented neurons. Therefore they respond beautifully to low doses of L-DOPA or bromocriptine. This and many other disorders involving abnormalities of receptor numbers or affinities are surveyed in what is still the only book on the subject, by Ted Melnechuk (9).

Meltzer: Why should schizophrenic patients have increased numbers of neuroleptic binding sites rather than less? If presynaptic dopamine activity is increased as the primary abnormality, one would expect to find postsynaptic subsensitivity; i.e., decreased numbers or affinity of postsynaptic receptors. Quik and Iversen (11) and Howletter and Nahorski (7) reported decreased numbers of [^{3}H]spiroperidol binding sites in rat striatal membranes after chronic administration of bromocriptine or *d*-amphetamine, respectively. This is what one might predict we should find in schizophrenic brains if there had been excessive presynaptic dopaminergic activity.

Seeman: There are more receptors. Whether they're there all of the time I don't know. And I don't know how the patient compensates for them during remission if they're present then.

Meltzer: After unilateral 6-hydroxydopamine-induced lesioning of the substantia nigra, which has been used by many investigators as a model for supersensitivity of the nigrostriatal dopaminergic pathway (13), there is an increase in the number of dopamine receptors (3). The rotation induced in these animals by dopamine agonists is blocked by neuroleptics but the doses required are relatively high compared with doses required to block other behaviors induced by these agents in nonlesioned, nonsupersensitive animals.

Seeman: But by denervating with 6-hydroxydopamine one removes the dopamine. Parkinson's disease patients have many dopamine receptors, but they're not psychotic, because they lack dopamine to bind. Psychiatrists tell us that if Parkinsonian patients are given L-DOPA, which restores dopamine, the patients have hallucinations.

Henn: Yet the literature shows that having Parkinson's disease doesn't protect against schizophrenia.

Meltzer: Why do you find three times as many binding sites for neuroleptics as for dopamine agonists, whereas Dr. Henn finds more binding sites for agonists than for neuroleptics?

Seeman: The two kinds of binding sites are physically separate and different in numbers. Some may be on glia.

Meltzer: Your data on sulpiride appears to disagree with that of other investigators. Howard et al. (6) find that it's about six to seven times less potent a dopamine antagonist than tritiated haloperidol, whereas you find it to be as potent as chlorpromazine.

Seeman: The sulpiride should be done on radio haloperidol binding.

Meltzer: You may be overemphasizing the micromolar versus nanomolar issue. One can show no effect of neuroleptics on pituitary prolactin secretion in the high micromolar range, because they have no direct action; instead, they antagonize dopamine. If used to antagonize the effect of a dopamine agonist, one can readily show neuroleptic effects in the nanomolar range. Lack of a direct effect of neuroleptics may mean nothing if they are really antagonists.

Seeman: Dopamine content is normal, but dopamine activity is higher, because of the increase in postsynaptic receptors.

Meltzer: You have suggested that the binding studies from bovine caudate may be extrapolated to humans. Could you provide more evidence for this?

Seeman: The original bovine data were too high by a factor of two but we have since regenerated the data and it's correct now.

Bird: You mentioned a binding difference between animal and human. In what animal?

Seeman: Wistar rats on massive doses of haloperidol for 3 weeks, which of course does not simulate the years of medication that human patients get. We wanted to see what the quality of the picture would be if animals received 10 mg per kilo per day for 3 weeks. Their receptors go up about 30% postsynaptically and 70% presynaptically.

K. Davis: Was the difference between rats and people given haloperidol that the presynaptic receptors go up in rats but do not go up in people?

Seeman: Yes. The binding of tritiated apomorphine, which selects presynaptic sites to bind to, does not go up in treated people. In rats getting long-term neuroleptics such as chlorpromazine, it always goes up.

K. Davis: Why?

Seeman: We know that neuroleptics have both pre- and postsynaptic actions in animals. We don't know if this is true in humans.

Baxter: What evidence is there that any of these receptors bind with high affinity?

Seeman: It's true that in human tissue we have not fully characterized them; thus we don't know for sure. We use radioactive haloperidol to tag whatever it tags. What needs to be done is to miniaturize these assays, with a full panoply of drugs, Scatchard analyses, and so forth, so that we can do a complete characterization of this one small piece of tissue.

Kleinman: In those patients whose receptor levels you've measured, have dopamine levels been measured as well?

Seeman: Yes, in some of those sent us by Dr. Bird, but overall the differences were small.

Bird: Dopamine *is* increased in the nucleus accumbens, but there is no significant increase in either the putamen or the caudate nucleus.

Matthysse: This suggests a project appropriate for the VA. You tried to control for the possible prior effect of neuroleptics by looking at some drug-free patients and also at pre- versus post-treatment cases. A nice way might be to look at patients who are young. Haloperidol is a good isotope for positron emission tomography (PET) because its constituent fluorine is a positron emitter. Repeat *in vivo* the experiment you now do *in vitro:* Give your patient haloperidol and then wash the blood system with either + or − butaclamol. The experiment would be reasonably safe. Then you could look at the binding before the patient has been on drugs for any length of time.

Seeman: Very interesting. I think it's being done by the McMaster group (5).

Buchsbaum: New ligands are being explored at the NIMH, but results are already reported with labeled chlorpromazine, by Comar et al. (4). The NIMH and Brookhaven groups are concentrating on labeled deoxyglucose, since they know better what happens to glucose than to labeled chlorpromazine or haloperidol. The field needs good radioactive ligands for those drugs. With our new scanner it will be a year or so before we have results with labeled neuroleptics. The NINCDS is supporting five PET centers, which will probably be used more for neurological than for psychiatric research.

Schooler: One possible way to control for neuroleptics is to find nonschizophrenic individuals who have received chronic neuroleptic treatment. It may be difficult in practice but it ought to be possible to accomplish.

Melnechuk: If only in those Soviet hospitals where dissenters are imprisoned, called schizophrenic, and given neuroleptics.

Seeman: You are reminding me to pursue with phenothiazines the allergists who put patients on long-term antihistamines.

Schooler: Are postmortem specimens usually looked at blind? Or do the dissectors also do the chemical analyses?

Seeman: A bit of both. When Dr. Bird sent us specimens, he told us what was what, but we also did some dissecting ourselves. But the time is coming when the two will be done by different people.

Hiatt: Was there a difference in the mode of death between the normals and the schizophrenics?

Seeman: No. Most died from pneumonia and car accidents; there was the same number of suicides, although there were fewer myocardial infarctions in the schizophrenics.

Weinberger: Here's an interpretation of your findings that fits in with our morphological work. Perhaps what you're seeing is the biological sequelae of a structural denervation. These postsynaptic cells may be losing their presynaptic inputs, whether neuronal or glial, and are behaving much as postsynaptic elements in Parkinsonian patients behave.

Seeman: It could be.

Weinberger: People with early Alzheimer's disease resemble psychotics.

Seeman: And so do many Huntington's patients, in the early stages, though dopamine receptors are down 50% in the late stages of HD.

Henn: If you think of tardive dyskinesia as being caused by dopamine supersensitivity, why don't we see exacerbations of psychosis in a condition where at least the motor system has an increase in dopamine receptors?

Seeman: Psychiatrists and neurologists have told us for years that schizophrenic patients have soft neurological motor signs that may stem from the basal ganglia. Still, I don't think that schizophrenia stems from basal ganglia in a hyperdopaminergic state. Dr. Meltzer tells us that the pituitary doesn't really show evidence of dopamine supersensitivity. Schizophrenia may not be a generalized dopaminergic disorder.

Brown: The dopamine hypothesis of schizophrenia, which has obviously had much heuristic value, rests primarily on two pieces of indirect evidence. One is that all effective neuroleptics block dopamine receptors, and the other is that if you give normal people enough *d*-amphetamine for a long enough period of time, they will behave something like schizophrenics. But neuroleptics don't cure schizophrenia, and amphetamine has other effects besides psychosis. So we needn't try to fit all of our findings to the Procrustean bed of the dopamine hypothesis.

Seeman: I agree.

J. Davis: There is more evidence for the hypothesis: L-DOPA makes patients paranoid, as do cocaine, Ritalin, amphetamine, and all drugs of that class; schizophrenics have their psychosis worsened by very small doses of intravenous Ritalin, and it happens only when they're symptomatic, not after they've recovered. Postsynaptic receptor stimulants also make schizophrenics worse. Granted, all of this evidence is indirect.

Meltzer: I closed my review (10) of the dopamine hypothesis with the remark that the theory had reached the point where it could explain any data, however an experiment turned out, by invocation of pre- and postsynaptic receptor effects, so that it had lost some of its heuristic value to a significant extent.

Singh: [Des-Tyr[1]]-γ-endorphin, which a Dutch group (14) has just reported to have antipsychotic properties, does not seem to have the neurochemical or neurophysiological effects associated with neuroleptics; so even if schizophrenia does have a dopaminergic component (or, more accurately, a neuroleptic-responsive component), which seems related to psychomotor activation, is worsened by antimuscarinics, and is most evident in catatonic schizophrenics, there is also at least one other component that is not neuroleptic-responsive and probably not dopaminergic (8).

Nasrallah: Have you done any work with Suzuki on non-receptor-blocking neuroleptics?

Seeman: No.

Nasrallah: We have been giving reserpine to drug-resistant chronic schizophrenics without changing their dose of neuroleptics. We find that some of those patients who never fully responded before to neuroleptics improve markedly after reserpine treatment. We also find that some patients who responded moderately well to reserpine doses of 4 to 8 mg did still better with reserpine doses of 12 to 16 mg. In terms of the dopamine hypothesis, giving reserpine makes sense because it depletes dopamine.

Seeman: It seems perfectly reasonable.

Yuwiler: You can interpret that another way: Giving reserpine may slowly desensitize the postsynaptic receptors because of constant low level stimulation by newly formed monoamine.

Nasrallah: I must add that reserpine depletes not only dopamine but also other monoamines, such as norepinephrine and serotonin. This may hearken back to the heterogeneity issue, for patients may be responding to changes in those monoamines.

Meltzer: The pharmacology is even more complicated than that. Although neuroleptics acutely increase dopamine turnover in the striatum, tolerance develops rapidly in animals and man. In man dopamine turnover is no longer increased after about a month of neuroleptic treatment, although recent studies by Bacopoulos et al. (2) suggest it may continue to be increased in various areas of the cortex.

The initial effect of a single dose of reserpine in rats is to decrease dopamine synthesis. Later you get an increase in dopamine synthesis. After chronic reserpine treatment, there appears to be no effect whatsoever on dopamine synthesis. So, if you are in fact demonstrating this kind of an interaction of reserpine and neuroleptics, rather than finding that in support of the dopamine hypothesis, I would consider looking elsewhere for the explanation, as you implied in your further remark.

Cole: In the early days, there was a belief, held mainly by George Brooks in Vermont, that giving chlorpromazine with reserpine was better than giving either one alone. I'm glad Dr. Nasrallah seems to be confirming that.

Savage: Our group at the VA in Baltimore has also found that reserpine is a useful additive (1,12). Dr. Nasrallah, have you found it necessary to go before your human rights committee? I used reserpine 25 years ago; it was safe and effective then, and it still is, but some reviewers required that we tell them exactly what we told the patient. Only then would they publish. Have you met a similar response?

Nasrallah: Not quite. We were able to document having very few side effects. It's amazing how stable blood pressures are, even at high doses of reserpine.

REFERENCES

1. Bacher, N. M., and Lewis, H. A. (1979): Addition of reserpine to antipsychotic medication in refractory manic patients. *Am. J. Psychiatry,* 136:811–814.
2. Bacopoulos, N. C., Spokes, E. G., Bird, E. D., and Roth, R. H. (1979): Antipsychotic drug action in schizophrenic patients: Effect on cortical dopamine metabolism after long-term treatment. *Science,* 205:1405–1407.
3. Creese, I., Burt, D. R., and Snyder, S. H. (1977): Dopamine receptor binding enhancement accompanies lesion-induced behavioral supersensitivity. *Science,* 197:596–598.
4. Comar, D., Zarifian, E., Verhas, M., Soussaline, F., Maziere, M., Berger, F., Loo, H., Cuche, H., Kellersholn, and Deniker, P. (1979): Brain distribution and kinetics of ^{11}C-chlorpromazine in schizophrenics: Positive emission tomography studies. *Psychiatr. Res.* 1:23–30.
5. Garnett, E. S., Firnau, G., Chan, P. K. H., Sood, S., and Belbeck, L. W. (1978): [^{18}F]Fluorodopa, an analogue of dopa, and its use in direct external measurements of storage, degradation, and turnover of intracerebral dopamine. *Proc. Natl. Acad. Sci. USA,* 75:464–467.
6. Howard, J. L., Large, B. T., Wedley, S. and Pullar, I. A. (1978): The effects of standard neuroleptic compounds on the binding of ^{3}H-spiroperidol in the striatum and mesolimbic system of the rat *in vitro. Life Sci.,* 23:599–604.

7. Howletter, D. R., and Nahorski, S. R. (1979): Acute and chronic amphetamine treatments modulate striatal dopamine receptor binding sites. *Brain Res.,* 161:173–178.
8. Kay, S. R., and Singh, M. M. (1979): Cognitive abnormality in schizophrenia: A dual process model. *Biol. Psychiatry,* 14:155–176.
9. Melnechuk, T. (1978): *Cell Receptor Disorders.* Western Behavioral Sciences Institute, La Jolla, CA.
10. Meltzer, H. Y., and Stahl, S. M. (1976): The dopamine hypothesis of schizophrenia: A review. *Schizophr. Bull.,* 2:19–76.
11. Quik, M., and Iversen, L. L. (1978): Subsensitivity of the rat striatal dopaminergic system after treatment with bromocriptine: Effects on [^{3}H]spiperone binding and dopamine-stimulated cyclic AMP formation. *Naunyn Schmiederbergs Arch. Pharmacol.,* 304:141–145.
12. Savage, C., and Day, J. (1958): Effect of a tranquilizer (reserpine) on psychodynamic and social processes. *AMA Arch. Neurol. Psychiatr.,* 79:590–596.
13. Ungersted, U. (1971): Postsynaptic supersensitivity after 6-hydroxydopamine-induced degeneration of the nigro-striatal dopamine system. *Acta Physiol. Scand. (Suppl.),* 367:69–93.
14. Verhoeven, W. M. A., van Praag, H. M., Ree, J. M. V., and de Wied, D. (1979): Improvement of schizophrenic patients treated with [des-tyr^1]-γ-endorphin (DTγE). *Arch. Gen. Psychiatry,* 36:294–298.

Perspectives in Schizophrenia Research,
edited by C. Baxter and T. Melnechuk.
Raven Press, New York, 1980.

Biological Concepts of Schizophrenia

Fritz A. Henn

Department of Psychiatry, University of Iowa School of Medicine, Iowa City, Iowa 52240

LAYPERSON'S SUMMARY

Early investigations of antipsychotic drugs led to a simple theory of the biochemical abnormality in schizophrenia. This theory stated that a possible neurotransmitter, dopamine, was found in excess in schizophrenic illness. This one abnormality explained how all of the drugs which alleviate schizophrenic symptoms might work. This unitary explanation must be evaluated in light of the clinical evidence suggesting schizophrenia is a label covering many illnesses. Closer investigations of dopamine's localization and sites of action suggest that it may not be acting only as a neurotransmitter in the brain. Our laboratory has shown that receptors for dopamine exist on astroglial cells, non-neuronal cells which surround nerve cells in the central nervous system. Furthermore, we feel that these receptors are metabolically coupled to control mechanisms regulating nerve cell activity. Other investigators have shown that dopamine is physically located in such a way as to suggest it acts as a neuromodulator. Putting these facts together suggests to us that dopamine may have a modulator role in the brain which could be compared to an amplifier in an electric circuit. Namely, this substance can regulate the amount of flow through the system. This is just like changing the volume control of a radio. Such a theory explains how drugs acting on one system might be effective in many differing illnesses. It also points to the need to get a better understanding of basic brain mechanisms before we can explain complex illnesses of the central nervous system. Biological investigations therefore need strong basic as well as clinical support. One further area which could be clinically helpful is the development of biochemical tests which would help identify patients with schizophrenia; one such study is reported and this area needs further investigations.

INTRODUCTION

In reviewing the clinical studies presented here on schizophrenia, one is struck with the ever-increasing complexity presented by this group of disorders. After contemplating the difficulties, I fear we may find ourselves in the youthful position of Alexander Throckmorton from Edgar Lee Master's *Spoon River Anthology:*

> In youth my wings were strong and tireless
> but I did not know the mountains.
> In age I knew the mountains but my weary wings
> could not follow my vision.

Our tools, both biochemical and clinical, are becoming ever more powerful, yet it appears we have not found the right mountains. The great contribution this volume is making is in helping us to focus on problems, whose solutions may lead to an unraveling of some of these complexities.

Biological investigations as we have already seen can focus on immunological, neurohumoral, endocrine, or metabolic studies. These, to be useful, ought to be aimed at an etiological understanding of schizophrenia or at providing a valid biochemical marker for some group of these disorders. In these two areas biological research can have its greatest impact on understanding the schizophrenic illnesses. Clinical studies repeatedly suggest that schizophrenia is not a unitary illness but rather a group of illnesses. Yet the strategy that has gone the farthest in defining possible biochemical abnormalities in schizophrenia is based on the opposite assumption. An analysis of therapeutically useful drugs and their biochemical effects assumes that these drugs are acting on the areas of etiological significance for all of schizophrenia. This has been a useful assumption resulting in the dopamine theory of schizophrenia (29,33,37). Simply stated, this theory suggests that schizophrenic symptomatology results from a functional excess of dopamine at certain central receptors. Since this is the currently accepted theory concerning the biological mechanism in schizophrenia, it might be helpful to review the evidence on which it is based. This evidence is pharmacological in nature and rests on the biochemical actions of neuroleptic drugs and the mechanism of amphetamine psychosis.

EVIDENCE SUPPORTING A DOPAMINE THEORY OF SCHIZOPHRENIA

Amphetamine Psychosis

Amphetamine psychosis is the best model psychosis for understanding schizophrenia. The rationale is that if a toxic psychosis can mimic schizophrenic symptoms, an understanding of the central effect of the toxin may aid in understanding schizophrenia. Initially, hallucinogens were thought to provide model psychosis, but early on it was shown that the psychosis produced by these compounds was quite different from that seen in schizophrenia (24). This is in contrast to amphetamine psychosis which can be misdiagnosed as acute paranoid schizophrenia unless a history of drug abuse is obtained (4). The amphetamine psychosis which mimics paranoid psychosis is usually found in a chronic user and is seen in the absence of delirium. Other reactions to amphetamines are acute and toxic showing a psychosis with confusion and disorientation; this is not the illness of interest in modeling schizophrenia. Chronic administration of *d*-amphetamine is able to produce a paranoid psychosis in healthy volunteers which resembles paranoid schizophrenia (2). The mechanism by which amphetamine causes such a psychosis could involve either norepinephrine or dopamine since amphetamines interact with both neurotransmitter systems centrally. However, since the norepinephrine molecule is asymmetric and has stereoisomers while dopamine does not, a study using both the *d* and *l* forms of amphetamine should differentiate between these two possibilities. The *d*-amphetamine isomer is a more potent norepinephrine uptake inhibitor while both *d* and *l* forms are equally potent in blocking dopamine uptake (13). This and numerous lesion studies suggest that *d*-amphetamine interacts preferentially with norepinephrine systems while both isomers are equally effective on dopamine systems. Angrist, Shopsin, and Gershon (3) studied the ability of the two isomers of amphetamine to mimic paranoid psychosis in healthy volunteers. In general, their conclusions suggest that *d*- and *l*-amphetamine are nearly equipotent in eliciting psychotic symptoms. Thus amphetamine psychosis suggests that dopaminergic systems may be involved in symptom production.

Neuroleptic Drug Action

The biochemical action of neuroleptic drugs has provided the principal support for the dopamine theory of schizophrenia. Very early on it was recognized that drugs with antipsychotic properties differed from sedatives in important ways. In fact, the term "neuroleptic drugs" was coined to describe the effects of chlorpromazine and reserpine (15), two very different drugs, that both exhibited antipsychotic properties. It was soon discovered that all neuroleptic drugs appeared to interact with central dopamine systems. Reserpine depleted monoamine stores, and chlorpromazine and haloperidol were shown by Carlsson and Lindquist (7) to elevate the brain levels of methoxylated metabolites of norepinephrine and dopamine. They suggested on the basis of these data that neuroleptic drugs block receptors for catecholamines resulting in increased turnover for these compounds. Gradually this idea has received more and more experimental support. It now appears that among the catecholamines, dopamine is the most important in mediating antipsychotic responses because of a better correlation of dopaminergic effects with the clinical potency of various drugs. For example, direct effects of dopamine applied iontophoretically can be reversed by neuroleptics (1). Many studies have examined the site of action of dopamine, and an initial choice was the dopamine-stimulated adenyl cyclase which has been described in both striatal and limbic tissues. Greengard and co-workers (12,27) have suggested that dopamine sensitive adenyl cyclase may be coupled to the dopamine receptor and mediate the action of dopamine postsynaptically. Although considerable evidence now suggests that this is not the case (28,30), this model served as another test for neuroleptic drug action. In this scheme dopamine is thought to cause the activation of adenyl cyclase with the production of the second messenger 3′, 5′-cAMP. This in turn activates a specific phosphokinase resulting in the phosphorylation of specific membrane proteins. It is postulated that these would affect the membrane properties of the cell. If the dopamine hypothesis is correct, one would expect neuroleptic drugs to inhibit the production of 3′, 5′-cAMP by the dopamine-stimulated adenyl cyclase with potencies having rank orders similar to the clinical efficacy of the drugs. This is true with one exception (25). The butyrophenones, a potent group of neuroleptics, do not block the enzyme found in brain homogenates with anywhere near the potency they display clinically.

Recently, more direct methods of examining dopamine receptors have become available. Seeman and his co-workers developed a receptor assay using radioactively labeled butyrophenones. These assays described in Dr. Seeman's chapter allowed a direct measure of dopamine receptors. Both Seeman (31) and Snyder's (14) laboratories were able to show that all neuroleptics inhibit the binding of labeled haloperidol in proportion to their clinical potency. This is the strongest support to date for dopamine's role in schizophrenia. The fact that all chemical classes of drugs tested for their ability to inhibit binding correlate with clinical potency, while butyrophenones do not correlate in inhibiting the dopamine-sensitive adenyl cyclase, points to the possibility of multiple drug receptors.

EVIDENCE AT ODDS WITH THE UNITARY DOPAMINE THEORY OF SCHIZOPHRENIA

Thus the evidence for dopamine playing a role in schizophrenia rests on the actions of neuroleptics and an analogy to amphetamine psychosis. Further examination of both these areas raises several questions. First, amphetamines in general only lead to paranoid delusions, a symptom complex seen in affective disorders, schizophrenia, and toxic psychosis. Amphetamines do not give rise to the picture of chronic process schizophrenia. In addition, drugs which should certainly increase dopamine such as levadopa have inconsistent effects in producing psychosis (8). Investigations of dopamine metabolites in cerebrospinal fluid of schizophrenic patients fail to support the idea that dopamine is elevated in schizophrenia, for decreased metabolite levels are found (5). An analysis of the principal symptoms of schizophrenia, which include thought disorder, delusions, hallucinations, and problems in relating to others, suggests that major areas of association cortex must be involved. This is also suggested by the studies of blood flow in schizophrenia (Ingvar, *this volume*). Dopamine, however, is distributed principally in three subcortical tracts: nigrostriatal, mesolimbic, and tuberoinfundibular. These, of course, correspond to the three effects seen when administering neuroleptic compounds: extrapyramidal motor side effects, antipsychotic action, and endocrine effects as a result of increased prolactin release.

So it appears the antipsychotic effects might be mediated by the limbic system influencing output to cortical structures.

The paradox of a unitary biochemical theory accounting for what most certainly appears to be an etiologically heterogeneous group of disorders may lead to a better theory of how dopamine may be acting in the CNS. It may be that limbic circuits are involved in modulating output to a variety of cortical centers, and regardless of why patterns are disordered, neuroleptics act to modulate a final common pathway. On closer examination it appears that dopamine itself may be acting as a neuromodulator rather than a neurotransmitter.

DOPAMINE AS A POSSIBLE NEUROMODULATOR

A theory favoring dopamine as a neuromodulator with multiple receptors is suggested by the discrepancy between the dopamine binding studies and the action of neuroleptics on the dopamine-sensitive adenylate cyclase. Dopamine or apomorphine, a dopamine agonist, can inhibit the firing of dopaminergic cells and this can be blocked by neuroleptic drugs (1). In addition, either of these compounds can block the synthesis of dopamine and this also can be blocked by neuroleptics (11,26). These actions point to dopamine or its analogues acting on the dopamine neurons themselves. Binding studies using ligands which are preferentially agonist or antagonists to dopamine also suggest multiple dopamine receptors (36). All of these studies suggest that dopaminergic neurons have autoreceptors.

In addition, our laboratory has used cell fractionation techniques which point to different classes of dopamine receptors (20,22). In a fractionation of bovine caudate nucleus we prepared astroglial, neuronal, and synaptosomal fractions and measured haloperidol binding in each. Surprisingly, the receptor is enriched in the astroglial cell fraction. Since these fractionation techniques are not widely used, I will briefly describe them.

The tissue is chopped into cubes and incubated in a balanced salt solution, under O_2. After 30 min the tissue is dissociated by passage through a 1 mm nylon mesh. It is then further dissociated using smaller meshes of 150 and 50 μm pore sizes. The dissociated tissue is centrifuged at low speed ($100 \times g$) to sediment intact cells which are then placed on a discontinuous Ficoll gradient to isolate enriched cell fractions. The problems with the fractions are that they may contain up to 25% by weight of other membranous material and that the cells are damaged and will not generally remain viable under culture conditions. Because of these problems, primary astrocytic cultures were examined for haloperidol binding, and were found to have a neuroleptic receptor (6). The properties of this receptor differed from those of a receptor obtained from adult brain, which may reflect the lack of complete differentiation under culture conditions. Since the problem of contamination can not easily be eliminated, we also examined fractions prepared using trypsin to dissociate tissue. This

TABLE 1. *Receptor binding*

Sample	Diazepam receptor (pmol/mg)	Spiroperidol receptor (specific): (pmol/mg)
Homogenate with trypsin	0.186	10.8
Homogenate without trypsin	0.879	76.3
Astroglia with trypsin	0.490	15.1
Astroglia without trypsin	1.310	142.5

results in a marked decrease in receptor activity, although the astroglial fractions contain no more than 10% contaminating material and enrichment of the receptor is still found (Table 1). This finding is puzzling unless glia have a metabolic response to dopamine. In order to examine this question, we chose to investigate the second messenger system in astroglial cells. We found that caudate astroglia have an adenylate cyclase which is sensitive to dopamine and not sensitive to α- or β-adrenergic stimulation. This enzyme and especially the dopamine-stimulated activity are sensitive to GTP as shown in Fig. 1. The enzyme appears to be inhibited by Ca^{2+} and also by neuroleptic drugs. Due to its sensitivity to guanosine triphosphate, we found it necessary to use a nonmetabolized analogue of GTP, 5′-guanylylimidodiphosphate Gpp(NH)p to measure 3′, 5′-cAMP reliably. When we measured a series of neuroleptics for their capacity to inhibit the enzyme, we found that in the presence of Gpp(NH)p the drugs were approximately 50-fold less potent than when using brain homogenate without GTP added. However, the rank order of the compounds matched their clinical efficacy

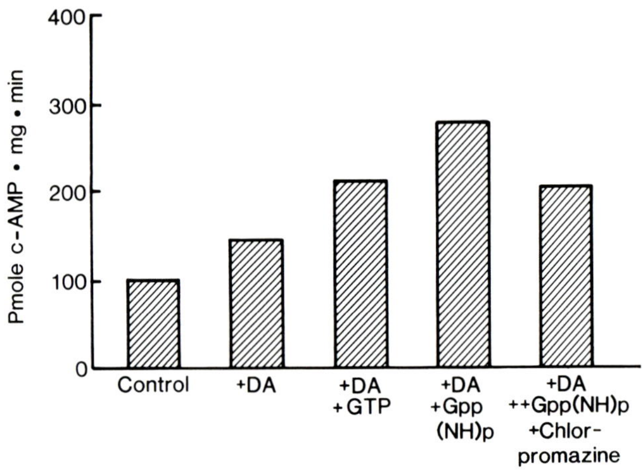

FIG. 1. Effect of GTP on cAMP formation is demonstrated in the presence of dopamine and chlorpromazine. The dopamine concentration was 40 μM, the GTP 20 μM, Gpp (NH) p μM, and chlorpromazine 30 μM.

as shown in Table 2. This illustrates that the glial receptor, which is presumably homogeneous, exhibits no discrepancy between binding properties of neuroleptic drugs and their ability to inhibit adenyl cyclase.

To further examine the effect of dopamine on glial cells, we looked at phosphokinase activity in these fractions. Caudate astroglia have a cAMP-stimulated phosphokinase, and we have recently found its specific activity to be higher in the glial cell fraction than in homogenate or isolated synaptosomal fractions. This enzyme appeared to phosphorylate specific membrane proteins. The electrophoretic pattern of phosphorylated proteins appeared similar to that seen when looking at synaptic fractions. We were interested to see if the proteins which are specifically phosphorylated are identical in synaptic and glial fractions. To test this ^{32}ATP and ^{33}ATP were synthesized and used as the substrate for phosphorylation of synaptic and astroglial membrane fractions, respectively. After incubation in the presence of cAMP, the fractions were combined and a crude membrane fraction was prepared for SDS-polyacrylamide disc gel electrophoresis. Gels were run and the gels were cut into 1-mm slices, dissolved, and counted for ^{32}P and ^{33}P. The results shown in Fig. 2 suggest that essentially the same proteins are phosphorylated in both fractions. This is of some interest since the specific activity of both enzymes, adenyl cyclase and phosphokinase, is higher in astroglia as is the specific activity of phosphorylated protein. In view of this and our finding that synaptic fractions contain 50% or more glial vesicles, the postsynaptic localization of the second messenger system is called into question.

The bulk of isolated cell studies point to a glial receptor with metabolic coupling to the second messenger system. However, before postulating an entirely new role for dopamine as a metabolic regulator, it is necessary (a) to obtain verification of the astroglial localization of a dopamine receptor and (b) to demonstrate how stimulation of this receptor might alter neuronal transmission. One technique which might allow an *in vivo* demonstration of the glial localization of the haloperidol receptor is an autoradiographic study of [^{3}H]haloperidol (22). We carried out such a study in rats using [^{3}H]haloperidol. Rats were given intra-

TABLE 2. *Comparison of clinical dosage and adenyl cyclase inhibition by neuroleptic drugs*

	Equivalent daily dose	IC_{50} (μM) brain homogenate caudate	IC_{50} (μM) glial homogenate caudate
Aliphatic phenothiazine Chlorpromazine	100	0.6	38.8
Piperidine phenothiazine mesoridazine	50		5.2
Piperazine phenothiazine trifluoperazine	5	0.1	2.0
Butyrophenone haloperidol	2	2.0	2.9

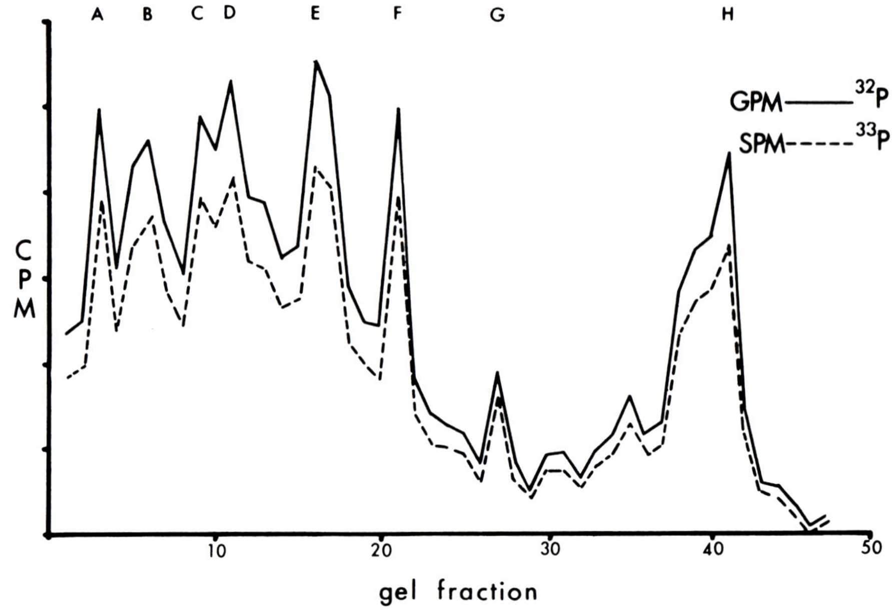

FIG. 2. An SDS-polyacrylamide gel containing glial plasma membrane (GPM) with ^{32}ATP and synaptic plasma membrane (SPM) with ^{33}ATP. This illustrates the similarity of protein phosphorylation patterns in the two membrane fractions.

peritoneal injections of 2.4 μg of [^{3}H]haloperidol and either unlabeled (+) or (−) butaclamol (500 μg). After 30 min the rats were perfused with a mixture of acrolein (1.0%) and glutaraldehyde (4.0%) through the carotid artery. The caudate nuclei were removed and sections cut. These were stained with lead citrate and uranyl acetate and coated with Ilford L-4 emulsion. After 6 weeks' development they were examined by electron microscopy. In sections with low background no counts were found over myelin, indicating little diffusion into lipophilic regions. The (+) butaclamol was clearly effective in displacing counts compared to the (−) form. A preliminary study resulted in approximately three-fourths of the counts being found on tissue processes adjacent to synaptic boutons or normal synaptic profiles (Fig. 3). About 20% of the counts appeared to be located on presynaptic neuronal membranes and less than 5% were found on postsynaptic membranes. This supports the suggestion of glial localization of a majority of dopamine receptors and fits in well with the detailed neuroanatomy of dopamine fibers.

The fine structure of all the catecholamine pathways provides a surprise when studied in detail. Hökfelt (23) carried out the first study on the striatum of rats, using the false transmitter 5-hydroxydopamine to visualize dopamine storage sites. He found that about 15% of the presynaptic areas identified in his sections contained dopamine. Few of the boutons found containing dopamine

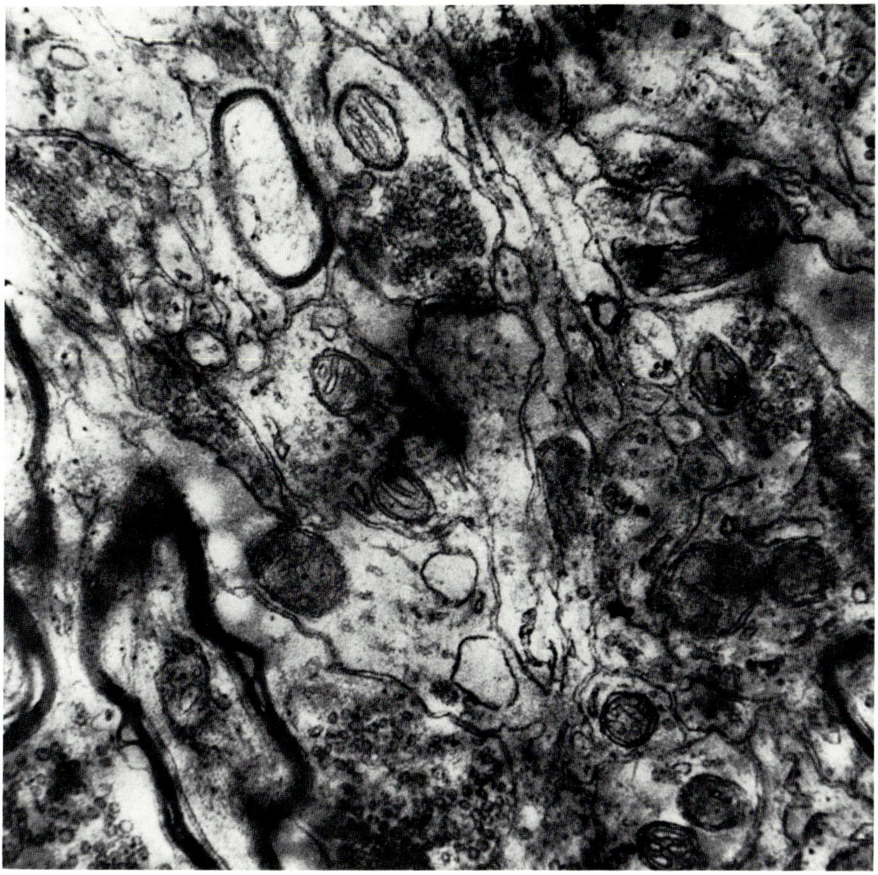

FIG. 3. An autoradiograph of [^{3}H]haloperidol showing a typical localization on a membranous process near but not on a synaptic region.

appeared to make contact with postsynaptic neurons. Tennyson and her co-workers (35) carried out a more quantitative study on rabbit striatum using 5-hydroxydopamine to visualize dopamine storage granules. She found about 9% of the striatal boutons in rabbit appeared to be dopaminergic boutons. Of these, few were found making contact with a clearly defined postsynaptic membrane. In fact, only about 2% of the dopaminergic boutons made clear contact with an obvious postsynaptic membrane. Although problems in the angle of sectioning may obscure some postsynaptic profiles, it is unlikely 98% would be missed. In addition, there was a much higher proportion of complete synaptic profiles in nondopaminergic boutons. Although dopamine is the least carefully studied of the catecholamines from the viewpoint of detailed fine structure, the published reports correspond to the findings for norepinephrine (17) and

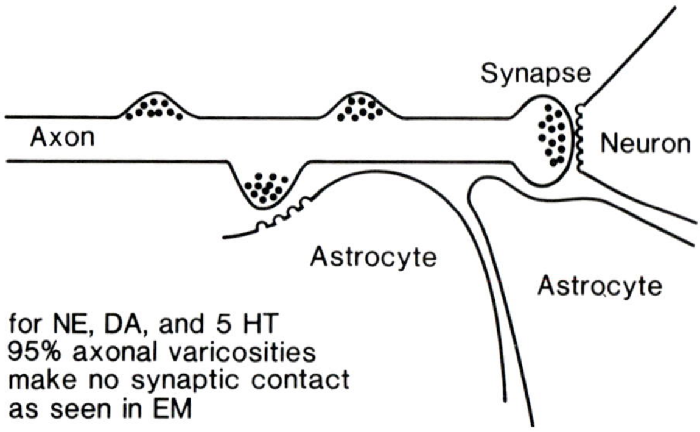

FIG. 4. Schematic representation of the suggested relationship between dopaminergic boutons and astroglial cells.

serotonin (10,16). This points to an anatomical structure fit more for the secretion of a neuromodulator than of a neurotransmitter. Since astroglia in general surround nonmyelinated axons and seal off areas of synaptic contact, they are located in the right place to receive inputs from neuromodulators secreted into the extracellular space. This is illustrated in Fig. 4, which suggests how the dopamine tracts and astroglial receptors may relate to one another. The data from structural studies and isolated astroglial fractions taken together point to the possibility that dopamine is acting as a modulator through the glia cells. This system could act as an amplifier, setting the gain or rate of transmission for other neurotransmitter systems. For example, the neuronal secretion of dopamine could activate the astroglial second messenger system and result in an altered K^+ handling capacity changing the extracellular K^+ and resulting in altered rates of neuronal firing. This might explain how neuroleptics affecting dopamine receptors might be beneficial to most schizophrenic patients regardless of the etiology of their disorders. In general, the drugs have the functional effect of turning down the gain for a variety of inputs to the cortex.

If such a modulator system exists, what might be its generality? Table 3 shows the type of receptor localization seen using bulk isolated cells and primary cultures from fetal brain. These studies suggest that the catecholamines and diazepam may have glial receptors, suggesting a modulatory role for these compounds. The amino acid receptors and peptide receptors, such as the opiate receptor, appear to be predominantly localized on postsynaptic membranes, suggesting these compounds have a principal role as neurotransmitters. The case of the diazepam receptors is particularly interesting. The cell isolation techniques clearly show receptors on astroglia (21) as do kainic acid lesion studies (9) when carried out on frontal cortex. Similar bulk cell isolations which we recently performed on cerebellar tissue suggest an enrichment of diazepam receptor on neurons, particularly Purkinje cells, and this is also suggested by kainic acid lesions of cerebellum (C. Braestrup, *personal communication*) and

TABLE 3. *Summary of cellular localization of various CNS receptors*

	Synaptic	Glia
Dopamine	++	+++
Norepinephrine (β)	?	+++
Acetylcholine (muscarinic)	++	++
Serotonin	++	+++
GABA	+++	+
Glutamate (kianic acid)	+++	+
Opiates	+++	+

studies on mutant mice (32). These studies using a variety of methods clearly suggest that the same or very similar receptors are predominantly localized on different cell types in different brain regions. The fact that the same receptor may serve a variety of functional purposes in the CNS illustrates the organizational complexity found in brain.

CLASSIFICATION OF SCHIZOPHRENICS ON THE BASIS OF BIOLOGICAL CRITERIA

Although the investigation of what neuroleptic drugs do and where they do it has led to the heuristically useful dopamine theory of schizophrenia and now to the hypothesis of dopamine acting via astroglia as a neuromodulator, this has not helped in classifying schizophrenic patients. Other types of biological investigations may prove to be of greater value for these purposes. Classifications according to treatment response are usually not very helpful, but this can be easily investigated. Perhaps of more help is a careful study of family histories of schizophrenic patients combined with a complete analysis of genetic markers in an effort to find groups of patients with apparent genetic linkages. Another approach is to find some metabolic or biochemical marker which would be unique to schizophrenia or to a subgroup of schizophrenics. This would be an enormous aid in classifying patients.

Our laboratory is beginning one such study following the pioneering work of Dr. John Stevens (34). Dr. Stevens was interested in the possibility that the genetic defect in schizophrenia might involve the plasma membrane and thus affect transport systems. As a model for his investigation he looked at the composition of red blood cells from schizophrenic and control patients. He was able to collect over 100 schizophrenic patient samples which included both long-term and newly admitted patients. In this group approximately one-quarter were untreated with neuroleptic drugs and three-quarters had been treated. The red blood cell phospholipids of controls and patients were determined after extraction and fractionation using thin-layer chromatography. The

TABLE 4. *Percentage of the phospholipid fractions in the red cells of controls and schizophrenics*

	Controls (20)			Schizophrenics (101)			Difference of means	T	*p*
	N	Mean	SD	*N*	Mean	SD			
Phosphatidylserine	20	13.23	1.52	101	18.09	2.58	4.86	8.14	< 0.0001
Sphingomyelin	20	27.41	4.49	101	28.13	3.08	0.72	1.06	ns
Lecithin	20	31.39	3.55	101	28.27	3.72	3.12	3.45	< 0.006
Phosphatidylethanolamine	20	27.97	3.10	101	25.51	4.13	2.46	2.52	< 0.012

From Stevens (34).

four major phospholipid fractions were analyzed; including phosphatidylserine, phosphatidylethanolamine, phosphatidylcholine, and sphingomyelin. Stevens calculated the sum of these and expressed each constituent as a percentage of that total. His results are shown in Table 4. These results suggest that phospholipid distribution may prove to be a marker of schizophrenia. Even more encouraging, he reports that the phospholipid distribution of treated and untreated patients is similar, suggesting that the drugs do not alter phospholipid distribution. In addition, he looked at seven patients with affective disorders including some manics and found essentially a normal phospholipid profile.

Phospholipids appear to form the stable core of cell membranes. They apparently lie in a bilayer configuration with their charged head groups on the surface of the bilayer. In general, the distribution of these base groups choline, ethanolamine, and serine tends to be quite stable throughout membranes of a given animal. The fatty acid constituents in general are more labile, and even can be altered by changing dietary patterns. The suggestion that the ratio of bases may be changed in a disease state is a new concept as far as I can determine. The finding that the acidic group serine is increased at the expense of the neutral zwitterions phosphocholine and phosphoethanolamine is remarkable for this would alter the charge distribution on the membrane surface considerably and would be expected to have significant functional effects especially on nerve cells.

In view of Stevens' results, we undertook a small-scale replication study using the techniques of phospholipid extraction and quantitative thin-layer chromatography. Our patients were selected on the basis of meeting the Feighner Research criterion and our controls were normal hospital employees. These preliminary results suggest that phospholipid distribution may indeed be a marker for schizophrenia (Table 5) and have encouraged us to begin a larger study aimed at examining both schizophrenic patients and their first-degree relatives.

In general, these studies point to the need for a more complete understanding of the integrative features of the mammalian CNS prior to attempting to delineate the neurobiological features of a complex disorder such as schizophrenia. Studies on the neuroleptic drugs may provide a tool for a more complete understanding

TABLE 5. *Phospholipid distribution in RBCs of Freighner-diagnosed schizophrenia*

	Controls ($N = 11$)	Patients ($N = 14$)
Phosphatidylserine	12.1	17.1
Sphingomyelin	27.8	29.7
Phosphatidylcholine	31.4	28.7
Phosphatidylethanolamine	28.6	24.5

Feighner criteria for schizophrenia include at least a 6 months duration of illness without return to normal, either delusions or disorganized thoughts making communication difficult, and at least three of the following five possibilities. (a) single; (b) poor premorbid social adjustment; (c) family history of schizophrenia; (d) absence of alcoholism or drug abuse; (e) onset prior to age 40.

of control mechanisms in the CNS just as marker studies may allow us to define etiologically homogeneous subgroups of patients. The real advances in understanding any medical disorder come when clinical findings can be related to information on the physiology and biochemistry of involved organ systems. In the CNS our knowledge of basic neurochemical and neurophysiological mechanism remains incomplete. For this reason efforts at attacking schizophrenia or other biological disorders of the CNS require a strong component of basic research. Only with this background can the details of neuropathology be understood. As work on neuroleptic drugs so well demonstrates, this effort must be a two-way street with pharmacological and clinical investigations often providing clues that lead to fruitful basic studies. This type of research when aimed at a clinical problem such as schizophrenia can, through the clues presented by pathology, open up new areas of research and provide surprising fundamental advances.

REFERENCES

1. Aghajanian, G., and Bunny, B. (1977): Dopamine "autoreceptors": Pharmacological characterization by micro-iontophoretic single cell recording studies. *Nauyn-Schniedeberg's Arch. Exp. Pathol. Pharmakol.,* 297:1–14.
2. Angrist, B., and Gershon, S. (1970): The phenomenology of experimentally-induced amphetamine psychosis. Preliminary observations. *Am. J. Psychiatry,* 126:95–107.
3. Angrist, B., Shopsin, B., and Gershon, S. (1971): The comparative psychotomimetic effects of stereo-isomers of amphetamine. *Nature,* 234:152–154.
4. Beamish, P., and Kiloh, L. (1960): Psychosis due to amphetamine consumption. *J. Ment. Sci.,* 106:337–343.
5. Bowers, M. G., Jr. (1974): Central dopamine turnover in schizophrenic syndromes. *Arch. Gen. Psychiatry,* 31:50–54.
6. Braestrup, C., Nissen, C., Squires, R. F., and Schousboe, A. (1979): Lack of brain specific benzodiazepine receptors on mouse primary astroglial cultures. *Neurosci. Lett.,* 9:45–49.
7. Carlsson, A., and Lindquist, M. (1963): Effect of chlorpromazine or haloperidol on formation of 3-methoxytyramine and normetanephrine in mouse brain. *Act. Pharmacol. Toxicol.,* 20:140–144.
8. Celesia, G. G., and Barr, A. N. (1970): Psychosis and other psychiatric manifestations of Levadopa therapy. *Arch. Neurol.,* 23:193–200.
9. Chang, R. S., Vinh, T. T., Poduslo, S. E., and Snyder, S. H. (1978): Glial localization of benzodiazepine receptors in the mammalian brain. *Soc. Neurosci. Abstr.,* 1632:511.
10. Chan-Palay, V. (1976): Serotonin axons in the supra- and subependymal plexuses and in the leptomeninges; Their roles in local alterations of cerebrospinal fluid and vasomotor activity. *Brain Res.,* 102:103–130.
11. Christiansen, J., and Squires, R. (1974): Antagonistic effects of apomorphine and haloperidol on rat striatal synaptosomal tyrosine hydroxylase. *J. Pharm. Pharmacol.,* 26:367–369.
12. Clement-Cormier, Y., Kebabian, J. W., Petzold, G. L., and Greengard, P. (1974): Dopamine-sensitive adenylate cyclase in mammalian brain: A possible site of action of anti-psychotic drugs. *Proc. Natl. Acad. Sci. U.S.A.,* 71:1113–1171.
13. Coyle, J. T., and Snyder, S. H. (1969): Catecholamine uptake by synaptosomes in homogenates of rat brain: Stereospecificity in different areas. *J. Pharmacol. Exp. Ther.,* 170:221–231.
14. Creese, I., Burt, D. R., and Snyder, S. H. (1976): Dopamine receptor binding predicts clinical and pharmacological potencies of anti-schizophrenic drugs. *Science,* 192:481–483.
15. Delay, J., Deniker, O. (1957): Caractéristiques psychophysiologiques des médicaments neuroleptiques. In: *The Psychotropic Drugs,* edited by S. Garattini and V. Ghetti, pp. 485–501. Elsevier Publishing Co., Amsterdam.

16. Descarries, L., Beaudet, A., and Watkins, K. C. (1975): Serotonin nerve terminals in adult rat neocortex. *Brain Res.,* 100:563–588.
17. Descarries, L., Watkins, K. C., and Lapierre, Y. (1977): Noradrenergic axon terminals in the cerebral cortex of rat III topometric structural analysis. *Brain Res.,* 133:197–222.
18. Feighner, J., Robins, E., Guze, S., Woodruff, R., Winokur, G., and Munoz, R. (1972): Diagnostic criteria for use in psychiatric research. *Arch. Gen. Psychiatry,* 26:57–63.
19. Henn, F. A. (1980): Separation of neuronal and glial cells and subcellular constituents. In: *Advances in Cellular Neurobiology,* edited by S. Federoff, and L. Hertz. Academic Press, New York *(in press).*
20. Henn, F. A., Anderson, D. J., and Sellström, Å. (1977): Possible relationship between glial cells, dopamine and the effects of antipsychotic drugs. *Nature,* 266:637–638.
21. Henn, F. A., and Henke, J. (1978): Cellular localization of [^{3}H]diazepam receptors. *Neuropharmacology,* 17:985–988.
22. Henn, F. A., Titler, M., Anderson, D. J., and May, K. (1978): Investigations concerning the cellular origin of dopamine receptors. *Life Sci.,* 23:617–622.
23. Hökfelt, T. (1968): *In vivo* studies on central and peripheral monoamine neurons at the ultrastructural level. *Z. Zellforsch,* 91:1–74.
24. Hollister, L. E. (1962): Drug induced psychosis and schizophrenic reactions—A critical comparison. *Ann. N.Y. Acad. Sci.,* 96:80–88.
25. Iversen, L. L. (1975): Dopamine receptors in brain. *Science,* 188:1084–1089.
26. Iversen, L. L., Rogawski, M., and Miller, R. (1976): Comparison of the effects of neuroleptic drugs on pre- and postsynaptic dopaminergic mechanisms in the rat striatum. *Mol. Pharmacol.,* 12:251–262.
27. Kebabian, J. W., and Greengard, P. (1971): Dopamine-sensitive adenyl cyclase: Possible role in synaptic transmission. *Science,* 174:1346–1349.
28. Libet, B. (1979): Which postsynaptic action of dopamine is mediated by cyclic AMP. *Life Sci.,* 24:1043–1058.
29. Mattysse, S. (1973): Antipsychotic drug actions: A clue to the neuropathology of schizophrenia? *Fed. Proc.,* 32:200–205.
30. Phillis, J. W. (1977): The role of cyclic nucleotides in the CNS. *Can. J. Neurol. Sci.,* 4:153–195.
31. Seeman, P., Chaw-Wong, M., Tedesco, J., and Wong, K. (1975): Brain receptors for antipsychotic drugs and dopamine: Direct binding assays. *Proc. Natl. Acad. Sci. U.S.A.,* 72:4376–4380.
32. Skolnick, P., Syapin, P. J., Paugh, B. A., and Paul, S. M. (1979): Reduction in benzodiazepine receptors associated with Purkinje cell degeneration in "nervous" mutant mice. *Nature,* 277:397–399.
33. Snyder, S., Banerjee, S., Yamamura, H., and Greenberg, D. (1974): Drugs, neurotransmitters, and schizophrenia. *Science,* 184:1243–1253.
34. Stevens, J. D. (1972): The distribution of the phospholipid fractions in the red cell membrane of schizophrenics. *Schizophr. Bull.,* 6:60–61.
35. Tennyson, V., Heikkila, R., Mytilineou, C., Côté, L., and Cohen, G. (1974): 5-Hydroxydopamine "tagged" neuronal boutons in rabbit neostriatum: Interrelationship between vesicles and axonal membrane. *Brain Res.,* 82:341–348.
36. Titeler, M., Weinreich, P., Sinclair, D., and Seeman, P. (1977): New detection of brain dopamine receptors with [^{3}H]dihydroergocryptine. *Proc. Natl. Acad. Sci. U.S.A.,* 74:3750–3753.
37. Van Rossen, J. M. (1966): The significance of dopamine-receptor blockade for the mechanism of action of neuroleptic drugs. *Arch. Int. Pharmacodyn. Ther.,* 160:492–494.

Discussion

Mason: Are there regional neurochemical differences in glia?

Henn: Yes. The simplest transmitter to look at was glycine, because it is clearly a neurotransmitter in the spinal cord, but does not seem to be one in the cortex. Glycine transport occurs in cord glia with a sodium-sensitive high-affinity system that is not found in astroglia isolated from frontal cortex (4). As for dopamine receptors on astroglia, we find low levels in frontal cortex and none in occipital cortex but do find them in striatal tissue, where most of our work has been done. The astroglial benzodiazepine receptors we've localized are in the same brain regions where Claus Braestrupp (2) has found them, except that our cortical ones are purely astrocytic whereas both his and our cerebellar receptors are on Purkinje neurons. Snyder's (3) lab has recently confirmed that astrocytic localization of benzodiazepine receptors in frontal cortex by showing that they are not sensitive to kainic acid, which destroys neuronal cell bodies.

Perez-Polo: Have you compared the effects of 6-hydroxydopamine on glia with those of 5-hydroxydopamine, which is a nice control?

Henn: No; it's clearly something we should do.

A word on where we're going technically: We've spent the last 6 months on the isolation of astrocytes. We are now developing two good techniques. One uses magnetic microspheres, which are little pieces of ferrite that stick to cells. In a high magnetic field, you can hold the cells with very little force and pour out everything that lacks your marker. The other technique is fluorescence-activated cell sorting, which was invented by Herzenberg (5). Cells bearing fluorescent-tagged antibodies are deflected from a stream containing all cells by electric charges added to them after a laser has identified them, so that the undeflected cells fall into a separate bin. In both cases, one needs a very specific membrane antibody, and that's where we're hung up. We've spent a year trying to develop a monoclonal antibody system that would generate large amounts of specific antibodies to some astroglial membrane antigen. When we get it, we'll be able to get pure preparations of viable glia.

Melnechuk: At the Salk Institute, there is a library of monoclonal antibodies, including antibody to Thy-1, which is also on Purkinje cells.

Henn: Like Elizabeth Bock (1), we can get neuronal antibodies, but the astrocyte has resisted our efforts. One problem is the assay: We may have the antibodies at low levels but can't find an assay to establish whether or not we have them.

REFERENCES

1. Bock, E. (1978): Nervous system specific proteins. *J. Neurochem.,* 30:7–14.
2. Braestrup, C., and Squires, R. F. (1977): Specific benzodiazepine receptors in rat brain characterized by high affinity ^{3}H-diazepam binding. *Proc. Natl. Acad. Sci. USA,* 74:3805–3809.
3. Chang, R. S., Tran, V. T., Poduslo, S. E., and Snyder, S. H. (1978): Glial localization of benzodiazepine receptors in the mammalian brain. *Soc. Neurosci. Abatr.,* 4:511. (Abstr. 1632)
4. Henn, F. A. (1976): Neurotransmission and glial cells: A functional relationship. *J. Neurosci. Res.,* 2:271–282.
5. Herzenberg, L. A., Sweet, R. G., and Herzenberg, L. A. (1976): Fluorescence-activated cell sorting. *Sci. Am.,* 234:110–117.

Perspectives in Schizophrenia Research,
edited by C. Baxter and T. Melnechuk.
Raven Press, New York, 1980.

Chronic Schizophrenia: Postmortem Studies

Joel E. Kleinman, Peter Bridge, Farouk Karoum,
Samuel Speciale, Jr., Richard Staub, Steven Zalcman,
J. Christian Gillin, and Richard Jed Wyatt

Adult Psychiatry Branch, Division of Special Mental Health Research, Intramural Research Program, National Institute of Mental Health, Saint Elizabeths Hospital, Washington, D.C. 20032

LAYPERSON'S SUMMARY

A number of lines of evidence suggest that chronic schizophrenia may be related to disorders of chemicals in the brain, such as dopamine and norepinephrine. Difficulty in measuring these substances in the brains of living subjects has led to studies of the brains of deceased schizophrenics. The following study briefly reviews this area of research and presents new results using advanced biochemical techniques to measure dopamine, norepinephrine, and some of the chemicals they are converted to in the brain. The results do not support the dopamine hypothesis of schizophrenia, but do suggest that concentrations of norepinephrine and its metabolites may be abnormal in schizophrenics. It is important to emphasize that these findings are preliminary and further studies are warranted in this area.

INTRODUCTION

One of the major hypotheses of schizophrenia research is that this syndrome is related to excess monoaminergic activity in the brain (13). Pharmacological studies which support this hypothesis include the findings that both L-DOPA and amphetamines can produce psychoses which resemble schizophrenic symptoms presumably by increasing activity of dopamine and norepinephrine in the brain (1,5). In addition, drugs such as phenothiazines reduce psychotic symptoms in proportion to their dopamine receptor binding capacity (6). Direct tests of these hypotheses require examination of the human brain which can be done through postmortem studies.

Initial studies of postmortem brains demonstrated increased dopamine concentrations in the nucleus accumbens of chronic psychotics (2). A second group found increased dopamine concentrations in the caudate and putamen of schizophrenic brains, but not in the nucleus accumbens (7). This same group reported increased dopamine receptor sensitivity in several regions of the basal ganglia of schizophrenics (14), a finding confirmed by other investigators (11).

Although initial postmortem reports focused on dopamine, subsequent studies have lent support to the norepinephrine hypothesis of schizophrenia. The first of these reports found increased norepinephrine concentrations in several brain regions of four paranoid schizophrenics (8). A second study, without subtype diagnoses, confirmed this finding in the nucleus accumbens of a larger number of schizophrenic subjects (3), whereas a third study demonstrated increased norepinephrine concentrations in the mesencephalon of three paranoid schizophrenics (4). A recent report failed to find an increase in the nucleus accumbens, but did find an increase in the putamen of chronic schizophrenics (7).

The following report adds our data to this growing body of postmortem studies, while attempting to emphasize the need for further studies of this type.

METHODS

Postmortem tissues were obtained from the District of Columbia Medical Examiner's Office and Saint Elizabeth's Hospital. Hypothalamus, nucleus accumbens, and substantia nigra were dissected, placed on either ice or dry ice immediately, and stored at −70°C until biochemical determinations could be made. Samples remained in the freezer for 3 days to 5 years for controls and 5 days to 5 years for psychotics. Prior to analysis, samples were placed in liquid nitrogen, pulverized, and a portion was removed.

Gas chromatography-mass spectrometry was used to measure dopamine, norepinephrine, dihydroxyphenylacetic acid (DOPAC), homovanillic acid (HVA), free 3-methoxy-4-hydroxyphenylglycerol (MHPG), and total MHPG on each of the specimens (9,10). Conjugated MHPG concentrations were determined by subtracting free MHPG from total MHPG. Proteins were also measured on each sample (12). All biochemical determinations and psychiatric diagnoses were made independently.

All psychiatric patients had chronic unremitting psychoses as determined by chart reviews, or in one case, by interviewing people familiar with the subject. Psychoses fell into the following subtypes using Research Diagnostic Criteria (15): chronic undifferentiated schizophrenia ($N = 4$); chronic paranoid schizophrenic ($N = 3$); unspecified functional psychosis ($N = 2$); chronic schizoaffective illness ($N = 1$); and manic-depressive illness ($N = 1$).

Normal controls were carefully screened to exclude alcohol, other drugs, and psychiatric history. In addition, blood, urine, and a number of tissues were screened for drugs with gas chromatography at the District of Columbia Medical Examiner's Office. All normals were drug-free at autopsy as determined by gas chromatography or chart review. One psychotic never received a neuroleptic. By history, others were drug-free for periods ranging from 2 weeks to 2 years. Normals and psychotics were matched for age, sex, and race. The mean ± standard error of the mean age for normals was 46.6 ± 6.1 years, whereas for psychotics it was 48.8 ± 5.9 years. Postmortem interval (from time of death to freezer) was 27.0 ± 4.7 hr for psychotics and only 10.5 ± 1.5 hr for normals (two-tailed *t*-test, $p < 0.01$).

RESULTS

There were no significant differences between psychotic patients and normal controls for dopamine or their metabolites in the three regions studied (Table 1). A different picture emerged for norepinephrine (Table 2). Free (MHPG) concentrations in the hypothalamus were 83% higher in psychotic patients than in normal controls ($p < 0.02$). There was a corresponding decrease in conjugated MHPG concentrations in the hypothalamus of psychotic subjects relative to controls ($p < 0.05$).

Although no other statistically significant differences were noted for norepinephrine or its metabolites, one particular item warrants further comment. Norepinephrine concentrations in the nucleus accumbens of two paranoid schizophrenics were 2.1 and 5.4 ng/mg protein. These concentrations represent a 3.5- to 10.5-fold increase relative to the closest patient. None of the other psychotic patients were paranoid schizophrenics. There was one normal control whose norepinephrine concentration in the nucleus accumbens was 7.5 ng/ml protein. However, this subject's postmortem interval was only 7 hr compared to 17 and 49.5 hr for the two paranoid schizophrenics.

DISCUSSION

These data do not support the dopamine hypothesis of schizophrenia. However, the long postmortem intervals in the psychotic group relative to the controls may be responsible for this negative finding. Moreover, dopamine receptor sensitivity has not as yet been measured in our samples.

These data do suggest a possible disorder of norepinephrine metabolism in chronic psychotic patients. Increases in free MHPG concentrations in the hypothalamus raise the possibility of deficient conjugation in these subjects. Although 8 of the 11 psychotic subjects were drug-free at the time of autopsy, all except one had a previous history of neuroleptics. As a consequence, the long-term effects of neuroleptics cannot be ruled out as a cause of increase in free MHPG concentrations or the decrease in conjugated MHPG. Another important factor may be postmortem interval. Free MHPG and postmortem interval do not correlate when all subjects are examined together (Spearman RHO = 0.08, $p =$ 0.72, $N = 21$). However, there are nonsignificant trends for the psychotic and control groups examined separately (RHO = 0.30, $p = 0.40$, $N = 10$; and RHO = 0.44, $p = 0.17$, $N = 11$, respectively). Although these are just trends, the negative correlations suggest that free MHPG goes down with increasing postmortem intervals, a direction which should have lowered, not increased, concentrations for the chronic psychotic subjects.

TABLE 1. *Concentrations of dopamine and its metabolites in postmortem brains of psychotic subjects and normal controls (ng/mg protein)*

		Dopamine		DOPAC		HVA	
Region		Normal controls	Psychotic subjects	Normal controls	Psychotic subjects	Normal controls	Psychotic subjects
Hypothalamus	*N*	10	11	10	11	10	11
	$\bar{x}$	8.9	10.8	1.53	0.96	37.7	30.4
	SEM	3.5	3.4	0.50	0.31	6.9	3.2
Nucleus accumbens	*N*	7	6	7	5	7	5
	$\bar{x}$	60.4	64.3	8.21	7.25	98.7	88.6
	SEM	11.9	4.9	2.21	2.17	5.3	8.2
Substantia nigra	*N*	8	8	8	8	8	8
	$\bar{x}$	14.2	10.0	1.92	1.16	74.9	55.9
	SEM	3.5	1.7	0.70	0.37	16.3	6.5

TABLE 2. *Concentrations of norepinephrine and its metabolites in postmortem brains of psychotic subjects and normal controls*

Region		Norepinephrine (ng/mg protein)		Free MHPG (pg/mg protein)		Conjugated MHPG (pg/mg protein)		Total MHPG (pg/mg protein)	
		Normal controls	Psychotic subjects	Normal controls	Psychotic subjects	Normal controls	Psychotic subjects	Normal controls	Psychotic subjects
Hypothalamus	N	10	11	10	11	10	11	10	11
	$\bar{x}$	8.7	14.2	658.1	1171.8[a]	677.0	444.7[b]	1335.0	1616.1
	SEM	1.9	4.2	134.2	175.0	120.1	52.5	170.0	196.3
Nucleus accumbens	N	7	6	7	6	7	6	7	6
	$\bar{x}$	1.65	1.54	327.0	311.8	505.2	603.0	832.2	914.8
	SEM	0.99	0.82	74.8	66.8	166.0	83.4	193.8	132.3
Substantia nigra	N	8	8	8	8	8	8	8	8
	$\bar{x}$	1.25	1.29	378.7	310.4	757.4	639.1	1136.0	949.5
	SEM	0.29	0.16	66.0	51.7	168.4	131.9	154.5	134.8

[a] $p < 0.03$. [b] $p < 0.05$.

A final point should be made about norepinephrine in the nucleus accumbens. Our study had an insufficient number of subjects to confirm this previous finding of increased norepinephrine (8), although the preliminary data do lend some support. It should be noted, however, that norepinephrine concentrations in the initial report (8) are an order of magnitude greater than those reported in this study or two others (3,7). Differences in dissection are one possible explanation. Preliminary data from anterior and posterior portions of rat nucleus accumbens do not support this explanation as they are essentially the same (J. E. Kleinman, D. Luchins, D. R. Weinberger, F. Karoum, and R. J. Wyatt, *unpublished observations*).

This study, as well as the work of others, attests to the feasibility of testing the dopamine and norepinephrine hypotheses of schizophrenia in postmortem material. One could readily improve on these initial efforts in several ways. Larger numbers of subjects and careful collection of data prior to death are two obvious sources of improvement. In addition, portions of the brain should be saved for histopathological studies, a re-emerging area of schizophrenia research. One possible problem in studies involving several hospitals and investigators could be variability in dissection and diagnosis. Thus standardization of procedures is essential for the Veteran's Administration and all researchers who pursue this promising area of schizophrenia research.

SUMMARY

Dopamine, norepinephrine, and some of their metabolites were measured in the hypothalamus, nucleus accumbens, and substantia nigra of chronic psychotic patients and normal controls using gas chromatography-mass spectrometry. No significant differences between psychotics and normals were detected with regard to dopamine and its metabolites. Free 3-methoxy-4-hydroxyphenylglycol was increased in the hypothalamus of psychotics relative to normals (two-tailed *t*-test, $p < 0.02$). A corresponding decrease in conjugated MHPG was also demonstrated in psychotics compared with normals ($p < 0.05$).

ACKNOWLEDGMENTS

This study was made possible by the District of Columbia Medical Examiner's Office (Dr. James L. Luke, Chief Medical Examiner; Dr. Brian D. Blackbourne, Assistant Chief; Dr. William S. Brownlee, Dr. Rak H. Kim, and Dr. LeRoy Riddick) and Blackburn Laboratory, Saint Elizabeths Hospital (Meta A. Neumann).

REFERENCES

1. Angrist, B. M., Sathanathan, G., and Gershon, S. (1973): Behavioral effects of L-DOPA in schizophrenic patients. *Psychopharmacology,* 31:1–12.

2. Bird, E. D., Spokes, E. G., Barnes, J., Mackay, A. V. P., Iversen, L. L., and Shepherd, M. (1977): Increased brain dopamine and reduced glutamic acid decarboxylase activity in schizophrenia and related psychoses. *Lancet,* ii:1157–1159.
3. Bird, E. D., Spokes, E. G., and Iversen, L. L. (1979): Brain norepinephrine and dopamine in schizophrenia. *Science,* 204:93–94.
4. Carlsson, A. (1980): The impact of catecholamine research on medical science and practice. In: *Catecholamines: Basic and Clinical Frontiers,* edited by E. Usdin, I. J. Kopin, and J. D. Barchas, pp. 4–19. Pergamon Press, New York.
5. Connell, P. H. (1958): *Amphetamine Psychosis.* Maudsley Monograph, No. 5. Chapman and Hall, London.
6. Creese, I., Burt, D. R., and Snyder, S. A. (1976): Dopamine receptor binding predicts clinical and pharmacological potencies of antischizophrenic drugs. *Science,* 192:481–483.
7. Crow, T. J., Baker, H. F., Cross, A. J., Joseph, M. H., Lofthouse, R., Longden, A., Owen, F., Riley, G. J., Glover, V., and Killpack, W. S. (1979): Monoamine mechanisms in chronic schizophrenia: Postmortem neurochemical findings. *Br. J. Psychiatry,* 134:249–256.
8. Farley, I. J., Price, K. S., McCullough, E., Deck, J. H. W., Hordynski, W., and Hornykiewicz, O. (1978): Norepinephrine in chronic paranoid schizophrenia. *Science,* 200:456–458.
9. Karoum, F., Cattabeni, F., Costa, E., Ruthven, C. R. J., and Sandler, M. (1972): Gas chromatographic assay of picomole concentrations of biogenic amines. *Anal. Biochem.,* 47:550–561.
10. Karoum, F., Gillin, J. C., Wyatt, R. J., and Costa, E. (1975): Mass-fragmentography of nanogram quantities of biogenic amine metabolites in human cerebrospinal fluid and whole rat brain. *Biomed. Mass. Spectrom.,* 2:183–189.
11. Lee, T., Seeman, P., Tourtellotte, W. W., Farley, I. J., and Hornykeiwicz, O. (1978): Binding of ^{3}H-neuroleptics and ^{3}H-apomorphine in schizophrenic brains. *Nature,* 274:897–900.
12. Lowry, O. H., Rosebrough, N. J., Farr, A. L., and Randall, R. J. (1951): Protein measurement with the folin phenol reagent. *J. Biol. Chem.,* 193:265–275.
13. Matthysse, S. M., and Kety, S. S. (1975): *Catecholamines and Schizophrenia.* Pergamon Press, Oxford.
14. Owen, F., Cross, A. J., Crow, T. J., Longden, A., Poulter, M., and Riley, G. J. (1978): Increased dopamine-receptor sensitivity in schizophrenia. *Lancet,* ii:223–226.
15. Spitzer, R. L., Endicott, J., and Robins, E. (1975): Clinical criteria for psychiatric disorders and DSM-III. *Am. J. Psychiatry,* 132:1187–1192.

Discussion

J. Davis: To what extent were your subjects in remission at time of death?

Kleinman: To the best of my knowledge, the subjects of this study were all chronically psychotic and unremitting. These patients did not have acute exacerbations.

J. Davis: You think they were symptomatic at death?

Kleinman: Yes.

Carpenter: Not just dysfunctional but with florid psychotic symptoms?

Kleinman: Nothing has ever led us to believe that they were anything but chronically psychotic.

Ewalt: Could you discuss why the Hornykiewicz group finds ten times more norepinephrine in the nucleus accumbens than the Bird (1) group finds? The discrepancy doesn't inspire confidence in the methods.

Kleinman: That issue needs resolution. I hope we will all exchange some brains.

Bird: I think I know why we disagree. I visited Dr. Hornykiewicz and dissected a brain with him. He takes his nucleus accumbens toward the midline and above where you and I take it, Dr. Kleinman. Dr. Crow also takes a slightly different area for nucleus accumbens; we taught his technician how to do it our way, but when he returned they unfortunately decided to change it. The discrepancy proves that we need standards for dissection.

Perez-Polo: I am concerned that postmortem times of dissection are not the same for schizophrenic and control brains, which are dissected sooner. Why not wait to dissect the control brain until the times are more comparable?

Kleinman: That's a possibility.

Uzman: Time isn't the only variable; condition of death is another.

Kleinman: It's very complicated. It depends on where the person died and where the body is stored before autopsy. And since some people are not sympathetic to the performance of these studies by psychiatrists, it is necessary to use what brains are available.

J. Davis: To reinforce that statement, when I was at the NIH, I had difficulty obtaining brains from the medical examiner's office. They would not call you to come for an available brain. I finally gave that source up as too nonproductive and turned to England as a source of brains. (Yes, my English supplier of 50 brains marked the container "operation brain drain.")

Kleinman: I too had to visit the medical examiner's office daily to be sure of not missing a brain, but after some years they have now included me on their team.

Buchsbaum: Dr. Kleinman and I had difficulty obtaining brains from the Jonestown, Guyana mass suicide. We thought someone should study brains from perhaps the largest mental health disaster of the century, and the NIMH was very supportive, but members of the State Department utterly opposed any medical study of this kind, saying it was "ghoulish." Had the hundreds died from a pneumonia epidemic or from some exotic infection, corps of doctors would have flown down from the Atlanta Contagious Disease Center and no one would have thought their postmortem studies ghoulish, but a mental health disaster was somehow felt to be off limits. We need to sensitize the rest of the medical community to the legitimacy of such research.

Kleinman: The rest of the psychiatric community, too. We meet with resistance even at St. Elizabeth's Hospital. We haven't been able to get brain tissue from them at times.

Ingvar: The public education aspect of this type of research is very important. We met difficulties when we wanted to study blood flow in schizophrenics. It took quite some time to convince colleagues, nurses, and administrators that this disease causes so much suffering and is so costly to society that it was unethical *not* to do the research. Perhaps the VA could mount a well-planned program of public information pointing out the consequences and costs of our ignorance about schizophrenia, and thus create a favorable climate for further research on this disease.

Seeman: The really cooperative people are the families of patients. After the death of someone whose life, like the life of his or her family, was extremely unhappy, we are invariably given postmortem consent with extreme grace by the family, who feel it is the least they can do for future generations. We work in Ontario with the Friends of Schizophrenics, a lay society, and with others, such as the Californian group of parents of schizophrenics. Families of VA patients could provide public support.

Kleinman: To second that: After our studies were underway, relatives of schizophrenics who died called to beg us to take the deceased's brain and do something useful with it.

Brown: I'm concerned by the direction our conference seems to be taking. Dr. Baxter started it by saying that schizophrenia is an organic disease, and we have been implying that we are going to find out what's wrong with the brain in schizophrenia. But, as in the case of such malignancies as uterine carcinoma, many advances have been made in the treatment of illnesses without understanding the basis for the treatment.

REFERENCE

1. Bird, E. D., Spokes, E. G., and Iversen, L. L.; Taylor, M. A.; Farley, I. J., Price, K. S., McCullough, E., Deck, J. H. N., Hordynski, W., and Hornykiewicz, O. (1979): Brain norepinephrine and dopamine in schizophrenia (Exchange of letters). *Science,* 204:93–94.

Perspectives in Schizophrenia Research,
edited by C. Baxter and T. Melnechuk.
Raven Press, New York, 1980.

Biochemical Correlates of Behavior: What Is a Neurochemist to Measure?

J. R. Perez-Polo, C. E. Beck, and M. Blum

Department of Human Biological Chemistry and Genetics, University of Texas Medical Branch, Galveston, Texas 77550

LAYPERSON'S SUMMARY

Although there is much evidence that schizophrenia is linked to perturbations of dopaminergic metabolism, the precise nature of the defect in schizophrenics is not known. In large measure this is due to the problems associated with correlating behavioral measurements on patient populations with biochemical measurements carried out on samples from their peripheral circulation, urine, etc. One such approach is to measure levels of nerve growth factor (NGF) like activity and protein in schizophrenic peripheral blood serum as compared to controls. Although absolute NGF levels could not be determined, the results were conclusive in showing a relative decrease in NGF-like activity and protein in schizophrenics when compared to sex-matched controls.

EVALUATION PROBLEMS

Although it has been possible in recent years to devise good strategies for the cataloging of patients suffering from a number of diseased states which have been labeled as schizophrenia, it is more difficult to arrive at quantitative measurements of behavior which would be clinically useful. Simultaneously, a growing awareness developed that many modes of chemotherapy produce results, leading to the practice of labeling patients as "responders" versus "nonresponders." Many correlative studies between the diagnostic classifications and the response to chemotherapy have been made with varying degrees of success. To a large extent the problems encountered in these studies arose because of the need for "bits" in behavioral analysis, the evidence for "degeneracy" in the nervous system, and the "nonlinearity" of response to drugs in the affected portions of the central nervous system.

In the above context, "bits" are defined as additive units of some variable with behavioral relevance. This is in contrast to the scheme of using exclusion and inclusion principles or the summation of responses on a behavioral scale where parameters are unlikely to be equivalent, although the validity of responses or their clinical interpretation is often definitive. Given the absence of behavioral "bits," it might be best to limit studies to those patient populations which exhibit a marked degree of homogeneity with respect to a specific clinical evaluation technique. An inherent shortcoming of such *a priori* assignments is that they entail an implicit one-to-one correlation between the assignment and the organic parameters such as, for example, the levels of a particular enzyme activity in plasma that are being measured.

The known degeneracy built into modes of operation of the mammalian central nervous system may account for some of the ambiguity in many investigations which have tried to establish organic correlates with behavioral disorders. That is, there are likely to be multiple organic causes to account for individual behavioral outcomes; the converse is also likely to be the case. A strategy which might be useful to deal with this problem would be to select, through appropriate pilot studies, only those patient subpopulations which display a homogeneous diagnostic response as well as providing homogeneity in the organic variable (be it neurochemical or electrophysiological) that is being measured. In chemotheraupeutic trials, this would involve studying, for example, only responders with a common diagnostic profile. The obvious shortcoming of this approach is the likehood that only small populations would be studied and statistical validity would be hard to attain.

Lastly, the nonlinear relationships between observed behavioral outputs and the organic dysfunctions leading to these responses might account for the large scatter observed in most experimental situations. Since in many instances the precise relationships between behavioral components are not fully understood, it is difficult to interpret the significance of results which markedly differ from some mean value observed in control groups.

ONE APPROACH TO EVALUATION

On the basis of the premise that there are genetic components which place some subpopulations at risk for manifestations of schizophrenia, one strategy has been to actively pursue the search for pharmacologic or neurochemical perturbations that are likely to be present in individuals diagnosed as schizophrenics. More recently, such studies have focused on some schizophrenic subpopulations established by explicit diagnostic protocols. As a result of these studies it was proposed that alterations in metabolic parameters responsible for dopaminergic neurotransmission across synapses were involved (6). At one time or another, anabolic and/or catabolic neurotransmitter enzymes also have been proposed as being altered in the diseased state (42). Alternatively, it has been proposed that the schizophrenic condition might involve differences in the state of presynaptic and/or postsynaptic dopaminergic receptors (19). On theoretical grounds, it was also suggested that the levels of activity of the developmental neurohormone, nerve growth factor (NGF), might be altered in schizophrenics (42). A preliminary report from our group indicated that indeed there appeared to be drastic reductions in the levels of NGF activity and/or protein in the serum of chronic schizophrenics of both sexes (29). It will be the purpose of this chapter to critically evaluate the hypothesis that nerve growth factor activity in human serum might be related to schizophrenia. The evaluation will be made in light of what we now know about measurements of NGF activity and/or protein.

NERVE GROWTH FACTOR STRUCTURE

The nerve growth factor protein (NGF), both as a growth promoting agent and as an antigen, has been found in all vertebrates investigated (5,39–41). However, the levels detected to this date have been low in most tissues (in the order of magnitude of a few nanograms NGF per mg protein), except in the submaxillary gland of sexually mature male random bred Swiss Webster mice (8) and in a number of snake venoms (2), in which a much higher percent of the total protein present may be recovered as NGF (7). More recently, NGF has been purified and characterized from human placenta at term (12) and guinea pig prostate (14). Most of the information regarding the chemical structure and nature of NGF is limited to the mouse or snake venom NGF, but studies of the biological effects of the substance and the detection of the molecule in tissues of numerous vertebrate species have been possible because of the nonspecific response of chick sensory ganglia to NGF from all sources. This universality of response by the chick sensory ganglia implies that there are certain similarities in the chemical structure of NGF in all vertebrates.

A number of purification schemes carried out under different ambient conditions have been devised for NGF from mouse submaxillary gland (4,36) as well as from a variety of snake venoms (18,27,28). In general, these results can be summarized as follows: when mouse NGF is isolated at neutral pH under simulated *in vivo* conditions, it is found as a protein of molecular weight 137,000 daltons called 7S NGF (37). 7S NGF is stable from $5 \leq \text{pH} \leq 9$ (38). Outside this pH range 7S NGF dissociates into three dissimilar subunits (36), one of which, called the β-subunit, has the ability to maintain sympathetic and embryonic sensory ganglia in a differentiated state (23). The two other subunits which make up the 7S NGF molecule have no biological activity (34), and it has been suggested that they serve a protective function for the β subunit, albeit the complexed 7S NGF is not active unless dissociation takes place.

The subunit β-NGF described above can be isolated directly from the purified 7S NGF complex (36). The existence of the 7S NGF complex as a typical subunit containing protein has been established by the fact that, after dissociation, the subunits demonstrate a specific and proportionately precise affinity for each other, even in the presence of a heterogeneous mixture of proteins (30). It seems likely that the NGF present in the snake is similar to that found in the mouse, although high molecular weight complexes are difficult to isolate and characterize due to partial degradation of the β-subunit. A high degree of sequence homology between mouse and snake NGF has been found in certain species comparisons (32), and antibodies to mouse β-NGF cross-react antigenically with snake NGF (1).

Other Sources

NGF from sources other than mouse or snake has not been as fully characterized. There is, however, good evidence that a high molecular weight form of NGF, which can be reversibly dissociated through pH shifts into smaller subunits, exists in human serum (29) and hamster brain (33). More recently, nerve growth factor protein has been isolated from human placenta and found to be made up of a high molecular weight complex which can be dissociated at low pH into a number of protein subunits (12). The biological activity in this instance, as in mouse NGF, is also found to reside in a basic protein, also called β-NGF (12).

In summary, the NGF protein has been successfully isolated from male mouse submaxillary gland, a number of snake venoms, guinea pig prostate, and human placental tissue. In addition, some characterization of the NGF activity found in rat serum, human sera, and hamster brain has been carried out.

NERVE GROWTH FACTOR

There is ample evidence that ambient levels of NGF are necessary for the production of neurites during innervation by catecholaminergic neurons of the peripheral nervous system (15). These effects can be elicited *in vitro* by organ culture of either excised mammalian sympathetic ganglia or dissociated sympathetic ganglia (21–24). In addition, the PC12 clone of rat pheochromocytoma has also been demonstrated to require NGF in order to display morphological differentiation (13), and two human neuroblastoma lines of sympathetic origin, SK-N-SH-SY-5Y and KA, have been shown to mimic all of the responses associated with neuronal differentiation for catecholaminergic neurons by the addition of NGF (31). Following innervation of target tissues, peripheral catecholaminergic neurons retain their differentiated state through the continuous retrograde transport of NGF, which is known to be present in target tissues such as the iris (17) and the pineal (33).

In the CNS, the results are not as consistent. It has been demonstrated that collateral sprouting of monoaminergic CNS neurons in rat, following experimentally induced lesions, is enhanced by murine NGF and abolished by antibodies to NGF when these are present at the lesioned site (3). Also there is evidence for the retrograde transport of exogenously added ^{125}I-labeled murine NGF in rat brain (9). For some time now it has been shown that there are differential levels of NGF in mouse (16) and hamster brain (33), and that receptors to NGF cells exist in rat brain (11). However, experiments aimed at determining differences in rat behavior or immunofluorescent labeling, following the addition of exogenously added NGF, did not yield conclusive results (20). This, in large measure, may be due to the lack of antigenic cross-reaction between antibodies to the murine NGF and endogenous NGF in rats. Also, the measurement of endogenous NGF activity levels or endogenous NGF protein in various tissues has been found to be fraught with problems.

MEASUREMENT OF NGF

NGF activity can be measured by the classic bioassay that was developed by Levi-Montalcini et al. (25). In this assay, a number of explanted embryonic dorsal root ganglia are embedded in a plasma clot and the different ganglia are exposed for 24 hr to serial dilutions of the sample being tested for NGF activity. If NGF is present the ganglia will extend a dense halo of neurites within the 24-hr incubation, otherwise the ganglia will degenerate. The protein concentration which when tested in a bioassay elicits the best neurite response is called a biological unit per milliliter (1 BU/ml). This response is referred to as NGF activity, NGF-like activity, or NGF biological activity (25). For pure murine NGF an optimal response is observed for protein concentrations of about 10 ng/ml (25,36). Similar values have been reported for pure NGF of snake origin (28) and of human origin (12). Although the response observed with purified NGF from mouse, snake, or human origin is unequivocal, the same is not true when measuring endogenous NGF levels found in tissue homogenates or body fluids of these same species. In fact, when either human or rat serum is tested in this fashion, there is little homogeneity of response (29,35). Therefore it is difficult to quantitate levels of NGF activity in whole serum using the bioassay. This is in part due to the inability to quantitate levels of serum which interfere with NGF activity. Since the bioassay depends on the response of a heterogenous group of cells isolated from their normally operating homeostatic controls, the response of the explanted ganglia to NGF is affected also by the degree of cell damage during ganglion excision in the sensory ganglion assay (36). Careful dissection and control of plasma clotting and ganglion excision can overcome this problem. However, two other problems are not as easily overcome. They are the sensitivity of responsive neurons to other inhibitors or effectors and the "sticky" nature of NGF due to its positive charges at neutral pH. For pure murine NGF, an optimal response is observed at 10 ± 3 ng/ml, where the high standard error makes comparison of values difficult.

In an attempt to solve these problems, whole serum can be fractionated by sucrose gradient centrifugation prior to assaying biological activity with the goal of separating endogenous NGF away from inhibitors or effectors (29). When this is done the levels of measurable NGF activity are much higher than for unfractionated serum but much lower than those obtained by a one-site radioimmunoassay (Table 1).

Currently there are two types of radioimmunoassay (RIA) techniques available

TABLE 1. *Levels of total NGF in serum*

	Bioassay (1 BU = 10 ng)[a]		
	Whole serum	Fractionated serum	One-site RIA (ng/ml)
Male	18[b]	94 ± 26	158 ± 21
Female	18[b]	116 ± 89	255 ± 35

[a] Since for pure mouse NGF a concentration of 10 ng/ml gives an optimal response (1 BU/ml), it was assumed that for every BU/ml there were 10 ng/ml of NGF protein.

[b] Given the variability in responses to whole serum, representative values of NGF activity found in those sera which gave a response are given.

to quantitate NGF. One type, called the one-site or competition RIA, is based on the competition between radiolabeled NGF and unlabeled NGF for the antibody. The amount of labeled NGF that will be bound to the antibody will be inversely proportional to the NGF concentration. Therefore, by adding varying amounts of unlabeled NGF to a constant amount of labeled NGF, one can establish a relationship between the concentration of unlabeled NGF and radioactivity, thus allowing determination of the concentration of NGF in a sample.

A second type of RIA, called the two-site RIA, involves an unlabeled antibody bound to a solid phase which is incubated with the samples containing NGF. After the NGF is bound, a second labeled antibody is added to the assay and is allowed to bind to the NGF. A "sandwich" is formed of antibody-antigen-antibody. The amount of radioactivity bound to the solid phase is directly proportional to the amount of NGF present in the sample. When rat serum was assayed by both techniques, different results were obtained (35).

In order to determine why the results from the different assays were not in agreement further analyses were undertaken. If ^{125}I-β-NGF was incubated with human serum prior to sucrose density gradient centrifugation, a shift in the apparent sedimentation of the labeled NGF resulted, indicating that some of the labeled NGF is bound to a serum component. Incubation of ^{125}I-NGF with varying amounts of serum showed the serum component to be saturable (Fig. 1), although at most only 49% of labeled NGF was found to bind to the serum component. These results are consistent with the hypothesis that the serum component may serve to maintain a constant serum level of the free NGF hormone as has been proposed for other serum binding protein–hormone interactions (such as between thyroxine and thyroxine binding protein). It has been reported elsewhere (35) that the binding between rat serum components and ^{125}I-NGF has a high affinity ($K_d = 10^{-7}$ M) and a very high capacity (0.5 mg NGF per ml of rat serum). This is an agreement with the findings for human serum. Thus the role of this particular serum component may be

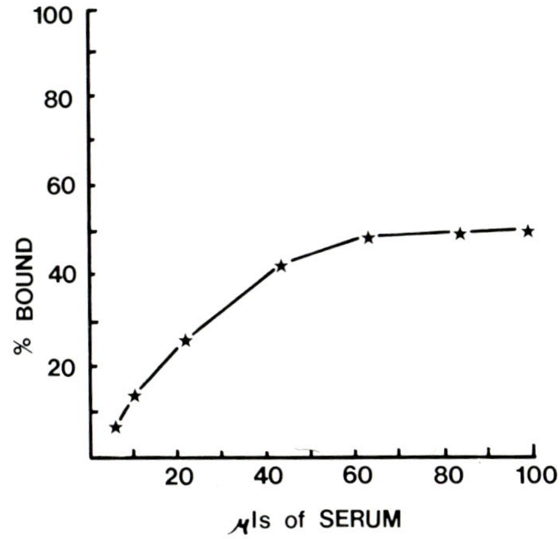

FIG. 1. Binding of ^{125}I-β-NGF to high molecular weight components as a function of added serum. Binding was determined as described in text.

regulatory, protective, or both; but in any event its binding to NGF interferes with NGF detection. Upon binding to the serum component, the labeled NGF may be rendered immunologically unreactive. The net effect of such binding would be a decreased binding of the radiolabel to antibodies, which would be interpreted as evidence for the presence of native NGF in the serum. Thus NGF values reported, using this technique, would be spuriously high due to the presence of the binding component in the serum. Support for this interpretation of results was obtained in experiments which showed that non-ionic detergents were able to break the bond between the binding component and NGF. When a one-site or competition RIA is performed in the presence of detergents, the apparent levels of NGF in serum samples decrease by more than 70% as compared to RIAs not done in the presence of detergents (35). The presence of the binding component would also explain why NGF values obtained with the two-site RIA are always lower than those obtained for the one-site RIA. In the two-site RIA, NGF concentrations are directly proportional to the amount of radiolabel bound, and interference in antigen binding ability will depress the amount of radiolabeled antibody bound in the final step of the assay.

Current methodologies available for radioimmunological quantitation of NGF are limited not only by the serum binding components discussed, but also by the unavailability of species-specific, high-affinity antibodies. The use of affinity chromatography for the preparation of monospecific antibodies (35) yields low-affinity antibodies. Consequently, when the two-site solid phase radioimmunoassay was used recently, no detectable endogenous NGF in either mouse or rat sera was demonstrated at detection levels of 5 ng/ml serum (35). The rat serum data can be assessed only as a relative measurement, since the relative affinities of mouse antibodies for the rat antigens are unknown. Endogenous rat serum

NGF levels would also have to be corrected by an amount proportional to the cross-reactivity found with the mouse antibody. Only when these different affinities and degrees of cross-reaction become known will it be possible to obtain absolute quantitative values of the levels of NGF in nonmurine tissues.

NGF LEVELS IN SCHIZOPHRENIC SERA

When a number of serum samples from schizophrenic patients at admission were compared to controls, an interesting pattern developed (Table 2). Regardless of whether NGF-like activity or NGF-like proteins are measured, there was a significant depression of both values in the serum of both female and male schizophrenics as compared to matched controls. In these patients free NGF-like activity measured by bioassay on the small molecular weight fraction of serum appeared reduced by eight- to nine-fold. NGF-like protein was also reduced although only by four-fold. It should be reemphasized that NGF levels as measured by RIA and reported in Table 2 are only relative. Exact levels of NGF binding proteins in human serum are unknown at this time, as is the precise role that circulating levels of NGF might play on the development and maintenance of adrenergic structures of both the CNS and the PNS. All that is clear is that NGF levels appear depressed in the peripheral circulation of schizophrenics.

The finding that the depression in NGF-like biological activity is greater than that observed for NGF-like proteins would suggest that the structure of NGF molecules in schizophrenics is not unique to the schizophrenic condition. Similar suggestions have been made for familial dysautonomia (26) and neurofibromatosis (10), in which fluctuations in NGF levels have also been reported. In conclusion, these findings argue that a better knowledge of the role of NGF in CNS maintenance and development coupled to precise measurements of absolute levels of circulating human NGF-like molecules are likely to provide suggestions as to organic events associated with schizophrenia.

TABLE 2. *Levels of NGF in schizophrenic serum (N = 58)*

	NGF-like activity[a] (low molecular weight)		NGF-like protein[b]
	(BU/ml)	(%)	(%)
Female (normal)	22.5 ± 9.7	100	100 ± 13
Female (schizophrenic)	2.5 ± 1.7	11	29 ± 13
Male (normal)	15.8 ± 4.3	70	62 ± 14
Male (schizophrenic)	1.9 ± 3.2	8.4	17 ± 14

[a] NGF-like activity measured by bioassay on active low molecular weight fraction (BU = biological unit).

[b] Relative values of NGF-like protein determined by competition RIA.

ACKNOWLEDGMENT

Research supported by grants from the National Institutes of Health.

REFERENCES

1. Angeletti, P., Levi-Montalcini, R., and Caremia, F. (1973): Analysis of the effects of the antiserum to nerve growth factor in adult mice. *Brain Res.,* 27:343.
2. Banks, B. C., Banthorpe, D. V., Berry, P. R., Davies, H. H. S., Doonan, S. S., Lamont, D. M., Shipolini, R., and Vernon, C. A. (1968): The preparation of nerve growth factors from snake venoms. *Biochem. J.,* 108:157.
3. Bjerre, B., Björklund, A., and Steveni, U. (1973): Stimulation of growth of new axonal sprouts from lesioned monoamine neurons in adult rat brain by nerve growth factor. *Brain Res.,* 60:161.
4. Bocchini, V., and Angeletti, P. U. (1969): Nerve growth factor, purification 30,000 M.W. protein. *Proc. Natl. Acad. Sci. U.S.A.,* 64:787.
5. Bueker, E. D., Schenkein, I., and Bane, J. L. (1960): The problem of distribution of a nerve growth factor specific for spinal and sympathetic ganglia. *Cancer Res.,* 20:1220–1228.
6. Carlsson, A. (1977): Does dopamine play a role in schizophrenia? *Psychol. Med.,* 7:583–597.
7. Cohen, S. (1959): Purification and metabolic effects of a nerve growth-promoting protein from snake venom. *J. Biol. Chem.,* 234(5):1129–1137.
8. Cohen, S. (1960): Purification of nerve growth factor from the mouse salivary gland and its neuro-toxic antiserum. *Proc. Natl. Acad. Sci. U.S.A.,* 46:302.
9. Ebbott, S., and Hendry, I. (1978): Retrograde transport of nerve growth factor in the rat central nervous system. *Brain Res.,* 139:160.
10. Fabricant, R. N., Todaro, G. J., and Eldridge, R. (1979): Increased levels of a nerve growth factor cross-reacting protein in "central" neurofibromatosis. *Lancet,* 1:4–7.
11. Frazier, W. A., Boyd, L. F., Szutowicz, A., Pulliam, M. W., and Bradshaw, R. A. (1974): Specific binding sites for ^{125}I-nerve growth factor in peripheral tissues and brain. *BBA,* 57:1096.
12. Goldstein, L. D., Reynolds, C. P., and Perez-Polo, J. R. (1978): Isolation of human nerve growth factor from placental tissue. *Neurochem. Res.,* 3:175–183.
13. Green, L. A., and Tischler, A. S. (1976): Establishment of a noradrenergic clonal line of rat adrenal pheochromocytoma cells which respond to nerve growth factor. *Proc. Natl. Acad. Sci. U.S.A.,* 73:2424.
14. Harper, G. P., and Thoenen, H. (1980): Nerve growth factor: Biological significance, measurement, and distribution. *J. Neurochem.,* 34:5–16.
15. Hendry, I. A. (1976): Control in the development of the vertebrate sympathetic nervous system. *Rev. Neurosci.,* 2:149–194.
16. Hendry, I., and Iverson, L. (1973): Changes in tissue and plasma concentrations of nerve growth factor following the removal of the submaxillary glands in adult mice and their effects on the sympathetic nervous system. *Nature,* 243:500.
17. Hendry, I. A., Stockel, K., Thoenen, H., and Iverson, L. L. (1974): The retrograde axonal transport of nerve growth factor. *Brain Res.,* 68:103–121.
18. Hogue-Angeletti, R. A., Frazier, W. A., Jacobs, J. W., Niell, H. D., and Bradshaw, R. A. (1976): Purification, characterization, and partial amino acid sequence of nerve growth factor from cobra venom. *Biochemistry,* 15:26.
19. Kety, S. S. (1978): The challenge and the prospects of biological research. *Birth Defects,* 14(5):5–95.
20. Kimble, D. P., Bremiller, R., and Perez-Polo, J. R. (1980): Nerve growth factor applications fail to alter behaviour of hippocampal lesioned rats. *Physiol. Psychol.,* 23:653–657.
21. Levi-Montalcini, R., and Angeletti, P. U. (1961): Essential role of the nerve growth factor in survival and maintenance of dissociated sensory and sympathetic embryonic nerve cells in vitro. *Dev. Biol.,* 7:653.
22. Levi-Montalcini, R., and Angeletti, P. (1966): Immunosympathectomy. *Pharmacol. Rev.,* 18:619.
23. Levi-Montalcini, R., and Angeletti, P. U. (1968): Nerve growth factor. *Physiol. Rev.,* 48(3):534–569.
24. Levi-Montalcini, R., Caramia, F., Luse, S. A., and Angeletti, P. U. (1968): In vitro effects of the nerve growth factor on the fine structure of sensory nerve cells. *Brain Res.,* 8:347–362.

25. Levi-Montalcini, R., Meyer, H., and Hamburger, V. (1954): In vitro experiments of effects of mouse sarcomas 180 and 37 on the spinal and sympathetic ganglia of the chick embryo. *Cancer Res.,* 14:49–57.
26. Mobley, W. C., Server, A. C., Ishii, D. N., Riopelle, R. J., and Shooter, E. M. (1977): Nerve growth factor. *N. Engl. J. Med.,* 297:1096–1104, 1149–1158, 1211–1218.
27. Pearce, F. L., Banks, B. C., Barthrope, D. V., Berry, A. R., Davies, H. H. S., and Vernon, C. A. (1972): The isolation and characterization of nerve growth factor from the venom of vipera russelli. *Eur. J. Biochem.,* 29:417.
28. Perez-Polo, J. R., Bomar, H., Beck, C., and Hall, K. (1978): Nerve growth factor from *Crotalus adamenteus* snake venom. *J. Biol. Chem.,* 253(17):6140–6148.
29. Perez-Polo, J. R., Dy, P., Westlund, K., Hall, K., and Livingston, K. (1978): Levels of serum nerve growth factor in schizophrenia. *Birth Defects,* 14(5):311–321.
30. Perez-Polo, J. R., and Shooter, E. M. (1974): Subunit affinities in the 7S nerve growth factor complex. *Neurobiology,* 4:197–209.
31. Perez-Polo, J. R., Werrbach-Perez, K., and Tiffany-Castiglioni, E. (1979): A human clonal cell line model of differentiating neurons. *Dev. Biol.,* 71:341–355.
32. Server, A. C., Herrup, K., Shooter, E. M., Hogue-Angeletti, R. A., Frazier, W. A., and Bradshaw, R. A. (1976): Comparison of the nerve growth factor proteins from cobra-venom *(Naja naja)* and mouse submaxillary gland. *Biochemistry,* 15(1):35–39.
33. Shine, H. D., and Perez-Polo, J. R. (1976): A recombination assay of high molecular weight nerve growth factor protein complexes. *J. Neurochem.,* 26:513–519.
34. Smith, A. P., Varon, S., and Shooter, E. M. (1968): Multiple forms of the nerve growth factor protein and its subunits. *Biochemistry,* 7(9):3259–3268.
35. Suda, K., Barde, Y. A., and Thoenen, H. (1978): Nerve growth factor in mouse and rat serum: Correlation between bioassay and radioimmunoassay determinations. *Proc. Natl. Acad. Sci. U.S.A.,* 75(8):4042–4046.
36. Varon, S., Nomura, J., Perez-Polo, J. R., and Shooter, E. M. (1972): The isolation and assay of the nerve growth factor proteins. In: *Methods in Neurochemistry, Vol. 3,* edited by R. Fried, pp. 203–216. Marcel Dekker, New York.
37. Varon, S., Nomura, J., and Shooter, E. M. (1967): The isolation of the mouse nerve growth factor protein in a high molecular weight form. *Biochemistry,* 6(7): 2202–2209.
38. Varon, S., Nomura, J., and Shooter, E. M. (1968): Reversible dissociation of the mouse nerve growth factor protein into different subunits. *Biochemistry,* 7(4):1296–1303.
39. Weis, J. S. (1968): The effects of nerve growth factor on the spinal ganglia of *Ambystoma maculatum. J. Exp. Zool.,* 170:481–488.
40. Weis, J. S. (1968): Analysis of the development of the nervous system of the zebra fish, *Brachydanio rerio:* In the normal morphology and development of the spinal cord and ganglia of the zebra fish. *J. Embryol. Exp. Morphol.,* 19:109.
41. Winick, M., and Greenberg, R. E. (1965): Appearance and localization of a nerve growth promoting protein during development. *Pediatrics,* 35:221.
42. Wise, C. D., Baden, M. M., and Stein, L. (1975): Post-morten measurements of enzymes in human brain: Evidence of a central noradrenergic deficit in schizophrenia. In: *Catecholamines and Their Enzymes in the Neuropathology of Schizophrenia,* edited by S. Matthysse and S. S. Kety, pp. 185–198. Pergamon Press, Oxford.

Discussion

Nasrallah: In relation to the dopamine hypothesis, would you please comment on how NGF might interact with tyrosine hydroxylase and DBH? Your finding that NGF activity drops in schizophrenia didn't make immediate sense to me because I expected it to rise.

Perez-Polo: So did we. Our reason for studying NGF is that there are many alterations in the dopaminergic systems of schizophrenics. Such a large degree of perturbation seemed bound to affect a key hormone that's involved in the regulation of the various neurotransmitter enzymes. So I'd have been surprised to find no change in its activity. As for the significance of the depressed NGF levels—whether it's a marker, like platelet monoamine oxidase—we can't say at this time.

Janowsky: Were these schizophrenics on drugs?

Perez-Polo: They had been on drugs, and had not been off them for more than a week. We are now looking at a better controlled population of patients and will repeat the measures on particular subpopulations.

Baxter: Have you looked for antibodies to NGF in schizophrenics?

Perez-Polo: No.

Cole: Are any neurological conditions known in which there are abnormalities of NGF?

Perez-Polo: Familial dysautonomia is one. Neurofibromitosis is another.

Carpenter: What are the effects of drugs on NGF activity in serum?

Perez-Polo: We cannot say.

Kleinman: Have you measured this NGF anywhere else in humans besides the blood?

Perez-Polo: Just in saliva, where the levels were not detectable. What we found to be much easier and are doing now is to culture human fibroblasts to look at rates of de novo synthesis of NGF.

Henn: Are there differences between normal and schizophrenic fibroblasts?

Perez-Polo: We don't know yet.

Henn: What is the ratio between CSF NGF and plasma NGF in adults?

Perez-Polo: No one has looked at that.

Henn: One would suspect that peripheral release is ganglionic, but one would wonder about central release. Since the known function of the molecule is in early development, its role in adults is worth looking at.

Yuwiler: Since NGF is a fairly large protein, you would hardly expect it to leak out of the brain; nor would you expect it to be extruded from sympathetic terminals, like DBH. Its site of origin may be important to the marked differences you find in blood. That is, the basis of the difference might be in its rate of release or degradation at its site of origin. What's the origin of the NGF in the serum—the salivary gland?

Perez-Polo: No. If you look at the salivary gland for NGF, it's almost entirely in the lumen for export in the saliva, where it is degraded. Our work shows that glial cells and fibroblasts can make NGF but this has been done only in culture. No one knows where serum NGF is synthesized.

Perspectives in Schizophrenia Research,
edited by C. Baxter and T. Melnechuk.
Raven Press, New York, 1980.

Immunological Components in Schizophrenia

[1]Allan L. Goldstein, [2]Jeffrey Rossio, [3]Galina I. Kolyaskina, [4]Lee E. Emory, [5]John E. Overall, [1]Gary B. Thurman, and [1]Janelle Hatcher

[1]*Department of Biochemistry, The George Washington University School of Medicine, Washington, D. C. 20037;* [2]*Department of Microbiology and Immunology, Wright State University School of Medicine, Dayton, Ohio 45431;* [3]*Institute of Psychiatry of Academy of Medical Science, Moscow, USSR;* [4]*Department of Psychiatry, University of Texas Medical Branch, Galveston, Texas 77550; and* [5]*Department of Psychiatry, Baylor College of Medicine, Houston, Texas 77025*

LAYPERSON'S SUMMARY

Several reports have suggested an association between abnormal immune function and psychosis, especially schizophrenia. The topic remains controversial, however, as many of the reported associations have not been reproducible. Attempts to clarify the relationship of immunity to schizophrenia are complicated by the substantial evidence that some of the drugs used to treat psychosis have an adverse effect on the immune system when used for prolonged periods. One such drug, chlorpromazine (CPZ), has been linked to the presence of atypical lymphocytes in the blood of schizophrenics and to the development of systemic lupus erythematosus (SLE) in psychotic patients. Lupus-like symptoms, including antinuclear antibodies and LE cells, have been seen in a large number of psychotic subjects on chronic CPZ therapy.

In reviewing the literature, it is apparent that the critical studies pertaining to the possibility of immunologic and/or virologic components have yet to be carried out. Previous studies, which failed to substantiate immunologic and/or virologic components in schizophrenia, were performed or reported before we had a clear understanding of the important role of slow viruses in several central nervous system diseases and before we knew the crucial role of the thymus-dependent immune system and immune complexes in the etiology of autoimmune diseases of the central nervous system. Thus, one of the potentially most attractive areas for new approaches in schizophrenia would appear to be that dealing with immunological and/or virological components.

In this chapter we have summarized recent studies that have been conducted in our laboratory which would indicate that CPZ by itself is a potent immunosuppressive agent, both *in vitro* and *in vivo,* in murine systems. In addition, we have completed a clinical study, the results of which indicate that a significant immunological imbalance exists in some patients with schizophrenia. These differences include abnormal lymphocyte responsiveness to selected mitogenic lectins and the presence in the serum of a cytotoxic factor(s) directed against murine thymocytes. Our studies also indicate that during a 28-day chemotherapy trial using CPZ, there was a tendency towards normalization of T-cell responses and significant decrease in serum cytotoxicity.

INTRODUCTION

Several reports have suggested an association between abnormal immune function and psychosis, especially schizophrenia (9,13,22,26,28,30,35,36). The topic remains controversial, however, as many of the reported associations have not been reproducible. In particular, literature reports emanating from the U.S.S.R. have frequently reported the presence of unusual factors in the serum of schizophrenic patients (28,30,36). These studies have been criticized primarily on the grounds that patient selection criteria were inadequate and that the methodologies used in these laboratories differ from those used in the United States. Attempts to clarify the relationship of immunity to schizophrenia are complicated by the substantial evidence that some of the drugs used to treat psychosis have an adverse effect on the immune system when used for prolonged periods. One such drug, chlorpromazine (CPZ), has been linked to the presence of atypical lymphocytes in the blood of schizophrenics (15) and to the development of systemic lupus erythematosus (SLE) in psychotic patients (3,8). Lupus-like symptoms, including antinuclear antibodies and LE cells, have been seen in a large number of psychotic subjects on chronic CPZ therapy (1–3,5,8).

In reviewing the literature, it is apparent that the critical studies pertaining to the possibility of immunologic and/or virologic components have yet to be carried out. Previous studies, which failed to substantiate immunologic and/or virologic components in schizophrenia, were performed or reported before a clear understanding of the important role of slow viruses in several central nervous system diseases (17), and the crucial role of the thymus-dependent immune system and immune complexes in the etiology of autoimmune diseases of the central nervous system (27) had been obtained. Thus, one of the potentially most attractive areas for new approaches in schizophrenia would appear to be that dealing with immunologic and/or virologic components.

Our own studies have documented a significant immunosuppressive effect of CPZ in the mouse (19) and a suggestion of subtle changes in lymphocytes and serum in patients with schizophrenia related to a defect in immune regulation (29). Although by no means conclusive, these data certainly suggest that it would be important to take a more critical look at the role of the immune system in the etiology and progression of the schizophrenias.

The following information is presented to briefly document recent studies that have been conducted in our laboratory which indicate that CPZ by itself is a potent immunosuppressive agent, both *in vitro* and *in vivo*, in murine systems, and secondly to report the results of a study in our laboratory indicating that a significant immunologic imbalance exists in some patients with schizophrenia. These differences include abnormal lymphocyte responsiveness to selected mitogenic lectins and the presence in the serum of a cytotoxic factor(s) directed against murine thymocytes. Our studies also indicate that during a 28-day chemotherapy trial using CPZ, there was a tendency towards normalization of T-cell responses and a significant decrease in serum cytotoxicity.

RESULTS

In Vitro Studies of the Effect of CPZ on In Vitro Antibody Response of Murine Spleen Cells

The effect of CPZ on the *in vitro* antibody response of murine spleen cells to sheep red blood cells (SRBC) is shown in Fig. 1. CPZ was added at the initiation of the SRBC immunized cultures, with final CPZ concentrations ranging from 1×10^{-6} M to 5×10^{-5} M. The cultures were assayed for direct (IgM) plaque-forming cells (PFC)/culture and for recoverable viable cells/culture after 5 days incubation. Each point represents the mean ± standard error of the mean (SEM) for a minimum of 4 and a maximum of 7 separate experiments. An inhibitory effect of CPZ on the production of IgM specific for SRBC is obvious, with close to 50% inhibition occurring at a final CPZ concentration of 5×10^{-6} M, and almost total inhibition at a final CPZ concentration of 5×10^{-5} M. This suppression of the immune response by CPZ cannot be attributed to a direct cytotoxic effect of CPZ on lymphoid cells as reductions in viability, when they occurred, were much less than corresponding reductions in PFC numbers.

The *in vitro* response to SRBC can be considered to occur in three phases. The first phase, occurring 0 to 24 hr after antigen is introduced into the cultures, is the inductive phase. The second phase, 24 to 48 hr after introduction of antigen, is related to proliferation of stimulated lymphocytes, primarily B cells. The third phase, usually occurring between 48 and 72 hr, involves differentiation of the antibody-producing plasma cells.

The comparative effect of CPZ on primary and secondary *in vitro* responses to SRBC is shown in Table 1. The secondary response appears to be much less sensitive than the primary response to the inhibitory effects of CPZ at the two lower drug concentrations. This result may reflect a difference in the sensitivities of memory cells (secondary response) and naive cells (primary response). These results are consistent with other data that suggest that once a responding cell is past a certain critical point, it is relatively insensitive to CPZ at concentrations up to 1×10^{-5} M and will become an antibody-producing cell even in the presence of the drug.

We have also tested the *in vivo* effect of CPZ on the immunity of C57B1/6 mice to see if it has immunosuppressive activity. C57B1/6 mice received daily

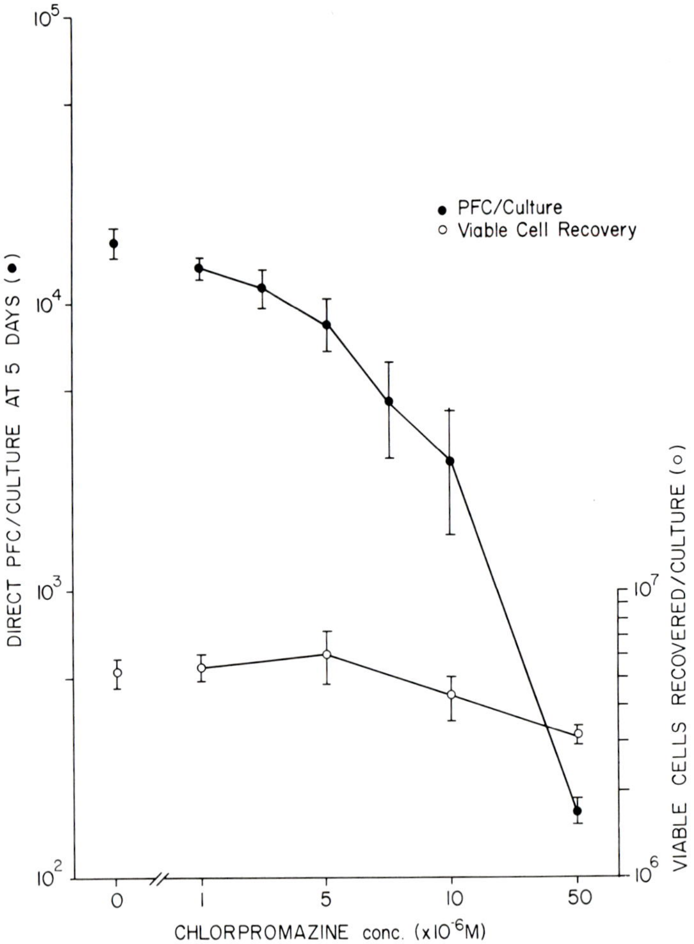

FIG. 1. Dose effect of chlorpromazine on the *in vitro* antibody response of C57B1/6 mouse spleen cells to SRBC. CPZ was added to spleen cell-SRBC cultures at the start of the 5-day incubation period. Points represent direct (IgM) PFC/culture (●) and viable cells recovered/culture (○) ± SEM after 120 hr at 37°C. From Lovett et al., ref. 29.

intraperitoneal injections of either saline or CPZ and were immunized with 3×10^8 M SRBC at various times. As can be seen in Table 2, the anti-SRBC response reached its highest level in saline-treated animals immunized 5 days prior to the PFC assay, while the response of CPZ-treated animals on the same immunization schedule was 95% suppressed. In CPZ-treated animals immunized 7 days prior to assay, the anti-SRBC response was inhibited much less (approximately 57%), suggesting that some cells may be relatively insensitive to CPZ and may continue to proliferate and differentiate into antibody-producing cells

TABLE 1. *Comparative effect of chlorpromazine on the primary and secondary* in vitro *antibody response to SRBC*

Chlorpromazine concentration	Primary response	Secondary response
0	24,506 ± 1,168[a]	66,700 ± 518
5×10^{-6} M	11,006 ± 870	57,850 ± 2,375
1×10^{-5} M	4,050 ± 1,212	34,300 ± 1,018
5×10^{-5} M	0	216 ± 35

From Lovett et al. (29).
[a] Mean direct PFC/culture ± SEM.

in its presence. The data in Table 2 show that CPZ as administered here has a marked inhibitory effect *in vivo* on the response of mice to SRBC. Moreover, the mice receiving CPZ appeared wasted and showed marked atrophy of both the spleen and thymus at the end of treatment.

Effect of CPZ on Immunological Correlates in Patients with Schizophrenia

Twenty-six patients, shown to be schizophrenic through satisfaction of stringent clinical and actuarial (psychometric) criteria, were examined for peripheral blood lymphoid cell responses to mitogenic agents, and for the presence of serum factors cytotoxic for murine thymocytes.

Blood was drawn for lymphocyte and serum testing prior to initiation of therapy (day 0). Patients were then started on a 28-day treatment protocol using chlorpromazine. The dosages of chlorpromazine varied from 400 to 1,200 mg/day, depending on the individual needs of the patient. Additional blood samples were drawn at 14 and 28 days following initiation of therapy. Of the 26 schizophrenic patients, 17 were analyzed at 0 day.

TABLE 2. In vivo *effect of chlorpromazine on the anti-SRBC response*

Treatment[a]	Day of PFC assay post-immunization	PFC/10^6 spleen cells	PFC/spleen
Saline	3	14 ± 2[b]	1,918 ± 227
CPZ	3	5 ± 1	210 ± 38
Saline	5	455 ± 24	63,895 ± 5,447
CPZ	5	56 ± 7	3,388 ± 516
Saline	7	215 ± 25	25,621 ± 4,966
CPZ	7	239 ± 12	11,188 ± 751

From Lovett et al. (29).
[a] C57B1/6 mice received intraperitoneal injections of either saline or CPZ (10 mg/kg body weight) daily for 21 days. Spleens were assayed for PFC on day 22.
[b] Mean direct PFC ± SEM.

Normal Control Group

Twenty-five normal, healthy volunteers (age, sex, and race matched), recruited from hospital or laboratory personnel and community members, served as controls in this study. Informed consent was obtained prior to participation in the study.

Lymphocyte Testing

Lymphocytes were separated from peripheral blood for use in a mitogen-induced transformation assay using the standard procedure followed in our laboratory; blood was centrifuged on Lymphoprep solution (Nyegaard and Co., density = 1.077 g/ml). Lymphocytes and other mononuclear cells remained at the plasma-separation fluid interface and were collected, washed, and dispensed in appropriate numbers for mitogen testing. The tissue culture medium for the mitogen test was supplemented with 5% human AB+ serum.

Lymphocyte mitogen responses were measured 3 and 4 days following treatment with phytohemagglutinin (PHA), concanavalin A (Con A), and pokeweed mitogen (PWM), by the uptake of ^{3}H-thymidine into DNA of dividing cells. Details of the assay method have been described previously (29).

Cytotoxicity Testing

Cytotoxicity of serum from schizophrenics and controls toward murine thymocytes (CBA/J, 3 to 4 weeks of age) was measured as follows: Heparin-free serum was collected, heat-inactivated (56°C, 30 min), and stored at 4°C. The serum was added to murine thymocytes for 30 min at room temperature. Serum was then removed and agar absorbed guinea pig complement added for an additional 60 min at 37°C. Viability of the thymocytes was then measured using trypan blue dye exclusion as the criteria. Details of this procedure have been described (4).

Mitogen-Induced Lymphocyte Transformation

Table 3 shows the results using 3- and 4-day incubations of 17 patient samples and 25 control samples with and without PHA, Con A, or PWM. Since counts incorporated in unstimulated cultures did not differ significantly between normals and schizophrenics, only counts following mitogen stimulation are noted. Sample means for each mitogen were compared by analysis of variance (ANOVA). At the 4-day incubation point, lymphocytes from schizophrenic individuals showed significantly elevated responses to both Con A ($p < 0.05$) and PHA ($p < 0.01$) compared to the normal controls. There was no difference in PWM response in the schizophrenic group.

TABLE 3. *Summary of adjusted means (from separate ANOVA) for 3- and 4-day PHA, Con A, and PWM responses of peripheral blood lymphocytes obtained from schizophrenic patients*

	Schizophrenics (17)	Controls (25)
3-Day		
PHA	88.8[a]	85.6
Con A	70.2	76.0
PWM	37.6	49.1
4-Day		
PHA	47.9	30.1[b]
Con A	54.6	36.0[c]
PWM	47.8	46.3

From Goldstein et al., ref. 19.
[a] cpm × 10^3.
[b] Difference significant, $p < 0.01$.
[c] Difference significant, $p < 0.05$.

Effect of CPZ on Lymphocyte Mitogenic Responses

Lymphocyte mitogenic response data for 14 evaluable patients who completed the 28-day chlorpromazine treatment protocol are shown in Table 4. F values derived from the ANOVA and the associated probability figures are given as well in this table. All mitogen responses were observed to increase over base line after 14 days of treatment with chlorpromazine. The increase was statistically significant in the case of the 3-day Con A response and 4-day PWM response. The response to PHA was observed to increase between days 0 and 14, but the change was not statistically significant. The combined response to all three

TABLE 4. *Mean mitogen responses for 14 schizophrenic patients prior to drug treatment (day 0) and after 14 and 28 days of chlorpromazine treatment*

	Day 0	Day 14	Day 28
3-Day PHA	78.8[a]	92.3	75.4
3-Day Con A[b]	60.8	76.8	70.7
3-Day PWM	32.7	43.0	44.3
4-Day PHA	43.7	46.2	40.1
4-Day Con A	48.3	53.3	47.3
4-Day PWM	38.0	56.4	38.8

From Goldstein et al., ref. 19.
[a] cpm × 10^3.
[b] *Significant contrasts:* 3-Day Con A—Across all 3 test periods $F_{2,24} = 4.15$, $p < 0.05$; Between day 0 and day 14 $F_{1,12} = 9.42$, $p < 0.01$. 4-Day PWM—Across all 3 test periods $F_{2,24} = 3.50$, $p < 0.05$; Between day 0 and day 14 $F_{1,12} = 13.59$, $p < 0.01$. 3-Day PHA, Con A, and PWM combined—Across all three test periods $F_{2,24} = 3.91$, $p < 0.05$; Between day 0 and day 14 $F_{1,12} = 8.52$, $p < 0.02$.

mitogens at 3 days' incubation was significantly increased between days 0 and 14.

Following the significant elevation at 14 days of treatment, the mitogen responses decreased, approaching day 0 values by the 28th day of drug treatment. The only exception was the 3-day PWM response, which at 28 days of treatment was still elevated above base line. Comparing earlier data (Table 3) with these data, it is relevant to note that the 3-day PWM response in the schizophrenic population was lower than that of normal controls at day 0. The increase observed during treatment then moved the 3-day PWM response toward normal. On the other hand, 4-day PHA and Con A responses were significantly elevated at day 0, compared with the normal control group, and drug treatment elevated these mitogen responses still further by day 14. By day 28, however, the 4-day PHA and Con A values in the schizophrenic population returned to day 0 values and even dropped slightly below day 0 values, which may suggest a trend toward normalization. Thus, by day 28 all mitogen responses which differed significantly from the normal control values at day 0 moved in the direction of normal.

Serum Anti-Thymocyte Cytotoxicity

The levels of serum anti-murine-thymocyte cytotoxicity for 28 normal controls and 26 patients evaluated at day 0 (i.e., prior to any drug therapy), and the 15 schizophrenic patients followed during chlorpromazine therapy are shown in Table 5 and Fig. 2.

TABLE 5. *Cytotoxicity indices of the serum of normal controls and schizophrenic patients during treatment with chlorpromazine*

Cytotoxicity	0–40%	41–100%
Normal controls ($N = 28$)	20	8
Patients (15)		
0 Day	6	9
14 Day	8	7
28 Day	11	4
Patients (26)		
0 Day	12	14

Chi square analysis of the cytotoxicity assay in schizophrenic patients treated with chlorpromazine

Control vs patients—day 0	$p < 0.05$
Control vs patients—day 14	$p < 0.24$
Control vs patients—day 28	$p < 0.75$
Patients—day 0 vs patients—day 14	$p < 0.13$
Patients—day 0 vs patients—day 28	$p < 0.48$

After Goldstein et al., ref. 19.

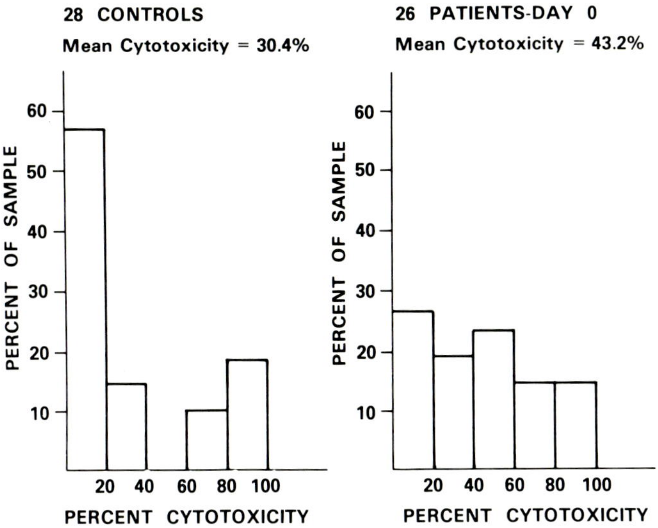

FIG. 2. Cytotoxicity indices of the serum of normal controls and schizophrenic patients. From Goldstein et al., ref. 19.

The normal control population segregated into two subgroups, those with indices of cytotoxicity ranging from 0 to 40%, and those with indices ranging from 41 to 100%. Most controls had cytotoxic indices of less than 20%. The significance of high cytotoxicity in the serum of some "normal" controls is not understood at this time. The normal control population exhibited a mean cytotoxicity of 30.4%, while the 26 schizophrenic patients evaluated at day 0 showed a mean cytotoxicity of 43.2% (Fig. 2).

In the group of 15 patients treated with chlorpromazine, the mean cytotoxicity fell from 45.5% at day 0 to 37.2% at day 28. As shown in Table 5, chi square analysis of the groups divided at the 40% level reveals a significant elevation in the cytotoxic indices of schizophrenic patients at day 0 ($p < 0.05$) which disappears during treatment ($p < 0.75$). These results appear to confirm the earlier observations of Luria and Domashneva (30) and seem to implicate a serum factor which may be associated with schizophrenia and which is decreased during treatment with chlorpromazine. This confirmation contradicts data published by Singal et al. (33) who failed to detect cytotoxic factors.

DISCUSSION

A great deal of controversy surrounds the question of the involvement of an immunologic component in schizophrenia. Two major types of immune aberrations have been reported. One is a decrease in the responsivity of peripheral blood lymphocytes from schizophrenics compared to normal individuals. For example, Vartanian et al. (36) have observed a decrease in mitogenic response to PHA from a mean of 40.9% dividing cells in normals to 27.2% in schizophrenics. A significant decrease was observed in 68% of the patients studied.

The second immunological change reported in schizophrenic patients is the appearance of unusual serum factors which, among other reactivities, are cytotoxic for murine thymocytes *in vitro* in the presence of complement. Numerous studies have implicated serum factors as important elements in the etiology or course of schizophrenic disease (4,9,13,19), although controversy certainly exists regarding these observations.

Our present study substantiates the presence of a serum cytotoxic factor or factors in schizophrenic patients (Table 5 and Fig. 2). The patient population showed significantly higher serum cytotoxic activity than controls. Of additional interest is the finding of high levels of similar cytotoxic substances in the sera of patients with a number of well-characterized autoimmune diseases (systemic lupus erythematosus, rheumatoid arthritis, and myasthenia gravis), as well as in patients with multiple sclerosis and anterior lateral sclerosis (ALS), two neurological diseases with suspected virologic and immunologic components *(unpublished observations)*. However, the range of values was large in both groups and it is difficult at this time to explain the observations of control individuals with high levels of serum cytotoxic factors.

An interesting and perhaps significant observation of this study, however, is the tendency toward a decrease in serum cytotoxic factors during treatment with the phenothiazine drug chlorpromazine (Table 5). This drug has been found to be associated with the development of antinuclear antibodies and, more recently, to have direct immunosuppressive effects *in vitro* and *in vivo* (10–12,29).

Of particular interest here, in the context of possible immunologic factors in schizophrenia, are the effects on the immune system of drugs commonly prescribed in the treatment of the disease. Attention is focused on CPZ as a prototype antipsychotic drug, introduced almost a quarter century ago and still in widespread use today.

Four years after the initial report on CPZ as an effective agent for the treatment of psychosis (38), Goldman (18) reported infections to be a major complication associated with use of the drug in treating more than 1,200 psychotic patients. Reports of similar observations by others soon followed (25,37).

In 1962 Van der Kamp (34) reported nuclear changes in white blood cells of patients with schizophrenia and suggested that the observed changes might be manifestations of a genetic defect associated with the disease. This report was followed by several papers, all confirming the presence of abnormal leukocytes in the blood of schizophrenics (6,14,23,32). Fieve et al. (15), noting that the appearance of atypical leukocytes in schizophrenia patients seemed to coincide with the introduction of CPZ as an antipsychotic agent, conducted a study of patients receiving and not receiving CPZ, concluding that the observed leukocyte abnormalities were associated with CPZ therapy.

Evidence of a possible effect of CPZ on the immune system began to appear as early as the mid-1950s. Studies with laboratory animals showed that treatment with CPZ decreased resistance to pneumococcal infections (7,31), *Salmonella enteritidis* (20,21), *Trypanosoma cruzi* (16), and nasally inoculated streptococci (24), but had no effect on resistance to *Salmonella typhimurium, Trypanosoma congolense, Trypanosoma brucei, Plasmodium berghei,* or intraperitoneally inoculated streptococci (20,31).

In a recent series of publications, Ferguson et al. (10–12) describe studies of the effects of CPZ on human peripheral blood lymphocytes and mouse spleen cells *in vitro.* Their investigations reveal that CPZ inhibits a number of *in vitro* parameters of the cellular immune response, including proliferation of human peripheral blood lymphocytes and mouse spleen cells in mixed lymphocyte culture (MLC), MLC generation of cytotoxic mouse spleen cells, and proliferation of human and mouse lymphoid cells in response to stimulation with a variety of mitogens. They also find that CPZ inhibits the Con A-induced aggregation of mouse spleen cells.

The studies we report here demonstrate that CPZ is a powerful inhibitor of the humoral immune response as well. CPZ at concentrations from 1×10^{-6} M to 5×10^{-5} M inhibits in a dose-dependent fashion one event or more in the generation of antibody-producing cells with specificity for thymus-dependent and thymus-independent antigens. CPZ does not inhibit synthesis, secretion, or binding of antibody to SRBC, nor does it have any effect on immune lysis in the presence of complement. The inhibition appears to be mediated through an effect of CPZ on an event (or events) late in the inductive phase or early in the proliferation phase of PFC generation. When CPZ is added later in the proliferation phase, PFC numbers are reduced correspondingly less. Our observation that the secondary antibody response was less sensitive to CPZ than the primary response is consistent with our finding that CPZ results in atrophy of lymphoid organs, and gives reason for caution in the interpretation of data on humoral immunity from schizophrenic patients. Moreover, the studies by Ferguson, Schmidtke, and Simmons (10–12) demonstrate that the same caution should apply to interpretation of data on cellular immunity in schizophrenics.

The observation of higher than normal levels of responses to PHA and Con A in the schizophrenic patients might suggest some intrinsic abnormality in the capacity of lymphocytes from schizophrenics to respond. It should be noted that there are reports that PHA responses are decreased in schizophrenics. The reasons for this discrepancy are not clear at the moment but may reflect different patient populations and a number of variables, including nutritional status and drug status. Whether these abnormalities are primary or secondary to drug abuse remains to be determined.

In this preliminary study, special care was taken to obtain truly reliable immunological baseline data concerning immune responses in schizophrenia through the choice of a carefully characterized patient group. There are indications that aberrant immune manifestations indeed exist in such patients. Whether these are involved in the etiology and/or course of the disease must await further study on additional well-defined populations of schizophrenic individuals.

SUMMARY AND PROJECTIONS FOR FUTURE RESEARCH

The results of our study indicate that a significant immunological imbalance exists in some patients with schizophrenia. The differences include abnormal lymphocyte responsiveness to selected mitogenic lectins and the presence in the serum of a cytotoxic factor directed against murine thymocytes. During a 28-day chemotherapy trial using chlorpromazine, there was an interesting tendency toward normalization of T-cell responses and a significant decrease in serum cytotoxicity. Our own studies in this area, as well as several new studies which are just appearing in the scientific literature, would suggest that there may be subtle changes in lymphocytes and serum in patients with schizophrenia related to a defect in immune regulation. Although by no means conclusive, these data certainly suggest that it would be worthwhile to take a more critical look at the role of the immune system in the etiology and progression of the schizophrenias. A few years ago it would have been almost heresy to suggest that diabetes and multiple sclerosis might have major immunological components, and yet we now know that this is indeed the case for both of these diseases. We would predict that if in depth studies of immunological systems of schizophrenic patients were carried out, we would see similar deficiencies and correlations.

Specific recommendations for new approaches to study immunologic and virologic components are presented in Table 6. Investigation of some of the questions identified in Table 6 should provide information regarding the role of viruses and the immune system in the schizophrenic process. If immunologic and/or virologic components of schizophrenia can be documented, it will provide the means to develop a whole new approach to the treatment and possible cure of this disease.

TABLE 6. *Recommendations for new immunological approaches to schizophrenia*

1. Critical studies should be carried out to evaluate immune functions in patients with schizophrenia and other psychiatric and CNS diseases using the most modern comprehensive immunological profile tests available. Immunological profile analyses have been developed in other disease categories such as the immunodeficiency diseases, cancers and autoimmune diseases, and could be easily adapted to projected schizophrenia studies.
2. Studies should be designed to correlate specific lymphocyte abnormalities in psychiatric patients with disease states.
3. Particular investigations should be carried out to search for the possible presence of viruses, including slow viruses, in the body fluids and, in particular, in the cerebrospinal fluids of patients with schizophrenia using readily available techniques presently being employed in the study of other CNS diseases.
4. Studies should be designed to determine whether chlorpromazine and other psychoactive drugs used in the treatment of patients with psychiatric disorders affect the immune system and contribute to lymphocyte malfunction in humans. Ongoing studies indicate that certain of the psychoactive drugs are indeed immunosuppressive.

ACKNOWLEDGMENTS

This study was sponsored in part by The Supreme Council 33° A.F.A.M. Scottish Rite Northern Masonic Jurisdiction, Schizophrenia Research Program, Lexington, Mass. Dr. Kolyaskina was a Visiting Professor in the laboratory of Dr. Allan Goldstein.

REFERENCES

1. Alarcon-Segovia, D., and Fishbein, E. (1975): Patterns of antinuclear antibodies and lupus-activating drugs. *J. Rheumatol.,* 2:167–171.
2. Alarcon-Segovia, D., Fishbein, E., Cetina, J. A., Raya, R. J., and Barrera, E. (1973): Antigenic specificity of chlorpromazine-induced antinuclear antibodies. *Clin. Exp. Immunol.,* 15:543–548.
3. Ananth, J. V., and Minn, K. (1973): Chlorpromazine-induced systemic lupus erythematosus. *Can. Med. Assoc. J.,* 108:680.
4. Baron, M., Stern, M., Anavi, R., and Witz, I. P. (1977): Tissue-binding in schizophrenic sera: A clinical and genetic study. *Biol. Psychiatry,* 12:199–219.
5. Bergland, S., Gottfries, C. G., Gottfries, I., and Stormby, K. (1970): Chlorpromazine-induced antinuclear factors. *Acta Med. Scand.,* 187:67–74.
6. Bucci, L., and Johnson, E. E. (1964): Lymphocytes and schizophrenia. *Dis. Nerv. Syst.,* 25:107–109.
7. Chernukh, A. M., and Tolmacheva, N. S. (1960): The effect of aminazine upon the course of experimental pneumococcal infection and the Schwartzman phenomenon. *J. Microbiol. Epidemiol. Immunobiol.,* 31:841–846.
8. Dubois, E. L., Tallman, E., and Wonka, R. A. (1972): Chlorpromazine-induced systemic lupus erythematosus. *J.A.M.A.,* 221:595–596.
9. Durell, J. D., Archer, E. G. (1976): Plasma proteins in schizophrenia: A review. *Schizophrenia Bull.,* 2:147–159.
10. Ferguson, R. M., Schmidtke, J. R., and Simmons, R. L. (1975): Concurrent inhibition by chlorpromazine of concanavalin A-induced lymphocyte aggregation and mitosis. *Nature,* 256:744–745.
11. Ferguson, R. M., Schmidtke, J. R., and Simmons, R. L. (1976): Differential effects of chlorpromazine on the *in vitro* generation and effector function of cytotoxic lymphocytes. *J. Exp. Med.,* 143:232–237.
12. Ferguson, R. M., Schmidtke, J. R., and Simmons, R. L. (1976): Inhibition of mitogen-induced lymphocyte transformation by local anesthetics. *J. Immunol.,* 116:627–634.
13. Fessel, W. J. (1961): Disturbed serum protein in chronic psychosis. *Arch. Gen. Psychiatry,* 6:154–160.
14. Fessel, W. J., and Hirata-Hibi, M. (1963): Abnormal leukocytes in schizophrenia. *Arch. Gen. Psychiatry,* 9:601–613.
15. Fieve, R. R., Blumenthal, B., and Little, B. (1966): The relationship of atypical lymphocytes, phenothiazines, and schizophrenia. *Arch. Gen. Psychiatry,* 15:529–534.
16. Friebel, H., and Kastner, H. (1955): Der einfluss von Megaphen auf den Verlauf von experimentellen Trypanosomenerkranghungen von Mausen (Tr. cruzi und evansi). *Arch. Exp. Pathol. Pharmacol.,* 225:210–236.
17. Gajdusek, D. C. (1978): The possible role of slow virus infection in chronic schizophrenic dementia. In: *Neurochemical and Immunologic Components in Schizophrenia,* edited by D. Bergsma and A. L. Goldstein pp. 81–87. Alan R. Liss, Inc., New York.
18. Goldman, D. (1956): The major complications of treatment of psychotic states with chlorpromazine and reserpine and their management. *Psychiatr. Res. Rep.,* 4:79–88.
19. Goldstein, A. L., Rossio, J., Kolyaskina, G. I., Emory, L. E., Overall, J. E., Thurman, G. B., and Hatcher, J. (1980): Immunological aberrations in schizophrenia: Effect of chlorpromazine on lymphocyte function and serum cytotoxicity. Submitted for publication.
20. Greenberg, L., and Ingalls, J. W. (1960): Influence of tranquilizing drugs on phagocytosis *in vivo. Nature,* 188:588.
21. Grosz, H. J., and Norton, J. (1959): Effect of chlorpromazine on *Salmonella enteritidis* infection in mice. *Science,* 129:784–785.

22. Haddad, R. R., and Robe, A. (1963): An antigenic abnormality in the serum of chronically ill schizophrenic patients. In: *Serological Fractions in Schizophrenia,* edited by R. G. Heath, pp. 151–157. Harper and Row, New York.
23. Hirata-Hibi, M., and Fessel, W. J. (1964): The bone marrow in schizophrenia. *Arch. Gen. Psychiatry,* 10:414–419.
24. Kahn, G., and Davis, B. P. (1970): *In vitro* studies on longwave ultraviolet light-dependent reactions of the skin photosensitizer chlorpromazine with nucleic acids, purines and pyrimidines. *J. Invest. Dermatol.,* 55:47–52.
25. Kline, N. S., Barsa, J., and Gosline, E. (1957): Management of the side effects of reserpine and combined reserpine-chlorpromazine treatment. *Dis. Nerv. Syst.,* 16:352–358.
26. Kolyaskina, G. I., and Kishner, G. G. (1969): Principles governing appearance of antibrain antibodies in serum of schizophrenics. *Zh. Nevropatol. Psikhiatr.,* 69:1679–1682.
27. Lampert, P. W., Garrett, R. S., and Oldstone, M. B. A. (1978): Immune complex deposits in the choroid plexus. In: *Neurochemical and Immunologic Components in Schizophrenia,* edited by D. Bergsma and A. L. Goldstein, pp. 237–244. Alan R. Liss, Inc., New York.
28. Liedeman, R. R., and Prilipko, L. L. (1978): The behavior of T-lymphocytes in schizophrenia. In: *Neurochemical and Immunologic Components in Schizophrenia,* edited by D. Bergsma and A. L. Goldstein, pp. 365–377. Alan R. Liss, Inc., New York.
29. Lovett, C. L., Ulrich, J. T., and Simms, B. G. (1978): Effects of chlorpromazine on antibody production *in vitro.* In: *Neurochemical and Immunologic Components in Schizophrenia,* edited by D. Bergsma and A. L. Goldstein, pp. 407–422. Alan R. Liss, Inc., New York.
30. Luria, E. A., and Domashneva, I. V. (1974): Antibodies to thymocytes in sera of patients with schizophrenia. *Proc. Natl. Acad. Sci. U.S.A.,* 71:235–236.
31. Maral, R., and Cosar, C. (1955): Etude de l'action de la chlorpromazine, de la promethazine et de la cortisone vis-a-vis de diverses infections experimentales. *Arch. Int. Pharmacodyn. Ther.,* 102:1–16.
32. Maznina, T. P., and Kushner, S. F. (1976): Studies on human brain thymus cross-reactive antigens. *J. Immunol.,* 117:818.
32. Pennington, V. M. (1963): A study to determine possible differences in the formed blood elements of normal and schizophrenic subjects. *J. Neuropsychiatry,* 5:21–27.
33. Singal, D. P., Graf, P., and MacCrimmon, D. (1975): Antibodies to thymocytes in sera of normal control and of patients with schizophrenia. *J. Immunol.,* 114:425–427.
34. Van der Kamp, H. (1962): Nuclear changes in the white blood cells of patients with schizophrenic reaction. *J. Neuropsychiatry,* 4:1–2.
35. Vartanian, M. E. (1963): Immunological investigation of schizophrenia. *Zh. Nevropatol. Psikhiatr.,* 63:3–12.
36. Vartanian, M. E., Kolyaskina, G. I., and Lozovsky, D. V. (1978): Aspects of humoral and cellular immunity in schizophrenia. In: *Neurochemical and Immunologic Components in Schizophrenia,* edited by D. Bergsma and A. L. Goldstein, pp. 339–364. Alan R. Liss, Inc., New York.
37. Wardell, D. W. (1957): Untoward reactions to tranquilizing drugs. *Am. J. Psychiatry,* 113:745.
38. Winkelman, N. W. (1954): Chlorpromazine in the treatment of neuropsychiatric disorders. *J.A.M.A.,* 155:18–21.

Discussion

Mosher: You presented two studies—one essentially *in vitro,* and the other *in vivo.* The *in vitro* study showed that chlorpromazine is an immunosuppressant, whereas the *in vivo* study showed, if anything, an activation of the immune system. Is that a fair summary?

Goldstein: Not altogether. You're right about the first study: Humoral and cell-mediated immunity is suppressed by chlorpromazine. In the clinical study with chlorpromazine, we saw what looked like decreased cytotoxicity, which could be interpreted as a suppression by chlorpromazine of plasma cells making too much of an antibody.

Mosher: At the baseline, when people had been off chlorpromazine for 4 weeks, you showed they had an elevation. But they had been previously suppressed by chlorpromazine, 4 weeks earlier. Now they're hyperactive, through a feedback system, and have higher levels than normal.

Goldstein: That could explain their elevation with respect to PHA and Con A, although not the pokeweed results. This study is not the critical study that should be done, but it suggests that there may be an immunological component in schizophrenia.

Canoso: Have you studied the effects on lymphocytes of phenothiazines other than chlorpromazine?

Goldstein: No, but Ferguson and his colleagues (10) at the University of Minnesota have done so, and found differential effects on human and animal lymphocyte responsivity.

Canoso: Because chlorpromazine is the only phenothiazine that produces antinuclear antibodies (3,5,17).

Weinberger: A Yugoslavian group (14) reported in *Lancet* about 2 years ago, in an article entitled "Cerebral atrophy. An immunological disorder?" an interesting experiment. They took a large group of patients who had been diagnosed by pneumoencephalography as having cerebral atrophy and injected them, intradermally, with an extract of human brain protein. As controls, they used a large sample of psychiatric patients who were given the same injections. An extract of hepatic protein served as a protein control. They found a heightened delayed hypersensitivity response to the brain protein in about 70% of the patients with alleged cerebral atrophy, 35% of the schizophrenics, and only 2.5% of the psychiatric outpatients ("neurotics").

Goldstein: I missed the paper but it could be relevant. The study is unusual. That so many of the patients with atrophy responded would seem to indicate that the brain antigens had somehow breached whatever mythical barrier there may be between brain and lymphocytes.

Cole: Some young people who develop catastrophic schizophrenia after an apparently excellent premorbid adjustment act as if they were bombed out by something, perhaps a virus. Could your technology pick this up, and would you have to find it in the first week, or if you studied them years later, could you tell whether the causation had been viral rather than, say, autoimmune?

Goldstein: That's a relevant question I wish I could answer. The sudden schizophrenia in young people who may have taken drugs or otherwise been stressed is very different from late-onset schizophrenia. It's similar to juvenile diabetes and other diseases that are increasingly being associated with a stress, possibly a viral infection. A drug could certainly cause stress that would allow a virus to gain a foothold. I think there are immunological techniques to address the question you raised, but I don't think that such studies are being done, for the NIMH does not seem to appreciate yet why there is so much excitement in other areas of medicine at this potential to approach schizophrenia from a new direction.

Singh: To support your plea for the study of schizophrenia by immunological methods, and also to persuade the VA that our (19) study of wheat gluten in schizophrenia makes sense, I'll mention a recent study done in Israel by Dr. Ashkenazi (4) and co-workers. They applied to celiac patients a leukocyte migration inhibition test they had developed. It was positive in 95% of the celiac patients but only in 5% of the healthy controls. It was positive in 50% of a group of 30 schizophrenic patients.

I recommend that in all such studies schizophrenics be prospectively subclassified in terms of their diagnostic and prognostic subtypes. In that way it may be possible to relate clinical presentations or forms of schizophrenia to biological indices of interest.

Goldstein: I agree that to think in terms of "schizophrenia" hurts our efforts. It's probably many different diseases. In the case of the primary immune deficiency diseases, immunologists are beginning to appreciate that putting everything under one umbrella made life unnecessarily difficult.

Janowsky: Many patients had their thymus glands irradiated half a century ago and since. Did they suffer any subsequent psychological aberrations?

Goldstein: No one has studied that.

Janowsky: What was the immunological impact of irradiating their thymuses?

Goldstein: A serious iatrogenic problem. At that time it was thought that the sudden death syndrome in children was caused by an enlarged thymus pressing against the trachea. Accordingly the syndrome was called "thymostatus lymphaticus" and, since the thymus was thought to be as useless as the appendix, the thymus was irradiated in thousands of children. This was thought to be good medicine, and papers were published in such good journals as *Lancet* and the *New England Journal of Medicine.* But the disease was fictitious; the thymus was enlarged in children who died suddenly because it is a barometer of stress, and unless there's a long-standing disease in which the glucocorticoids have been elevated for a time the thymus will tend to be enlarged; had they compared thymus sizes in cases of accidental death they would have found no differences. Now the literature reports thyroid cancer and other types of malignancy and other diseases associated with thymic malfunction. Schizophrenia may be one of the results and perhaps the VA could study it.

Janowsky: What happens if you knock out the thymus?

Goldstein: What's critical is the damage done to the thymic epithelial cells that produce the thymic factors that maintain various critical subpopulations of lymphocytes. Many diseases of aging are thought to be caused by a breakdown of those cells.

Hays: Thymic and tonsil irradiation began in 1920. When I started training we were beginning to see thyroid cancer as a result of it. I'm not sure that other dramatic clinical changes have been reported in the literature.

Goldstein: I agree that the only good papers so far have been on the thyroid cancer but I am hearing more and more of other consequences. One problem is that it's difficult to learn whether a person's thymus was irradiated.

Hays: The histories are hard to get but the first of those babies would now be in their 60s if they've survived.

Goldstein: Thymocytes, like brain cells, have a long life time—anywhere from 10 to 30 years. I've just learned from Dr. T. Makinodan that a group at his institution (the Wadsworth VA) has found evidence of chromosomal damage in thymocytes in people with senile dementia.

Melnechuk: : Issidorides et al. (12) found altered chromatin structure in neutrophils of schizophrenics about 4 years ago. Now I wish to pose a question: Since it appears that the thymus directs the hypothalamus to instruct the gonads to initiate adolescence, which is when schizophrenia appears, what happened to the sexual development of the children whose thymuses were irradiated?

Goldstein: This is a virgin group in the sense of not being studied. However, there is evidence that the thymus is involved with steroid sex hormones. Recent studies at the Weizman Institute by Weinstein (24) and colleagues have found that thymocytes contain a high concentration of 20alpha-steroid dehydrogenase (20αSDH), an enzyme that breaks down progesterone to an inactive analog. It's not known why thymocytes contain this enzyme.

Melnechuk: Progesterone has been reported (8) to be the hormone with which embryos resist the maternal immune system.

Goldstein: Also, a group from Japan (16) has reported, and it's been confirmed by Sandy Michael (15) in the United States, that thymectomy done at an early critical time in female mice induces premature ovarian dysgenesis with destruction of germinal centers and the growth of many interstitial cells. It's thought to be caused by an immune imbalance that leads to an autoimmune attack.

Berger: You spoke of reconstituting immunity in thymus-deprived organisms with thymosin. Might thymosin be an experimental therapy for schizophrenia?

Goldstein: I'm afraid not. Thymosin has been used experimentally for the last 5 years to treat children with various immune-deficiency disorders—DiGeorge's, Nezelov, Wiskott-Aldrich—and its use in oat-cell cancer of the lungs has been reported by Dr. Paul Chretien (7) and a group at the Washington VA led by Dr. Martin Cohen. We've incubated lymphocytes with thymosin to enhance T-cell numbers *in vitro,* and we've since attempted to do this *in vivo* in schizophrenic patients, with negative results.

Baxter: A recent article (18) in *Science* claimed that schizophrenic patients have a much lower incidence of cancer.

Goldstein: If true, it could be an actuarial artifact, for schizophrenic patients may not live as long as other groups; but if there were a relationship, it would probably be mediated by the suppressor T-cells, which are thought to be the offender in cancer by suppressing cytotoxic T-cells, but a lack of which may be the offender in schizophrenia.

Ewalt: At the University of Texas in the late 1940s, a young resident named Ainsworth had the idea that psychosis protected against cancer and tested it by studying patients at the Austin State Hospital. When they were matched for age, he didn't find decreased incidence.

Nasrallah: The literature suggests an increased mortality in schizophrenics from all causes of death, by a factor of two or three. Perhaps it is an iatrogenic effect.

Ewalt: You have to correct for nutritional factors, life style, suicide, and so forth.

Weinberger: Can the abnormalities that you reported be nonspecific indicators of an immune system in disequilibrium, caused perhaps by an autoantigen load, as in rheumatoid arthritis, systemic lupus erythematosus (SLE), and so forth?

Goldstein: An immune irregularity would conform in part with what seems to be seen with some of the slow virus diseases, where you can easily miss an immune imbalance unless you look very carefully.

Brown: Do you know how chlorpromazine suppresses immunity? Some unclear data suggest that the drug stimulates the pituitary-adrenal system. Some better data indicate that schizophrenics, during psychotic episodes, have very high cortisol levels.

Goldstein: The glucocorticoids determine thymic function in a major way, as reviewed by Fauci (9). All of the suppressor T-cells are very sensitive to glucocorticoids, and there are different species of such cells for other T-cells, B-cells, and macrophages, so that the set is analagous to the complement system, where many controlling factors are involved. Other endocrine glands regulate thymic function, according to current evidence (25). Whether, and how, chlorpromazine affects hormones has not been critically analyzed.

Perez-Polo: Some neuroactive peptides were first found in the gut, and nerve growth factor, which plays a role in the development of the sympathetic nervous system, is found in saliva, where its role is unknown. Many hormones regulate more than one system, and, in disease, can alter either levels or structures, throwing some systems out of balance. So that perhaps the perturbations you see in another system, such as the immune system, may be side effects of the disease, having no direct relationship with the etiology of that disease.

Now your hypothesis is that some malfunction of the immune system leads to schizophrenia or to an aspect of it. Isn't the inverse hypothesis also tenable—not that the immune system may modulate the nervous system, but that the nervous system may modulate the immune system, as it does the endocrine system?

Goldstein: I believe very strongly that the nervous system regulates the immune system, in part by affecting the thymus. Uncontrolled studies claim that hypnosis can modulate aspects of inflammation, and in Yugoslavia, the Jankovič (13) group has manipulated immune responses by lesioning brain regions.

Melnechuk: Two reviews have been published, and at least four are in press or in preparation, on psychological and neural modulation of immunity by means of hormonal—and possibly autonomic—mediation (1,11,20–23). At the behavioral level, stress affects immunity at least by means of the glucocorticoids, but recent American confirmation by Ader (2) of older Russian claims for the conditionability of immune responses seem not to involve those steroids. At the neural level, hypothalamic and other limbic and brainstem lesions and stimulations appear to modulate immune responses (21,22), and older Russian claims of an immediate feedback to the hypothalamus from the onset of an immune response seem to have been confirmed by Sorkin's group (6). A new biomedical field could arise—psycho-neuro-immunology—that may subsume some of what has been called psychosomatic medicine and the sound parts of holistic medicine in a new synthesis with profound implications for a general theory of health.

REFERENCES

1. Ader, R., editor (1981): *Psychoneuroimmunology.* Academic Press, New York. *(In press)*
2. Ader, R., Cohen, N., and Grota, L. J. (1979): Adrenal involvement in conditioned immunosuppression. *Int. J. Immunopharmacol.,* 1:141–148.
3. Alarcon-Segovia, D., Fishbein, E., Cetina, J. A., et al. (1973): Antigenic specificity of chlorpromazine-induced antinuclear antibodies. *Clin. Exp. Immunol.,* 15:543–548.
4. Ashkenazi, A., Krasilowsky, D., Levin, S., Idar, D., Kalian, M., Or, A., Ginat, Y., and Halperin, B. (1979): Immunologic reaction of psychotic patients to fractions of gluten. *Am. J. Psychiatry,* 136:1306–1309.
5. Berglund, S., Gottfries, C. G., Gottfries, I., et al. (1970): Chlorpromazine-induced antinuclear factors. *Acta. Med. Scand.,* 187:67–74.
6. Besedovsky, H., Sorkin, E., Felix, D., and Haas, H. (1977): Hypothalamic changes during the immune response. *Eur. J. Immunol.,* 7:323–325.
7. Chretien, P. B., Lipson, S. D., Makuch, R., et al. (1978): *Cancer Treat. Rep.,* 62:1787–1790.
8. Clemens, L. E., Siiteri, P. K., and Stites, D. P. (1979): Mechanism of immunosuppression of progesterone on maternal lymphocyte activation during pregnancy. *J. Immunol.,* 122:1978–1985.
9. Fauci, A. S. (1978–79): Mechanisms of the immunosuppressive and anti-inflammatory effects of glucocorticosteroids. *J. Immunopharmacol.,* 1:1–25.
10. Ferguson, R. M., Schmidtke, J. R., and Simmons, R. L. (1976): Inhibition of mitogen-induced lymphocyte transformation by local anesthetics. *J. Immunol.,* 116:627–634.
11. Hall, N. R. S. (1980): Behavioral and neuroendocrine interactions with immunogenesis. In: *Behavioral Neuroendocrinology,* edited by A. J. Dunn and C. B. Nemeroff. Spectrum, New York.
12. Issidorides, M. R., et al. (1975): Altered chromatin ultrastructure in neutrophils of schizophrenics. *Nature,* 258:612–614.
13. Jankovič, B. D., and Isakovič, B. D. (1973): Neuro-endocrine correlates of immune response. I. Effects of brain lesions on antibody production, arthus reactivity, and delayed hypersensitivity in the rat. *Int. Arch. Allergy,* 45:360–372.

14. Jankovič, B. D., Jakulič, S., and Horvat, J. (1977): Cerebral atrophy. An immunological disorder? *Lancet,* ii:219–220.
15. Michael, S. D. (1979): The role of the endocrine thymus in female reproduction. *Arthritis. Rheum.,* 22:1241–1245.
16. Nishizuka, Y., and Sakakura, T. (1977): Thymus and reproduction: Sex-linked dysgenesis of the gonad after neonatal thymectomy in mice. *Science,* 166:753–754.
17. Quismorio, F. P., Bjarnason, D. F., Kiely, W. F., et al. (1975): Antinuclear antibodies in chronic psychotic patients treated with chlorpromazine. *Am. J. Psychiatry,* 132:1204–1206.
18. Roppel, R. M. (1978): Cancer and mental illness. *Science,* 201:398.
19. Singh, M. M., and Kay, S. R. (1976): Wheat gluten as a pathogenic factor in schizophrenia. *Science,* 191:401–402.
20. Solomon, G. F., Amkraut, A. A., and Rubin, R. T. (1980): Stress and psycho-immunological response. *(in press).*
21. Spector, N. H. (1980): The central state of the hypothalamus in health and disease; III: Does the hypothalamus regulate or influence immune responses? In: *Handbook of the Hypothalamus,* edited by P. Morgane and J. Panksepp. Marcel Dekker, New York.
22. Stein, M., Schiavi, R. C., and Camerino, M. (1976): Influence of brain and behavior on the immune system. *Science,* 191:435–440.
23. Rogers, M. P., Dubey, D., and Reich, P. (1979): The influence of the psyche and the brain on immunity and disease susceptibility: a critical review. *Psychosom. Med.,* 41:147–164.
24. Weinstein, Y. J. (1977): 20-Alpha-hydroxysteroid dehydrogenase: A T-lymphocyte-associated enzyme. *J. Immunol.,* 119:1223–1229.
25. White, A., and Goldstein, A. L. (1973): Hormonal control of immunity. In: *Immunogenicity,* edited by F. Borek, pp. 334–364. Elsevier, Amsterdam.

Perspectives in Schizophrenia Research,
edited by C. Baxter and T. Melnechuk.
Raven Press, New York, 1980.

Chronic Schizophrenia from the Standpoint of Vulnerability

Joseph Zubin

VA Medical Center, Pittsburgh, Pennsylvania 15206

LAYPERSON'S SUMMARY

The original view of schizophrenia as a persistent, progressive chronic disorder leading to complete deterioration of the personality has been challenged by a new outlook. This new approach regards schizophrenia as occurring only in *vulnerable* individuals who are subjected to stresses and strains of such magnitude that they develop a crisis. While all of us develop crises to stressful events, we can usually adjust to them and overcome them in a salutary way. However, the vulnerable individual cannot absorb the crisis and an episode of illness results. Such episodes, however, need not persist permanently, but disappear either with or without treatment in time, and then the patient returns to his pre-episode level of adjustment.

While some patients appear to have persistent chronic episodes, a careful examination indicates that the majority are victims of iatrogenic (due to type of treatment and hospitalization) and ecogenic (due to noxious environmental factors) circumstances rather than of the natural consequences of the disorder itself, and at most not more than 6 to 10% fall into the chronic category.

If we could identify the individuals who are vulnerable by discovering specific characteristics or markers that characterize the vulnerable (just as insulin deficiency identifies diabetics) and could also determine the specific contingencies which trigger episodes in these vulnerable individuals (like the presence of pollen in allergy), the way would be open for preventive intervention. This would enable us to abort episodes and thus prevent the chronic phase from developing. Current research directed at the discovery of markers and triggers has begun to show some promise, and it is to be hoped that with continued research in this direction, the scourge of mankind known as schizophrenia may yield to preventive interventions.

INTRODUCTION

The purpose of this chapter is to:

1. Indicate that the view of schizophrenia as a persistent progressive debilitating chronic disorder leading invariably to unremitting impairment or deteriora-

tion is no longer tenable. It has been challenged by a more benign outlook which regards schizophrenia as a time-limited episode of either a single or repeated occurrence.

2. Review the accumulating evidence for the episodic nature of schizophrenia.

3. Propose the hypothesis that the episodic nature of schizophrenia emerges from the graded vulnerability of individuals to triggering events (life event stressors) of either exogenous or endogenous origin.

Based on the assumption that schizophrenia is episodic, and that episodes are elicited by triggering events in vulnerable individuals, a program of research will be outlined to test this formulation and draw its implications for schizophrenia in general and for its chronic phase in particular.

As a result of the application of such a program, we may be able to identify the individuals who stand in high risk of developing an episode of schizophrenia and also identify the contingencies which trigger episodes in these vulnerable individuals. This information can provide the means for determining the most suitable preventive intervention strategies for aborting even the initial episode or recurrent episodes and in this way eliminate the development of chronic schizophrenia at its very source.

EVIDENCE FOR THE EPISODIC NATURE OF SCHIZOPHRENIA

We have postulated that schizophrenia is not a continuing condition leading to a chronic state of either deterioration or unremitting impairment and that the only persistent characteristic of the schizophrenic is his *vulnerability,* not his *disorder.* This, however, flaunts the usual view regarding schizophrenia and makes no allowances for chronic conditions. Is there any evidence favoring the episodic nature of schizophrenia?

A survey of recent studies of schizophrenia (48) indicates that the evidence for the chronic and unremitting nature of all schizophrenic illness is rather sparse and that the episodic hypothesis, at the very least, is tenable. Hospital statistics indicate that the average duration of hospitalization has dropped from several years in the custodial period before the mid 1950s to some 37 days in 1975, and this is a worldwide trend. Most of the chronic cases in our hospitals have been admitted as long as 20 years ago and probably reflect the iatrogenic influences of long-term incarceration rather than the course of the disorder itself. More recently, randomly selected experimental brief therapy groups lasting only 4 weeks have shown results as good as or better than those groups consigned to long-term therapy. In 2 to 4 weeks of therapy, symptoms subsided in the majority of cases, and the episode seemed well on its way to termination. This is additional evidence for the episodic nature of schizophrenia. Reports from England (33) indicate that the relapse rate of patients returned to hostile home environments is far greater than that of those returned to benign home environments. Thus, the relapse rate of patients, if not the rate of new episodes, may be a function not of the natural course of their illness but of the niche they occupy in life. Perhaps the most telling comment on the disappearance or gradual reduction of the chronic unremitting schizophrenic is Manfred Bleuler's follow-up of his 208 schizophrenic probands over their lifetime.

In the Second Rochester International Conference on Schizophrenia, Manfred Bleuler (4) summarized the long-term course for the different groups of patients that he and others studied. He reported that at least 25% were fully recovered without further relapse and without requiring drug maintenance. Only a minority required welfare agency attention, and only about 10% remained permanently hospitalized.

He further pointed out that at any given point in time during the follow-up, 50% of the patients were fully recovered, though some of these relapsed later and their course fluctuated. After the fifth year of follow-up, 75% of the patients resided in the community at any given point in time and only 25% were hospitalized. This is a far cry from the persistency with which schizophrenia has been endowed. More than half worked to maintain themselves. Bleuler's study gave a conservative estimate of the outcome of all schizophrenic patients in Switzerland since it included only a small proportion of first admissions, the majority being readmissions who comprised a larger number of more severe cases. Furthermore, many young patients and those with strong church affiliations tended to be hospitalized in private institutions.

One finding based on Bleuler's follow-up (5) and regarded by him as most important showed that 5 or 10 years after onset, the relationship between recoveries (30%), mildly chronic (38%), moderately (17%) and severely (15%) chronic remained constant throughout the subsequent follow-up period. However, this constancy did not apply to the individual probands. The probands constantly changed back and forth between the various stages of recovery. Apparently the probands were in dynamic equilibrium, like ions in a solution: when one entered an episode, another exited from it. This dynamic equilibrium is additional evidence that the alleged persistence of the schizophrenic episode is a myth. Since the episode does not persist, what does persist in schizophrenia? This chapter suggests that the permanent feature in schizophrenia is the vulnerability of the individual to the development of episodes.

Wing (55) found in a 5-year follow-up of first admission schizophrenics that about 75% had a good outcome (mild or no disability).

Even patients with a poor prognosis as determined by Vaillant's 6 factors and Shepherd et al.'s 11 factors (3) showed a favorable outcome (mild or no disability) in 53% of the cases. If we take into consideration not only the hospitalized schizophrenics, but also those seeking help in outpatient clinics and community mental health centers, the proportion of permanently disabled is reduced to a small minority. The reason why schizophrenia was regarded as malignant is attributed by Manfred Bleuler to the fact that earlier generations of psychiatrists saw only the patients who returned to the clinic after discharge and never again laid eyes on those who recovered successfully without relapsing.

Even the hard core chronic schizophrenics do not need to remain hospitalized continuously if proper treatment is provided. Thus, Paul and Lentz (38) investigated the effect of social-learning programs on a group of 137 hard core chronic schizophrenics who were selected on the basis of the following criteria: (a) aged 18 to 55; (b) average duration of hospitalization 17 years (nearly two-thirds of their adult life spent in a mental institution); (c) low socioeconomic status; (d) process schizophrenics without organic involvement; (e) non-sudden onset or precipitant for first episode; (f) less than 15% married without being divorced; (g) maintained on psychotropic drugs; and (h) rejected for extended care community placement because of low level of self-care and excess of bizarre behavior. The results indicated that even among these recalcitrant patients, with the lowest probability of release, a significant rate of release could be achieved. About 91% of the released patients continued to stay in the community and only 5% required rehospitalization during a 2-year follow-up period. Furthermore, by phasing the transition to the community with the help of social work follow-up, the readjustment to community living was so successful that they functioned at a level indistinguishable from that of their community peers in fully one-third of the cases. Fully 90% of the patients in the original chronic group were able to function well enough to fulfill their basic needs for food, shelter, socialization, and recreation, and 10% of these were able to live completely independently in the community.

In summary, chronic unremitting schizophrenics, certainly those of the catastrophic variety, are becoming increasingly rare, and it seems reasonable to assume that the permanent factor in schizophrenia is not the episode, but the vulnerability to the disorder.

The hypothesis appears to be consistent with two well-known characteristics of schizophrenics: (a) they do not exhibit schizophrenic behavior all the time, and even when they are in the hospital they are not always in their episode; (b) schizophrenics who exhibit good premorbid adjustment tend to recover. When the good premorbids' episodes end, they return to their good premorbid level and resume their place in society. When the poor premorbids' episodes end, they too return to their premorbid status, but it is difficult to recognize that they have actually been freed from their episode since they were unable to cope with life's exigencies premorbidly, and postmorbidly they still cannot cope. The hospitalization episode is often no promoter of better coping efforts. In such patients the episode may appear to persist, thus giving schizophrenics a bad name.

Other workers also have entertained the possibility that schizophrenia occurs in self-limiting episodes. Bockoven and Solomon (6) concluded that pre-drug-era follow-ups showed results as good as drug-era follow-ups. They discussed the common philosophy that permeated the clinical and social management of patients in the two eras:

> This philosophy is based on the idea that the majority of mental illnesses, especially the most severe, are largely self-limiting in nature if the patient is not subjected to demeaning experiences or loss of rights and liberties. Therapeutic management consists first and foremost of removing these negative influences

> and replacing them with a positive attitude of respect for the patient's needs for human companionship and interest-holding activity. Somatic treatments are prescribed in this context to relieve specific kinds of suffering and thereby to expedite the spontaneous healing process. (p. 796).

Extein and Bowers (13) considered the functional disorders as "states" (episodes) rather than "traits." They indicated that:

> State disorder refers to those qualitatively different mental conditions which tend to be time-limited and autonomous in that, once present, they are relatively insensitive to environmental input. They respond poorly to verbal or other psychosocial treatment but usually respond to medication or other somatic treatment. Specifically, state disorders include schizophrenic and other functional psychoses, mania, major depression, severe anxiety, acute organic brain syndrome, and seizures. Most of these state disorders probably involve a variety of environmental stressors acting on genetic or other biological vulnerability.

The more benign outlook on schizophrenia has not yet been accepted universally. This is made clear by the neo-Kraepelinian character of the newly proposed DSM-III. The reason for this may rest on the premise that codification of diagnosis, like codification of laws, must not keep up too closely with science but must stay discretely behind it, especially when the scientific results are still tentative. The more basic conception of schizophrenia provided by Kraepelin may still be the firmest thing we can offer for diagnostic codification, but not the best we can offer for research.

RELATION OF EPISODIC NATURE OF SCHIZOPHRENIA TO VULNERABILITY

In order to find an explanation for the episodic nature of schizophrenia we must first examine the causes of the schizophrenic disorder. Considerable advances have been made in the investigations of the phenomenology of schizophrenia by the development of more objective and reliable methods for describing the deviant behavior of the schizophrenic in the setting of structured and semistructured interviews. The data obtained in this manner can be systematically organized into dimensions of psychopathology, which provide the basis for matching behavior with the diagnostic criteria required for assigning a patient to a specific category.

Description of behavior, however, is not enough to find the causes of mental disorder or to intervene successfully in the rehabilitation or even prevention of mental disorders. Ever since early man trephined skulls to eject the evil demons, attempts have been made to divine the sources of mental illness and these attempts can now be formulated as scientific models on the basis of which hypotheses are projected and experimental work done to test their tenability.

At least six models have been proposed to explain the etiology of mental disorders. They range from a molecular-biological model, primarily influenced by genetic factors, to a field-theory model which is primarily influenced by ecological factors. Models favoring the internal environment and neurophysiology as determinants of mental disorders are more closely related to the genetic factors, whereas models favoring development and learning are more closely related to the ecological factors (58) (Fig. 1.).

The *genetic model* is perhaps the most advanced model in terms of tenability. It is based on the belief that predisposition to schizophrenia is inherited. This model suffered a setback when the concordance rates for monozygotic twins reported by Kallmann (26) to be between 0.69 and 0.86 were found to be considerably lower by other investigators who used more representative samples of monozygotic twins. However, the model regained strength from the adoption studies begun by Heston (21) in Minnesota and by Kety, Rosenthal, Wender, and Schulsinger in Denmark (28). It is acceptable now to state that genetics may be a necessary but not a sufficient cause for schizophrenia, although not all researchers (including some geneticists) subscribe to the necessity of a genetic etiology for schizophrenia (29). At the opposite pole is the *ecological model.* It has not yet gained as much general scientific acceptance. One advantage the genetic model has over the ecological model is its use of consanguinity as a measure of degree of genetic similarity. There is, as yet, no comparable measure for assessing degree of similarity of ecological factors, though one will be suggested in this chapter. Nevertheless, some components of the ecological model have been generally accepted as being associated with schizophrenia: i.e., socioeconomic status, physical and social characteristics of the milieu, social network supports, minority status, etc. Claims that these components are necessary or sufficient to elicit a schizophrenic episode have not been pressed as hard as the claims for the genetic model.

The *developmental model* dealing with the ontogenesis of behavior has focused attention on perinatal factors, nutritional factors, and lag of maturational development as indicators associated with the development of schizophrenia. Recently, research by Kinney and Jacobsen (29) revealed that the season in which an individual is born and cerebral injury after birth increase the likelihood of schizophrenia in probands of low genetic risk (i.e., those with no known schizophrenia in their immediate family). They conclude that schizophrenia in at least some of the low-risk probands is environmentally induced or a phenocopy, thus giving the developmental model and the other nongenetic models considerable etiological support. But there is no conclusive evidence yet that the developmental factors are either necessary or sufficient as etiological agents in the occurrence of schizophrenic episodes.

The eminent Adolf Meyer was a progenitor of the *learning theory model* for the etiology of schizophrenia. He stressed that the accumulation of faulty habits in reacting to life's exigencies could become a cause for the initiation of dementia praecox. Accordingly, the development of ineffectual social and interpersonal relationships, whether learned actively in maladaptive situations or passively through modeling on inappropriate models, can render individuals

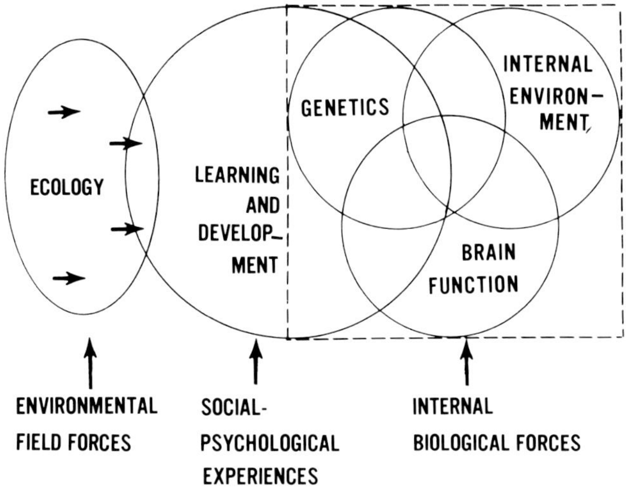

FIG. 1. Scientific models of etiology of mental disorders.

more vulnerable to later life-stressors. In this way early learned helplessness may lead to depression in adulthood under sufficient stress. The family unit, which transmits attitudes, habits, values, and communication patterns, is an important etiological agent according to this model. Yet there is still no cogent evidence for causality here.

The *internal environment model* has perhaps been the most prolific in providing hypotheses for the etiology of schizophrenia. It stimulated the search for biochemical abnormalities in schizophrenia. To date, research conducted in this area has probably done more for biochemistry than for psychopathology. However, considerable progress has been made in psychopathology as well. A search began in the 1940s for peripheral metabolic correlates of schizophrenia, observable in the blood and the urine (27). It failed primarily because the metabolic changes which were found turned out to be nonspecific. More recently the search has shifted to an investigation of central synaptic mechanisms. Our improved understanding of synapses was summarized recently by Kety (27) as follows: "The recognition that these are chemical switches provides crucial loci at which metabolic processes, hormones, and drugs may affect these junctions and influence the psychologic processes they mediate" (p. 85). The psychological processes which are mediated through the biochemical reactions occurring at synapses include perception, cognition, attention, motivation, mood, and other emotional and mental states. Kety concluded that: "Although . . . the mechanisms of action of the drugs effective in the treatment of mental disorders are becoming well defined, the metabolic and biochemical factors involved in schizophrenia and the affective disorders have not been elucidated." Here again, we have no definite evidence.

The *neurophysiological model* has been instrumental in stimulating investigators to use a considerable array of techniques for examining deviations in those functions of the schizophrenic's brain which affect information processing and to probe how the central nervous system and the autonomic nervous system might deviate from normal expectations. Deviations could occur at any level of information processing, beginning with: (a) reception of the energy and information in the stimulus; (b) encoding and processing of the information in higher centers; (c) interaction of the arriving information with stored memories of previous experiences and wired-in patterns of networks, and (d) emission of the final response. Among the techniques which have been found useful in differentiating schizophrenic from other mental patients and normals according to Spring and Zubin (49) are various reaction time measures including Shakow's crossover index and our own cross-modality effect and Steffy's redundancy effect; event-related potentials, especially Sutton's P300; pupillography à la Hakerem and Steinhauer and Rubin; and smooth pursuit eye movements à la Philip Holzman. Thus far the results are still only promising. A more recent review of the neurophysiological and psychophysiological techniques has been provided by Spohn and Patterson (47).

ETIOTYPES

The advanced state of the genetic model based on consanguinity as a measure of genetic similarity and on well-developed biologically anchored genetic theories had cast a pall on etiological claims of the other five models. But the preeminent position which genetics held in the etiology of schizophrenia until recently has been eroded by the new evidence that suggests that phenocopies for schizophrenia may exist so that the disorder may develop in individuals who do not possess the genotype for schizophrenia (29).

Thus we can now postulate other etiological types or "etiotypes" to represent the other scientific models in a manner analogous to the way the genotype

TABLE 1. *Etiotypes and their potential markers*

Model	Etiotype	Example of potential markers
Genetic	Genotype	Consanguinity
Internal environment	Chemotype	Monoamine oxidase level
Neurophysiological	Neurophysiotype	Evoked potentials
Ecological	Ecotype	Constricted social network
Developmental	Auxeinotype[a]	Parental loss in early childhood
Learning theory	Mathetotype[b]	Communication disorder
Vulnerability	Schizotrope[c]	Profile of etiotype markers

[a] Suggested by E. I. Burdock from the Greek root for growth.
[b] Suggested by K. Salzinger from the Greek root for learning.
[c] Because Rado and Meehl have preempted the term schizotype, a new term had to be provided for one prone to schizophrenia without exhibiting schizotypy.

represents the genetic model. This is shown in Table 1. Each of the etiotypes in Table 1 characterizes individuals vulnerable to schizophrenia on the basis of the model from which it is derived. Some of the potential markers which might identify these etiotypes are also shown in Table 1.

CURRENT IMPASSE

Having described the advances made possible in the past by considering the implications of each model, and having postulated etiotypes for each of them, we will now turn to their current status.

The genetic model represents the most advanced etiological approach to schizophrenia. According to this model the etiological agent is the genotype which is transmitted from one generation to the next. If we accept a monogenic model, this genotype contains the genetic "anlage" for schizophrenia in the form of a deviant allele in a particular location on a specific chromosome. If we accept a polygenic model, the genotype is the result of deviant alleles in various locations. It is clear that the person possessing the genotype for schizophrenia does not always develop the phenotype.

It has been demonstrated that some individuals have a higher risk for developing an episode of schizophrenia by virtue of their consanguinity with probands, but no further advances on the basis of the genetic model have been made in locating any allele or alleles presumably responsible for the disorder. Nor has it been possible to explain why some genotypes develop into phenotypes while others do not. Nor has it been possible so far to link the DNA structure of the genes with the biochemical action of the internal environment. Despite the notable advances made with the use of each of the models, we have not yet found any necessary or sufficient causes for schizophrenia. To overcome this impasse is our immediate problem.

VULNERABILITY MODEL

In trying to fathom why we have reached the current impasse, I realized that the six etiological models have been working until very recently in relative isolation from each other. Thus, although each model has the common goal of finding the etiology of schizophrenia, each fails to provide the means for either confirming or negating hypotheses emanating from competing models. But is there a common thread that may bind them together?

A logical analysis of all these models would indicate that it is the interaction of these models rather than their individual main effect which produces the schizophrenic episode. If we squeezed all of these models into a goblet, what would their common elixir contain? I suggest that it would contain the common denominator of vulnerability. This vulnerability is composed of contributions from the various etiological models. The vulnerable individual—the schizotrope—may bear the genotype for schizophrenia, any one of the other five etiotypes discussed earlier, or any combination of these etiotypes. Thus, though no single etiotype is in itself a necessary and sufficient etiological agent, the interaction between these etiotypes can produce a schizotrope who may suffer an episode if triggered by a sufficiently stressful life event.

Once an episode has occurred and the symptoms of the disorder are visible, what maintains the symptoms? Do such episodes have a natural history which runs its course, or are there certain life events or contingencies which tend to maintain the episode and whose elimination or prevention would tend to shorten the episode? A behavioral analysis of episodes seems necessary to answer this question.

It is important to determine the various kinds of events which trigger a crisis. Specifically, a triggering event is defined as an event which elicits a crisis in a vulnerable individual, this crisis leading to an episode depending on the degree of vulnerability. Triggering life events should not be confused with etiological life events which give rise to the various etiotypes (ecological, developmental, learning). The latter are long-term influences formative of vulnerability. An example given by van Praag (53) of such a long-term influence is the long continued exposure to serious emotional neglect during childhood which results in the "deprivation dwarfism" syndrome. In this condition somatic growth and mental development are retarded despite normal and even excessive food intake, but this retardation is quickly overcome after hospitalization without hormonal substitution. In comparison, the "triggering" life events are recent life event stressors of short duration which induce sufficient stress to produce a crisis. They can be either somatic or psychosocial in nature. Thus, the somatic effect of childbirth may be a sufficiently stressful life event to serve as a trigger, or the psychosocial loss of a beloved relative may trigger a crisis.

A useful distinction has been made by van Pragg (53) between "stable" and interactional life events. By stable life events he refers to immutable or irreversible events like the loss of a spouse. Interactional events involving interpersonal interactions such as sharp exchange of words, hatred, jealousy, or rejection may be quite potent in triggering a crisis but are not as easily traceable. Thus, the critical attitude of family members towards a returned patient may hasten either a relapse or a new episode. Brown and Rutter (7a) have developed techniques for monitoring such life events.

In searching for criteria to distinguish between life events that serve as triggers and those that do not, the following classification has been suggested: those that (a) produce losses; (b) are undesirable; (c) are novel; (d) are unexpected; (e) are unanticipated; (f) are uncontrollable; and (g) require considerable readjustment of daily routine. It would be well to find a common denominator for these criteria. It has occurred to the writer that the impact of the life event on the social network support system that surrounds the individual may serve as the common denominator which triggers the crisis and episode. One could argue that the other criteria bring about their stressor effects only insofar as they overwhelm the defenses provided by the social network supporting system.

This is why, for example, the presence of a confidant protects against depression (7) and the reason why certain losses can be withstood as long as the social network remains intact. It is interesting to note that of the 43 items in the life event schedule provided by the Social Readjustment Rating Scale of Holmes and Rahe (22), fully 37 or 86% involved reduction in the social interconnections of the individual (death of spouse, divorce, etc.).

As long as the stress is below the threshold of vulnerability, the individual responds to the stressor with a minor crisis in an elastic homeostatic way and remains well within the limits of normality, his coping ability remaining intact. When the stress exceeds the threshold, his coping ability collapses and he is likely to develop a major crisis, followed by a psychopathological episode. Furthermore, we postulate that the episode is time limited. When the stress sinks below the vulnerability threshold, the episode ends and the patient returns to his pre-episode level of coping.

A considerable amount of evidence has been collected on the role that triggering life event stressors play in the elicitation of both physical and mental disorders (7,12,40). The strain of readjustment to the consequences of the life event, if

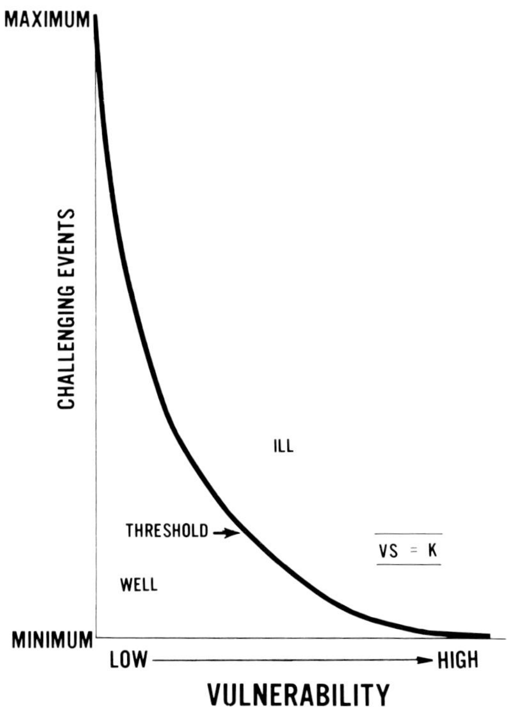

FIG. 2. Relation between vulnerability and challenging events. (The equation for this hypothetical curve is VS = K, where V is the degree of vulnerability, S is the degree of stress induced by the challenging event, and K is a constant.)

severe enough, appears to trigger first a crisis, which in the case of a vulnerable person—schizotrope—then leads to an episode of illness as shown in Fig. 2, relating life event stressors to vulnerability.

VULNERABILITY MARKERS

In order to test the tenability of the vulnerability model and of the hypotheses emerging from it, markers are needed that will identify the vulnerable individual.

A marker is an identifying indicator of a specific condition such as a disorder. In genetics it indicates a gene of known location and effect, which makes possible the determination of the distribution of other less conspicuously effective genes. In psychometrics it denotes a test of known factorial structure which can be used to identify the presence of the factor with which it is highly correlated. Here we shall use the term marker to designate a specific performance or characteristic which characterizes individuals who have demonstrated vulnerability specifically to schizophrenia. To assure the validity of a marker we must establish its presence in individuals who have already exhibited vulnerability by succumbing to at least one episode of schizophrenia and establish its absence in matched controls. Once the marker is established as an index of vulnerability, it can be used to discover vulnerable individuals who have never had an episode.

It should be pointed out here that we have extended the term marker beyond its usual more limited boundaries as used in genetics where, strictly speaking, a marker denotes a condition but is itself not associated in any direct way with the condition (e.g., color blindness and manic-depressive psychosis). Because of the open-ended definition of schizophrenia, it is unrealistic to expect that every schizophrenic patient will exhibit a marker, and we must, therefore, investigate every differential characteristic between schizophrenia and other conditions to determine whether the characteristic can serve as a potential marker of vulnerability.

At present, most research is conducted with patients during an episode, hence, it is difficult to determine without further follow-up whether a given marker is a vulnerability marker or an episode marker. If the marker persists after the end of the episode there is a greater chance that it will be a vulnerability marker, while those markers which disappear with the episode are episode markers. A further check for a vulnerability marker is possible by examining unaffected siblings of patients. If these siblings show the marker with a frequency higher than would be expected in a normal population, it would be evidence in favor of a vulnerability marker.

The vulnerability markers can be classified in accordance with the etiological model from which they spring. In addition the descriptive approach also provides certain marker-like characteristics which are claimed to be unique to schizophrenia. Among these are Schneider's (45) first-rank symptoms, Jasper's (25) concept of ununderstandability, and a variety of other phenomenologically based claims which could eventually be exploited as markers if they could be established on a more objective basis. The Chapmans (11), for example, have shown that the clinical concept of anhedonia and of body-image distortion can be quantitatively scaled through an inventory. Some day, perhaps, we can establish the physiological underpinnings of "thought insertion" or "thought stealing" in the manner that we established the underpinnings of dreams through the discovery of rapid eye movement (REM) which accompanies dreaming.

Investigations of vulnerability markers are still in their infancy. A review of the current status of these markers as of 1977 was published in 1979 (59). The following discussion will be confined to two opposite models—the ecological and the neurophysiological.

Ecotype Markers

We have already discussed life event stressors as immediate, short-term ecological triggers of episodes in the vulnerable. Now we shall deal with long-term ecological factors in the formation of vulnerability and try to find markers for identifying those who are vulnerable on ecological grounds. Among the potential factors formative of vulnerability are low socioeconomic status, degree of community disorganization, crowding, minority status in the community, high mobility, migration, ethnicity, and cultural influences. All of these factors and many others have been implicated as etiological agents in the development of schizophrenia. The controversies regarding the relative importance of these factors and whether they are causes or effects are too well known to be discussed here. It would be highly desirable to find a common denominator for integrating the impact of these forces so that this common denominator could provide the markers we are seeking.

As was previously suggested by us and by Hammer et al. (20), the social network of the individual and the degree of support, constraint, or freedom imposed on it by the ecological niche may be such a common denominator. The relationships that make up the social network "may be thought of as the basic building blocks of social structure; and their formation, maintenance, and severance are universal and fundamental social processes" (20). They may provide insight into the relationship of various social factors with psychiatric disorders. Thus, a ghetto niche may impose restraints on the size and mutual intimacy of the network by having poor physical facilities which discourage network development. Bereavement and other losses due to such factors as moving away from a neighborhood also tend to disrupt networks.

Just as the vascular network serves to nourish and maintain the homeostasis of the internal environment, the social networks serve similar functions for the external environment. The vascular network provides some biological bases for identifying and classifying an individual by indicators such as blood types and other genetic markers. In a similar fashion, the social network could provide by its branching structure, density, quality, and quantity of interconnectedness, indicators to classify and identify individuals in the social sphere. It is possible that the social network analysis could do for the ecological model what consanguinity did for the genetic model.

The importance of the social networks is not limited to the social sphere. Berkman and Syme (2) report that social network ties are an important determinant of survival even when the other important determinants of mortality are kept constant: (a) self-estimate of physical health; (b) year of death; (c) socioeconomic status; (d) smoking; (e) consumption of alcohol; (f) obesity; (g) physical activity; (h) utilization of preventive health services and health practices.

Since the impact of any ecological factor depends on the stress it induces, we may postulate that unless the stress is more powerful than the countervailing effects of the social network in which the individual is imbedded, a schizophrenic episode may not develop.

Is there any evidence that social networks are important in the etiology of episodes of schizophrenia?

Though the literature on the relationship between network characteristics and schizophrenic disorder is not entirely consistent, some trends are emerging. Individuals with schizophrenic disorders seem to have smaller networks than those nonpsychiatrically ill (37a,46a,52a). Schizophrenics who have small, low-density, nonmultiplex networks run a higher risk of rehospitalization (46a).

Hammer et al. (20) have summarized the evidence for the relation between social network characteristics and the development of schizophrenic episodes from the point of view of the ecological model. The following ecological factors have been found to be associated with higher risks of schizophrenia: migration, social marginality, lack of acculturation, underprivileged ethnic origin, and social isolation. These factors tend either to prevent the development of normal social networks or to disrupt them. They are also highly associated with lower socioeconomic status. This may be the reason why lower socioeconomic status brings with it a higher risk of schizophrenia.

Thus, it is quite clear that a benign social network may be the bulwark against the development of vulnerability to episodes, and an inadequate or malignant social network may be etiological in the development of vulnerability.

How to classify social networks into benign and malignant and how to quantify their protective or malignant influence is a task facing the psychopathologist, and fortunately there is a growing literature on this question (1,20).

Neurophysiotype Markers

The neurophysiological model deals with the way the brain processes information, a field in which considerable work is going on both in normals and in patients.

Regardless of which etiotypes contribute to the schizotrope status, the end result is aberrant behavior, which may be the result of an aberrant nervous system. The neurophysiological model is eminently suited to detect such aberrations in a systematic, objective fashion. Therefore, we have focused our efforts in this direction. We must, however, not attribute all aberrant behavior to endogenous biochemical or genetic influences on the nervous system. We are cautioned by the possibility presented by the learning model that deviant patterns of behavior may have occurred through learning without involving genetic or endogenous biochemical influences. That such a possibility exists has been indicated by the evidence that chronically hospitalized schizophrenics sometimes exhibit behaviors that are iatrogenic (17), having been learned as appropriate during their hospitalization, and are not related to the illness directly (38).

Neurophysiological markers involving psychomotor control which have been found to characterize mental patients as well as their first degree-relatives have recently been summarized by Zubin (59). Among them are: (a) Cancro's measures of eye movements during visual mental tasks; (b) Holzman's recording of smooth pursuit eye movements; (c) Kornetsky and Orzack's vigilance task of continuous performance. Among other neurophysiological markers that have been proposed, the EEG, evoked potential, and autonomic markers have been most prominent (57,60).

It appears most likely that the evoked potentials, which have smaller amplitudes in schizophrenics than in depressives and normals, are episode rather than vulnerability markers. The amplitude of all the components tends to be universally related to the severity of clinical symptoms, returning to their normal size during periods of remission. Whether they become entirely normalized is not clear yet.

However, there is some evidence that the pattern of augmentation or reduction as a function of stimulus intensity, as reported by Buchsbaum (10), may indeed be a vulnerability marker. This author defines augmentation as the tendency for the amplitudes of the early components of the cortical evoked potential to increase with the intensity of the stimulus. Reduction refers to the opposite tendency.

Haier, Buchsbaum, and Murphy (18) sampled a college population to obtain blood samples for MAO determination and applied the Minnesota Multiphasic Personality Inventory (MMPI) and the Schedule for Affective Disorders and Schizophrenia (SADS) as well as the Research Diagnostic Criteria (RDC) for determining the presence of psychopathology. They found that individuals with the pattern of either low MAO and an augmented average evoked potential or high MAO and a reduced average evoked potential showed sufficient psychopathology to qualify as affective disorder patients on the RDC.

In connection with a series of ongoing studies of vulnerability launched while the author was Chief of the Biometrics Research Unit of the New York State Psychiatric Institute (NYSPI), several techniques have shown some evidence of serving as potential markers. (These studies are continuing under the direction of Dr. Samuel Sutton, Department of Psychophysiology at NYSPI, Dr. Bonnie Spring, Department of Psychology and Social Relations at Harvard University, Dr. Harvey Babkoff, Bar Ilan University, Israel, and the author at the VA Medical Center, Highland Drive, Pittsburgh, and the Department of Psychiatry,

University of Pittsburgh School of Medicine.) Some of the results of these studies follow:

Sensory Thresholds

Schizophrenia is supposed to exist in an intact sensorium, and no evidence was available until recently that the sensory thresholds of schizophrenics differed from those of normals. Recent studies, aided by the new signal detection and forced-choice techniques, have shown the original supposition to be in doubt (8,37).

The vision laboratory of the Department of Psychophysiology at the New York State Psychiatric Institute, Dr. Mitchel Kietzman, director, has collected detection threshold data in two separate studies involving 101 subjects—55 patients (schizophrenics and depressives), 15 siblings of schizophrenic patients, and 31 nonpatient control subjects. Results from these studies indicate that approximately 50% of the patients have higher visual thresholds (are less sensitive) than any of the nonpatient subjects. Furthermore, five clinical factors obtained from semi-structured interviews—auditory hallucinations, hypomania, reported belligerence, bizarre behavior, and grandiose delusions—are significantly and positively correlated with higher visual thresholds.

These visual threshold findings are unique and can not be extended to other modalities as shown by the findings of the audition laboratory of NYSPI, Dr. Gerard Bruder, director. Bruder, Sutton, Babkoff et al. (8) used a forced-choice staircase procedure to measure thresholds for detecting a click. High click thresholds in patients were associated with a diagnosis not of schizophrenia but of affective psychosis. The click thresholds were significantly and positively correlated with the factor based on degree of speech retardation ratings. Ratings on other clinical factors usually associated with affective disorders (depression or hypomania) and those usually associated with schizophrenia (delusions, hallucinations, flat affect, incomprehensibility) were not significantly correlated with click thresholds. These findings have been recently replicated in two additional studies (8,9).

Yozawitz, Bruder, Sutton et al. (56) have also tested patients and controls on measures of central auditory processing and lateralization. They used a forced-choice threshold procedure to measure summation of dichotic two-click stimuli. The ear asymmetries for affective psychotic patients were similar to those for right temporal lesioned controls and differed from those of schizophrenic patients and normal controls. The implication of their findings for cerebral asymmetry in psychopathology falls in line with recent research linking affective disorders and right hemisphere involvement.

Pupillary Response

Reduction in the amplitude of the pupillary contraction to light and the related dilation to the onset of darkness has been reported consistently for schizophrenic patients as contrasted with normals (19). The data indicating that such response decrements are maintained even after the end of an episode suggest that the pupillary response may serve as a vulnerability marker. The influence of phenothiazenes on pupil contraction has been discounted in most studies, although scattered reports suggest that long-term phenothiazene administration may produce additional reduction temporarily, which rebounds after withdrawal of drugs (23,35,41,42).

Schizophrenic patients also show a marked deviation in psychosensory dilation to nonvisual stimuli (pupil contracts only to light—to other stimuli it dilates). Under "uncertain" conditions when they guess whether the coming stimulus will be one or two clicks, schizophrenics fail to show dilation while normals have a marked dilation.

Pupillary reactions of acute schizophrenics and their healthy siblings were studied by Steinhauer, Hakerem, and Spring (50). Most normal subjects and siblings showed a large dilation to auditory stimuli under uncertain conditions when guessing, as compared to the smaller response produced when subjects were certain of the nature of the stimulus. All patients, as well as several siblings and control subjects, failed to show a dilation when guessing, and the evoked potentials in these subjects were also reduced. Further study of individuals with aberrant pupillary and evoked potential characteristics is in progress. Whether this is an episode marker or a vulnerability marker remains to be demonstrated.

EPISODE MARKERS

Thus far we have dealt with markers that presumably earmark vulnerability. The markers which indicate the onset, duration, and offset of an episode have not been studied as actively as the vulnerability markers. The difficulties in pursuing such studies have been described elsewhere (61). Since most of our investigations deal with patients during their episodes, we must be able to distinguish episode markers before we can find vulnerability markers.

Episode markers can be classified in accordance with the etiological models from which they emanated.

Ecological Markers

It has been shown, using the Holmes and Rahe scale, that an accelerated rate of occurrence of life events forebodes the development of episodes. Thus, if we were to monitor the rate we could use this as an index of a forthcoming episode and by the same token use it to indicate the end of an episode when the rate normalizes (39).

The beginning of an episode often follows close on the heels of a period of coping failure. Similarly, once the episode of disorder has subsided, one may expect the patient once again to be able to resume coping at his characteristic premorbid level and style. The concurrence of periods of coping dysfunction and restoration with episodes of psychiatric disorder and recovery opens the way for investigation of another type of episode marker. If we were to have knowledge of the patient's premorbid level of coping ability, we could use evidence of a sharp plummeting of coping effectiveness and a return to the usual capacity for efficiency as rough boundaries to index the course of a psychopathological episode. Following Goldfried and D'Zurilla's (15) behavior-analytic model for assessing competence, Goldsmith and McFall (16) have experimented with simulated interpersonal contexts to evaluate the effectiveness of patients' social coping strategies. The entire spectrum of role performance should actually be sampled to see whether the capacity to cope has returned to its premorbid level. Weissman (54) has recently reviewed 15 scales available for assessing performance in occupational, marital, extended family, and community roles. These might serve to probe for fluctuations in coping capacity that occur during hospitalization, particularly if it were possible to tap the significant role contexts in simulated situations (15).

Learning and Developmental Markers

The speech and thought processes of the patient, which may be highly dependent on learning and reinforcement, are often found to deviate from the usual during an episode. Monitoring the speech and thinking characteristics at the onset, duration, and offset of an episode can provide markers useful for our purposes. Schmale (44) suggests that giving in to feelings of helplessness and hopelessness is the earmark of a beginning episode. Luborsky and Auerbach (36) have derived another potential mini-episode index by examining speech samples of patients in psychoanalysis taken just before instances of momentary forgetting or just prior to reports of migraine headaches or stomach pain. When these passages are rated for expression of content, helplessness ratings are found to be much higher than for samples taken at other times during therapy sessions. It is not entirely outside the realm of possibility that mild transient mini-episodes might also be provoked experimentally by psychological or biochemical challenges. The ethics of such experimental procedures must be carefully investigated so as not to interfere with the civil rights and freedom of the patient, but under skilled personnel, mindful of the ethical issues involved, perhaps some salutary solution can be found. It should be no more hazardous than a challenge with a glucose tolerance test in diabetes.

Internal Environment Markers

Janowsky et al. (24) have shown that if methylphenidate (Ritalin®) is injected in a patient undergoing an episode of schizophrenia, an exacerbation of the episode will occur briefly, but if the episode is ended, no exacerbation is induced. Thus, challenging a patient with methylphenidate can be used as a probe for determining the state of the episode.

Another strategy may be to monitor mini-episodes or acute periods of symptom exacerbation in patients during their hospital stay. These may, in microcosm, reveal some properties of onset and offset of maxi-episodes. Some progress has been made in this area. Although most of it has concerned a search for indicators of the onset and offset of mini-episodes in depressed patients, it is likely that comparable indexes can be found for schizophrenic mini-episodes induced by visitors, peer conflicts, and so on. In a study of the rise and fall of corticosteroid levels in reactive depression by Sachar, MacKenzie, Binsback, and Mack (43), it was observed that hormonal stress levels rise when the patient actively struggles with the confrontation of the loss of a love object or when his defense mechanisms falter temporarily. On the other hand, when his defenses are operating adequately and he seems clinically comfortable and adjusted, the hormonal level drops to normal. After the patient has adjusted to the hospital regime and achieved stable hormonal levels, perturbations in corticosteroid levels may therefore index the eruption of mini-episodes.

Neurophysiological Markers

Just as the beginning and end of episodes of epilepsy can be indexed by electroencephalographic characteristics before and after seizure, so in depression there have been findings indicating that changes in sleep characteristics (30) and motility (32) serve to mark the beginning and end of episodes. In schizophrenia, too, a reduction in rapid-eye-movement sleep accompanies acute episodes (31).

VULNERABILITY: RECOMMENDATIONS FOR ITS STUDY IN SCHIZOPHRENIA RESEARCH

As a result of the research work now going on in various laboratories, it is expected that we will have available in the not too distant future a series of vulnerability and episode markers together with a group of triggering contingencies which elicit episodes in the vulnerable. Some of these may turn out to be predictors of episodes in the vulnerable.

It would thus be possible to detect individuals in the general population who stand in high risk of developing episodes. As a first step, it would be advantageous to study a group of siblings of schizophrenics because of the increased risk they represent, to determine which of them exhibit the markers. These siblings could then be followed for several years to determine who succumbs to an episode. The circumstances which surround developing episodes, the life events, and the social networks that surround the individuals could be analyzed to determine the triggering events leading to the episode. The siblings who do not show the markers can also be followed for control purposes and their development compared with those who have markers. A comparison of those who show the markers with those who do not, and a comparison of those with markers who develop episodes with those who do not, ought to shed light on the question of what kind of intervention may be possible.

Eventually, with the results of such a study in hand, it will be possible to sample the general population for the vulnerable individuals and institute possible therapeutic interventions for preventing the development of episodes. A beginning in screening the general population by Haier, Buchsbaum, and Murphy (18) has already been described. Similarly, the Chapmans (11) found that individuals with high scores on their anhedonia scale and on their body-image scale (two standard deviations above the mean) reported symptoms of rather severe psychopathology. It is important to develop such techniques for screening out individuals with deviant characteristics in order to provide them with prophylactic intervention against the development of episodes and to eliminate such individuals in selecting control groups in studying schizophrenics. Among the specific gains that the discovery of markers can achieve are the following:

1. *Aid to diagnosis:* The availability of objective markers of psychopathology for the various mental disorders can help validate the diagnostic categories into which patients are placed.

2. *Differential diagnosis:* One of the perennial problems facing the diagnostician is how to separate affective disorders from schizophrenia. The availability of specific markers can help in their differentiation.

Individual differences in the behavioral, physiological, or biochemical indicators within the psychiatric population may themselves become the basis for delineating more specific patient subgroupings. Sutton has emphasized the possible advantages of utilizing such an iterative approach (51,52) in which the independent variables are interchanged. Individuals who exhibit similar patterns or profiles of behavioral, physiological, and biochemical responses can constitute a new subgroup. These subgroups may be identified by cluster analysis. Subgroups can then be compared for their clinical characteristics as determined by the clinical assessment procedures. That is, response differentiation in the laboratory test profiles is assumed to reflect some characteristic difference between the patient groups which can be verified by examining their clinical profiles. The newly found clinical profile which characterizes these subgroups can now become the independent variable for classification. The profile of laboratory test performance becomes the dependent variable to see how clearly the new clinical subgroups live up to the expected laboratory profile differentiation.

This iterative process can continue until a stable set of subgroups is established and replicated on new data. For example, the iterative approach can be applied to the study of EEG patterns to distinguish psychiatric subgroups, much as they have been used for identification of individuals prone to seizures or having focalized neural pathology (14).

3. *Objective indicators of episodes:* Objective episode markers can provide indicators of the beginning and end of episodes and provide objective indications for initiating and terminating treatment, and thus avoid errors in delay of treat-

ment or in prolonging it unduly with the danger of incurring unnecessary side effects.

4. *Avoiding the stigma of mental illness:* If we can alter the public image of schizophrenia from that of being a persistent deteriorative disease to that of being a vulnerable state, the stigma of schizophrenia, which now attaches to former patients and which prevents the majority of them from resuming their place in society, can be mitigated.

5. *Prophylaxis for the vulnerable:* Individuals who belong to the vulnerable group can be educated to deal with their vulnerability in the same way that diabetics or hypertension cases can be educated to live more normal lives by preventing or avoiding situations which may catapult them into an episode. Furthermore, if the staff could be taught to regard the patient as vulnerable rather than as sick, and proceed to relieve him of the stressors which elicit his vulnerability, there would be no need to label him as ill and induce him to accept the label. The label of vulnerability is probably much easier to take and live with since it presages a brief episode from which the patient will soon recover without being labeled schizophrenic the rest of his life. Furthermore, the episode could hopefully be prevented by proper intervention.

6. *Other advantages:* There are several other baffling problems which the vulnerability hypothesis can help explain. The apparently spontaneous recovery of long-standing patients falls into this category. The patient may have emerged from his episode much earlier but the recognition of this fact may occur suddenly and the recovery consequently may be regarded as miraculous. Some patients develop and mature in the hospital and increase competence and coping efforts under its protective environment. These too fit into the vulnerability hypothesis since it is often reported that suddenly, patients who have been hospitalized for many years make a miraculous recovery. As a matter of fact, the episode has long since passed and the primary change has been not in the disease process but in further development of coping skills. The observation of Manfred Bleuler (5) that as decades passed, there was a tendency toward improvement, rather than deterioration, falls into this category.

Perhaps the most trenchant reason for investigating the vulnerability hypothesis stems from the fact that advances in health are likely to come in the future, as in the past, from modification of conditions which lead to psychopathology rather than from therapeutic intervention after it has occurred. We need to tackle the conditions leading to the disorder, whether they be internal or external, before the disorder develops. Notable examples of such an approach are the "high-risk" studies of the offspring of the mentally ill. However, these "high-risk" studies are perforce longitudinal and the payoff in terms of actual cases is low. Only a minority of schizophrenics belong to families with a history of schizophrenia (46). Only about 5% of the parents of schizophrenics and about 9% of the siblings of schizophrenics suffer the same disorder. Whether they are representative of schizophrenia as a whole is highly debatable. Bleuler (5), for example, has reported that those with family histories tend to have milder disorders. Another problem is the fact that "only" offspring of fertile, married, cooperative, and sustaining parents, often lodged in intact families, constitute the sample in high-risk studies. In our vulnerability study we are certain that the patients we study are diagnosed schizophrenic and any markers we discover can be used to detect individuals in the population and initiate effective intervention even before an episode develops.

SUMMARY

Schizophrenia today is no longer the deteriorative disorder which it appeared to be 40 years ago. The vast majority of schizophrenics seem to spend the majority of their lives in the community. If the community were to provide better facilities, Manfred Bleuler's follow-up studies (5) suggest that probably only 6 to 10% would remain chronically ill.

Schizophrenia is not basically a continuous disorder. What is continuous is the vulnerability to the disorder. This vulnerability can remain latent for life, or be elicited by life event stressors of both the exogenous and endogenous variety. It resembles an allergy rather than a persistent disease.

The underlying causes of the vulnerability depend on the etiotype or types which characterize the person, and these range from ecotype to auxeinotype (development), mathetotype (learning), genotype, chemotype, and neurophysiotype. The impact of a life event stressor produces a crisis in all of us. Depending on our degree of vulnerability, we can contain the crisis homeostatically, as long as the stress produced is below our threshold. If it exceeds our threshold of vulnerability, an episode of illness will develop. When the episode ends, and all of them are time limited, we return to our pre-episode coping level. If that was good to begin with, we are regarded as recovered. If it was on a poor premorbid level, we are often mistakenly regarded as still disordered even though the episode has ended. The primary therapeutic problem is not so much to cure the disorder—it is self-limiting—but to provide the means for preventing the initial occurrence or recurrence of the episode.

To accomplish this end we need to find markers of vulnerability for the various etiotypes, and markers for the beginning and end of episodes. Once these are available we can through the use of screening tests identify the vulnerable and provide them with techniques for preventing initial or recurrent episodes, through the use of therapeutic psychological and/or pharmacological or other somatic intervention.

What is preventing the discovery of the markers today and what is causing the logjam? It is unlikely that any one etiological model will provide pathognomonic markers by itself. Even the advocates of the most highly developed model—the genetic—seem to have given up such a claim. Only the patterning of the markers across the etiological models can break the current logjam. Whether such patterns will require the subdivision of schizophrenia into separate subcategories or whether schizophrenia can remain polythetically defined even though it may lose its monothetic character remains an empirical though challenging question.

The implications of the vulnerability hypothesis for chronic schizophrenia are only vaguely discernible at this time because the hypothesis is still in the process of being tested. If the hypothesis proves tenable, only a small fraction of schizophrenia (some 6 to 10%) need ever become chronic. Even these cases need not remain in their chronic state for life (38). As for the recidivists to whom the revolving door pattern applies, a monitoring of their home atmosphere for its emotional quality can give the clues to the triggering events which initiate relapses or new episodes (34). As for those who are no longer in their episode but are still kept in the hospital mistakenly, the discovery of episode markers may hasten their delivery from overtreatment or prevent too early release.

But the most important implication of the vulnerability hypothesis is that the future discovery of the markers of vulnerability and of the beginning and end of episodes, as well as of the triggering contingencies which elicit episodes in the vulnerable, may halt the development of chronicity by providing means of identifying the vulnerable even before an episode develops. In this way the march toward chronicity can be halted even before it begins, just as it is now possible to abort episodes of diabetes by education and proper safeguards in the vulnerable.

ACKNOWLEDGMENTS

The preparation of this chapter was assisted by a VA grant "Vulnerability to Episodes of Functional Disorder in Adults" and by the Department of Psychiatry of the University of Pittsburgh Medical School. The author wishes to acknowledge the assistance of the following colleagues, formerly members of the Biometrics Research Unit of the New York State Department of Mental Hygiene: Drs. Muriel P. Hammer, Barry Gurland, Ruth Bennett, and David Wilder, formerly of the sections on Diagnosis and Psychopathology, section on Gerontology, and section on Sociology, respectively, and now of the Center for Geriatrics and Gerontology of the College of Physicians and Surgeons of Columbia University; Drs. Samuel Sutton, Gad Hakerem, Mitchel Kietzman, and Gerald Bruder of the Department of Psychophysiology, New York State Psychiatric Institute and Dr. Bonnie Spring of the Department of Psychology and Social Relations, Harvard University. Special thanks go to my two colleagues Stuart Steinhauer and Ira Bernhaus in the Biometrics Research Unit at the VA Medical Center, Highland Drive, Pittsburgh, Pennsylvania.

REFERENCES

1. Beels, C. C. (1978): Social networks, the family, and the psychiatric patient: Introduction to the issue. *Schizophr. Bull.*, 4:512–521.

2. Berkman, L. F., and Syme, S. L. (1979): Social networks, host resistance, and mortality: A nine-year follow-up of Alameda county residents. *Am. J. Epidemiol.*, 109:186–204.
3. Bland, R. C., Parker, J. H., and Orn, H. (1978): Prognosis in schizophrenia. *Arch. Gen. Psychiatry*, 35:72–80.
4. Bleuler, M. (1978): The long-term course of schizophrenic psychoses. In: *The Nature of Schizophrenia: New Approaches to Research and Treatment*, edited by L. C. Wynne, R. L. Cromwell, and S. Matthysse, pp. 631–636. John Wiley & Sons, New York.
5. Bleuler, M. (1978): *The Schizophrenic Disorders: Long-Term Patient and Family Studies*, translated by S. M. Clemens. Yale University Press, New Haven, Conn. (Translation of *Die Schizophrenen Geistesstörungen im Lichte Langjähriger Kranken-und Familiengeschichten*, Intercontinental Medical Book Corp., New York, 1972.)
6. Bockoven, J. S., and Solomon, H. C. (1975): Comparison of two five-year follow-up studies: 1947 to 1952 and 1967 to 1972. *Am. J. Psychiatry*, 132:796–801.
7. Brown, G. W., and Birley, J. L. T. (1968): Crises and life changes and the onset of schizophrenia. *J. Health Soc. Behav.*, 9:203–214.
7a. Brown, G. W., and Rutter, M. (1966): The measurement of family activities and relationships: A methological study. *Hum. Relations*, 19:241–263.
8. Bruder, G. E., Sutton, S., Babkoff, H., Gurland, B. J., Yozawitz, A., and Fleiss, J. L. (1975): Auditory signal detectability and facilitation of simple reaction time in psychiatric patients and non-patients. *Psychol. Med.*, 5:260–272.
9. Bruder, G., Spring, B., Yozawitz, A., and Sutton, S. (1980): Auditory sensitivity in psychiatric patients and non-patients: Monotic click detection. *Psychol. Med. (in press)*.
10. Buchsbaum, M. (1975): Average evoked response augmenting/reducing in schizophrenia and affective disorders. In: *The Biology of the Major Psychoses: A Comparative Analysis*, edited by D. Freedman, pp. 129–142. Raven Press, New York.
11. Chapman, L. J., and Chapman, J. P. (1979): Scales of traits of the schizophrenia-prone. *Psychopharmacol. Bull.*, 15:9–10.
12. Dohrenwend, B. S., and Dohrenwend, B. P. (1972): Social class and the relation of remote to recent stressors. In: *Life History Research in Psychopathology, Vol. 2*, edited by M. Roff, L. Robins, and M. Pollack, pp. 170–185. University of Minnesota Press, Minneapolis.
13. Extein, I., and Bowers, M. (1979): State and trait in psychiatric practice. *Am. J. Psychiatry*, 136:690–693.
14. Fink, M. (1978): EEG response strategies in psychiatric diagnosis. In: *Critical Issues in Psychiatric Diagnosis*, edited by R. Spitzer and D. Klein, pp. 253–263. Raven Press, New York.
15. Goldfried, M. R., and D'Zurilla, T. J. (1969): A behavior-analytic model for assessing competence. *Curr. Top. Clin. Commun. Psychol.*, 1:151–196.
16. Goldsmith, J. B., and McFall, R. M. (1975): Development and evaluation of an interpersonal skill-training program for psychiatric inpatients. *J. Abnorm. Psychol.*, 84:51–58.
17. Gruenberg, E. M. (1967): The social breakdown syndrome—Some origins. *Am. J. Psychiatry*, 123:12–20.
18. Haier, R. J., Buchsbaum, M. S., and Murphy, D. L. (1979): Screening young adults for psychiatric vulnerability: A preliminary comparison of biological and clinical measures. *Psychopharmacol. Bull.*, 15:7–9.
19. Hakerem, G., Sutton, S., and Zubin, J. (1964): Pupillary reactions to light in schizophrenic patients and normals. *Ann. N.Y. Acad. Sci.*, 105:820–831.
20. Hammer, M., Makiesky-Barrow, S., and Gutwirth, L. (1978): Social networks and schizophrenia. *Schizophr. Bull.*, 4:522–545.
21. Heston, L. L. (1976): Psychiatric disorders in foster home reared children of schizophrenic mothers. *Br. J. Psychiatry*, 112:819–825.
22. Holmes, T. H., and Rahe, R. H. (1967): The social readjustment rating scale *J. Psychosom. Res.*, 11:213–218.
23. Ikushima, M., and Matsunaga, K. (1977): *Pupillary light reactions of schizophrenics.* Paper presented at the Tenth Pupil Symposium, New York City, June 1977.
24. Janowsky, D. S., Davis, J. M., Huey, L., and Judd, L. L. (1979): Adrenergic and cholinergic drugs as episode and vulnerability markers of affective disorders and schizophrenia. *Psychopharmacol. Bull.*, 15:33–34.
25. Jaspers, K. (1963): *General Psychopathology*, translated by J. Hoenig and M. W. Hamilton. Manchester University Press, Manchester.

26. Kallmann, F. J. (1946): The genetic theory of schizophrenia. *Am. J. Psychiatry,* 103:309–322.
27. Kety, S. S. (1978): Introduction: Section II. Biochemical approaches. In: *The Nature of Schizophrenia: New Approaches to Research and Treatment,* edited by L. C. Wynne, R. L. Cromwell, and S. Matthysse, pp. 85–86. John Wiley & Sons, New York.
28. Kety, S. S., Rosenthal, D., Wender, P. H., and Schulsinger, F. (1968): The types and prevalence of mental illness in the biological and adoptive families of adopted schizophrenics. In: *The Transmission of Schizophrenia,* edited by D. Rosenthal and S. S. Kety, pp. 345–362. Pergamon Press, London.
29. Kinney, D. K., and Jacobsen, B. (1978): Environmental factors in schizophrenia: New adoption study evidence. In: *The Nature of Schizophrenia: New Approaches to Research and Treatment,* edited by L. C. Wynne, R. L. Cromwell, and S. Matthysse, pp. 38–51. John Wiley & Sons, New York.
30. Kupfer, D. J. (1976): REM latency: A psychobiologic marker for primary depressive disease. *Biol. Psychiatry,* 11:159–174.
31. Kupfer, D. J., and Foster, F. G. (1975): The sleep of psychotic patients: Does it all look alike? In: *Biology of the Major Psychoses: A Comparative Analysis,* edited by D. X. Freedman, pp. 143–159. Raven Press, New York.
32. Kupfer, D. J., Weiss, B. L., Foster, F. G., Detre, T. R., Delgado, J., and McPartland, R. (1974): Psychomotor activity in affective states. *Arch. Gen. Psychiatry,* 30:765–768.
33. Leff, J. P. (1976): Assessment of drugs in schizophrenia. *Br. J. Clin. Pharmacol. [Suppl.],* pp. 75–78.
34. Leff, J. (1978): Social and psychological causes of the acute attack. In: *Schizophrenia: Towards a New Synthesis,* edited by J. K. Wing, pp. 139–166. Academic Press, New York.
35. Lidsky, A., Hakerem, G., and Sutton, S. (1971): Pupillary reactions to single light pulses in psychiatric patients and normals. *J. Nerv. Ment. Dis.,* 153:286–291.
36. Luborsky, L., and Auerbach, A. (1969): The symptom-context method: Quantitative studies of symptom formation in psychotherapy. *J. Am. Psychoanal. Assoc.,* 17:68–99.
37. Mannuzza, S., Spring, B., Gottlieb, M. D., and Kietzman, M. L. (1980): Visual sensitivity in relation to the diagnosis and symptoms of psychiatric patients, their siblings, and normal controls. In preparation.
37a. Pattison, E. M., deFrancisco, D., Wood, P., Frazier, H., and Crowder, J. (1975): A psychosocial kinship model for family therapy. *Am. J. Psychiatry,* 132:1246–1251.
38. Paul, G. L., and Lentz, R. J. (1977): *Psychosocial Treatment of Chronic Mental Patients; Milieu Versus Social Learning Programs.* Harvard University Press, Cambridge, Mass.
39. Paykel, E. S. (1979): Causal relationships between clinical depression and life events. In: *Stress and Mental Disorder,* edited by J. E. Barrett, R. M. Rose, and G. L. Klerman, pp. 71–86. Raven Press, New York.
40. Rahe, R. H., Meyer, M., Smith, M., Kjaer, G., and Holmes, T. H. (1964): Social stress and illness onset. *J. Psychosom. Res.,* 8:35–44.
41. Roth, W. (1977): Late event-related potentials and psychopathology. *Schizophr. Bull.,* 3:105–120.
42. Rubin, L. S. (1974): The utilization of pupillometry in the differential diagnosis and treatment of psychotic and behavioral disorder. In: *Pupillary Dynamics and Behavior: Proceedings of the University of Manitoba Symposium on Pupillometry,* edited by M. P. Janisse, pp. 75–134. Plenum Press, New York.
43. Sachar, E. J., MacKenzie, J. M., Binsback, W. A., and Mack, J. E. (1968): Corticosteroid responses to the psychotherapy of reactive depressions: II. Further clinical and physiological implications. *Psychosom. Med.,* 30:23–44.
44. Schmale, A. H. (1972): Giving up as a final common pathway to changes in health. *Adv. Psychosom. Med.,* 8:20–40.
45. Schneider, K. (1971): *Klinische Psychopathologie, 9th Ed.* Thieme, Stuttgart.
46. Slater, E., and Cowie, V. (1971): *The Genetics of Mental Disorders.* Oxford University Press, London.
46a. Sokolovsky, J., Cohen, C., Berger, D., and Geiger, J. (1978): Personal networks of ex-mental patients in a Manhattan S.R.O. hotel. *Hum. Organization,* 37(1):5–15.
47. Spohn, H. E., and Patterson, T. (1979): Recent studies of psychophysiology in schizophrenia. *Schizophr. Bull.,* 5:581–611.
48. Spring, B., and Zubin, J. (1977): Vulnerability to schizophrenic episodes and their prevention

in adults. In: *Primary Prevention of Psychopathology, Vol. 1: The Issues,* edited by G. W. Albee and J. M. Joffee, pp. 254–284. The University Press of New England, Hanover, Mass.

49. Spring, B. J., and Zubin, J. (1978): Attention and information processing as indicators of vulnerability to schizophrenic episodes. In: *The Nature of Schizophrenia: New Approaches to Research and Treatment,* edited by L. C. Wynne, R. L. Cromwell, and S. Matthysse, pp. 366–375. John Wiley & Sons, New York.
50. Steinhauer, S. R., Hakerem, G., and Spring, B. J. (1979): The pupillary response as a potential indicator of vulnerability to schizophrenia. *Psychopharmacol. Bull.,* 15:44–45.
51. Sutton, S. (1973): Fact and artifact in the psychology of schizophrenia. In: *Psychopathology: Contributions from the Social, Behavioral, and Biological Sciences,* edited by M. Hammer, K. Salzinger, and S. Sutton, pp. 197–213. John Wiley & Sons, New York.
52. Sutton, S., and Tueting, P. (1978): Evoked potentials and diagnosis. In: *Critical Issues in Psychiatric Diagnosis,* edited by R. Spitzer and K. Klein, pp. 265–279. Raven Press, New York.

52a. Tolsdorf, C. C. (1976): Social networks, support and coping: An exploratory study. *Fam. Process,* 15:407–418.

53. van Praag, H. M. (1979): Psychopsychiatry: Can psychosocial factors cause psychiatric disorders? *Compr. Psychiatry,* 20:215–225.
54. Weissman, M. (1975): The assessment of social adjustment: A review of technique. *Arch. Gen. Psychiatry,* 32:357–365.
55. Wing, J. K. (1966): Five year outcome in early schizophrenia. *Proc. R. Soc. Med.,* 59:17–18.
56. Yozawitz, A., Bruder, G., Sutton, S., Sharpe, L., Gurland, B., Fleiss, J., and Costa, L. (1979): Dichotic perception: Evidence for right hemisphere dysfunction in affective psychosis. *Br. J. Psychiatry,* 135:224–237.
57. Zahn, T. P., Carpenter, W. T., Jr., and McGlashan, T. H. (1979): Autonomic variables related to short-term outcome and clinical improvement in acute schizophrenia. *Psychopharmacol. Bull.,* 15:42–43.
58. Zubin, J. (1972): Scientific models for psychopathology in the '70s. *Semin. Psychiatry,* 4:283–296.
59. Zubin, J. (Chairman) (1979): Markers of vulnerability to mental disorders. *Psychopharmacol. Bull.,* 15:7–49.
60. Zubin, J. (1979): Summary of Session: Markers of vulnerability to mental disorders. *Psychopharmacol. Bull.,* 15:47–49.
61. Zubin, J., and Spring, B. (1977): Vulnerability—A new view of schizophrenia. *J. Abnorm. Psychol.,* 86:103–126.

Discussion

Bird: Huntington's disease (HD) can serve as a model for studying schizophrenia, since many patients with HD originally present with psychotic episodes. HD patients who present with schizophrenia usually do so early in life, and probably have a severe biochemical deficit, whereas those who present later in life rarely present with schizophrenia. Here, then, schizophrenic vulnerability is relevant to the degree of biochemical defect, but some environmental effect probably brings it out.

Ingvar: I would like Dr. Zubin to be more precise in defining the vulnerable entity. Is it the whole mental apparatus of the patient, or specific parts of it, say the perceptual or emotional machinery, or the behavioral programming?

Zubin: That question is difficult to answer, but I'd say that in schizophrenics studied thoroughly from the very beginning, we would probably find that they had small losses, perceptually and motorally; they'd be slower than their peers and wouldn't respond as readily; and they might be preoccupied more with their own thoughts. But although they had these measurable differences from their peers, these would not be the differences that brought them to the mental hospital, for they could have gone through life with those deviations without too much trouble. But when they become noticeably deviant in the eyes of their peers they develop a different self-image, which brings about a feeling of not belonging, of not being "with it," and that may be the phenomenon we finally see as schizophrenia. There are probably deviations in the various models I pointed out—the biochemical, the ecological, the developmental, the learning—but based on them, as a superstructure, is the phenomenology we come to see, the hallucinations and delusions, and so forth.

Henn: The issue I'm concerned with is that of the return to premorbid level by schizophrenics. I suggest that part of the difference between Bleuler's and Kraepelin's data depended not only on the populations examined but also on the initial diagnosis. My Iowa colleague Dr. Tsuang is finishing a 40-year follow-up study of 200 patients in the Iowa 500, which, although a little different from Dr. Carpenter's, points to the same result—that chronicity resides in about 50% of the patients, if you define them narrowly by strict Kraepelinian criteria, and if you measure outcome not only in a psychiatric sense but also in terms of occupation and personal relationships. In this narrowly defined population, premorbid levels are not achieved with any regularity. I think your vulnerability model still holds up, but the axes are shifted over and set down a bit.

Zubin: Do both the psychopathology and social relationships improve with time?

Henn: No. I would say what Dr. Bird said: that those people who express schizophrenia early—and that's one of the Kraepelinian criteria—are probably going to have a more severe defect and will not return to anywhere near premorbid levels of functioning.

Zubin: The question that arises is: What are the contingencies that elicit an episode in a vulnerable individual? Why does one twin of a monozygotic pair develop a schizophrenic episode whereas the other does not? We haven't yet discovered what differentiates the two. Perhaps the VA could launch a study of siblings of schizophrenics, even though they are not in need of psychiatric help, to find out what keeps them from experiencing a breakdown, and if they eventually do, the cause. What we might learn could provide a better approach to prevention than high-risk studies, which have the severe limitations of the long wait involved and of coming from families that are too well integrated to be representative of schizophrenics generally.

Yuwiler: Disease periodicity could result from undamped interactive oscillations between compensatory systems set in motion by some initial stimulus. If this were the case, then psychotic episodes should occur with some regularity and the manifest symptoms of every other episode should be similar. A likely site for genetic vulnerability in this case might be a defect in mechanisms involved in neuronal feedback, especially feedback interactions between sets of neurons. Direct identification of the environmental psychogenic trigger initiating the sequence might be impossible.

On the other hand, periodicity could result from intermittent reexposure to a psychotogenic environmental trigger acting on a genetically hypersensitive neural system. In this case the occurrence of psychotic episodes should be randomly distributed and symptom patterns should be similar each time. The genetic defect might be expressed in sensitivity of a particular neural system but direct identification of the environmental trigger may again be difficult because overtly different stimuli may have similar emotional meanings to one individual but not another, even if the other is his identical twin. Nor need initial and subsequent stimuli be of equal strength. For example, neonatal exposure to stress hormones can alter development of several metabolic and neural systems and may alter their response to hormonal release by subsequent stresses.

Brown: One of the few things we know about schizophrenia is that it is a disease that has its onset in young adulthood. Not many conditions are like that. How do you integrate that knowledge into your notions of periodicity and vulnerability?

Zubin: Some children are born with a mild brain defect they don't show until they begin school and are found to have a reading disability. The difficulty doesn't appear until it is elicited. The particular life stresses of early adulthood—finding one's identity, one's career, one's mate—elicit crises in all young people, and, in the vulnerable, episodes. Schizophrenia may emerge in young adults because those crises may be the severest crises people experience.

I love the concept of vulnerability because it opens up possibilities for interaction between the various approaches in the field that may lead to the synthesis we desire, for serendipity will strike the mind that's open to all of the factors.

Perspectives in Schizophrenia Research,
edited by C. Baxter and T. Melnechuk.
Raven Press, New York, 1980.

Clinical Research Methods Applicable to the Study of Treatment Effects in Chronic Schizophrenic Patients

William T. Carpenter, Jr.

Maryland Psychiatric Research Center, Catonsville, Maryland 21228

LAYPERSON'S SUMMARY

Schizophrenia is a common illness (about 1% of the population) with onset during adolescence and early adulthood, and for many patients is progressively devastating. Schizophrenia is psychiatry's most important unsolved problem. In the United States, it is a medical problem almost without rival in terms of economic cost, and the human burden to patients and family is incalculable. Chronic schizophrenia is, no doubt, a heterogeneous disorder comprised of several distinct disease entities sharing certain common features. The causes remain unknown, and prevention and current treatments are woefully inadequate. Many chronic patients are unresponsive to any presently available treatment and others have only a limited response.

Certain principles should guide selection of patients for treatment research. The clinician's diagnosis should be supplemented (not replaced) by one of several sets of specified criteria used in schizophrenia research. These criteria depend on cross-sectional symptomatology, so measures of premorbid functioning or course of illness must also be used to ensure that the focus on chronic forms of schizophrenia is maintained. Finally, investigators should attempt to eliminate the doubtful cases from study by using alternate explanations for the manifest psychopathology whenever possible, and by using follow-up evaluations to give the benefit of hindsight to classification.

Since schizophrenia is associated with a broad range of dysfunction, no single treatment is likely to be sufficiently comprehensive to be used to the exclusion of others. Various treatments purport to be therapeutic in some, but not all, schizophrenics. In designing treatment studies, a clinical judgment as to suitability of each patient for each treatment is required. In an illness with little effective therapy, it is important not to conclude that a treatment is ineffective based on testing in the wrong subjects.

Previous treatment has been so narrowly conceptualized as to leave major gaps in information relevant to understanding long-term consequences of present treatment techniques. Clinical assessment of change should include factors expected to improve with treatment, any factors on which the treatment may have a deleterious effect, and other factors considered crucial to understanding the course of illness whether or not a treatment change is hypothesized. Such a broad battery of assessment will be more generously informative to the future clinician than the last generations of studies which relied too heavily on unidimensional assessment.

Since we assume chronic schizophrenia to be a syndrome comprised of several illnesses, efforts to identify treatment-relevant subgroups are advised. Some illustrative examples are presented.

INTRODUCTION

Chronic schizophrenia is a prevalent illness whose etiology and pathogenesis remain enigmatic, and whose treatment is usually limited to a variety of interpersonal therapeutic strategies of uncertain efficacy and pharmacotherapy of demonstrated, but limited, usefulness. The cost of the illness in human and economic terms is unrivaled in all of medicine. Peak onset is in adolescence and early adulthood, and patients face the disruptions and anguish associated with psychotic episodes and (for most) impaired social functioning and restricted intrapsychic life, dimming the personal gratifications and productivity that most of us take for granted. Recognizing the patient's pain and disability, the family's burden, and the cost to society, one would expect schizophrenia research to be at the top of the nation's health research priorities. However, the chronically ill, generally, and the chronically insane, in particular, are disenfranchised citizens. Hospital care is often provided in low-prestige hospitals with custodial rather than therapeutic intent, and community-based support and therapeutic services are inadequate and often fail to reach patients in need. Similarly, national research funding is woefully inadequate, failing even to approximate in priority the importance of the illness itself (32,44).

Any research initiative in chronic schizophrenia should be applauded. The points discussed in this chapter call attention to some research methods in psychopathology which can guide patient selection to preserve a focus on chronic schizophrenia, and which will enhance assessment of change so that treatment studies will be more generously informative than studies of the past two decades. For convenience, the discussion is divided into four major categories: patient selection, assignment to treatment, special subgroups for treatment studies, and principles for assessing treatment effects.

DIAGNOSIS AND PATIENT SELECTION

Before Kraepelin (22) and since Bleuler (3), we have assumed that the patient population referred to as schizophrenic not only is heterogeneous in its clinical manifestations, but is comprised of at least several discrete syndromes or illnesses.

For many years, acute schizophrenic episodes with a good outcome have been distinguished from insidious psychoses with a chronic course. In recent years, this distinction has been validated with genetic, drug response, and premorbid factor assessments, although the cross-sectional symptom manifestations overlap extensively. Criteria are readily available to divide schizophrenia on this dimension, but it is still common practice to speak of schizophrenia as a unitary entity, permitting clinicians and investigators to gravitate toward those forms of illness they find most gratifying to treat or propitious for investigation. If an initiative in the study of chronic schizophrenia is to be successful, the first step is to establish diagnostic criteria for the illness, criteria that identify valid study cohorts and simultaneously preclude the witting and unwitting dilution of attention to chronic illness. Too often studies of schizophrenia are informative about acute schizophrenic psychoses, atypical psychoses, psychogenic psychoses, manic-depressive psychoses, reactive psychoses, schizoaffective psychoses, and others, without being generalizable to chronic schizophrenia.

The following methods are recommended for patient selection:

Clinician's Diagnosis

With present day emphasis on various sets of research diagnostic criteria, there is a disturbing tendency to ignore the clinician's best overall judgment. It is mindless to make an investigative effort in a population not judged suitable for the study by a seasoned clinician. There is good reason not to rely solely on the clinician's judgment, but the first step in forming a study cohort should be a clinical synthesis of all available information relevant to classification of the individual patient. This not only increases prior probability that patients finally selected for study will belong to the appropriate diagnostic group, but also provides the best method for avoiding mistakes. A patient with a past history of two depressive episodes and a manic episode should not be included in a schizophrenic study, even if present symptomatology satisfies some research criteria for schizophrenia. Clinicians vary as they synthesize information into diagnostic judgment, but no other method is available to consider all the data and all the alternate explanations for the manifest psychopathology.

Criteria for Research Diagnosis

Investigators may utilize any of a number of sets of specified criteria for diagnosis. Six systems were recently reviewed and critically evaluated by Kendell et al. (20), and other empirical guides have been reported (13,43). The New Haven Schizophrenia Index (1), relying extensively on disturbed thinking, defines schizophrenia broadly with the most inclusive criteria. Schneider's first-rank symptoms (12,34), and a computerized diagnostic system overlapping with Schneider's concepts (i.e., CATEGO) (45,47) define nuclear schizophrenia in terms of a few positive or productive symptoms and are less inclusive than the New Haven Schizophrenia Index. These three systems have weak prognostic significance (18,20,40).

Langfeldt (24,25) discriminated between "true" schizophrenia and schizophreniform psychosis, believing that course of illness differentiated the two. This distinction is germane to this discussion, and earlier reports by Langfeldt and his students confirmed the concept. However, recent studies which keep diagnostic and outcome judgments independent have failed to confirm (18,20,40) or have revealed only limited prognostic validity (20).

The Research Diagnostic Criteria (RDC) (37) and 12-point flexible system (10) proved more predictive in the Kendell et al. study (20), but even here prognostic significance was modest and less successful in predicting social functioning than symptomatic course. Our assessment of predictive power of the 12-point flexible system produced marginal results (18). DSM-III is now approved as the official nomenclature of the American Psychiatric Association, and overlaps with the RDC, as does an earlier effort by the St. Louis group (14).

Most investigators will use one of these to assist in the reliable identification of schizophrenic patients and in the description of their study cohort for purposes of replication and communication. However, it should be appreciated that these systems are not impressive in distinguishing chronic schizophrenia from other forms of schizophrenic illness. DSM-III is likely to be most successful in that it requires a minimum of 6 months of illness before schizophrenia can be diagnosed and relegates schizoaffective disorders and briefer psychoses to other nosologic classes.

Prognostic Status

Since cross-sectional symptom criteria are not successful in delineating chronic schizophrenia, it is necessary to employ other criteria in our classification. Course of illness or prognostic variables can be employed. Poor prognosis associated with chronic schizophrenia can be defined in the following terms: impaired premorbid functioning, childhood asociality, early age of onset, insidious onset, long duration since onset of illness, decreased affectivity, and no compelling relationship to precipitating social factors (15,19,38). Although a broad range of prior social functioning criteria have been implicated in predicting chronic course of illness, it is most feasible to ascertain recent social functioning. Discussion and schedules are available in recent issues of the *Schizophrenia Bulletin* (33,42).

Course of Illness

Chronic schizophrenia implies perseverance of psychopathology, and course variables can supplement or replace prognostic variables to distinguish between episodic, nondeteriorating psychotic illness and chronic schizophrenia. Particular

TABLE 1. *Item headings from the Quality of Life Interview Schedule*

Section I: Interpersonal relations and social network
1. Rate intimate relationships with household members
2. Rate intimate relationships with people other than household members
3. Rate active acquaintances
4. Rate level of social activity
5. Rate involved social network
6. Rate social initiatives
7. Rate social withdrawal
8. Rate sociosexual relations
9. Rate subjective satisfaction with interpersonal relations
Section II: Occupational role functioning
10. Rate extent of occupational role functioning
11. Rate level of accomplishment
12. Rate degree of underemployment
13. Rate satisfaction with occupational role functioning
Section III: Other residual symptoms
14. Rate sense of purpose
15. Rate degree of motivation
16. Rate curiosity
17. Rate anhedonia
18. Rate time utilization
19. Rate commonplace objects or activities
20. Rate capacity for empathy
21. Rate capacity for rapport
22. Rate appearance and personal hygiene

attention is directed towards social deterioration with incomplete recovery following psychotic episodes, and to negative or deficit symptomatology. Manfred Bleuler (4) refers to the latter as degeneration in the imaginative world: These impairments are at the very core of human functioning involving initiative, spontaneity, curiosity, range of the ideational field, capacity to experience pleasure, to modulate affect, and to experience gratification in the ordinary events of life.

Clinical assessment techniques are poorly developed in this area. Undue attention has been placed on certain measures (e.g., readmission to hospital) to the exclusion of others (e.g., quality of functioning). This situation has been addressed in some recent work (18,20,35,36,39–41). Table 1 provides a list of variables rated in the Quality of Life Scale developed at the Maryland Psychiatric Research Center. Judgments are made following 30 to 60 min interviewing, using a semi-structured interview schedule. Preliminary psychometric evaluation of the scale indicates quite satisfactory interrater reliability. This schedule is mentioned to illustrate a critical need in clinical methods. A definitive recommendation for its use must await further testing, but the instrument is available on request.[1]

[1] Address request to Douglas Heinrichs, M.D., Maryland Psychiatric Research Center, Box 3235, Catonsville, Maryland 21228.

A final comment on prognosis and course criteria. If the intent of study is to examine treatment effects in chronic patients with schizophrenia, the course variables are used with or without prognostic variables. There is no reason to rely on prognostic variables alone in this instance since they are imperfect predictors. However, many studies wish to identify patients with chronic schizophrenia prior to established chronicity, and the prognostic criteria can be used for this purpose (e.g., first break chronic schizophrenia). The word "chronic" is nominal in this volume, but is adjectival as course criteria.

Alternate Explanations for Psychopathology

Except for epidemiologic and survey work, clinicians and investigators place different demands on classification. The clinician strives to make the most likely diagnosis and to appreciate the reasonable alternatives and the implications of uncertainty. The investigator need not reach a diagnosis in every instance, but rather strives to enhance his confidence that the group of patients selected for study are appropriately classified. In short, the clinician must deal with the doubtful case whereas the clinical investigator must exclude the doubtful case. In practical terms this means that investigators must make every effort to explain manifest psychopathology with alternatives to a diagnosis of chronic schizophrenia.

Additional Diagnostic Considerations

In addition to usual procedures of differential diagnosis, the following considerations are cogent:

1. The investigator should avoid the study (under the rubric of chronic schizophrenia) of nonpsychotic social breakdown syndromes. The deterioration associated with schizophrenia is not pathognomonic of schizophrenia. There is no reason to doubt that nonpsychotic forms of schizophrenia exist, but the investigator will be wise to include only patients who manifest psychotic symptoms highly discriminating of schizophrenia (11,46).
2. Patients with stereotyped episodic illnesses where a set progression of decompensation can be defined, and where the medical history raises a suspicion of epilepsy, or where an altered state of consciousness is associated with psychosis should be considered as possible episodic behavioral dyscontrol syndrome patients distinguished from schizophrenia and affective disorders by Monroe and others (2,28,29).
3. Follow-up data are particularly relevant to diagnosis in that more information is available and the diagnostician can use hindsight. Course of illness, treatment response, and development of new symptoms may serve to affirm the index diagnosis and, more importantly, may be used as a basis for reconsidering the original psychopathologic formulation.

ASSIGNMENT TO TREATMENT STUDY

Schizophrenia is a multifactorial disease(s), and there is no acceptable rationale for unidimensional treatment. There are, in fact, many extant therapies. Some are used simultaneously or sequentially with others, and practitioners often emphasize one approach to the exclusion of others. Many therapeutic approaches may have merit, but none represents a comprehensive therapeutic approach for the schizophrenic patient. In fact, many treatments presently used still require scientific demonstration of efficacy, and little information is available to guide the clinician in judging what combination of treatments will be most advantageous in the individual case. We look forward to the day therapeutic techniques are derived intuitively, empirically, or theoretically. In chronic schizophrenia particularly, therapeutic efforts are woefully inadequate and an emphasis on designing and testing treatments of the chronic patient merits the highest priority.

Several important errors are often made when assigning patients to treatment studies. These errors usually bias against finding the hypothesized treatment effect, an unfortunate design problem in an illness where little effective treatment exists. The following points should be considered:

1. All patients assigned to an experimental treatment group should be judged suitable recipients of such treatment. This issue is not important when the treatment is presumed applicable to all chronic schizophrenic patients, or if no criteria are available to judge which patients might benefit from treatment. However, many treatments require a clinician's judgment as to suitability for therapy. This may be theoretically or practically derived. Mute patients are not likely to profit from verbal expressive therapies, and an interpersonal strategy aimed at altering attitude toward illness based on insight may require a capacity for establishing a therapeutic alliance in order to generate relevant information. Such a treatment would be feasible in some, but not all, patients. To test psychotherapeutic efficacy in patients unwilling or unable to establish a therapeutic alliance results in misleading negative results. If monoamine oxidase (MAO) activity could be induced, such an alteration might be beneficial only in low MAO chronic schizophrenic patients. To test the treatment in all patients and find it wanting reveals limits in applicability, but this must be distinguished from a test of therapeutic efficacy *per se.* Type II errors are common in heterogeneous illness populations.

The same reasoning applies when two or more distinct treatment strategies are being compared. All patients studied must be judged suitable recipients of all therapies. Two types of errors occur here. First, all patients may be judged suitable candidates for one treatment (e.g., a program of social activation). Random or stratified assignment biases in favor of one treatment and a type II error affects the other. Second, a strategy which assigns patients to the treatment for which they are best suited creates another problem. If a group of patients were assigned to different experimental treatments according to presence or absence of neurological soft signs, any differential treatment outcome might be accounted for by inherent differences between the groups. Similarly, a lack of discernible difference in treatment effects may lead to the erroneous conclusion that the two treatments are of equal effect, but in fact, one treatment group may have a more severe form of the illness and are made comparable to the other group by receiving a more effective therapy.

2. The duration of treatment must fit conceptually with the treatment modality and the patient population under study. Turning to a comparative study of aftercare for another example, let us suppose that the protective effect of antipsychotic drugs is effective immediately, whereas a protective effect with psychotherapy aimed at reducing vulnerability to stress may become effective after many months of treatment. A proper test of the latter may require 2 years. Results of this comparative study will be determined, in part, by the timing of posttreatment assessment.

3. It is obvious that assignment to treatment groups in comparative studies should not impose a prior bias on outcome. Since studies necessarily involve fairly small numbers, random assignment is risky. If a random assignment technique is used, it is imperative that careful assessment of prognostic status and other factors known to relate to treatment effect be conducted. It can be retrospectively determined whether these factors are balanced between the two groups. It is more desirable to use matching techniques or stratified random assignments to ensure that the two treatment groups will be similar on key dimensions most predictive of outcome or treatment response.

4. Patients must be in a phase of illness appropriate to the treatment under study. Many treatment maneuvers are intended as phase specific, and schizophrenic patients have changing therapeutic requirements over time. If a situational crisis occurs in a patient vulnerable to decompensation under stress, prudent management requires reduction of stress (e.g., social therapy), reduction in idiosyncratic reactions to stress (e.g., psychotherapy), or a reduction in the physiologic consequences of stress (e.g., antipsychotic medication). Each of these three treatments might prove helpful if used in a phase-specific manner. However, these same patients may have impaired functioning based on understimulation, social isolation, overmedication, etc. during another phase of illness. Under these circumstances treatments aimed at stress reduction might actually increase dysfunction. Hence, phase of illness can determine treatment response and bears special monitoring since changes are expected over time. Some workers have concluded that certain treatments are harmful to schizophrenic patients, when we may simply be observing phase-inappropriate therapy (e.g., "total push therapy" during a period of stress).

SELECTED SUBGROUPS FOR TREATMENT STUDIES

Heterogeneity in schizophrenia is now taken for granted, and attention has turned to the identification of special subgroups. This is especially characteristic of current biologic research, where deviations in some patients are taken seriously as possible guides to etiologically relevant subtypes. Using this strategy in treatment studies promises to make the 1980s an exciting period for the acquisition of new knowledge directly applicable to clinical practice. Various investigative groups will use their ingenuity to determine subgrouping, but several examples are provided to illustrate.

Clinical Subtypes

Traditional subtypes (simple, catatonic, paranoid, and hebephrenic) have not proven useful in identifying treatment requirements. This may be due to the absence of crisp psychopathologic distinctions during the early stages of illness (5,47) and the absence of potent treatments during the later phases of chronic illness. To some extent two more recent subtypes may be distinguished by therapeutic response (i.e., acute schizophrenia and schizoaffective schizophrenia), but this may simply be a differential between the chronic schizophrenias and the acute or episodic psychoses (8,9,31). The investigator attempting to determine if clinical subtypes based on cross-sectional psychopathology can be differentiated by treatment response will wish to consider the descriptive subtypes in DSM-III and experimental subtypes derived by cluster analysis from International Pilot Study of Schizophrenia data (47).

Prognostic subgroups appear more promising and keep the problem of chronic schizophrenia in focus. In pharmacology trials, there is some agreement that poor prognosis patients tend to do badly regardless of treatment (16,27). The English group found therapeutic benefits in the mid-prognosis range and found that good prognosis patients did well with or without antipsychotic drugs (27). Gittelman-Klein et al. (16) found the good prognosis patients the best responders. Studying hospital treatment of psychotic patients, Goldstein (17) mixed cross-sectional and prognostic variables and found that good prognosis, nonparanoid patients responded better off medication whereas poor prognosis, paranoid patients showed a decisive advantage on drug treatment. These findings have received some support in other studies (7,30).

Pharmacologic Response Subgroups

An ever-increasing number of drugs are available for altering those neurotransmitter systems relevant to affect, cognition, and behavior. Pharmacologic response profiles may be predictive of response to drug treatment since the same systems are presumed relevant to mode of therapeutic action. The clinician already uses history of drug response in planning treatment. The investigator can test a wide array of pharmacologic probes and determine the relation between acute response and therapeutic response. For example, amphetamine infusions worsen psychosis in some patients, improve behavior in others, and have no effect in some. Can therapeutic response to antipsychotic drugs be predicted from these data? If an acute dose of physostigmine provided symptom relief, would antipsychotic drugs with minimal anticholinergic activity be preferred? Could a test battery developed to test behavioral and physiologic consequences of antagonists and agonists in dopaminergic, cholinergic, serotonergic, noradrenergic, and gabaminergic neurons produce distinct profiles which would identify treatment-relevant subgroups?

Genetic and Biologic Subgroups

Do patients who develop schizophrenia with no family history of the illness have a different etiology from those with a genetic association? If so, genetic subtyping may be informative as to treatment requirements. This approach is limited since it is difficult now to establish what the genetic component is in any particular patient. However, as the search for heritable biologic markers of illness comes to fruition, we can expect greater clinical research leverage in this area. Biochemical, anatomical, and psychophysiological subgroups are already being defined independent of genetics, and some examples are found in other chapters of this volume. Several workers have linked psychophysiologic variables with course of illness if not treatment response *per se* (21,23,50).

Psychosocial Subgroups

Leff (26) has reviewed the important studies by Brown and later by Vaughn and Leff defining an environmental factor which is a potent predictor of relapse and whether or not maintenance drug therapy is required. These studies require replication in this country, and their specific relevance to chronic schizophrenia must be determined. Subgroups based on deviant patterns of communication in families of schizophrenic patients can be formed according to dimensions defined by Wynne and Singer and their colleagues (48,49). It is reasonable to hypothesize treatment relevance (e.g., families with high deviancy may not be able to gain insight from family therapy, and drug treatment may protect the patient from the disorganizing effects of such communication).

Multidimensional Subtypes

Variables such as those discussed above can be examined within a patient cohort to determine whether a multidimensional approach to typing would offer more power in predicting treatment requirements than the use of single dimensions in subtyping. The patient with neurologic soft signs, low platelet MAO, and high scores on communication deviancy may have very different treatment requirements from a patient without signs of neurologic disorder, with high platelet MAO activity, who lives alone.

PRINCIPLES FOR ASSESSING TREATMENT EFFECTS

For many years, American psychiatry was divided between those interested in somatic etiology and treatment and those postulating social and intrapsychic factors. The former too narrowly conceptualized the clinical data germane to investigative work whereas the latter eschewed systematic and controlled clinical studies. We have described the origins and clinical consequences of this split elsewhere (6), and will simply adumbrate the issue here. Despite three decades of methodologically "sound" pharmacotherapeutic investigations, we remain uninformed as to the long-term consequences of antipsychotic medication on critical aspects of the schizophrenic patient's functioning. Pervasive deterioration of the personality reflected in declining interpersonal and intrapsychic functioning is the hallmark of chronicity in schizophrenia, but treatment research has not yet been informative as to the interaction between long-term neuroleptic exposure and deficit or negative symptomatology in schizophrenia. The few variables routinely used to reflect course of illness in drug studies do not permit generalization to other areas of functioning. Hospital readmission and psychotic symptom status typify outcome measures, but these variables have only a modest association with social or work functioning (18,20,36,39–41).

This section will be used to articulate several principles in assessing change which can enhance the generation of new knowledge in treatment studies. Modification or extension, depending on study goals, will be required.

Timing of Assessment

A minimum of four time periods for assessment are required: (a) average functioning during the period preceding the psychotic episode to which treatment is given; (b) the baseline assessment during psychotic period prior to initiation of treatment; (c) functioning at the end of the treatment period; and (d) follow-up study to assess whether treatment effects are sustained beyond the period of active therapy.

Quality of Variables Chosen to Reflect Change

Meaningful clinical dimensions not subject to rapid and spontaneous change should be relied on in assessing treatment results. Many aspects of psychotic functioning change abruptly without evident relationship to treatment. Such ephemeral phenomena create noise in the assessment system, and can cause type I and type II errors when small populations are studied. The clinical significance of change variables should also be clear. Increased agitation may not be informative, since it can be associated with either deterioration or improvement. A common fallacy in chronic mental illnesses is to value quiescence and mistake disquietude for illness. If (to use an extravagant example) L-DOPA therapy evoked bizarre speech and anxiety in a previously catatonic, mute patient, we would have an interesting but difficult-to-interpret change.

Types of Variables Chosen to Reflect Change

Three types of change criteria should be assessed in treatment studies. First, aspects of manifest psychopathology hypothesized to improve with treatment must be observed in order to test the hypothesis. Second, we should designate those aspects of illness which may worsen with the treatment. This is routinely done by the sensitive clinician concerned with risks of any treatment and is clearly relevant in a multifaceted illness such as schizophrenia in which there is no suggestion that a unidimensional pathophysiology is basic to all dysfunction. Third, aspects of illness broadly informative of course and outcome should be measured even if no change is predicted.

Such a range of measurement would provide the needed information to understand the benefits and risk associated with each treatment, and the aspect of illness not responsive to the therapeutic approach.

Setting Conclusive to Therapeutic Results

In many situations clinical improvement is associated with negative consequences, and the Veterans Administration is no exception. Antitherapeutic forces may counterbalance the innate therapeutic efficacy of the treatment. For example, a patient unable to sustain himself in the community may be resistant to hospital treatment if improvement means discharge. If periodic rehospitalization is required to keep a pension, a prophylactic program intended to eliminate the need for subsequent hospitalization may prove a failure.

Reliability of Clinical Observations

During recent years the field has appreciated the necessity of reliable clinical observations in studies of psychopathology. Reliability in clinical judgments usually implies a capacity of two or more observers to reach the same conclusion from the same data. This should be demonstrated for critical variables within each study. It is usually insufficient to use a "reliable" scale without some demonstration of the investigators' capacity to use it reliably.

SUMMARY

Clinical methods used in investigating schizophrenia have improved considerably during the past two decades. Data are now more likely to be systematically collected, criteria for diagnosis specified, and many instruments which lend themselves to reliable use have been promulgated. One unfortunate consequence of these developments is the proclivity to focus on highly specifiable phenomena, forgetting that schizophrenia is a complex illness and clinical judgments of subtle and difficult-to-specify manifestations are necessary to assure comprehensive assessment of patients. Some measures which increase the breadth and depth of evaluation have been discussed above.

Research in chronic schizophrenia is disadvantaged when prestigious institutions and accomplished investigators select more acute forms of illness for treatment studies. Hence, the application of prognostic and/or chronicity variables in designating the populations which fit the concept of chronic schizophrenia is advised.

Treatment research in chronic schizophrenia should blossom, in part because there are many psychosocial strategies which have never been tested for therapeutic efficacy, in part because of missing information on the consequences of present pharmacotherapy, and because new drug development promises other profiles of therapeutic response. The principles which govern the selection of study patients for treatment research and the assessment of clinical variables associated with change have been discussed.

This author is excited that the Veterans Administration is taking a research initiative in chronic schizophrenia. It is hoped that both the assessment techniques employed and the variables under investigation will be a valid reflection of the complexity and heterogeneity of chronic schizophrenia.

REFERENCES

1. Astrachan, B. M., Harrow, M., Adler, D., Brauer, B., Schwartz, A., Schwartz, C., and Tucker, G. (1972): A checklist for the diagnosis of schizophrenia. *Br. J. Psychiatry,* 121:529–539.
2. Ballenger, J. C., and Post, R. M. (1978): The therapeutic effects of carbanizine in affective illness: A preliminary report. *Commun. Psychopharmacol.,* 2:159–175.
3. Bleuler, E. (1950): *Dementia Praecox or the Group of Schizophrenias,* translated by J. Zinkin. International University Press, New York.
4. Bleuler, M. (1978): *The Schizophrenic Disorders.* Yale University Press, New Haven.
5. Carpenter, W. T., Bartko, J. J., Langsner, C. A., and Strauss, J. S. (1976): Another view of schizophrenia subtypes: A report from the International Pilot Study of Schizophrenia. *Arch. Gen. Psychiatry,* 33:508–516.
6. Carpenter, W. T., and Heinrichs, D.: The role for psychodynamic psychiatry in the treatment of schizophrenic patients. In: *Psychotherapy of Schizophrenia: Current Status and New Directions,* edited by J. S. Strauss, S. Fleck, M. Bowers, I. Levine, T. W. Downey, and S. Jackson. Plenum Publishing Corp., New York *(in press).*
7. Carpenter, W. T., McGlashan, T. H., and Strauss, J. S. (1977): The treatment of acute schizophrenia without drugs: An investigation of some current assumptions. *Am. J. Psychiatry,* 134:14–20.
8. Carpenter, W. T., and Stephens, J. H. (1980): An attempted integration of information relevant to schizophrenic subtypes. *Schizophr. Bull.,* 5:490–506.
9. Carpenter, W. T., and Strauss, J. S. (1979): Diagnostic issues in schizophrenia. In: *Disorders of the Schizophrenic Syndrome,* edited by L. Bellak. Basic Books, New York.
10. Carpenter, W. T., Strauss, J. S., and Bartko, J. J. (1973): A flexible system for the identification of schizophrenia: A report from the International Pilot Study of Schizophrenia. *Science,* 182:1275–1278.
11. Carpenter, W. T., Strauss, J. S., and Bartko, J. J. (1974): Use of signs and symptoms for the identification of schizophrenic patients: A report of the International Pilot Study of Schizophrenia. *Schizophr. Bull.,* 11:37–49.
12. Carpenter, W. T. Strauss, J. S., and Muleh, S. (1973): Are there pathognomonic symptoms

in schizophrenia? An empiric investigation of Kurt Schneider's first-rank symptoms. *Arch. Gen. Psychiatry,* 28:847–852.

13. Endicott, J., Forman, J. B., and Spitzer, R. L. (1978): Research approaches to diagnostic classification in schizophrenia. In: *Neurochemical and Immunological Components in Schizophrenia,* edited by D. Berasma and A. L. Goldstein, pp. 41–57. Alan R. Liss, New York.
14. Feighner, J., Robins, E., Guze, S., Woodruff, R., Winokur, G., and Munoz, R. (1972): Diagnostic criteria for use in psychiatric research. *Arch. Gen. Psychiatry,* 26:57–63.
15. Garmezy, N. (1968): Process and reactive schizophrenia: Some conceptions and issues. In: *The Role and Methodology of Classification in Psychiatry and Psychopathology,* edited by M. M. Katz, J. O. Cole, and W. E. Barton, Superintendent of Documents, pp. 419–466. U.S. Government Printing Office, Washington, D.C.
16. Gittelman-Klein, R., and Klein, D. F. (1969): Premorbid asocial adjustment and prognosis in schizophrenia. *J. Psychiatr. Res.,* 7:35–53.
17. Goldstein, M. J. (1970): Premorbid adjustment, paranoid status, and patterns of response to phenothiazine in acute schizophrenia. *Schizophr. Bull.,* 3:24–37.
18. Hawk, A. B., Carpenter, W. T., and Strauss, J. S. (1975): Diagnostic criteria and 5-year outcome in schizophrenia: A report from the International Pilot Study of Schizophrenia. *Arch. Gen. Psychiatry,* 32:343–356.
19. Kantor, R. E., and Henron, W. G. (1966): *Reactive and Process Schizophrenia.* Science and Behavior Books, Palo Alto, California.
20. Kendell, R. E., Brockington, I. F., and Leff, J. P. (1979): Prognostic implications of six alternative definitions of schizophrenia. *Arch. Gen. Psychiatry,* 36(1):25–34.
21. Klasman, R., Strauss, J. S., and Kokes, R. F. (1977): Premorbid adjustment in schizophrenia: Part IV. Some biological approaches to research on premorbid functioning in schizophrenia. *Schizophr. Bull.,* 3(2):226–239.
22. Kraepelin, E. (1919): *Dementia Praecox,* translated by R. M. Barclay. E & S Livingstone Ltd., Edinburgh.
23. Landau, S. G., Buchsbaum, M. S., Carpenter, W. T., Strauss, J. S., and Sacks, M. (1975): Schizophrenia and stimulus intensity control. *Arch. Gen. Psychiatry,* 32:1239–1245.
24. Langfeldt, G. (1939): *The Schizophrenic States.* E. Munksgaard, Copenhagen.
25. Langfeldt, G. (1969): Schizophrenia, diagnosis and prognosis. *Behav. Sci.,* 14:173–182.
26. Leff, J. P. (1976): Schizophrenia and sensitivity to the family environment. *Schizophr. Bull.,* 2(4):566–574.
27. Leff, J. P., and Wing, J. K. (1971): Trial of maintenance therapy in schizophrenia. *Br. Med. J.,* 3:559–604.
28. Mitsuda, H. (Ed.) (1967): *Clinical Genetics in Psychiatry: Problems in Nosological Classification.* Iquaku Shoin, Tokyo.
29. Monroe, R. R. (1970): *Episodic Behavioral Disorders: A Psychodynamic and Neurophysiologic Analysis.* Harvard University Press, Cambridge.
30. Mosher, L. R., and Keith, S. J. (1979): Research on the psychosocial treatment of schizophrenia: A summary report. *Am. J. Psychiatry,* 136:623–631.
31. Pope, H. G., and Lipinski, J. F. (1978): Diagnosis in schizophrenia and manic depressive illness. *Arch. Gen. Psychiatry,* 35:811–828.
32. *Report to the President from the President's Commission on Mental Health* (1978): Superintendent of Documents, U.S. Government Printing Office, Washington, D.C.
33. *Schizophr. Bull.,* (1977): 3(2):180–182.
34. Schneider, K. (1959): *Clinical Psychopathology,* translated by M. W. Hamilton. Grune & Stratton, New York.
35. Schooler, N. R., Hogarty, G. E., and Weissman, M. M. (1977): The Social Adjustment Scale. In: *Resource Materials for Community Mental Health Program Evaluation,* edited by W. Hargreaves, L. Attkisson, and R. Sorenson, pp. 290–303. U.S. Public Health Service, Washington, D.C.
36. Schwartz, C. C., Myers, J. K., and Astrachan, B. M. (1976): Concordance of multiple assessments of outcome of schizophrenia. *Arch. Gen. Psychiatry,* 32:1221–1227.
37. Spitzer, R. L., Endicott, J., and Robins, E. (1975): *Research Diagnostic Criteria.* Biometric Research Unit, New York State Department of Mental Hygiene, New York State Psychiatric Institute.
38. Stephens, J. H., and Astrup, C. (1963): Prognosis in "process" and "non-process" schizophrenia. *Am. J. Psychiatry,* 119:945–953.

39. Strauss, J. S., and Carpenter, W. T. (1972): The prediction of outcome in schizophrenia. I: Characteristics of outcome. *Arch. Gen. Psychiatry,* 27:739–746. (Published as a chapter in: *Annual Review of the Schizophrenic Syndrome, Vol. 3,* edited by R. Cancro, Brunner/Mazel, New York, 1973.)
40. Strauss, J. S., and Carpenter, W. T. (1974): Characteristic symptoms and outcome in schizophrenia. *Arch. Gen. Psychiatry,* 30:429–434.
41. Strauss, J. S., and Carpenter, W. T. (1977): Prediction of outcome in schizophrenia. III. Five-year outcome and its predictors: A report from the International Pilot Study of Schizophrenia. *Arch. Gen. Psychiatry,* 34:159–163.
42. Strauss, J. S., and Carpenter, W. T. (1978): The prognosis of schizophrenia: Rationale for a multi-dimensional concept. *Schizophr. Bull.,* 4:56–67.
43. Strauss, J. S., and Gift, T. E. (1977): Choosing an approach for diagnosing schizophrenia. *Arch. Gen. Psychiatry,* 34:1248–1253.
44. Talbott, J. A. (Ed.) (1979): *The Chronic Mental Patient: A Report of a Conference Held in January, 1978.* American Psychiatric Association, Washington, D.C.
45. Wing, J. K., Cooper, J. E., and Sartorius, N. (1974): *The Description and Classification of Psychiatric Symptoms: An Instruction Manual for the PSE and Catego System.* Cambridge University Press, London.
46. Wing, J. K., and Nixon, J. (1975): Discriminating symptoms in schizophrenia: A report from the International Pilot Study of Schizophrenia. *Arch. Gen. Psychiatry,* 30:853–859.
47. World Health Organization (Eds.) (1973): *International Pilot Study of Schizophrenia, Vol. 1.* World Health Organization Press, Geneva, Switzerland.
48. Wynne, L. C., Singer, M. T., Bartko, J. J., and Toohey, M. L. (1977): Schizophrenics and their families: Recent research on parental communication. In: *Developments in Psychiatric Research,* edited by J. M. Tanner, pp. 254–286. Hodden & Stoughton, Ltd., London.
49. Wynne, L. C., Toohey, M. L., and Doane, J. A. (1979): Family studies. In: *The Disorders of the Schizophrenic Syndrome,* edited by L. Bellak. Basic Books, New York.
50. Zahn, T. P., Carpenter, W. T., and McGlashan, T. H. (1978): Short-term outcome, clinical improvement, and reaction time performance in acute schizophrenia. In: *The Nature of Schizophrenia,* edited by L. C. Wynne, R. L. Cromwell, and S. Matthysse, pp. 273–279. John Wiley & Sons, New York.

Discussion

Melnechuk: With regard to assignment of patients to treatment studies, please expand a bit on stratification by sex.

Carpenter: One needs either to study only one sex, or match for sex in comparative groups.

Melnechuk: And on the relationship of stratifying to randomizing?

Carpenter: I meant a "stratified random" technique. A group should be balanced on key dimensions before randomization.

Baxter: In discussing special cohorts for treatment studies, you suggested using pharmacology as a means of diagnosis rather than of treatment. Since drugs tend to interact with each other and modify each other's effects, do you suggest a particular order in which drugs should be used, and what would you use as a control?

Carpenter: The sequence is, first, to establish a group of chronic schizophrenic patients with clinical judgment and specified criteria and, second, to use the pharmacological probes to subdivide the study cohort. If neurochemical theories of antipsychotic drug action are reasonably correct, then information about the functioning status of these may be predictive of drug responsivity. For example, patients with symptom exacerbation during an amphetamine infusion may be good subjects for antipsychotic medication, whereas patients who improve clinically with dopamine agonists may be poor subjects for neuroleptic therapy.

Itil: In your biological subtypes, I miss some of the biochemical and other physiological variables. For example, in earlier times, Kretschmer (6,7) and others described body types and other physiological patterns employed in subclassifications used not so much for diagnosis as for selection of patients.

Carpenter: I didn't give many examples of physiological variables because you, Zahn, Buchsbaum, and other speakers have addressed the subject. To briefly illustrate, chronic schizophrenic patients trichotomized with ANS variables into low, normal, and high physiologic arousal, or subjects with augmenting or reducing patterns of evoked potentials, may constitute treatment-relevant subgroups. Body type receives little current attention. There were problems in achieving reliable judgments as to somatotype, and its importance as a clinical dimension has not been convincingly demonstrated.

Melnechuk: Toward the end of the biological subtypes you did list, you mentioned patients who had suffered perinatal complications. With regard both to that and to the role of endorphins in mental illness (8) discussed by Dr. Buchsbaum, Dr. Roger Guillemin of the Salk Institute is collaborating in an ongoing study with Dr. J. P. Gautray (3) and others that preliminarily seems to have found twofold to 20-fold elevations of the beta-endorphin in human amniotic fluid in cases of fetal distress.

Turning to your exemplifications of psychosocial subtypes, you spoke mainly of psychological variables and of family size. What is your opinion of epidemiological surveys like Schwab's (10) and of social class analysis?

Carpenter: Socioeconomic class analysis has yielded some of the most consistent findings in psychiatry. Lower socioeconomic groups and inner-city environments provide a disproportionately large number of schizophrenics, in whom the course and outcome seem to be worse. The downward drift hypothesis is only a partial explanation, and Kohn (5) has reviewed these data and provided an explanatory hypothesis for socially-induced vulnerability relevant to schizophrenia and to chronicity. My presentation was focused on the individual patient who may participate in treatment studies; hence special emphasis was given to familial interactive variables of immediate relevance to course of illness and treatment response. Socioeconomic status is clearly important in characterizing a study cohort, establishing prognosis, and in large-scale studies dealing with epidemiologic and service delivery data. It may also be a variable in matching or stratifying in treatment study designs.

Yuwiler: Many of our strategies and speculations on schizophrenia derive from data obtained on subpopulations that may not be representative of all schizophrenics. Who goes to a Veterans Administration (VA), university, county, or private hospital is determined by complex social and economic factors including hospital admissions policy. Similar factors influence who is released and who is studied. If the population studied is not representative but preselected, our data may be skewed and our strategies erroneous. The late Ralph Gerard carried out an unpublished study showing that both schizophrenics and sociopaths at one state hospital did, indeed, have poor family environments. However, when Helen Fritz and Eira Mattsson, the sociologist and psychologist in the study, visited the ethnic neighborhoods from which these schizophrenics came, they found similar behaviors in the families of their neighbors: that is, first-generation Polish fathers beat their children, first-generation Ashkenazi Jewish mothers were oversolicitous of theirs, broken and fatherless homes were common, parental conflict was high, and so forth. If we are to avoid confounding preselection factors with attributes of disease we have to either be more careful in matching control and diseased populations or derive our experimental populations from hospitals with differing catchment areas and different selection criteria.

Ewalt: Until 25 to 30 years ago, the supposed contribution of broken families to schizophrenia was much studied. Then Thomas Rennie and Leo Serole (9) showed that the controls had more broken families than the troubled children had. Most subsequent studies have verified their conclusions.

Cole: Our experience at McLean Hospital in Belmont, Massachusetts, which receives a greater number of patients from middle and upper classes than do VA hospitals, is that high-density schizophrenic families are hard to find. We find many high-density families with regard to manic-depressive illness, epilepsy, brain disorders, and undiagnosable syndromes, but the number of high-density schizophrenic families seems lower than is suggested by studies of Danish cohorts (4).

Melnechuk: In discussing the assessment of treatment effects, you mentioned as one variable that did not seem meaningful to you the number of minutes a patient's eyes were open. But since the loss of rapid-eye-movement sleep was once thought to be related to some psychotic episodes, and since Dr. William S. Condon (2) of the Boston University School of Medicine has filmed episodes of independent eye movements in patients with multiple personality or with schizophrenia, at least some optical characteristics may be meaningful. Therefore, could you please expand on your comment?

Carpenter: I apologize for being cavalier, for the eye is truly a window to the brain, and many dysfunctions including those you mention have been linked to schizophrenia, the eye-blinking data of Stevens (11) being most relevant, had my comment really been focused on the eye. My remark was an association to a lecture I recently attended where numerous behavioral variables were used to reflect change in chronic schizophrenic patients, some of which were not intuitively obvious as to their meaning. For example, length of time eyes open per unit time was emphasized to an audience who would surely have been judged replete with psychopathology by this criterion. Fortunately, those in attendance showed a remarkable recovery to the simple phrase "slides off, lights on," although with an explosion of blinks that would have confused even the most adroit limbic system dopaminologist. I only intended to convey that while some behavioral variables have a clear relationship to psychopathology, others do not. In the latter, it is encumbent on the investigator to make the relationship explicit.

Perez-Polo: I wonder if the term "variable" is appropriate for such complex and integrated changes, in trying to classify patients. Could you comment on the possibility of quantifying the variables that one looks at in classifying patients, using quantifiable criteria?

Carpenter: Schizophrenia is an extraordinarily complex phenomenon. If we use methods that belie that complexity, we're unlikely to validly represent the illness, or guide the clinician in selecting treatment methods, so complexity of models and diagnostic methods must be maintained. However, quantification can be accomplished in part. Diagnostic criteria lend themselves to estimates of the extent to which one's diagnosis concurs with principles commonly used across cultures and diagnostic schools. False positive diagnoses can be minimized by requiring stringent criteria for schizophrenia, although any standard is conditional in the individual patient as long as we lack external criteria to validate diagnoses. Prognosis and course-of-illness measures are also quantifiable, at least in the sense that you can take a measure of social functioning and can either dichotomize or scale it—that is, a person is paranoid or not, or has a certain score on a dimension of paranoia. Quantifying data makes judgments more explicit, but not necessarily more "objective." We deal in inferences concerning another person's subjective experience and observations of multi-determined behavior. Quantification does not render one subject matter less complex, but does facilitate systematic data collection, data analysis, and psychometric assessment of reliability.

K. Davis: I have a practical suggestion. We in Palo Alto have a multiple correlation analysis protocol for patients admitted with depression. In it, we do a very large battery of chemical tests and psychological assessments, all of which are repeated when the patient gets well. We've administered the protocol over the last 5 years to 60 patients. The amount of data already generated, and the amount of data we're talking about generating in various types of analysis, is massive. We must analyze it by fairly sophisticated methods. We will have different degrees of success in analyzing such data at different stations, depending on our access to the computer facilities of large centers.

Meltzer: What have you found?

K. Davis: We need to look at twice the number of patients we've already examined to start to say anything meaningful. In 5 years, when we have a larger *n*, we'll see what cross-correlates.

Schooler: What I've heard here is that our assay methodology and our hypotheses are far more equal to the task than are our data-analytic capacities. However, I don't think correlational techniques and multiple regression, however nicely applied, are the answer. We need far more sophisticated techniques of data analysis. I suspect they exist, but most of the investigators in our research community probably don't have them. We'll have to go outside to get them.

K. Davis: I agree. Our group's experience has been that the more complicated the data becomes, the more we have to go beyond those methods that psychopharmacologists and biological psychiatrists usually use. The people we brought in to analyze our data have had a degree of sophistication in statistics far beyond our own training. Therefore, one practical action the VA might consider is to make available to investigators terminals and other appropriate hardware so that we can do the kinds of analyses that may be necessary.

J. Collins (VA Cooperative Studies Program): The VA medical research service has set up a system that will make statisticians available for more sophisticated data handling and analysis.

Hays: I'm a mathematical modeler, using data based on theoretical models, and I don't see how you're going to assault problems like these without improving your theoretical methodology for such interactions as those of hormones and getting good mathematical models which can then be perturbed with all of the various stimuli you are going to contribute. Mere cluster analyses or various correlational analyses are not going to answer the problem. You're going to have to get cause-and-effect models in various types of circumstances.

Zubin: The modeling approach *is* the answer. Factor analysis is certainly not the answer, because nonlinear relationships have to be dealt with. Even though there are methods for doing nonlinear factor analysis, they squeeze the data into a mass that is not very useful. But cluster analysis may be an answer, even before you prepare a specific model. It clusters people, rather than factors, and people who belong together can be examined for other things in common.

Beck: I reviewed E. Roy John's book on neurometrics, which uses cluster and other types of analysis (1). It reminded me of an admonition by Dr. Zubin that the Eleventh Commandment is "Thou shalt not correlate." Perhaps the data are so prodigious that we shouldn't expect magic analytical tools to provide us the answers not provided by familiar tools.

Meltzer: I suggest asking your consultant statistician's advice on appropriate ways to handle the data *before* you gather it, rather than presenting one with some accomplished fact that may violate requirements or demand the development of new methods, when some preliminary consultation might have handled it.

I'm distressed at the tone of some of this discussion: Now that we have high technology available to us, let's start collecting variables. I'd prefer more emphasis on hypothesis generation and conceptual frameworks.

Hiatt: I agree. We've heard pessimism arising from measuring every aspect of the responding organism. We can narrow down the large number of variables to those crucial variables it is important to look at, then do cluster analysis as a first way to look at the data, to judge how to proceed.

Yuwiler: Dr. Zubin's cluster analysis of patients may turn up groups that can be tested for treatment modalities but that's a different sort of cluster analysis than that required to determine interactive influences of hormones on homeostatic balance.

REFERENCES

1. Beck, E. C. (1978): (Review of: *Functional Neuroscience, Vol. 2. Neurometrics: Clinical Application of Quantitative Electrophysiology,* edited by E. R. John. Wiley, Somerset, NJ, 1977.) *Electroencephalogr. Clin. Neurophysiol.,* 45:679–680.
2. Condon, W. S., Ogston, W. D., and Pacoe, L. V. (1969): Three faces of Eve revisited: A study of transient microstrabismus. *J. Abnorm. Psychol.,* 74:618–620.
3. Gautray, J. P., Jolivet, A., Vielh, J. P., and Guillemin, R. (1977): Presence of immunoassayable beta-endorphin in human amniotic fluid: Elevation in cases of fetal distress. *Am. J. Obstet. Gynecol.,* 129:211–212.
4. Kety, S., Rosenthal, D., Wender, P., Schulsinger, F., and Jacobsen, B. (1975): Mental illness in the biological and adoptive families of adopted individuals who have become schizophrenic: A preliminary report based on psychiatric interviews. In: *Genetic Research in Psychiatry,* edited by R. Fieve, D. Rosenthal, and H. Brill, pp. 147–165. Johns Hopkins Press, Baltimore.
5. Kohn, M. L. (1976): The interaction of social class and other factors in the etiology of schizophrenia. *Am. J. Psychiatry,* 133:177–180.
6. Kretschmer, E. (1927): *Der Sensitive Beziehungswahn. 2nd ed.* Springer, Berlin.
7. Kretschmer, E. (1936): *Physique and character. 2nd ed.* Routledge, London.
8. Melnechuk, T. (1978): Endorphins in mental illnesses. In: *Cell Receptor Disorders,* pp. 134–152. Western Behavioral Sciences Institute, La Jolla, California.
9. Rennie, T. A. C., and Serole, L. (1962): *Midtown Manhattan Study.* McGraw-Hill, New York.
10. Schwab, J. J. (1978): *Sociocultural Roots of Mental Illness: An Epidemiologic Survey.* Plenum Press, New York.
11. Stevens, J. R. (1978): Eye blink and schizophrenia: Psychosis or tardive dyskinesia. *Am. J. Psychiatry,* 135:223–226.

Perspectives in Schizophrenia Research,
edited by C. Baxter and T. Melnechuk.
Raven Press, New York, 1980.

Strategies for Applied Research in Chronic Schizophrenia: Choosing the Right Treatment and Measuring Outcome

Philip R. A. May

Health Services Research and Development Laboratory, Veterans Administration Medical Center, Brentwood, Los Angeles, California 90073; and Neuropsychiatric Institute, Center for the Health Sciences, University of California at Los Angeles, Los Angeles, California 90024

LAYPERSON'S SUMMARY

Better ways are needed to treat schizophrenia, to select the correct treatment methods, and to improve drug treatment, particularly to reduce unwanted side effects on the nervous system.

There is a need to find means by which individuals who may be at risk for developing schizophrenia can be identified so that something can be done to prevent the disease in these persons, or catch it at its inception.

Additional insight is required to prevent schizophrenia from becoming chronic when it occurs and to prevent relapses. The gaps in support systems provided by federal, state, and local agencies for patients recovering from episodes of schizophrenia must be found, so as to decrease the risk of relapse. Other suggested directions for research are as follows:

1. New, better, and more cost-efficient ways must be found to measure concentrations of neuroleptic medication in the bloodstream so that the dose can be adjusted for optimal results with minimal toxic effects. Methods must be devised to detect side effects of medication on the nervous system at the earliest possible moment.
2. To prevent relapse, the best combinations of psychological and drug treatment for the recovering patient must be explored, as well as better ways to help family situations.
3. Racial and cultural differences in response to treatment must be ascertained so as to adapt treatment to individual needs.
4. Little is known concerning the relationship of alcohol to schizophrenia, and this relationship should be explored.
5. Better ways must be found to measure and follow-up the results of treatment. Special note should be taken of unusual cases that do not react to standard

treatments and they should be studied. Information should be generated that will result in the improvement of the quality of life of the schizophrenic patient—just drug administration and follow-up studies in the clinic are not enough.

INTRODUCTION

Knowledge, no matter how useful it may be for academic or heuristic purposes, attains clinical relevance only when it has been translated into a classification or a measurement that can be used to describe or monitor a patient's condition; or to make reliable references about his past, present, or future state; or to predict his possible response to a treatment. In short, the problem is one of detecting differences between individuals and between groups. From the clinical point of view, a strategy for future research should be to focus on differences between patients and how these relate to treatment outcome; how better to choose the right treatment for a particular patient; and how to measure progress.

A few areas have been chosen for discussion that seem particularly promising, and will refer mainly to the future rather than to work that has already been done.

The thrust should be to prevent, reduce, or remedy chronicity, and not merely to palliate symptoms while abandoning the patient to chronicity.

AREAS OF RESEARCH THAT ARE PARTICULARLY APPLICABLE TO MEDICAL RESEARCH CENTERS SUCH AS THE VETERANS ADMINISTRATION

Identification of "High-Risk" Individuals

In psychiatry there is much talk of prevention, even a certain amount of action, but few hard data and tangible results. It would, therefore, be easy to assert that preventive measures are not a part of our mission and probably would not work. This would be a grave mistake and a disservice to patients. If we know anything for sure about schizophrenia, it is that after the first attack there is often residual scarring and vulnerability—schizophrenic psychosis tends to recur. Research should be directed therefore towards identifying patients who are at "high risk" and are particularly likely to be hospitalized at some future date for treatment of schizophrenia.

There are two groups of patients that are obviously at high risk: (a) Those who have had a prior schizophrenic episode and (b) those whose parents or siblings have had a schizophrenic episode. But there are probably more subtle indicators of "high risk" that could be developed. For example, the literature indicates that certain measures of attention, perception, and information processing may be persistently abnormal in persons who have seemingly remitted from their illness and also in genetically related persons who have not (yet) had a schizophrenic episode (1,4,5,11–13,15,21). And there is an obvious challenge to look for valid biochemical markers.

Research of this type poses administrative problems, not the least of which is likely to be the difficulty in establishing effective collaboration between organizations which make the original diagnosis of schizophrenia and those which are called on to provide subsequent support. A good example would be the Armed Forces and the V.A. Given the necessary impetus by interested scientists, it should be possible, however, to organize collaborative research studies involving two separate bureaucracies.

The legal and regulatory issues should not be insurmountable.

Integration of Preventive Measures and Support Systems

Having classified certain persons as "high risk," the next logical step would be to develop programs and interventions that might prevent them from developing a schizophrenic episode in the future, or at least reduce its severity if it occurs.

The care given by private practitioners, local community clinics, and other support and welfare services significantly affects the outcome of schizophrenia, the quality of the patient's life, and the risk for relapse. Yet these services are usually beyond the control of the medical research center which is attempting to develop preventive measures and support systems. The fragmentation is a major obstacle for the development of an integrated care system for post hospital treatment and the follow-up of high risk patients in the United States. Regrettably, our compartmentalized system tends to encourage and perpetuate fragmented treatment. Departments, institutions, agencies, and private therapists guard their boundaries jealously, often to the detriment of a comprehensive and rational plan for the patient. There is a sort of schizophrenia in the system. In this respect the patient's internal splitting, which is his schizophrenia, mirrors—and often unwittingly accentuates—the splitting and lopsided attitudes in the treatment and research support systems.

A recent report on the Mental Health System in California addressed itself to this issue. It found that in California the mental health treatment system was inherently fragmented and unstable. Numerous agencies were concerned with one or another aspect of helping the mentally ill, yet there was nowhere a comprehensive listing of these agencies and their responsibilities; nor did any single person or agency possess information about what resources were available, much less informed insight about the quality of services that might be available. The report concluded that it was hardly surprising to find that patients and their families had little or no knowledge as to where to go for the different kinds of help they needed (22).

It could be hypothesized that fragmentation in the mental health and support services is itself a cause for relapses of schizophrenics and that correction of this deficit will lead to fewer schizophrenic episodes. One research strategy might be to start with epidemiologic studies to identify and classify the sources of fragmentation; next, to develop corrective techniques; and finally, to perform controlled experiments to evaluate these techniques, their value to the patient, and their cost-effectiveness to society.

In the United States, V.A. Medical Centers have a unique opportunity to study the effects of coordinating services to meet the needs of the chronic schizophrenic patient. The V.A. accepts responsibility in the case of service-connected illness for the patient's psychiatric care, rehabilitation, and subsistence. It, therefore, has the opportunity to study the costs and benefits of coordinating all the various elements required for overall care of "high-risk" individuals. For example, the V.A. might, for research purposes, establish special facilities and services for the chronic care and rehabilitation of these particular veterans and compare the costs and benefits of this treatment with the costs and benefits of the present system.

The major obstacles to such an evaluation are likely to be administrative and inherently conservative inertia. This is an obviously difficult and sensitive issue, but if we can avoid precipitating defensive attitudes about present conditions, it should be relatively easy to identify and classify the sources of fragmentation and to determine the practical needs and requirements for improvement. Once this point has been reached, major administrative interagency reorganizations should not be necessary for optimal deployment of resources. Instead, it may become desirable to use "Case Helpers" or "Case Managers" whose role will be carefully defined in accordance with the needs that have been disclosed by prior research. This approach would be different from the currently fashionable concept of "Advocates" whose role seems to be limited largely to legalistic battling with the treatment staff about civil rights and with refusing treatment and research, rather than constructively attempting to see that the patient gets the positive help that is needed.

AVOIDABLE PITFALLS IN APPLIED STUDIES OF SCHIZOPHRENIA

There is overwhelming evidence that antipsychotic drugs have profound and widespread effects in schizophrenia. The evidence is strong that such drugs are not anti-anxiety agents and do more than merely relieve secondary symptoms. Such drugs influence the primary symptoms of schizophrenia. It is mandatory, therefore, that research studies of schizophrenia be rigorously controlled for the effects of these drugs. Indeed, it is unethical to conduct studies without the necessary controls: it would expose patients to risk without the likelihood of answering the research question accurately. Agencies, therefore, should not support any research on schizophrenic patients in which drug treatment is inadequately controlled, a judgment which can be made only by persons with experience in psychopharmacologic research. Such guidelines should apply to a wide range of different types of clinical research—biochemical, neurophysiological, psychological—not just to treatment outcome studies. In some instances, a valid answer to a particular question can be obtained only when patients are taking no drugs at all: in other instances it may be sufficient to limit, measure, and record drug intake and take this into account when the results are evaluated by statistical analysis.

BLOOD AND TISSUE LEVELS OF ANTIPSYCHOTIC DRUGS AND OTHER SUBSTANCES

A major research question is whether knowledge of blood and tissue levels of drugs can be used to predict clinical outcome of the disease or side effects of the drug, or if such data can be used to monitor progress.

When Curry (6) discovered a sensitive method to measure chlorpromazine, it seemed to herald the dawn of a new era in which drug dosage could be adjusted on a scientific basis. The invention of radioimmunoassay added to this hope. Unfortunately, even for the most studied drug, chlorpromazine, we are as yet uncertain as to the relationship between blood levels and clinical outcome (3,14,17,23). To some extent, this lack of understanding is attributable to the difficulty and cumbersomeness of the chemical methods, but it is mainly due to a number of weaknesses in the design of the experiments (17). Thus present research needs are as follows:

1. To develop better (i.e., more accurate, more reliable, and less costly) methods to measure antipsychotic drugs and relevant biological substances (hormones, metabolites, neurotransmitters) in body tissues and fluids. Considerable basic research is still necessary to bring these methods to the point of practical utility and to establish a scientific basis for their use in clinical practice.
2. To conduct clinical studies to probe the relationships between blood and tissue levels of these substances and psychological and physiological parameters that might be clinically relevant (EEG, measures of attention and perception, etc.).

INDIVIDUAL DIFFERENCES IN RESPONSE TO DRUG TREATMENT

In the past, psychopharmacologic research, both animal and clinical, has tended to concentrate on overall group means and standard errors rather than on individual differences and standard deviations. Yet it is the individual differences that count in medical practice—for the patient and for the clinician, the primary objective is to find ways of adjusting treatment to benefit the patient. The strategy, therefore, should be to stimulate examination of this neglected area.

One can "predict" that most schizophrenics will improve if given drug treatment; yet a substantial number will do satisfactorily also without drugs and some will develop adverse physical or behavioral effects as a result of drug treatment. Our present state of knowledge in the area of prediction of response to treatment is not impressive, epitomized by Hollister's observation that we can predict that drug treatment is unlikely to make a patient play the violin if he has never played the violin before, and by the old adage that you can't make a silk purse out of a sow's ear (16). We should count it no great feat that we can make self-evident statements such as: "Results will be less favorable if a person has been ill for a long time"; or "Those who, at their best, before they became ill were never able to read or write (hold a job) (enjoy life) (be a good parent) (mix freely in society) (form a lasting relationship) etc. will be unlikely to improve on drug treatment alone or with any combination of treatments above their pre-illness performance level." Such statements are hardly "predictions." The issue, therefore, is whether, over and above such crude statements of the obvious, one can predict if drug treatment is likely to be of advantage to a particular person.

More than a decade ago we embarked on research in this area. After 7 years of painstaking research, we failed to develop methods that were any better in predicting the outcome of drug treatment for a specific patient than merely using the average (mean) outcome of all other patients treated with drugs, and we came to the unhappy conclusion that we could not predict from pretreatment demographic, history, and clinical status variables. Perhaps, we reasoned, we might learn something relevant to the eventual clinical outcome by studying individual differences in the patient's immediate response to a single dose of a drug. In such a case the best predictors of outcome might be individual differences in drug levels that one retained in the body after a specified period of time, or individual differences in some measure of the patient's immediate clinical or physiological response to the drug. This reasoning led to the development of procedures for monitoring the immediate pharmacokinetic, physiological, psychological, and clinical responses to a single test dose of a drug (e.g., changes of drug levels in blood and saliva, measurements of EEG, skin resistance, attention, perception, and clinical ratings). Hopefully, individual differences in response to a test dose might be useful in predicting the blood levels and clinical responses that would be expected from an optimal dosage of the same drug during the course of therapy (18).

Our preliminary experience with this test dose model has been most encouraging. An extremely wide range of individual differences in plasma and saliva chlorpromazine levels and in subjective and objective reactions to a test dose of drug was found. A few patients seemed to respond quite differently from the rest. These differences were so striking that one could not avoid the inference that they must have some relevance to clinical outcome. Indeed, we found that a patient's subjective response to a single test dose—i.e., whether they became dysphoric or whether they perceived the drug as helpful and syntonic—had distinct bearing on the development of extrapyramidal side effects, or compliance with drug therapy, and with the eventual clinical outcome (18,19,24,25).

We also found that chlorpromazine can be measured easily in the saliva and that there was a statistically significant relationship between plasma and saliva levels (18). We have also found evidence that chlorpromazine binds locally in the mouth, most probably to the oral mucosa *(unpublished data)*. This observation opens up the exciting possibility of a noninvasive method for examining individual differences in human tissue binding of antipsychotic drugs.

OUTPATIENT DRUG AND PSYCHOSOCIAL THERAPY: ASSESSMENT OF FAMILY FACTORS

A critical issue in outpatient therapy is how to prevent relapse, how to hold the patient in the community and improve the quality of his life and that of his family and those around him. It has been well established that antipsychotic drugs reduce the risk of relapse (10), but they do not work in all cases. They can have cumulative toxic effects, and need to be supplemented for optimal results by social therapy, social support, training in the activities of daily living, and psychotherapy or behavior therapy. The research task is to identify optimal dosages for maintenance pharmacotherapy and the indications for optimum combination with non-drug therapies.

It is particularly important to establish optimal outpatient treatment. In the inpatient situation, the toxic effects of moderate doses of drugs may be of relatively minor significance since the patient is usually hospitalized for only a relatively brief period of time. Outpatients, however, tend to receive neuroleptic drugs for much longer time periods, and even subtle akinesias or akathisias which may develop have the potential for being of far greater significance with regards to the patient's ability to be rehabilitated. The concept of possible toxic effects also applies to social therapy and psychotherapy. If these treatments have either positive or toxic effects, it seems most likely that these effects would show up in studies of a long-term ability of individuals to adjust to their environment.

It is also important to identify different kinds of individual vulnerabilities. Recent research has underlined the importance of stresses, burdens, and interactions within the family that provoke relapse (2,26). At present, however, the methods for measuring family factors are primitive in content and cumbersome in use. It would, therefore, seem important to develop practical, reliable scales to assess and categorize the different types of stresses, burdens, problems, and interactions within the family and to record in a useful fashion the differing goals and perceptions of the various parties. If we can develop a practical and useful methodology and obtain data that can be used to categorize patient and family problems in a clinically meaningful way, then further research can be aimed at developing and evaluating specific family and social intervention techniques.

It is particularly important to evaluate the interacting effects of drugs and psychosocial and behavioral forms of therapy. We need to develop non-drug therapies that will potentiate and improve the effects of drug therapy.

RACIAL AND CULTURAL DIFFERENCES IN RESPONSE TO TREATMENT

Chronic schizophrenia occurs in persons of all races and in all cultures and at every level in society. Yet there is little knowledge of the potential influence of racial and cultural differences (dietary, genetic, and attitudinal) on the outcome of treatment.

For example, Japanese regulatory agencies will not approve a drug for use in that country without data from Asiatic subjects, maintaining that data from Occidentals are insufficient and may be misleading because they fail to take into account the possibility of genetic differences in metabolism and of drug-diet interactions. This is by no means fanciful—the interaction of monoamine oxidase inhibitors with Italian wine and certain types of Scandinavian, Italian, and English cheeses and with certain British meat and vegetable extracts is well known (14a), as is susceptibility to the peripheral vascular effects of alcohol in Asiatic persons and the tendency for Chinese food to contain large amounts of glutamic acid. Sociocultural studies show that attitudes of Oriental and Hispanic persons towards phychotherapy and drug therapy differ from those of Anglos; there are even obvious differences among Anglo subcultures and socioeconomic levels.

It would be appropriate, therefore, to investigate the impact on drug treatment, psychotherapy, and social treatment, of social, cultural, racial, and dietary factors. Such information could be crucial to developing treatment programs that would be more appropriate for minority groups.

The chief obstacle to this kind of research may be the widespread belief that any kind of research into racial differences is discriminatory. In this particular case, however, the research would, in fact, be antidiscriminatory, for the objective is to focus directly on the special needs of minorities and to discover whether or not the usual "majority treatment" is not in fact an inferior form of treatment in their particular case.

MONITORING AND EARLY DETECTION OF DRUG SIDE EFFECTS

This subject is covered here quite briefly, since it is the focus of another chapter in this volume.

Extrapyramidal side effects, particularly akinesia, akathisia, and tardive dyskinesia, are of major concern in the pharmacotherapy of schizophrenia: they have been of particular interest to our research group. We have found that these side effects have a definite relationship to drug-induced depression and to noncompliance with treatment, both findings of obvious importance to clinical outcome (24,25).

One of the difficulties for research in this area is measuring extrapyramidal symptoms objectively. The rating scales that are available are not entirely satisfactory, and there is an obvious need for less subjective and more reliable measurements. We have recently been attempting to develop nonintrusive apparatus to measure tremors, involuntary movements, and extrapyramidal effect; so far we have prototype electromagnetic and ultrasound transducers that will measure hand tremors and general body movement *(unpublished).* We plan to use the equipment to monitor movement of other parts of the body. Our instrumentation is sensitive enough to detect the effect of smoking a single cigarette on hand tremor.

Following leads from Wetterberg *(personal communication)* and Denber (7), we are developing a method for analyzing a patient's voice, using power spectrum analysis. Their work in Stockholm and Louisville indicates that such "voice-prints" can differentiate schizophrenic subjects from normals and from alcoholics. In Los Angeles we are attempting to apply this technique to measuring the effect of a single dose of antipsychotic drug on extrapyramidal side effects. This approach is based on the well-known clinical observation that the voice is affected in Parkinson's disease and in drug-induced parkinsonism.

ALCOHOLISM, PATHOLOGIC INTOXICATION, AND SCHIZOPHRENIA

A substantial proportion of patients with chronic schizophrenia have trouble with alcohol, yet our understanding and treatment of this double problem leave much to be desired. Research might be directed at several different levels:

1. Biochemical, psychological, and neurophysiological studies of the interactions between antipsychotic drugs and alcohol. For example, the effect of levels of antipsychotic drugs and alcohol in the blood on pathways of metabolism. This applies particularly to the depot neuroleptics (such as fluphenazine decanoate and enanthate), which are becoming widely used in the outpatient setting.
2. Neurobiochemical studies of persons who develop "pathological intoxication"—i.e., psychotic (or near psychotic) symptoms that appear usually abruptly, after relatively small amounts of alcohol. A useful model may be Wetterberg's studies of hematoporphyrinuria, in which the sudden onset of psychotic symptoms has been shown to be due to a number of genetically determined defects in porphyrin metabolism, specifically triggered by certain drugs—and by alcohol (27–30).
3. Clinical studies, largely epidemiologic, of the extent and nature of alcoholism in schizophrenia.
4. Controlled trials of different treatment methods for the double problems.

MONITORING TREATMENT OUTCOME

Apart from measurement of extrapyramidal side effects, the existing methods for measuring a patient's symptoms, behavior, and psychological and clinical status are probably sufficient for most research in the immediate future.

One prominent difficulty, however, is that treatment outcome is seen by many as involving much more than symptoms and behavior—it is, they say, a matter of quality of life. "What," the critics ask, "have you done to improve the patient's quality of life?" The implication is, of course, that we have done nothing. Nor can we even begin to answer that question in a scientific manner until we devise an instrument to assess "quality of life."

Such assessment is irrelevant for some types of schizophrenia research. It is possible to take the narrow attitude that the main purpose of medical intervention is to relieve symptoms and that relief of illness is part of the "quality of life." This is, however, an attitude that will not satisfy the critic. The "quality of life" has many different parameters; all of which taken together can measure the outcome of treatment. It would be helpful, therefore, to define the parameters that enter into "quality of life," and to develop a systematic approach to their measurement.

Preliminary collaborative work with investigators in Wisconsin, Britain, Sweden, and Greece has given reasonable ground for hope that a suitable scale can be developed to facilitate this objective.

STATISTICAL TECHNIQUES

For some research purposes, traditional statistical techniques such as simple *t*- and *F* tests, will suffice. But in clinical research every group of patients is likely to contain a few extreme or unusual cases, so-called outliers. Particularly in schizophrenia, the variability is great. In clinical research we must be interested in the unusual values, particularly when prediction of therapeutic outcome may be an issue. The "outlier" is precisely the type of patient who may have a deviant outcome. It is extremely important, therefore, to find out whether a particular treatment works in the same way for everybody, or only for a few unusual individuals.

Various methods of statistical analysis have been suggested for studying the influence of "outliers," but this is a greatly neglected area (8,9). Thus it is important to do the fundamental statistical research that will provide a basis for meaningful studies of unusual clinical cases.

SUMMARY

In selecting targets for research that seem most likely to benefit patients suffering from chronic schizophrenia, the thrust should be to prevent, reduce, or remedy chronicity, and not merely to palliate symptoms. A strategy is formulated that focuses on individual differences and vulnerabilities; on selecting the right treatment for a patient; and on measuring therapeutic progress. To attain these objectives, the following areas require study:

1. Identification of individuals at high risk for a future schizophrenic episode.
2. Integration of the treatment and support systems.

3. Development of better methods for the rapid and economical measurement of blood and tissue levels of antipsychotic drugs and other substances.
4. Evaluation of individual differences in response to treatment and the relationship to optimal treatment modalities and outcome predictability.
5. Evaluation of optimal outpatient drug and psychological therapy.
6. Assessment of family factors in aggravating schizophrenia.
7. Evaluating racial and cultural differences in response to treatment.
8. Research in the monitoring and early detection of side effects.
9. Defining objectively the borderline between alcoholism and schizophrenia.
10. Developing methods for monitoring treatment outcome.
11. Statistical techniques for dealing with "outliers" or unusual cases.

REFERENCES

1. Asarnow, R. F., Cromwell, R. L., and Rennick, P. M. (1978): Cognition and evoked response measures of information processing in schizophrenics with and without a family history of schizophrenia. *J. Nerv. Ment. Dis.,* 166:719–730.
2. Brown, G., Birley, J., and Wing, J. (1972): Influence of family life in the course of schizophrenic disorders. A replication. *Br. J. Psychiatry,* 121:241–258.
3. Cooper, T. B., Simpson, G. M., and Lee, J. H. (1976): Thymoleptic and neuroleptic drug plasma levels in psychiatry: Current status. *Int. Rev. Neurobiol.,* 19:269–309.
4. Cromwell, R. J. (1972): Strategies for studying schizophrenic behavior. *Psychopharmacologia,* 24:121–146.
5. Cromwell, R. J. (1978): Problems in applying information processing methodology to schizophrenia (Discussion). *J. Psychiatr. Res.,* 14:327–331.
6. Curry, S. H. (1968): Method for the estimation of nanogram quantities of chlorpromazine and some of its relatively non-polar metabolites in plasma, using gas chromatography with an electron capture detector. *Anal. Chem.,* 40:1251–1256.
7. Denber, M. J. A. (1978): *Sound Spectrum Analysis of the Mentally Ill.* Thesis prepared for the University of Rochester, Rochester, New York.
8. Dixon, W. J. (1960): Simplified estimation from Censored Normal Samples. *Ann. Math. Stat.,* 31:385–391.
9. Dixon, W. J., and Tukey, J. W. (1968): Approximate behavior of the distribution of Winsorized *t. Technometrics,* 10:83–89.
10. Gardos, G., and Cole, J. O. (1978): Maintenance antipsychotic therapy: For whom and how long? In: *Psychopharmacology: A Generation of Progress,* edited by M. A. Lipton, A. DiMascio, and F. Killam, pp. 1169–1178. Raven Press, New York.
11. Garmezy, N. (1978): Attentional processes in adult schizophrenia and in children at risk. *J. Psychiatr. Res.,* 14:3–45.
12. Holzman, P. S., Kringlen, E., Levy, D. L., Proctor, L. R., and Haberman, S. (1978): Smooth eye pursuit movements in twins discordant for schizophrenia. *J. Psychiatr. Res.,* 14:111–120.
13. Holzman, P. S., Levy, D. L., and Proctor, L. R. (1978): The several qualities of attention in schizophrenia. *J. Psychiatr. Res.,* 14:99–110.
14. Kane, J., Rifkin, A., Quitkin, F., and Klein, D. (1976): Antipsychotic drug blood levels and clinical outcome. In: *Progress in Drug Treatment,* pp. 399–408. Brunner/Mazel, New York.

14a. Klein, D. F., and Davis, J. M. (1969): *Diagnosis and Drug Treatment of Psychiatric Disorders,* pp. 231–236. Williams & Wilkins, Baltimore.

15. Kornetsky, C., and Orzach, M. H. (1978): The effects of antipsychotic medication and diagnostic criteria on distractibility in schizophrenia. *J. Psychiatr. Res.,* 14:81–91.
16. May, P. R. A., and Goldberg, S. C. (1978): Prediction of schizophrenic patients' responses to pharmacotherapy. In: *Psychopharmacology: A Generation of Progress,* edited by M. A. Lipton, A. DiMascio, and K. F. Killam, pp. 1139–1153. Raven Press, New York.
17. May, P. R. A., and Van Putten, T. (1978): Plasma levels of chlorpromazine in schizophrenia: A critical review of the literature. *Arch. Gen. Psychiatry,* 35:1081–1086.

18. May, P. R. A., Van Putten, T., Jenden, D. J., and Cho, A. K. (1978): Test dose response in schizophrenia: Chlorpromazine blood and saliva levels. *Arch. Gen. Psychiatry,* 35:1091–1097.
19. May, P. R. A., Van Putten, T., Yale, C., Potepan, P., Jenden, D. J., Fairchild, M. D., and Dixon, W. J. (1976): Predicting individual responses to drug treatment in schizophrenia: A test dose model. *J. Nerv. Ment. Dis.,* 162:177–184.
20. Neuchterlein, K. H. (1977): Reaction time and attention in schizophrenia: A critical evaluation of the data and theories. *Schizophr. Bull.,* 3:373–428.
21. Salzman, F., Klein, R. H., and Strauss, J. S. (1978): Pendulum eye tracking in remitted psychiatric patients. *J. Psychiatr. Res.,* 14:121–126.
22. Teknekron, Inc. (1977): Improving California's Mental Health System: A framework for public contributions. Report prepared for California Assembly Permanent Subcommittee on Mental Health and Developmental Disabilities, September 30.
23. Usdin, E. (1971): The assay of CPZ and metabolites in blood, urine and other tissues: Critical review. *Clin. Lab. Sci.,* 2:347–391.
24. Van Putten, T., and May, P. R. A. (1978): Akinetic depression in schizophrenia. *Arch. Gen. Psychiatry,* 35:1101–1107.
25. Van Putten, T., and May, P. R. A. (1978): Subjective response as a predictor of outcome in pharmacotherapy: The consumer has a point. *Arch. Gen. Psychiatry,* 35:477–480.
26. Vaughn, C., and Leff, J. P. (1976): The influences of family and social factors on the course of psychiatric illness. *Br. J. Psychiatry,* 129:125–137.
27. Wetterberg, L. (1964): Oral contraceptives and acute intermittent porphyria. *Lancet,* ii:1178–1179.
28. Wetterberg, L. 1966): Acute porphyria and lead poisoning. *Lancet,* i:498.
29. Wetterberg, L. (1967): *A Neuropsychiatric and Genetical Investigation of Acute Intermittent Porphyria,* pp. 1–87. Svenska Bokforlaget, Stockholm.
30. Wetterberg, L. (1978): Schizophrenia as an inborn error of metabolism. Paper presented at Second World Congress, Barcelona, Spain, August 31, Sept. 6.

Discussion

Cole: You have a good place for making films and videotapes at UCLA. What about producing training and reference films to show people: "This is +1 tremor, this is +2 cogwheeling, this is choreoathetoid movement," going through the examination to show examples of mild, moderate, and severe neurological side effects?

May: With regard to technological aids, we are working on diagnostic instruments that are sufficiently sensitive to tell from tremor in your outstretched hand whether or not you've smoked a cigarette.

Freed: You described what I might call a tertiary prevention program for the VA to prevent recidivism. Can we do better and move it up to secondary prevention?

May: You mean, could we take people at risk who have not yet had a schizophrenic break? Actually, that's what I had in mind: whether we could identify, by psychophysiological or biochemical markers, people being discharged from the military or veterans who have the susceptibility but haven't yet had a break.

Freed: People who are not yet VA clientele—

May: But are real candidates to become so, because they have a vulnerability that we can identify. Some of the speakers on this program are experts on attention and perception and biochemical markers. This is a challenge to them, to develop markers that identify patients at risk.

Meltzer: Turning to research strategies: You pointed out that schizophrenia can be episodic; if so, those patients who have psychotic breaks and then recover might be good subjects for high-risk strategies. On the other hand, Dr. Carpenter seemed to be saying that the episodic patient might not be a good subject for research. However, I disagree with this, for three reasons: One, such patients provide a chance to study those state dependent processes that might be relevant to the illness; two, they provide an opportunity to study what might be a less malignant form of the disease; and three, they may provide an opportunity to study its earlier stages. Medicine gives many examples where studies of end stages or the most malignant forms are less valuable than studies of the early.

Kleinman: On one topic you mentioned—neuroleptic blood levels—we've done several studies with haloperidol and chlorpromazine. Our collaborators, Dr. Perel and Dr. Forrest, cautioned us about trying to collect plasma or serum levels in Vacutainer tubes, because the stoppers may contain a substance that alters the plasma by pulling the neuroleptics up into red blood cells (5).

May: Thank you; we've heard about that.

Brown: About your groups who had syntonic and dysphoric responses to a loading dose of antipsychotic: Can you say more about the outcome, and were there any differences in diagnosis between the people who responded with dysphoria and those with syntonia?

May: All were diagnosed as schizophrenic by reasonable criteria. The difference seemed to be that the people who responded in a dysphoric way were less disorganized and seemed to have more insight. (I'm not convinced that schizophrenic patients ever have real insight.) Being in better shape, they could complain more effectively. The outcome of being kept on the drug was either that they didn't comply or, if they did, that the outcome was poor.

Carpenter: Concerning dysphoric and syntonic affective response to drugs, our patients, treated for sustained periods off drugs, reported in similar terms when contrasting previous psychotic episodes treated with drugs with the present episode treated off medication. We didn't determine whether there was a predictive relationship to treatment outcome, but patients' subjective experience of sustained medication dichotomized similar to your test dose responses.

Nasrallah: What about the placebo effect of that thiothixine (Navane) shot you gave the patients? Would they have responded the same way to a shot of saline?

May: I'd like to see someone design the perfect experiment, which, in one patient, would disentangle the effects of placebo and a single dose of antipsychotic drug. One can't give a placebo on a battlefield, and we're in battlefield conditions, so we'll do our predicting from one dose of the drug, which undoubtedly has a placebo effect also.

Cole: Is there any objection to trying a series of drugs if patients don't like the first one? We have schizophrenics who can't tolerate thioridazine (Mellaril), but are reasonably comfortable on fluphenazine (Prolixin).

May: Absolutely right. Chlorpromazine was the first drug we used. Navane happened to be the second; we've finished collecting data on that, and we're about to study a depot drug, I'm not sure which. If haloperidol made a patient feel terrible, I'd try a dose of another drug.

Itil: We recently completed a study within the VA system of the sort just suggested by Dr. Cole. To a group of chronic therapy-resistant schizophrenic patients, we gave test dosages of four different neuroleptics and placebo, with findings I have shown in my talk. Unfortunately, these patients were not communicative enough to provide any kind of clinical responses. However, we have also conducted a large study in three countries giving test dosages of five different neuroleptics, with placebo control, to normal volunteers. Our preliminary results show that at least two neuroleptics produce dysphoric reactions in normals—namely, thiothixine (Navane) and Molindone, whereas chlorpromazine is not so dysphoric in its effect. However, a single test dose of neuroleptic causes much more side effect in a Turkish population than in American patients, with a German population intermediate.

Carpenter: In regard to racial or regional differences in drug response, many psychiatrists from Asian and African countries have insisted that much smaller doses of neuroleptics are required in their countries to obtain an antipsychotic effect.

Meltzer: I was fascinated by your mention of racial differences, because I've been restudying serum dopamine beta-hydroxylase (DBH) activity in schizophrenia. Previously, I and others found no difference in serum DBH between schizophrenics and normals (4), but Nagatsu in Japan, who literally invented the DBH assay, collaborated with Japanese psychiatrists in a large-scale study of serum DBH in schizophrenics and found a striking decrease in their DBH compared to normals (2). The Fujita study employed a reliable DBH assay; and the clinical assessment seemed reliable—they used Schneiderian criteria, so I repeated a large series of schizophrenics and controls and generally replicated my earlier finding of no overall difference, except that we did find a small subset of chronic paranoid schizophrenics whose serum DBH activity was well below the median of our controls. In writing up the work, I suggested a possible evidence for the discrepancy was that DBH is genetically determined and that in Japan there may be a linkage between DBH and schizophrenia that doesn't occur in other populations. Did I hear that the Japanese don't permit the use of psychotropic or neuroleptic drugs until there have been dose-finding studies done in Japan? Perhaps there is a genetic factor.

May: The Chinese tell me that they're susceptible to alcohol. Apparently it causes a facial flush.

Meltzer: Interestingly, there are some data suggesting a relationship between alcoholism and serum DBH activity. Ewing and Rouse (1) reported that normal volunteers with lower plasma DBH activity had fewer positive mood states after a standard dose of ethanol than those with higher DBH activity who had much more positive responses to alcohol ingestion. However, Sullivan et al. (6) found normal serum DBH activity in chronic alcoholics. Lerner et al. (3) found normal DBH activity in the CSF of alcoholics.

Nasrallah: Regarding the relationship between alcoholism and depot fluphenazine (Prolixin Decanoate), I *(unpublished data)* found in 35 patients on Prolixin and about 50 patients on lithium that 80% of the lithium patients but only 1% of the Prolixin patients were heavy drinkers.

May: You seem to be saying either that schizophrenics don't drink or that the depot drug does something to alcoholism.

Nasrallah: Apparently, those who used to drink gave up drinking once on Prolixin. I think the depot drug population is different from the oral drug population, perhaps because of the enforced compliance, or because the depot blocks the euphorogenic effects of alcohol, or because its side effects synergize with those of alcohol so that the patients avoid it.

REFERENCES

1. Ewing, J. A., and Rouse, B. A. (1978): Alcohol susceptibility and plasma dopamine-b-hydroxylase activity. *Res. Commun. Chem. Pathol. Pharmacol.,* 8:551–554.
2. Fujita, L, Ito, T., Maruta, K., Teradaira, R., Beppu, H., Nakagami, Y., Kato, Y., Nagatsu, T., and Kato, T. (1978): Serum dopamine-b-hydroxylase in schizophrenic patients. *J. Neurochem.,* 30:1569–1572.
3. Lerner, P., Goodwin, F. K., van Kammen, D. P., Post, R. M., Major, L. F., Ballenger, J. C., and Lovenberg, W. (1978): Dopamine-b-hydroxylase in the cerebrospinal fluid of psychiatric patients. *Biol. Psychiatry,* 13:685–694.
4. Meltzer, H. Y., Cho, H. W., Carroll, B. J., and Russo, P. (1976): Serum dopamine-b-hydroxylase activity in the affective psychoses and schizophrenia. *Arch. Gen. Psychiatry,* 33:585–591.
5. Midha, K. K., Loo, J. C. K., and Rowe, M. L. (1979): The influence of blood sampling techniques on the distribution of chlorpromazine and tricyclic anti-depressants between plasma and whole blood. *Res. Commun. Psychol. Psychiatr. Behav.,* 4:193–203.
6. Sullivan, J. L., Stanfield, C. N., Schanberg, S., and Cavenar, J. (1978): Serum dopamine-b-hydroxylase in chronic alcoholism. *Psychol. Med.,* 8:505–508.

Perspectives in Schizophrenia Research,
edited by C. Baxter and T. Melnechuk.
Raven Press, New York, 1980.

Pharmacological Studies of Tardive Dyskinesia: Implications for Future Research

*,**Philip A. Berger and **,†Kenneth L. Davis

**Department of Psychiatry and Behavioral Sciences, Stanford University School of Medicine, Stanford, California 94305; **Stanford Psychiatric Clinical Research Center, Veterans Administration Medical Center, Palo Alto, California 94304; and †Department of Psychiatry, Mount Sinai School of Medicine, Veterans Administration Medical Center, Bronx, New York 10468*

LAYPERSON'S SUMMARY

Tardive dyskinesia is an involuntary movement disorder, most often involving the mouth, lips, and tongue (sucking and smacking, chewing motions, tongue-thrusting) and sometimes extending to the limbs or trunk (rocking and swaying, shoulder shrugging, pelvic rotation, grunting, abnormal breathing). It is a socially embarrassing and sometimes disabling condition, interfering with speech, manual dexterity, eating, and breathing. The movements are involuntary, and any attempts to control them may actually make the movements more severe.

Tardive dyskinesia is the most severe side effect of the best drug treatment known for chronic schizophrenia, the long-term use of antipsychotic medications (neuroleptics). No clear relationship has been found between duration or dosage of treatment and the onset of tardive dyskinesia. About 15 to 20% of hospitalized psychiatric patients are reported to have tardive dyskinesia. All classes of antipsychotics seem to be capable of causing tardive dyskinesia; and there have been cases reported following the use of antihistamines, antidepressants (tricyclics), amphetamines, anticonvulsants, and anticholinergics.

Schizophrenia has been hypothesized to be caused by an overabundance of the brain chemical dopamine, which serves as a transmitter or chemical messenger in the nervous system. Antipsychotics seem to work by blocking dopamine receptors (the places in the brain where dopamine attaches to transmit its message). The dopamine receptor blockade results in underactivity in the dopamine receptors; the body is thought to react by increasing the number of dopamine receptors. The increased number of dopamine receptors eventually would cause overactivity in dopamine systems, resulting in an imbalance between dopamine and another neurotransmitter, acetylcholine. This increase in dopamine receptors and the resulting imbalance is thought to cause tardive dyskinesia.

Dopamine-blocking agents, including the antipsychotics, and dopamine-depleting drugs suppress the movements of tardive dyskinesia; but, while masking the symptoms, such medications actually make the tardive dyskinesia worse by increasing the dopamine overactivity. Anticholinergic medications which block acetylcholine in the nervous system also worsen tardive dyskinesia by further upsetting the balance of dopamine and acetylcholine. Acetylcholine-like drugs (cholinomimetics), then, would be expected to improve tardive dyskinesia. Two cholinomimetics, physostigmine and choline chloride, have been tested with some success; studies indicate, however, that such drugs are effective in the treatment of only some of the cases of tardive dyskinesia. Even when improvement is seen, it is sometimes more statistically significant than clinically significant (e.g., a reduction of chewing movements from 30 to 20 per minute does not mean much to a patient's life). However, any improvement is important in suggesting the possibility of an effective treatment.

An important question raised by the incidence of tardive dyskinesia deserves immediate and urgent attention. The antipsychotic-induced increase in dopamine receptors in the nigrostriatal area thought to account for the movements of tardive dyskinesia might also be developing in other dopamine pathways in the nervous system, the mesolimbic system. The mesolimbic system has been proposed as the brain area from which schizophrenic symptoms arise: the overabundance of dopamine in this system causes psychotic symptoms until the dopamine is blocked by neuroleptics. If an increase in dopamine receptors in this area were to occur, however, the long-term effect of antipsychotic drugs actually may be to make the psychosis more severe. The increased severity of the psychotic symptoms, like the tardive dyskinesia, could be masked by the antipsychotic dopamine-blocking action of the drugs, becoming apparent only when the medication was discontinued. If an increase in dopamine receptors in the mesolimbic brain area was caused by antipsychotics, a nonpsychotic patient treated with antipsychotics could be expected to develop psychosis; such a case has been reported.

A carefully designed, multicenter prospective study is needed to address these important issues:

1. To determine the true prevalence and incidence of tardive dyskinesia; to develop strict, uniform diagnostic criteria and assessment techniques.
2. To determine the relationship of tardive dyskinesia to other movement disorders, to discriminate and study the different subtypes of tardive dyskinesia, some of which improve or remit spontaneously while others are irreversible or untreatable.
3. To correlate the onset and severity of tardive dyskinesia with specific neuroleptics or multiple neuroleptic use (polypharmacy), unique EEG patterns, age, sex, brain disease, early extrapyramidal side effects of antipsychotics, the contribution of other drugs (especially anticholinergics), and the importance of "drug holidays."
4. To develop and test new potential treatments for tardive dyskinesia, includ-

ing cholinomimetics and GABA-like compounds thought to decrease dopamine activity, and to study the possible preventive effect of lithium treatment.

5. To develop and study new antipsychotic agents that may not cause tardive dyskinesia.

6. To determine whether there is a mesolimbic equivalent to tardive dyskinesia, i.e., to determine whether long-term treatment with antipsychotic medications may worsen schizophrenia in some patients.

7. To further expand our knowledge, on a basic science level and with the use of animal and clinical studies, of tardive dyskinesia and schizophrenia.

INTRODUCTION

Tardive dyskinesia is a complex syndrome of hyperkinetic involuntary movements of the mouth, lips, and tongue, sometimes accompanied by choreiform movements of the limbs or trunk. The so-called buccolinguomasticatory triad is most commonly seen and consists of sucking, smacking movements of the lips, lateral jaw movements, chewing movements, tongue-thrusting, and at times tic-like motions of the lips, eyes, and eyebrows. Extremities may show choreiform or athetoid movements and the trunk may also move. Lordosis, rocking and swaying, axial dystonias, shoulder shrugging, rotatory pelvic movements, grunting, and respiratory arrhythmias are also seen. Similar to choreoathetosis in general, movements in tardive dyskinesia may worsen with anxiety and decrease with relaxation or sedation. They disappear in sleep. Volitional motor activity or attempts to voluntarily inhibit portions of the dyskinesia often enhance the movements (1,5,18,48,51,61).

Tardive dyskinesia causes social embarrassment. It can also interfere with speech, manual dexterity, eating, and respiration, and it can occasionally produce significant disability. Tardive dyskinesia is a major problem because it is the most important side effect limiting the use of maintenance neuroleptics, which is the best pharmacological treatment for chronic schizophrenia (7).

EPIDEMIOLOGY OF TARDIVE DYSKINESIA

The literature presents a confusing picture regarding the incidence and prevalence of tardive dyskinesia. The reported prevalence in institutionalized patients has varied between 0.5% and 56%, with a mean value of about 15 to 20% (1,5). The differences in methods of diagnosis and assessment obviously complicate accurate determination of prevalence. Tarsy and Baldessarini (5) report that 5% of patients in mental hospitals and about 20% of elderly, chronically institutionalized patients exhibit drug-induced tardive dyskinesia. Simpson and colleagues (66) found that 11% of their population had the syndrome. Crane (18) reported 17.6% incidence of tardive dyskinesia in his 1973 review of 22 reported series involving 22,399 neuroleptic-treated patients. Obviously, further studies using strict diagnostic criteria are needed. These studies will also be needed to sort out the epidemiology of the illness. The evidence for the role of neuroleptics in tardive dyskinesia is mainly epidemiological, but it is convincing. Although tardive dyskinesia is usually seen after several years of treatment, onset within the first 6 months has been reported (5). Attempts to determine the amount of drug exposure necessary to produce tardive dyskinesia have been inconclusive. Many studies report an association between the duration of drug treatment, the total dosage, and tardive dyskinesia (5). Others are unable to confirm these findings (47,66).

Gardos et al. (34) used a discriminant function analysis and could distinguish patients with tardive dyskinesia from those without on the basis of duration of low-potency neuroleptic treatment, previous electroconvulsive therapy (ECT), length of neuroleptic therapy, total long-acting fluphenazine, and abnormal electroencephalographs (EEGs). Some of the original studies suggested that tardive dyskinesia was more common in the elderly, in women, and in patients with preexisting organic brain disease, but each of these associations has been challenged (5,51,66). Wegner and colleagues (78) report a high incidence of the B-mitten EEG in patients with tardive dyskinesia. Simpson and colleagues (66) in 1978 compared a group with tardive dyskinesia to a hospitalized control group. The tardive dyskinesia patients were older, more often female, and had been hospitalized for slightly longer, but this study could not confirm higher total neuroleptic intake or find significant differences in anticholinergic, antianxiety, or antidepressant medication use and no difference in duration of multiple neuroleptic use (polypharmacy). The Simpson study also could not implicate specific neuroleptic classes (66). Ayd in 1973 (4) reported that long-acting fluphenazine was less liable, whereas Gardos et al. (34) in 1977 reported it was more liable, to be associated with tardive dyskinesia. There may or may not be an association between tardive dyskinesia and the severity of early parkinsonian symptoms. All classes of antipsychotics seem to be capable of causing tardive dyskinesia, but interestingly, occasional cases are reported following only antihistamine medications (73), large doses of tricyclics (32), anticholinergic medications (9,30), diphenylhydantoin (16), and amphetamines (55).

Thus, epidemiology of tardive dyskinesia is imperfectly characterized. The possible association with specific neuroleptics, unique EEG patterns, age, sex, organic brain disease, early extrapyramidal reactions, use of anticholinergic medications, polypharmacy, and the contribution of other drugs will have to be carefully studied.

DIFFERENTIAL DIAGNOSIS

It is necessary to distinguish between tardive dyskinesia and other choreoathetoid movement disorders. For example, the movement disorders of schizophrenia can mimic tardive dyskinesia. Kraeplin (52,68) observed that:

> There is still another type of convulsive movement, involving the muscles of the eye and speech, which is both characteristic and of frequent occurrence

> in dementia praecox. Some of these movements correspond exactly to the movements of expression; wrinkling of the eyebrow, distortion of the mouth, rolling the eyes, and those other facial movements which are characterized as grimacing. These movements remind one of choreic movements and are quite independent of ideas and feelings. There may be associated with them smacking of the lips, clucking the tongue, sudden grunting, sniffing, and coughing. Furthermore, in the lips we observe very rapid rhythmical movements. More often there exists a peculiar choreiform movement of the mouth which may be described as an athetoid ataxia.

Bleuler in 1911 (10) reported "grimaces of all kinds, peculiar ways of shrugging the shoulder, extraordinary movements of the tongue and lips." These early descriptions of unmedicated schizophrenic patients are obviously similar to drug-induced tardive dyskinesia.

Some patients with Parkinson's disease who are on high doses of levodopa develop symptoms that can be indistinguishable from tardive dyskinesia. Gerlach (36) reports that levodopa hyperkinesia shows an increased tendency to oral preponderance with age, whereas tardive dyskinesia gets worse with age, without any changes in distribution. Levodopa dyskinesia does not cause a problem with differential diagnosis, but it may help in understanding the pathophysiology of tardive dyskinesia. Spontaneous orofacial dyskinesia, however, can be difficult to distinguish from neuroleptic-induced tardive dyskinesia (2). Some patients with the tardive dyskinesia syndrome have no history of drug exposure. Spontaneous orofacial dyskinesia may be rare. Some studies suggest that 1 to 2% of tardive dyskinesia is actually spontaneous dyskinesia, but other studies suggest that as many as 10 to 20% of patients in mental institutions, of the elderly, or of nursing home residents have spontaneous dyskinesia (5,29,39). Spontaneous orofacial dyskinesia may be the correct diagnosis in the reports of tardive dyskinesia following tricyclic antidepressants, antihistamines, or other medications. The natural history and epidemiology of spontaneous orofacial dyskinesia, indistinguishable clinically from tardive dyskinesia, must be studied.

In pure form, Huntington's chorea can easily be distinguished from tardive dyskinesia by examining the family history and noting a progressive dementia with no neuroleptic history. But in many cases, there is no reliable paternal family history, and patients with Huntington's disease may be using neuroleptics. Therefore, in some patients the differential diagnosis of Huntington's disease from tardive dyskinesia is difficult to make (14).

The so-called rabbit syndrome refers to another distinguishable movement disorder. It is a late onset neuroleptic-induced extrapyramidal syndrome, characterized by rhythmic 5.0 to 5.5 per second involuntary movements of the masticatory musculature that mimic the chewing movements of a rabbit (77). The syndrome is readily reversible when neuroleptics are discontinued. The rabbit syndrome responds to anticholinergics and persists in stage I non-rapid eye movement (NREM) sleep whereas tardive dyskinesia does not (67,77). This suggests that it is a syndrome distinct from tardive dyskinesia, but its relationship to tardive dyskinesia should be studied.

The subtypes of tardive dyskinesia have also been poorly defined. Categories such as physostigmine responsive versus nonresponsive, reversible versus irreversible, remitting versus nonremitting, orofacial versus orofacial plus truncal, and dyskinesias of the extremities are dichotomies that, among others, should be considered.

NEUROPHARMACOLOGY OF TARDIVE DYSKINESIA

Tardive dyskinesia is proposed to result from a state of dopaminergic overactivity or supersensitivity which is the striatal response to long-term neuroleptic blockade (49,50). The result of the dopamine overactivity is an imbalance between dopamine and acetylcholine in the nigrostriatum (19,28,37,49,50).

The dopamine-acetylcholine imbalance proposed in tardive dyskinesia is the opposite of the imbalance seen in Parkinson's disease (19,28,37). The evidence for both the dopamine supersensitivity and the dopamine-acetylcholine imbalance comes from pharmacological studies with both animals and humans (19,24,37,50). Chronic administration of neuroleptics to animals results in an enhanced behavioral sensitivity of these animals to dopamine agonists such as apomorphine or methylphenidate (71), and to an increase in striatal dopamine receptor sites or affinity, as demonstrated by ^{3}H-spiroperidol binding (13,60).

An example of the dopamine hyperactivity is seen in the animal model used in our studies (24,25). Rats are given 0.5 mg/kg subcutaneously of haloperidol for 28 consecutive days. On days 36 to 39 animals are challenged with 0.125 to 1.0 mg/kg of apomorphine subcutaneously. Animals treated for 29 days with haloperidol have more severe apomorphine-induced stereotypy. Other investigators such as Burt et al. (13), Muller and Seeman (60), and Pert et al. (62) have shown that animals treated chronically with neuroleptics bind more ^{3}H-spiroperidol in the striatum as well. In this proposed animal model of tardive dyskinesia, we find that choline chloride administered by gavage for 11 days immediately following the discontinuation of haloperidol is superior to water in preventing the severity of apomorphine-induced stereotypic behavior (24,25).

PHARMACOLOGICAL STUDIES IN HUMANS WITH TARDIVE DYSKINESIA

The evidence for dopamine supersensitivity and dopamine-acetylcholine imbalance in humans comes mainly from pharmacological studies (19). Dopamine-blocking agents, including all chemical classes of neuroleptics, suppress tardive dyskinesia. Unfortunately, they are not the ideal treatment since they are the original cause of the syndrome and should eventually exacerbate the dopamine supersensitivity.

Dopamine-depleting agents, such as reserpine and tetrabenazine, and blockers of catecholamine synthesis also suppress tardive dyskinesia (5), and theoretically could also add to dopamine supersensitivity. The opposite approach, that is, levodopa, worsens tardive dyskinesia (49).

The cholinergic pharmacology of tardive dyskinesia is not clear-cut. However, in general, anticholinergic agents worsen or exacerbate tardive dyskinesia (19, 28,37). Treatment with cholinomimetics could be expected to improve tardive dyskinesia (19).

In our study, five patients with tardive dyskinesia were improved by treatment with physostigmine (19,21). This is consistent with some reports (31), but not all investigators agree. For example, Tarsy et al. (72) report that patients with tardive dyskinesia are not improved with physostigmine. Casey and Denney (15) find some patients with tardive dyskinesia are improved by physostigmine and others are not.

Other cholinomimetics such as choline chloride also may improve tardive dyskinesia. The literature on treatment of tardive dyskinesia is filled with positive reports that have never been confirmed by subsequent investigations. Methodological problems abound in assessing the efficacy of drug treatments for this disorder. The gradual improvement seen in many patients with tardive dyskinesia is often overlooked (21,58). Slow improvement in the symptoms of tardive dyskinesia have occasionally been seen in patients who have been neuroleptic-free for years; furthermore, early signs of tardive dyskinesia often completely remit. Therefore, positive effects often attributed to the experimental drug may actually be manifestations of the natural history and progression of tardive dyskinesia. In order to control for the possibility of a slow, steady improvement process, a placebo period should follow as well as precede the period of investigational drug administration. Protocols in which the movement frequency at the end of the period of experimental drug administration is compared to that in the preceding base-line or placebo period, rather than to movement frequency in a subsequent placebo period, bias toward finding a positive drug effect (21).

To date, two double-blind controlled studies have been conducted to test the efficacy of choline chloride in tardive dyskinesia. We have now administered choline chloride to six patients with tardive dyskinesia (19,24). These patients have had an average duration of buccolinguomasticatory movements of over 12 months. All patients were significantly improved by choline chloride treatment. However, three patients had no exacerbation of their movements when placebo was substituted for choline at the end of the choline chloride treatment period. These three patients were also the patients who showed the largest improvement over baseline movement frequencies. It is impossible to know if these three patients were actually improved by choline chloride. They may have displayed a process of natural remission, or a combination of a positive choline effect and an underlying trend toward spontaneous improvement. Thus, from our data, it can be definitely concluded that three patients were unequivocally improved by choline chloride (21).

The other double-blind study of choline chloride in tardive dyskinesia, by

Growden et al. (41), used either an A-B or B-A design. Half of the patients received a placebo followed by choline, and the other half received choline followed by placebo. Obviously an unambiguous statement about the efficacy of choline in this study should be based on the latter group of patients; nine of the 20 patients improved, five markedly and four moderately. It is obvious from the case descriptions that at least two patients got worse when placebo was substituted. Thus, if a strict analysis of the effect of choline on tardive dyskinesia is applied, in which movement frequencies during choline treatment must be significantly less than during the subsequent placebo period, then a relatively small number of patients can actually be included as unequivocal responders. Therefore, some patients with tardive dyskinesia respond to choline chloride, whereas others do not. For some patients this response is more statistically significant than clinically significant. To reduce chewing movements from 30 to 20 per minute may not mean much to a patient's life. However, the statistically significant response of some patients with tardive dyskinesia to choline chloride suggests that the movement disorder can be treated.

Whether choline is a cholinomimetic is an important consideration. On the positive side, choline was reported to cause increased tyrosine hydroxylase activity in the corpus striatum and in the adrenal gland (74,75). This increase in activity was blocked by atropine. When given subcutaneously, we find that choline reverses stereotypy (25). Furthermore, our studies have shown a perfect correlation between physostigmine and choline response in all patients with tardive dyskinesia and Huntington's disease (19,21,24). Finally, another study reported that choline, like the cholinomimetics oxytremorine and physostigmine, increases striatal homovanillic acid (HVA), an effect which is blocked by atropine (42). Conversely, oral administration of choline chloride in our studies to non-haloperidol-treated animals did not reverse stereotypy (25). Our studies also report an imperfect correlation between the effects of physostigmine and choline chloride in studies of cholinergic mechanisms of human memory (8,26). In addition, morphine analgesia is potentiated by cholinomimetics but not by choline chloride (11,57). Thus, only if choline chloride is indeed a cholinomimetic, and if indeed its positive effect on tardive dyskinesia is mediated by this cholinomimetic activity, would the search for more effective cholinomimetics be expected to yield more efficacious treatments for tardive dyskinesia.

Other compounds such as lecithin (phosphatidyl choline) and deanol deserve mention as possible cholinomimetic treatments for tardive dyskinesia. Gelenberg et al. (35) report that lecithin is as effective as choline in tardive dyskinesia without producing the occasional objectionable odor of trimethylamine caused by choline chloride treatment. Further study is clearly needed here. Deanol (dimethylaminoethanol), the precursor of choline, was not found to be effective in our studies, perhaps because the dose (2.5 g) was too low (20). Casey and Denney (15) report that deanol is effective in some patients with tardive dyskinesia. Even if lecithin and deanol prove to be effective in tardive dyskinesia, it is not clear whether they in fact increase cholinergic activity.

The relationship between GABA and acetylcholine in the nigrostriatum is the subject of considerable controversy in neurochemistry. One simple hypothesis of this relationship has been proposed by Groves et al. (40), who suggest that GABA and acetylcholine inhibit dopaminergic neurotransmission. This hypothesis predicts that cholinomimetics and GABA agonists would act to decrease dopamine hyperactivity in nigrostriatal dopamine neurons. Several compounds have been proposed to act as GABA agonists including baclofen, muscimol, and sodium valproate. Baclofen is probably not a GABA agonist, but it may act on substance P or be a phenylethylamine analogue (22). Muscimol does seem to increase GABA activity and has been used as an experimental treatment for tardive dyskinesia (69). Preliminary investigations report that sodium valproate and muscimol may improve tardive dyskinesia (54,69). If these two compounds in fact increase GABA activity, they are worthy of study in patients with tardive dyskinesia.

UNANSWERED QUESTIONS CONCERNING TARDIVE DYSKINESIA

More research is needed to determine the true prevalence and incidence of tardive dyskinesia. The observation that many patients with tardive dyskinesia spontaneously improve and that some completely remit raises the question of a possible separate subtype of the disorder. Other questions to be answered include the possible benefit of drug holidays and the effect of administering anticholinergics during early neuroleptic treatment on the development of tardive dyskinesia. In addition, it would be important to determine whether a correlation exists between tardive dyskinesia and plasma neuroleptic concentrations. This last question might also be approached more efficiently by using a measurement of plasma neuroleptic activity, rather than actually measuring plasma neuroleptic concentrations. For example, it should be possible to determine the prolactin-stimulating ability or ^{3}H-spiroperidol-displacing ability per ml of plasma in a patient receiving neuroleptics. These measures should be highly correlated with plasma neuroleptic concentrations but would offer several advantages. For example, measuring plasma neuroleptic activity would theoretically account for all active metabolites of neuroleptics and simultaneously account for the activity of more than one neuroleptic.

To answer these questions, a carefully designed, multicenter prospective study is necessary. The fluphenazine injection clinics could provide the ideal population for this difficult study. Uniform, strict diagnostic criteria will be needed, with meticulous record keeping for these essential data. Careful assessment techniques for improvement will be needed. One way of establishing uniform criteria for improvement or worsening in tardive dyskinesia would be to provide videotapes which had been rated in a standardized manner to all centers that participate in a collaborative investigation. Another method would be to develop a mechanical or electronic device which automatically records the abnormal involuntary movements of tardive dyskinesia. Such a device would greatly facilitate research of this disorder.

It is essential that new potential treatments for tardive dyskinesia continue to be developed and tested. Studies of new treatments using careful study design should be given a high priority. The importance of a pre- and post-experimental treatment placebo period in studies of tardive dyskinesia cannot be overemphasized. In addition, the relationship between cholinomimetics and GABA agonists should be further explored in basic and animal neuropharmacological studies. These studies are extremely important since it is possible that cholinomimetics and GABA agonists may improve tardive dyskinesia by decreasing dopamine release and thus providing the receptor with less dopamine. The net result would be that cholinomimetics and GABA agonists would ultimately cause dopamine supersensitivity and in the long run exacerbate tardive dyskinesia. Thus cholinomimetics and GABA agonists might be no better than neuroleptics in treating tardive dyskinesia. However, cholinomimetics and GABA agonists may improve tardive dyskinesia by mechanisms totally unrelated to dopamine neurons. Determining whether cholinomimetics and GABA agonists would eventually worsen tardive dyskinesia is not a trivial question. Both basic and clinical studies are urgently needed to better understand tardive dyskinesia and its improvement during cholinomimetic and GABA-agonist treatment. Use of the animal model of tardive dyskinesia and further human pharmacological and biological studies are essential to solve this problem.

Another question concerns the possible prophylactic effect of lithium on tardive dyskinesia. Pert et al. (62) used the animal model of tardive dyskinesia and ^{3}H-spiroperidol binding to show that in at least one experimental condition, pretreatment with and concomitant lithium administration prevented dopamine supersensitivity. The clinical implication of this study is that pretreatment and concomitant treatment with lithium carbonate in all patients given neuroleptics could prevent the development of tardive dyskinesia. This idea, with its practical implications, should be tested immediately.

Another important question is to determine if it is possible to develop an antipsychotic agent that does not cause tardive dyskinesia. To answer this question, we need to develop and test new antipsychotic agents that do not have the pharmacological profile of the standard neuroleptics. β-Endorphin and des-tyrosine-gamma-endorphin (DTγE) are two potential antipsychotics that deserve a high priority for clinical trials (6).

IS THERE A MESOLIMBIC EQUIVALENT TO TARDIVE DYSKINESIA?

There are numerous animal studies demonstrating that neuroleptics can cause dopamine supersensitivity in the nigrostriatal dopamine tract as described above (13,17,25,59,60,71). It is logical to ask whether the other major dopamine pathways also develop supersensitivity during neuroleptic administration. The evidence that demonstrates dopamine supersensitivity following neuroleptic administration in the tuberoinfundibular dopamine tract is contradictory (3, 53,56,64,70).

The mesolimbic dopamine pathway, which has been proposed as the neuroanatomical substrate of the schizophrenic symptoms, might also develop supersensitivity. The evidence for mesolimbic supersensitivity comes from both animal and human studies. The animal evidence has been predominantly indirect, since in most animal studies apomorphine is given systemically rather than directly into the mesolimbic system (45,76). The increased locomotion caused by apomorphine is assumed to be due to dopamine receptor supersensitivity in the nucleus accumbens. However, this assumption may not be justified. One animal study offers more direct evidence for mesolimbic dopamine supersensitivity (46). This study used a systemic MAO inhibitor followed by the intracerebral injection of apomorphine. We have also used this animal model (22). Haloperidol was given to rats for 28 days and dopamine was injected directly into the nucleus accumbens. Dopamine injections into the nucleus accumbens normally cause hyperactivity. However, in the haloperidol-treated animals, the hyperactivity produced by dopamine was significantly enhanced, suggesting nucleus accumbens supersensitivity (23). Recently, Muller and Seeman (60) have reported increases in the ^{3}H-spiroperidol binding in the accumbens in a similar animal study, also suggesting that neuroleptic treatment can induce mesolimbic dopamine supersensitivity in animals.

We and other investigators have suggested that there is a mesolimbic equivalent of tardive dyskinesia in humans treated with neuroleptics (27). The manifestation of such a syndrome might include sleeplessness, anxiety, and agitation since these symptoms were reported in many studies in the 1950s and 1960s as "neuroleptic withdrawal symptoms" (12,33,38,44). Far worse is the possibility that the long-term effect of neuroleptics may be to exacerbate schizophrenia in the very patients who initially had an improvement using these medications.

If a mesolimbic equivalent of tardive dyskinesia existed, it would predict that long-term neuroleptic treatment in a nonpsychotic patient might eventually cause psychosis. There is one report of a patient on neuroleptics without psychosis who developed psychosis for the first time when neuroleptics were withdrawn (65). This might represent one end of the spectrum of mesolimbic dopamine hypersensitivity. The large collaborative studies that established the efficacy of neuroleptics, done by both the Veterans Administration and the National Institute of Mental Health, always reported a group of patients who relapsed as soon as neuroleptics were withdrawn (43,63). Is it possible that these patients had mesolimbic dopamine supersensitivity? Collaborative studies involving longitudinal evaluations of the same patients on neuroleptics, biochemical and pharmacological studies on patients who are withdrawn from neuroleptics, and further animal studies will be needed to determine whether there really is a mesolimbic equivalent to tardive dyskinesia. The implications of such a syndrome would be enormous, suggesting that these studies are urgently needed.

ACKNOWLEDGMENTS

This work was supported by the Medical Research Service of the Veterans Administration and by the National Institute of Mental Health Specialized Research Center Grant MH-30854.

REFERENCES

1. ACNP-FDA Task Force (1973): Medical intelligence—Drug therapy. *N. Engl. J. Med.,* 289:20–24.
2. Altrocchi, P. H. (1972): Spontaneous oral-facial dyskinesia. *Arch. Neurol.,* 26:506–512.
3. Annunziato, L., and Moore, K. E. (1978): Increased ability of apomorphine to reduce serum concentrations of prolactin in rats treated chronically with alpha-methyltyrosine. *Life Sci.,* 21:1845–1849.
4. Ayd, F. J., Jr. (1973): Neuroleptic-induced extrapyramidal reactions: Incidence, manifestations and management. In: *The Future of Pharmacotherapy New Drug Delivery System,* edited by F. J. Ayd, Jr., pp. 77–88. International Drug Therapy Newsletter, Baltimore.
5. Baldessarini, R. J., and Tarsy, D. (1978): Tardive dyskinesia. In: *Psychopharmacology: A Generation of Progress,* edited by M. A. Lipton, A. DiMascio, and K. F. Killam, pp. 993–1004. Raven Press, New York.
6. Berger, P. A. (1978): Investigating the role of endogenous opioid peptides in psychiatric disorders. *Neurosci. Res. Program Bull.,* 16:585–599.
7. Berger, P. A. (1978): Medical treatment of mental illness. *Science,* 200:974–981.
8. Berger, P. A., Davis, K. L., and Hollister, L. E. (1979): Cholinomimetics in mania, schizophrenia and memory disorders. In: *Nutrition and the Brain,* edited by A. Barbeau, J. Growdon, and R. Wurtman, pp. 425–441. Raven Press, New York.
9. Birket-Smith, E. (1974): Abnormal involuntary movements induced by anticholinergic therapy. *Acta Neurol. Scand.,* 50:801–811.
10. Bleuler, E. (1950): *Dementia Praecox or the Group of Schizophrenics,* translated by J. Zinkin, from 1911 German Edition. International University Press, New York.
11. Botticelli, L. J., Lytle, L. D., and Wurtman, R. J. (1977): Choline-induced attenuation of morphine analgesia in the rat. *Commun. Psychopharmacol.,* 1:519–523.
12. Brooks, G. W. (1959): Withdrawal from neuroleptic drugs. *Am. J. Psychiatry,* 115:931–932.
13. Burt, D. R., Creese, J., and Snyder, S. H. (1977): Antischizophrenic drugs: Chronic treatment elevates dopamine receptor binding in brain. *Science,* 196:326–328.
14. Buxton, M. (1976): Diagnostic problems in Huntington's chorea and tardive dyskinesia. *Compr. Psychiatry,* 17:325–333.
15. Casey, D. E., and Denney, D. (1977): Pharmacological characterization of tardive dyskinesia. *Psychopharmacology,* 54:1–8.
16. Chadwick, D., Reynolds, E. H., and Marsden, C. D. (1976): Anticonvulsant-induced dyskinesias: A comparison with dyskinesias induced by neuroleptics. *J. Neurol. Neurosurg. Psychiatry,* 39:1210–1218.
17. Christensen, A. V., Fjalland, G., and Moller-Nielsen, I. (1976): On the supersensitivity of dopamine receptors, induced by neuroleptics. *Psychopharmacology,* 48:1–6.
18. Crane, G. E. (1973): Persistent dyskinesias. *Br. J. Psychiatry,* 122:395–405.
19. Davis, K. L., and Berger, P. A. (1978): Pharmacological investigations of the cholinergic imbalance hypotheses of movement disorders and psychosis. *Biol. Psychiatry,* 13:23–49.
20. Davis, K. L., Berger, P. A., and Hollister, L. E. (1977): Deanol in tardive dyskinesia. *Am. J. Psychiatry,* 134(7):807.
21. Davis, K. L., Berger, P. A., and Hollister, L. E. (1979): Clinical and preclinical experience with choline chloride in Huntington's disease and tardive dyskinesia: Unanswered questions. In: *Nutrition and the Brain,* edited by A. Barbeau, J. Growdon, and R. Wurtman, pp. 305–315. Raven Press, New York.
22. Davis, K. L., Hollister, L. E., and Berger, P. A. (1976): Baclofen in schizophrenia. *Lancet,* 1:1245.

23. Davis, K. L., Hollister, L. E., and Fritz, W. C. (1978): Induction of dopaminergic mesolimbic receptor sensitivity by haloperidol. *Life Sci.,* 23(15):1543–1548.
24. Davis, K. L., Hollister, L. E., Vento, A. L., and Berger, P. A. (1980): Cholinergic aspects of tardive dyskinesia: Human and animal studies. In: *Tardive Dyskinesia,* edited by J. M. Davis and R. C. Smith. Spectrum Press, New York *(in press).*
25. Davis, K. L., Hollister, L. E., Vento, A. L., and Simonton, S. (1978): Choline chloride in methylphenidate- and apomorphine-induced stereotypy. *Life Sci.,* 22:2171–2178.
26. Davis, K. L., Mohs, R. C., Tinklenberg, J. R., Hollister, L. E., Yesavage, J. A., and Kopell, B. S. (1979): The treatment of memory deficits in the aged with choline chloride. In: *Brain Acetylcholine and Neuropsychiatric Disease,* edited by K. L. Davis and P. A. Berger, pp. 253–262. Plenum Press, New York.
27. Davis, K. L., and Rosenberg, G. (1980): Is there a limbic system equivalent of tardive dyskinesia? *Biol. Psychiatry (in press).*
28. De Fraites, E. G., Davis, K. L., and Berger, P. A. (1977): Coexisting tardive dyskinesia and Parkinsonism: A case report. *Biol. Psychiatry,* 12:267–272.
29. Degwitz, R. (1969): Extrapyramidal motor disorders following long-term treatment with neuroleptic drugs. In: *Psychotropic Drugs and Dysfunctions of the Basal Ganglia,* edited by G. E. Crane and R. Gardner, pp. 22–32. Public Health Service Publication No. 1938, Washington, D.C.
30. Fahn, S., and David, E. (1973): Oral facial-lingual dyskinesia due to anticholinergic medication. *Trans. Am. Neurol. Assoc.,* 97:277–279.
31. Fann, W. E., Lake, C. R., Gerber, C. J., and McKenzie, G. M. (1974): Cholinergic suppression of tardive dyskinesia. *Psychopharmacologia (Berl.),* 37:101–107.
32. Fann, W. E., Sullivan, J. L., and Richman, B. W. (1976): Dyskinesias associated with tricyclic antidepressants. *Br. J. Psychiatry,* 128:490–493.
33. Gallant, D. M., Edwards, C. G., Bishop, M. P., and Galbraith, G. C. (1964): Withdrawal symptoms after abrupt cessation of antipsychotic compounds: Clinical confirmation in chronic schizophrenics. *Am. J. Psychiatry,* 121:491–493.
34. Gardos, G., Cole, J. O., and La Brie, R. A. (1977): Drug variables in the etiology of tardive dyskinesia, application of discriminant function analysis. *Prog. Neurol. Psychopharmacol.,* 1:147–154.
35. Gelenberg, A. J., Wojcik, J. D., and Growden, J. H. (1979): Use of lecithin in tardive dyskinesia. In: *Nutrition and the Brain,* edited by A. Barbeau, J. Growden, and R. Wurtman, pp. 285–303. Raven Press, New York.
36. Gerlach, J. (1977): Relationship between tardive dyskinesia, L-dopa-induced hyperkinesia and Parkinsonism. *Psychopharmacology,* 51:259–263.
37. Gerlach, J., Reisby, N., and Randrup, A. (1974): Dopaminergic hypersensitivity and cholinergic hypofunction in the pathophysiology of tardive dyskinesia. *Psychopharmacologia (Berl.),* 34:21–35.
38. Greenberg, L. M., and Roth, S. (1966): Differential effects of abrupt versus gradual withdrawal of chlorpromazine in hospitalized chronic schizophrenic patients. *Am. J. Psychiatry,* 123:221–226.
39. Greenblatt, D. L., Dominick, J. R., Stotsky, B. A., and DiMascio, A. (1968): Phenothiazine-induced dyskinesia in nursing-home patients. *J. Am. Geriatr. Soc.,* 16:27–34.
40. Groves, P. M., Wilson, C. J., Young, S. J., and Rebec, G. V. (1975): Self inhibition by dopaminergic neurons: An alternative to the "normal feed-back loop" hypothesis for the mode of action of certain psychotropic drugs. *Science,* 190:522–529.
41. Growden, J. H., Hirsch, M. J., Wurtman, R. J., and Wiener, W. (1977): Oral choline administration to patients with tardive dyskinesia. *N. Engl. J. Med.,* 297:524–527.
42. Haubrich, D. R., and Chippendale, T. J. (1977): Minireview: Regulations of acetylcholine synthesis in nervous tissue. *Life Sci.,* 20:1465–1478.
43. Hogarty, G. E., Ulrich, R. F., Mussare, F., and Aristigneta, N. (1976): Drug discontinuation among long-term, successfully maintained schizophrenic outpatients. *Dis. Nerv. Syst.,* 37:494–500.
44. Hollister, L. E., Eikenberry, D. T., and Raffel, S. (1960): Chlorpromazine in nonpsychotic patients with pulmonary tuberculosis. *Am. Rev. Respir. Dis.,* 81:562–566.
45. Iversen, S. D., Kelly, P. H., Miller, R. J., and Sevior, P. (1975): Amphetamine and apomorphine responses in the rat after lesion of mesolimbic or striatal dopamine neurones. *Br. J. Pharmacol.,* 54(2):2448.

46. Jackson, D. M., Anden, N. E., and Dahlstrom, A. (1975): A functional effect of dopamine in the nucleus accumbens and in some of the dopamine rich parts of the rat brain. *Psychopharmacologia,* 45:139–149.
47. Jus, A., Pineau, R., Lachance, R., Relchat, G., Jus, K., Pires, P., and Villeneuve, R. (1976): Epidemiology of tardive dyskinesia, I and II. *Dis. Nerv. Syst.,* 37:210–214; 257–261.
48. Klawans, H. L., Jr. (1973): The pharmacology of tardive dyskinesias. *Am. J. Psychiatry,* 130:82–86.
49. Klawans, H. L., Jr., and McKendall, R. R. (1971): Observations on the effect of levodopa on tardive lingual-facial-buccal dyskinesia. *J. Neurol. Sci.,* 14:189.
50. Klawans, H. L., Jr., and Rubovits, R. (1974): Effect of cholinergic and anticholinergic agents on tardive dyskinesia. *J. Neurol. Neurosurg. Psychiatry,* 37:941–947.
51. Kobayashi, R. M. (1976): Orofacial dyskinesia—clinical features, mechanisms and drug therapy. *West. J. Med.,* 125:277–288.
52. Kraepelin, E. (1907): *Clinical Psychiatry,* translated by A. Ross Deifendorf, p. 229. Macmillan Company, New York.
53. Lal, H., Brown, W., Drawbaugh, R., Hynes, M., and Brown, G. (1977): Enhanced prolactin inhibition following chronic treatment with haloperidol and morphine. *Life Sci.,* 20:101–105.
54. Linnoila, M., Viukari, M., and Hietala, O. (1976): Effect of sodium valproate on tardive dyskinesia. *Br. J. Psychiatry,* 129:114–119.
55. Mattson, R. H., and Calverley, J. (1968): Dextroamphetamine-sulfate-induced dyskinesias. *J.A.M.A.,* 204:108–110.
56. Meltzer, H. Y., Goode, D. J., Paul, S., Fang, V. S., and Kadjan, B. (1976): Lack of development of supersensitivity of pituitary dopamine receptors following chlorpromazine. *Neurosci. Abst.,* 2(2):873.
57. Metys, J., Wagner, N., Metysova, J., and Herz, A. (1969): Studies on the central antinociceptive action of cholinomimetic agents. *Int. J. Neuropharm.,* 8:413–425.
58. Moline, R. A. (1975): Atypical tardive dyskinesia. *Am. J. Psychiatry,* 132:534–535.
59. Moller-Nielsen, I., Fjalland, B., Pedersen, V., and Nymard, M. (1974): Pharmacology of neuroleptics upon repeated administration. *Psychopharmacologia (Berl.),* 34:95–104.
60. Muller, P., and Seeman, P. (1977): Brain neurotransmitter receptors after long-term haloperidol—Dopamine, acetylcholine, serotonin, alpha-noradrenergic and naloxone receptors. *Life Sci.,* 21:1751–1758.
61. Paulson, G. W. (1975): Tardive dyskinesia. *Annu. Rev. Med.,* 26:75–81.
62. Pert, A., Rosenblatt, J. E., Sevel, C., Pert, C. B., and Bunney, W. E., Jr. (1978): Long-term treatment with lithium prevents the development of dopamine receptor supersensitivity. *Science,* 201:171–173.
63. Prien, R. F., Cole, J. O., and Belkin, N. F. (1968): Relapse in chronic schizophrenics following abrupt withdrawal of tranquilizing medication. *Br. J. Psychiatry,* 115:679–686.
64. Ravitz, A. J., and Moore, K. E. (1977): Lack of effect of chronic haloperidol administration on the prolactin lowering actions of peribedil. *J. Pharm. Pharmacol.,* 29:384–386.
65. Sale, I., and Kristall, H. (1978): Schizophrenia following withdrawal from chronic phenothiazine administration: A case report. *Aust. N.Z. J. Psychiatry,* 12:73–75.
66. Simpson, G. M., Varga, E. J., Lee, J. H., and Zoubok, B. (1978): Tardive dyskinesia and psychotropic drug history. *Psychopharmacology,* 58:117–124.
67. Sovner, R., and DiMascio, A. (1977): The effect of benztropine mesylate in the rabbit syndrome and tardive dyskinesia. *Am. J. Psychiatry,* 134:1301–1302.
68. Stevens, J. R. (1974): Motor disorders in schizophrenia. *N. Engl. J. Med.,* 290:110.
69. Tamminga, C. A., Evans, H., and Chase, T. N. (1979): GABA agonist therapy in tardive dyskinesia. Scientific Proceedings of the American Psychiatric Association Annual Meeting, 1979, p. 147.
70. Tamminga, C. A., Smith, R. C., Pandee, G., Frohmm, L. A., and Davis, J. M. (1977): A neuroendocrine study of supersensitivity in tardive dyskinesia. *Arch. Gen. Psychiatry,* 34:1199–1203.
71. Tarsy, D., and Baldessarini, R. J. (1973): Pharmacologically-induced behavioral supersensitivity to apomorphine. *Nature,* 245:262–263.
72. Tarsy, D., Leopold, N., and Sax, D. R. (1974): Physostigmine in choreiform movement disorders. *Neurology (Minneap.),* 24:28–33.
73. Thach, B. T., Chase, T. N., and Bosma, J. F. (1975): Oral facial dyskinesia associated with prolonged use of antihistaminic decongestants. *N. Engl. J. Med.,* 293:486–487.

74. Ulus, I. H., Scally, M. D., and Wurtman, R. J. (1977): Choline potentiates the transynaptic induction of adrenal tyrosine hydroxylase by reserpine, probably by enhancing the release of acetylcholine. *Life Sci.,* 21:145–148.
75. Ulus, I. H., and Wurtman, R. J. (1976): Choline administration in activation of tyrosine hydroxylase in dopaminergic neurons of rat brain. *Science,* 194:1060–1061.
76. Ungerstedt, U., and Ljungberg, T. (1977): Behavioral patterns related to dopamine neurotransmission: Effect of acute and chronic antipsychotic drugs. Nonstriatal dopaminergic neurons. *Adv. Biochem. Psychopharmacol.,* 16:193–199.
77. Villeneuve, A., Jus, K., and Jus, A. (1973): Polygraphic studies of tardive dyskinesia and of the rabbit syndrome during different stages of sleep. *Biol. Psychiatry,* 6:259–275.
78. Wegner, J. T., Struve, F. A., and Kane, J. M. (1977): The B-Mitten EEG pattern and tardive dyskinesia: A possible association. *Am. J. Psychiatry,* 134:1143–1145.

Discussion

Schooler: I wish to comment on early incidence and prevalence studies, and about the kinds of problems they had in establishing the range of the disorder. One of the first reviews of incidence and prevalence studies was by Kazamatsuri, Chien, and Cole (6). From their table of prevalence studies, which shows rates ranging between 0.5% and 41.3%, I calculated a negative correlation between the size of the study and the prevalence rate found. This suggested that you see high rates in small, selected, very chronic populations but much lower rates once you broaden criteria and screening.

Carpenter: Tom McGlashan first pointed out to me a particular concern about the prophylactic effect of antipsychotic drugs in aftercare. All studies had been done on patients previously treated with neuroleptics and who presumably responded to neuroleptics and were discharged to aftercare. Dr. McGlashan wondered if maintenance drug therapy was superior to placebo in part because of an iatrogenic effect (i.e., drug-induced supersensitivity in limbic system dopaminergic neurons) (2).

Please discuss the recent finding of much higher prevalence of tardive dyskinesia and the problems of using AIMS scale scores to identify tardive dyskinesia. How would you establish a diagnosis of tardive dyskinesia that would include the early or minimal forms but exclude false positives?

Berger: We have to establish criteria in the way suggested earlier by Dr. Cole: We should make and share videotapes, and use standardized videotapes that define scale steps for movements rated by the AIMS scale.

Carpenter: Would you conceptualize those people who have mild abnormal involuntary movement disorders after prolonged neuroleptic treatment as having an early form of tardive dyskinesia or as being irrelevant to it?

Berger: Whether this is a continuum or separate syndromes will require a longitudinal study of patients who have the mild form. Some of them will presumably continue to be treated with neuroleptics because the possibility of exacerbating the tardive dyskinesia will be judged a lesser risk than the continuation of the psychosis.

Cole: It's difficult to prove the presence or absence of tardive dyskinesia. Patients in whom I see no abnormal movements report that their family members see them making unconscious chewing movements. When I do see even only a little bit of tongue and finger hyperactivity I rate them as 1's on the AIMS scale and assume they have early tardive dyskinesia. We do need to follow a large series of such patients longitudinally.

Berger: It is difficult to judge minimal movements. While I was giving my presentation, I glanced around this room and saw that some of you had mouth movements that would qualify for a score of 1 on the AIMS scale.

Itil: A longitudinal effort would be very important. I have been videotaping biweekly interviews with tardive dyskinetic patients. The videotapes show a tremendous variability in the dyskinetic movements even though the treatment procedures never changed.

Regarding your finding of mesolimbic high sensitivity, we have just compared 32 patients with and without tardive dyskinesia, matched by computer, based on nine different criteria. We found that the patients who have tardive dyskinesia have significantly more acute psychotic symptoms and more symptoms of the chronic brain syndrome, as established by BPRS rating, neurological findings, and experimental psychological findings (5).

Carpenter: Concerning lithium and dopaminergic hypersensitivity, in both Pert et al.'s (8) and in the earlier work of Klawans (7), I think lithium pretreatment was used to prevent haloperidol induced supersensitivity. It wasn't simply concomitant treatment with lithium but pretreatment.

Berger: I remember it as being both pretreatment and concomitant treatment (8).

Cole: Klawans certainly didn't give it before.

Carpenter: In a recent conversation, Bunney stressed the importance of pretreatment in his work with Pert.

Itil: I thought Baclofen was a GABA agonist. At least the company that makes it suggests that. We have just completed a study with Baclofen and found that it is not effective in tardive dyskinesia (4).

Berger: We assumed also that it was a GABA agonist when we used it as an experimental treatment for schizophrenia but we were unable to get positive results; instead, we saw an exacerbation, as we reported in *Lancet* (3). The molecule resembles phenylethylamine to me; others have suggested that it acts through substance P. I don't think the company would now claim it has GABA agonist activity.

Cole: You mentioned one treatment that might work differently from suppressing dopamine by an indirect route—the Friedhoff-Alpert (1) method of desensitizing dopamine receptors by high-dose L-DOPA.

Berger: In schizophrenic patients, the improvement was followed for only 2 months.

Cole: They have some patients who have been fine for 2 years.

Berger: That's true, but only for patients with tardive dyskinesia.

Schooler: Concerning your issue of post-treatment study, in certain kinds of treatments, one regards the persistence of the effect after discontinuing the treatment as positive proof that the treatment had a real effect. For example, psychotherapists feel that a treatment with an effect that was reversed immediately on discontinuation didn't really have an effect. Pharmacologists tend to feel the opposite, but ought to consider the possibility that a treatment is effective even though the effect persists after you stop giving it, as with penicillin.

Berger: I agree. We would like to call all six of our patients responders, and we'd like to say we cured the last three, but I'm glad you said it first.

Meltzer: Dr. Buchsbaum's earlier presentation on the antipsychotic effects of naloxone indicates that after 2 years of investigation of this issue we're no closer to a definitive answer than when this line of inquiry started; and I see nothing happening that will prevent a repetition with other novel antipsychotic drugs that may be useful for only a subgroup of patients. We all accept, or at least give lip service to, the heterogeneity of schizophrenia, and yet continue to carry out small-sample studies where we look for group differences that generally are not statistically significant. Perhaps this VA conference will spark the organization and design of collaborative research efforts, when appropriate for the further study of issues that appear ripe for such an approach because of preliminary results or theoretical import. Dr. Berger's work with naloxone gives a clue at least to dosage, even if we can't determine the relevant features of those patients who respond.

Dr. Berger's work also persuades me that it's not enough any longer to deal with simple treatment outcome. We have to utilize a within-patient research design more frequently. You reported the effects of giving a patient naloxone twice with good replication of the result. It would also be useful to know if the patients who improve on naloxone would worsen if they would agree to take an opiate agonist. (I believe such an experiment is ethical, because the effect would be transient and reversible.) Such inpatient designs are needed in place of group designs.

Schooler: One of the problems with the strategy that Dr. Meltzer suggests is that the same patient is not in the same state at different times. Dr. Buchsbaum illustrated that point nicely with the very clear power curves he showed us. There's another kind of power in terms of the *n* you need when you have a small difference as opposed to a large one. Some recent treatment studies (9) capitalize in a useful way on subgroups of responders by using individuals who have shown a clinical response to a particular treatment; they are put into a classic between-groups design, but at least you're focusing on a particular population where you have reason to believe there's an effect. I would say that any treatment that hasn't been shown effective in an open or single-blind form isn't likely to be demonstrated effective under more controlled conditions.

K. Davis: A paradigm we're starting to use at Palo Alto and will use again in the Bronx bears on the comments of Dr. Meltzer and Dr. Schooler. One advantage of the VA is that patients who leave the inpatient service go to the outpatient service, and, when rehospitalized, return to the same setting. That makes possible longitudinal assessments of the patients at different phases of their illness. Even with a small-*n* design, we can do within-patient studies. One kind of study not done before but beginning to be done now uses recently developed techniques to see what is the neurochemical difference in a given individual in remission and in relapse. Such within-patient comparisons may tell us, from chemical clues in the urine, or plasma or cerebrospinal fluid, whether or not dopamine metabolism does change from remission to relapse.

Yuwiler: In biochemistry it generally turns out that if 20 assays are available for a single compound, not everyone works in every laboratory because of unspecified critical variables. The same pattern likely holds true for a great deal of our data on schizophrenia in that different results reflect critical differences in environment or populations.

Hiatt: How are we to decide whom to include in our group? We have no a priori way to decide that. But no matter what research strategy we employ, we ought to know at least whom we've been studying, so we ought to be fully characterizing our populations beyond age, sex, and diagnostic subtypes, on a wide range of variables.

Zubin: Usually, when you try to learn the effect of some treatment, you take a random sample of schizophrenics, and come up against the problem of heterogeneity. I suggest concentrating on families. A family will usually have similar conditions for its various members. It is true that it's not always easy to find a family heavily loaded with schizophrenia, but the search is worthwhile, for in a family you can minimize heterogeneity.

REFERENCES

1. Alpert, M., and Friedhoff, A. (1979): Clinical applications of receptor modification. In: *Tardive Dyskinesia—Research and Treatment,* edited by R. Smith and J. Davis. Spectrum Publications, New York.
2. Carpenter, W. T., McGlashan, T. H., and Strauss, J. S. (1977): The treatment of acute schizophrenia without drugs: An investigation of some current assumptions. *Am. J. Psychiatry,* 134:14–20.
3. Davis, K. L., Hollister, L. E., and Berger, P. A. (1976): Baclofen in schizophrenia. In the correspondence section of *Lancet,* 5:1245.
4. Itil, T. M., Herkert, E., Schneider, S. J., Luhar, J., Fredrickson, J., and Roffman, M. (1979): Baclofen in the treatment of tardive dyskinesia: Open label study. *(in press)*
5. Itil, T. M., Reisberg, B., Huque, M. F., and Mehta, D. (1979): Clinical profiles of tardive dyskinesia. *In press.*
6. Kazamatsuri, H., Chien, C. P., and Cole, J. O. (1972): Therapeutic approaches to tardive dyskinesia. *Arch. Gen. Psychiatry,* 27:491–499.
7. Klawans, H. L., Weiner, W. J., and Nausieda, P. A. (1977): The effect of lithium on an animal model of tardive dyskinesia. *Prog. Neuropsychopharmacol.,* 1:53–60.
8. Pert, A., Rosenblatt, J. E., Sivit, C., Pert, C. B., and Bunney, W. E., Jr. (1978): Long-term treatment with lithium prevents the development of dopamine receptor supersensitivity. *Science,* 201:171–173.
9. Rimland, B., Callaway, E., and Dreyfus, P. (1978): The effect of high doses of Vitamin B_6 on autistic children: a double-blind crossover study. *Am. J. Psychiatry,* 134:472–476.

Perspectives in Schizophrenia Research,
edited by C. Baxter and T. Melnechuk.
Raven Press, New York, 1980.

Prevention of Tardive Dyskinesia and Other Drug-Related Adverse Effects

Jonathan O. Cole

Psychopharmacology Program, McLean Hospital, Belmont, Massachusetts 02178

LAYPERSON'S SUMMARY

Tardive dyskinesia is a growing problem in patients, mainly chronic schizophrenics, who may require prolonged-maintenance antipsychotic drug therapy to prevent serious psychotic relapses. Much larger scale studies relating past drug exposure to present dyskinesia are needed to determine whether any of our present antischizophrenic drugs are more or less likely to be associated with tardive dyskinesia. We also need to learn more about the course of tardive dyskinesia over time. The disease often appears to be static or slowly progressive, and to fade if caught early and the patient can be taken off antipsychotic drugs. But these are impressions, not documented facts.

Studies are needed to determine whether low-dose antipsychotic drug therapy can achieve as good remissions in schizophrenia as do the currently more prevalent high-dosage regimens. New drug therapies for schizophrenia (propranolol, polypeptides, and clozapine-like drugs) urgently need to be studied as potentially dyskinesia-free alternatives to our present antipsychotic drugs.

In addition, the epidemiological relationships between other potentially drug-related, serious adverse effects (agranulocytosis, sudden death) and the use of specific antipsychotic drugs need study.

INTRODUCTION

There is currently general professional and public concern about the apparently increasing prevalence of "tardive dyskinesia" (TD), or late-appearing abnormal movements in chronic schizophrenics as well as other patients exposed to dopamine-blocking antipsychotic drugs for prolonged periods. Although this problem has more current publicity, other possible, serious, adverse effects of antipsychotic drugs also exist. All of them pose epidemiological problems which have, to date, not been adequately handled. Are such adverse effects more closely associated with the use of one drug than another? How does the incidence of the adverse effects in patients at risk relate to the frequency with which the related drug is used? Studies need to be conducted which relate the numerator of adverse effects to the denominator of patients being treated with the various available drugs as well as other patient characteristics, which may increase vulnerability to the adverse effect.

Large psychiatric systems with good patient records should be particularly useful in this regard. The Veterans Administration is ideal but other large state systems are also appropriate, and, with greater effort to standardize data bases and ensure the reporting of adverse effects, regional or urban psychiatric facility networks could be evolved drawing in both private and public facilities.

ADVERSE EFFECTS OTHER THAN TD

Although tardive dyskinesia occupies the present limelight, other rare but serious medical conditions exist which may be related to drug therapy. Agranulocytosis occurs in patients on antipsychotics; it is believed to be most common, though very rare—one case in 3,000 to 5,000 chlorpromazine-treated patients (6,18). Thioridazine also has been associated with this disorder. However, there is currently no national system for collecting data on drug-related agranulocytosis and relating it to the number of patients exposed to the drug presumed to be involved. Large psychiatric hospital systems could collect systematic data on agranulocytosis and, if the incidence warranted it, could relate this numerator to an appropriate denominator, probably the number of patients exposed to the drug per year or, better, the number of patients on that and related drugs for an initial 6 months, since agranulocytosis has been reported to almost always occur early in antipsychotic (AP) drug therapy.

Sudden death is another rare condition in psychiatric patients which is sometimes attributed to AP drugs (15). To be sure, sudden unexplained death occurs in the general nonpsychiatric population as well; and some "sudden" deaths in psychiatric patients are attributed to lethal catatonia (17), both before and after the advent of drug therapy, or to asphyxiation (30) secondary to aspiration of food or vomitus. In one series of sudden deaths culled from the literature after the advent of neuroleptic drugs, only 9 of 58 were clearly due to aspiration (15), whereas 49 were on chlorpromazine (24), thioridazine (17), or both (6) at the time of death. Both drugs can cause electrocardiographic changes of unknown significance. I happen to have encountered 4 cases of unexplained sudden death in nonelderly patients on thioridazine in the last 20 years and recall only 2 on other antipsychotics. Hollister (14) has gone on record as believing that association between phenothiazines and sudden death is spurious.

The area is certainly complex and full of problems. Autopsies, when done on patients with sudden unexplained deaths, are often negative. Only occasionally are cardiac arrhythmias noted before death. Even when aspiration is found, it could be a terminal event after cardiac arrest. The state of knowledge in this area is inadequate, at best. Von Brauchitsch and May estimate deaths from aspiration at about 2 per 1,000 in hospitalized psychiatric patients and found them most common in patients with chronic brain syndrome (30). Presumably, if one-sixth of sudden deaths are due to aspiration [an overinterpretation of the data of Leetsma and Koenig (15)], then sudden deaths might occur in about 12 patients per 1,000 per year. If the incidence were really that high and if such deaths were reported regularly by a range of psychiatric facilities in sufficient number, and if the drug treatments to which the patients were exposed were known, then the larger epidemiological question as to the degree of risk associated with specific AP drugs could be answered. At less serious levels, the tendency of AP drugs to be associated with convulsions, lupus erythematosus, breast cancer, etc. could be assessed. I do not believe that any of these problems are major enough to necessitate or warrant keeping ongoing records of all medications given all psychiatric patients plus all side effects and intercurrent physical illnesses on a computer file; but governmental agencies might consider the Jick-Slone model for drug side effect monitoring (16) on selected acute and chronic psychiatric wards to collect better data on the relationship of various side effects with specific drugs. Perhaps the FDA would be interested in funding such a program as part of its post-marketing surveillance program. It should be noted that this model has been well worked out for acute admissions to psychiatric services by Swett and Cole (27) but has never been thought through for chronic patients.

TARDIVE DYSKINESIA

It would be valuable to make new cases of TD a reportable event within one or more psychiatric hospital or clinic systems. From my limited experience in the Boston area, I suspect that new dyskinesia emerges more commonly on depot fluphenazine, thioridazine, loxapine, and molindone, but this "observation" may be only a result of my biased experience. Large-scale data on this issue might reveal unsuspected associations once the numerators and denominators were known. Also, such cases of newly emerging dyskinesia could provide the basis of a more focussed study in a few hospitals of the course of dyskinesia over 2 or more years. At present we really do not know the course of early dyskinesia or how to predict worsening or disappearance. Even a naturalistic study, with periodic videotapes of the dyskinesia and an adequate record of ongoing drug therapy and drug-free periods in 300 to 500 patients, would be very helpful to clinicians in advising patients about their likelihood of developing severe dyskinesia and about the likely consequences of various drug treatment strategies in such patients. At the moment, the best one can say is that some patients lose their dyskinesia if kept off AP medication or on very low dosages of such drugs, particularly if this is done soon after the dyskinesia appears (20). If I see 30 such new cases a year in a 250-bed private hospital with 1,500 admissions, single V.A. or other public mental hospitals with larger numbers of somewhat more chronic patients should see even more.

For this purpose and for a variety of other research purposes described below, a major need is some way to teach and standardize the clinical assessment of dyskinetic movements. Existing films and tapes illustrate the phenomena but do not tie into existing rating scales, such as the Abnormal Involuntary Movement Scale (AIMS) or the Simpson Dyskinetic Rating Scale, in any quantitative manner. Detailed tapes illustrating specific movements which deserve a specific rating (e.g., borderline tongue movements versus mild, versus moderate or severe tongue movements) tied to scores on the AIMS would do a great deal to allow such a scale to be used with better reliability across hospitals and raters. For such general use, the AIMS is the most feasible of the existing instruments though the Simpson is more detailed and precise (10,24).

The project would require the availability of a large number of patient tapes, a first-class video studio, and a major time commitment by a psychiatrist or neurologist experienced in this area to select appropriate movement segments. An advisory committee of other experts in the field would be useful.

There are a number of other unsettled and important issues growing out of the problem posed by TD in chronic schizophrenics. These include:

1. *The exact relationships existing between drug exposure and the presence of TD:* At present the studies relating TD to drug history are relatively small, usually about 50 to 100 patients at a time. These studies yield heterogeneous results, probably due to both small sample size and differences in the specific populations sampled. The only partially consistent finding is that duration of drug therapy is weakly but positively correlated with TD (7–9,11,19). Occasional studies have suggested relationships with age (25), sex, periods off AP drugs, depot prolixin exposure or even amount of low-potency drugs (i.e., chlorpromazine and thioridazine) used (11), and there is a suspicion that antiparkinsonian drug use may correlate with TD. This area is well reviewed in the APA Task Force Report on Tardive Dyskinesia which is now in press (2). If a much larger study were done in 500 to 1,000 VA schizophrenics with detailed neurological and medication histories and dyskinesia ratings, substantially better and more stable estimates of the relationships between various drugs, dosages, and durations and the presence of TD could be derived. If depot prolixin really causes more dyskinesia (4,11) and thioridazine were really to cause less, because it has fewer neurological side effects, this might be a helpful guide to drug therapy. At any rate, such a large and thorough multi-hospital and clinic survey could provide definitive and helpful data.

2. *Drug holidays:* Recommendations in the emerging report of the APA Task Force on Tardive Dyskinesia (2) will probably include the suggestion that schizophrenic patients be taken off AP medications for 6 weeks every year or two. This suggestion is made for two purposes: to make sure that no "covert" dyskinesia is being covered over by AP medication and to make sure AP drugs are really necessary. This approach has not been widely pretested. Gardos and I have studied about 40 schizophrenics in aftercare programs in this manner and find that about 20% show emergence or exacerbation of dyskinesia; we have not encountered serious exacerbations of psychosis within the 6-week period. Nevertheless, if this procedure becomes a semi-official recommendation

of the APA, it will deserve systematic evaluation in larger patient samples. In our small study we included only patients judged by their clinicians to be stable. It is hard to tell what would happen if more overtly psychotic patients were taken off medication, especially the chronically disturbed inpatients who are seriously ill despite high doses of medication. Some such patients might be no worse, or even better, off AP drugs; while others might become even more disturbed. The area deserves systematic study.

3. *Evaluation of low-dose AP drug therapy:* America is, in general, a high-dose country. We use large doses of drug readily to try to speed the remission of psychosis in schizophrenics. This practice may well account for the high prevalence of TD in our hospitals and clinics. I know of only one small systematic study, by John Davis's group (3), which compared early high-dose AP drug therapy with steady low-dose therapy in newly admitted patients. The two groups were equally improved after 6 weeks. I believe it is time to do a larger test of the hypothesis that, in the end, low AP drug dosage is as beneficial as high dosage. This study should be done in newly admitted or readmitted schizophrenic patients as a multi-unit collaborative study. The related question of the use of antiparkinsonian drugs could also be studied. Many patients receive AP drugs at a level that induces neurological side effects. These symptoms are then treated by antiparkinsonian drugs rather than by lowering AP drug dosage. Perhaps the latter approach is as good or better in the long run.

4. *Establishing lowest effective maintenance dosage:* It is clear from Hogarty's studies, among others, that maintenance AP medication averts relapse in schizophrenia (80% relapse over 2 years on placebo versus 48% on drug), although the placebo patients look as well adjusted, prior to relapse, as do the drug patients (13).

Concern over TD has led to strong recommendations that chronic schizophrenics be maintained on the "lowest effective dose" of AP drugs. This suggestion is well intentioned, but fraught with problems. Adjusting maintenance dosage in schizophrenics in the community places the clinician in a situation where no clear feedback can occur until the patient relapses. If all drug treatment is stopped, patients begin to relapse gradually, at a steady, slightly decreasing rate of from 12 to 5% a month for 2 years (12). The only way to find out whether low maintenance dosages are worse than higher ones or better than placebo would be to do formal studies. Rifkin at New York State Psychiatric Institute and Kane at Hillside Hospital have begun such a study comparing 100% depot fluphenazine with 10% depot fluphenazine double blind. A pilot study (J. Kane, *personal communication*) has shown fairly convincingly that the 10% dose is, in fact, more effective than a comparable placebo trial in a non-concurrent control group and that patients stable on the 10% dose relapse when taken off medication. They also have formulated the hypothesis that the low-dose patients will have less akathisia and akinesia and may function better between relapses, even if relapses are more common on the minimal dosage. A related hunch, not being formally tested, is that keeping chronic schizophrenics on low AP drug dosages in the community makes it easier to abort relapses by increasing the drug dose; drug-free patients are guessed to be harder to bring under control once they relapse.

The consequences of all four strategies in terms of community adjustment, relapse, and emergence of TD could be the basis of a collaborative study, perhaps with some NIMH support.

TREATMENT OF TARDIVE DYSKINESIA

At present the only effective treatment of emerging dyskinesia is to stop AP drugs and wait for the dyskinesia to fade. It seems likely, but not proven, that if dyskinesia is detected early and AP drugs stopped within the first few months, the dyskinesia will gradually disappear (20). To date, no large series of such patients have been followed; thus, factors influencing the disappearance are unknown. I have seen both sudden severe dyskinesia and insidious minor dyskinesia fade. I cannot tell whether the duration of prior AP drug treatment, or its dose, is a factor.

Given patients with marked dyskinesia of long duration or patients with newer dyskinesia who become psychotic rapidly when AP drugs are withdrawn, some attempt to modify the dyskinesia is necessary. Currently choline and lecithin and, by extension, other cholinergic drugs are worth further study. Benzodiazepines probably have a mild ameliorative effect. Reserpine may be helpful but could exacerbate the underlying dyskinesia. Lithium could conceivably be helpful. None of these therapies are proven (2). Controlled clinical trials aimed at assessing efficacy in the short- and long-term are needed.

ALTERNATE DRUG THERAPIES FOR SCHIZOPHRENIA

The best solution to the TD problem is the development of new AP drugs which do not cause TD. In addition, it is obvious that many schizophrenics receive only slight benefit from our current drugs. New and more effective and safer therapies are needed. It is hard to predict what drugs may emerge in the next few years, but the following approaches are reasonable:

1. High-dose propranolol. This treatment was discovered by Atsmon and has been improved by Yorkston (5,22). One controlled study is clearly positive and Yorkston claims that at least some chronic patients are markedly improved. The odds that this is a real drug effect are increased by the tendency of patients to relapse rapidly when the drug treatment is discontinued. This approach deserves serious study, despite Berger's early negative pilot work (P. Berger, *personal communication*).

2. The Organon polypeptide, studied in patients by Van Praag's group in Holland, looks promising (29). It is alleged to have AP potency without neurological side effects.

3. Clozapine, despite its many side effects, was an effective antipsychotic, almost completely free of neurological side effects and perhaps working only on presynaptic dopamine receptors (6,23). The drug industry should be able to develop similar safe compounds. Sulpiride, or related drugs in that series, may also be useful and have less danger of neurological sequelae. Units to study such new treatment approaches systematically should be funded.

4. Perhaps some schizophrenics are lithium responders and could be maintained on lithium rather than dopamine-blocking drugs. One suspects that patients resembling bipolar schizoaffectives or chronic manics would be most likely to benefit, but other chronic patients might also respond (21,26,28).

If TD becomes a larger issue and no better treatments emerge, electroconvulsive therapy (ECT) is an alternate option for treating catatonic excitements and other disturbed psychotic states (1). Perhaps the efficacy of ECT in schizophrenia deserves reassessment, at least in patients with clear TD.

CONCLUSION

Public mental hospital systems including the V.A. have large and sometimes well-staffed psychiatric facilities which provide care on both an intermittent and continuing basis for large numbers of chronic schizophrenics. They are therefore in a potentially good position to do both epidemiological studies and clinical trials relevant to long-term side effects presumably due to drugs. Rare events such as agranulocytosis and sudden death as well as more common problems such as tardive dyskinesia could and should be studied.

In tardive dyskinesia, the most prominent and controversial current side effect, the following studies are warranted:

1. newly emerging dyskinesia, its antecedents and course;
2. large-scale epidemiology of tardive dyskinesia;
3. the feasibility of 6-week drug holidays;
4. the efficacy of low-dose antipsychotic drug therapy, in both acute and maintenance therapy;
5. treatments of tardive dyskinesia; and
6. alternative newer drug therapies for schizophrenia not based on dopamine blockade.

Some of these warrant multi-hospital collaborative studies based on a single protocol while others are more appropriate for research units in single hospitals. In the latter case, the V.A. and the NIMH should consider providing stable program support for a few units doing drug studies in schizophrenia relevant to tardive dyskinesia.

REFERENCES

1. A.P.A. Task Force #14 on Electroconvulsive Therapy (1978): American Psychiatric Association, Washington, D.C.

2. Baldessarini, R., Cole, J., Davis, J., Gardos, G., Preskorn, S., Simpson, G., and Tarsy, D. (1979): Tardive dyskinesia: A task force report of the American Psychiatric Association.
3. Brickson, S. E., Hurt, S. W., and Davis, J. M. (1976): Dosage of antipsychotic drugs (continued). *N. Engl. J. Med.,* 294:1296.
4. Chouinard, G., Annable, L., Ross-Chouinard, A., and Nestoros, J. N. (1979): Factors related to tardive dyskinesia. *Am. J. Psychiatry,* 136:79–83.
5. Cole, J., Altesman, R., and Weingarten, C. (1979): Beta-blocking drugs in psychiatry. *McLean Hosp. J.,* 4:40–68.
6. Cole, J., Swett, C., and Pope, H. (1976): Agranulocytosis revisited. *McLean Hosp. J.,* 1:34–39.
7. Crane, G. E. (1970): High doses of trifluoperazine and tardive dyskinesia. *Arch. Neurol.,* 22:176–180.
8. Degkowitz, R., and Wenzel, W. (1967): Persistent extrapyramidal side effects after long-term application of neuroleptics. In: *Neuropsychopharmacology,* edited by H. Brill, pp. 608–615. Excerpta Medica, Int. Congress Series 129, Amsterdam.
9. Faurbye, A., Rasch, P. J., Peterson, P. B., et al. (1964): Neurological symptoms in pharmacotherapy of psychoses. *Acta Psychiatr. Scand.,* 40:10–27.
10. Gardos, G., and Cole J. (1980): Problems in the assessment of tardive dyskinesia. In: *Tardive Dyskinesia: Clinical and Basic Research,* edited by R. C. Smith, W. E. Fann, J. M. Davis, and E. Domino. Spectrum Press, New York *(in press).*
11. Gardos, G., Cole, J. O., and LaBrie, R. A. (1977): Drug variables in the etiology of tardive dyskinesia: Application of discriminant function analysis. *Neuropsychopharmacology,* 1:147–154.
12. Hogarty, G. (1977): Temporal effects of drug and placebo in delaying relapse in schizophrenic outpatients. *Arch. Gen. Psychiatry,* 34:297–304.
13. Hogarty, G., Goldberg, S., and Schooler, N. (1974): Drug and sociotherapy in the aftercare of schizophrenic patients. II. Two year relapse rates. *Arch. Gen. Psychiatry,* 31:603–608.
14. Hollister, L. (1965): Unexpected asphyxial death and tranquilizing drugs. *Am. J. Psychiatry,* 114:366–367.
15. Leetsma, J. and Koenig, K. (1968): Sudden death and phenothiazines. *Arch. Gen. Psychiatry,* 18:137–148.
16. Miller, R. (1972): Drug surveillance utilizing epidemiological methods: A report from the Boston Collaborative Drug Surveillance Programs. *Am. J. Hosp. Pharmacy,* 30:584–592.
17. Peele, R., and Von Loetzen, I. (1973): Phenothiazine deaths: A critical review. *Am. J. Psychiatry,* 130:306–308.
18. Pisciotta, A. V. (1969): Agranulocytosis induced by certain phenothiazine derivatives. *J.A.M.A.,* 208:1862–1868.
19. Pryce, I. G., and Edwards, H. (1966): Persistent oral dyskinesia in female mental hospital patients. *Br. J. Psychiatry,* 112:983–987.
20. Quitkin, F., Rifkin, A., Gochfeld, L., and Klein, D. F. (1977): Tardive dyskinesia: Are first signs reversible. *Am. J. Psychiatry,* 134:84–87.
21. Rapp, M., and Edwards, P. (1977): A high prevalence of affective disorder in a "schizophrenic clinic." *Can. Psychiatr. Assoc. J.,* 22:181–183.
22. Robert, E., and Amacher, P. (eds.) (1978): *Propranolol and Schizophrenia.* Liss, New York.
23. Shopsin, B., Klein, H., Aaronson, M., and Collora, M. (1979): Clozapine, chlorpromazine and placebo in newly hospitalized, acute schizophrenic patients. *Arch. Gen. Psychiatry,* 36:657–664.
24. Simpson, G. M., Lee, J. H., Zoubok, B., and Gardos, G. (1979): A rating scale for tardive dyskinesia. In: *Tardive Dyskinesia: Clinical and Basic Research,* edited by R. C. Smith, W. E. Fann, J. M. Davis, and E. Domino. Spectrum Press, New York *(in press).*
25. Simpson, G. M., Varga, E., Lee, J. H., and Zoubok, B. (1978): Tardive dyskinesia and psychotropic drug history. *Psychopharmacology,* 58:117–124.
26. Small, J., Kellams, J., Milstein, V., and Moore, J. (1975): A placebo controlled study of lithium combined with neuroleptics in chronic schizophrenic patients. *Arch. Gen. Psychiatry,* 36:657–664.
27. Swett, C., and Cole, J. O. (1976): Drug side effects on psychiatric wards. *McLean Hosp. J.,* 1:141–149.
28. Van Putten, T., and Sanders, D. (1975): Lithium in treatment failures. *J. Nerv. Ment. Dis.,* 161:225–264.

29. Verhoeven, W., Van Praag, H. M., Van Ree, J. N., and DeWied, D. (1979): Improvement of schizophrenic patients treated with [DES-TYRL]-gamma-endorphin (D T gamma E). *Arch. Gen. Psychiatry,* 36(3):294–298.
30. von Brauchitsch, H., and May, W. (1968): Deaths from aspiration and asphyxiation in a mental hospital. *Arch. Gen. Psychiatry,* 18:129–136.

Discussion

Baxter: You mentioned the possibility that drugs like lithium carbonate might be causing interstitial nephritis, and asked whether that was worse than the tardive dyskinesia that lithium may help to prevent. Your comment made me wonder whether drugs like lithium affect the nervous system first or second. It's quite possible that a drug might affect the kidney or liver first and the CNS second.

Cole: As far as I can tell, lithium affects the brain first and the kidney second.

Brown: The feasibility of developing neuroleptic assays is an important issue.

Regarding tardive dyskinesia, you said that prolixin may be particularly prone to causing it. Has anyone looked at the relationship between early appearing pyramidal symptoms—acute dystonia and akathisia—and later development of tardive dyskinesia?

Cole: About the only way you can study it retrospectively is to survey charts for the proportion of time a patient was on any anticholinergic drug, which may not be a good measure. Documentation of dystonia is hard to find in medical records. Maybe we haven't looked hard enough.

Brown: You would certainly predict a relationship.

Cole: It's a good hypothesis.

Berger: We need prospective studies to quantitate the amount of anticholinergics and carefully document each case of extrapyramidal movement disorder.

Carpenter: Crane (1) argues that persistent Parkinsonian symptoms identify patients at higher risk for tardive dyskinesia, and Jus et al. (2) find a positive relationship between anti-Parkinsonian drugs and tardive dyskinesia.

K. Davis: Relating to your studies of treating senile psychosis with choline, we've now given choline in various doses to about 20 elderly people, all in a double-blind cross-over paradigm, and we can find no efficacy at any dose for choline in the elderly. That's in contrast with physostigmine, which in small doses has remarkable effects in patients with Alzheimer's disease and in normal elderly people with an age-related dementia.

On your notion of collaborative studies of what happens to schizophrenics in remission: We began a study of schizophrenics in remission who are drug-free, but we had a methodological problem. It wasn't clear how to define when a person is in remission and when in relapse. We decided to define a person as being in remission when the patient was once judged positive for schizophrenia by RDC criteria, is now diagnosed as having schizophrenia in remission by RDC criteria, has a BPRS scale score below 30, and has been living in the community for 6 consecutive months. Then we reviewed more than 1,000 patients in VA outpatient clinics by these criteria. We found that probably less than 5% of the VA outpatient population meets the criteria. I'm not sure whom we're going to study.

Cole: In the chronic wards I work in, some people are more psychotic and others are less psychotic, but there's no one whom I can consider as being in good remission. Operationally, being in relative remission means having ground privileges.

REFERENCES

1. Crane, G. E. (1972): Pseudoparkinsonism and tardive dyskinesia. *Arch. Neurol.,* 27:426–430.
2. Jus, A., Pineau, R., Lachance, R., Pelchat, G., Jus, K., Pires, P., and Villeneuve, R. (1976): Epidemiology of tardive dyskinesia, Part II. *Dis. Nerv. Sys.,* 37:257–261.

Perspectives in Schizophrenia Research,
edited by C. Baxter and T. Melnechuk.
Raven Press, New York, 1980.

Clinical Strategies for Antipsychotic Drug Treatment, Tardive Dyskinesia, and the Training of Research Psychiatrists

John M. Davis, Philip G. Janicak, and Grant A. Killian

Illinois State Psychiatric Institute, Chicago, Illinois 60612

LAYPERSON'S SUMMARY

This chapter looks at the issue of neuroleptic treatment and tardive dyskinesia from the viewpoint of developing clinical research strategies to improve our treatment and minimize side effects. This review serves as an introduction to the problem of training psychiatrists in clinical research. Several suggestions including rare patient protocols, registries, and record keeping are discussed in the context of "mini" collaborative projects which are deemed feasible in both the state and federal systems of psychiatric care. Such a model could alleviate the critical shortage of psychiatrists trained in good clinical research.

INTRODUCTION

Tardive dyskinesia is the most important problem facing long-term psychiatric care in state and federal treatment centers. Tardive dyskinesia can develop in patients of all ages treated with antipsychotics for prolonged periods of time (3 months or longer). It is reported most often in hospitalized patients, but it has occurred also with outpatients on maintenance therapy. Because there is no effective treatment for tardive dyskinesia, prevention becomes particularly important, and since tardive dyskinesia is caused by prolonged exposure to antipsychotic drugs, the question is: Can these patients be effectively treated without antipsychotics? Clearly, methods for treatment without antipsychotics should be developed for long-term, partially remitted patients in sustaining care clinics and on the wards of state and federal hospitals.

This chapter outlines research to prevent tardive dyskinesia by utilizing strategies that reduce the intake of antipsychotic drugs. Since tardive dyskinesia is caused by drugs, we must first re-examine the evidence supporting our belief that prolonged treatment with drugs is effective in treating schizophrenia. Second, it is our contention that conventional methods for statistical analysis of such drug trials is conceptually insensitive and that a survival distribution analysis, rather than a fourfold chi square test, be used to analyze maintenance studies. Correct basic mathematics underlying relapse studies is necessary for an understanding of how maintenance drug studies should be designed and analyzed. Third, we will suggest some protocols to develop alternate treatment strategies for long-term patients at risk for tardive dyskinesia. Ideally, these strategies can be carried out by psychiatric researchers in one of many institutional settings.

NECESSITY FOR SURVIVAL ANALYSIS OF ANTIPSYCHOTIC RELAPSE STUDIES

The principal concern with maintenance medication in schizophrenia is the prevention of relapse. At present 29 maintenance studies have compared the efficacy of antipsychotic drugs versus placebo (Table 1). These studies report that schizophrenics on medication have fewer relapses than those maintained on placebo. Because these studies address the identical hypothesis, their separate results can be statistically combined. The probability of similarity in the results occurring by chance is substantially less than 10^{-100}. A common belief is that since 50% of these patients do not relapse on placebo, then 50% of the patients do not need drugs. We find this proposition dubious, and challenge the view that 50% of patients do not relapse. We maintain that this latter conclusion is based on an insensitive conceptual appraisal of the data. We were the first to consider the exponential nature of a relapse rate (9), and this chapter will develop our argument in greater detail.

As an example, Hogarty and Goldberg (20) compared maintenance medication with placebo in outpatient schizophrenics. Cumulative relapse rates are recorded in their paper and are expressed in Fig. 1 as the percentage of patients unrelapsed after 24 months. The percentage of patients unrelapsed plotted against time yields a curve (Fig. 1) which flattens out at 18 months, leaving about 20% of the patients unrelapsed. On first analysis, this curve might suggest a first-order function with the percentage of patients who relapsed per unit time as a constant. However, this analysis is not satisfactory. As patients relapsed, they were dropped from the study so that the number of patients left with the potential to relapse decreased with time, leaving at 18 months a group of patients (about 20% of the original group) with an exceedingly low relapse rate. Data from all three studies (5,20,26) on the number of patients relapsing per unit of time are plotted as a logarithm of the percentage of patients unrelapsed over time (see Figs. 2–4). Prien and Cole (26) presented data only for the effect of placebo with time and did not present what happens to patients maintained on drugs, whereas Hogarty and Goldberg (20) and Caffey et al. (5) did present the number of patients relapsing on drug and on placebo. Thus, it is easy to see that far more patients relapsed on placebo than on drug. To calculate the rate of relapse, the fraction of the patient population relapsing per unit time was divided by the number of patients in that study within that period of time (see bottom panels of Figs. 2–4). The number of patients unrelapsed was corrected for the decreasing sample size by calculating the natural logarithm of that percentage

TABLE 1. *Prevention of relapse in schizophrenia by antispychotic drugs*

Authors	Year	Drug	Dose (mg CPZ[a])	No. of patients: Placebo	No. of patients: Drug	Percent relapse on placebo	Percent relapse on drug
Schawver et al. (31)	1959	Chlorpromazine	200	40	40	18	5
Diamond & Marks (10)	1960	Phenothiazines	468	20	20	70	25
Blackburn & Allen (4)	1961	Phenothiazines	—	28	25	54	24
Gross & Reeves (16)	1961	Phenothiazines	—	73	36	58	14
Schiele et al. (32)	1961	Phenothiazines	1,044	20	60	60	3
Adelson & Epstein (1)	1962	Phenothiazines	max 2,900	90	191	90	49
Freeman & Alson (12)	1962	Chlorpromazine	220	42	44	31	14
Troshinsky et al. (33)	1962	Phenothiazines	150–200	19	24	63	4
Whitaker & Hoy (34)	1963	Chlorpromazine	284	26	13	65	8
Caffey et al. (5)	1964	Phenothiazines	375	171	88	45	5
Kinross-Wright & Charalampons (22)	1965	Fluphenazine	300	20	20	70	5
Garfield et al. (13)	1966	Chlorpromazine	610	16	9	31	11
Melynk et al. (24)	1966	Phenothiazines	100–600	20	20	50	0
Engelhardt et al. (11)	1967	Chlorpromazine	200	142	152	30	15
Prien & Cole (26)	1968	Chlorpromazine	300 or 2,000	189	573	42	16
Morton (25)	1968	Phenothiazines	—	20	20	70	25
Prien et al. (27)	1969	Trifluperazine	540 or 2,860	107	218	56	20
Baro et al. (3)	1970	R-16341	10–40[b]	13	13	100	0
Rassidakis et al. (29)	1970	Various drugs	—	43	41	58	34
Clark et al. (8)	1971	Pimozide	—	10	9	70	44
Leff & Wing (23,35)	1971	Various drugs	418	12	18	83	33
Hershon et al. (18)	1972	Trifluperazine	575	32	30	28	7
Hirsch et al. (19)	1973	Fluphenazine	—	38	36	66	8
Hogarty & Goldberg (20)	1973	Chlorpromazine	282	174	187	67	31
Clark et al. (7)	1975	Pimozide	10–20[b]	9	26	78	27
Chien et al. (6)	1975	Fluphenazide	—	15	16	87	12
Gross (15)	1975	Chlorpromazine	625	20	41	65	34
Andrews et al. (2)	1976	Chlorpromazine	216	17	14	35	7
Ritkin et al. (30)	1977	Fluphenazine	5–30	19	43	68	7

[a] Dose was determined by transforming all drugs to CPZ equivalents; if there was more than one drug, the CPZ equivalents were averaged and these drugs were classified as phenothiazines.

[b] These drugs are not transformed to CPZ equivalents.

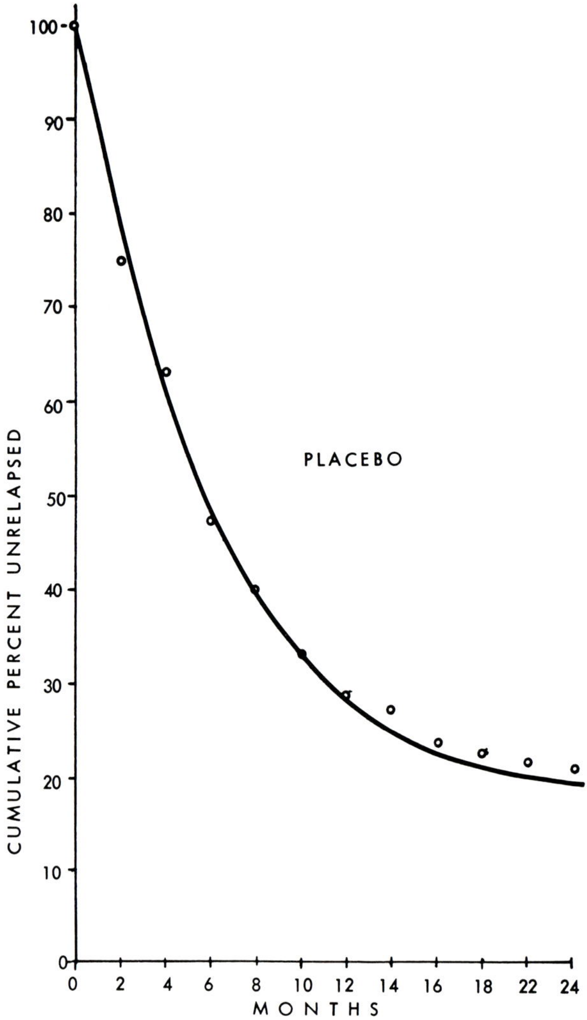

FIG. 1. Cumulative relapse over time is expressed as the percent of patients unrelapsed vs. time. Data from Hogarty and Goldberg, ref. 20.

of patients unrelapsed. In Figures 2, 3, and 4, all these curves show approximate linearity.

Consider the case of determining whether a drug is more effective than a placebo. The chi-square statistic, utilizing a fourfold table with the number of patients relapsed or not relapsed with drug and placebo, is invalid for this purpose because it is excessively conservative. More appropriate ways of thinking about such data were published in 1693 by Halley (17). At present, a number of methods are available for dealing effectively with such survival curves. These

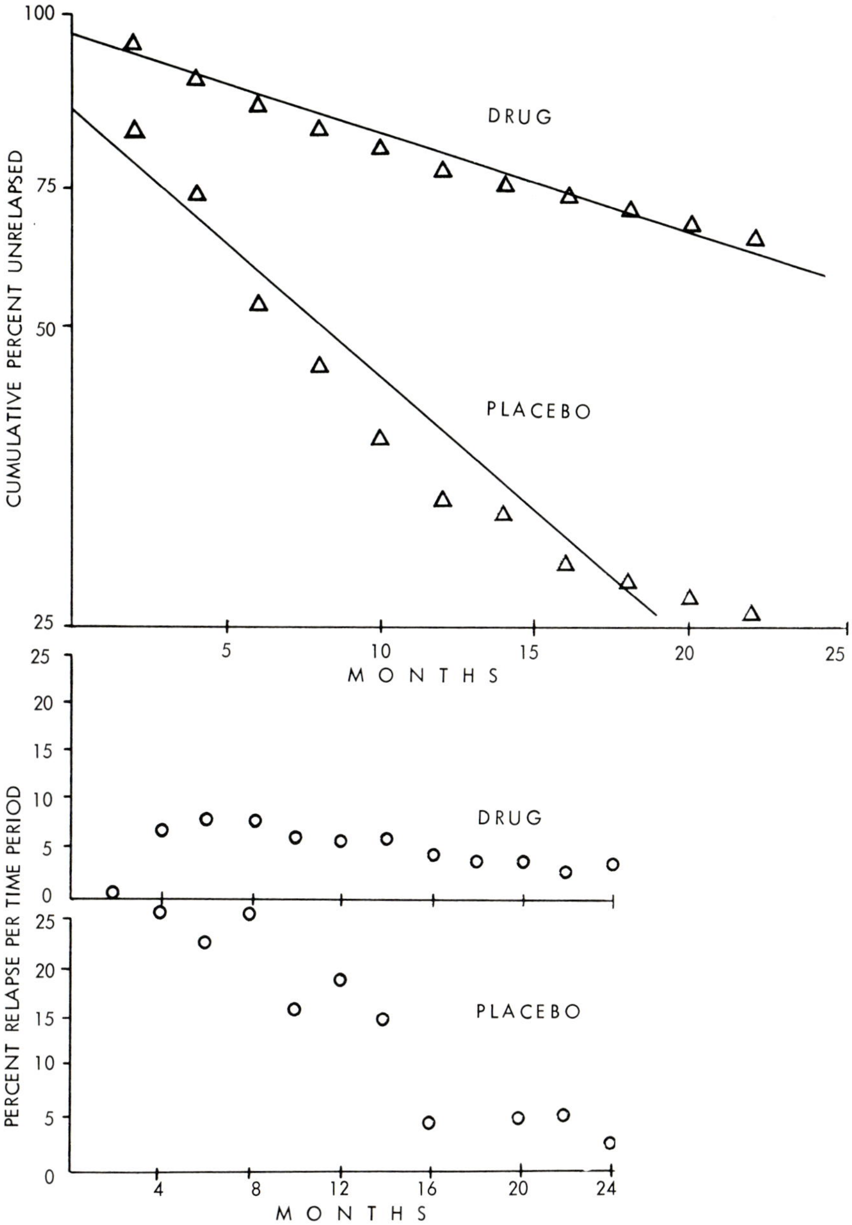

FIG. 2. Survival distribution of cumulative relapse over time is expressed as the Ln_e of the percent of patients unrelapsed vs. time. Data from Hogarty and Goldberg (20). *Bottom panel:* hazard rates, same data. Number of relapses divided by the number of patients being studied (expressed as a percent) at each time interval.

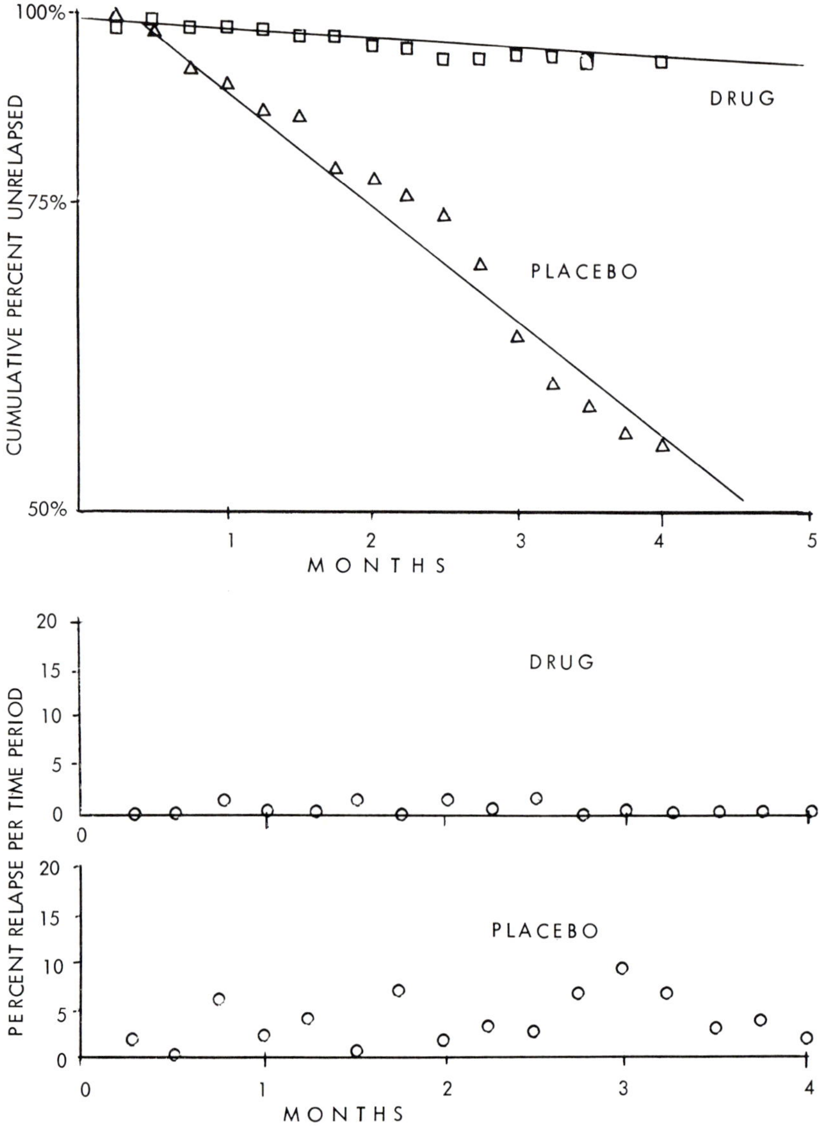

FIG. 3. Survival distribution of cumulative relapses over time is expressed as the Ln_e of the percent of patients unrelapsed vs. time. Data from Caffey et al., ref. 5. *Bottom panel:* hazard function, same data.

have been developed in a wide variety of areas concerned with survivor distribution, e.g., insurance policies, reliability of manufacturing goods over time, radioactive decay, or other measures based on concepts of half-life. Both parametric and nonparametric methods have been used by Kaplan and Meier (in 1958;

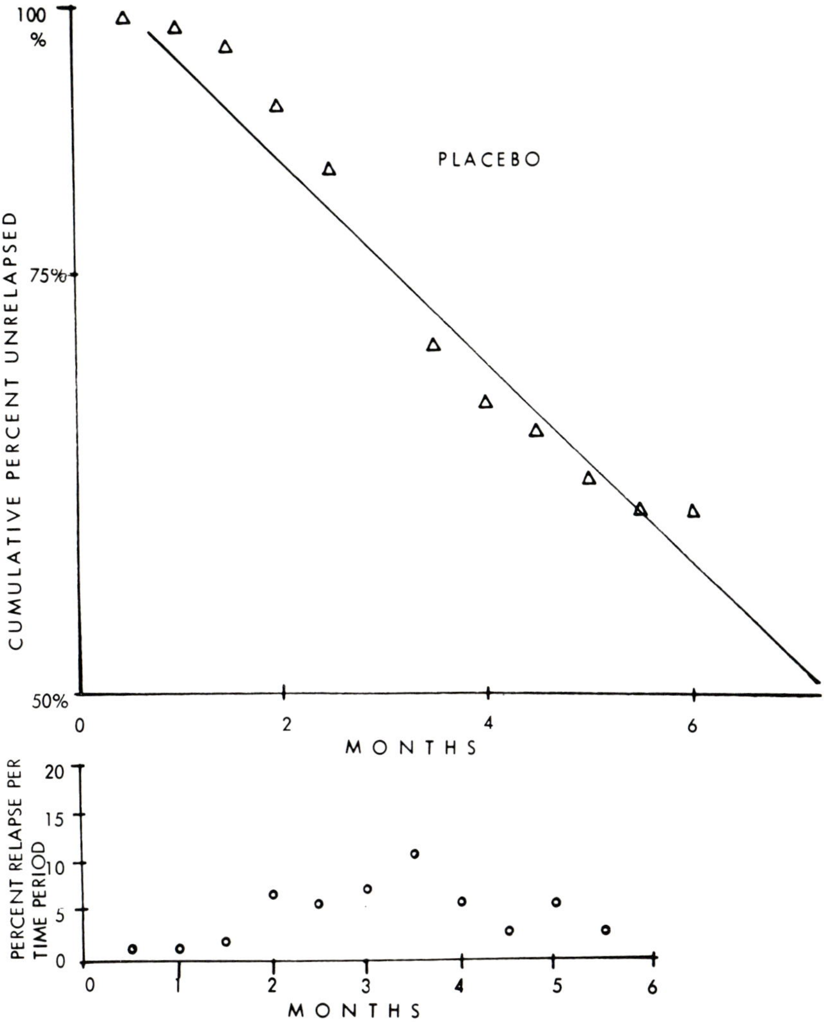

FIG. 4. Survival distribution of cumulative relapses over time expressed as the Ln_e of patients unrelapsed vs. time. *Bottom panel:* hazard function. Data from Prien and Cole, ref. 26.

21) and Gehan (in 1965; 14). Nonparametric methods are useful in situations when a distribution is not assumed, whereas survival analysis is appropriate in parametric methods for a variety of statistical models and is not limited to exponential functions. Note that normal distributions are not typically observed in survivor-type data, so the appropriate parametric survival technique provides a better statistical fit of the data.

The next step after plotting the data for description as survival functions and significance testing is to view the curve in a quantitative sense. A logical point of departure is to inquire as to the consistency of the rate of relapse per unit of time. The rate of relapse in most of these curves does appear to be constant per unit of time. If this is fitted to Ln_e percent of relapse per unit time, as we did by the least-squares method, the fit is really quite good. In the Prien placebo data (26), for example, the correlation coefficient is 0.98 ($r^2 = 0.96$, with a relapse rate of 10% per month), in Caffey's placebo data (4), the correlation coefficient is 0.99 ($r^2 = 0.97$, with a relapse rate of 14% per month), and in Hogarty's placebo group (20), the correlation coefficient is 0.96 ($r^2 = 0.93$, with a relapse rate of 7.1% per month). It is obviously important for the clinician to know whether a patient should be on prophylactic medication for periods longer than this. Since most of the research on relapse rates has studied patients for only the first 4 to 6 months, the empirical data showing relapse rates over 2 years collected by Hogarty are particularly important and his data are consistent with a constant relapse rate for the first 18 months. In the Hogarty and Goldberg study there is a curvature apparent in the line at 16 to 22 months (the end of the study), which suggests that the relapse may be decreasing slightly with time. It may be that the constant relapse rate applies only to the initial phases. Since the exponential function neatly fits, it provides a reasonable approximation for describing the relapse survival function for the first 18 months. Another plausible interpretation of the data suggests that there are two types of schizophrenic patients: one type that relapses at the rate of approximately 15% a month, and a small population of good prognosis schizophrenics who never relapse. In other words, this relapse-rate curve is composed of two components: one component with a relatively rapid rate and a second component that has either a very slight relapse rate or a relapse rate of zero.

DRUG-FREE MAINTENANCE FOR THE PREVENTION OF TARDIVE DYSKINESIA

To prevent tardive dyskinesia, a logical goal is to develop alternate treatment strategies for long-term schizophrenics. The appropriate treatment for chronically relapsing but partially remitted schizophrenics is maintenance antipsychotic therapy to sustain the gains that have been made and prevent further deterioration. There is an important conceptual distinction between continued therapy and prophylactic therapy to prevent relapse in a symptomatic, partially remitted patient or in an asymptomatic remitted patient. These two types of patients to some degree tend to overlap each other. In general, the therapeutic efficacy of drugs is comparable in both situations. However, a relapse for an outpatient can have a more serious impact than for an inpatient who is under continuous medical supervision in an environment where treatment can be reinstituted rapidly. Continuing therapy in the hospital can be a model for what happens in the outpatient situation, and work in both settings must be done because of the necessity of proving that generalizations from one to the other are valid.

In view of the adverse side effects of permanent drug therapy and the exponential nature of relapse, we suggest alternate treatment modes. If a patient is under careful supervision to detect signs of relapse, it should be possible to discontinue medication entirely during periods of quiescence and move in vigorously with drug treatment only when a relapse occurs. The research question is: Can such relapses be detected early and can vigorous treatment check the relapse so that it is relatively minor?

If the process involved in the decompensation of schizophrenia is difficult to reverse once it starts, then this method of treatment would be impractical. On the other hand, if early drug intervention can abort a schizophrenic episode, then the strategy outlined above might provide a method of management with a much lower incidence of tardive dyskinesia.

Research shows that relapse rates are much lower among inpatients who are maintained on relatively low antipsychotic doses, whereas relapse rates are greater among inpatients treated with higher antipsychotic doses (28). If techniques to treat patients who are on low levels of antipsychotics without medication could be developed, they might be extended to sicker patients who usually need high levels of medication. Designing a protocol for this research would involve identifying by the Research Diagnostic Criteria those patients with a diagnosis of schizophrenia or schizoaffective illness who require relatively low doses of a drug (under 600 mg, CPZ equivalent) for maintenance. Extremely violent patients or "brittle" patients requiring higher doses of medication for stabilization would be excluded.

A selected patient would enter four treatment groups in a double-blind random assignment study. Two groups would receive maintenance antipsychotic medication and the other two groups would receive placebo. These two groups would be crossed with two treatment procedures: one with an early identification of relapse with rapid treatment, and the other procedure would be a conventional psychiatric ward without early identification and rapid treatment (Table 2). In the early identification, rapid intervention groups, patients would be followed by a special team that would carefully monitor their status and watch for early signs of relapse. In the case of early signs of relapse, non-blind emergency medications would be added to abort the relapse. Such vigorous treatment would continue until the relapse was clearly prevented, a period which could be as long as several weeks. In the study, it would be necessary to specify the maximum period that such an extra treatment procedure could be administered. Under all conditions, the psychiatric status would be assessed at periodic intervals. In evaluating the outcome of all groups, if a patient relapsed to a clinically significant degree (as defined by certain criteria) there would be two different factors which would be assessed: First, the number of patients who deteriorated to such a degree that they were considered to have relapsed and had to be dropped

TABLE 2. *Drug-free vs. maintenance design*

	Special monitoring and early vigorous drug treatment	No special monitoring or extra medication
Maintenance drug	A	B
Placebo	C	D

Selected inpatients who require under 600 mg CPZ equivalents for maintenance and who do not pose a significant risk of violence or suicide, or other management problem.

Random assignment to treatment group according to design above.

from the study; and second, the degree of psychiatric illness would be calculated over time and the area under the curve summated. Consequently, an index could be calculated which would quantitate how unrelapsed patients remaining in the study were doing. Of course, both measures could be combined in the final global score.

Since the research program would require spotting relapses early, it would be necessary to develop a methodology for their detection to make rapid intervention possible. Built into this study would be a natural history component. Whenever a relapse occurred, there would be a staffing in order to determine if there were any signs which indicated that the patient was relapsing. The problem would be to identify the prodrome of a schizophrenic relapse and its early warning signals, such as perhaps a slight increase in bizarre behavior and bizarre nightmares. Patients would have to be rated at frequent intervals on a behavioral evaluation form. The data then could be analyzed to determine if such prodromal signs did, in fact, herald any major relapse. The development of such predictive measures is an important part of the study, and provisions should be made to permit changes in the behavioral evaluation form (if needed) as the study progresses.

If the drug-free strategy is ineffective, one might consider using extremely low doses of antipsychotic drugs, supplemented by occasional moderate-dose treatment during exacerbations, or electroconvulsive therapy (ECT) which could be valuable in controlling an acute exacerbation of schizophrenia. A pilot study could compare conventional maintenance treatment for continuously ill inpatients versus a low-dose treatment which is supplemented by a high-dose treatment during exacerbations with the judicious use of small amounts of ECT given unilaterally to the nondominant hemisphere. Since one must be concerned about memory loss as a side effect of ECT, this mode of treatment is suggested only as a pilot trial to test its efficacy.

If mildly to moderately ill patients can be managed by a drug-free model of early detection, then the same strategy might be applied first to sicker inpatients and then second to outpatients. Since many chronic schizophrenics are no longer maintained exclusively in an acute treatment hospital, but rather in halfway houses or sheltered care facilities, such a study could be done in a wide variety of inpatient and after care settings.

If the early detection of relapse is possible and such relapse is containable and reversible by vigorous drug treatment, then the drug-free maintenance of schizophrenics may become feasible and the risk of tardive dyskinesia decreased accordingly.

RARE PATIENT PROTOCOLS

In order to compare the effectiveness of one treatment against a placebo and/or another treatment, it is necessary to have a population of at least 10 to 15 patients in each experimental group. Although this minimal sample size does not yield results which are "written in stone," it is clear that one cannot do a treatment evaluation study with only one or two patients in each group. In psychiatry, there are some rare conditions that occur with insufficient frequency so that no single medical center will have a sufficient number of patients to conduct a valid study. However, several centers collaborating may generate enough patients for a valid study. Thus, there is a need for a mechanism by which investigators in several hospitals can get together to conduct low-budget minicollaborative studies on rare patients. For example, some patients have an acute onset of a highly "reactive" psychosis with a good premorbid personality. These episodes are now called either "brief reactive psychosis" or "schizophreniform psychosis." Is antipsychotic drug treatment necessary or will these patients remit spontaneously? In the latter case, drugs may not be necessary for this type of psychosis.

Tourette's disease provides another example. It is a rare but serious disorder, and one medical center seldom sees enough cases to make a treatment study feasible. Another example would be acute psychotic emergencies. Many of these emergencies, involving highly disturbed or violent patients, constitute crises which seem to preclude even minimal research interventions. Nevertheless, there are infrequent occasions when highly disturbed patients could undergo alternate but effective treatment programs for the purpose of comparison. Comparing sedative antipsychotics to nonsedative antipsychotics is one example. Other examples would be treatment of temporal lobe epilepsy, or use of lithium alone for prophylactic purposes in schizoaffective disorders, strictly defined so as not to include manics and atypical manics. Another possible project would be to find out if methadone is an effective antipsychotic agent (methadone may be a dopamine blocker). Occasionally, narcotic addicts are also psychotic, and with a collaborative study it would be possible to compare methadone versus placebo in treating their psychosis.

RARE PATIENT REGISTRY

An idea related to the rare patient protocol is the rare patient registry. A system could be established so that psychiatric services would be notified of rare diagnostic entities: When patients with rare clinical problems or side effects are identified, this central registry could be informed. Any researcher could then contact the facility concerning treatment, clinical care, and/or research.

RARE PATIENT RECORD KEEPING

Many other types of studies can be conducted in a large hospital system that has high-quality medical, computer and clerical facilities. A computerized mechanism for systematically recording rare side effects could be instituted. Side effects might include agranulocytosis, fatal hyperpyrexia, sudden death during treatment with tricyclics and/or phenothiazines, or renal failure with chronic lithium treatment. At present, a medical event could occur in a schizophrenic patient and be falsely attributed to a drug. On the other hand, rare, but true, side effects could occur which are true side effects of a drug, but go unnoticed. For example, fatal hyperpyrexia has been falsely attributed to drugs received by schizophrenics. Records have been found that show that some reactions attributed to the drugs occurred before neuroleptic drugs were in use. A systematic way of recording rare side effects will require the construction of a list that would be circulated with a comment-reporting format attached. This would allow for the first time an accurate evaluation and computation of the incidence of side effects, together with background data, the descriptions and the course of rare effects, as well as clinical data, laboratory data, and outcome. These compilations should result in new and useful knowledge.

LOW-BUDGET COLLABORATIVE STUDIES

In the VA medical center system, collaborative studies have been used successfully both in general medicine and in psychiatry. Additional collaborative studies with schizophrenic patients may prove important to the resolution of other important clinical questions. It may be possible to conduct some of these studies with a low budget and minimal risk. For example, it is not known whether some antipsychotics have a greater propensity for causing tardive dyskinesia than other antipsychotics. A prospective investigation of tardive dyskinesia would require a long-term study. In state and federal care facilities (chronic hospitals, nursing homes, and halfway houses where chronic schizophrenics in a quasi-inpatient setting are receiving drugs), it would be possible to randomly assign patients to several different neuroleptics to see if certain neuroleptics have a higher propensity for causing tardive dyskinesia. We know that some drugs cause more sedation, whereas others cause greater extrapyramidal side effects; however, the overall risks are approximately equal. If a given neuroleptic causes less tardive dyskinesia, it would clearly be the preferred drug for maintenance therapy. Patients could be randomly assigned for maintenance purposes to thioridazine, fluphenazine in tablet form, or fluphenazine decanoate. They could be evaluated once annually with the AIMS Scale and the BPRS. Over the course of several years, it could be determined whether there was more tardive dyskinesia associated with one or the other drug. A low-budget, multihospital study focusing just on the essential measurements could accomplish this purpose. The problem in such a long-term prospective study is to maintain sufficient enthusiasm to obtain valid data over such a long period of time.

DEVELOPMENT OF RESEARCH PSYCHIATRISTS

The types of research we have discussed require the enthusiasm and motivation of young researchers. Both state and federal hospital systems have some difficulty recruiting psychiatrists into their facilities. The field of psychiatry, in general, has experienced a great deal of difficulty developing research psychiatrists. Only 2% of the National Institute of Mental Health's training dollars goes toward the development of training research psychiatrists, and a good proportion of these trainees are physicians doing work in basic science, so that there is virtually no support for psychiatrists doing clinically oriented research.

Most university medical schools do not have psychiatrists whose primary orientation is research and they lack specific research units for psychiatric studies. In contrast, every university medical school has research endeavors in almost all the other specialties of medicine, surgery, and pediatrics. In addition, there is substantial support for research in the basic sciences (e.g., physiology, biology, biochemistry, psychology, and sociology).

From an educational point of view, the basic science graduate student is in a peer group with other students, and as a postdoctoral fellow he is in a laboratory working in a peer group with other postdoctoral trainees and other members of the department. At every level, there are individuals who can teach the student substantive knowledge and with whom he can identify. Thus there is a social infrastructure where an individual can "master his trade." A similar type of infrastructure has also been developed for the training of researchers in the areas of medicine and surgery, but not in psychiatry. By and large, no research hierarchy exists in psychiatry. There is clearly a need to develop such an infrastructure for training research psychiatrists. This should be one of the highest priorities for all state and federal hospital systems.

Psychiatric research has never been fully established as a specialty. Yet, it is necessary to promote research in psychiatry so that new knowledge can become available for better clinical practice.

We particularly advocate the need for small starter grants for young researchers in psychiatry. There is often a "catch 22," that keeps psychiatrists out of psychiatric research: an investigator is not really eligible for a psychiatric research grant unless he is a proven researcher with a given productive "track record," yet, there is no social infrastructure for psychiatrists to develop such a record. At the present time, a high priority should be assigned to funding earmarked for the career development of young psychiatrists and their initial research work.

A psychiatrist in training should be salaried as a research psychiatrist. Funds for a research assistant and some supplemental equipment should be available so that he may work as an apprentice on an existing research ward. In short, what is needed is the development of a research training infrastructure for the clinical psychiatrist, similar to that which exists in basic science, medicine, surgery, and pediatrics.

SUMMARY

Tardive dyskinesia must be a high research priority in both state and federal hospital systems. We have suggested the development of treatment strategies for schizophrenics that would include drug-free intervals, viz-à-viz, understanding the exponential process of research. This may not work, but it has to be tried as it may lead to a much safer method of treating patients. In a system of hospitals, it is easier to work out collaborations between several units, and we have suggested a number of ways. The existence of a system of hospitals under a common management allows an organizational solution to some of the difficult problems of collaboration, and we have outlined several ways in which such cooperation among facilities could be useful. Stimulation of research in schizophrenia should be seen in the context of a necessity for developing research wards for clinical investigations and the development of suitable research psychiatrists who actually participate in the work.

REFERENCES

1. Adelson, D., and Epstein, L. A. (1962): A study of phenothiazines in male and female chronically-ill schizophrenics. *J. Nerv. Ment. Dis.,* 134:543–554.
2. Andrews, P., Hall, J. N., and Snaith, R. P. (1976): A controlled trial of phenothiazine withdrawal in chronic schizophrenic patients. *Br. J. Psychiatry,* 128:451–455.
3. Baro, F., Brugmans, J., Dom, R., et al. (1970): Maintenance therapy of chronic psychotic patients with a weekly oral dose of R 16341. *J. Clin. Pharmacol.,* 10:330–341.
4. Blackburn, H., and Allen, J. (1961): Behavioral effects of interrupting and resuming tranquilizing medication among schizophrenics. *J. Nerv. Ment. Dis.,* 133:303–307.
5. Caffey, E. M., Diamond, L. S., Frank, T. V., Grasberger, J. C., Herman, L., Klett, C. J., and Rothstein, D. (1964): Discontinuation or reduction of chemotherapy in chronic schizophrenics. *J. Chronic Dis.,* 17:347–358.
6. Chien, Ching-Piao, and Cole, J. O. (1975): Drugs and rehabilitation in schizophrenia. In: *Drugs in Combination with Other Therapies,* edited by M. Greenblatt, pp. 13–34. Grune & Stratton, New York.
7. Clark, M. L., Huber, W., Hill, D., Wood, F., and Costiloe, J. P. (1975): Pimozide in chronic outpatients. *Dis. Nerv. Syst.,* 36:137–141.
8. Clark, M. L., Huber, W., Serafetinides, E. A., and Colmore, J. P. (1971): Pimozide (Orap): A tolerance study. *Clin. Trial J. [Suppl.]* 2:25–32.
9. Davis, J. M. (1975): Maintenance therapy in psychiatry. *Am. J. Psychiatry,* 132:1237–1245.

10. Diamond, L. S., and Marks, J. B. (1960): Discontinuance of tranquilizers among chronic schizophrenic patients receiving maintenance dosage. *J. Nerv. Ment. Dis.,* 131:247–251.
11. Engelhardt, D. M., Rosen, B., Freedman, D., et al. (1967): Phenothiazines in the prevention of psychiatric hospitalization. *Arch. Gen. Psychiatry,* 16:98–99.
12. Freeman, L. S., and Alson, E. (1962): Prolonged withdrawal of chlorpromazine in chronic patients. *Dis. Nerv. Syst.,* 23:522–525.
13. Garfield, S., Gershon, S., Sletten, L., et al. (1966): Withdrawal of ataractic medication in schizophrenic patients. *Dis. Nerv. Syst.,* 27:321–325.
14. Gehan, E. A. (1965): A generalized Wilcoxon Test for comparing arbitrarily singly-censored samples. *Biometrika,* 52:203–223.
15. Gross, E. S. (1975): A double-blind comparison of once-a-day pimozide, trifluoperazine, and placebo in the maintenance care of chronic schizophrenics. *Curr. Ther. Res.,* 16:696–705.
16. Gross, M., and Reeves, W. P. (1961): Relapse after withdrawal of ataractic drugs. In: *Mental Patients in Transition,* edited by M. Greenblatt, pp. 313–321. Charles C Thomas, Springfield, Ill.
17. Halley, E. (1693): An estimate of the degree of mortality of man. *Philos. Trans. R. Soc. Lond.,* 17:596–610.
18. Hershon, H. I., Kennedy, P. F., and McGuire, R. J. (1972): Persistence of extrapyramidal disorders and psychiatric relapse after withdrawal of long-term phenothiazine therapy. *Br. J. Psychiatry,* 120:41–50.
19. Hirsch, S. R., Gaind, R., Rohde, P. D., et al. (1973): Outpatient maintenance of chronic schizophrenic patients with long-acting fluphenazine double-blind placebo trial. *Br. Med. J.,* 1:633–637.
20. Hogarty, G. E., and Goldberg, S. E. (1973): Drugs and sociotherapy in the aftercare of schizophrenic patients. One year relapse rates. *Arch. Gen. Psychiatry,* 28:54–62.
21. Kaplan, E. L., and Meier, P. (1958): Nonparametric estimation from incomplete observations. *J. Am. Statis. Assoc.,* 53:457–481.
22. Kinross-Wright, J., and Charalampous, K. D. (1965): A controlled study of a very long acting phenothiazine preparation. *Int. J. Neuropsychiatry,* 1:66–70.
23. Leff, J. P., and Wing, J. K. (1971): Trial of maintenance therapy in schizophrenics. *Br. Med. J.,* 2:599–604.
24. Melynk, W. T., Worthington, A. G., and Laverty, S. G. (1966): Abrupt withdrawal of chlorpromazine and thioridazine from schizophrenic inpatients. *Can. Psychiatr. Assoc. J.* 11:410–413.
25. Morton, M. R. (1968): A study of withdrawal of chlorpromazine or trifluoperazine in chronic schizophrenia. *Am. J. Psychiatry,* 124:1585–1588.
26. Prien, R. F., and Cole, J. O. (1968): High dose chlorpromazine therapy in chronic schizophrenia. Report of National Institute of Mental Health. Psychopharmacology Research Branch Collaborative Study Group. *Arch. Gen. Psychiatry,* 18:482–495.
27. Prien, R. F., Levine, J., and Cole, J. O. (1969): High dose trifluoperazine therapy in chronic schizophrenia. *Am. J. Psychiatry,* 126:305–313.
28. Prien, R. F., Levine J., and Switalski, R. W. (1971): Discontinuation of chemotherapy for chronic schizophrenics. *Hosp. Comm. Psychiatry,* 22:4–7.
29. Rassidakis, N. C., Kondakis, X., Papanastassiou, A., et al. (1970): Withdrawal of antipsychotic drugs from chronic patients. *Bull. Menninger Clin.,* 34:216–222.
30. Rifkin, A., Quitkin, F., Rabiner, C., et al. (1977): Fluphenazine decanoate, oral fluphenazine and placebo in the treatment of remitted schizophrenics: I. Relapse rates after one year. *Arch. Gen. Psychiatry,* 34:43–47.
31. Schawver, J., Gorham, D. R., Leskin, L. W., et al. (1959): Comparison of chlorpromazine and reserpine in maintenance drug therapy. *Dis. Nerv. Syst.,* 20:452–457.
32. Schiele, B. C., Vestre, N. D., and Stein, K. E. (1961): A comparison of thioridazine, trifluoperazine, chlorpromazine, and placebo: A double-blind controlled study on the treatment of chronic hospitalized, schizophrenic patients. *J. Clin. Exp. Psychopathol.,* 22:151–162.
33. Troshinsky, C. H., Aaronson, H. G., and Stone, R. K. (1962): Maintenance phenothiazine in the aftercare of schizophrenic patients. *Pa. Psychiatr. Q.,* 2:11–15.
34. Whitaker, C. B., and Hoy, R. M. (1963): Withdrawal of perphenazine in chronic schizophrenia. *Br. J. Psychiatry,* 109:422–427.
35. Wing, J., and Leff, J. (1971): Trial of maintenance therapy in schizophrenia. *Br. Med. J.,* 2:599–604.

Discussion

Perez-Polo: Obtaining informed consent is a practical problem, as most patients come in at a time of crisis, but it's also a problem in ethics and the protection of patients. How would you go about getting informed consent for the violence protocol you suggest?

J. Davis: To do a violence protocol study in the outpatient situation is almost impossible, but in the inpatient situation you have a patient whose history you know. You can get your informed consent from the patient when he or she is in a good period, or from family members, or, if necessary to do research that's clearly in the patient's benefit, you could get a court order. When an episode occurs, you can go right into the protocol. No one hospital has enough patients to do the overall study, but it could be done in a set of hospitals cooperatively.

Cole: Where populations are large, most places will have a proportion able to give informed consent that will be large enough to study.

Schooler: We (2) did a withdrawal study that compared patients who had been treated with fluphenazine decanoate or fluphenazine hydrochloride for a year and then had been withdrawn from medication, double-blind, for 15 weeks. Using the survival-curve technique that you recommended, what we considered as the "death" in terms of lifetable analysis was the development of a global Abnormal Involuntary Movement Scale (AIMS) rating above a threshold of 2, which is "mild." In the patients discontinued from oral fluphenazine a higher percentage of cases reached this threshold than among patients discontinued from the decanoate. Most cases who developed movements did so within 3 weeks of discontinuation. This represents prospective evidence *against* the claim that fluphenazine decanoate leads to tardive dyskinesia. This drug is particularly likely to be present in the histories of chronic patients. Similarly, chlorpromazine, the prototypic phenothiazine, is likely to be present in most patients' histories, which may account for the observed association in nonprospective studies. In this study, where treatment was experimentally manipulated, the decanoate was not associated with greater development of movements. A final point that this study makes is that the placebo was the experimental condition and continuation of drug treatment was the control. In the consent form provided to patients, we assured them that if they fell into the continued medication group they would have an opportunity to have medication withdrawn after the study was over.

J. Davis: If, for a naturalistic study, all patients are nonrandomly assigned to different groups, the most severely ill patients would get the decanoate, and maybe the most severely ill were on it the longest.

Schooler: Relapse curves look similar to those for development of movements, but we do not find a correlation between development of abnormal movements and subsequent relapse in individuals.

Carpenter: Drug withdrawal from decanoate is gradual and from oral is abrupt. Could this factor account for both the abnormal movements and the psychiatric relapse?

Schooler: If that were the case, then the decanoate-discontinued group should simply shadow the oral discontinued group, only being 3 or 4 weeks later in development of movements and relapse; but that is not the pattern we saw.

Janowsky: Blood levels are probably different in the two groups, since only the fluphenazine was given orally. Thus, there may have been a lower decanoate level to start with, and therefore less of the movements when you stop, than in your oral medication group.

Schooler: To support that, the baseline levels of the abnormal movements were slightly although not significantly higher in the decanoate group. A larger number of cases in the decanoate group had movements we considered above threshold, which would be consistent with lower blood levels.

Kleinman: Both Dr. Cole and Dr. Davis mentioned sudden deaths on neuroleptics. Working with the local medical examiner's office I've come across many such cases. The VA might not be an appropriate place to study this.

Ewalt: With VA outpatients, that would be true; but with VA inpatients, these cases come to my desk and they are very rare. Every one is examined. Usually the hospital tries to give the case to the local medical examiner but doesn't always succeed.

J. Davis: If you had ready a common protocol for the cardiologists at all your VA hospitals, who would be notified of a sudden death, whatever data the experts wanted to study could be collected over the course of several years.

Kleinman: The medical examiner draws from a population different from VA inpatients and we see many unexplained sudden deaths.

Cole: I wonder if they are associated with any particular drug?

Yuwiler: Earlier, Dr. Zubin mentioned the episodic nature of schizophrenia and questioned whether a steady state existed in which the size of the schizophrenic population remained constant but its composition was ever changing. This implies an equivalence between rates of schizophrenic breakdown and recovery. Your first order falls in the population remaining asymptomatic after drug withdrawal would fit that model, since the decrement in the asymptomatic is matched by the increase in those with recurrence of disease. However, the abrupt break in that curve to yield a small permanently asymptomatic population should, if the steady-state model were correct, match the incidence of fresh cases. Further, if the experiment were repeated using only those who had a recurrence of symptoms on drug withdrawal, it would be interesting to see if the slope of the decline remained the same and, additionally, if that slope was maintained down to zero or if it, too, abruptly broke to leave a residual of essentially "cured" subjects.

Ethnic populations reportedly differ in sensitivity to psychotherapeutic drugs. For example, we have mentioned being told that the acceptable clinical dosage of phenothiazine in Japan is much lower than routinely used here. This difference could be due to cultural differences in defining improvement, or it could be due to real biological differences between groups. Among such differences may be environmental and genetic alterations in concentrations of blood constituents binding drugs, and drug binding could affect the transport of the drug from blood to brain. That is, most psychotherapeutic drugs are relatively nonpolar and would freely permeate into brain if they were not bound to blood constituents. If bound, however, entry into brain is some function of the binding equilibrium of the various binding materials in blood. Given this, studies attempting to relate clinical response to blood levels of drugs might usefully include some measures of drug binding to blood constituents. Gross static measures could be obtained from ultrafiltration or equilibrium dialysis measurements of free and bound drugs. Perhaps even better estimates of dynamic processes could be obtained using Oldendorf's (3) technique for assessing penetrance of substances from blood into brain. Essentially this consists of injecting a mixture of differently labeled test and reference substances into the carotid artery of a rat and comparing the ratio of isotopes in brain with that in the mix 5 sec after injection. By substituting blood from a patient for the usual carrier in these studies, Oldendorf's procedure could provide a bioassay of the relationship between total blood drug levels and that fraction available for entry into brain.

J. Davis: By using such a technique we (1,4) have shown that lithium transport abnormalities associated with affective disorders may be in the lithium-sodium exchange system.

Mosher: I'm surprised at the presentations on tardive dyskinesia. We know how to prevent it. The method is very simple and straightforward, but it was never suggested: you just don't treat people with neuroleptics. I'm surprised that it was never suggested, because the first rule of Hippocrates is to do no harm.

J. Davis: I did suggest that.

Mosher: You suggested treating them only when they're symptomatic.

J. Davis: And I also suggested that acute reactive patients, one of the small special populations, be studied without drugs.

Mosher: We ought to return to what Dr. Zubin said, and what Dr. Gordon Paul has done, and remember that in fact people get better without drugs. We have, or can establish and use, techniques for dealing with people without neuroleptic drugs. It's a viable alternative.

Schooler: You cannot compare the population in your study with the population Gordon Paul looked at. They were different, different things were probably happening there, and the treatment was not the same. The difficulty with nondrug treatment is in specifying what about a particular manipulation is having the direct effect. Psychopharmacology is so much easier to do, since it's substantially easier to specify the independent variable.

Mosher: Remember that 85% of Dr. Paul's patients were obtained from the 3% return rate over 2 years, all off medication. You can do it even in chronics without medication.

Perez-Polo: Dr. Davis, you mention checking psychological tests done 20 years ago. Will you also study the effects of being institutionalized for such a long time?

REFERENCES

1. Dorus, E., Pandey, G. N., Shaughnessy, R., Gaviria, M., Val, E., Ericksen, S., and Davis, J. M. (1979): Lithium transport across red cell membrane: a cell membrane abnormality in manic-depressive illness. *Science,* 205:932–934.
2. Levine, J., Schooler, N. R., et al. (1979): Discontinuation of oral and depot fluphenazine in schizophrenic patients after one year of continuous medication. In: *Long-term Effects of Neuroleptics: Pharmacological Basis and Clinical Implications,* edited by G. Racagni, F. Cattabene, S. Gorini, and P. F. Spano. Raven Press, New York.
3. Oldendorf, W. H. (1971): Brain uptake of radiolabeled amino acids, amines, and hexoses after arterial injection. *Am. J. Physiol.,* 221:1629–1639.
4. Pandey, G. N., Ostrow, D. G., Hars, M., Dorus, E., Casper, R. C., Davis, J. M., and Tosteson, D. C. (1977): Abnormal lithium and sodium transport in erythrocytes of a manic patient and some members of his family. *Proc. Natl. Acad. Sci. USA,* 74:3607–3611.

Perspectives in Schizophrenia Research,
edited by C. Baxter and T. Melnechuk.
Raven Press, New York, 1980.

Some Thoughts Concerning the Influence of Environmental Factors and Placebo Treatment on Schizophrenia

Earl X. Freed

Medical Research Service, Veterans Administration Central Office, Washington, D.C. 20420

As we explore the impact of environmental factors, placebo treatment, and noninvasive therapy on schizophrenic patients, we should consider experimental approaches that could reveal any "organic basis" for the effect of such modalities. The latter is akin to what Astrup (1) called "a need for physiological explanations of how social and psychological factors act on the mind." That these environmental factors play a significant role in the development of schizophrenia is broadly acknowledged. That noninvasive therapies and environmental manipulations often help to improve the schizophrenic syndrome appears equally evident. That some of the improvement noted may constitute a nonspecific placebo reaction, however, in no way helps us to understand what is going on. Placebo effects are notoriously variable (13), and placebo dynamics are a mystery.

Over and above a possible placebo reaction, there is a similar nonspecificity about the personality and environmental factors associated with the schizophrenic patient. This is not to mention the absence of clarity about personality and environmental variables associated with the schizophrenic's caregivers. Even the crucial interpersonal relationship between patient and therapist is replete with nonspecific factors. In the literature on schizophrenia one sees descriptions of a disorder which is biogenic and psychogenic in causation; has many underlying processes; is multifactorial, variable, complex, and diverse in etiology, manifestations, and therapy; differs in precursors and antecedents; and has varying outcomes and treatment requirements. The overall vagueness to which I have alluded is better illustrated by a 1935 quotation of Macfie Campbell (4) recently cited by Grinker (5): "Instead of considering patients with the diagnosis of dementia praecox as having a 'disease,' I prefer to think of them as belonging to a Greek letter society, the conditions for admission to which are obscure; inclusion in and exclusion from the fraternity are determined by considerations which may vary from year to year and from place to place, and the directing board is not known." It is to be noted that this paradigm neatly handles—among others—spontaneous remission, the response to therapeutic milieu, and the psychopharmacological effect of taking antipsychotic medication.

It also broadly includes the therapeutic response to placebos. The placebo reactions are so special that they deserve separate mention as we study the secret society of schizophrenia. Outlining a history of behavioral pharmacology which has shown phenomenal advances, Pickens (10) delineated four stages—the first which he called the "early years," and then the periods from 1800 to 1940, 1940 to 1955, and, finally, 1955 to the present. He wrote, only 2 years ago, that most of the drugs used "far back" in the "early years" were placebos. Yet we continue to ponder placebos today. For example, Dr. Ewalt and his colleagues (6), reviewing an earlier psychopharmacological study with schizophrenic patients, asked, "How are we to account for the differences among the placebo-treated patients who deteriorate to such a marked degree, those who do not deteriorate, and those who show significant improvement?" And a recent report in *The Journal of Family Practice* (2) called attention to the fact that "any agent effective 35 percent of the time or causing side effects in one out of ten is a powerful tool. The fact that such agents are frequently placebos discomforts the more scientifically minded among us." Even the lay press has taken notice of the placebo dilemma, as witness a recent headline in the *New York Times* (3): "Placebos Work, but Survey Shows Widespread Misuse." A recent editorial in *Science* (9), discussing the implicit risk factors that accompany "informed consent," includes the following admonition: "And when a specific risk is disclosed, it should be discussed in the context of placebo effects in general, why they occur, and how to guard against them."

Just 2 months ago, I attended a 2-day conference on pain at the National Institutes of Health. I had the placebo problem with schizophrenics in mind as I listened to the program which focused on understanding and treating chronic pain and the terminally ill. I was struck by the applicability to schizophrenia of the NIH topic, "Pain, Discomfort, and Humanitarian Care." I was impressed by the analgesic role of placebos and I wrote some questions on my program as I listened to the presentations: Do schizophrenics who demonstrate a placebo effect have different plasma levels of beta-endorphin (which appears to rise during a painful situation) than schizophrenics who are unresponsive to that placebo? Can we identify placebo reactors among schizophrenics? Why are placebo effects not more stable or uniform?

In their "Special Report: Schizophrenia 1976" (8), researchers at the NIMH Center for Studies of Schizophrenia concluded that there is "new interest in the evaluation of the psychosocial therapies with and without adjunctive treatment" as well as a need for "sorting out patients who are responders or nonresponders to a given treatment." Suggesting that broader social factors and attitudinal changes may even underlie "the dramatic pharmacologic response of many schizophrenics to the newly introduced antipsychotic agents," Stephens (14) concluded that "Questions concerning the long-term effects of both psychosocial and drug treatments of the schizophrenias remain unresolved and warrant continued investigation. . . ."

Implicit and explicit situational aspects of the therapeutic environment influence the placebo effect (7). Surely, too, expectations and convictions of both the patient and the therapist can render a placebo an effective treatment. They have to be believers. Thus an important research question concerns what we can do in the therapeutic milieu to effectively influence the eye of the beholder. The spectrum which this eye perceives covers a literary range from Shakespeare's glowing:

> I am giddy, expectation whirls me round,
> The imaginary relish is so sweet
> That it enchants my sense

to Pope's gloomy: "Blessed is the man who expects nothing for he shall never be disappointed."

We are not talking only of the patient's expectancies. Romano (11), discussing schizophrenia from the point of view of "changes in the observer as well as the observed," pointed out that "what one sees and hears is dependent, in some part, on expectations, and these are determined by one's *a priori* ideas of the nature of the distress."

Two little boys, ages 5 and 7, who live next door to us are at that stage of intellectual curiosity where everything is expressed as a riddle. They prefix every verbalization with "Guess what? Guess what?" I have a few riddles about schizophrenia. Additional riddles about schizophrenia are what is meant by the expression, "Carrying coals to Newcastle." One riddle is, "When is a treatment for schizophrenia not a treatment?" There are at least four answers to this question. The first is, "When it's a control." The second is, "When it's a failure." The third is, "When it wasn't needed because of spontaneous remission." The fourth is, "When it's a placebo that didn't work." It should be clear that one of the tricks in answering a riddle is shifting one's frame of reference. For example, here is another riddle: "When is a placebo not a placebo?" One answer is, "When it's an effective treatment." That's why Trousseau wrote 146 years ago (12), "You should treat as many patients as possible with the new drugs while they still have the power to heal."

REFERENCES

1. Astrup, C. (1973): Proposal for a prophylactic psychiatry. *Biol. Psychiatry,* 6:107–108.
2. Berg, A. O. (1977): Placebos: A brief review for family physicians. *J. Fam. Pract.,* 5:97–100.
3. Brody, J. E. (1979): *New York Times,* April 3, Section C, p. 1.
4. Campbell, C. Macfie (1935): *Destiny and Disease in Mental Disorders with Special Reference to the Schizophrenic Psychoses.* W. W. Norton, New York.
5. Grinker, R. R., Sr. (1975): *Psychiatry in Broad Perspective.* Behavioral Publications, New York.
6. Grinspoon, L., Ewalt, J. R., and Shader, R. I. (1972): *Schizophrenia: Pharmacotherapy and Psychotherapy.* Williams & Wilkins, Baltimore.
7. Gryll, S. L., and Katahn, M. (1978): Situational factors contributing to the placebo effect. *Psychopharmacology,* 57:253–261.
8. Keith, S. J., Gunderson, J. G., Reifman, A., Buchsbaum, S., and Mosher, L. R. (1976): Special report: Schizophrenia 1976. *Schizophr. Bull.,* 2(4):510–565.
9. Loftus, E. F., and Fries, J. F. (1979): Informed consent may be hazardous to health. *Science,* 204:11.

10. Pickens, R. (1977): Behavioral pharmacology: A brief history. In: *Advances in Behavioral Pharmacology, Vol. 1,* edited by T. Thompson and P. B. Dews, pp. 229–257. Academic Press, New York.
11. Romano, J. (1977): On the nature of schizophrenia: Changes in the observer as well as the observed (1932–77). *Schizophr. Bull.,* 3(4):532–558.
12. Shapiro, A. K. (1960): A contribution to a history of the placebo effect. *Behav. Sci.,* 5:109–135.
13. Shapiro, A. K., Struening, E. L., Barten, H., and Shapiro, E. (1975): Correlates of placebo reaction in an outpatient population. *Psychol. Med.,* 5:389–396.
14. Stephens, J. H. (1978): Long-term prognosis and followup in schizophrenia. *Schizophr. Bull.,* 4(1):25–47.

Perspectives in Schizophrenia Research,
edited by C. Baxter and T. Melnechuk.
Raven Press, New York, 1980.

Placebo Effect: From Control to Experimental Condition

Nina R. Schooler

Psychopharmacology Research Branch, National Institute of Mental Health, Rockville, Maryland 20857

LAYPERSON'S SUMMARY

The use of placebos (inert medications designed to provide an experimental control for the act of taking medication in studies of drugs) is discussed from a novel vantage point. Can administration of such inert substances provide information about the biological state of individuals being studied? By drawing on several examples, this chapter tries to suggest that this is possible and offers an example of a type of study with schizophrenic patients that might prove productive. The major thrust of the chapter, then, is to raise methodological issues about the design of such studies which need to be addressed if they are to be useful.

Finally, it is suggested that our understanding of both the positive and negative effects of drugs used in the treatment of schizophrenia makes studies which use placebo treatments innovatively both clinically desirable and ethically appropriate.

INTRODUCTION

Researchers who study the effects of therapeutic drugs on clinical response usually consider the "placebo" as an experimental tool to control for nonspecific effects of time, expectancy, and environment. By subtracting "placebo" effects from observed drug effects, they are left with specific effects attributable to the pharmacological action of the drug that is being studied. The assumption that response to placebo requires a nonbiological interpretation has been extended by analogy to etiology. Thus patients whose symptoms improve on hospitalization without specific drug intervention are seen as providing evidence in favor of a nonorganic or environmental etiology of their distress. There is also a body of literature which links a nonorganic etiology to a variety of psychotherapeutic, milieu-oriented treatment strategies, both for a wide range of schizophrenic individuals and for certain subgroups. However, the effectiveness of a nonorganic treatment strategy does not necessarily indicate that etiology should be sought in nonorganic factors, or conversely, that the efficacy of organically based treatments implies an organic etiology. Recent treatment research in schizophrenia provides numerous examples of environmental mediators of drug response (2,4,17) and behavioral treatments for biologically based disorders (1,15).

For purposes of the present discussion, placebo will not be considered as a control condition, but rather as an experimental condition in which nonorganic, noninvasive manipulations of the patient and his environment are translated within the individual into organic events or sequelae. The assumptions of such an approach, the definition of independent variables (including the placebo), and the outcome criteria may differ from those used in placebo-controlled clinical drug trials.

The study by Levine et al. (8) of the analgesic effect of a placebo provides a model and example of how a "placebo" can be used to reveal an underlying biological substrate. These investigators hypothesized that the analgesic effect of placebo was mediated by endorphins (endogenous opiates). To test this hypothesis, they administered placebo and naloxone (an opiate antagonist) to patients whose wisdom teeth had been extracted. Subjects received one of three treatment sequences: placebo followed by naloxone, placebo followed by placebo, or naloxone followed by placebo. Results indicated that in patients who initially were placebo "responders," naloxone reduced the analgesic effect of the placebo. No change was seen in patients who did not experience pain relief with placebo. The extent of the subsequent placebo response was smaller in patients who had received naloxone prior to placebo. Since administration of an opiate antagonist both reversed placebo analgesia and blocked its occurrence, the investigators concluded that placebo analgesia is mediated by elevation of endorphins (a biological response). It is of interest to consider that in the absence of prior knowledge of an endogenous opiate, these findings would have been virtually uninterpretable and probably the experiments would never have been conceived.

The design of the foregoing study is similar to designs used in studies in which pharmacological challenges are used to predict the effectiveness of a subsequent treatment or to assess the biological state of an organism (6,13). An early example of the use of response to placebo to predict subsequent treatment response is provided by a study by Hankoff, Engelhardt, and Freedman (5). They found that schizophrenic patients who showed no response or a negative response to a 3-week treatment with placebo were more likely to drop out of a subsequent course of neuroleptic treatment or be hospitalized while on neuroleptic treatment than those who responded positively to the placebo treatment. The design of the study is much like that used in studies employing a pharmacological challenge, i.e., the placebo intervention elicits a response which provides information about how the individual will respond to subsequent interventions. However, the search for variables which affected subsequent response was directed toward factors such as denial of illness and whether patients had been treated previously as inpatients or as outpatients, rather than the possibility of a biological mechanism which mediated the response to placebo.

More recently, responses to pharmacological challenges have been used to predict subsequent response to drug treatment by schizophrenics. In their studies with "test doses" of neuroleptic drugs (chlorpromazine and thiothixene), May, Van Putten, and co-workers (10,16) found that the most successful predictor of treatment outcome was the patient's subjective response to the drug. Patients who had dysphoric responses 4 hr after a single drug dose showed poorer response to drug treatment as measured by clinical rating scales at the end of their hospital stay. Moreover, this subjective response was not related to symptom levels prior to the start of treatment. The utilization of this "test dose" design with a placebo challenge rather than with pharmacologically active agents is one example of how placebos could be used to study individual biological functioning.

METHODOLOGICAL ISSUES

Future studies which use placebo conditions in studies of underlying biological mechanisms will be successful only if they are specific in defining the nature of the population studied, in defining placebo (the independent variable), in specifying the nature of the effects (the dependent variables), and in hypothesizing the mechanism for those effects (the intervening variables).

Identification of the Population

As in most experimental studies, in investigations of neuroleptic effects with a placebo control, design of the study is affected by the population being investigated. In one design, a patient population receiving neuroleptics is identified and drug withdrawal is placebo controlled. In the second, a patient population receiving no drug treatment is selected and either a drug or a placebo is administered. This difference in design will affect the interpretation of placebo effects.

Results obtained in one population cannot be translated to another. For example, it was found by Paul, Tobias, and Holly (11) that there was no effect of phenothiazine withdrawal in a population of chronic hospitalized schizophrenic patients. The subjects in this study had been rejected for community placement because of their deteriorated and severely regressed condition. Although these results have been cited as an indication of a general lack of effectiveness of phenothiazines, they are valid only for chronically hospitalized non-drug-responsive individuals, and need to be qualified still further because the patients tested had been transferred quite recently to wards with active psychosocial treatment programs. Thus effects observed in withdrawal studies are dependent on variables that reflect the nature of the population studied, including prior dosage (12) and degree of chronicity.

Application of diagnostic or demographic selection criteria will also vary depending on whether patients selected for study are or are not currently receiving drug treatment. Because schizophrenic patients will generally be receiving drugs and may not show florid symptoms, greater reliance on records to establish a diagnosis of schizophrenia in such patients according to Research Diagnostic Criteria will be needed.

Thus the simple question of whether schizophrenic subjects are selected when on or off drugs reflects a major issue of sampling and therefore will have an inpact on the general applicability of a diagnosis, subsequent choice of dependent variables, and interpretation of the results. The definition of the population is of even greater importance in studies concerned with biological effects. Lack of attention to this parameter may be a significant factor that accounts for variability of results from one study to another.

Definition of the Placebo

"Placebo" has its origin in the Latin word *placere*—to please. In the first person future indicative, *placere* becomes placebo, "I shall please." Which aspect of the placebo treatment causes the "pleasing" effect? As long as the placebo condition is simply a control, that question is not very important. Only when the placebo is the experimental condition, as proposed here, or when the placebo has an effect which calls for an explanation does the need for specificity of the placebo condition become important. In a follow-up study of the effects of neuroleptics in schizophrenics, we observed a reduced likelihood of rehospitalization during the first year following discharge in patients who had been treated with placebo (14) compared with those treated with drug. Multiple interpretations of such a finding are possible. It is possible, for example, that the staff responded with an extra measure of care and devotion to the placebo-treated subjects because of "guilt" feelings at having withheld drug treatment. This attention may have resulted in the better outcome. Alternately, the longer hospitalization experienced by the placebo-treated patients as compared to the drug-treated patients may have resulted in better reintegration at the time of discharge, and therefore a reduced risk of returning to the hospital. A third possibility requires the assumption that treatment with neuroleptics predisposes patients to relapse when drugs are withdrawn because patients do not develop alternative inner resources. Most patients in this study did not receive continuous maintenance drug treatment following discharge. Thus, if the assumption of dependence is true, the placebo-treated patients, having developed less dependence, were less vulnerable to relapse following discontinuation.

One might also consider possible artifacts in the design of the study which could have led to biased results. For example, it is possible that the patients who were able to complete the 6-week clinical trial on placebo were less severely ill than those in the drug-treated group and therefore less likely to relapse subsequently. The major point to be drawn from this range of possibilities is that the placebo condition in this study does not provide us with any good and rigorous way to discriminate among these alternate interpretations.

Determination of Outcome Measures

In studies of neuroleptic effects with a placebo control, the definition of outcome varies, of course, with the nature of the study. The most frequently employed clinical measures are as follows: (a) relapse (defined as a simple binary variable); (b) time to relapse (or risk of relapse per unit time); (c) symptom status (indexed by global measures of change); and (d) ratings of psychopathology based on behavioral observations. Perhaps because of the assumption referred to earlier, that response to placebo requires a nonbiological interpretation, there has been little systematic investigation of biological responses to defined placebo interventions. This lack of attention to hypotheses linking biological sequelae to nonbiological interventions reflects the same logical fallacy involved in linking an organic etiology to organic treatment and nonorganic etiology to nonorganic treatment.

Ethical Considerations

A factor that must be considered in the design of studies involving placebos in chronic schizophrenia is the ethics of research with the "institutionalized mentally disabled." The population of interest here, chronic schizophrenic patients, includes many who would meet that designation. The uncertain magnitude of the risk of tardive dyskinesia and other possible side effects of neuroleptic drugs offers excellent clinical justification for studying the effects of placebo, drug withdrawal, and specific environmental treatments. Placebo, drug withdrawal, and specific environmental treatments need not be defined as the control conditions necessary for the study of drug effects, but as experimental strategies needed for estimating risk for tardive dyskinesia and for assessment of alternatives to drug treatment. Recently, we have conducted such studies (7). The consent document for a double-blind study in which neuroleptics were withdrawn informed patients that they were being given an opportunity to have medication withdrawn to assess both development of abnormal involuntary movements related to tardive dyskinesia and the stability of clinical remission. Subjects who fell in the control group (continued neuroleptic) were assured that they would have a subsequent opportunity to have their drug treatment discontinued. As expected, the results of the study indicated that neuroleptic withdrawal is associated with increased risk of both relapse and development of abnormal movements associated with tardive dyskinesia. However, its significance lies in the nature of the consent negotiated with the subjects in the study.

CONCLUSION

We have come in a full circle. In commenting on Philip May's landmark clinical trial described in *Treatment of Schizophrenia* (9), Jonathan Cole said, "The handful of controlled studies of specific nondrug treatments (psychotherapy, intensive milieu therapy) . . . would make most clinical investigators reluctant to place acutely ill schizophrenics even on psychotherapy without drugs for any prolonged period. The . . . results of this study serve, in fact, to make any replication attempt improbable." It is now clear that both extrinsic questions about risks with neuroleptic treatments and intrinsic questions about the limits of efficacy of these drugs require renewed attention and should include research with placebos or focused noninvasive treatments.

When fashions change and neckties become more narrow again or skirts become longer again, the old narrow ties and long skirts in our closets do not look quite right. Similarly, the new generation of scientific questions about placebo effects cannot be answered by dusting off our old data. New research which addresses the questions in contemporary terms with greater emphasis on internal biological mechanisms and attention to issues of experimental design represents the direction we will have to take.

REFERENCES

1. Albanese, H., and Gaarder, K. (1970): Biofeedback treatment of tardive dyskinesia. *Am. J. Psychiatry,* 134:1149–1150.
2. Brown, G., Birely, J., and Wing, J. (1972): Influence of family life on the course of schizophrenic disorders: A replication. *Br. J. Psychiatry,* 121:241–258.
3. Goldberg, S., Schooler, N., Davidson, E., and Kayce, M. (1966): Sex and race differences in response to drug treatment among schizophrenics. *Psychopharmacologia,* 9:31–47.
4. Goldberg, S., Schooler, N., Hogarty, G., and Roper, M. (1977): Prediction of relapse in schizophrenic outpatients treated by drug and sociotherapy. *Arch. Gen. Psychiatry,* 34:171–184.
5. Hankoff, L., Engelhardt, D., and Freedman, N. (1960): Placebo response in schizophrenic outpatients. *Arch. Gen. Psychiatry,* 2:43–52.
6. Janowsky, D., El-Yousef, M., Davis, J. M., and Sekerke, H. (1973): Provocation of schizophrenic symptoms by intravenous administration of methylphenidate. *Arch. Gen. Psychiatry,* 28:185–191.
7. Levine, J., Schooler, N., Severe, J., Escobar, J., Gelenberg, A., Mandel, M., Sovner, R., and Steinbook, R. (1980): Discontinuation of oral and depot fluphenazine in schizophrenic patients after one year of continuous medication: A controlled study. *Long-term Effects of Neuroleptics,* edited by E. Costa, F. Cattabeni, G. Racagni, and P. F. Spano, pp. 483–493. Raven Press, New York.
8. Levine, J. D., Gordon, N., and Fields, H. (1978): The mechanism of placebo analgesia. *Lancet,* II, 8091:654–657.
9. May, P. R. A. (1968): *Treatment of Schizophrenia.* Science House, New York.
10. May, P. R. A., Van Putten, T., Yale, C., Potepan, P., Jenden, D., Fairchild, M., Goldstein, M., and Dixon, W. (1976): Predicting individual responses to drug treatment in schizophrenia: A test dose model. *J. Nerv. Ment. Dis.,* 162:177–183.
11. Paul, G., Tobias, L., and Holly, B. (1972): Maintenance psychotropic drugs in the presence of active treatment programs. *Arch. Gen. Psychiatry,* 27:106–115.
12. Prien, R., Cole, J., and Belkin, N. (1968): Relapse in chronic schizophrenics following abrupt withdrawal of tranquilizing medication. *Br. J. Psychiatry,* 115:679–686.

13. Rotrosen, J., Angrist, B., and Paquin, J. (1978): Neuroendocrine studies with dopamine agonists in schizophrenia. *Psychopharmacol. Bull.,* 14:14–17.
14. Schooler, N., Goldberg, S., Boothe, H., and Cole, J. (1967): One year after discharge: Community adjustment of schizophrenic patients. *Am. J. Psychiatry,* 123:986–995.
15. Topoff, M. (1972): Massed practice, relaxation and assertion training in the treatment of Gilles de la Tourette's Syndrome. *J. Behav. Ther. Exp. Psychiatry,* 4:71–73.
16. Van Putten, T., and May, P. R. A. (1978): Subjective response as a predictor of outcome in pharmacotherapy. *Arch. Gen. Psychiatry,* 35:477–480.
17. Vaughn, C., and Leff, J. (1976): The influence of family and social factors on the course of psychiatric illness. *Br. J. Psychiatry,* 129:125–137.

Discussion

Brown: The placebo effect in patients who have been treated with drugs and then put on placebo is often discussed as if it involves suggestion, but it may involve classic conditioning, which could be tested in an animal model.

Beck: I did test that idea in an animal. I injected a cat several times with a drug, bulbocapnine, that caused it to salivate, then I injected it with saline, and it salivated profusely.

Freed: We (4) tested the idea in rats, with an injection of alcohol, which caused a decrement from baseline in measures of activity. Some reacted a week later to an injection of saline as if they had been given alcohol. Of course other aspects of the experience—being held, injected, and put on an activity platform—had meaning, too.

Nasrallah: On the role of suggestion in the placebo effect, the evidence so far shows that hypnotic analgesia is not reversible with naloxone.

Cole: The placebo effect in schizophrenia may barely exist as a phenomenon. It's almost never been studied. Don Gallant (1) claims that chronic schizophrenics get no benefit from placebo. However, Olson and Peterson (5) showed that people maintained on placebo relapsed less than people maintained on nothing, but whether placebo does anything but help prevent relapse is another question.

Singh: In 1970 we (7) did a study of the first break in acute schizophrenics. Within an active therapeutic program, patients received placebo for 4 weeks, preceded in most cases by 2 weeks of receiving neither drugs nor placebo. A 6-week study found no significant improvement in any of the 50 or so parameters we studied—psychopathology, sleeplessness, directed and nondirected participation in activities, and so forth. I think we can safely say that the placebo effect does not exist in schizophrenia.

Schooler: I wouldn't say that, because studies in different kinds of populations have shown very definite nonspecific effects. Paul (6) and colleagues conducted a triple-blind withdrawal study in which they showed a lack of deterioration on drug removal in very chronic schizophrenic patients. Some placebo effect was surely involved in that.

Carpenter: Extrapyramidal side effects have been reported in placebo-treated schizophrenic patients.

Hiatt: There must be some difference between those people who are acutely psychotic, are admitted to the hospital, and the next day are well, and those people who enter the hospital acutely psychotic and the next day are worse, with no drug in either case.

Mosher: Dr. Singh, I can show you data from the inpatient multidimensional psychiatric rating scale showing that a group of newly admitted schizophrenic patients' symptoms remitted as quickly over 6 weeks without any neuroleptics at all as did a similar group treated with neuroleptics. It was clearly not a drug effect, and it was contrary to my hypothesis that it would not happen in 6 weeks, but it did happen. However, I dislike calling it a placebo effect, for we see it as an effect of an environment specifically designed to deal with those patients.

Yuwiler: I think the key to the placebo response is in the biological individuality of the patient, but we lack tools to approach it. Ours is a biology of means, and of mean differences between populations. But the idosyncratic meaning of a stimulus to a particular individual may uniquely affect him both physiologically and psychologically.

Schooler: The methodological issue is that little research has been done that fills in the complete paradigm, which includes a no-pill condition. If you're simply concerned with *controlling* for nonspecific effects, the placebo pill itself sums them all up very neatly.

Cole: A psychiatrist friend of mine to whom a patient once complained about auditory hallucinations told him to put cotton in his ears and the hallucinations went away.

Yuwiler: Most children, when blood is drawn, show a corticoid response. But some autistic children have no corticoid rise in response to blood drawing, and they behave as if they didn't know they were being given a needle.

Carpenter: Ed Fink and I looked at 24-hr 17-OHCS and free cortisol in urine of acute schizophrenics on the day of admission (all studies show a first day elevation) and found no values higher than normal limits (despite acute psychosis and first day effects!). Marvin Orne discusses a negative "placebo" response that may help explain effects opposite to those expected in drug and other treatments. Has that been important?

Schooler: I haven't considered it.

Cole: It's hard to unscramble. In a hospital study of antipsychotics versus placebo, more of those getting placebo got worse than got better, but whether it's a negative placebo effect or the natural course of the illness is the problem.

Carpenter: Orne's point is somewhat different. He observes that a small proportion (up to 20%) of subjects have responses contrary to those expected with a non-placebo intervention (e.g., a hypnotic subject told to relax may become excited, an analgesic drug may be followed by increased pain). Schizophrenic negativity is what I have in mind in this regard. Some of this work has been summarized by Evans (3).

May: I have no data but it is clinical lore that some schizophrenics will, when told to do something, do just the opposite. So, to get them to *do* anything, you must use negative psychology. I think paranoid people might show a *negative* placebo effect related to the paranoia.

Schooler: That suggests the utility of the no-pill control.

J. Davis: Did you say that in Engelhart's work there was a good prophylactic effect of placebo?

Schooler: The placebo response in the early weeks predicted good subsequent response to drugs.

Perez-Polo: In talking about the placebo effect, we are using a highly simplistic misnomer, an enormous umbrella that covers changes in concentration at different time sequences, as well as psychosocial factors. Unfortunately, we cannot do with people what is done in certain animal preparations where the stimulus used is white noise. With people we cannot ask for such extreme uniformity of treatment, and to take into account all of the environmental factors is not a realistic task. In order to separate the environmental factors from the placebo effect, is there some way to create the equivalent of a white-noise condition?

Zubin: Thus far in this conference, the use of white noise as a factor is all that anyone has offered on the question of a noninvasive approach. In that regard, what about such things as life events and social support networks—these very important factors that serve noninvasively either to elicit an episode or to protect a person from an episode? We need to think more about life events, even though we don't understand how a threatening life event produces a central nervous system reaction. It's easy enough to understand how a chemical put into the body can affect the CNS, but how is the birth or death of a relative transduced and insinuated into the CNS? The problem is in defining a life event. I think an event is a life event when it constricts your social network. We need to study this. Dr. George Brown (2) has found that the presence of a confidant prevents depression.

REFERENCES

1. Bishop, M., and Gallant, D. (1966): Observation on placebo response in chronic schizophrenic patients. *Arch. Gen. Psychiatry,* 14:497–503.
2. Brown, G. W., and Harris, T. (1978): *Social Origins of Depression: A Study of Psychiatric Disorder in Women.* Free Press, New York.

3. Evans, F. J. (1977): The placebo control of pain: A paradigm for investigating nonspecific effects in psychotherapy. In: *Psychiatry: Areas of Promise and Advancement,* edited by J. P. Brady, J. Mendels, W. R. Reiger, and M. T. Orne, pp. 129–136. Spectrum, New York.
4. Freed, E. X., Carpenter, J. A., and Riley, E. (1976): Illustration of a control problem in alcohol research designs. *Behav. Neuropsychiatr.,* 7:67–70.
5. Olson, G., and Peterson, D. (1962): Intermittent chemotherapy for chronic psychiatric inpatients. *J. Nerv. Ment. Dis.,* 134:145–149.
6. Paul, G. L., Tobias, L. L., and Holly, B. L. (1972): Maintenance psychotropic drugs in the presence of active treatment programs. *Arch. Gen. Psychiatry,* 27:106–115.
7. Singh, M. M., and Smith, J. M. (1973): Kinetics and dynamics of response to haloperidol in acute schizophrenia: A longitudinal study of the therapeutic process. *Compr. Psychiatr.,* 14:393–414.

Perspectives in Schizophrenia Research,
edited by C. Baxter and T. Melnechuk.
Raven Press, New York, 1980.

A Brain Tissue Resource Center to Promote Research in Schizophrenia

Edward D. Bird

McLean Hospital, Harvard Medical School, and Ralph Lowell Laboratories, Belmont, Massachusetts 02178

LAYPERSON'S SUMMARY

The remarkable growth in new biochemical knowledge of animal brain has stimulated an interest in applying this knowledge to neuropsychiatric disorders in man. Contrary to popular belief, a number of important chemical substances are very stable in human brain and can still be measured 3 days after death, when proper handling of tissues is observed. Useful information has come from the study of several disorders involving the brain when the neurochemical data are compared to that in the brain of control subjects handled similarly after death. Ehringer and Hornykiewicz's discovery of a decreased concentration of the chemical substance dopamine in postmortem Parkinson's disease brain led to the development of useful drugs for this crippling disorder. Huntington's disease (HD), an autosomal dominant inherited neurological disorder, has also come under neurochemical investigation, and a very large number of chemical alterations in the brain have now been reported in this tragic genetic disease.

Since HD is not a common disorder, it was necessary to organize a system for the collection, shipping, and suitable storage of postmortem tissues. The author initiated a collection in England and was able to collect over a 6-year period more than 250 brains from patients dying with the disorder. The success of this scheme allowed the author to send over 50 shipments of tissues to neuroscientists throughout the world and, as a consequence, there are now more neurochemical data published on the Huntington brain than on any other brain with a specific neurological disorder.

This collection scheme served as a model for the acquisition of postmortem brains from dying patients with a history of schizophrenia. Early data from the author's laboratory and from neuroscientists who received some of these tissues indicate that schizophrenia is accompanied by specific neurochemical alterations in the brain.

The establishment of a Brain Tissue Resource Center at the McLean Hospital in Belmont, Massachusetts, now provides a center on the East Coast of the United States where brain tissues from patients dying with neuropsychiatric diseases may be sent for storage, dissection, and ultimate disbursement to active neuroscientists throughout the country. The success of such a collection scheme is dependent on a cooperative team that involves not only the families of patients that have been afflicted with this disorder, but also a number of allied health professionals.

In this chapter the procedures for handling such tissues are described. Some of the data obtained with postmortem schizophrenic brain are presented to indicate that there is scope for further studies in the investigation of schizophrenia.

The extensive clinical records on veterans and the close contact that the Veterans Administration keeps with its patients make this health care organization ideal for promoting and being involved in research on schizophrenia.

INTRODUCTION

During the last two decades, there has been a remarkable growth in the field of neurochemistry. New tools and methods have been designed to measure an ever increasing number of molecular substances within the brain. In animals with discretely placed lesions, neurochemical methods have expanded our knowledge regarding various pathways in the brain. The development of new neuropharmacologic agents that are effective in certain disorders has stimulated neuroscientists to apply their expertise to the investigation of possible neurochemical disturbances in a variety of neuropsychiatric disorders in man.

Carlsson et al. (7) developed a method for measuring catecholamines in brain tissue, and this method was applied by Ehringer and Hornykiewicz (11) to the examination of postmortem brain tissue from patients dying with Parkinson's disease. They found that the basal ganglia of the brain from Parkinson's disease was deficient in dopamine, and this led to the development of various neuropharmacologic agents to correct this deficiency.

This study stimulated a number of investigators to carry out neurochemical measurements on postmortem brain from patients dying with other neuropsychiatric disorders. These include Huntington's disease (1), Alzheimer's disease (16), and more recently schizophrenia (3). Huntington's disease (HD) is the rarest of these disorders, and it has been difficult to collect a series of postmortem brains from patients dying with this disorder in a local region. The author decided that in order to collect significant data on brain tissue from patients dying with HD, it would be necessary to collect tissues from a wide region. This led to the development of a brain tissue bank at the University of Cambridge, England.

The term "Brain Bank" was adopted following the example set by Dr. Wallace Tourtellotte, who for many years had collected tissues from patients who died with multiple sclerosis. This "Brain Bank" later expanded to include tissues from a number of other disorders. Since Dr. Tourtellotte's center and the present bank that has now been established in Boston at the McLean Hospital make tissues available to other researchers throughout the country, a more suitable term might be a "Brain Tissue Resource Center."

The advantage of having such resource centers throughout the country is to maximize the number of tissues that could be collected from one disorder at each center so as to provide tissues to any one of a number of established investigators. Furthermore, a center can establish reliable methods for distribution of such tissues by the frequent utilization of the delivery systems. The collection of tissue can be standardized and thereby reduce the variable conditions that might affect neurochemical data.

If a brain tissue resource center is established in a large academic center, then a large source of controlled material to match the abnormal tissues will be available. Academic centers would become well-known throughout the country for their special interest in certain diseases and thereby increase the referrals from pathologists and physicians around the country. Occasionally, there is a local need by neuroscientists for unfrozen tissues obtained quickly from the postmortem, and these probably would be available only in a large city. It is the author's opinion that the collection of postmortem tissues by a center should be specialized for two reasons: (a) the Director of such a collection will be more enthusiastic and personally involved with a disorder that represents his special area of interest, and (b) as mentioned above, a center that specializes will eventually become nationally known for that disorder, and will lead to a continual referral of specimens.

Huntington's Disease Brain Tissue Resource

The development of the Brain Tissue Resource Center for Huntington's Disease and Schizophrenia in Cambridge, England, will be described since this may serve as a model for others to follow in the development of brain banks elsewhere.

In England and Wales there are few nursing homes for the chronic care of choreic patients, and therefore most patients with HD are admitted to psychiatric hospitals in the terminal phase of the disease. Visits by the author to a number of mental hospitals throughout England and Wales were made to discuss arrangements for postmortems on patients dying with HD.

Prior to my visit to the United Kingdom, few patients with HD were being autopsied, but psychiatrists and pathologists were enthusiastic and helpful regarding the plan to collect postmortem brain tissue, and they alerted their staff regarding this new endeavor.

There was an immediate increase in the number of autopsies carried out on patients dying with HD which probably was a result of my visits to the various mental hospitals. However, two other factors, I think, played a role in this immediate response; pathologists were not asked to perform autopsies outside of general working hours, although on a number of occasions they did autopsies at unusual hours, and secondly, I always made it my responsibility to collect the tissues from the pathologists.

The United Kingdom Committee to Combat Huntington's Chorea, a lay organization of families afflicted with this disease, informed their members through their "Newsletter" about the Brain Tissue Bank in Cambridge and the benefits of donating postmortem tissue for HD research. When a patient with HD died, families immediately asked the attending physician to organize an autopsy and to alert the Brain Bank in Cambridge.

I had the cooperation of Dr. J. A. N. Corsellis, Professor of Neuropathology at the Institute of Psychiatry, University of London, who undertook to examine each fixed hemisphere histopathologically. It soon became apparent that some patients diagnosed as having HD, in fact, had other inherited neurological disorders, such as familial Alzheimer's disease or autosomal dominant cerebellar ataxia. The local physicians and psychiatrists were given a full histopathological report and neurochemical results for their hospital records, and this provided a stimulus for further referrals to our facility.

Schizophrenia

Patients with HD sometimes have psychotic features that may be indistinguishable from those of schizophrenia. After reviewing a large number of clinical records on HD patients who had died in mental hospitals in England, I was impressed by the number of patients originally admitted with a diagnosis of schizophrenia who had the diagnosis changed to HD after choreiform movements appeared and a more extensive family history was elicited.

If the neurochemical imbalance present in HD brain could be associated with a psychotic illness, it seemed important to examine the neurochemistry of the postmortem brain from patients dying with the diagnosis of schizophrenia. Having established a brain tissue collection from a number of mental hospitals in the United Kingdom, it was fairly easy to include the collection of postmortem tissue from patients who died with a hospital diagnosis of schizophrenia. Also, the National Schizophrenia Fellowship in the United Kingdom, a lay organization of concerned family members with this disorder, was enthusiastic regarding the importance of the neurochemical examination of postmortem brain tissue. Within 18 months, 75 postmortem brains from patients who had a hospital diagnosis of schizophrenia were collected at the Brain Bank in Cambridge. In addition to carrying out our own studies, we were able to distribute these tissues to neuroscientists in the United Kingdom, Canada, and the United States who were interested in studying schizophrenia.

McLean Hospital Brain Tissue Resource Center

As it was apparent that there was an increased need in the United States for postmortem brain tissues to investigate both Huntington's disease and schizophrenia, the author, in collaboration with Dr. Alfred Pope and Dr. Steven Matthysse, established a Brain Tissue Resource Center at the Ralph Lowell

Laboratory of the Mailman Research Center at McLean Hospital in Belmont, Massachusetts. The location of the resource center at McLean follows the principles outlined earlier since the McLean Hospital is well-known for its research into psychiatric disorders and is attached to a large academic community by being a division of the Massachusetts General Hospital within the Harvard Medical School. The center is supported by NIMH and NINCDS at NIH and the Huntington's Chorea Foundation, the Hereditary Disease Foundation, and the Scottish Rite Foundation.

The procedure for collecting tissue is basically similar to that worked out previously by the author in the United Kingdom. The Huntington's Disease Lay Societies in the United States have been informed of the existence of this bank, and they in turn have alerted their members through their newsletters and, as a result, a number of choreic brain tissues have been collected.

Preliminary contacts have been made with lay chapters concerned with schizophrenia in regard to the collection of postmortem brains from patients dying with this disorder.

I anticipate a great deal more difficulty collecting schizophrenia brain tissue in the United States than in England, since a trend to discharge many schizophrenia patients to the community results in such patients losing contact with the local authorities.

There does exist, however, in the United States within the Veterans Administration a system in which patients with schizophrenia do keep in contact with their local hospitals or with another Veterans Administration facility. When veterans become seriously ill, they are usually admitted to a Veterans' hospital. There are a number of reasons why one might look toward the Veterans Administration for future research in schizophrenia; the first and probably the most important is the accurate recording of the initial psychotic episode in the service record of a veteran along with a continual extensive follow-up throughout the years. Secondly, the drug history on each patient is recorded in the clinical notes that are invaluable in the final interpretation of the neurochemical data.

It is the author's opinion that for future research postmortem brain tissue from patients dying from schizophrenia will need to be carried out in the United States under the auspices of or in collaboration with the Veterans Administration.

As noted in other chapters throughout this volume, there are a number of basic scientists working at various VA hospitals throughout the United States who are eager to apply their expertise to the study of schizophrenia.

GENERAL PROCEDURE FOR ORGANIZING A POSTMORTEM BRAIN COLLECTION

Autopsy Permit

One aim in collecting brain tissue for neurochemical or histopathological studies should be to collect such tissues as quickly after death as possible. When postmortem brain studies on Huntington's disease, schizophrenia, or other neuropsychiatric disorders are contemplated, plans can be made years before death by having the afflicted person sign a donor card, just as plans are made by many individuals to donate their eyes or kidneys for transplantation or to medical research. It is recommended that the family discuss this among themselves in order that they will be clear regarding what is to be done when death occurs. An organ donation signature by a donor is legal after death according to the Anatomical Gift Act, and most legally responsible next of kin will concur with the wishes of the donee. However, if the next-of-kin voice an objection to an autopsy, then, I believe, it wise to concur with their wishes, since to do otherwise would only create bad public relations for medical research on autopsy tissues. When a donee has not signed a card, the consent form for an autopsy is not legal until signed by the next-of-kin after death. This can sometimes be given by telephone with two witnesses at the hospital or by telegram from the next-of-kin.

The primary physician caring for the case also needs to be made aware of the family's wishes. Physicians will more likely arrange postmortem examinations if they have received previous information regarding the importance of studying brain tissue after death. It, therefore, falls upon the organizer of a postmortem brain resource to institute an education program for physicians, psychiatrists, neurologists, and pathologists in order that they will be continually alerted to the latest research developments in understanding disorders of the brain.

The pathologist is the key person to make certain that the autopsy is properly carried out. We need to remember that the postmortem is an important aspect of total medical care. Attending physicians and house officers need to communicate with the pathologist and visit the autopsy suite at the time of the postmortem in order that the full benefit of the autopsy can be derived. Many of the clinical features that may or may not appear in the written record may be vital to the pathologist who is continually searching for new knowledge regarding various disorders. Statistics have been compiled showing that in 40% of the autopsies carried out today, the diagnosis arrived at by the pathologist differs from the clinical diagnosis. However, since the autopsy rate has decreased in recent years, this percentage may be biased by the fact that more of the autopsies carried out recently were requested by clinicians because they doubted the clinical diagnosis and wanted a pathologist's diagnosis. This revealing statistic also indicates the importance of autopsy procedures and the need to retain them in clinical practice. Unfortunately, there appear to be fewer autopsies performed in hospitals throughout the country. The importance of the pathologist and his department within our hospitals needs to be recognized and adequately supported by the government and the hospital administration.

Medical Examiner's Office

The autopsies of a number of patients dying with neuropsychiatric disorders are handled by the medical examiner's office. We hope that, in the future, both the neurochemical and histopathological examination of brain tissue might help not only the medical examiner in his final assessment of the case, but also bereaved families who, for the first time, may be given the exact diagnosis of their deceased kin. A recent patient with a diagnosis of schizophrenia, who came to the attention of a medical examiner, was found at autopsy to have Huntington's disease. This new diagnosis raised many new problems for the family who, for the first time, were made aware that they were "at risk" for this tragic inherited disorder. One might wonder how often a diagnosis for HD is missed, since few autopsies are carried out on patients with "schizophrenia." If the diagnosis of schizophrenia is made sometime early in the course of HD, it is conceivable that some patients receiving heavy doses of neuroleptics may never really show some of the signs of Huntington's disease and may, therefore, remain undiagnosed as having HD.

Nurses' Protocol

It is important to have a standardized protocol included within the clinical record, preferably inside the front cover of the patient's chart, so that all old and new staff, at all hours of the day, will be aware that everyone has agreed that an autopsy should be done after death. The protocol should indicate that the corpse needs to be taken promptly to the mortuary suite and placed in a 4°C refrigerator in preparation for the autopsy. The ward staff need to alert the attending physician and the pathologist in order that arrangements for the autopsy can be made without delay. Should the corpse need transporting to a nearby hospital, the arrangements for transportation need to be made in advance so that whenever the call comes, there will be no question of reimbursement or responsibility for transportation.

Pathologists' Protocol

A complete autopsy should be performed, since information derived from other organs of the body may be vital to an understanding of the neurochemical or histopathological findings in the brain.

The brain should be removed promptly along with the pituitary gland with as much of the pituitary stalk attached to the brain as possible in order to preserve the median eminence. The brain should then be sliced sagittally in the midline through the brainstem, cerebellum, and cerebral hemisphere. One-half of the brain should be placed into a suitable fixative, usually neutral formalin. The other half should be placed in a plastic box with the flat medial surface of the brain down in order to maintain the anatomical configuration of the brain when it freezes. The box should be sealed with a lid and placed in a deep freeze at −20°C or lower.

It is important to be aware that, frequently, the brain is the last organ of the body to be examined, in which case the diener may remove the brain and lay it in a bowl at room temperature until the complete autospy is done. For the purposes of neurochemistry, one should resist removing the brain from the skull until it is to be examined, since certain neurochemical substances deteriorate rapidly after being exposed to air at room temperature. Once the tissues have been placed in formalin, and one-half has been sealed in a plastic box in a freezer, then the respective brain bank can be called regarding pick-up of the tissues.

Formalin-Fixed Hemisphere

The brain may be examined histopathologically by a local neuropathologist. Alternately, if there is no local neuropathologist available, the brain bank will provide a histopathological report after the fixed brain has been sent to the bank. The brain should remain in formalin at the donating institution for 1 month, until firm, in order to withstand the stress of transportation through the mail. The formalin should be changed at least one or twice during the month, and then the brain should be drained and wrapped in damp formalin paper toweling. The wrapped brain should be placed in a plastic box, sealed with tape, and then placed in a suitable container for mailing.

It is important to try to obtain a histopathological report fairly promptly for the benefit of the investigators carrying out the neurochemical studies. It is equally important to get the report back to the donating institution in order that they can complete their records. It is imperative, also, to provide information to the family through their physician.

Frozen Hemisphere

Although dry ice is sometimes available, many hospitals do not have access to dry ice. The pathologist, who has already been generous in giving his time to arrange the autopsy, should not be overburdened by being asked to search for dry ice. My policy has been to prepare a styrofoam box with dry ice for the pathologist; a courier agency then collects the box, takes it to the airline, and it is delivered to the donating hospital, usually within 24 hr. The hospital technicians remove the brain from the plastic box that has been stored in the freezer, seal the brain in a plastic bag, and place it on the dry ice for return shipment to the brain bank. A complete two-way trip time of 48 hr, or at the most 72 hr, is required for this procedure.

Once the frozen tissues arrive at the brain bank, they are stored at −70°C or colder until they are dissected. Once they are ready for dissection, the brain can be removed for 24 hr to a freezer at −10°C to −15°C, which is a suitable temperature for slicing frozen brain. The brain can be sliced in 3 or 4 mm large coronal sections, usually starting at the anterior pole. The coronal sections are laid on a frozen surface so that the tissues never reach the melting point. The frozen surface ought to be at −7°C or colder; the slices usually maintain this temperature, making it possible to differentiate white from gray matter and to dissect neuroanatomical areas. Lower temperatures make it more difficult to differentiate nuclear gray matter.

Neuroanatomical Dissection

The dissection of the brain can proceed using standard atlases. The atlas being utilized at present in our laboratory is the Schaltenbrand and Wahren Stereotaxic Atlas (18). Starting with the anterior area of the cortex, the various Brodman (6) regions of the cortex can be dissected, chopped with a fine blade to produce a homogeneous mix, and then placed into suitable tubes. The tissues going into the various tubes need to be representative aliquots from the area being dissected, and it is important to keep the tubes on dry ice. I have found that tubes containing 1 g are suitable for storage and can be removed to send *in toto* to prospective investigators without the need to remove aliquots.

The anatomical dissection of the brain is performed on the frozen coronal slices starting with Brodman cerebral cortical area 10, dissected at the most anterior pole of the brain, followed by areas 9,8 on subsequent slices, and then areas 11, 12 on the orbital surface of the frontal cortex. Finally, in the subcallosal region, Brodman area 25 can be removed.

At this point the very anterior tip of the striatum will appear. The most medial and ventral areas of the anterior striatum form the nucleus accumbens, which is part of the limbic system, and this area extends back to the anterior commissure. Proceeding posteriorly, the internal capsule makes its appearance in subsequent slices with the caudate and putamen separated by the internal capsule.

At this level, the anterior tip of the temporal lobe can be seen and the cortical Brodman area 34 can be removed. In the midline extending ventrally from the corpus callosum, rostral to the anterior commissure, the ventral and dorsal parts of the septal nuclei can be dissected. At this level, tissue, dorsal and medial to the caudate, near the midline, is lighter in color, more firm than the caudate, and forms the bed nucleus of the striae terminalis. Also at the level of the anterior commissure, the suprachiasmic and preoptic regions of the hypothalamus are seen. The basal ganglia contain the globus pallidus, and then as one proceeds more posteriorly, the globus pallidus is divided into the lateral and medial regions that can easily be separated from one another. In addition, at this level the amygdala makes its appearance in the temporal lobe and can be divided into the nuclear and cortical areas. In the more posterior sections, regions of the thalamus can be seen and can be divided into the ventral medial, ventral lateral, dorsal medial, and more posterior regions. In the midline again, the hypothalamus continues to make its appearance as far back as the mammary body and the median eminence, just above the pituitary stalk, if this indeed can still be found. At this stage, the median eminence has frequently been destroyed, either carried away with the hemisphere that is placed in formalin or pulled off with the pituitary stalk when the brain was removed. In the temporal lobe the hippocampus makes its appearance. In the brainstem, the red nucleus, the subthalamic nucleus, the dorsal and ventral aspects of the substantia nigra with zona reticulata ventrally and the zona compacta dorsally can be divided based largely on the dark pigment seen in the zona compacta as distinct from the more lightly colored zona reticulata. The interpeduncular nucleus can also be seen at this level. Extending down the brainstem, the olive makes its appearance and at this level, the cerebellum is present, and the dentate nucleus, vermus, and cerebellar cortex can then be removed.

At least 75 sections can be sampled, but this number is really dependent on the limit one sets on dissecting the brain. To dissect a full brain usually takes anywhere from 8 to 16 hr. All tissues, once collected in the tubes, should be returned to the −70°C freezer and filed in trays so that any specific samples can be easily retrieved for shipping, or for utilization locally. The shipping of tissues to investigators can be accomplished using the same system described earlier for collecting the brains. Samples are less likely to go astray if the local courier system is used regularly. It is important for the brain bank to keep accurate records of shipments, including the recording of the weigh bill number of each shipment, so that packages that are delayed more than 24 hr can be traced.

A large number of postmortem brains were collected from cases that had a diagnosis of Huntington's disease or schizophrenia and from cases that had died without a history of a psychoneurological disorder. A number of factors need to be considered when collecting postmortem brain tissue, and these will be reviewed.

Clinical Diagnosis

Huntington's Disease

Within the National Health Service in the United Kingdom, it is possible to exchange clinical notes between hospitals. This allowed us to carry out a thorough review of all the records. An IBM card was devised to summarize all the relevant clinical and drug data, and this information was recorded under a code number for each patient. This information was then available to all recipients of tissue samples so that they could correlate their neurochemical data with the clinical and/or pharmacologic history. Review of the clinical records on some patients with Huntington's disease were not typical for this disorder and, indeed, histopathology failed to confirm HD in about 7% of these cases.

Schizophrenia

It is necessary to have well-trained clinical psychiatrists to collaborate in any study involving the evaluation of neurochemical data in postmortem brain from cases in which a diagnosis of schizophrenia has been made.

In our original study of postmortem material from cases that had a psychotic illness during life, we had two psychiatric colleagues assess independently the case notes. They then classified each case either as "schizophrenia" or as "schizophrenia-like psychosis." When there was disagreement, the opinion of a third, more senior, psychiatrist became the determinant for a final classification (3). The main factors determining the diagnosis of schizophrenia were the following: (a) first psychiatric episode under the age of 30; (b) a chronic illness with repeated hospital admissions or, as in many cases, uninterrupted hospital care after the first admission; (c) the core symptoms of schizophrenic illness, as included in the nuclear syndrome of the Wing symptom check list, which roughly correspond to Schneider's first-rank symptoms; and (d) the absence of significant organic illness or psychotogenic drug abuse. We found on review of the clinical notes from 75 autopsied cases who had a history of schizophrenia that approximately two-thirds of the cases could be considered as having had a typical schizophrenic illness and one-third to have had a schizophrenic-like illness.

Again, it is crucial to this evaluation to be able to extensively review the clinical notes, particularly to be able to review the notes of the first psychotic episode.

Time Period Between Death and Freezing of the Brain Tissue

The general policy was to handle abnormal brain tissues in the same way as tissue from control brains. This includes similar postmortem temperatures and time periods from death to freezing of the tissues for both groups. A corpse is usually taken to a mortuary and placed in a refrigerator at 4°C within 4 hr of death. For the group of brains from schizophrenics and controls that we collected, the average time period for the corpse to be placed at 4°C was 3.0 ± 2.2 hr versus 1.9 ± 1.5 hr, respectively, and the average time period between death and the time that the brain was removed from the skull and placed at −20°C was 40.6 hr for a schizophrenic group and 43.5 hr for the control group (Table 1). Similar postmortem time intervals were noted in the choreic and control cases that were collected.

In order to determine the actual temperature change occurring near the center of the human brain when still intact in the skull, Spokes and Koch (21) passed thermocouples through the skull and the brain to measure the temperature on

TABLE 1. *Time period between death and storage of tissues from patients with a hospital diagnosis of schizophrenia and controls*

	Control	Schizophrenia
Time from death (hr) average (± SD) corpse to 4°C	1.9 ± 1.5	3.0 ± 2.2
Tissues to −20°C (hr)	43.5 ± 23.2	40.6 ± 25.9

TABLE 2. *Influence of the interval between death and necropsy on measured GAD values in control brain*

	GAD activity (μmol/hr/g protein)	
Region	1–48 hr	48–72 hr
Caudate	47.9 ± 3.9 (31)	45.2 ± 6.2 (14)
Putamen	58.9 ± 5.3 (33)	56.9 ± 7.0 (16)
Nucleus accumbens	82.8 ± 9.1 (22)	80.0 ± 11.4 (10)

Values are means ± SEM for number of brains in parentheses.

the surface of the basal ganglia. During the cooling period in the 4°C refrigerator, the basal ganglia took approximately 18 hr to reach 4°C. When mouse brain was cooled slowly at 4°C over the same period of time, the activity of the enzyme glutamic acid decarboxylase (GAD) decreased over 12 hr to about 75% of the activity found when compared to that in the mouse brain examined immediately after death. The activity remained stable for 72 hr (21). Therefore, for studies where there is reasonable stability of the chemical substance that is to be tested, it would seem best to handle all tissues similarly and not to remove the brain from the skull until at least 12 hr after death. By that time, most enzyme activities would be stabilized. GAD is the biosynthetic enzyme that produces the neuroinhibitory transmitter γ-aminobutyric acid (GABA) in the central nervous system. The concentration of GABA and the activity of GAD have been found to be reduced in the basal ganglia of choreic brain (1,17). Evidence that GAD is fairly stable in postmortem brain is supported by comparisons of postmortem GAD values obtained from patients in which the interval between death and autopsy was more than or less than 48 hr (Table 2). Measurements from a large series of cases show no significant reduction in GAD activity in those cases in which autopsy was delayed. It thus seems unlikely that postmortem delays and storage conditions play an important role in determining differences in GAD activity.

However, permissible postmortem delays need to be assessed for each individual assay; and if it is found that postmortem stability is not adequate, then it may be necessary to remove the brain quickly after death in both controls and abnormal cases. It is often administratively difficult to complete autopsies in abnormal disease states within 6 hr; furthermore, it is difficult to collect control tissues within a few hours of death. Since control tissues need to be collected in the same way as abnormal tissues, this is a good reason to delay removing the brain in abnormal cases until the time periods are the same in both groups. I would caution neurochemists interested in studying postmortem brain tissue of a critical time period between removing the brain from the skull and placing the brain in the deep-freeze, which may contribute to instability of neurochemical substances in postmortem tissue.

Agonal Effects

Although postmortem changes do not present insurmountable problems in the postmortem analysis of GAD, another uncontrollable factor, the immediate premortem condition, appears to be of crucial importance in determining postmortem GAD activity. Bowen et al. (5) reported that low postmortem GAD values were obtained from patients dying with conditions likely to lead to cerebral hypoxia. Perry et al. (16) also drew attention to the influence of premortem status on postmortem GAD activity. In a group of chronically hospitalized patients, they found that GAD activity was significantly lower in several brain regions, as compared to activity in the same regions in brains of a group of normal people who had suffered sudden deaths. This suggested that spuriously low GAD activities may easily be recorded as a result of various pathological conditions in which postmortem brain samples are obtained from elderly patients, whose immediate cause of death is often bronchial pneumonia. The results obtained in our own laboratory strongly support this conclusion and show that death from bronchial pneumonia in control and schizophrenia patients does lead to lower GAD activities in various brain regions. Because of the preponderance of death with bronchial pneumonia in the HD and schizophrenia patient groups, GAD values may be unusually low as a result of circumstances unrelated to the primary neurological disease.

Pharmacologic Agents

Since a number of agents are effective in altering behavior, neurochemical substances in the brain may be substantially altered by these agents. The possible effect of neuroleptic drugs on catecholamines would be the most relevant for the assessment of data on postmortem schizophrenic brains.

The data on choreic brain tissues might be cited here, since chronic neuroleptic drug administration is a common practice in the treatment of chorea. Spokes (20) found significant increases in dopamine concentrations in the corpus striatum, substantia nigra, and nucleus accumbens of choreic brains. However, these increases could not be attributed to chronic neuroleptic drug administration, since normal striatal dopamine values were found in patients dying with a hospital diagnosis of schizophrenia, who also had been taking neuroleptics (4). Moreover, other drug-treated chorea subjects had dopamine values similar to those of their drug-free counterparts (20). Animal studies also support the view that chronic treatment with neuroleptic drugs does not influence striatal dopamine levels (13,15).

By contrast, there is in the postmortem schizophrenic brain an increased dopamine concentration in the nucleus accumbens and anterior perforated substance, regions of the limbic system (4). This finding might be related to chronic neuroleptic treatment, as suggested by animal studies in which long-term administration of neuroleptic drugs selectively increased dopamine concentrations in limbic areas (13).

Further studies will need to be carried out on the brain from psychotic patients that have not received neuroleptic drugs in order to assess the alterations of dopamine that have now been reported.

Standardization of Brain Dissection

When large nuclei are being dissected, there is little difficulty in defining the boundaries of the various brain regions. However, as interest shifts in the future to smaller nuclei, whose neuroanatomical boundaries have not been well defined, it will be important to standardize the dissection of human brain tissue to assure some uniformity in reports on the neurochemical data in human brain. I have proposed that those involved with the dissection of brain tissue meet to reach some consensus on a standardized way of dissecting the human brain.

NEUROCHEMICAL DATA IN SCHIZOPHRENIA

The availability of frozen tissue from patients dying with HD and schizophrenia allowed us to investigate certain neurochemical substances in the brain. Dr. Leslie Iversen, Director of the Medical Research Council's Neurochemical Pharmacology Unit at the University of Cambridge, collaborated by developing a number of methods for the measurement of neurotransmitters in human brain tissue.

The large number of HD brains that were collected (250 brains in 6 years) enabled us to distribute tissue to various investigators who had neurochemical expertise; and within a period of 2 to 3 years, over 50 shipments of brain tissue were sent to medical centers around the world. A number of publications ensued from the studies on these tissues, and as a result, more neurochemical data have now been published on the brain in Huntington's disease than in any other neurological disorder (2). In addition, for every Huntington's brain examined, the brain from a patient who died from a non-neurological disorder was examined. Consequently, a great deal of new neurochemical information has been generated on normal human brain.

Data obtained on postmortem schizophrenic brains collected in Cambridge, England, will be reviewed here. Neurotransmitters and related enzymes were measured in more than 50 control and schizophrenic brains.

Dopamine

There was a highly significant increase in dopamine concentration in the nucleus accumbens and in the anterior perforated substance (a limbic forebrain area which includes the dopamine-rich olfactory tubercle) in the psychotic group. No significant differences in dopamine concentration were found in other areas of limbic forebrain (septal nuclei and central nucleus of amygdala) or in the putamen and caudate nucleus (Table 3). The dopamine concentration in the nucleus accumbens was positively correlated with the dopamine concentrations

TABLE 3. *Dopamine and norepinephrine concentrations in postmortem brain from psychotic patients*

Region	Dopamine (μg/g protein)	Norepinephrine (μg/g protein)
Nucleus accumbens		
Control	12.2 ± 0.95 (46)	1.3 ± 0.13 (40)
Schizophrenic	16.3 ± 1.03 (51)[a]	1.8 ± 0.18 (47)
Anterior perforated substance		
Control	1.9 ± 0.30 (32)	0.7 ± 0.11 (25)
Schizophrenic	3.7 ± 0.58 (37)[b]	1.5 ± 0.24 (35)[c]
Caudate		
Control	17.3 ± 1.27 (51)	0.7 ± 0.10 (47)
Schizophrenic	19.7 ± 1.35 (50)	0.5 ± 0.06 (44)
Putamen		
Control	22.0 ± 2.30 (29)	
Schizophrenic	22.9 ± 2.20 (37)	
Septal nuclei		
Control		4.2 ± 0.71 (35)
Schizophrenic		4.2 ± 0.10 (32)

Values are means ± SEM for the number of samples in parentheses.
[a] $p < 0.02$, Student's *t*-test.
[b] $p < 0.05$, Student's *t*-test.
[c] $p < 0.05$, Student's *t*-test.

in the anterior perforated space ($r = 0.38$, $p < 0.05$) and in the caudate ($r = 0.68$, $p < 0.001$) in the schizophrenia but not in the control series. The increased dopamine concentrations in nucleus accumbens and anterior perforated substance in schizophrenia were statistically significant by both parametric and nonparametric statistical procedures used.

Increased dopamine concentrations in schizophrenic brain have been found by Crow et al. (9). However, the increase was noted in the caudate nucleus, whereas normal concentrations of dopamine were found in the area dissected as nucleus accumbens. A comparison of dissecting techniques revealed that Crow et al. (9) defined a much smaller area of striatum as the nucleus accumbens, and this tissue would represent the center of a larger region in the head of the striatal tissue taken by Bird et al. (3) as nucleus accumbens. Also for the data of Crow et al. (9), caudate tissue consisted mainly of the head and anterior body of the caudate nucleus, whereas Bird et al. (3) took the whole of the caudate nucleus. Therefore, a greater amount of the tissue defined by Bird et al. (3) as nucleus accumbens would be included in the tissue called caudate by Crow et al. (9).

An accurate definition of the boundaries of the nucleus accumbens in the human brain has not been described, so it is not surprising that different neurochemical data are being reported for this region of the brain. It is, therefore, important to define accurately anatomical areas during the dissecting procedure.

The increases in dopamine in nucleus accumbens and anterior perforated substance appear to be highly selective, since no changes in catecholamine content were observed in other limbic brain areas (septal nuclei and central nucleus of amygdala) or in the striatum.

The increases in dopamine in limbic forebrain areas in schizophrenia may be taken as evidence in favor of the "dopamine hypothesis" of schizophrenia, and particularly of the view that abnormalities in mesolimbic dopamine pathways may be involved (22). The present results, however, must be interpreted with caution since a large majority (all except three cases in the present series) of patients dying with schizophrenic illness received chronic medication with neuroleptic drugs prior to death.

Animal studies show that chronic treatment with neuroleptic drugs can lead to a selective increase in brain dopamine and norepinephrine. In particular, significant increases in the concentrations of dopamine and norepinephrine in rat nucleus accumbens and septum were found after 167 days of treatment with haloperidol (5 mg/kg) (13), whereas chronic drug treatment failed to influence dopamine or norepinephrine concentrations in the the basal ganglia (13,15).

Norepinephrine

The same brain regions from patients with schizophrenia which exhibited significantly higher dopamine concentrations also contained elevated concentrations of norepinephrine (nucleus accumbens and anterior perforated substance) (Table 3). As was the case with dopamine, the increase in norepinephrine was proportionally greater in anterior perforated substance (100% increase) than in nucleus accumbens (38% increase). No differences in norepinephrine were observed in any other areas (septal nuclei, putamen, or caudate nucleus) (Table 3).

The observation of increased norepinephrine levels in limbic areas confirms in part the report by Farley et al. (12) who observed selective increases in norepinephrine in nucleus accumbens, bed nucleus of stria terminalis, ventral septum, and mammillary body in postmortem brain tissue from four schizophrenic subjects.

The finding that norepinephrine levels are unchanged or even increased does not support the hypothesis of Wise and Stein (23) who proposed that noradrenergic "reward" pathways are damaged in schizophrenia, on the basis of their finding that the biosynthetic enzyme dopamine-*p*-hydroxylase was significantly reduced in postmortem specimens of diencephalon from 18 schizophrenic patients. This finding has, however, not been confirmed in other biochemical studies on postmortem brain tissue from patients dying with schizophrenic illness (8,24).

Glutamic Acid Decarboxylase

Glutamic acid decarboxylase activity was decreased in the postmortem brain of psychotic cases that had bronchopneumonia as a terminal event. When the

GAD activity in the brain of psychotic cases that had acute death was compared to control cases that had acute death, there were no significant differences in GAD activity in any of the areas examined (Table 4).

Although the preterminal condition plays an important role in determining postmortem GAD activity, it does not have any significant effect on postmortem norepinephrine, dopamine, or choline acetyltransferase values in control of psychotic cases (19).

Choline Acetyltransferase

Choline acetyltransferase (CAT) activity was measured and no significant differences were observed between the control and psychotic groups in any of the regions examined (Table 4).

The failure to detect any significant changes in choline acetyltransferase does not support the findings of Domino, Krause, and Bowers (10) who reported a significant increase in choline acetyltransferase activity in medial amygdala samples from five chronic schizophrenic patients, or McGeer and McGeer (14) who reported significant increases in choline acetyltransferase in nucleus accumbens, caudate, putamen, and hippocampus from eleven patients with schizophrenia.

The above studies in schizophrenic postmortem brain tissue are not as extensive as those that have been carried out on HD tissue. When more postmortem brain tissue from patients dying with a diganosis of schizophrenia are collected

TABLE 4. *Glutamic acid decarboxylase and choline acetyltransferase activities in postmortem brain from psychotic patients*

Region	GAD (μmol/hr/g protein)	CAT (μmol/hr/g protein)
Nucleus accumbens		
Control	78.5 ± 6.6 (40)	221.0 ± 10.77 (47)
Schizophrenic	80.7 ± 8.34 (14)	198.1 ± 10.71 (48)
Anterior perforated substance		
Control	36.2 ± 4.93 (25)	62.8 ± 8.59 (37)
Schizophrenic	36.1 ± 2.06 (13)	63.9 ± 7.61 (37)
Caudate		
Control	46.2 ± 2.94 (55)	259.0 ± 12.76 (67)
Schizophrenic	52.5 ± 5.15 (20)	255.5 ± 15.41 (53)
Putamen		
Control	58.0 ± 4.1 (51)	351.0 ± 14.2 (59)
Schizophrenic	60.4 ± 7.34 (13)	308.8 ± 18.5 (41)
Septal nuclei		
Control		17.8 ± 1.73 (27)
Schizophrenic		18.4 ± 2.09 (31)

Values are means and SEM for the number of samples in parentheses.

and distributed to neuroscientists, further neurochemical data will be reported. In order to promote this, it will be important to develop a systematic collection of postmortem tissues as described.

REFERENCES

1. Bird, E. D., and Iversen, L. L. (1974): Huntington's chorea: Post-mortem measurement of glutamic acid decarboxylase, choline acetyltransferase and dopamine in basal ganglia. *Brain,* 97:457–472.
2. Bird, E. D., and Spokes, E. G. S. (1980): Huntington's chorea. In: *Disorders of Neurohumoural Transmission,* edited by T. J. Crow. Academic Press *(in press).*
3. Bird, E. D., Spokes, E. G. S., Barnes, J., Mackay, A. V. P., Iversen, L. L., and Shepherd, M. (1977): Increased brain dopamine and reduced glutamic acid decarboxylase and choline acetyltransferase activity in schizophrenia and related psychoses. *Lancet,* ii:1157–1159.
4. Bird, E. D., Spokes, E. G. S., and Iversen, L. L. (1979): Increased dopamine concentration in limbic areas of brain from patients dying with schizophrenia. *Brain,* 102:347–360.
5. Bowen, D. M., Smith, C. B., White, P., and Davison, A. N. (1976): Neurotransmitter-related enzymes and indices of hypoxia in senile dementia and other abiotrophies. *Brain,* 99:459–496.
6. Brodman, K. (1909): *Vergleichende Lokalisationlehre der Grosshirnrinde in ihren Prinzipien dargestellt auf Grund des Zellenbaues,* p. 324. J. A. Barth, Leipzig.
7. Carlsson, A., and Waldeck, B. (1958): A fluorometric method for the determination of dopamine (3-hydroxytyramine). *Acta Physiol. Scand.,* 44:293–298.
8. Cross, A. J., Crow, T. J., Killpack, W. S., Longden, A., Owen, F., and Riley, G. J. (1978): The activities of brain dopamine-beta-hydroxylase and catechol-O-methyl transferase in schizophrenics and controls. *Psychopharmacology,* 59:117–122.
9. Crow, T. L., Owen, F., Cross, A. J., Lofthouse, R., and Longden, A. (1978): Brain biochemistry in schizophrenia. *Lancet,* i:36–37.
10. Domino, E. F., Krause, R. R., and Bowers, J. (1973): Various enzymes involved with putative neurotransmitters. Regional distribution in the brain of deceased mentally normal, chronic schizophrenics or organic brain syndrome patients. *Arch. Gen. Psychiatry,* 29:195–201.
11. Ehringer, H., and Hornykiewicz, O. (1960): Verteilung von noradrenalin und dopamin (3-hydroxytyramin) im gehirn des menschen und ihr verhalten bei herkrankundgen des extrapyramidalen systems. *Klin. Wochenschr.,* 38:1236–1239.
12. Farley, I. J., Price, K. S., McCullough, E., Deck, J. H. N., Hordyinski, W., and Hornykiewicz, O. (1978): Norepinephrine in chronic paranoid schizophrenia: Above-normal levels in limbic forebrain. *Science,* 200:456–458.
13. Lloyd, K. G., Shibuta, M., Davidson, L., and Hornykiewicz, O. (1977): Chronic neuroleptic therapy: Tolerance and GABA systems. In: *Advances in Biochemical Psychopharmacology, Vol. 16,* edited by E. Costa and G. L. Gessa, pp. 409–415. Raven Press, New York.
14. McGeer, P. L., and McGeer, E. G. (1977): Possible changes in striatal and limbic cholinergic systems in schizophrenia. *Arch. Gen. Psychiatry,* 34:1319–1323.
15. O'Keefe, R., Sharman, D. F., and Vogt, M. (1970): Effects of drugs used in psychoses on cerebral dopamine metabolism. *Br. J. Pharmacol.,* 38:287–304.
16. Perry, E. K., Gibson, P. N., Blessed, G., Perry, R. H., and Tomlinson, B. E. (1977): Neurotransmitter enzyme abnormalities in senile dementia. *J. Neurol. Sci.,* 34:247–265.
17. Perry, T. L., Hansen, S., and Kloster, M. (1973): Huntington's chorea: Deficiency of γ-aminobutyric acid in brain. *N. Engl. J. Med.,* 288:337–342.
18. Schaltenbrand, G., and Wahren, W. (1977): *Atlas for Stereotaxy of the Human Brain,* Second Revised and Enlarged Edition. Georg Thieme Publishers, Stuttgart.
19. Spokes, E. G. S. (1979): An analysis of factors influencing measurements of dopamine, noradrenaline, glutamate decarboxylase and choline acetylase in human post-mortem brain tissue. *Brain,* 102:333–346.
20. Spokes, E. G. S. (1979): Brain dopamine in Huntington's disease: A study of post-mortem tissue. *Adv. Neurol.,* 23:481–493.
21. Spokes, E. G. S., and Koch, D. J. (1978): Post-mortem stability of dopamine, glutamate decarboxylase and choline acetyltransferase in the mouse brain under conditions stimulating the handling of human autopsy material. *J. Neurochem.,* 31:381–383.

22. Stevens, J. R. (1973): An anatomy of schizophrenia. *Arch. Gen. Psychiatry,* 29:177–189.
23. Wise, C. D., and Stein, L. (1973): Dopamine-beta-hydroxylase deficits in the brain of schizophrenic patients. *Science,* 181:344–347.
24. Wyatt, R. J., Schwartz, M. A., Erdelyi, E., and Barchas, J. D. (1975): Dopamine-beta-hydroxylase activity in brains of chronic schizophrenic patients. *Science,* 187:368–370.

Discussion

Zubin: Your evidence for the dopamine hypothesis, which shows small but significant differences between schizophrenic and control brains, is striking. What sort of matching was done? Were the people really equivalent?

Bird: It's difficult to match controls with abnormal subjects unless you take them from the same mental hospital, where they have the same environment and food; but even if you do, they usually have been hospitalized for different reasons. I think you need many controls, for example, acute accidents, sudden death, dying slowly from bronchial pneumonia, hospitalization in a mental institution, receiving phenothiazine, etc. Obtaining good controls is a difficult problem. That's one reason why I use a large number of subjects, because then you usually end up with at least the same number of males and females at about the same ages. Dr. Crow's schizophrenics were somewhat older than his controls (1).

Cole: Some of your Huntington's patients were psychotic and some were not. Do they differ biochemically?

Bird: We haven't studied that yet. However, in the nucleus accumbens, dopamine is increased just as it is in schizophrenia, perhaps even more so. One must generally be cautious about dopamine and noradrenaline increases, part of which is caused by the loss of other neurons in the region, so that concentrations may reflect tissue shrinkage. However, in the nucleus accumbens, there is less shrinkage than in the other areas, yet the dopamine increase is greater. So I think this increase may be significant and related to psychosis. However, one must be cautious; the nucleus accumbens wouldn't have to shrink much for dopamine to increase, so we don't really know why the increase occurs.

K. Davis: How might you reconcile the increased dopamine concentration that you found in the nucleus accumbens with the increased haloperidol receptor binding that Dr. Seeman found? If the increased haloperidol and spiriperidol binding is a manifestation of increased dopamine receptor sensitivity, one would expect *decreased* dopamine concentrations.

Bird: That was part of an earlier discussion. We've actually looked at the homovanillic acid in the nucleus accumbens and it does not increase, so the dopamine there may be bound, without increased turnover, which receptor binding would depend on. We've never found any increase in tyrosine hydroxylase, which also should be increased if dopamine production increases, so the dopamine increase has some other cause that needs explaining.

Yuwiler: If you normalize your data three ways—relative to protein, cholesterol, and DNA—you might get a better idea as to whether the changes are associated with alterations in cellular number, or size, or with changes in axonal mass.

Melnechuk: In view of such claims as that by Oke et al. (5) that the brain has an asymmetrical distribution of a neurotransmitter—they report that the left pulvinar region and the right somatosensory input area of the thalamus is rich in norepinephrine, whereas the mirror-image areas are low—do your results reflect a random mixture of left and right hemispheres?

Bird: In England, I wasn't fortunate enough to have enough pathologists around who could look at schizophrenic brains, and in this country I was surprised to find that neuropathologists guard their postmortem brains, so that I've had to make arrangements with them. I'm pleased that we are now going to cut each schizophrenic brain in half, so that at least one hemisphere of each brain will be examined biochemically and one hemisphere histologically. I'm hoping that the sharing will be randomized and that we'll end up with 50 right and 50 left halves in every 100 brains.

Ingvar: I suspect that schizophrenia is not per se a mortal disease; and so I ask, what do schizophrenics die of? Could the immediate cause of death be affecting your results?

Bird: Bronchopneumonia is quite common for schizophrenics, as it is for Huntington's patients, 90% of whom die of the pneumonia. Glutamic acid decarboxylase (GAD) is quite sensitive to anoxia prior to death. If you look at the acute deaths in Huntington's disease, GAD is very significantly down as compared to acute deaths in normals. In our original paper (2) on GAD in schizophrenia, we found some decreases, which were attributable to a greater number of pneumonias in our schizophrenic group than in controls, but when we looked at our acute schizophrenic deaths—accidents, suicide, heart attacks—there was no difference in GAD levels. Choline acetyltransferase is very stable to agonal effects; so is dopamine, but dopamine decreases after you take the brain out of the skull and expose it to air.

Melnechuk: Dr. Fred Plum (6) once suggested that some catatonics who die suddenly may be hyperthermic, since acute catatonics often combine the hyperthermic-like symptoms of dehydration, autonomic changes, and hyperactivity, whereas focal lesions resembling ischemic changes compatible with hyperthermia have been found in the inner cortical layers of acute catatonics.

Uzman: About the tissue procurement, the NCI has had a national cancer tissue procurement program. Dr. Gajdusek's laboratory at the NINCDS has requested by a nationwide inquiry that brain and tissues be submitted to his laboratory. In each instance, contributors have received advice and assistance concerning temperature or fixation, including provision of proper containers, to maximize preservation during shipping. Does the current NIMH program help with this aspect?

Bird: The NIMH and the NINCDS in collaboration have been aiding two tissue resource centers—I don't like to call them "banks" because banks are places where you lock things up; a better term is "resource center," which is a place where you get tissues to use. One, on the west coast, is run by Dr. Wallace Tourtellotte; it's called the Human Tissue Bank, at the Wadsworth VA Hospital Center, Los Angeles, CA 90073. The other is a new Tissue Resource Center we've established on the east coast, at the Mailman Research Center, McLean Hospital, Belmont, MA 02178, telephone (617)855–2405. It is funded to collect and distribute brain tissue to neuroscientists everywhere.

Uzman: Do you provide containers and instructions?

Bird: Yes.

Canoso: I would like to affirm the importance of the brain tissue resource center to another field than those already mentioned—immunology. We have found evidence of autoimmune disorder in 30% of the patients exposed to chronic chlorpromazine therapy, the majority of whom are schizophrenic. I am referring to a syndrome characterized by the presence of a lupus-like circulating anticoagulant, antinuclear antibodies (3), and high levels of IgM (4). It would be extremely useful to study brain sections for deposition of immunoglobulins and complement.

Bird: One of the advantages of a tissue resource center is that one schizophrenic brain can be dissected into a number of pieces, and small aliquots from these can be sent to every VA hospital in the country. With 100 brains, one could send out all 100 brains and controls and the investigators could have their data in a week or two, whereas if they collected such brains independently there would probably be no more than five brains in each institution.

Schooler: I want to argue for thoughtful sampling in procuring brains. One problem with collection strategies such as the one that's been described is that people think of you only when they think they have an "interesting" case, so you may not really be sampling from the entire population of schizophrenic patients, and the brains may not be representative. It's hard to control what people send you. It may be wise in any VA-wide collection program to collect parallel information about the deaths in VA hospitals that do not result in brains received at the center, so you would know if the samples you were receiving at the tissue resource center were typical.

Uzman: You should speak directly to the clinical staff, since they obtain permissions, and might devote additional effort to study a broad spectrum of patients.

Nasrallah: I think we should all try to document good neurological examinations for all of our patients, as close as possible to the time they are admitted, mainly because of the neurological abnormalities that are coming into focus now, but also because of the large literature on neurological findings that we in psychiatry have generally ignored.

REFERENCES

1. Bird, E. D., Spokes, E. G., and Iversen, L. L. (1979): Brain norepinephrine and dopamine in schizophrenia. *Science,* 204:93–94.
2. Bird, E. D., Spokes, E. G. S., and Iversen, L. L. (1979): Brain norepinephrine and dopamine concentration in limbic areas of brain from patients dying with schizophrenia. *Brain,* 102:347–360.
3. Canoso, R. T., and Sise, H. S. (1977): High prevalence lupus-like anticoagulant and antinuclear antibodies associated with phenothiazines (Abstr.). *Blood,* 50(Suppl.):261.
4. Hutton, R. A. (1977): A chlorpromazine-induced inhibitor of blood coagulation. *Am. J. Hematol.,* 2:183–191.
5. Oke, A., Keller, R., Mefford, I., and Adams, R. N. (1978): Lateralization of norepinephrine in human thalamus. *Science,* 200:1411–1413.
6. Plum, F. (1972): Neuropathological findings. In: *Prospects for Research in Schizophrenia,* edited by S. S. Kety and S. Matthysse, pp. 384–388. *Neurosci. Res. Program Bull.,* 10:369–507 + vii.

Perspectives in Schizophrenia Research,
edited by C. Baxter and T. Melnechuk.
Raven Press, New York, 1980.

New Initiatives in Schizophrenia Research

* Claude F. Baxter and ** Theodore Melnechuk

** Neurochemistry Laboratories, Veterans Administration Medical Center, Sepulveda, California 91343; Department of Psychiatry and Brain Research Institute, UCLA School of Medicine, Los Angeles, California 90024; **Western Behavioral Sciences Institute, La Jolla, California 92037; and Department of Neurosciences, UCSD, San Diego, California 92093*

No short summary of the preceding conference could do justice to the many interesting and provocative data and ideas presented by the participants, especially during the long discussions. Thus, this summary chapter is intended to provide a distillate of the essence, not the substance, of the conference. It presents a condensed and integrated view of some of the more important issues raised by conference participants, together with a few unabashed views and ideas of our own.

The content of this symposium volume provides ample evidence that the definition of "schizophrenia" as a single or multiple disease entity is neither neat nor precise. Man is the only vertebrate species in which the disease (as currently defined) can be identified and, within the family of Man, schizophrenia appears in all races and cultures. Symptoms of the disease include disturbances of thought, abnormal speech patterns, catatonic motor behavior, systematized and unsystematized delusions, paranoid traits, visual and auditory hallucinations, blunted or inappropriate emotions, disturbances of social relationships, and disturbances of behavior. Although a predisposition to the disease appears to have some genetically inherited determinants, its onset and the way it manifests itself may be influenced by cultural, social, and environmental factors.

LONGITUDINAL VERSUS CROSS-SECTIONAL STUDIES

Some investigators emphasize the "undulating" or "phasic" nature of the disease; others view it more in terms of a permanent underlying condition. Thus, psychological studies presented at the conference emphasized the periodic (undulating) nature of the affliction, whereas electrophysiological studies focused on the persistent nature of abnormalities in schizophrenic patients.

Whether one regards schizophrenia as a phasic or as a permanent condition is not academic, since it will influence profoundly the research strategies used in attempting to discover underlying causes. If the substrate of schizophrenia is undulatory in nature, it seems logical that these undulations and their biological correlates should be studied in a small, select number of patients for long periods of time (longitudinal studies). On the other hand, if the substrate of schizophrenia is permanent, such as a genetically coded biological trait that causes or predisposes individuals to the disease, then discovery of the cause should be possible by cross-sectional studies in which biological parameters are studied in large patient populations for short periods of time. A sizable number of studies have been conducted in this latter manner. On the whole, they have been disappointing in that no consistent cause for the disease has been found. It is not yet clear whether this is because the critical parameters have not been examined, identification of a critical factor has been obscured by environmental and technological variables, the disease and its underlying causes are truly episodic, or more than a single cause exists for the disease.

LESSONS LEARNED FROM PAST BIOLOGICAL STUDIES IN SEARCH OF AN ETIOLOGY

Studies in the 1950s and 1960s yielded a plethora of papers suggesting that blood, urine, and other accessible tissues from schizophrenic patients contained unusual levels of some metabolites, unknown toxic factors, or other abnormal metabolic features. Virtually all of these early studies are now discredited. Most of the abnormalities were shown to be related to peculiarities of environment, nutrition, and habit patterns that are common in institutionalized schizophrenic patients but are not shared by the control subjects with whom they were compared.

More recent clinical studies, conducted under far better controlled conditions and with more appropriate comparison subjects, were designed to avoid some of these pitfalls. Nevertheless, the results obtained remain contradictory: Statistically significant differences between schizophrenic and control populations have been reported, as have flat contradictions of such reports. However, at best, even differences with high statistical significance may have little predictive value for the treatment of individual patients. Contradictory studies may be the result of methodological inconsistencies, varying patient populations, or unknown artifacts. The cause of contradictory results often remains unknown.

Because of this discouraging situation, most of the participants at the conference agreed that progress in *biological* schizophrenia research would require (a) even more stringent controls, the measurement of new parameters, and the use of new technology, and (b) a concerted effort to divide the population of patients with schizophrenia into subgroups on the basis of shared *biological* abnormalities. The more biologically oriented specialists suggested that the new groupings of schizophrenics be based upon physiological, pharmacological, biochemical, immunological, and, probably, morphological criteria. Researchers will have to critically ascertain whether individuals in each group have common characteristics, such as the course of their disease and their response to specific treatment modalities. Although this approach to the grouping of schizophrenic patients is a reversal of the usual dependent and independent variables in schizophrenia research (i.e., the groupings of patients on a behavioral and mentation basis and then attempting to find biological commonalities), it is more common in epidemiological research. Diagnostic categorization of schizophrenic patients, by operationally identified biological or behavioral criteria, should not be an abstract exercise in classification, but should produce higher predictive accuracy for the outcome of the disease and greater assurance in selecting, without trial and error, the most effective mode of therapy.

APPLICATION OF NEW TECHNOLOGIES AND THE MEASUREMENT OF NEW PARAMETERS IN SCHIZOPHRENIA RESEARCH

Presentations at the conference indicated that chronic schizophrenic patients can be distinguished from control subjects on the basis of quantitative differences in blood circulation in the forebrain and structural abnormalities in size and thickness of brain ventricles, cortical sulci, and cerebellar vermis, as visualized by computerized tomographic scanning techniques. These differences from control subjects appear to be unrelated to drug therapy. Whether they are markers of vulnerability to the disease or reflect the result of the disease cannot be answered at this time. However, the unusual initial success in finding *in vivo* techniques for measuring regional changes in the brain that correlate with mental activity represents a landmark in schizophrenia research. It will encourage further studies of regional cerebral blood flow measurements with ^{133}Xenon, the use of positron emission tomography with 18-fluoro-2-deoxyglucose for the measurement of regional metabolism, and CAT scanning, as well as other physical and physiological techniques that permit the *in vivo* exploration of the central nervous system of man.

There are a number of recent observations that show the applicability of relatively noninvasive techniques in the demonstration of abnormalities in schizophrenic patients. Abnormalities were found in scalp-recorded, computer-analyzed electroencephalograms, some specific functions of the autonomic nervous system, rates of habituation, levels of growth hormone during sleep, levels of nerve growth factor in blood serum, and the immune responsiveness of lymphocytes to mitogenic lectins. All these may provide possible markers for schizophrenia. The presence of some of these abnormalities also appeared to aid in the prediction of outcome for and identification of individuals in the high-risk group for contracting schizophrenia.

Other abnormalities were revealed by studies of some well-preserved postmortem brains of schizophrenics and control subjects (collected, processed, and distributed by a brain-tissue resource center). These retrospective studies revealed that in the brain tissue of schizophrenics, either the number of dopamine receptors or their affinity constants for dopamine had increased. This provocative finding was challenged by another report which stressed the involvement of abnormal noradrenergic rather than dopaminergic mechanisms in schizophrenia. The conference accurately mirrored the disagreements in results and interpretation in the field and left no doubt that the time to narrow the biochemical focus for compounds related to the etiology of schizophrenia has not yet arrived.

SUGGESTIONS FOR NEW RESEARCH APPROACHES TO THE BIOLOGY OF SCHIZOPHRENIA AND ITS TREATMENT

Many new biological parameters were suggested to help pinpoint and classify schizophrenics and those at risk for contracting schizophrenia. Some endocrine systems have been implicated as potential mechanisms to trigger the precipitation of schizophrenic episodes, and the close interrelationship between some hormones and the catecholamines (suspected as one group of compounds involved in the etiology of schizophrenia) enhances this possibility. The involvement of the immune system in schizophrenia has been suggested both by the finding that chlorpromazine is an effective immunosuppressive agent and by scattered data suggesting an altered immunoresponsiveness in schizophrenia. Advances in immunohistochemical procedures now permit identification and detailed histochemical mapping of key enzymes in the fine structures of the brain. Together with the availability of computerized microscopic techniques for the analysis of geometric patterns and other organizational characteristics of brain tissues, these technical advances suggest that the time is opportune to renew retrospective postmortem studies in search of distinctive morphological and biochemical differences between the brain tissues from schizophrenic and those from normal subjects.

New biological approaches to the study of schizophrenia are suggested also by the slow but continual revision of some fundamental concepts in neurobiology. A case in point is the reevaluation of the role of glial cells in the nervous system. The recent discovery of receptor sites for putative neurotransmitters, on glial cells as well as on neurons, opens up a new area of inquiry into the mode of action of neuroleptic drugs in schizophrenia. Similarly, the discovery in recent years of many new neuroactive peptides in brain tissues and the development of related pharmacological agents is having an impact on research in schizophrenia. The finding of abnormal callosal connections between the cerebral hemispheres of schizophrenic brains suggests the possibility of an important relationship between psychosis and laterality. Since the sexes differ in their hemispheric specialization, a reexamination of sexual differences in schizophrenia is indicated. Disorders of language in schizophrenics also need to be reexamined from the perspective of contemporary linguistics; for example, the extent to which schizophrenic neologisms obey phonological constraints might help illuminate the nature and even the location of aberrant functioning. Videotapes of psychiatric interviews now used only for refining therapeutic skills contain a mine of information awaiting content analysis.

Clearly, the search for the biological roots of schizophrenia can start at psychological levels. One long-familiar but tantalizingly elusive psychobiological concept that may apply to schizophrenia research is the "placebo effect." It is possible that patients whose symptoms remit spontaneously, or who improve when given a biologically inactive compound as a drug, form distinctive subgroups. Discussion at the conference made clear that the placebo is not a passive control. It may elicit both positive and negative effects, and the direction of change is not always the same. Conditioning may be involved, at least in some cases, and there are biological concomitants—such as endorphin release—that may be of brief or of long duration. A placebo, like psychotherapy or other modes of noninvasive treatment, may trigger biological changes in some patients. If the effects of placebos upon patients with schizophrenia are real, then future studies must include a search for the biological substrates that might mediate such effects.

The biochemical properties of neuroleptic drugs have, in the past, provided valuable starting points for inquiries into the biological nature of schizophrenia. These drugs and their apparent mechanisms of action were instrumental in the formulation of specific biochemical theories concerning the etiology of schizophrenia. Whereas these drugs help many schizophrenics, their continual use has resulted in unacceptable side effects, notably tardive dyskinesia, in many patients. A large number of practical ideas were voiced at the conference, suggesting possible ways to minimize such side effects while maintaining pharmacological control over the schizophrenic behavior. Suggestions were made for intermittent drug use (drug holidays), the use of lower drug dosages, and the use of new drugs, drug cogeners, and drug combinations. All these parameters will have to be tested in clinical settings. They are of practical importance even if they do not open up new conceptual initiatives for an understanding of the basic nature of schizophrenia.

One supplementary, innovative approach was mentioned: It was suggested that the differential response of schizophrenic patients to specific drugs and the patients' susceptibility to tardive dyskinesia may itself be useful in classifying patients into biological subgroups.

STUDIES OF SCHIZOPHRENIA AS A FAMILY OF DISEASES WITH DIFFERENT ETIOLOGIES

As already stated, there is at this time no generally accepted biological marker for schizophrenia. If, as is generally agreed, there are genetic factors that predispose certain individuals to contracting schizophrenia, it is surprising that the large amount of time, effort, talent, and money expended on the finding of a marker has yielded no consistent positive biological finding. This could indicate that the aberrant expression of the genetic defect is in some control system that does not manifest itself as an overt, easily observable, metabolic change. A popular premise holds that the inconsistency of experimental results may indicate that there is no single common biological marker or etiology for schizophrenia. Many of the symposium participants expressed their views, directly or indirectly, concerning this vexing problem. Without doubt, the most popular belief today is that schizophrenia (like cancer) is not a single disease entity but, rather, a family of diseases with similar outward manifestations but differing etiologies. Such a belief is based not only on the failure to find a common etiology to date, but also on precedents in neurobiology. Not so long ago, mental retardation in children was considered a single medical entity. Only through the discovery of the differing biochemical etiologies responsible for galactosemia, phenylketonuria, and other aminoacidurias has it become clear that common behavioral manifestations may be produced by different mechanisms. It has become possible, with early detection, to alleviate or prevent the mental retardation that is common to all these diseases. Similarly, it is hoped that the discovery of different biological etiologies of schizophrenia will lead not only to a greater intrinsic understanding of the different causes of schizophrenia, but will also result in greater protection for those who are vulnerable and at risk to the disease and lead to a more rational approach for the treatment of those afflicted.

The assumption that schizophrenia has multiple etiologies requires totally new strategies for studying the disease. Whereas in the past the inconsistencies of relating the disease to a single biochemical abnormality or drug response led to the rejection of many hypotheses concerning the biological etiology of schizophrenia, these very inconsistencies may in the future prove to be guidelines for the differentiation of biological etiologies causing the mental and behavioral abnormalities.

Some contributors to the conference indicated that DSM III (the third edition of the American Psychiatric Association's Diagnostic and Statistical Manual of Mental Disorders, published in 1980) is not likely to be the last word in the descriptive classification of the schizophrenic syndrome. It would be fortuitous if further classification of patients into psychiatric subgroups related in some way to the projected biological classification, but any experiments designed to uncover biological markers for subgroups of schizophrenia should not be based on such an assumption!

Furthermore, all of the biological parameters that were rejected in the past on the assumption that schizophrenia had a single etiology now deserve to be reexamined on the basis of multiple etiologies. Using the endorphin hypothesis of schizophrenia as a practical example, it was demonstrated at the conference that conventional experimental design and conventional statistical analyses will miss detecting subgroups of schizophrenic patients with a distinctive biological abnormality. Thus, new statistical methods are being devised for the analysis of clinical data in a way that will permit detection of such subgroups.

OTHER POSSIBLE REASONS FOR THE FAILURE TO FIND A COMMON ETIOLOGY

Although the multiple etiologies of schizophrenia could account for the difficulties encountered in the search for a single unique biological marker, it is by no means the only explanation for past failures. Some of the conferees addressed themselves to other possibilities.

Even under carefully controlled conditions, equivalent environments for different patients and control subjects are almost impossible to achieve. Thus, subtle environmental differences may affect the experimental results. Several participants described evidence that suggested quite persuasively that the social environment of a human subject (or a monkey), stress factors, and a variety of placebos could help precipitate or alleviate the schizophrenic syndrome and possibly affect the biological balance of factors that may cause or control or are secondary concomitants of the disease.

Another reason for the wide scattering of biological results in schizophrenic subjects might be a quantitative relationship of the biological marker to the phase or stage of the illness. Since quantitation of behavioral and mental abnormalities is still rather subjective, it is difficult to establish a systematic relationship between quantitative, nonparametric, psychiatric evaluations and quantitative, parametric, biological variables (biochemical, immunological, pharmacological, hormonal, physiological, or anatomical), unless a single patient is studied longitudinally by the same team of investigators. Many of the contradictory studies reported in the literature were conducted by different investigators in different environments using different groups of schizophrenic patients for comparison with different groups of controls, thereby compounding the potential complications we have enumerated.

Even when longitudinal studies are conducted with a single patient, there is the inherent assumption, in many studies, that changes in the biochemistry of body fluids reflect in some way some changes in the CNS. Yet we know, on the basis of animal experiments, that this assumption is likely to be true for only a very limited number of chemical parameters. Thus, the absence of a correlation between the disease and biochemical parameters in tissue fluids does not exclude the possibility that such correlations do exist and might be demonstrable retrospectively in the analysis of postmortem brain tissues.

It is obvious that a large number of biological parameters that could be functionally related to schizophrenia remain to be tested. The record of the conference abounds with new suggestions and preliminary observations concerning such compounds. Further research is bound to lead into other areas that we have not mentioned.

THE QUESTION OF COMPENSATING MECHANISMS IN THE CONTROL OF THE SCHIZOPHRENIC SYNDROME

The great bulk of the literature and presentations at the conference suggest that schizophrenia may be correlated with biological factors such as genetic predisposition, changes in cerebral circulation, morphological abnormalities, biochemical defects, and immunological abnormalities. It is difficult to conceive of some of these factors as phasic. Consequently, the phasic nature of the disease must be explainable by some other mechanism. One attractive possibility that should be explored is that undulations are the result of more or less effective *compensating mechanisms.* Such a concept is in line with the undulating nature of regulatory feedback systems that have been demonstrated in many areas of biology. *It follows that it may be the compensating mechanisms that are reinforced by neuroleptic drugs or other therapy, leaving the basic lesion of the disease unchanged.* If this concept of variable compensating mechanisms is taken as a working hypothesis, then it follows that longitudinal studies of variables are as likely to yield information about compensating mechanisms as they are to yield information about the underlying etiology of schizophrenia. On the other hand, cross-sectional studies should yield clear-cut answers for variables related to the disease's etiology, with a wide scatter of results if the variables studied are more closely related to the compensatory mechanisms. This too might be an explanation for the wide variability of past studies.

PSYCHOLOGICAL AND BEHAVIORAL STUDIES

Testing biological hypotheses of mental disease is predicated on the ability to relate biological measurements to psychological and behavioral criteria of the disease syndrome. This is true regardless of whether the etiology of schizophrenia, the markers of vulnerability to schizophrenia, the course of tardive dyskinesia, or the nature of compensating mechanisms is being studied. Consequently, it is essential that such studies have a set of well-defined standards and criteria for diagnosis and measurement of the disease. Furthermore, the availability of objective and reproducible outcome measurements appears to be indispensable, particularly the establishment and maintenance of uniform appraisals by different evaluators (inter-rater reliability) and a reference system for maintaining some uniformity in the evaluations by different research teams. Only in this way will it be possible to make sure that the same parameters are being evaluated. Needed also are experimental designs that take into account the possible multiple etiologies of the disease as well as the many extrinsic and intrinsic variables entering into biological and psychiatric measurements. A number of conference participants tackled some of these problematic issues and made general recommendations concerning the mode and execution of future research in these areas. They concerned themselves not only with the experimental details but also with psychosocial factors, informed consent, the training of research psychiatrists, and the design of cooperative studies.

Finding the biological etiology or etiologies of schizophrenia will be only one of many steps in the conquest of this disease. New modalities for the early identification of those at risk, new methods of prevention, and new modalities of treatment have to be devised. Means must be found to measure the less obvious and subtle signs of improvement or impending relapse. At the same time, psychosocial, cultural, ethnic, environmental, and nutritional factors that are suspected of triggering or exacerbating the disease must be more clearly and quantitatively identified, so that those at risk can avoid, or be protected from, such factors as much as possible. Some humble beginnings in these areas were detectable in the reports and comments of some of the conference participants.

Perhaps the most obvious and important conclusion of the conferees was that the study of schizophrenia requires a truly interdisciplinary approach and that no single discipline can work in isolation on this important, peculiarly human, disease.

Subject Index

Abnormal Involuntary Movement Scale (AIMS), 349, 356, 386
Acetylcholine
  and γ-aminobutyric acid, 341
  -dopamine imbalance, in tardive dyskinesia, 333, 334, 338
  and prolactin, 151
Adaptation, *see* Autonomic nervous system functioning
Adenyl cyclase
  dopamine-sensitive, 196, 211–212, 213, 214
  inhibition of, by neuroleptics, 215
Adrenal cortical adenomata, and paranoid symptoms, 135
Adrenal cortical hormones; *see also specific hormone*
  and denial, 140
  and stress, 20–22, 146
  treatment with, 132, 133
Adrenocorticotrophic hormone (ACTH), 5, 147
Advocates, 320
Affective blunting, and phenothiazines, 98
Affective disorders; *see also specific disorder*
  and pain insensitivity, 185
Afferent functions, *see* Sensory-gnostic functions
Age
  and stressors, 20
  and structural brain abnormalities, 31, 34, 39
Agranulocytosis, antipsychotic-induced, 353, 354
Akathisia, antipsychotic-induced, 323, 324, 357, 363
Akinesia, antipsychotic-induced, 323, 324, 357
Alcoholism
  and chronic schizophrenia, 325
  and dopamine beta-hydroxylase activity, 330–331
  and fluphenazine, 331
Aldosterone, and response patterns, 137
Alzheimer's disease
  physostigmine for, 363
  rapid progression of, 39
  resembling psychosis, 205
γ-Aminobutyric acid (GABA)
  and acetylcholine, 341
  in choreic brain, 412
  and tardive dyskinesia, 341
γ-Aminobutyric acid agonists, for tardive dyskinesia, 341, 342
Amphetamine
  and computer-analyzed EEG response, 73, 74
  effect of, on psychotic symptoms, 157, 305, 313
  and increase in locomotion, 18
  neuroleptic blocking of psychotomimetic effects of, 196
  tardive dyskinesia caused by, 336
Amphetamine psychosis, 210–211, 212, 227
d-Amphetamine
  and dopamine systems, 211
  and growth hormone response, 155, 166
  and norepinephrine systems, 166, 211
  and prolactin response, 155, 164–165, 174
  psychosis caused by, 205
  and ^{3}H-spiroperidol binding sites, decrease in, 203
l-Amphetamine, and dopamine systems, 211
Androgens
  neonatal exposure to, 23
  and paranoid symptoms, 135
Androgeny score, 8
Anger, styles of handling, 140
Anhedonia, 193, 281, 288
Anterior perforated substance
  choline acetyltransferase activity in, 417
  dopamine in, 413, 414, 415–416
  glutamic acid decarboxylase in, 417
  norepinephrine in, 413, 414, 415–416
Anticholinergics; *see also specific name*
  and EEG, 77, 78
  with neuroleptics, 106, 341
  tardive dyskinesia caused by, 336, 339
Antidepressants
  EEG response to, 78
  tricyclic, tardive dyskinesia caused by, 336, 337
Antihistamines, tardive dyskinesia caused by, 336, 337
Antinuclear antibodies, and chlorpromazine, 250, 258, 263, 422
Antiparkinsonian drugs

Antiparkinsonian drugs (*cont'd*)
and EEG, 77
and tardive dyskinesia, 356, 357, 363
Antipsychotic drugs; *see also* Drug response; Outcome, treatment; *specific type; specific name*
action of, 211–213, 218
and adenyl cyclase, 214–215
adverse effects of, 307, 321–322, 323, 324–325, 353, 354–355, 376, 382; *see also* Tardive dyskinesia
and anticholinergics, 106
and apomorphine, 196, 338
and attentional capacity, 87–88, 100
and autonomic nervous system activity, 97–99, 100, 106
computer-analyzed EEG effects of, 61, 62, 66–69, 70, 71, 72–74, 77–78
and dopamine, 211–213, 413, 416
dyskinesia-free, 353, 358–359
and growth hormone, 154
and hormonal changes, 145–146, 154, 212
low dose, 353, 357, 373, 374
maintenance on, 349, 357–358, 366–372, 377
measurement of blood and tissue levels of, 321, 322–323, 329, 341
and α-methyl-*p*-tyrosine, 163–164
and norepinephrine, 416
and postmortem brain, 413–414
and prolactin, 151, 163–164, 173–174, 175, 203, 212, 341
psychosis produced by, in nonpsychotics, 343
and sudden death, 353, 354, 382
Antitherapeutic forces, 308
Anxiety, and EEG response, 78, 79
Anxiolytics, 77, 78
Apomorphine
binding of, 204
and growth hormone response, 155–158, 173, 174, 175
and neuroleptics, 196, 338
and prolactin response, 149, 155–158, 173, 175
Applied research, 317–331
Aspiration, death from, 354–355
Astrocytes, 225
Astroglial cells, 213–219, 225
Atropine, 77
Attentional functioning, 81, 82, 83–88, 121, 129, 182, 275, 284
and clinical state, 86–87
deficits of, as traits, 85–86
and drugs, 87–88, 100
and prediction of outcome, 83–85, 99–101
Autism, reversal of neuroanatomical asymmetries in, 29, 35
Autonomic nervous system functioning, 81, 82, 88–99, 108, 121, 128, 275, 313
and clinical change, 92–93, 97–99
and brain lesions, 105–106
disturbances of, as traits, 93–95
and drugs, 97–99, 100, 106
and MAO activity, 95–97, 105
and prediction of outcome, 89–92, 99–101, 105, 106

Baclofen, 341, 350
Basal ganglia, dopamine receptor sensitivity in, 228
Behavior, and EEG, 65–66, 72
Behavioral "bits," 237–238
Benzodiazepines; *see also specific name*
for tardive dyskinesia, 358
Big adrenocorticotrophic hormone (Big ACTH), 147
Biological parameters, 426, 428–431
Birth, season of, 274
Birth complications, 19, 95, 274, 313
"Bit," behavioral, 237–238
Blood-brain barrier, delayed development of, 22, 23
Blood flow, cerebral, 107, 109–130, 212
Blood sampling device, 146
Body awareness, 128
Body-image distortion, 281, 288
Body type, 306, 313
Brain abnormalities, structural, 29, 41, 108, 116, 117, 284
Brain asymmetries, 34–35, 116, 117, 284
Brain atrophy, 30, 33–34, 35–36
and immunology, 36, 263
Brain tissue resource center, 401–414, 422–423
Brain tumors
and autonomic nervous system activity, 105–106
and cerebral blood flow, 127, 129
schizophreniform symptoms caused by, 40
Brainstem mechanisms, 108
Breast cancer, antipsychotic drugs associated with, 355
Brief Psychiatric Rating Scale (BPRS), 161, 178, 179
Brief reactive psychosis; *see* Schizophreniform psychosis
Bromocryptine
and ^{3}H-neuroleptic/dopamine receptors, 199, 203
for Parkinson's disease, 203
and prolactin, 151
Bronchial pneumonia
as cause of death in Huntington's disease, 421
as cause of death in schizophrenia, 413, 422
Bufotenine, and computer-analyzed EEG, 64
Butaperazine, and prolactin, 161
Butyrophenones, *see also specific name* action of, 212
and serum prolactin levels, 212

California, mental health treatment system in, 319
Cancer
  breast, antipsychotic drugs associated with, 355
  incidence of, and schizophrenia, 265
Carphenazine, and attentional capacity, 87
Case helpers, 320
Catatonia
  acute, and hyperthermia, 422
  and catecholaminergic transmission, 122
  lethal, 354
Catecholamine pathways; *see also specific catecholamine*
  fine structure of, 216–218
CATEGO, 299
Caudate nucleus
  choline acetyltransferase activity in, 417
  dopamine in, 227, 414, 415
  glutamic acid decarboxylase activity in, 417
  and ^{3}H-neuroleptic binding, 195, 196, 197, 198, 199
  norepinephrine in, 415, 416
Cell fractionation technique, 213–215
Cerebellar vermis, atrophy of, 35–36
Cerebral blood flow, 107, 109–130, 212
Cerebral cortex
  abnormalities of, 30, 33–34, 39, 40
  resting functional landscape of, in chronic schizophrenia, 114, 120–121
    in normals, 114, 118–120
Cerebral metabolic rate of oxygen ($CMRO_2$), 113
Chapman scale, 193, 194
Children; *see also* High-risk children
  psychotic, computer-analyzed EEG in, 61, 63, 72
Chlorgyline, behavioral effects of, 13, 17
p-Chlorophenylalanine (PCPA), behavioral effects of, 12, 13, 15, 17
Chlorpromazine
  and adenyl cyclase, 215
  agranulocytosis caused by, 354
  and attentional capacities, 87
  and autonomic nervous system activity, 98, 106
  and dopamine, 211
  and effect of guanosine triphosphate on cyclic adenosine monophosphate formation, 214
  and electrocardiogram, 354
  endocrine contraindications to use of, 135–136
  and growth hormone, 154, 173
  immunosuppressive effect of, 253, 254–257, 258–259, 263, 265, 422
  maintenance studies of, 367
  measurement of, in blood, 321, 322–323, 324
    in saliva, 322–323
  and norepinephrine, 211
  and prevention of relapses, 367
  and prolactin levels, 153, 158–159, 160, 164, 173
  with reserpine, 206
  and sudden death, 354
  therapeutic dose of, 160
Choline
  for senile psychosis, 363
  for tardive dyskinesia, 358
Choline acetyltransferase (CAT) activity, 417, 422
Choline chloride, for tardive dyskinesia, 334, 339–340
Cholinomimetics, for tardive dyskinesia, 334, 339–341, 342
Chronic brain syndromes, and aspiration deaths, 354
Classic conditioning, and placebo effect, 397
Clozapine
  absence of neurologic side effects with, 359
  computer-analyzed EEG profile of, 69, 77
  and prolactin, 161
Collaborative studies, low-budget, 376–377
Compensating mechanisms, 431–432
Computed tomography (CT), and structural brain abnormalities, 29, 30–41, 427
Computer-analyzed electroencephalogram (CEEG), 61–80
  in adult schizophrenics, 62–63, 71, 72
  and hallucinogens, 61, 64, 72, 73
  in high-risk children, 61, 63–64, 72
  and neuroleptics, 61, 62, 65
  and prediction of outcome, 66–69, 70, 71, 72–74
  in psychotic children, 61, 63, 72
  in sleep, 64
Computer microscope, quantitative neurohistology with, 43–59
Computerized diagnostic system, 299–300
Conceptually driven behavior, 127–128
Contingent negative variation, 122
Continuous Performance Task, 86, 87
Convulsions, antipsychotic drugs associated with, 355
Coping dysfunctions, 285–286, 290
Corpus callosum, thickness of, 40
Corticosteroids; *see also specific name*
  levels of, in reactive depression, 287
Cortisol, and response patterns, 137, 139
Cortisone, 133
Creatinine excretion, 5, 6
Culture
  and definition of improvement, 382
  and response to treatment, 324
Cyclic adenosine monophosphate, 212, 214, 215
Cypropheptadine, and growth hormone secretion, 154

Cytotoxic factors in schizophrenia, 250, 251, 254, 254–257, 258, 259, 260, 263, 265

Data analysis, 3, 9–10, 315–316, 326, 366–372
Data-driven responses, 127–128
Deanol, for tardive dyskinesia, 340
Death, sudden, 354–355
  antipsychotics causing, 353, 354, 382
  from aspiration, 354–355
  from catatonia, 354
Delirium, EEG correlates of, 77, 78
Dementia
  age-related, physostigmine for, 363
  and brain atrophy, 39
  schizophrenic, 110
  and ventricular enlargement, 33
Dendrites, computer microscopic study of, 43, 44, 45–59
Denial, and hormones, 140
Depression
  drug-induced, 324
  effects of MAO inhibitors in, 96, 97
  and pain insensitivity, 185
  reactive, corticosteroid levels in, 287
Des-tyrosine-gamma endorphin (DtγE), 205, 342, 358
Developmental markers, 276, 286
Developmental model, 274, 276, 277
Diagnosis
  criteria for, 298–300, 315
  functions of, 2
  and Gerard paradigm, 1, 2–10, 27
  and patient selection in clinical research, 297, 299–302
  and postmortem studies, 410–411, 422
  vulnerability and episode markers as aid in, 288
Diazepam, and EEG response, 78
Diazepam receptors, 218–219, 225
Diet-drug interactions, 324
(1,12-Diethylaminoethyl) phenobarbital, 64
Dimethylaminoethanol, for tardive dyskinesia, 340
Diphenylhydantoin, tardive dyskinesia caused by, 336
Ditran, 64, 72, 77, 78
DOPAC, location of, 230
Dopamine
  and adenyl cyclase, 211, 212
  and autonomic nervous system activity, 96, 97, 105
  and chronic neuroleptic treatment, 413, 416
  and growth hormone, 149, 151
  location of, 196, 204, 227, 230, 413, 414, 415–416, 421
  as neuromodulator, 209, 213–219
  in Parkinson's disease, 401, 402
  and prolactin, 149, 151
  and reserpine, 206
  urinary, 96
Dopamine-acetylcholine imbalance, in tardive dyskinesia, 333, 338
Dopamine agonists; *see also specific name*
  behavioral sensitivity to, and chronic neuroleptic administration, 338
  and growth hormone, 151, 155–158
  and prolactin, 155–157
Dopamine antagonists; *see also specific name*
  response to, and basal prolactin levels, 152–154
Dopamine beta-hydoxylase (DBH), 330–331, 416
Dopamine hypothesis of schizophrenia, 122, 149, 237, 238
  definition of, 195, 210
  and EEG, 72
  and endocrinology, 149, 162, 174
  evidence at odds with, 212–213, 229
  evidence for, 195–207, 209, 210–212, 227, 416, 421
Dopamine pathways, mesolimbic, 153, 334, 342–343, 349, 416
Dopamine receptors
  and antipsychotic drugs, 161, 162, 163, 166, 338, 342–343
  on astroglial cells, 209, 218, 225
  and ^{3}H-neuroleptic binding, 195–205, 212
  in Parkinson's disease, 203
  reduction in, 199
  sensitivity of, 149, 155–158, 173, 174, 228
    and γ-aminobutyric acid agonists, 342
    and cholinomimetics, 342
    and lithium, prophylactic, 342, 349–350
    in Parkinson's disease, 203
    in tardive dyskinesia, 174, 199, 205, 333, 338, 342–343
Drug addiction, 194, 375
Drug-diet interactions, 324
Drug holidays, 341, 356–357, 429
Drug response; *see also* Antipsychotic drugs; Outcome, treatment; *specific drug*
  and culture, 324
  individual differences in, 321–323, 329
  and McGuire-Raleigh-Brammer paradigm, 1, 11–18, 27
  serum prolactin levels as predictor of, 158–161
  and subgroups in clinical research, 305–306, 313
  and ventricular enlargement, 37
Drug surveillance, 354, 355
DSM-III, 273, 300, 305, 430
Duchenne-type muscular dystrophy, 39
Dyslexia, reversal of neuroanatomical asymmetries in, 29, 35
Dystonia, acute, 363

Ecological model, 274, 276, 277
Ecotype markers, 276, 281–282, 285–286
Efferent functions, *see* Motor-behavioral functions
Electroconvulsive therapy (ECT)
  prognosis of, and cerebral blood flow, 129
  for schizophrenia, 359, 374
Electroencephalogram (EEG), 70–74, 121; *see also* Computer-analyzed electroencephalogram (CEEG)
  and anxiety, 78, 79
  and anxiolytics, 77, 78
  and behavior, 65–66
  and cerebral blood flow, 121–122
  and delirium, 77, 78
  in tardive dyskinesia, 336
Emergencies, acute psychotic, 375
Emission tomography, 109, 121, 127
Endocrine equilibrium, 133–134, 136, 137–138, 140, 142, 145, 147
Endocrine stigmata, 132
β-Endorphin, 147, 342
Endorphin hypothesis of schizophrenia, 167, 177–194, 313
  direct evidence for, 178–180, 185
  indirect evidence for, 180–184
Endorphins
  in amniotic fluid, and fetal distress, 313
  antipsychotic effects of, 205, 342
  and placebo effect, 386, 390
  and prolactin, 151
Enkephalins, 147, 151
Environment; *see also* Ecological model; Ecotype markers; Stress and stressors
  and drug response, 11–14
  in Gerard paradigm, 7–9
  and placebo effect, 385–388, 398
  state-dependent characteristic of, 5
Enzymes; *see also specific name*
  and autonomic nervous system activity, 81
  induction of, 20–22, 146
  neurotransmitter, 238
Epinephrine
  and anger, 140
  and response patterns, 140
  urinary, and autonomic nervous system activity, 96
Episode markers, 280, 283, 285–287
  use of, 287–290, 291
Estradiol, and response patterns, 137
Estrogens
  and prolactin, 151
  and response patterns, 137
Estrone, and response patterns, 137
Ethics
  and challenge tests, 286
  and informed consent, 381, 386, 393
  and placebo studies, 393
N-Ethyl-3-piperidyl phenylcyclopentylglycolate, 64, 72, 77, 78
Etiology of schizophrenia, 134; *see also specific hypothesis*
  biological studies, 426, 429–430
  failure to identify, 430–431
  models of, 273–278, 295; *see also specific model; markers*
  and Schapiro paradigm, 1, 18–24
  and structural brain abnormalities, 36
Etiotypes, 276, 278, 290
Euphoria, 193
Evoked potentials, 121–122, 128, 283, 313
  and pain sensitivity, 180, 182, 183–184, 193
  and pupillary response, 285
Eye movements
  independent, 314
  smooth pursuit, 185, 275, 283

Familial dysautomia, and nerve growth factor, 244, 247
Family
  broken, 314
  interaction in, 306, 313, 314
  and relapses, 101, 323
Family studies; *see also* Genetics
  and minimization of heterogeneity, 351
Fluorescence-activited cell sorting, 225
α-Flupenthixol, and serum prolactin levels, 160
Fluphenazine
  computer-analyzed profile of, 67, 71, 73
  maintenance studies of, 357, 367
  and relapses, 367
Fluphenazine decanoate
  and alcoholism, 331
  for outpatient treatment, 325
  and tardive dyskinesia, 355, 356, 363, 381
  withdrawal study of, 381
Fluphenazine hydrochloride, withdrawal study of, 381
Formalin-fixed hemisphere, 407, 408
Fourier transform, 54, 55, 56, 57, 58
Free fatty acids, and growth hormone, 154
Frozen hemisphere, 407, 408–409, 411–412

Genetic model, 274, 276–277, 296
Genetic subgroups, in clinical research, 306, 313
Genetics; *see also* High-risk children
  and attentional functioning, 81, 86
  and autonomic nervous system functioning, 94–95, 96, 105
  and biogenic amines, 72
  and endorphin hypothesis, 189
  and mental disease, 19

trait-dependent characteristic of, 4–5
and vulnerability, 128, 146
Gerard paradigm, 1, 2–10, 27
Glandular extracts, 132, 133
Glucocorticoids; *see also specific name*
and environmental challenge, 5
and immunological system, 265, 266
and thymic function, 265
Glucose uptake, cerebral, 109, 121, 127
Glutamic acid decarboxylase (GAD), in postmortem brain, 412, 413, 416–417, 422
Glycine, 225
Golgi method, 44, 47, 48, 51–52, 59
Gonadal abnormalties, 132, 133, 135–136
Gonadal steroids, and growth hormone, 154
Growth hormone
and dopamine agonists, 151, 155–158, 166, 174
and duration of illness, 149, 156–157
and environmental challenge, 5, 137, 139, 140
levels of, 153
and maternal rejection, 23
and methylphenidate, 166
and neuroleptics, 154
and psychological influences, 5, 137, 139, 140
regulation of secretion of, 149, 150, 151
and tardive dyskinesia, 173
Growth hormone release inhibiting hormone, 151
Growth hormone releasing hormone, 151
Guanosine triphosphate (GTP), and cyclic adenosine monophosphate formation, 214
5′-Guanylylimidodiphospate, 214

Habituation, *see* Autonomic nervous system functioning
Haldol, *see* Haloperidol
Hallucination
and cerebral blood flow, 120, 128
naloxone for, 188, 194
in Parkinson's disease, 203
Hallucinogens; *see also specific name*
and computer-analyzed EEG, 61, 64, 65, 72, 73, 77, 78
and prolactin, 164–166
psychosis produced by, 210
Haloperidol
and adenyl cyclase inhibition, 215
and autonomic nervous system activity, 98, 106
and computer-analyzed EEG, 67, 71, 73
and growth hormone, 154
and prolactin, 174
^{3}H-Haloperidol binding, 195, 196–199, 204, 212, 215–216, 217, 421
Halsted-Reitan neuropsychological tests, and brain atrophy, 37
Heart rate, *see* Autonomic nervous system functioning
Hematoporphyrinuria, 325
Heterogeneity of schizophrenia
problem of, 134–135, 142, 186
attempts to solve, 27, 178, 187–188, 209–210, 298, 304–306, 350, 351
and treatment, 206, 297, 298
Hexamid, 64
High-risk children
and attentional functioning, 86
and autonomic nervous system functioning, 81, 94–95
and birth complications, 19, 95
and computer-analyzed EEG, 61, 63–64, 72
identification of, 318–319, 329
and pregnancy complications, 95
and relaxation techniques, 79
and vulnerability, 19, 289–290
Hippocampal granule cells, murine, 47–51
Hippocampus, choline acetyltransferase in, 417
Histocompatibility antigen profile, and brain atrophy, 36
Homovanillic acid (HVA)
brain concentrations of, 173, 230, 340, 421
and cholinomimetics, 340
Hormones; *see also specific hormone*
and drugs, 145–146
evolution of, 27
and immune system, 265–266
and stress, 5, 146, 296
treatment with, 132, 133, 134
Hospitalization
continuous, as unnecessary for chronic schizophrenia, 271–272
iatrogenic influences of, 9, 270, 283
length of, average, 6
and physical dysplasias, 8
and urinary creatinine excretion, 6
voluntary, 7–8
Huntington's disease
brain tissue resource center for, 401, 403–404, 405
bronchial pneumonia as cause of death in, 421
Huntington's disease
correlation between physostigmine and choline response in, 421
diagnosis of, 407, 410
as model for studying schizophrenia, 295
postmortem studies of, 402, 412, 413, 421
presenting as psychotic episode, 295
tardive dyskinesia differentiated from, 337
17-Hydroxycorticosteroid
in acute schizophrenia, 141

17-Hydroxycorticosteroid (*cont'd*)
and response patterns, 140
6-Hydroxydopamine-induced lesion of substantia nigra, 203
5-Hydroxytryptamine, *see* Serotonin
5-Hydroxytryptophan (5-HTP), behavioral effects of, 13, 17
5-Hydroxytryptophan decarboxylase, 20
Hypertermia, 422
Hypothalamus
DOPAC in, 230
dopamine in, 230
and growth hormone secretion, 151, 157–158
homovanillic acid in, 230
methoxy-hydroxyphenylglycol in, 229, 231
norepinephrine in, 231

Immaturity syndrome, male, 135–136
Immunology, and schizophrenia, 249–267, 422
Infections, and chlorpromazine, 258, 259
Informed consent, 381, 386, 393
Inpatient Multidimensional Psychiatric Scale (IMPS), 87
Insulin, and response patterns, 137, 139, 140
Insulin coma treatment, endocrinological contraindications to, 135
Internal environment markers, 276, 287–287; *see also specific marker*
Internal environment model, 275, 276, 277, 296
Intralaminar thalomocortical projection system, 122

Kety technique, 108, 113, 118, 127

Learning theory markers, 276, 286
Learning theory model, 274–275, 276, 277, 283
Lecithin, for tardive dyskinesia, 340, 358
Levodopa
and autonomic nervous system activity, 97
and growth hormone, 155, 156
hyperkinesia induced by, 337
and ^{3}H-neuroleptic/dopamine receptors, 199, 350
for Parkinson's disease, 203
and prolactin, 151, 155, 156
psychotic symptoms caused by, 157, 203, 205, 227
tardive dyskinesia exacerbated by, 339
Life event stressors, 278–280, 281, 290, 296, 398; *see also* Environment; Stress and stressors
β-Lipotropin, 147
Lithium
as antipsychotic, 359, 363
and dopamine supersensitivity, 342, 349–350
interstitial nephritis caused by, 363
in schizoaffective disorders, prophylactic use of, 375
for tardive dyskinesia, 358, 363
Longitudinal vs cross-sectional studies, 425
Loxapine
and prolactin, 161, 162
tardive dyskinesia caused by, 355
Lupus erythematosus, antipsychotic drugs related to, 249, 250, 355
Lupus-like anticoagulant, 422
Luteinizing hormone-releasing factor, 147
Lymphocytes
and chlorpromazine, 249, 250, 254–257, 259, 263
in schizophrenia, 249, 250, 251, 254, 255–256, 257–258, 259, 260, 263, 264, 265
Lysergic acid diethylamide
and computer-analyzed EEG, 64, 72
and prolactin, 150, 164–165, 166
and serum growth hormone, 166

McGuire-Raleigh-Brammer paradigm, 1, 11–18, 27
McLean Hospital Brain Tissue Resource Center, 404–405
Magnetic microspheres, 225
Manic episodes, acute, cerebral blood flow in, 129
Maternal deprivation, and growth hormone, 21, 23
Maternal rejection, and enzyme induction, 20
Mellaril, *see* Thioridazine
Melperone, and prolactin, 162
Menstrual cycle, and psychotic episodes, 134, 135
Mental disorders, etiological models of, 273–278; *see also specific model*
Mental retardation, 39, 43, 45
Mescaline, and computer-analyzed EEG, 64
Mesencephalon, norepinephrine in, 228
Mesolimbic dopamine pathways, 153, 334, 342–343, 349, 416
Mesoridazine, adenyl cyclase inhibited by, 215
Metanephrine, urinary, and autonomic nervous system activity, 96
Methadone, 193, 194, 375
3-Methoxy-4-hydroxyphenylglycol (MHPG)
and autonomic nervous system activity, 97
location of, 229, 231
α-Methyl-*p*-tyrosine (AMPT)
and dopamine, 149
and neuroleptic effects on serum prolactin levels, 151, 163–164, 165

Methylphenidate
and chronic neuroleptic administration, 338
and growth hormone, 166, 174
and prolactin, 165, 166, 174
psychosis exacerbated by, 157, 338
Methylphenidate challenge, 286
Methysergide, and growth hormone, 154
Metoclopramide, and prolactin, 150, 162
Mini-episodes, 286, 287
Moban, *see* Molindone
Molindone
and computer-analyzed EEG, 71, 73
dysphoric response to, in normals, 330
and tardive dyskinesia, 355
Monoamine oxidase activity
in affective disorders, 185, 283
and autonomic nervous system activity, 95–96, 105
in schizophrenia, 152, 185
and vulnerability, 283
Monamine oxidase inhibitors
and blood pressure, 96–97
and food interactions, 324
and heart rate, 96–97
and urinary amine excretion, 97
Morphine, 193
Mothering; *see also* Maternal deprivation; Maternal rejection
inadequate, and serotonin-*N*-acetyltransferase, 23
Motor-behavioral functions, 108, 110, 118, 119, 120–121, 123
Motor neurons, alpha, 39, 59
Movement disorders of schizophrenia, 336–337; *see also specific disorder*
Muscimol, 341

Naloxone, 178, 179, 183–184, 188, 194
Naltrexone, 178, 179, 182, 193
Narcotic addicts, 194, 375
National research funding, 298
Navane, *see* Thiothixine
Neonates, and stress, 20, 21–23
Nerve cell activity, *see* Cerebral blood flow
Nerve growth factor (NGF), 237–247
measurement of, 241–244
in schizophrenia, 244, 247
sources of, 239–240, 265
structure of, 239–240
Neuroanatomical asymmetries, 34–35, 116, 117, 284
Neurofibromatosis, and nerve growth factor, 244, 247
Neurohistology, quantitative, with computer microscope, 43–59
Neuroleptic drugs, *see* Antipsychotic drugs; *specific group; name*
Neuroleptic receptors, 195–207
Neuromodulator, dopamine as, 209, 213–219
Neurophysiological markers, 276, 282–285, 287; *see also specific marker*
Neurophysiological model, 275, 276, 277
Neurotic processes, 140
New Haven Schizophrenia Index, 299, 300
New technologies, application of, in research, 427
Norepinephrine
and amphetamine psychosis, 211
and *d*-amphetamine, 166
and anger, 140
and circadian rhythm, 22, 23
and growth hormone, 150, 151
location of, 228, 229, 231, 232, 235, 415, 416, 421
and prolactin, 151
and reserpine, depletion of, by, 206
and response pattern, 140
urinary, and autonomic nervous system, 96
Norepinephrine hypothesis of schizophrenia, 228, 229, 232
Normetanephrine, and autonomic nervous system activity, 96
Nucleus accumbens
choline acetyltransferase activity in, 417
of choreic brain, dopamine in, 413, 421
DOPAC in, 230
dopamine in, 204, 227, 230, 413, 414, 415–416
glutamic acid decarboxylase activity in, 417
homovanillic acid in, 230, 421
methoxy-hydroxyphenylglycol in, 231
and ^{3}H-neuroleptic binding, 196, 198
norepinephrine in, 228, 229, 231, 232, 235, 415, 416
supersensitivity of, 343
Nurses' protocol, in postmortem brain collection, 407

Opiate antagonists, 177, 178–180; *see also specific name*
and evoked potential amplititude, 182–184
Opiates, 193, 194
Outcome, treatment; *see also* Drug response
assessment of, 307–308, 315–316
definition of, 393
and endocrine function, 135–136
and measurement of blood and tissue levels of antipsychotic drugs, 321
predicting
and additional functioning, 83–85, 99–101
and autonomic nervous system functioning, 83, 89–92, 99–101, 105
and patients' subjective response to drug, 391

Outcome, treatment
predicting (*cont'd*)
and placebo response, 390–391
Outlier, 326
Outpatient treatment, 323, 325, 357–358, 372–373
Oxytremorine, 340

Pain sensitivity, 180–182, 185–187
in affective disorders, 185
evoked potential studies of, 182–184
Paradigms, for studies on schizophrenia, 1–27
Parkinsonism, drug-induced, 325
Parkinson's disease
and dopamine, 203, 401, 402
and hallucinations, 203
postmortem studies of, 402
and voice, 325
Pathological intoxication, 325
Pathologists' protocol, in postmortem brain collection, 407–408
Patient selection, in clinical research, 299–302, 314–315
Perinatal complications, 19, 95, 274, 313
Perphenazine, computer-analyzed EEG profile of, 67
Pharmacological challenges, 322, 323, 329, 330, 390–391
Phasic characteristics, 425
Phenothiazines; *see also* Antipsychotic drugs; *specific drug*
and affective blunting, 98
antipsychotic properties of, 227
and attentional capacity, 87
and autonomic nervous system activity, 97, 98–99
maintenance studies of, 367
and prevention of relapses, 367
and serum prolactin levels, 159–160
Pheromones, 27
Phosphokinase activity, in glial cells, 215
Phospholipid fractions, 219–221
Physostigmine
for Alzheimer's disease, 363
and EEG patterns, 77
for tardive dyskinesia, 334, 340
Pimozide, 367
Pineal gland, maturation of, 22–23
Placebo
analgesic effect of, 386, 390
as experimental condition, 389–399
and extrapyramidal side effects, 397
and relapses, 366–372
Placebo challenge, 391
Placebo effects, 330
and classic conditioning, 397
and environmental factors, 385–388, 398
negative, 398
and suggestion, 397
Pneumoencephalography, 30, 39, 40
Positron emission tomography, 204
Postmortem brain collection, 401–402, 405–414, 427, 431
and agonal effects, 413
and autopsy permit, 405–406
and clinical diagnosis, 410–411, 422
and formalin-fixed hemisphere, 407, 408
and frozen hemisphere, 407, 408–409
and medical examiner's office, 407
and neuroanatomical dissection, 409–410, 414, 415
and nurses' protocol, 407–408
and pharmacologic agents, 413–414
and standardization of dissection, 414, 415
and time period between death and freezing tissue, 411–412
Postmortem studies
of cerebellar pathology, 36
of choline acetyltransferase, 417
of chronic schizophrenics, 227–236
and consent, 235–236, 405–406
of corpus callosum thickness, 40
of dopamine concentrations, 415–416, 421
of endocrine glands, 132
of glutamic acid decarboxylase, 416–417, 422
methodological problems of, 30
of neurolpetic/dopamine receptors, 157, 195, 196–202, 205
of norepinephrine, 416, 421
of Parkinson's disease, 402
pattern analysis in, 43, 51–54
Postpartum mental disorders, 134
Pregnancy complications, 19, 95
Prevention of schizophrenia, 318–320, 323
and support systems, 319–320
and vulnerability, 289
Prolactin
and dopamine agonists, 149, 151, 155–157, 174, 175
and dopamine antagonists, 152–154
and psychotropic drug action, 146, 161–166, 173–174, 212, 341
regulation of secretion of, 149, 151
and response patterns, 5, 137, 139
serum levels of, as predictor of clinical response, 150, 158–161, 174, 175
and sleep, 154, 174
and tardive dyskinesia, 173
Prolactin-inhibiting factor (PIF), 151
Prolixin, *see* Fluphenazine
Promethazine, and EEG, 77–78
Propranolol
as adjunct to treatment, 98
high-dose, 353, 358
Prostaglandins, and prolactin release, 151
Psychiatrists, research, development of, 365, 377–378

Psychoendocrine research, 131–147; *see also specific hormone*
basic, 137–140
clinical, 132–136
Psychological defense mechanisms, 140
Psychosocial subgroups, in clinical research, 306, 313–314
Psychotherapy, 136, 303, 323, 324, 386
Puberty, and onset of schizophrenia, 135, 298
Pupillary response, 284–285
Purkinje cells, 44, 59
Putamen
choline acetyltransferase activity in, 417
dopamine in, 227, 414, 415
glutamic acid decarboxylase in, 417
and ^{3}H-neuroleptic binding, 195, 196, 198, 199
norepinephrine in, 228
Pyridoxine, and prolactin release, 151

Q-sort, in Gerard paradigm, 3, 9–10
Quality of life, 326
Quality of Life Scale, 301

R-16341, 367
Rabbit syndrome, 337
Race
and dopamine beta-hydroxylase activity, 330
and treatment response, 324, 330, 382
Radioimmunoassay, and nerve growth factor, 241–244
Rare patient protocol, 375
Rare patient record keeping, 375
Rare patient registry, 376
Reaction time, *see* Attentional functioning
Red blood cell phospholipids, 219–221
Regional cerebral blood flow, 107, 109–130, 212
Relapse
and familial climate, 101
prediction of, 100, 101
prevention of, 318, 319–320, 323, 366–375
rate of, 270–271, 366–375
Remission, definition of, 363
Research Diagnostic Criteria (RDC), 300
Research funding, 298
Research methods
applied, 317–331
clinical, 297–316
Research psychiatrists, development of, 365, 377–378
Reserpine
and dopamine hypothesis, 206, 211, 338–339
neuroleptics combined with, 206
and prolactin, 151
tardive dyskinesia suppressed by, 338–339
Ritalin, *see* Methylphenidate
RMI-81, 161
Rockland-Pollin (RP) scale, 110, 111, 112–113, 115, 118

Schapiro paradigm, 1, 18–24
Schizoaffective disorders, prophylactic lithium for, 375
Schizophrenia
acute and chronic, distinction between, 299
chronicity of, arguments against, 269–270, 271–272
duration of, and growth hormone, 149, 156–157
episodic nature of, 269, 270–273, 295–296, 300, 329, 382
heterogeneity of, *see* Heterogeneity of schizophrenia
incidence of, 297
and mortality, 265, 353, 354–355, 382, 413, 422
paradigms for study of, 1–27
public image of, 289
schizophreniform psychosis differentiated from, 300
symptoms of, principal, 212
Schizophreniform psychosis, 40, 300, 375
Schizotrope, 277, 278, 280
Schneider's first-rank symptoms, 299–300
Seizures, and cerebral blood flow, 128
Senile psychosis, choline for, 363
Sensory-gnostic functions, 108, 109, 119, 120, 123
Sensory motor functions, 108
Septal nuclei
choline acetyltransferase activity in, 417
dopamine in, 414, 415, 416
norepinephrine in, 415, 416
Serotonin
and behavior, 13, 17–18, 27
blood, as trait-dependent marker, 5, 15–16
and growth hormone, 150, 151, 154
and prolactin, 151
reserpine depletion of, 206
Serotonin receptor blockers, 166
Serotonin receptors, 199
Serotonin-*N*-acetyltransferase (SNAT), 22–23
Sex differences
in attentional functioning, 91, 105
in serum chlorpromazine, 173
in serum prolactin levels, 160
Sex hormones; *see also specific hormone*
and prolactin release, 151
and thymus gland, 265
Simpson Dyskinetic Rating Scale, 356
Skin conductance level, *see* Autonomic nervous system functioning
Sleep
EEG findings in, 287

Sleep (*cont'd*)
computer-analyzed, 64
and episodes, 287
and growth hormone, 154–155
and neuroleptics, 65
and prolactin, 154
Social functioning criteria, 300, 301
Social Readjustment Rating Scale, 279, 285
Social role, and drug responses, 11–16
Social support systems, 278–279, 281, 398
Social therapy, 323
Socioeconomic class, 282, 313
Sociological factors, in Gerard paradigm, 7–9
Sodium valproate, 341
Speech onset, delayed, 35
Speech processes, in episodes, 286
^{3}H-Spiperone binding, 195, 196, 198, 199, 203
^{3}H-Spiroperidol binding, 162, 163, 338, 341, 342, 343, 421
Spleen cells, murine, effect of chlorpromazine on *in vitro* antibody response of, 251–253
Spontaneous orofacial dyskinesia, 337
Stress and stressors; *see also* Environment; Life event stressors
and age, 20
and autonomic nervous system activity, 101
and catastrophic schizophrenia, 263
early exposure to, 18–19, 21–24
and hormones, 20–24, 146, 147, 296
and vulnerability, 278–280, 281
Subcortical mechanisms, and cerebral blood flow, 108, 122–123, 129
Substantia nigra
of choreic brain, dopamine in, 413
DOPAC in, 230
dopamine in, 230, 413
homovanillic acid in, 230
methoxy-hydroxyphenylglycol in, 231
norepinephrine in, 231
Sulpiride
and computer-analyzed EEG response, 77
neurological side effects absent with, 359
and prolactin, 150, 162
Support services, and preventive measures, 319–320, 329
Survival distribution analysis, 365, 366–372, 381
Sweat substance, 27
Symptoms, presenting, 2
Syndromes, 2
Syphilis, 40

Tardive dyskinesia, 333–351
clinical assessment of, 355–356
definition of, 333, 335
differential diagnosis of, 336–338, 349
EEG pattern in, B-mitten, 336
epidemiology of, 333, 335–336, 349, 353
mesolimbic equivalent to, 342–343
neuropharmacology of, 173, 174, 199, 205, 334, 338, 429
pharmacological studies of, 334, 338–341, 349, 358, 363
prevention of, 353–354, 355–358, 359, 363, 365, 372–375, 382–383, 393
research needed on, 334–335, 341–342, 355–359
subtypes of, 338, 341
Temporal lobe epilepsy, 375
Testosterone
and anger, 140
and response patterns, 137, 139, 140
thioridazine suppression of, 174
Tetrabenazine, and tardive dyskinesia, 338–339
Thalamus, norepinephrine in, 421
Thiethylperazine, and serum prolactin levels, 160
Thioridazine
agranulocytosis induced by, 354
computer-analyzed EEG profile of, 67, 77
and electrocardiogram, 354
and sudden death, 354
and tardive dyskinesia, 355
testosterone suppressed by, 174
Thiothixine
computer-analyzed profile of, 67, 70, 71, 73
dysphoric response to, in normals, 330
and placebo effect, 330
Thought processes, in episodes, 286
Thymectomy, 265
Thymocytes, murine, and cytotoxic factor, 250, 251, 254–258, 260, 263, 264, 265
Thymosin, 265
Thymus gland
irradiation of, 264–265, 266
removal of, 265
Thyroid-stimulating hormone, and response patterns, 139
Thyroxine, and response patterns, 137, 139, 140
Tourette's disease, 375
Trans-3-methyl-2-hexenoic acid, 27
Transmitter systems; *see also specific system*
and behavior, 16–18
Treatment; *see also* Outcome, treatment
fragmented, 319–320
and culture, 324
and race, 324, 330, 382
Trebenzomine, 162
Tremor, hand, measurement of, 325, 329
Tricyclic antidepressants, tardive dyskinesia caused by, 336, 337
Trifluoperazine
adenyl cyclase inhibited by, 215
maintenance studies of, 367

and relapses, 367
Tryptophan
behavioral effects of, 12, 13–14, 17, 18
blood level of, 5
and growth hormone, 154
loading, 5
Tryptophan hydroxylase, and stress, 20, 22
Tryptophan oxygenase, 21–22
Tuberoinfundibular dopaminergic (TIDA) neurons, 150, 152, 153, 154, 159, 164, 173, 343
12-Point flexible system, 300
Twin studies, and autonomic nervous system functioning, 95, 96, 105
Tyrosine hydroxylase, 421
Tyrosine transaminase, and stress, 20

Valium, *see* Diazepam
Vanillylmandelic acid (VMA), and autonomic nervous system activity, 96, 97
Ventricular enlargement, in chronic schizophrenia, 30, 31–33, 34, 37, 39–40
Vervet monkey, and drug response, 11–14
Vigilance techniques, *see* Attentional functioning
Violence protocol study, 381
Viruses, and schizophrenia, 249, 263
Vitamins, and prolactin, 151
Voice analysis, 325
Volatile materials, in schizophrenia, 27
Vulnerability
and attention deficits, 81
and episodic nature of schizophrenia, 271, 272, 273–275, 278
and genetics, 19, 128
and socioeconomic class, 313
Vulnerability markers, 280–285, 287–290, 291
Vulnerability model, 276, 277–280

Wheat gluten, as pathogenic factor in schizophrenia, 106, 264
White blood cells, 258

^{133}Xenon clearance technique, 109, 110, 112, 116, 118, 127, 128–129